PENGUIN BOOKS

RIVER RUN RED

Andrew Ward is the author of numerous books, including the award-winning *Dark Midnight When I Rise: The Story of the Jubilee Singers* and *Our Bones Are Scattered: The Cawnpore Massacres in the Indian Mutiny of 1857*. A former contributing editor at *The Atlantic Monthly*, commentator for National Public Radio's *All Things Considered*, columnist for *The Washington Post*, and screenwriter, he lives in the state of Washington.

RIVER
RUN
RED

The Fort Pillow Massacre
in the American Civil War

ANDREW WARD

PENGUIN BOOKS

PENGUIN BOOKS

Published by the Penguin Group
Penguin Group (USA) Inc., 375 Hudson Street, New York, New York 10014, U.S.A.
Penguin Group (Canada), 90 Eglinton Avenue East, Suite 700, Toronto,
Ontario, Canada M4P 2Y3 (a division of Pearson Penguin Canada Inc.)
Penguin Books Ltd, 80 Strand, London WC2R 0RL, England
Penguin Ireland, 25 St Stephen's Green, Dublin 2, Ireland (a division of Penguin Books Ltd)
Penguin Group (Australia), 250 Camberwell Road, Camberwell,
Victoria 3124, Australia (a division of Pearson Australia Group Pty Ltd)
Penguin Books India Pvt Ltd, 11 Community Centre,
Panchsheel Park, New Delhi–110 017, India
Penguin Group (NZ), cnr Airborne and Rosedale Roads, Albany,
Auckland 1310, New Zealand (a division of Pearson New Zealand Ltd)
Penguin Books (South Africa) (Pty) Ltd, 24 Sturdee Avenue,
Rosebank, Johannesburg 2196, South Africa

Penguin Books Ltd, Registered Offices:
80 Strand, London, WC2R 0RL, England

First published in the United States of America by Viking Penguin,
a member of Penguin Group (USA) Inc. 2005
Published in Penguin Books 2006

10 9 8 7 6 5 4 3 2 1

THE LIBRARY OF CONGRESS HAS CATALOGED THE HARDCOVER EDITION AS FOLLOWS:
Ward, Andrew, date.
    River run red : the Fort Pillow massacre in the American Civil War / Andrew Ward.
        p. cm.
    Includes bibliographical references and index.
    ISBN 0-670-03440-1 (hc.)
    ISBN 0 14 30.3786 2 (pbk.)
    1. Fort Pillow, Battle of, Tenn., 1864.   I. Title.
    E476.17.W37 2005
    973.7'36—dc22   2005043058

Printed in the United States of America
Set in Fairfield LH Light
Designed by Daniel Lagin

This book is dedicated with all my heart
to the former
Deborah Lathrop Huntington

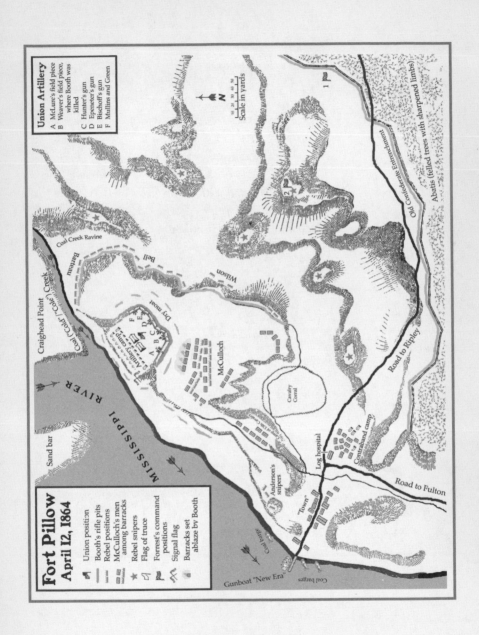

Fort Pillow
April 12, 1864

- Union position
- Booth's rifle pits
- Rebel positions
- McCulloch's men among barracks
- Rebel snipers
- Flag of truce
- Forrest's command positions
- Signal flag
- Barracks set ablaze by Booth

Union Artillery

A McLure's field piece
B Weaver's field piece, where Booth was killed
C Hunter's gun
D Epeneter's gun
E Bischoff's gun
F Mullins and Green

N

10 20 30 40 50
Scale in yards

MISSISSIPPI RIVER

Craighead Point Creek

Sand bar

Coal Creek Ravine

Coal "Coal" "Cole" Creek

Barton

Bell

Wilson

Dry moat

Fort Pillow

McCulloch

Cavalry Corral

Anderson's snipers

Log hospital

Contraband camp

"Town"

Road to Ripley

Road to Fulton

Old Confederate Entrenchment

Abatis (felled trees with sharpened limbs)

Coal barge

Coal barges

Gunboat "New Era"

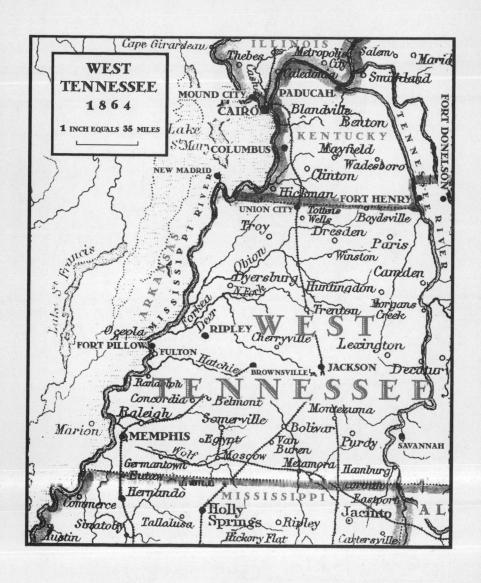

CONTENTS

PREFACE

I HAVE A FASCINATION—MY CHILDREN SAY A MORBID FASCINATION—
with nineteenth-century massacres. I have written two books—a novel and
then a historical narrative—about the carnage at Cawnpore, India, in the
Great Indian Mutiny of 1857; and an article about Custer's debacle at Little
Big Horn in 1876; and my shelves are packed with books about Kabul, the
Alamo, Khartoum, and Isandhlwana. This fixation derives, I suppose, from
my growing up a vastly outnumbered white boy in India and my formative
hero-worship of the Disney version of Davy Crockett, combined with an ir-
religious but nonetheless apocalyptic anxiety about death that draws me to
accounts of its wholesale form. But, for an American, the story of the Civil
War Battle of Fort Pillow in April 1864 contains elements at once more
frustrating and more edifying than any of the others, for Northerners and
Southerners, not to mention blacks and whites, have never agreed on what
transpired there.

When a battle is not completely one thing or another, partisans will subject it to enormous pressure to force it into one definition or another. In this
sense, the Confederate and Federal versions of what transpired at Fort Pillow are to varying degrees mistaken. Each side's efforts to define the Fort
Pillow affair as either a hard-won victory on the one hand or a premeditated
massacre on the other have led otherwise sagacious writers to commit an
uncharacteristic number of sins of commission and especially omission,
discarding the other side's evidence by the most tortured and sometimes
precipitate means. The job of creating a true picture of the battle demands
a capacity to embrace or in any case try to reconcile the apparent contradictions in various participants' memories of what they endured.

Few agree about what transpired at Fort Pillow—many authorities still balk, as I initially did, at calling it a massacre. But it is impossible to make sense of it without understanding the atmosphere in which it played itself out: the corruption of Union occupation, the horrors of guerrilla warfare, the rebel triumphs and defeats that immediately preceded it. And it is necessary, I think, to get some sense of who the players were: the liberated slaves and their ambivalent white comrades who constituted the Yankee garrison, and Nathan Bedford Forrest's men: perhaps the most dedicated and ferocious warriors in the entire Confederate army.

The men who served in the Civil War called going into battle "meeting the elephant." No one knows exactly why. Perhaps, from a distance, the smoke roiling up from a battle resembled an elephant, but it seems to me just as likely that they could have been referring to the old saw about the blind men and the elephant, each feeling a small portion and none able to describe the beast as a whole. I expect that most men tell the truth as they see it, and that just because they see it from different perspectives and draw different conclusions does not necessarily mean that those conclusions are contradictory or mutually exclusive.

The gaps that complicate the task historians take on—and the temptation to fill them with what we may desire or suspect of our ancestors—are formidable. What follows is a kind of cross between a narrative history of Fort Pillow and a portrait gallery of the people who converged upon it, because I determined early on that it is no more enlightening to characterize the battle as a case of white against black than to characterize the collision at Gettysburg as a case of white against white. In these pages there are slaves and masters and Yankees and rebels of all kinds, none of whom lived his or her life to fit the roles we may want to assign to them out of our retrospective pride or shame. There were soldiers of the noblest intentions who proved cowardly, and soldiers capable of the most terrible atrocities who proved brave.

No investigation of the battle can be undertaken without trying to arrive at some understanding of American slavery. Despite the centrality of race in American history, and especially the history of the Civil War, and even though, by the time the guns opened up at Fort Sumter, one out of every eight Americans and two out of every five Southerners were black, what gets left out of a lot of the mainstream histories of the Civil War is a proportionate representation of the experience of African Americans. The terms we employ to recount the war suggest why. In most histories, Northerners and

Southerners are equated with whites, and the South with the Southern cause, even though many Northerners were African Americans and a significant proportion of the South was black and rooting and in some cases fighting for the Union. It is difficult to overcome this problem. Read enough histories, diaries, letters, memoirs, and biographies and even the most conscientious of us slips into the same pitfalls. Someday I hope a more integrated account of the war will be written, but in the meantime I have chosen a battle and its aftermath whose recounting must of necessity encompass some measure of the slave experience.

Though when considering slavery we may want to think of suffering as necessarily ennobling, one reason we do not wish suffering upon ourselves is because it is more likely to be degrading. There are African Americans in these pages who were noble, and others who were merely trying to get by, some who were kind and some who were brutal, and it should be enough to state simply that they were human beings, which is to say as contradictory and complicated as we should understand ourselves to be. Every one of them was more interesting in his or her actuality than in the form black people took in either side's propaganda.

It should come as no surprise that the rebel cavalry who committed terrible acts at Fort Pillow would afterward deny them, because especially in the American Civil War men judged themselves not according to the crimes they may have committed in the heat of battle, but by the aggregate of what they considered themselves to be: responsible citizens, patriots, brave soldiers, hardworking farmers, honest merchants, devout Christians, faithful husbands and fathers, loyal and loving brothers and sons. Nor did such acts cost them the respect of their friends and neighbors, because in peace, war, and defeat the South deemed it paramount—and by the 1850s it had become a conditioned reflex—to hunker down and defend their slave society against the calumny of the abolitionist propagandists whom they blamed for the onset of the Civil War.

It seems to be true of most people who have committed a crime that they deny it not because they did not commit it but because they refuse to be defined by it. They know that the basically decent person they try to be, or believe themselves to be, would not—*could* not—have done what they are accused of doing, even if they did it. The crimes they commit, especially in extremity, do not suit their conception of themselves, and so to keep from shooting themselves or going mad, they must deny the one if they are to salvage the other. But it is not enough to say that the brutal acts depicted in these pages were committed by ordinary men caught up in extraordinary circumstances, because the story of Fort Pillow begs the question of what, exactly, was an ordinary man in the mid-nineteenth century and what the ordinary circumstance was for a society that had predicated itself on 250 years of uninterrupted slavery.

At the New-York Historical Society some years ago, I saw an exhibit of postcards of lynchings from the Jim Crow era. In these nightmare images individually ordinary white folks—farmers, small-town merchants, churchgoers, housewives, children—were captured gathering to celebrate the atrocious killing of a fellow human being, gazing and even grinning into the camera as they stood around the body of a black man or woman they had tortured, shot, burned, hanged. Perhaps because I could hardly bear to look upon the corpses of their victims, I concentrated instead on the individuals standing among the mobs and wondered if, when they made their way home and finished the dishes and tucked their children into bed, they returned to their ordinary "decency." Or did the lynching mark the end of their normality and humanity?

These are the kinds of questions that haunted their fathers and grandfathers who served in the war. Americans have never been good at embracing contradictions, so we tend to deny the inevitable discrepancies between ideal and reality, intention and effect. But we are all shaped by circumstance, and the circumstance of slavery had as profound an effect on the whites who owned slaves as it had on the African Americans they held in bondage.

———

Though I have felt a boyish thrill walking Pickett's charge at Gettysburg and have tried in these pages to consort with the ghosts of Fort Pillow, I have come to believe that apart from individual acts of heroism, mercy, and generosity, there was nothing glorious about the Civil War. The propertied class on one side of the Mason-Dixon Line profited from the war, and on the other side fought to defend the obscene extension of property rights to their fellow human beings. Most of the generals were of this class; many of them were the very politicians who had brought the nation to this pass in the first place, thus compounding the sheer unseemliness of their often corrupt and incompetent command with their self-interested demagoguery.

As I researched this book I had to keep reminding myself that it would have been far more glorious had our politicians avoided expending hundreds of thousands of young men's lives and laying waste to half of the country by mustering the courage and decency to legislate an end to slavery and divert a proportionate measure of the resources of a burgeoning nation into providing African Americans with an equal chance at life, liberty, and prosperity. But then it would have been more glorious still had the "peculiar institution" never taken root in North America in the first place.

A final note on my approach to the material upon which this book is based: Much of my examination of the Fort Pillow affair has been devoted to pruning away the flourishes that partisans on both sides of the Mason-Dixon Line added to the combatants' testimony. I have tried to give every account— rebel and Federal—the benefit of the doubt while at the same time separating eyewitness testimony from hearsay, questioning or excluding from my account any incident for which no eyewitness can or could be found, and severely scrutinizing accounts of the battle composed for political purposes and public consumption.

In order to better acquaint myself with Forrest's men I have leaned hard on the five-volume *Tennessee Civil War Veterans Questionnaires* compiled between 1915 and 1922 by Gustave W. Dyer and John Trotwood Moore. An even more significant resource was the collection of Union pension records I reviewed at the National Archives, many of which contained transcripts of the oral reminiscences of the former slaves and illiterate whites who took part in the Battle of Fort Pillow. I have tried to approach the latter material critically and to allow for the vagaries of old men's memories, but what strikes me most about them is how closely they adhere to the testimony they gave immediately following the battle.

Perhaps it is my reliance on pension records that has compelled me to dwell with unusual emphasis on the wounds and illnesses that either killed men outright or plagued them for the rest of their lives. But it seems to me that such aftereffects of war are underreported in even the most epilogic military histories, despite their profound impact on not only the men who fought but their families, neighbors, and employers. Besides, in order to explain why one side suffered exponentially more casualties than the other, I am obliged to describe the horrors of this battle in full, especially where the nature and circumstances of men's wounds and deaths are so central to defining the lethal dynamics that made such a catastrophe possible. Or perhaps I simply need to justify to myself the weeks I have spent reading reports of rheumatism, dementia, senility, yellow eyes and black tongues, cattarh, piles, boils, and missing digits and limbs, and the nights I have staggered out of the National Archives like some weary small-town general practitioner.

None of the dialogue in this book is invented: all of it comes from firsthand accounts. In quoting from written diaries and letters I have not made any changes in spelling except occasionally to substitute the correct spelling in brackets or to add a punctuation mark for clarity's sake. In employing oral quotes from blacks as represented by white writers in dialect form, I have retained all idiomatic usages ("knowed," "Marse," etc.) but otherwise corrected the spelling (from "dem" to "them" and "dar" to "there," and so on). I regard the dialect form of transcription as degrading, gratuitous, obtrusive, and almost invariably false; I too slur my speech and drop my g's, but I don't expect to be represented in caricature when I am interviewed, and neither should anyone quoted here. Nor should readers be required to impersonate the characters in a book or conspire with their ancestors in denigrating blacks and poor whites.

Andrew Ward
Seattle, Washington
June 22, 2004

ACKNOWLEDGMENTS

THE FORT PILLOW AFFAIR HAS BEEN THE SUBJECT OF RELENTLESS controversy, and none of those to whom I owe a particular debt of gratitude will agree with all of my interpretations of it. Some, I am afraid, may be affronted, even appalled, by my conclusions. But I am nonetheless grateful for their generosity in providing me with much of the primary material that led me, for better or worse, to those conclusions. So many people and institutions assisted and advised me during my research for this book that I must list them by state.

Alabama: I am especially indebted to Derek Frisby for his generous and collegial assistance as we reviewed together some of the material on which this book is based. His perspective on the war in West Tennessee has been invaluable, and his discovery of the letters of Samuel Henry Eells has shed a new and troubling light on the relations between blacks and Northerners in occupied Hardeman County. Also thanks to Nancy Gooch for her help investigating the Boddie and Key families of Lauderdale County, Alabama; Karl F. Schaeffer for information regarding George S. Palmer and Norwood A. Kerr; and the Alabama Department of Archives and History for the letters of Charles S. Stewart and Mark Lyons. **Arkansas:** My thanks to Dr. Robert C. Mainfort, professor of anthropology at the University of Arkansas and sponsored research administrator and series editor with the Arkansas Archaeological Survey for sharing his extraordinary collection of material relating to the history of Fort Pillow. I did not manage to visit him until after my research time and resources had just about run out. In fact, I finally met him on my return home from my last visit to the National Archives, from which I emerged still nagged by the miscellany of stray items I no longer had the time or the resources to find, but Dr. Mainfort provided me with almost every missing part. If this account of Fort Pillow even begins to verge on the comprehensive, it is thanks to Dr. Mainfort. **California:** Michele Sensano of the Fresno Historical Society for material relating to Tyree Bell; Stanford University Library; Los Angeles Public Library. **Delaware:** Professor Thomas J. Reed of the Widener University School of Law for help researching the 20th Tennessee Cavalry. **District of Columbia:** My special thanks to my nephew Sam Heldman, my honorary niece Hilary Ball, and my learned grandnephew Julius for putting up with me during the many weeks I spent at the National Archives. At the archives, I am especially indebted to Michael Musick (since retired from his position as head of the National Archives Department of Old Military and Civil Records) for his tireless assistance and many tips, and to Rebecca Livingston for her assistance reviewing naval records. I also wish to thank Joellen El Bashir, curator of manuscripts at the Moorland-Spingarn Research Center at Howard University. **Florida:** Bob Mays for the autobiography of William Tapley Mays, and to W.T.'s granddaughter, Lois Mays Rizzo, and her son, Robert M. Hudson, for permitting me to employ portions of it. **Illinois:** The Research Center of the Chicago Historical Society and the staff of the Manuscripts Department of the Illinois State Historical Library in Springfield. **Indiana:** Susan Truax for her research on my behalf at the Indiana State Library. **Kansas:** The staff of the Kansas History Center in Topeka. **Kentucky:** Joe Williams of Radcliff for information relating to his ancestor Peter Williams, ex-slave from Savannah, Tennessee, and Fort Pillow survivor from the 6th USCHA; Shelia E. Heflin of the Daviess County Public Library for editions of the *Owensboro Monitor;* Ray Parrish of Scottsville. **Louisiana:** April Ayto of the Hill Memorial Library of Louisiana State University for the papers of Aaron Charter Harper, John Forman, George Baylor, and Samuel Wragg. **Massachusetts:** My old friend Mario Valdez for reviewing the coverage of Fort Pillow in the African American press. **Michigan:** Evelyn Leasher, public services librarian, Clarke Historical Library, Central Michigan University, for John Ryan's "Reminiscences"; the staff of Carolyn E. Hart, curatorial assistant at the William Clements Library; the staff of the Michigan Historical Collections of the Bentley Historical Library at the University of Michigan at Ann Arbor. **Mississippi:** The staff of the Archives and Library Division of the Mississippi Department of Archives and History at Jackson; Andrew Gladman of the J. D. Williams Library at the University of Mississippi for the papers of Lionel Baxter, and the Dean and Juanita Brown collections; George and Patricia Weeks for their research on the postwar career of James Chalmers; Bobs M. Tusa of the McCain Library and Archives of the University of Southern Mississippi for the letters of W. L. Chatham and Captain John P. Worthing; Margaret Hardee Roseborough for her assistance in locating the original diary of Dewitt Clinton Fort; Jeff Giambrone of Bolton for his book on the 38th Mississippi Cavalry. **Missouri:** C. W. and Betty Browning for their assistance in tracing the lives of the McCulloch family; George and Linda McCollum of Sedalia for their assistance in contacting the descendants of the fighting McCulloch cousins; C. W. Browning and his wife, Betty McCulloch, the colonel's distant cousin, for providing me with biographical material about the two Bobs; Muriel Brewer of the Cooper County Historical Society; Gerald Early, Merle Kling Professor of Modern Letters and director of the African and Afro-American Studies Program at Washington University in St. Louis; Dr. Glen E. Holt, executive director of the St. Louis Public Library; James Joplin of Springfield; Terrell Dempsey of Hannibal; the staff of the G-3 Curtis Laws Wilson Library at the University of Missouri at Rolla; Dr. John A. Wright of University City; Roger Baker of Cole County, Missouri, for his assistance researching the 2nd Missouri Cavalry; Tom Pearson of the St. Louis Public Library for various issues of Missouri publications relating to Fort Pillow and the 2nd Missouri Cavalry, including the *Pioneer Times,* the *Prairie Gleaner,* and several St. Louis newspapers. **Nevada:** Stan Armstrong for sharing with me his documentary on Fort Pillow. **New Jersey:** Richard L. Fuchs, Esquire, the author of *Unerring Fire* (1994), the first serious twentieth-century book on the Fort Pillow massacre. **New York:** My brother, the historian Geoffrey C. Ward, for many commiserations and much sound advice; Richard Snow, editor of *American Heritage;* the Chatauqua County Historical Society in Westfield, **North Carolina:** Janie C. Morris of Duke University for the letters of General Mosby Monroe Parsons, Hubert Saunders, and William Wylie. **Ohio:** The staff of the Jerome Library at Bowling Green State University; the staff of the Oberlin College Archives. **Oklahoma:** Peggy Truesdell of Tulsa for the memoir of William L. Ridgeway of the 20th Tennessee Cavalry (CSA). **Pennsylvania:** The U.S. Army Military History Institute for the letters of Jonas D. Elliott and John P. Brownlow. **Tennessee:** Special thanks to my cousin Marilyn Tomlinson and her sons Jon and Andrew for their generosity and hospitality during my weeks researching the Fort Pillow story in Memphis and Nashville. Thanks also to my excellent researchers Jim Havron (Nashville) and Debra Burrell (Memphis); Bonnie Brooks of the Benton County Education Association; Earl Willoughby for his advice and for sharing his excellent articles on the Civil War history of West Tennessee; Ed

Frank of the Mississippi Wilderness Collection at Memphis State University for his assistance and sound advice; Jennifer Goforth of the Fort Pillow State Park Interpretive Center; Edward F. Williams III of Memphis; Jere Cox at the Gordon Browning Museum of the Carroll County Historical Society for the letters of Captain John A. Crutchfield and miscellaneous documents and articles relating to the Civil War in West Tennessee; the staff of the Memphis and Shelby County Room of the Memphis and Shelby County Public Library for miscellaneous clippings regarding Nathan Bedford Forrest and Fort Pillow, especially articles from the *Memphis Commercial Appeal* and *Memphis Bulletin;* genealogist Arthur L. Webb of Memphis; Virginia Morton for directing me to the journal of Dewitt Clinton Fort; Marilyn Tillman and the staff of the Lauderdale County Library; the staff of the Lauderdale County courthouse; the staff of the Fort Pillow State Historic Park; Ralph Babin of La Place for information about the Bowles men who served under Forrest; Mayor Russell Bailey of Covington; Rebel C. Forrester, Obion County historian in Union City; Natalie Huntley of the Dyer County Historical Society; Charles Yates of Gibson County; Rick Tuck; Milton Webb; Dr. Calvin Dickinson and the staff of the Putnam County Main Library at Cookeville; the staff of the McIver's Grant Public Library in Dyersburg; the staff of the Giles County Historical Society in Pulaski; Dr. James Jones of the Tennessee Historical Commission in Nashville; Ken Feith of the Nashville Metropolitan Archives of Nashville and Davidson County; R. M. Price of the 20th Tennessee Cavalry Web page; Richard Saunders, curator of Special Collections, Paul Meek Library, University of Tennessee at Martin; the staff of the Special Collections at the Jean and Alexander Heard Library at Vanderbilt University in Nashville; Benny Smith; Gary Overall for permission to quote from his ancestor Isaac Overall's letters; Marie Kleeberg for information about the 8th Tennessee Cavalry. **Texas:** Peggy Fox, director, Research Center, the Harold B. Simpson Hill College History Complex of Hillsboro, Texas, for A. J. Grantham's reminiscences; Laura Garcia, supervisor, Local History Department, Corpus Christi Public Library; Julie Holcomb, archivist at the Navarro College Library and Learning Resource Center at Navarro College for letters by Nathan Bedford Forrest defending his actions at Fort Pillow; Peggy Scott Holley for sharing with me her research into the treatment of Tennessee Unionists in Confederate prisons; Troy Groves for his marvelous Web site devoted to Terry's Texas Rangers, aka the 8th Texas Cavalry; Dr. B. D. Patterson of Hillsboro; Gary P. Whitfield of Fort Worth. **Virginia:** Thomas P. and Beth Lowry of the Index Project Inc., a wonderful service that provides an index for the general court-martial records at the National Archives and enabled me to examine records of courts-martial at Fort Pillow. **Washington:** John Thorne and Gordon Lingley for their faithful transcriptions of the voluminous materials I brought back from my researches; Jacqueline E. A. Lawson of the Black Genealogy Group of Seattle for her researches on my behalf; Quintard Taylor, the Bullitt Professor of History at the University of Washington, for his friendship, sage advice, and helpful introductions; Jeff Coopersmith for his insights and for sharing his collection with me; the naval historian John W. Hinds for his many kindnesses in sharing the records of Andersonville prisoners from the Fort Pillow garrison, including the pension records of Thomas W. McLure, and for reviewing portions of my manuscript.

I also want to thank my vigilant and loyal friend and agent Ellen Levine for all her encouragement and support, and my long-suffering friend and editor Kathryn Court, president of Penguin Books, for her help in cutting this book down to something approaching reasonable size. Finally, my love and thanks to my wife, Debbie, who kept me more or less sane through four years of highs and lows.

RIVER RUN RED

PROLOGUE
FORT PILLOW

Dawn, April 12, 1864

BEFORE SUNRISE ON TUESDAY, APRIL 12, 1864, THE UNION GARRISON at Fort Pillow was beginning to stir. Its zigzag parapet fort occupied a West Tennessee bluff forty miles north of Memphis—eighty if you followed the Mississippi's meander—where a small, swift stream called Coal Creek emptied into the great river. The bluff itself stood some eighty feet above the Mississippi's springtime flow. A welcome if fleeting relief from the monotonous flats upriver, its face was striped with undulant veins of loess, gravel, and orange sand perforated, in turn, by rifle pits and trenches.

A relic of the Confederacy's initial burst of overconfidence, Fort Pillow had been designed by rebel engineers, built by large teams of requisitioned slaves, and named after the preening and incompetent General Gideon Pillow. Abandoned by the rebels the previous spring after a grueling and prolonged gunboat siege, it was to forts what Pillow himself was to generals: extraneous and indefensibly grandiose.

If "fort" was supposed to conjure up vaunting watchtowers and imposing battlements bristling with guns, then this was something else: a camp, a fortified town, a station, a river port, a trading post, or some doubtful combination. Whatever it was, once the Union river fleet neutralized the rebel rams and gunboats that had once steamed freely up and down the Mississippi, Fort Pillow was deemed so useless and vulnerable that General William Tecumseh Sherman had ordered it abandoned. But the Union commander at Memphis, the crapulous and corrupt General Stephen Augustus Hurlbut, had ignored his old friend's order and not only permitted William Bradford's 13th Tennessee Cavalry—some two hundred Tennessee recruits—to employ it as a recruiting station, but then, at the end of March, added about three hundred black artillerists to the garrison, under the command of Major Lionel F. Booth.

From Fort Pillow's long, denuded bluff, Booth's newly trained gunners halfheartedly scanned the river for rebel boats. But behind the bluff, on the outskirts of a broad abatis—a tangled defensive zone of felled trees with sharpened limbs—white cavalry pickets kept a more anxious vigil, for the fort was far more vulnerable from the land side than from the river. Rainwater ran in rivulets along the bare flanks of the bluff this morning, pooling in the old rebel trenches and filling the craters from Yankee shelling two years past. A few black artillerists and white Unionist cavalrymen ducked around the post in oilcloth coats and limp hats with dripping brims. The earliest risers stood or sat in their cabin doorways or squatted just under the flaps of their Sibley tents smoking pipes, spitting tobacco, sipping diluted drafts of last week's coffee, oiling their carbines against rust, currying their horses, stoking their greenwood fires to keep the buffalo gnats at bay.

Perhaps thirty of Bradford's men picketed here and there east of the fort, along its outermost horseshoe boundary, huddled against the rain under makeshift tents and shelters, and anxiously awaited a dawn that seemed long in coming. Over the past few days, rumors had flown from barrack to tent to picket post that a vast rebel cavalry force was approaching under the brilliant and audacious command of General Nathan Bedford Forrest himself— Tennessee's own natural-born dog of war and the conflict's most formidable and successful cavalry commander, North or South, East or West—come to chastise white turncoats and disloyal slaves for taking up arms against their kith and kin, and masters.

Rumors of Forrest's approach had been roiling around camp ever since he had launched the second of his raids into West Tennessee in January and headquartered himself at Jackson, not fifty miles east of Fort Pillow. The garrison's officers had tried to reassure their men that the fort was impregnable; that the supposedly insuperable Forrest had recently met with disaster upriver at Paducah, Kentucky; that the humiliation of that defeat had taken the starch out of his men; that instead of attacking any more Union posts, Forrest would soon be hightailing it back to Mississippi to lick his wounds.

Local people, however, whispered that far from withdrawing in defeat, Forrest was preparing to cap his raid up the Mississippi with a victory that would teach Fort Pillow's "homegrown Yankees" and their "niggers" an everlasting lesson. About a dozen of Bradford's troopers had fled the night before, part of a white tide of desertions that had afflicted the garrison since it occupied Fort Pillow. In fact, this very morning, others were preparing to follow suit.

Bradford had stationed his lookouts at the edge of the abatis, almost a mile from camp. Their vigilance had flagged—another night had passed without a hint of trouble—and so for these last few minutes of their stint, they played cards and drank coffee under improvised tents and lean-to shelters, looking forward to riding back, returning to their barracks, and drying off.

As dawn approached, the rain began to flee before a strong river wind. But the sky would remain overcast all day. Even if the pickets had been listening closely, the rustle and tread of an advancing foe would have been lost in the wind that blustered through the popple woods, the constant patter of rainwater dripping and spraying from the feathery spring foliage overhead, and the gurgling from the rivulets that ran down the sloping abatis behind them.

By some pocket watches it was 5:30 in the morning, at the very crack of dawn, when someone suddenly called out from the edge of the woods. For a moment Bradford's boys merely gaped into the darkness, catching perhaps a shadow here, a glint of metal there.

Then a row of carbines opened fire.

Two pickets fell dead and several more fell wounded, while the rest scrambled onto their horses and galloped toward the fort, blindly firing their pistols behind them and shouting, "The rebs are coming! The rebs are coming!"

The rebs were indeed coming, and what was about to follow would be a suppuration, an eruption of all the toxins that had been festering throughout the Western theater since the war began: bigotry, anarchy, brutality, corruption, incompetence, feuds, and betrayals. A collision of Southerners—white and black—was about to provide the American Civil War with its most notorious atrocity.

"THIS UNNATURAL WAR"

WEST TENNESSEE

1682–1864

THE MORNING FORT PILLOW WAS ATTACKED MARKED THE THIRD AN-niversary of the first firing on Fort Sumter and the onset of the Civil War. There were no celebrations. It seemed to both sides that the war would never end. In the East, the conflict was at a stalemate. Though the South crackled with the sporadic gunfire of guerrillas and skirmishers, the two great armies had not collided since the previous fall. Lee had summoned Longstreet's corps back from the West, where it had been detached since Chickamauga. Grant was preparing his army for an enormous coordinated campaign to corral all the armies of the Confederacy: George Meade to pursue Lee wherever he went, Sherman to confront Joe Johnston in Georgia, Benjamin Butler to move on the Confederate capital at Richmond, Franz Sigel to scour the Shenandoah Valley.

Northerners struggled to puzzle out the purpose and meaning of the war upon which they had embarked so confidently thirty-six months before. Neither regional odium nor objections to high-handed Federal mandates could account any longer for the nation's bloody bifurcation or the South's phenomenal obstinacy. Throughout the young nation's history North and South had struggled over the nature of their Union, raising questions that, as Robert Selph Henry would write, "had gone unanswered through more than one crisis," including the controversy over the propriety of the Louisiana Purchase; "and, again, when the right of state nullification was asserted in opposition to the application of tariff laws; and then, only fifteen years before the Civil War itself, when the right to dissolve the Union was proclaimed by those who objected to the annexation of Texas." But the nation had weathered these crises without warfare, "for the issues which arose did not have behind them the forty years of crimination and recrimination over the question of African slavery." The rebels believed that the North was out to subjugate them by destroying slavery. And yet most of the white Southern and Northern rank and file hotly maintained that they were not fighting to defend or destroy slavery, but to stand up against tyranny on the one side and preserve the Union on the other.[1]

As the Northern army penetrated the slaveholding states, however, and recruited escaped slaves first as laborers and then as soldiers, it was harder and harder for either side to cling to such abstractions. Yankees looting the slave quarters of an abandoned plantation and even nonslaveholding rebels ducking artillery fire from a black Union battery began to see that, for better or worse, the core of the conflict was the destiny of the Southern slave, the runaway, and the armed black soldier. No matter how the war might end, not only the South but the entire country would be forever changed.

Any civilian who judged the cause of the war solely on the basis of political rhetoric might never have guessed at slavery's centrality. Hoping he might yet bring the fastidious British to the Confederacy's aid, an increasingly isolated and desperate President Jefferson Davis kept explicit references to slavery out of most of his speeches, couching the Southern cause as a struggle for liberty, identity, chivalry, destiny.

For much of the war Lincoln too had tried to keep the question of slavery at arm's length. It had been divisive enough in peacetime; in war it threatened to destroy all the political alliances he had carefully crafted to restore the Union, without which, after all, there could be no hope of emancipation. Determined to keep the slaveholding Border States out of the Confederacy's thrall, Lincoln had equivocated about the destiny of African Americans, and embraced for a time the old Southern white moderates' myopic notion of sending them all abroad. "I am naturally anti-slavery," Lincoln had lately written. "If slavery is not wrong, nothing is wrong." Nevertheless, he had "never understood that the Presidency conferred upon me an unrestricted right to act officially upon this judgment and feeling."[2]

The only way to defeat the South, Lincoln had decided, was to overwhelm its armies with massively superior numbers. But enlistments were lagging, and after his imposition of the draft triggered horrendous race riots in Chicago and New York, Lincoln reluctantly adopted a course he had long regarded as too risky: to recruit and train escaped slaves to serve in the Union army. It was a matter of military necessity, especially in the West, from which Sherman was siphoning off regiment after regiment of veteran white troops for his Meridian campaign, dangerously thinning out the garrisons along the Mississippi. And if enlisting them was a matter of military necessity, so was offering freedom to any black who volunteered. Tens of thousands of Southern blacks filed up to be inducted—some volunteering, some lured by recruiters with false promises of high pay and lavish rations, others rounded up by Yankee press gangs and the commandants of the Union camps to which they had fled from bondage.

When Lincoln celebrated New Year's, 1863, by issuing his Emancipation Proclamation, he freed only those slaves in Confederate territory, ostensibly leaving the slaves in Union-occupied or neutral states in bondage. South-erners scoffed that the proclamation was meaningless, for it could not free slaves under Confederate control and declined to free slaves under Yankee control. "Abraham Lincoln, the wily wretch," rhymed a Mississippi wag, "Freed the slaves he couldn't catch." But wiser heads North and South rec-ognized that despite its limitations, Lincoln's proclamation had created a fis-sure that could never be repaired. For all Americans, the earth was shifting underfoot.[3]

With western Kentucky above and the state of Mississippi brooding below, West Tennessee is bounded on two sides by great rivers. The broad Missis-sippi snakes along its western edge, while the Tennessee veers down through Kentucky to form the region's eastern boundary. Five capillary and nearly equidistant rivers bristle eastward from the Mississippi into West Tennessee. The Reelfoot is northernmost, then the Obion, the Forked Deer, the Hatchie, and finally the southernmost Wolf, with streams and creeks spreading from each of their trunks like the branches of fallen trees. The re-gion is divided into three fairly distinct parts. In the east, along the Ten-nessee River, the land ripples and buckles into hills and ridges bristling with pines; the midlands are marked by a verdant plateau; and the western por-tion comprises the overawing Mississippi's banks and bottoms.

Along the Mississippi's bluffs, prehistoric tribes had hunted and fished, piled their funerary mounds, and then mysteriously disappeared. Then the Chickasaw of Mexico, following the lean of a sacred pole, found their way to the lower Mississippi, where their pole held fast in the valley's yielding al-luvial loam. For centuries they camped along the bluffs in dwellings of wat-tle and daub; fished in the great river and its tributaries; exchanged volleys of arrows and stones with the rival tribes that occasionally paddled up and down the river; and hunted elk and bear, deer and beaver in poplar forests carpeted by lilies, orchids, and rye, and entangled in a twisting calligraphy of hickory.

On a chill February day in 1682, the indefatigable René-Robert Cavelier

La Salle had paused on his exploratory voyage down the Mississippi to raise a cross and erect a crude fort atop a promontory on the eastern bank that became known as the First Chickasaw Bluff. Over the next century and a half, the lower Mississippi Valley ostensibly passed from the French to the Spanish, back to the French, and at last to the fledgling American Republic as part of the Louisiana Purchase.

In 1798, a North Carolinian named Henry Rutherford and two black chain bearers had made their way to present-day West Tennessee to mark off large tracts of land for his investors. After Thomas Jefferson announced his Louisiana Purchase, Rutherford dusted off his deeds in the Hillsborough courthouse and counted the days until he and his friends could lay claim to their land.

The lower valley was regularly inundated by floods of Old Testament proportions, reconfiguring its topography so dramatically that portions of it were unrecognizable from year to year. Nor was that all. In the winter of 1811–1812, the Lower Mississippi Valley was rocked by earthquakes and aftershocks of such magnitude that the river actually flowed backward for a time, razing the forests of poplar and chestnut along its banks. Here and there the earth collapsed under the flood's weight, dotting the land with lakes that survive to this day.

When, in the late spring of 1812, the floodwaters receded from West Tennessee, they revealed some eighty thousand acres of rich bottomland conveniently scoured of trees and underbrush and covered by a thick, rich layer of alluvial soil. The flood so devastated the Chickasaw that they could resist the whites no longer. Three years later they were ready to sign a treaty with Andrew Jackson and his real estate crony Isaac Shelby, clearing the way for North Carolinians like Henry Rutherford to immigrate. What followed was one of the most squalid landgrabs in the squalid annals of American real estate speculation.

Not only the Chickasaw were shoved aside, but the common North Carolinians as well. When the state offered the land for sale, it required that anyone who wanted title had to travel to West Tennessee first, survey his claim, and then register it in person back in Hillsborough. But the law also called for the closing of the land office seven months later, making it impossible for anyone but insiders who were already in place to purchase parcels. Within those seven months, four million acres were sold, much of it to big speculators.[4]

In 1832, Rutherford arrived with his slaves from middle Tennessee in a small flotilla of keel boats and laid claim to five hundred acres of the land he had surveyed thirty-four years before. Others followed, forming a settlement they called Fulton a couple of miles south of the First Chickasaw Bluff. By now deer, wolves, bears, and panthers had returned, and slaves had to cut down the high cane and second growth that had reclaimed the scoured bottoms from quake and flood. They floated their logs to the tub water mills that soon popped up by every creek and stream. Toiling alongside their African bondsmen, pioneers of predominantly Scotch-Irish descent raised sheep; cultivated honey; and planted fruit trees, corn, wheat, tobacco, and cotton so dense and fine that it would soon become famed the world over.[5]

In Tennessee, the seeds of secessionism, like slavery, were river-borne, taking most stubborn root among the slaveholding plantations along the Mississippi. The concentration of Tennessee slaves decreased not the farther north one went, but the farther east. In East Tennessee the ratio of slaves to whites was only one in twelve, in Central Tennessee one in three. But in West Tennessee the proportion rose to three to every five whites. Over a thousand plantations boasted more than five hundred acres, and about thirty-seven thousand slaveholders controlled the destinies of almost 276,000 slaves. But even within West Tennessee, there were considerable differences from county to county. The richest cotton-growing counties were in the low-lying southwestern quadrant, where vast plantations run by overseers and worked by slaves produced some of the finest cotton in the world. But in hill counties like McNairy, the ratio of slaves to whites fell to only one in ten.

In 1836, a county at the center of the Tennessee bank of the Mississippi River was assembled from contiguous chunks of Tipton, Dyer, and Haywood counties and named after Colonel James Lauderdale, a colonel who had fallen by Jackson's side at the Battle of New Orleans. Until it was bypassed by the railroad, Lauderdale County's principal settlement at Fulton had hoped to give Memphis a run for her money. But Fulton got off to a rough start. The town was cyclically beset by epidemics of what was probably yellow fever, and the approach to the landing was so treacherous that boatmen dubbed a nearby bar "Flour Island" after all the flour boats that had been wrecked upon it.[6]

As Fulton faltered, the rowdy inland settlement of Ripley became the Lauderdale County seat. With a population of about four thousand, Lauderdale formed a militia that mustered twice a year, and sent a company of men to the Mexican War, half of whom never returned. Unless you counted the occasional passing navy boat with its Stars and Stripes fluttering in the river breeze, or the grizzled old vets of the War of 1812 who sat on their porches, surveying their land grants and telling their tales of Jackson at New Orleans, there was not much of a military presence in the county. But the boys of West Tennessee breathed an atmosphere of guns and horses and Bowie knives that would soon make warriors of them all.[7]

The future Fort Pillow would encompass much of the property of one A. G. Bragg of St. Louis, whose holdings extended over some 2,500 acres. But in 1858, a portion of the site was bought by the unlikeliest of the county's émigres: a Vermont native and New York lawyer named Edward B. Benton, who "through indomitable energy and unceasing labor" established a trading post on the First Chickasaw Bluff and lured "a number of settlers to locate with a view of building up a town."[8]

His tract was bounded by two minor contributors to the Mississippi's flood: the Hatchie River (*hatchy* being the Chickasaw word for river) and a creek sometimes misnamed Cole or Cold Creek, but originally dubbed Coal Creek because of the veins of coarse black gold that ran along its defile. The Mississippi and the Hatchie joined about three miles east of Benton's farm, creating, with Coal Creek, a veritable peninsula.[9]

Though the Mississippi threatened to lop away a few more yards of his property every year, Benton had the giddy faith and rigor of a transplanted urbanite, and continued to establish a barrel factory on his 215-acre share of the bluff. In 1860 he sailed to Europe "for the purpose of making contracts for the delivery of oak staves," but when war broke out and Tennessee seceded, he returned to the States, shelved his barrel-making plans, and holed up in Albany, New York, to wait for the Union army to sweep the rebels off his land.

Tennessee was the last state to join the Confederacy. In fact, it had voted against secession when the matter was first put up to a vote. But the subsequent fall of Fort Sumter and Lincoln's call for volunteers had now turned most of the county's whites against the Union. The secessionist movement in Tennessee owed a lot of its ardor to the machinations of its voluble, partisan governor, Isham Harris. For this second referendum on secession, Harris was taking no chances. He required that the balloting be conducted by voice vote and under the intimidating eye of his own enforcers, or "Homeguards," as he called them: gangs of secessionist vigilantes who had gleefully raided Unionist assemblies at His Excellency's behest, brandishing guns, torches, ropes, and whips, and chasing hundreds of Northern sympathizers into neutral Kentucky and Unionist Illinois.[10]

On a hot June day in 1861, the free white men of Tennessee converged on their county courthouses to vote on secession for a second time as the governor's sullen henchmen lounged around the steps. A lot of Union men stayed home. But not fifty-year-old Fielding Hurst. One of the biggest slave-holders in the county, Hurst lived in the grandest house; served as worship-ful master of the local Masonic lodge; and, with his brothers, ruled an estate so vast—sixty square miles traversing the Tennessee River—that it was lo-cally known as "Hurst Nation." But unlike the majority of his class, Hurst opposed secession. "One country, one language, one flag" was his credo.

Tall, wiry, with a prominent jaw and an icy gaze, Hurst was accustomed to having his way. He had not the slightest intention of allowing the gover-nor's ruffians to keep him from the polls. When his turn came to vote, Hurst not only declared himself for the Union but denounced Harris's henchmen to their faces as thugs, thieves, and traitors to the nation for which his an-cestors had bled and died.

This time around, those white males who dared to go to the polls would vote for secession by a large margin. But Harris's henchmen did not wait for the final tally before clapping Fielding Hurst in irons and carting him off to Nashville, where for the next seven months the lord of Hurst Nation would lie shivering in the penitentiary, nursing a lethal grudge.

It is a wonder he was not lynched. Before the war, on the region's north-eastern edge, the good citizens of Henry County nearly strung up West Ten-nessee's leading Unionist, Congressman Emerson Etheridge. Feelings ran so high that later, during the war, when a Confederate soldier revealed to his comrades that he was Etheridge's distant relation, they tried to lynch him as well.

The flames of secession had been fanned most effectively by outside ag-itators from the Deep South who riled up the more hesitant and divided cit-izenry of the Upper South with dire predictions: that Lincoln and his allies intended not just to keep slavery out of the territories but to deprive them of their slaves, force racial equality upon the South, instigate a race war, and encourage miscegenation. As Confederate brigadier general Felix Kirk Zolli-coffer warned, the object of "this unnatural war" was to "set at liberty your slaves," and eventually "to put arms in their hands and give them political and social equality with yourselves." He declared that "the honor of your wives and daughters, your past renown, and the fair name of your posterity forbid that you should strike for Lincoln and the abolition of slavery against those struggling for the rights and independence of your kindred race."[11]

In the bustling capital city of Nashville, in the center of the state of Tennessee, a larger-than-life-size bronze effigy of Andrew Jackson sat atop his rearing horse on a stone pedestal that proclaimed in deeply chiseled capitals, OUR FEDERAL UNION: IT MUST BE PRESERVED. Old Hickory was Tennessee's special pride and joy, and his legacy had encouraged Tennessee's beleaguered moderates in their hope that their state might at least remain neutral and serve as an agency of sanity and peace. But all they accomplished was to delay the inevitable. The secessionists' warnings of slavery's abolition and the equality of the black man painted Southern moderates as sentimental naïfs or, far worse, traitors to their race.

On the day Fielding Hurst was clapped in irons, West and Central Tennesseeans voted to secede from the Union in such numbers that they overwhelmed the Unionists to their east. Within a few months, a hammer-wielding secessionist would desecrate Andrew Jackson's statue by chipping FEDERAL and UNION from its pedestal.[12]

BEDFORD
NATHAN BEDFORD FORREST
1821–1864

TENNESSEE WOULD EARN THE DISTINCTION OF BECOMING NOT ONLY the last state to leave the Union but in effect the first to rejoin it, thanks to an unlikely and as yet unsung brigadier general named Ulysses S. Grant, who, with a fleet of Union gunboats and a force of fifteen thousand troops, laid siege to the Confederate strongholds of Fort Henry and Fort Donelson that commanded the Cumberland and Tennessee rivers.

It is an irony of American history that the same battle that would arguably spell the Confederacy's doom also saw the emergence of perhaps its most extraordinary warrior. At the time, Nathan Bedford Forrest was an untutored and, for the most part, untested forty-year-old lieutenant colonel of cavalry who, as a bootstrap frontier entrepreneur, Memphis alderman, compulsive gambler, and hugely successful slave trader, was earning a reputation for pugnacity and ingenuity.

"With his powerful frame, high cheek-bones, light gray eyes, and straight black hair," recalled a Virginian who served under him, Forrest "was in physical powers superior to all men." To another admirer, Forrest "appeared an apparition, the most inspiring personage my eyes had ever beheld." Forrest rarely sat in his saddle, but preferred to stand in his stirrups, accentuating his six-foot frame. His countenance could be dour and forbidding in repose, and at his gloomiest he reminded some of his older recruits of Andrew Jackson. Unlike Old Hickory, however, Forrest had a dazzling smile set off by a fine set of pearly whites that he never fouled with tobacco and was always picking clean with a pen knife.[1]

He and his ferocious brothers had joined as privates, but within weeks

his old pal and poker buddy Governor Isham Harris arranged that he be promoted to lieutenant colonel and commissioned to raise his own cavalry. Forrest soon rewarded Harris with intimations of his future brilliance. In one
episode he deterred a large force of Union home guards from pursuing him
by arraying his fresh and poorly armed recruits and their visiting relatives
along a railroad track at dusk so that the passengers on a passing train would
report back to the Union command that a vast Confederate force awaited
them. Outside Sacramento, Kentucky, in his first significant engagement,
Forrest and his men bluffed and bullied a superior Yankee force into beating
a headlong retreat.

There were disturbing portents, too, however. At Sacramento, Forrest
and his men pursued their panicked foe in a "promiscuous sabre slaughter
of their rear," as his gleeful dispatch described it, leaving "their bleeding and
wounded strewn along the whole route." Even his admirers were alarmed by
what came over Bedford in battle: a glandular or cardiovascular surge that
caused him visibly to darken and swell, like a serpent mustering its poisons.
His back straightened, his eyes blazed, and his face became "the colour of
heated bronze." "Ordinarily his manner was mild, his speech rather low and
slow," recalled one of his men, "but let him once be aroused and the whole
man changed; his wrath was terrible, and few, if any, dared to brave it." Racing after him as he charged into every fray, even his most loyal subordinates
worried that Forrest would prove injudicious and short-lived. But he learned
quickly, devised his own shrewd brand of backwoods tactics, and in any case
led an apparently charmed life.[2]

In February 1861, Lieutenant Colonel Forrest arrived at Fort Donelson leading a battalion of eight cavalry companies. About half of his troopers hailed
from Tennessee, the rest from Kentucky, Alabama, Texas, Mississippi, and
Arkansas. After his little triumph at Sacramento, his men already wor-
shipped at Forrest's altar, but it was at Fort Donelson that he would prove
himself worthier of command than any of his genteel superiors.[3]

Grant's gunboats and overwhelming force made Union victory inevitable, but Confederate brigadier general John Buchanan Floyd's dither-
ing was costing the Confederacy's vaunted western army its only means of
escape. Trying to navigate a middle path between the remonstrances of Simon Bolivar Buckner and the hollow bravado of Gideon Pillow, Floyd had
managed to squander the momentum of field commanders like Forrest,
whose cavalry had battered and scattered the Federals with repeated hell-

for-leather charges that at the very least should have opened the way for a rebel escape to Clarksville.[4]

For most of the garrison, however, it would prove to be a road not taken. In their low-comedic councils of war, the Confederates' jealousy of generals achieved first stasis and then a sequence of reverses. By the evening of February 16, the garrison was besieged by not only Grant and his Yankees but a whirling blizzard. Suspected of smuggling Federal matériel to his secessionist friends as Buchanan's secretary of war, Floyd was convinced that if he fell into Union hands he would be hanged for treason. So after he and his fellow generals decided they had no choice but to surrender the garrison, Floyd handed his command over to Pillow and prepared to escape by steamboat, whereupon Pillow pronounced himself so essential to the Confederate cause that he passed the buck to his old nemesis Buckner and arranged to flee in a purloined scow.[5]

Disgusted, appalled, Forrest declared that he had not joined the army to surrender, and demanded the right to lead his boys through the Federal lines to Nashville. Convinced that mere human beings could not survive such a journey through the swirling snow, traversing as it would a road submerged by the frigid overflow of the Cumberland River, the generals tried to talk him out of it. But Forrest would not be denied.

J. R. Miles of the 20th Tennessee Cavalry recalled that Forrest "got as many of the boys together as he could with[out] creating any excitement" and told them "he hadent surrendered and that if he had been in authority he would not surrender the fort." He told his men that he was "going away that night and as many as was willing to follow him he would carrey them away from there. All that was willing saddled up and fell in line. He sent too pickets ahead to give them instructions," Miles continued. "They was gone a short while, come dashing back, said, 'General Forrest, we are surrounded by [a] solid line of Yanks with fixed beyonets, so it is imposable to get away.'"

Trusting only what he could see with his own eyes, Forrest rode off and established that the bayonets were wooden fence pickets gleaming with ice, however, and as Floyd and Pillow made their ignominious getaways, the Wizard escorted three hundred of his own men, a company of artillery horses, and a defiant miscellany of infantry—some five hundred men all told—through the howling blizzard and Cumberland brash and onto the road to Nashville, without drawing a single shot or losing a single man. By the next morning, when the rest of the garrison had surrendered to the Yankees, Forrest and his men "were thirty mile away."[6]

Convinced that had it not been for the pusillanimity of Floyd, Pillow, and Buckner, "two-thirds of our army could have marched out without loss," Forrest led his "badly broken-up" but nonetheless undaunted contingent down to Nashville.[7]

Donelson's fall was a bitter blow to the Confederacy, costing it the control not only of its Tennessee and Cumberland lifelines but most of Kentucky and middle Tennessee. Now the rebels would have to rely more and more on their uneven, unreliable, and easily disrupted railways. The bitterest blow, however, fell upon Fort Donelson's rank and file, some of whom became so disillusioned with the Confederacy that they would end up fighting at Fort Pillow on the Union side.[8]

As the Yankees transported their captives north, Captain Robert I. Hill and his 23rd Mississippi Infantry expected the people of Illinois to "be very much enraged against us" for killing 1,800 of their boys. "But such was not the case. In fact the troops of Illinois seem to be proud of the terrible battle that we gave them." The Yankees seemed "to be very honorable and friendly, mixing with our men and talking over the incidents of the battle with great glee." They seemed to direct "no personal enmity at us."[9]

This combination of betrayal by incompetent commanders and decent treatment at the hands of their foes would utterly demoralize a great many Tennesseans as they marched under guard through the streets of Chicago and climbed aboard a train to the Federal prison at Johnson's Island in Ohio. Eventually scores of them would beg Andrew Johnson to allow them to take the Oath of Allegiance and go home to their farms and families. Among the signers were members of the 42nd and 47th Tennessee Infantry who would one day don Union uniforms at Fort Pillow and take up arms against the one man who might have led them to safety.[10]

To explain Nathan Bedford Forrest, a psychologist might go back to his frontier upbringing, his parents' deafness to his infant cries, or the regular whippings his ferocious and enormous mother, Mariam, used to administer. But he was not the only frontier baby to be so neglected, and whipping children was the order of the day. Perhaps he was driven to extremes by the death of his infant twin. But psychology seems a puny, mewling endeavor when it tiptoes up to Nathan Bedford Forrest.[11]

He was born in 1821 to a landless pioneer in Bedford County, Ten-

nessee, about fifty miles southeast of Nashville. Though some said the Forrests were decent, high-minded folk, others recalled that the women of the
family "chewed tobacco, went to the horse races, and spit as big as a man."
When Forrest was twelve years old, his family moved to "rough, hopeless,
God-forsaken" Tippah County, Mississippi, where four years later his father
died, leaving his oldest son to manage their farm: clearing trees, cultivating
crops, trading livestock, sewing buckskin leggings for his brothers.[12]

Even as a boy, Forrest always made good on his threats. After a couple
of warnings, he shot down a neighbor's chronically wayward ox, and at least
shot at its armed and indignant owner. Determined never to make a fool of
himself in public, Forrest gave liquor a single try while sitting alone in the
woods. After a few swigs he passed out and awoke feverish with pneumonia.
He promised his Maker that if he survived he would never touch the stuff
again, and apparently he never did; once, brandishing garden shears, Forrest
menaced some local gawks who jokingly tried to force liquor on him.

As soon as he could entrust his family's care to his younger brothers,
Forrest went into business with his uncle Jonathan in Hernando, Mississippi.
Together they opened a brickyard to supply the farmers and planters as they
moved from cabins into houses, and from houses into mansions. Forrest had
a genius for numbers that he would put to use in business, at cards, and on
the battlefield. He was wary and frugal, and his severe economies extended
even to his spelling. He would not waste his ink on silent letters nor write
double consonants where he reckoned one would suffice.[13]

His uncle proved a feckless business partner, and in early 1845, Forrest
had to protect him from an exasperated creditor named Matlock who had
ridden into town with his two sons and an overseer to recover what was
owed him. One of the junior Matlocks fired his gun, missing Forrest but
striking his hapless uncle, who toppled to the ground in a heap. All four then
turned on Forrest, but he felled two of them with his pocket pistol while the
other two merely singed him with their shots, whereupon an onlooker
tossed Forrest a Bowie knife with which he now charged the last Matlock,
disabling him with a few contemptuous slashes as the overseer prudently
shinned it down the street. Recognizing an enforcer when it saw one, the
town appointed Forrest to serve as Hernando's coroner, peacemaker, and
slave catcher.

His appointment could not have been made without the approval of
one of the county's leading planters: former U.S. senator Joseph Williams
Chalmers, the father of James Ronald Chalmers, the general Forrest would
deploy as field commander of the assault on Fort Pillow.[14] The impressive
young Nathan Bedford Forrest had already come to the senator's attention.

"In February, 1841," wrote James, "when I was but ten years of age, I re-member well a small company of volunteers who marched out of the town of Holly Springs, Mississippi, for the relief of Texas, then threatened by in-vasion from Mexico. In that little band stood Bedford Forrest, a tall, black-haired, gray-eyed, athletic youth, scarce twenty years of age, who then gave the first evidence of the military ardor he possessed." Forrest may have ac-companied the expedition to locate his younger brother John, who had been gravely wounded and semiparalyzed by a Mexican sniper. But by the time he got to Texas the fighting was over, and Forrest had to work his way home splitting rails for ranchers.[15]

It may have been during his constabulary rounds through De Soto County, chasing thieves and runaway slaves, that Forrest acquired the am-bition of obtaining a plantation for himself. Certainly the Chalmers planta-tion, with its slaves and manor house, must have inspired him. "In the South of that time," wrote Frank Montgomery of Mississippi, a man's "highest am-bition" was to become a planter and live out his life "surrounded by his slaves." To accomplish this, "the merchant invested his profits, the lawyer his earn-ings, and indeed everybody saved all he could to attain to this ideal life."[16]

In the 1850 census, Bedford Forrest gave his occupation as "none," but he actually had many: liveryman, horse trader, brick maker, lawman. In north-ern Mississippi, however, few joined the planter class by trading horses, sell-ing bricks, or keeping the peace. For men like Bedford Forrest, the straightest route to riches was lined with slaves.

The Forrests were no strangers to slavery. It is believed that before his death, Bedford's own father possessed a slave or two. Forrest's great-grandfather owned a slave, and his mother's people were slaveholders. After marrying Mary Montgomery, the petite and pious daughter of a Methodist minister, Forrest moved into a respectable double log cabin in Hernando, not unlike the house in which, after years of glory, turmoil, and ruin, they would end their days. After several more years of building on his expertise as a slave catcher, his reputation as a constable, and his contacts among north-ern Mississippi's elite, Forrest embarked on a full-time career as a slave speculator by moving to Memphis with his wife and son.[17]

A bustling river port perched on a high bluff over the Mississippi, Mem-phis was no paradise. Soggy and muddy when it was not hot and dusty, be-set by epidemics of cholera and yellow fever, the city was a Darwinian jungle "infested with gamblers at cards and dice." But it was prosperous, and much of the wealth it did not owe to slave-grown cotton it derived directly from the slave trade. With boats arriving daily from Arkansas, Kentucky, and Missouri, and the prospect of a railway terminal connecting the city to much of the rest of the South, Memphis was fast becoming the thriving hub of the Tennessee trade.[18]

A slave named Betty Simmons recalled standing on the riverfront one day and counting 258 slaves filing out of the city's slave pens and boarding a southbound boat. "In 1852, one of the first things that a traveler saw from the lower steamboat landing was a large sign on what had been the Herron House: 'Bolton, Dickins & Co., Slave Dealers.' And on a principal street, nearly opposite each other, were these: 'Byrd Hill, Slave Market' and 'Ben Little, Slave Market And Livery Stable.'" In fact, these represented only three of a dozen Memphis slave dealers, and that does not include the self-described agents, general merchants, and auctioneers who did not openly advertise the dismal source of their principal income.

With branch offices in at least half a dozen Southern cities, Bolton, Dickins & Company was Memphis's leading slave dealer. "Call and make your purchases to gather your crop," the firm urged its customers, "and then call quick again and buy to make another crop. By those means if you will keep up your purchases for ten years there is no telling how much you may be worth. This is the true Road to Wealth, and if you neglect the present offer of becoming wealthy it's your own [fault] and not ours as the Road is laid out plainly."

Forrest saw the road plainly enough. He and his industrious brothers became well known to just about every slaveholder within hundreds of miles of Memphis. The sociologist Frederic Bancroft gave an idea of the trade the Forrest brothers pursued with such alacrity. The typical dealer "watched for bargains at the public and the private jails; he started the bidding at auctions, but dropped out if there was ambitious competition" because he only bought low to sell high.

He often had, and always pretended to have, ample cash, but seemed meanly sparing of it. He was conspicuous and inquisitive in public places and on public occasions—on sale-days and during the session of the county court, at the musterings, the barbecues, the joint debates and even the Fourth of July celebrations, where "liberty," "freedom" and "State sovereignty" were on every tongue—collecting scraps of news or gossip about the fortunes and misfortunes of farmers, planters, professional men and merchants [who] might be induced to buy or compelled to sell. He was intrusive and impertinent privately,

eager to argue that a certain sum of money would be much more useful than the services of some boy or girl, cook or hostler, or that a
"breeder," a carpenter, a blacksmith, a drayman, or a hair-dresser
would surely be a good investment.

"Imagine a compound of an unscrupulous horse-trader," Bancroft concluded, "a familiar old-time tavern-keeper; a superficially complaisant and
artful, hard-drinking gambler; and an ignorant, garrulous, low politician, and
you will get a conception that resembles the Southern antebellum notion of
the 'nigger trader.'" And yet, as Bancroft himself pointed out, the successful
trader maintained good relations with his customers, advertised in city
newspapers and directories, and thanked his "friends and patrons" by name
and in print. How could they be so despised by planters and merchants who
constantly speculated in every after-dinner conversation about the current
market value of their Negroes? The Southerners who most despised slave
traders were not slaveholders but slaves.[19]

Forrest's brother Aaron opened a branch in Jackson, Mississippi, while
his fearsome brother William and his crippled brother John held down the
fort in Memphis, and it was said that it was hard to pass through what were
then the Southwestern states without encountering one or another of the
Forrest boys as they bought up prime, Virginia-bred slaves from the border
states of Kentucky and Missouri to sell to the sugar planters of Louisiana
and the cotton growers of East Texas.[20]

Unbeknownst to Forrest, his slave trading rounds were helping to prepare him for military command, for they taught him how to transport large
bodies of people while maintaining their health and conserving their
strength for some future dispensation. By 1854 he had purchased sixty feet
of frontage along one of Memphis's busiest commercial streets and established a full-fledged slave-trading yard. Within three years he could boast of
"one of the most complete and commodious establishments of the kind in
the Southern country" where "regulations, exact and systematic cleanliness,
neatness and comfort" were "strictly observed and enforced," so that he
might furnish his customers with "no. 1 servants and field hands, sound and
perfect in body and mind."[21]

A former slave named Horatio Eden recalled accompanying his mother
to Forrest's establishment: "a kind of square stockade of high boards" with
about five "two room negro houses" along "three sides of it & [a] high board
fence too high to be scaled on the other side. We were all left in these rooms
but when an auction was held & buyers came we were brought out and pa-

raded two by two around a circular brick work in the center of the stockade,"
Eden remembered. "The buyers would stand near by and inspect us as we
went by, stop by & Examine us & our teeth, & limbs and a doctor generally
if there were sick negros." His mother remembered how they "looked to see
if there were any scars on her body from a whip," which might be evidence
of "a vicious temper or as they [say] a 'bad nigger.' My mother said they always tried to keep us together & sell us together; that some man wanted to
buy her & another wanted me, but the master held us together."

Drawing on the testimony of escaped slaves, a wartime correspondent
for the *New York Tribune* would paint a gruesome picture of Forrest's yard:

> The slave pen of old Bedford Forrest, on Adams street, was a perfect
> horror to all negroes far and near. His mode of punishing refractory
> slaves was to compel four of his fellow slaves to stand and hold the
> victim stretched out in the air, and then Bedford and his brother John
> would stand, one on each side, with long, heavy bull whips, and cut
> up their victims until the blood trickled to the ground. Women were
> often stripped naked, and with a bucket of salt water standing by, in
> which to dip the instrument of torture, a heavy leather thong, their
> backs were cut up until the blisters covered the whole surface.[22]

One weakness of this account is that Forrest's brother John had been so
crippled in the Mexican War that he could not stand. But Forrest had other
brothers to assist him, and he did not shrink from using the lash. An admiring Tennesseean recalled how during the war Forrest once pointed at a slave
currying a mule and remarked that if "he had a good bull-whip he would
show this negro how to do it right." "I remember one day," Horatio Eden related, "when the slaves were being paraded. One negro got out of the line of
walk & kicked over a chamber that was near & broke it. The guard—I do not
know whether it was Gen Forrest or not, but I remember it well—picked up
another chamber & broke it over the negro's head. I remember seeing an old
negro woman washing his head at a pump."[23]

Forrest claimed in later life that he bought an interest in a slaving ship
called the *Wanderer*, on which he and his partners had illegally shipped over
four hundred blacks, of whom "only" a couple of dozen had died. "They were
very fond of grasshoppers and bugs," Forrest bragged, "but I taught them to
eat cooked meat, and they were as good niggers as any I ever had."[24]

The *New York Tribune* pictured a "mean, vindictive, cruel and unscrupulous" Forrest sporting "a stovepipe hat set on the back of his head at
an angle of forty-five degrees" and accounted him the husband of "two

wives—one white, the other colored (Catharine), by each of which he had two children. His 'patriarchal' wife, Catharine, and his white wife," the reporter continued, "had frequent quarrels or domestic jars."[25]

There is no way of knowing the truth of the matter, but such arrangements were commonplace. Forrest's Southern contemporaries, white and black, would not have made much of it. Some masters did not regard intercourse with their slaves as adultery, exactly, but one of many practices that were not so much unspeakable as unspoken.

Forrest was strong, vital, often absent from home; the former Mary Montgomery was a small, pious, upright woman whom he had married in part to reform himself. Though Forrest was an unusually solicitous husband who pitched in with the dishes after meals, over the course of their marriage this son of the frontier, himself the oldest of a multitude of children, sired only one daughter, who died of dysentery at the age of six, and one son, William, who as an adolescent would serve under his father in the cavalry. During the war, Forrest traveled with his black cook; in fact, he was criticized for hauling a heavy iron cookstove with him on his campaigns. It was common for rebel officers to travel with their cooks, but Forrest's was somewhat unusual in that she was a female and apparently indefatigable. A Union soldier recalled watching her drive her buggy team hard to catch up to her retreating master, oblivious of the jeers of the Yankee troops she passed.[26]

Forrest apparently impregnated at least one of his slaves: an ancestor of playwright Douglas Turner Ward of the Negro Ensemble Company. In 2005, Ward reluctantly revealed that the general was his great-great-grandfather through his slave Elnora, with whom Bedford sired a daughter named Dicey. When Forrest tried to sell Dicey away from her, Elnora escaped with their child to Union-occupied Louisiana. To those who would disbelieve the story, Ward pointed out that the last person he and his family ever wanted to count among their forebears was Nathan Bedford Forrest.[27]

Nevertheless, Forrest's champions have tried to swallow the indigestible lump of his slave trading by insisting that he was a deeply humane speculator who refused to separate slave families or sell them to cruel slaveholders, and that he even permitted his slaves to go out into the city "and choose their own masters."

The claim that he did not separate slaves, however, is feeble in at least three respects. First, it is probably not true. An otherwise admiring Judge J. P. Young recalled his "childish indignation" when Forrest came by his parents' house and took away his nursemaid Emaline, a mother of two. According to a former slave named Louis Hughs, whose illegally enslaved wife and family were sold in Forrest's yard, he did separate families. Though abolitionist lawyers had obtained their freedom in Kentucky, Hughs's wife and family were spirited away to Memphis, separated, and sold in Forrest's "traders' yard," and in later years Hughs would ascribe what he believed to have been Forrest's role in the massacre at Fort Pillow to "the debasing influences of his early business." Priscilla Parker would testify that Forrest sold her sister to a New Orleans trader; two brothers to buyers from Covington and Lebanon, Kentucky; and a third to a man from rural Louisiana.[28] Thomas Hooper, future corporal in the 6th United States Colored Heavy Artillery, would have an even more fateful rendezvous with Forrest at Fort Pillow. But as a boy he was bought with his mother by Forrest and then sold away from her.[29]

Some Tennessee masters did indeed request that traders not break up the slave families they put up for sale. One master had a policy of not selling any of the slaves he had raised from infancy. Another insisted that his three slaves—a stout man, his wife, and son—could be separated only if they remained in the same county. But in the heat of bidding, such stipulations often went by the board. When Isaac Johnson's mother was put up for bid with her baby son, "no one responded for some time, and it looked for awhile that they were to escape being sold. But someone called out: 'Put them up separately.' Then the cry was, 'How much do I hear for the woman without the baby?'"[30]

There is no evidence that Forrest refused to buy individual slaves from their owners. In fact, any trader who declined to do so would quickly have gone out of business, as most masters sold their slaves piecemeal. Even if Forrest had been reluctant to separate the families he sold, he would have gone broke refusing to separate the slaves he bought. Far from going broke, Forrest made a fortune.

Finally, the meaning of "family" in slave society renders this most far-fetched of Forrest's mercies moot. The peculiar institution did all in its power to destroy slaves' parental authority and filial devotion. Slaveholders took it upon themselves to name, discipline, feed, house, employ, pair off, and otherwise determine the fates of their slaves' children. Like most Southern states, Tennessee forbade slaves the legal right to marry lest their marital rights interfere with their owners' power to breed and dispose of their chattel as they saw fit. Children were often raised not by their mothers but by elderly slaves unfit for field work, and in any case sales and the high mortality among slaves turned many slave children into orphans. The result was that the wider slave community, and in some cases even the slaveholder's family itself, became the slave's only family, so that any separation from one's kith was as profoundly damaging as separation from one's kin.[31]

As for Forrest's allowing some trusted slaves to go out into the city to seek their own masters, slave traders, like prison wardens, cultivated their "trustees." They saved Forrest the care and keeping of slaves if they went out and found a buyer for themselves. Forrest's trade consisted largely of selling Upper South slaves to buyers in the Deep South, where conditions were so harsh that many slaves regarded their exportation downriver as a death sentence. They also believed that the kindliest masters did not attend auctions. It is therefore little wonder that slaves would apply to find masters for themselves. In any case, this ostensible nicety may be not a measure of Forrest's kindness so much as further evidence that slaves were so terrified of Forrest and his brothers that even when given an opportunity they dared not risk the consequences of trying to run away. Even some of Forrest's admirers admit that his slaves feared him "exceedingly." "I knowed Mr. Forrest before the war," declared a contraband from Columbus, Kentucky. "I knowed him as well as I knowed Master Jim. He was hard on niggers before the war."[32]

After his chief competitor, Isaac Bolton, bore witness to the squalid nature of the trade by murdering a rival dealer, Forrest became the preeminent slave speculator in the city: a man of such consequence and respectability that his Third Ward neighbors elected him alderman. Neither the frontier nor the slave trade, however, had endowed Forrest with a parliamentary temperament. He was always storming out of meetings or threatening to quit. Touring Memphis after the war, a Northern newspaperman reported that Forrest's "ferocity and reckless temper" had made him "actually quite unpopular with a large portion of the community, who feared and disliked him about evenly." He was not above trying to feather his own nest by proposing slave traders' licenses for competing newcomers or a paupers' cemetery to eliminate the cost—some fifty dollars a head—of burying the slaves who did not survive his mercies. One Memphis plutocrat described him as "fierce and terrible" and "one of the most arbitrary, imperious and determined" men that it was "possible to conceive of as holding a high position in a civilized community."[33]

Forrest expanded his thriving slave-dealing operation into a new brick building down the street. But after it collapsed in a driving rain, burying six slaves in the rubble, he began to leave much of the family's slave trading to his brothers. Though he had somewhat depleted his assets with his gambling—at one point he was actually indicted for playing at cards—Forrest set out to fulfill his dream of becoming a planter. In the late 1850s, he moved himself and his family down to his vast holdings in Coahoma County, Mississippi, where in 1860 a census taker found him living in a six-room house at the head of an avenue of cabins housing thirty-six slaves.[34]

To explain Forrest's volatility, most biographers concentrate on the hardships and perils of his frontier upbringing. But the hardships and perils faced by pioneers in, say, Minnesota, were at least as formidable, and compounded by a crueler climate and the depredations of the Sioux, whose Southwestern counterparts—Cherokee, Choctaw, Chickasaw—had been either removed or pacified by the time of Forrest's birth. A more likely precondition of Forrest's temper and even that of his men who did not own slaves was having to navigate as a free white in a slave society. A white man in what was then the American Southwest had to be willing not only to stand up for himself and his family, but to protect his own place in society by keeping slaves in theirs.

If slaves were to be extensions of a master's will, then his will had to be sufficiently steely to keep them captive to it. In order to prevent his slaves from shirking, stealing, running away, or rising up against him, a master had to project at least a capacity for violence. Even the most reluctant and best-intentioned slave owners operated under increasingly restrictive laws that required that they prevent their slaves from assembling, even for religious observances, without an overseer; from leaving their master's property without passes; from learning to read and write. The penalties were often stiff: fines, confiscation, even imprisonment. Though these laws were enforced haphazardly, and a few slaveholders were brave enough, decent enough, or secure enough to defy such sanctions, nevertheless they encircled the peculiar institution in an ever tightening grip.

The history of slavery is a paradox of intimacy and alienation. In downplaying or denouncing slavery, some try to deny its contradictions—the apparently happy, faithful slaves versus their abused, degraded fellows; contented slaves versus rebels and runaways; intelligence versus ignorance; courage versus cowardice; base exploitation versus benign paternalism; contempt, brutality, and distrust versus affection, kindness, and loyalty—as though the extremes of slavery had suspended the inherent ambiguities and contradictions of human nature. But for many of those who were born into the system—be they slaves or masters—life was a muddle.

Forrest apparently conceived of himself as the protector of a childlike, ignorant, credulous people. For the sake of their own survival, most of his slaves had in turn disguised themselves to him, to one another, and sometimes even to themselves as his passive, tractable agents. Forrest was probably grateful for this disguise, the happy mask of slavery: the courtesies of his house slaves; the men's vitality; the girls' fertility, and their offspring's endearing antics; the field slaves' ceaseless toil; and the great things they were achieving together in the Mississippi bottoms. If slavery sometimes represented a burden to Forrest, if he had to house and feed and care for his slaves, and occasionally resort to the lash to remind them of their place, it was never so heavy a burden as to eclipse the peculiar institution's promise of gracious living and ever expanding wealth. A young hand's recalcitrance, or the hint of a slave girl's dangerously inquiring intelligence, might hector Forrest in his sleep, but with the tools at his disposal such troublemakers could usually be subdued or redirected. And if such tools were unavailing, he could always sell them or destroy them, and comfort himself that he had done it not just for his good but for their own.

"BONDS OF WICKEDNESS"

SLAVERY IN TENNESSEE

1820-1861

IN THE 1820S A FEW DISTINGUISHED TENNESSEEANS HAD OPENLY ESpoused the gradual emancipation of slaves. One legislator urged his fellows to "loose the bonds of wickedness. Undo the heavy burdens. Let the oppressed go free." Francis Brown insisted to his fellows that freed blacks would make good citizens, and Andrew Jackson's brother-in-law, Alexander Donelson, emancipated all of his slaves in the belief that his afterlife depended on it. But over the next forty years these voices died away in the din from proslavery advocates who feared their neighbors' naïve machinations would result in slave uprisings and economic ruin, and the Northern abolitionists who denounced their proposals as overly gradual and conditional, though in most cases, once initiated, they would have been no more gradual or conditional than New England abolition had been.[1]

The slave insurrectionist Nat Turner drove the final nail into the coffin of Southern emancipationism. For two days in August 1831, he and his comrades hacked and stabbed to death fifty-five white men, women, and children. His followers were killed almost immediately, but Turner himself eluded his captors for two months. Whites mustered all through the South, sending squads of "country bullies and poor whites" to plantations to hunt for weapons in the slave quarters. Slaves were dragged off, flogged, and shot to death by gangs of whites who "exulted in such a chance to exercise a little brief authority, and show their subserviency to the slaveholders." "The brightest and best" slaves, said Charity Bowen, "were killed in Nat's time."[2]

It didn't take much to set whites off. George L. Knox recalled the 1856 insurrection panic that gripped Wilson County, just east of Nashville. According to one version, about a month before Christmas a slave named

Wash Smith traded with somebody for a bugle. Soon the rumor circulated that Wash intended to blow his bugle to signal the slaves to rise up, and as Christmas approached "the excitement grew." Most Southern states had already passed legislation denying slaves a virtual Bill of Rights' worth of freedoms, including literacy, assemblies, unmonitored religious observances, travel without passes, and contact with freedmen. Now slaves were forbidden to leave their masters' premises "unless sent for the doctor." Patrollers stepped up their inspections, and "orders were issued that two colored men were not to be seen talking together," nor were slaves allowed to talk to poor whites "for fear that they would take the Negro's part and aid him in the uprising." Violators were to be given "thirty-nine licks with a raw cow-hide on their bare backs." Just before Christmas, a white doctor reported that weapons had been found hidden in haystacks. In the ensuing panic, five slaves were lynched and "a few thousand" were whipped. According to one slave, the whites "shot niggers and chopped their heads off, and stick their heads on poles and throw their bodies in the river."[3]

After John Brown's abortive raid on Harpers Ferry, the Southern press got hold of a letter apparently from one of Brown's more deluded operatives claiming that in Arkansas and Tennessee there were not only "an immense number of slaves ripe and ready at the first intimation to strike a decided blow" but an astoundingly "large number of whites" in Memphis "ready to aid us." In West Tennessee, authorities intercepted a letter from a Northern teacher in Brownsville urging others to come south in the guise of schoolteachers and spread the gospel of abolitionism. The result was another panic. Vigilantes attacked everybody from "aged eccentrics and itinerant piano-tuners to substantial citizens of long residence." Northern laborers were special targets, and various states expelled dozens of schoolteachers. Others were flogged, tarred and feathered, and even lynched. There were public book burnings of abolitionist works, mobs attacked printing offices, and sheriffs closed down newspapers. Editorialists blacklisted Northern companies and urged a boycott of all Northern goods, driving Unionists and antislavery advocates out of the state.[4]

The slaves, however, suffered most. In Paris, Tennessee, a young black boy first realized that he was a slave when a white mob "cut darkies' heads off in a riot. They put their faces up like a sign board," he recalled, and threatened "to burn the niggers by the hundreds." In the late 1850s, when a seer named Fredonia Gallatin announced that the slaves of Tennessee were about to rise, whites sought out any slave who could read and whipped several of them to death. They lashed a black preacher named Henry King and beheaded an antislavery white named "Red Head" Bill Martin, displaying his head on the end of a stick until one of his comrades was forced to bury it.[5]

After these panics ebbed away, the slaves "began to talk over the great wrong that had been done," recalled a former slave named George Knox. "Many wondered what would next take place" and whether they could stand it. But they also saw in the white man's savage desperation that something was shaking the peculiar institution to its foundations. "In the midst of all the oppression," wrote Knox, "I could feel that freedom was not far away."[6]

Though often isolated and mostly illiterate, slaves did not lack for information. They were among the very first, for instance, to get wind of the Emancipation Proclamation. A visitor to the South once asked a group of Confederate officers what effect Lincoln's "Proclamation of Freedom" had had on slave owners.

"It had made hell with them," they replied.

But how could that be possible, asked the visitor, since the negroes could not read?

"One of them replied that one of his negroes had told him of the proclamation five days before he heard it in any other way. Others said their negroes gave them their first information of the proclamation."[7]

House slaves especially kept their eyes and ears open. Thomas Rutling's mistress always made him promise never to repeat her family's dinner table conversation, "but—well—in less than half an hour," Rutling joked, "some way, every slave on the plantation would know what had been said up at massa's house." Even field slaves used to listen at the windows when their masters read the paper aloud or talked with their neighbors about Lincoln and Jefferson Davis.[8]

Some slaves divined freedom's approach like a trembling in their bones. The mistress of a woman called Aunt Tilda told her that "God would visit the colored people with His displeasure for rejoicing at the success of the Yankees." Aunt Tildy "could not read, and perhaps we colored people did not understand the thing, and Missus was right. But as I went about my work I prays, and when I was in the kitchen, taking up the dinner, a voice said, 'Stand still, and see what I will do.'"[9]

For the most part, slaves were pragmatic country people. Their bondage had made them shrewd judges of where power lay. Before they would trade homes that were familiar and in many cases ancestral, and masters who at least clothed and fed and sheltered them, they first needed to settle in their own minds certain fundamental questions.

First of all, what was freedom? Slaves had been hearing about the promise of freedom for generations, and by 1861 some of them were heartily sick of it. "I thought it was foolishness then," recalled one. "Free? Is anybody ever free?" asked Patsy Jane Bland. "Ain't everybody a slave to some one or something or other?" Passing peddlers sometimes agitated slaves by telling them they would "be free someday." Louis Hughs recalled how "the down-trodden slaves, some of whom were bowed with age, with frosted hair and furrowed cheek, would answer, looking up from their work: 'We don't believe that. My grandfather said we was to be free, but we ain't free yet.'"[10]

For many others, however, freedom, like literacy and religion, was made all the more precious by the savage lengths to which their masters would go to deny it to them. "We had a man on our place named George," recalled Charlotte Brooks. "Master did not like him very much, no how, and one day he overheard George talking about freedom; and, I tell you, he half killed him that day. He beat George awhile, and then would make the driver beat him awhile," until the whip had put out one of his eyes.[11]

"We knowed freedom was on us," Felix Haywood explained, "but we didn't know what was to come with it. We thought we was going to be richer than the white folks, because we was stronger and knowed how to work, and the whites didn't, and they didn't have us to work for them any more. But it didn't turn out that way," Haywood continued. "We soon found out that freedom could make folks proud, but it didn't make them rich." Some slaves understood this going in, however. "Freedom," explained Charlie Davenport, may have "meant us could leave where us had been born and bred, but it meant, too, that us had to scratch for us own selves."[12]

Their next question was What was this war all about? Their answers ranged from the metaphorical ("Somebody from across the water sent a shipload of money to us colored folks and somebody stole it; and now they gwine fight it out") to the biblical ("Some of the old folks said it was near the end of time, because of folks being so wicked"). "It was the old story of the captivity in Egypt repeated," concluded L. M. Mills. "The slaveholders were warned time and again to let the black man go, but they hardened their hearts and would not, until finally the wrath of God was poured out upon them, and the sword of the great North fell upon their first-born." Whatever they may have guessed about the war's causes, however, they quickly understood what was at stake. For whites the war might mean Union or Confederacy, victory or defeat, prosperity or ruin, even life or death. But for slaves it meant all this and more: freedom at last or generations more of bondage.[13]

To their next question—Who were these Yankees?—masters hastened to provide answers. Union soldiers were devils, they warned their slaves: baby-killing, cannibalistic monsters with claws in their gloves, tails in their trousers, and horns erupting under their blue caps. Others claimed they were bent on stealing slaves and selling them in Cuba, depositing them in chains on the coast of Africa, or drowning them in the ocean.[14]

A wiser master might have trusted a little more in his slaves' intelligence, for their first encounters with real Yankees quickly dispelled such bogeyman notions, destroying the last shreds of their masters' credibility. "Why," a slave exclaimed on first meeting a squad of Yankees, "they's folks!" Among the fugitive slaves who escaped above Fort Pillow to the Union navy's river fleet was a man who said his master had described Lincoln to him as a man-eating ogre "with tail and horns" who intended to "devour every one of the African race," and lay waste to the South. "Lord," the slave exclaimed, "I don't know nothing, but I knows too much for that there. I knows Master Lincoln wasn't that kind of a person. Them there horns and tails," he said, laughing out loud at his master's belief in his slaves' credulity, "I—I couldn't swallow the horns and tails. Them was too much for *this* black man, sure."[15]

Early in the war, few Yankee soldiers saw themselves as agents of black liberation, and many treated slaves and slave owners with equal contempt. Some slaves reciprocated. "Now, if you please," an elderly slave remarked to his mistress as his fellow slaves rushed to greet the Yankees, "look at the poor, white trash them niggers is running after. If they was in the gutters," he said, they "wouldn't pick them up, unless they wanted them to fight for them. I tell you now they won't get this nigger," he assured his mistress. "And I thank God I know who my friends are."[16]

Many slaves were outraged by the rapacity with which Yankee foragers scoured their masters' plantations, hauling away every scrap of food, digging about the grounds for the family silver, overturning slaves' mattresses in search of their paltry savings. "Lincoln freed us," said Patsy Perryman, "but I never liked him because of the way his soldiers done in the South." Willie Doyle remembered that when the Yankees thundered onto his plantation, his master, who had been reading the paper, "throwed back his head and was dead. Just scared to death." With "Old Master Jim stretched dead in his chair" the Yankees began hurling meat out of his smokehouse and commanding the slaves to "Come and get it. Take it to your houses." The frightened slaves obeyed, but as soon as the Yankees left they returned the meat to the smokehouse.[17]

"You nasty, stinking rascal," Sam Ward's slave mother scolded a Yankee forager. "You say you come down here to fight for the niggers, and now you're stealing from them."

"You're a god damn liar," replied the Yankee. "I'm fighting for fourteen dollars a month and the Union."[18]

Slaves weighed such encounters against the knowledge that the Yankees had marched down from the North, where so many fugitive slaves had found freedom. Whatever an individual soldier's views on slavery, he was a member of the Army of the Lord.[19]

"I wanted to be free," said Jack Daniels, "and I was glad the Federal army was so lucky as to free me." Though he had "no influence," he had "wanted to see the Yankees come," and "just prayed with my whole heart that the Yankees might come and overcome my old masters, and whip them out."[20]

Having established at least that the Yankees were human (if not always humane), slaves asked, as a corollary, who this Abraham Lincoln was. The former slaves who were interviewed in their old age would prove surprisingly divided in their opinion of Lincoln. A good many revered his memory. "Abraham Lincoln?" asked Nancy Gardner of Oklahoma. "Now you is talking about the niggers' friend! Why that was the best man God ever let tramp the earth!"[21]

For some slaves he was an almost biblical figure. James Southall called him "God's emmissary." "I thought he was partly God," said Angie Garrett. Annie Young thought Lincoln was a greater man than Moses. "He done more for us," declared Charles Willis, "than any man done since Jesus left." But others were not so sure. Hannah McFarland "didn't care much about Lincoln. It was nice of him to free us," she admitted, "but 'course he didn't want to." George Strickland agreed. "It was the plans of God to free us niggers, and not Abraham Lincoln's."[22]

That was all in retrospect, however. The name "Abraham" had a special resonance for the slaves who first heard it. "Father Abraham" many called him, and only "Moses" would have seemed a more fitting name for this lofty entity who had promised, they believed, to lead them out of bondage. But would he win? Was he wise? Did he mean what he said?

Southern whites asked blacks what they thought freedom was, and entertained each other recounting their quaint replies: never having to work again, living in a mansion, sailing back to Africa. But the replies whites cited as proof of their slaves' ignorance revealed instead that what freedom meant to them at least in part was the right to dream, to hope, to fancy.

Out of pity, loyalty, a horror of losing touch with their families, or slavish habits of mind, some slaves stuck by their masters through the war. "Master was too old to work when they set us free," Nicey Kinney recalled, "so for a long time us just stayed there and run his place for him." J. W. Stinnett's mother pleaded with the Yankees not to make her quit her owner's place. Her husband was in the South, she told them, "and I'll never see him again if I leave the old home place, for he won't know where to find me." But the Yankees took her anyway.[23]

Robert Glenn of North Carolina recalled, "I took my freedom by degrees," and had a hard time "taking myself into my own hands and getting out of the feeling I was still under obligations to ask my master and mistress when I desired to leave the premises." Other slaves—some house slaves, or solitary slave families who lived with their masters on isolated farms—regarded themselves as members of the family, and in some cases actually were their owners' sons and daughters, brothers and sisters. "The Negroes knew as well what was going on as other people did." Though "at this late day he is spoken of by the coarse and profane class as the 'dam Nigger,' with no right to standing room on God's blessed foot stool," declared James Thomas, "while the Negroes' superiors were trying to break up the best government on earth, the Negro was caring for the defenseless."[24]

Locked with their masters in the agricultural cycle of the seasons, some slaves could not bring themselves to abandon the crops they had planted and tended, or the storehouses they had taken such pains to fill. Some third-, fourth-, and fifth-generation slaves of the same family believed they had traditions to honor, standards to uphold, even as their masters galloped off to sustain their bondage.

To such slaves' dismay, however, many masters betrayed those traditions and standards as the feudal code of honor that the old order had exalted began to crumble before the Yankee onslaught. "Sometimes a spy would come along in advance of an army," recalled Rachel Cruze,

> and I'd call to Old Major, who was sitting on the porch, "Major, here comes a spy." And Old Major, he'd start up from his chair and bawl, "Who-o-w-a-at?" If I said, "It's Johnny," and he was in a Rebel suit, he'd throw out his chest and prepare to greet them. But if I said, "Union," he'd sneak to his room, change into the blue uniform with its red-lined cape, and come back out on the porch. As he sat down, he'd throw back the corner of his blue cape to show its red lining.[25]

Slaves who had derived their sense of dignity and worth from their owners' pride and prosperity were appalled by the rapidity with which even their most aristocratic owners fell apart toward the end of the war. "Old Mistress never get well after she lose all her niggers," recalled Katie Rowe, "and one day the white boss tell us she just drop over dead setting in her chair, and we know her heart just broke." One slave owner said he "no longer went about his slaves any more" and would have "nothing to do with any of them as long as I can not control them."[26]

Bob Maynard's kindly master accepted emancipation "pretty good," Maynard recalled, "losing us niggers and all," but "lots of men killed theirselves." Tom Wilson's owner became so distraught that he "went off to a little stream of water and broke the ice and jumped in." Two weeks later he died of pneumonia. Declaring that "he don't want to live in a country where the niggers am free," Anna Miller's former master moved to Texas and "kills hisself about a year after they moves."[27]

Other masters were more extrovert. "'The faithful slave' is about played out," a slave owner wrote in July of 1863. "They are the most treacherous, brutal, and ungrateful race on the globe." "The negroes care no more for me," wrote one Texas mistress during the war, "than if I was an old free darkey," adding that she got "so mad sometimes" that she no longer cared whether her brutal and turbulent overseer beat the "last one to death." A slave in Davidson County who had remained with her owner was shocked when he started fulminating about emancipation. "He was gonna kill me 'cause I was free," she recalled sadly. "I got shame about it, they talked about it so."[28]

The presence of Union troops, however, sometimes forced masters to watch their step around their slaves. Harriett Robinson's mistress used to beat her slaves during the war. "You master's out fighting and losing blood trying to save you from them Yankees," she used to tell them, "so you can get your'n here." One morning a master hit his slave. But "he didn't know the Yankees were in town," an ex-slave recalled, "and when he found out, he come back beggin' me to stay with him, and said he was sorry."[29]

Slaveholders sometimes tried with what passed for logic to get slaves to see things their way. "Now look," James Thomas remembered a white explaining, "them blue bellied scoundrels went to Africa, stole the niggers, brought them here, sold them to us, then stole them from us, starved them and otherwise mistreated them," and now the Yankees "want to tell us what to do with the balance of them." Many Southern whites "said they never thought the 'peculiar institution' right, but they did not want the Dam bluebellied sons of bitches to tell them what to do with their property."[30]

Others simply tried to sell their slaves off while they could. "That old Yankee has got elected," declared one master after Lincoln's election, "and I am going to sell every nigger I got because he is going to free them." When George W. Harmon's master tried to sell his slaves during the war, he told them they were being appraised because "the Government was thinking of buying us free." Some sold their slaves at greatly reduced prices, not necessarily because they had given up their hopes of a rebel victory but because, for the time being, they could not afford to feed them.[31]

Masters took to hiding their slaves in the woods when Yankee patrols came near. Some spirited them down to the Deep South or all the way west to Texas, where they believed there was at least some hope that the peculiar institution might survive a Yankee victory. "They'd always had them Negroes," explained Allen V. Manning, "and lots of them had mighty fine places back in the old states," but in Texas, "they had to go out and live in sod houses and little boxed shotguns." Some slaveholders tried to move their slaves behind rebel lines deep in the mountains of northeastern Tennessee, where their slaves were kept in such isolation that they never heard about emancipation until the war was long over.[32]

But how and when should a slave escape to the Union lines? If freedom was coming, did it make sense to risk one's life just to hasten the day of liberation by a few months, weeks, even days? For many slaves the answer was an emphatic yes.

Slaves had been running away from their masters ever since the first African set foot on American soil. Running away had become something of an art in the South, but usually amounted to a kind of job action. If by the degraded standards of bondage, slaves deemed themselves unfairly treated, they would run into the woods and remain there, with their fellows' furtive help, until their masters promised to ease up on them. The storied northbound flights to freedom were much rarer, for they required of a slave not only an unusual degree of desperation, imagination, and courage, but a knowledge of geography, a trust in strangers, and access to the Underground Railroad's network of safe houses without which a successful journey north was nearly impossible.[33]

Slaves had developed ingenious techniques to confound slave catchers and their hounds. Tracking dogs were fearsome enforcers of human bondage. An elderly former slave recalled that whites regarded the crying of bloodhounds as the "sweetest music in the world." Mississippi slaves said that when "anybody would come for the hounds to run a nigger, the hounds would say, 'Our Father, I've got a heavenly home up yonder, hallelujah, hallelujah.'" Plomer Harshaw recalled how, as his master was about to strike him, a slave snatched away his hickory club and ran off into the bushes. "But that was far as he got. The dogs leap on him and tear him to pieces."[34]

Gaunt, ragged, desperate, crazed by deprivation, exposure, isolation, and the never ending fear of capture, runaways reinforced slaves' animist beliefs in ghosts and banshees. "A runaway Negro was the greatest bugaboo to all the boys and girls in the country," recalled E. L. Davison of Kentucky. "We had been taught that they would keep us in a cave and cut off a limb at a time and cook it whenever they became hungry, keeping us alive as long as possible." Runaways also provided larcenous, rapacious, and even homicidal whites with scapegoats for any crime they might choose to commit in a runaway's vicinity.[35]

Slaves were nevertheless so expert at hiding out that white boys hoping to elude rebel or Yankee press gangs turned to them for guidance. The son of a slave owner named Hawkens returned on furlough from service in the Confederate army and spent the rest of the war living in a runaway's cave. Lee Guidon of South Carolina recalled how his master's son used to "lay out in the woods" to avoid Confederate recruiters. "He say no need in him getting shot up and killed. He say, 'Let the slaves be free.' Mr. Jim say, 'All they fighting about was jealousy.'"[36]

Masters were shocked by how readily even their oldest slaves ran off, and the risks they would take to find freedom. A planter made his elderly slaves, Uncle Si and Aunt Cindy, promise that they would not go to the Yankee lines. "Oh no, Master," replied Uncle Si. "I is going to stay right here with you." But the next morning, he and Aunt Cindy and all the rest of the slaves had vanished. Searching for them in the woods, the planter came upon Uncle Si weeping over the body of his wife, who had died in the night of exposure. "Uncle Si," asked the planter, "why on earth did you so cruelly bring Aunt Cindy here for, through all such hardship, thereby causing her death?"

"I couldn't help it, Master," replied Uncle Si. "But then, you see, she died free."[37]

When a Yankee advised an elderly fugitive to return to the comfort and security of his master's house, he answered "that if he lived only one day," he would "live that day as a free man."[38]

Free, but uprooted in a land of ruins. "The last time I seed the home plantation," recalled William Colbert, "I was standing on a hill. I looked back on it for the last time through a patch of scrub pines, and it look so lonely. There weren't but one person in sight: the massa. He was setting in a wicker chair in the yard looking out over a small field of cotton and corn," and there were "four crosses in the graveyard in the side lawn where he was setting."[39]

HOOSIERS AND IOWANS

THE FIRST UNION GARRISON AT FORT PILLOW

1862–1864

THE CONFEDERACY'S ARCHIPELAGO OF RIVER FORTS FELL TO THE Union in rapid succession: Paducah, Columbus, New Madrid, Island No. 10. On April 14, 1862, the Union navy's river fleet anchored around a bend just north of Coal Creek and laid siege to Fort Pillow, lobbing round after round of lethal shells over Craighead Point. The Confederate navy tried to come to Fort Pillow's rescue, and fought over its destiny in the Battle of Plum Run, one of the fiercest gunboat clashes of the war. Each side claimed victory, but the Confederate rams and gunboats would eventually prove no match for the Union navy, which chased them down to Memphis and decimated the rebel fleet.

In early June, the rebel garrison evacuated the shell-pocked bastion and limped south. As the Yankees cautiously rowed up to the abandoned works, they could see that the rebels had done a thorough job of stripping and demolishing the place. On works designed for fifty guns, "only ten remained, three of them exploded" and the rest "carefully spiked and their muzzles wedged with ball or stands of grape."[1] The Yankees scoured the abandoned fort, salvaging what little they could from the flames. In one tent they found a table with a defiant note pinned to it by a rebel lieutenant. "I know you will exult over the occupation of this place," it said, "but our evacuation will hurt you from another point with disastrous effect. Five millions white men fighting to be relieved from oppression will never be conquered by twenty millions actuated by malice and pecuniary gain, mark that," the lieutenant declared. "The day of retribution is approaching and will fall upon you, deadly as a bolt from heaven; may your sojourn at this place be of few days and full of trouble."[2]

The Yankee occupation of Fort Pillow would last for years, not days. But he was right about the trouble.

From September 1862 to February 1864, Fort Pillow was garrisoned by a carousing Hoosier regiment under the command of Colonel Edward H. Wolfe. Wolfe's men had so often found themselves stationed at trestles and switches or roosting on Union freight cars with their muskets across their knees that his 52nd Indiana Infantry became known as the "Railroad Regiment."[3] Joined by a detachment from the 2nd Illinois Cavalry and equipped with a single field piece, the 52nd's mission was to fight guerrillas, guard railroads, requisition supplies, and prevent the rebels from firing on river traffic from the bluff.[4]

The fort's ruins still bore evidence that the Confederates and their slaves had built their facilities with considerable skill and care. Here and there among the wreckage the Hoosiers could still make out the vestiges of stables, bakeries, and a blacksmith shop. Determined to turn the fort into a substantial military post, Wolfe's men crossed the Mississippi to Arkansas, more or less dismantled the entire town of Osceola, and piled it onto a steamboat: walls, beams, rafters, roofs, windows, furniture—the works. "As the town was deserted," a soldier explained with a wink, "nobody objected to us moving it."[5]

Each company's officers were provided with a "very comfortable" cabin, with four or five more for their men, laid out on either side of a little cul-de-sac that ran eastward off the road to Fulton. Near the two mounted companies' barracks, stables were constructed to keep their ever expanding herd of requisitioned horses out of the wind. Atop the central bluff, perhaps half a mile from his men's barracks, they built Wolfe a sixteen-by-twenty-two-foot headquarters and two more cabins for his staff, one of which—Provost Marshal J. H. Parker's headquarters—included a meeting room, an office, and a bedroom. The 2nd Illinois Cavalry built barracks and stables southeast of the 52nd, on either side of the Fulton Road, just before it exited through the half-mile abatis of fallen timber.[6]

Wolfe began to send squads of cavalry and infantry off into the interior to exchange potshots with rebel guerrillas, visit nearby farms, and command leading citizens to take the loyalty oath even as the Yankees hauled away their slaves, mules, wagons, and supplies. The oath took several forms over the course of the war, evolving eventually into this version, written at the behest of Brigadier General Andrew Johnson, who in March 1862 had arrived in Nashville as military governor of Tennessee.[7]

I solemnly swear, that I will henceforth support the Constitution of
the United States, and against the assaults of all its enemies defend
it, that I will hereafter be and conduct myself as a true and faithful
citizen of the United States freely and voluntarily claiming to be subject to all the duties and obligations, and entitled to all the rights and
privileges of such citizenship; that I ardently desire the suppression
of the present insurrection and rebellion against the Government of
the United States, the success of its armies, and the defeat of all
those who oppose them, and that the Constitution of the United
States, and all laws and proclamations, made in pursuance thereof,
may be speedily and permanently established and enforced over all
the people, States, and Territories thereof; and further, that I will
hereafter heartily aid and assist all loyal people in the accomplishment of these results. So help me God.[8]

"Some take the federal oath to avoid pillaging," observed a local woman,
"but it doesn't work, and federals do not trust them." "Most locals," sniffed
a Yankee captain, "just *acted* neutral." It was common, in fact, for the Yankees to find loyalty oaths, duly sworn and signed, tucked into the jeans of
captive rebel soldiers and guerrillas.[9]

Though the Union might at least hope to keep rebel trading boats from
operating freely along the Mississippi, its tributaries were another matter. In
full flood, they afforded flatboats and skiffs a maze of swamped woods and
bayous to shelter them on their rounds, and in the dry season they were too
shallow for Union gunboats to navigate safely. Thus the Hatchie, the Forked
Deer, and the Obion became the preferred supply routes for rebel partisans,
smugglers, and farmers hoping to sell their cotton before the rebels could
burn it or the Yankees requisition it.[10]

A treasury agent was stationed at Fort Pillow to purchase the bales of
cotton brought in by local farmers and escaped slaves. "He has a permit
from the provost marshal to buy," wrote a visitor, "but has to take a bill of sale
of the men from whom he buys, and buys only from those who have taken
the oath of allegiance" in which most Yankee officers put so little faith. In
fact it seemed to some locals that the Yankees judged a citizen's loyalty not
by his devotion to the Stars and Stripes but by the value of his property or
the size of the bribes he could afford to pay.[11]

As a Hoosier soldier named Addison Sleeth recalled, mysterious little
packets of cash—hush money, some of it, the rest shares of the graft their
officers had negotiated—made their way into everyone's pockets. A couple
of nights after his company seized a smuggler's boatload of odds and ends, a

comrade handed him two dollars with the admonition, "Say nothing." When Sleeth pressed him, his buddy replied, "You remember that trip up the river? Now say no more about it." Sleeth never did find out "who sent the two dollars, nor how much the other boys got, if any." But, he concluded, "one thing I *do* know." Somebody higher up "did not care to offer it to me direct."[12]

In December, a lieutenant from the 52nd was accused of fraudulently condemning a shipment of salt pork as unfit for human consumption and then selling it to local smugglers. "A great many Cotton buyers were scatered all along the lines of the Armey," recalled John Ryan of the 2nd Illinois Cavalry, "and a goodly share of them were at fort Pillow. I do not know if any post of the Union Army was used to protect those speculators, but circumstantial evidence was strong to that effect." In any case, trade was brisk, and the beneficiaries too numerous, and furtive, to count.[13]

The 2nd Illinois clashed with guerrilla bands throughout Tipton, Dyer, and Lauderdale counties, with varying degrees of success. But the only rebel who posed any serious threat to Fort Pillow that fall was the Wizard of the Saddle himself, Nathan Bedford Forrest. For weeks Yankee commandants had wired each other in growing panic: "Look out for Forrest." "Watch for Forrest." "Forrest preparing a raid into central Kentucky."[14] Their panic was understandable. Ordered by General Braxton Bragg to cross the Tennessee and destroy the railway linking Grant at Columbus to his forces in northern Mississippi, Forrest had protested that his men were mostly green recruits, poorly armed and meagerly supplied—which only makes Forrest's first West Tennessee raid all the more remarkable.

With a battalion numbering some 2,500 men, he left Columbia, Tennessee, on December 11, crossed the Tennessee River, defeated a detachment of Union cavalry at Lexington, and then, as Bragg had instructed, began to chew up and spit out the railroad between Humboldt and Jackson. Following the line up into Kentucky, his men gleefully burned and toppled railroad trestles. In mid-December, a day after the local Yankee commandant had imposed martial law, Forrest thundered into Trenton and thundered out again, shooting up the Union camp and adding its livestock to his ever expanding herd of purloined hogs, horses, and mules.[15]

"While an enemy ten thousand strong was attempting to cut off his retreat," wrote James Ronald Chalmers, "he returned to his camp on the 1st of January, 1863, with a command stronger in numbers than when he started, thoroughly equipped with blankets and oil cloths, their shot guns replaced with Enfield rifles, and with a surplus of five hundred rifles and eighteen hundred blankets and knapsacks."[16]

Chalmers exaggerated somewhat. Forrest and his staff tended to keep an inflated count of their victims and their spoils, omitting their failures. This was not just a matter of vanity, but part of his strategy of representing himself and his forces as more formidable than they were, the better to bluff his foe. Forrest had been unable to take Jackson, Tennessee, for instance, and had suffered a defeat at Parker Crossroads that cost him most of his booty. He did indeed recruit an enormous number of farm boys, but he had lost five hundred men in battle, and many of his new conscripts—some of them paroled infantry, others boys from Unionist families—deserted as soon as they could, and worked their way home, only to fall into Yankee custody, pleading that "they were forced &c." ("What shall I do with such cases?" an officer asked Hurlbut. "They are mostly poor devils that are of no account to any body & say they have Families to support.") The most significant unintended consequence of Forrest's destruction of the line to Columbus, however, was that it forced Grant to move his headquarters southward to what turned out to be a far more advantageous position in Memphis.[17]

Nevertheless, Forrest's first West Tennessee raid was so audacious and so shocking that as he galloped off it seemed almost biblically appropriate that nature should mark his departure by convulsing West Tennessee in a terrifying earthquake, toppling trees and imbuing the sky over the lower Mississippi with a strange, smoky haze.[18]

Rebel forays into West Tennessee so rattled the already unstable Union general Thomas Davies that he ordered the destruction of the Union fortification at New Madrid and the evacuation of its garrison. New Madrid was manned by six companies of the 32nd Iowa Infantry, whose colonel was former state senator and future lieutenant governor John L. Scott, a square-built man with a full salt-and-pepper beard. He was a man of considerable empathy, and took his role as protector of the fugitive slaves at New Madrid so seriously that before abandoning the post he and his officers raised funds to transport them to Iowa to work on their families' farms.[19]

With the approach of the 32nd, Yankees of two very different stripes were about to collide at Fort Pillow, enacting in microcosm the deep divisions that plagued the Northern war effort. The rollicking, proslavery 52nd Indiana Infantry and the rampaging 2nd Illinois Cavalry were an unhappy match for the comparatively well-disciplined and high-minded 32nd Iowa.

"There being no immediate prospect of removal from Fort Pillow," wrote Scott, his Iowans laid claim to a number of abandoned slave cabins "that had been discovered in the neighborhood, and removed them to the regimental camping ground, rebuilding them better than they had previously been, and occupying them as quarters." The cabins were sided with rough wood and roofed with battened sticks and clay, and each boasted a fine brick chimney. Some Iowans "split 'shakes,' in pioneer Iowa style, with which they covered the roofs in lieu of shingles," and one captain "even made his house more comfortable with green blinds—which he found somewhere." Scott's headquarters were built from logs taken from abandoned slave cabins on the nearby farm of Samuel Lanier, and illuminated by windows pried from the walls of Lanier's mansion house.[20]

On a site just south of the northernmost earthen breastworks that black artillerists would occupy a year later rose barracks, hospitals, and storehouses, "and a pleasant camp was the result." Within the breastworks themselves, Scott's company of German recruits from the 2nd Missouri Artillery occupied what the rest of the garrison called a "Dutch Camp." Germans from St. Louis, they were apparently so disconsolate about their transfer, enraged by the destruction of their batteries at New Madrid, and bitter about the scant allotment of warm clothing they had received, that they refused with Teutonic resolve to drill or perform any military duty whatsoever.[21]

The Iowans were shocked by the corruption and lax discipline that seemed to plague Wolfe's command. Lieutenant Amos Collins of the 32nd wrote an insinuating letter to Memphis to inquire whether it was proper for Fort Pillow's provost marshal to pocket the fifty cents he charged for cotton-trading permits, and whether it was all right for field officers to purchase cotton from the quartermaster and sell it. Their chaplain fretted that his men would be corrupted by the Indianans. "Drill was not neglected," wrote an officer, "but it is not to be denied that the surroundings were disagreeable to the officers, and would have had a demoralizing effect upon the men but for constant resistance, and the labors and prayers of the chaplain, Rev L. S. Coffin." The Iowans were appalled by the pyromaniacal zeal of the Illinois boys as they laid waste to the farms and houses of suspected secessionists.[22]

The Illinoisans gave even the Hoosiers pause. "One cold evening," wrote John Ryan of the 52nd, Captain Moore of the 2nd Illinois stopped his command at the house of a local guerrilla named Cushman. Ordering Cushman's wife and children out into her yard, they burned her house to the ground. "I am willing to give Capt. Moore much praise as a industerious officer," wrote Ryan. "But I Condemned the act then and I Condem it now as I think of that poor woman with her children standing in the street in the

Snow, Crying and Shivering with Cold. Capt Moore may have done this By order of Col Wolf, But it was not nessesary. It was cruilty: only that and nothing more."[23]

Nonetheless Fort Pillow seemed secure enough to the Yankee Edward Benton that he returned to his property on the bluff, established a trading post under Colonel Wolfe's protection, and cultivated some acreage with contraband labor. According to his biographer, Benton rendered "many and valuable services to the Southern people in the vicinity, whom he knew by a previous residence in their midst, and whose respect and esteem he had secured by uniform kindness and correct deportment." Though he may not have converted any die-hard secessionists with his services, he probably helped persuade their more ambivalent neighbors that the road to survival began at Fort Pillow.[24]

CONTRABANDS
WEST TENNESSEE
1861–1863

ONE OF THE FIRST QUESTIONS WHITE MEMPHIANS ASKED WILLIAM Tecumseh Sherman when his forces occupied their fair city was "What will you do with the negroes, after you have freed them?" What indeed. The destiny of these living "contrabands of war" became a gnawing preoccupation for the Union army's Western command. The first blacks to be dubbed "contrabands" were three refugee slaves who had entered Benjamin Butler's camp at Fortress Monroe, Virginia, in May 1861. They proved to be the first trickle of a great flood of humanity that would deluge the Union encampments to which they fled. In August 1861, Congress passed a law providing for the seizure of all property used to aid the rebels, including slaves. Thus slaves who had been employed fortifying rebel positions or serving rebel officers were not to be returned to their masters but became not free, exactly, but the property, or "contraband," of the Union.[1]

Men debated whether their exodus was likelier to weaken the Union or the Confederacy. Andrew Johnson thought it would encumber the Federal government; Grant's superintendent of contrabands, John Eaton, believed it would destroy the Southern economy. In November 1862, Henry Halleck ordered his officers not to admit any more fugitive slaves into their lines and to expel any who were not already working for the army. Believing this would condemn runaway slaves to death from starvation and exposure or, at best, abandon them to the tender mercies of masters, slave catchers, kidnappers, and rebel home guards, abolitionists decried Halleck's order and tried to persuade Congress to override it.[2]

For the next seven or eight months, officers struggled with the order's implications. "If I turn them away," wrote Colonel George E. Waring,

I inflict great hardship upon them, as they would be homeless and helpless. Furthermore, such a course would occasion much personal inconvenience and sincere regret, to other officers no less than to myself. These people are mainly our servants, and we can get no others. They have been employed in this capacity for some time, long enough for us to like them as servants, to find them useful and trustworthy, and to feel an interest in their welfare.[3]

Some officers openly defied Halleck's order. One lieutenant colonel went so far as to threaten to punish any officer who obeyed it.

In the end, it hardly mattered. The floodgates had opened, and no one, least of all Halleck, could ever pull them closed. "The moment the Union army moved into slave territory," wrote W. E. B. DuBois, "the Negro joined it," and "it made no difference what the obstacles were, or the attitudes of the commanders. It was 'like thrusting a walking stick into an ant hill,' says one writer. And yet the army chiefs tried to regard it as an exceptional and temporary matter, a thing which they could control, when as a matter of fact it was the meat and kernel of the war."[4]

Many Union and civil authorities treated contrabands no better than slaves: exiling them, even whipping them for carrying weapons, assembling, hiring themselves out, or trading without their owners' permission. They fined free blacks and even whites for harboring fugitives or selling them liquor. But eventually the contrabands' sheer numbers made assemblies inevitable, and in their appalling poverty they had to find jobs and sell produce and merchandise in order to survive.

The old Black Code receded slowly from Tennessee's courts. At Nashville, Police Recorder William Shane fined Federal contractors for housing fugitive slaves and condemned two contrabands to nine lashes each for holding a dance, despite the fact that it had been authorized by the post commander. But at last the army ordered him to stop enforcing the old code altogether. Andrew Johnson began openly to push for outright abolition in Tennessee. The old unilateral antimiscegenation law remained in force, but Johnson issued licenses to contrabands to sell merchandise, and some military courts began to allow blacks to testify against whites. By 1864, the slave code in Tennessee had effectively passed into history.[5]

No one seems to have bothered to count the number of runaway slaves who first made their way to the ruins of Fort Pillow. There probably weren't many. Slaves elsewhere had escaped to Union lines where Union victories appeared decisive and Union occupation permanent. But even as the Confederates retreated from West Tennessee in early June 1862, slaves could see that there was no guarantee they would not be back, for the Yankees had shown little intention of staying.

All that changed in early September with the arrival of Colonel Wolfe and his 52nd Indiana Infantry. Once word circulated that the Yankees had occupied the bluff, slaves forsook their owners in droves, walking, riding, driving their masters' wagons and teams up from Fulton and westward from Ripley and greeting one another in a camp they slapped together where the two roads met, within the fort and a half mile back from the river. This would place them about equidistant to the landing and to the camps of the the 52nd, the 32nd Iowa Infantry, and the 2nd Illinois Cavalry up the Fulton Road: a convenient location for the men and women who would work once more on the fortifications, cook and launder for officers and men, and tote freight to and from the steamboats that docked at the post's landing. Most of the refugees who gathered at Fort Pillow were evidently slaves who had absconded from nearby plantations on both sides of the Mississippi, or rescued runaways deposited at Fort Pillow Landing by passing Union boats. Some of them had undoubtedly worked on the fortifications for the rebels, little knowing that their labor, by Yankee edict, would set them free.

There is scant record of conditions in the contraband camp at Fort Pillow; but the little "negro cemetery" indicated on a soldier's map, and the fact that at Nashville that winter some 1,400 contrabands died of disease, exposure, and starvation, suggest that conditions must have been dire. It is impossible to estimate how many would gather at Fort Pillow by the spring of 1863, but subsequent efforts to remove them suggest there were several hundred.[6]

The 52nd put them to work almost immediately, repairing the damage from the Yankee bombardment and trying to make a fortification that had originally been designed to be defended by twenty thousand rebels defensible by one thousand Federals. They filled the burrows the rebels had dug to protect themselves from Yankee mortar fire, reported a Yankee correspondent, repaired the "ghastly breaches which we made during its bombardment," replaced "the loose lumber and crumbling earthworks which we found," leveled the parapets and properly angled the casements, and finished the intermediary entrenchment the rebels had begun, until "no traces of the damage which our fearful shells inflicted" remained, "save a few deep scars upon the easterly face."[7]

A great many contrabands brought some of their masters' property along with them, claiming it as their due after lifetimes of unrewarded toil. They furnished their tents and lean-tos with their masters' dining chairs and brica-brac, furnished their kitchens with their mistresses' pots and pans, sold tools and books and silverware to Yankee soldiers. Three Lauderdale County refugees turned up hauling four of their master's cotton bales, which a Dr. Taliaferro obligingly sold for them at Fort Pillow Landing.[8]

Indignant local masters took their complaints to Henry Cage, the Lauderdale County justice of the peace, who in February arrested five slaves for stealing cotton from a man named Austin. Cage then took his case to Wolfe. "The Civil Law of this state as you are aware has been long since suspended," he wrote Wolfe. "You will please inform me what you will or I must do in the matter."

It beat hell out of the colonel, who passed the buck to General Lionel Sandor Asboth of Hurlbut's 6th Division. "The question raised is one of frequent occurance," wrote Wolfe, "and Liable to occur again." His own opinion was that it should fall to the local provost marshal to adjudicate such matters. Asboth apparently agreed, for the provost marshal was thereafter "instructed to punish such offenders by fines, imprisonment & hard labor, either or all at his discretion."[9]

This was not necessarily what their masters had in mind, however. Under the old order, if a man's slave committed such a crime he might be flogged but he was rarely imprisoned for very long because, like an errant mule that kicks down a neighbor's well house, the slave was regarded as brute property, and the sooner he returned to work, the better. But for a slave, imprisonment was not much worse than a field hand's living conditions at home and deprived his owner of his labor. The mere fact that Union officers listened to slave testimony flew in the face of centuries of Southern jurisprudence, in which slaves had been prohibited from testifying, especially against whites.

The plight of the contrabands and the demands of their owners seemed to tie Colonel Wolfe into knots. "Many negroes have applied to me for some assistance to get their families," he wrote. "I have told all such that I could not send a force out for that purpose alone, but invariably suggested to all such applicants that they accompany the Cavalry expedition from the Post and by this means bring in their families, frequently notifying negroes myself when the cavalry were going out."[10]

During Wolfe's absence the previous fall, a Lieutenant Benoni Beale had been dismissed from the service for helping a citizen seize a contraband. In March 1863, a white man flourishing a writ from a justice of the peace rode into Fort Pillow's contraband camp and seized two slaves he claimed as his own. "These negroes were tied and taken out without my knowledge or consent," Wolfe reported, "and when informed of the matter," Wolfe said, he had sent men out "and had the negroes returned to the Fort together with the gentleman who took them."[11]

That was not, however, how the Iowans of the 32nd saw it. They claimed that it was only after they protested "vigorously against this high-handed outrage" that Wolfe sent "a small detachment to fetch back the Negroes." "The Fifty-Second Indiana Infantry was really a pro-slavery regiment," Scott wrote, "always ready to drive the Negroes who came to the post back into slavery," whereas the 32nd Iowa, he said, was always eager "to espouse the cause of the loyal against the disloyal, regardless of the color line": so eager that the 52nd referred to the Iowans as the "abolition regiment."[12]

By January 1863, so many refugees had gathered at Fort Pillow that a reluctant Colonel Wolfe, under orders from General Grant, detailed Second Lieutenant B. K. Logan of the 52nd as "post superintendent of the colored men." Thanks to the men of the 32nd, his responsibilities would expand exponentially, for the Iowans seemed to regard it as part of their duty to collect slaves from the surrounding area. Local whites were outraged by the encouragement they gave slaves to evacuate their masters' farms and plantations. But the Iowans blandly replied that slaves simply followed them to the fort and never had to be compelled. As the 32nd headed back from a scout around the dismantled town of Osceola, Arkansas, with sixty slaves, a master protested that he would be ruined without his slaves. "You will only have to work with your own hands," their officer loftily replied, "as we have to do in the North," and there, he said, would be an end to treason.[13]

Some Union volunteers liberated slaves merely to debase their owners. A Nashville barber recalled, "All the soldiers as a rule were willing to break up that easy life of the owners of the Niggers." In Memphis, local whites who tried to fetch their slaves were subjected to "humiliating treatment— such as riding the rail horse, or carrying a barrel up the hill and rolling it down again, and they would continue this process for hours." Simply by association with the Iowans, Wolfe's Hoosiers were accused by the locals of abolitionism. Addison Sleeth of the 52nd recalled how local people accused them of harboring "'Nigger' loving propensities." In September 1863 a letter written by a visiting photographer from Rushville, Indiana, bitterly denounced the 52nd's officers as "Judases" who had turned from good Democrats into "nigger lovers" in hopes of currying favor with the Lincoln administration. The letter caused such a stir that Wolfe had it read aloud at dress parade, eliciting indignant groans from his men. When the colonel asked if any of his men agreed with the letter's appraisal, not a single man stepped forward.[14]

The way the Hoosiers saw it, for the sake of the Union they had endured the perils and privations of army life for almost two years, only to find themselves pressed into a crusade to free "ignorant, promiscuous slaves," who, if liberated, would only move north and take their jobs. "Tha niger was in is right plase before tha War commenced," wrote a Union private, "and i hope to god they will let im Stay there. But Still," he said, "if freeing them will Stop this war then i say free them. But it is not for me to say what tis right nor what is rong. I came here to fight tha battels of this my adopted country and I Am willing they Should be free if there is know other way to stop tha war."[15]

A Hoosier captain wrote home from Fort Pillow that even the Republicans among his men had renounced the party and were actively preventing contrabands from entering Fort Pillow, though another soldier later wrote to deny it. An Iowan reported in mid-February that the Emancipation Proclamation was only going to make the war last longer, and that if the Yankees tried to conscript contrabands they would sooner run back to their masters than serve in the Union army, for the blacks at Fort Pillow did not seem to them anxious to volunteer for anything, though they stole the Iowans' firewood, received fresh army tents, and were doled out the same rations as the men who were now expected to fight to set them free.[16]

Some of the poor country boys who served in the Union army did not think the slaves had had it so bad in the first place. "Niggers are thicker here in this country than catapillars on an apple tree," Joe Edwards of the 12th Michigan Infantry reported to his sister from his hospital bed in Helena, Arkansas. "All along the Mississippi you can see large villages of nigger huts arranged nicely in rows, the chimneys built outside & the house whitewashed. Some are log & some are very nice frame buildings." Yet it is hard to imagine men barracked in battened cabins that winter envying the barefoot contrabands as they shivered with their families in their icy, windwhipped tents.[17]

Though Yankees deplored the amount of thievery that went on around contraband camps, it was often necessary to the residents' survival. Theft had a curious place in the protocols of the South, for while some slaves deemed it only just to steal back at least a slice of the fruits of their labor, some masters actually encouraged their slaves to steal from their neighbors' larders. The result was that contrabands proved accomplished foragers on their Yankee employers' behalf, and some Union soldiers paid their black cooks and servants to steal.[18]

The necessary deceptions and constant monitoring of their masters' behavior and intentions turned many blacks into excellent spies and informers for the Union army. Posing as a Southerner, Allan Pinkerton, the chief of the United States Secret Service, went to Memphis on a spying mission in 1861. "Here, as in many other places," he recalled, "I found that my best source of information was the colored men, who were employed in various capacities of a military nature which entailed hard labor." Pinkerton mingled with them, and found them "ever ready to answer questions and to furnish me with every fact which I desired to possess." Slaves used their networks—Underground Railway systems, the hiding places runaways established in the woods surrounding their masters' plantations—to spirit escaped Yankee prisoners northward. A Union soldier escaping from Andersonville passed from black hand to black hand, and was refused help by only one slave: a woman who told him that she hated all whites so much that she had promised herself never to help a white man, not even a Yankee.[19]

As the contrabands continued to find their way to Union posts, officers desperately wired Memphis for instructions. No sooner had Cairo, Illinois, been cleared of refugees than three hundred more limped in, most of them "helpless women and children." Union general Napoleon Bonaparte Buford asked Hurlbut "how to support them & what to do with them."[20]

Colonel Wolfe's solution was to send as many of his contrabands to Island No. 10 as he could. On October 22, 1863, he ordered their superintendent, B. K. Logan, to evacuate "all negroes now at this Post not legally employed," leaving only the officers' body servants, company cooks, laundresses, wood choppers, and teamsters, since by now the repairs to Fort Pillow were all but complete. But apparently Logan had grown so devoted to the contrabands, or so attached to his position as their superintendent, that he reacted bitterly to Wolfe's order, calling him and his officers "a set of asses." The colonel relieved him of duty and replaced him with deputy provost marshal Lieutenant J. C. Alden, whereupon Wolfe's evacuation proceeded apace.[21]

None of Wolfe's papers indicate that the contrabands had caused him any significant problem; in fact, he could not have repaired his post without them. But their condition affronted the colonel's military desire for order, and their mere presence had been divisive. Though the contrabands themselves had been little trouble, the same could not be said of their white champions or their former owners, who had precipitated the war in the first place. Nevertheless, over five hundred contrabands, many of them transferred from Fort Pillow, were banished to Island No. 10.[22]

Even self-proclaimed abolitionists harbored profoundly contradictory feelings toward the contrabands they encountered. A Michigan surgeon named Samuel Henry Eells professed outrage at the way blacks were neglected in their camps. "Whenever they are gathered in together in any large numbers and kept at government expense," he wrote, "they are neglected by those whose business it is to take care of them, and die off rapidly in consequence, and everybody seems to feel as if that was about the best way to get rid of them." But Eells abhorred tending to the Hardeman County slaves who sought refuge in his camp. "I would as less doctor hogs," he wrote home, "and would much rather horses." He made himself a beneficiary of their high rate of mortality. "We intend to keep a dead nigger or two this winter for analytical purposes," he cheerfully declared. With contrabands at the camp at Bolivar, Tennessee, "dying at the rate of three or four a day," he hoped to obtain "plenty of subjects in Bolivar from the Negro 'corral,' as they call it there, and have got one already."[23]

Slaves nevertheless elicited a measure of sympathy from many Northern soldiers. "If a dog came up wagging his tail at sight of us," explained Colonel John Beatty of Ohio, "we could not help liking him better than the master, who not only looks sullen and cross at our approach but in his heart desires our destruction."[24]

Their sympathy was reciprocated. "I could not express to you the whole of my feelings and hopes and regard I had for the Federal Army," wrote Jack Daniels. "As sure as you are born it was a great thing, and as they first passed along—as long as I had milk or anything I carried it to them, and my wife sot up all night a-cooking for them, and we never charged them nothing for it."[25]

Once wrenched loose from their masters' thrall, even the most reluctant slaves sensed that something in their own hearts and minds had changed forever. Hemmed in, exploited, abused, overworked they might be by the Union army, but they were nevertheless regaining entire dimensions of their humanity that had been denied them for centuries: freedom from captivity, sale, separation, and the lash; the right to act as agencies of their own will; the right to choose their own spouses and name and raise and protect their own children; the right to be rewarded for work with more than an occasional buttered biscuit or a pass to visit the next farm over; the right to learn to write their names, count their wages, read the ballot and the Bible.

Expecting no consideration from white strangers, they were astonished and touched by sympathetic soldiers' little acts of kindness. "By and by" Tennessee slaves found Yankee soldiers "to be much nicer" than rebel troops, "and they treated everybody more courteously." One slave remembered how the Yankees would go from slave shack to slave shack, calling slaves out to follow them on their march, and distributing their masters' clothes to them as they followed the regiments down the road. Shared rations, the gift of a blanket, even a soldier's hand placed gently on a child's head elicited from many slaves paroxysms of relief, joy, and gratitude.[26]

Relations between the Hoosiers and the Iowans continued to deteriorate. Colonel Wolfe took a certain pleasure in recommending the dismissal from the service of the 32nd's revered Chaplain Lorenzo S. Coffin, whom he accused of being absent without leave. An outspoken abolitionist, Coffin had been a thorn in Wolfe's side. Perhaps Wolfe hoped to divert attention from the rampant venality at Fort Pillow, for which he was ultimately responsible. Loyal to the Union and probably not personally corrupt, Wolfe was nonetheless precipitate and neglectful. He allowed traders, informers, smugglers, and spies to infiltrate Fort Pillow, and in the process made a good many enemies out of men who should have been, if not his friends, his allies.[27]

In June 1863, Hurlbut removed the 2nd Illinois Cavalry from Fort Pillow. Stranded, sullen, idle, Wolfe's men grew slovenly, strewing garbage around their camps. After the cavalry's departure, the garrison fell into a rocky, contentious period marked by soldiers taking "French leave," and engaging in fistfights and drunken sprees. Wolfe's scouts indulged in a round of depredations, stealing cash from local farmers.[28]

Scott reported to Memphis that a number of local people had testified to him that they had been robbed by Wolfe's men. Other officers weighed in as well, and the cumulative accusations of corruption began to gather over Wolfe's head like a toxic cloud. It was charged that Wolfe had allowed traders to bring some twenty-three barrels of whiskey into Fort Pillow "by Government Teams and Guarded by soldiers at this post," and eventually to transport it all down to Fulton under escort to be sold. It was also "believed and asserted by some" that Wolfe ordered "the cavalry and Mounted Infantry at this Post" to escort a trader to the Fort, and that officers had received illegal payments for captured horses of from thirty-five to forty dollars a head.[29]

Seeing his chance to vent his outrage over Wolfe's management of the garrison and dismissive treatment of the 32nd, Colonel John Scott weighed in with his own charges against the commandant. Though Scott primly prefaced his allegations by asserting that he had not "encouraged criticisms of my immediate Commanding officer" or kept a "black book of his administration of affairs," Scott alleged that Wolfe had "the confidence of the disloyal of this section to a degree that is especially uncomplimentary to a man professedly loyal." Under Wolfe's command, Fort Pillow had become a leaky sieve out of which wagonloads of contraband salt and barrels of whiskey were frequently and mysteriously hauled off into the interior. Blankets and shoes that passed through the post were routinely found scattered around captured rebel posts. Wolfe had ordered the provost at Fulton "to pass the goods of a man who buys large quantities of 'family supplies' every month. I saw the June supply at Fulton to-day. Under his statement it is a shameless farce, and the man is indubitably disloyal."[30]

Scott's most serious charges, however, related to Wolfe's treatment of contrabands. He accused Wolfe, the provost marshal, and other officers of the 52nd Indiana of "want of sympathy" for refugee slaves that was "openly expressed." Scott backed up this allegation with several instances of neglect and abuse. The first involved a former Confederate soldier named Jones who manacled two runaway slaves who had taken refuge in the fort and led them off to a whipping post with the intention of flogging them to death. "They were rescued on the following day," Scott reported, but Wolfe had initiated "no investigation of this matter" despite its notoriety "throughout this whole region of country." In another case, a black man was "enticed without the guard lines and carried into slavery." His abductors were briefly imprisoned but "released with assurances that their conduct was not improper." An officer's servant was shot while traveling upcountry to visit his family, but "though his murderers are known and could be arrested without difficulty, no notice has been taken of the outrage."

Scott said that Wolfe had provided "no assistance or protection" to blacks who reached his lines, nor any assistance in retrieving their families "though frequently asked for and by men who wish to be enlisted as soldiers as soon as their families can be rescued." Wolfe refused to allow officers of the 32nd Iowa to round up slaves who wished to escape from rebel masters, and discouraged recruitment of black soldiers. When one of the officers of the 52nd Iowa volunteered to recruit black troops, one of Wolfe's lieutenants remarked in the colonel's presence that he "ought to be shot," to which "Wolfe expressed no dissent or reproof."[31]

Trying to keep the noise down, General Asboth summarily transferred Colonel Scott and his 32nd Iowa to Columbus with all their "camp and Garrison Equipage and Stores." However earnestly Scott may have wanted Wolfe brought to justice, he made no more accusations, delighted, under any circumstances, to be out from under the colonel's thumb.[32]

The 32nd's transfer was bad news for the contrabands. Nevertheless, it was with a giddy sense of renewal that John Scott and his men departed in stages on June 17 and 18, 1863, bidding Fort Pillow and the busy smugglers at Fulton Landing a hearty good riddance, relieved, as one of their captains put it, that they would no longer have to allow a "Hoosier colonel to abuse and vilify us."[33]

Scott and his men may have hoped that the army or the fates might reward them for their long-suffering service in West Tennessee. But as their steamer pulled away from the landing and chugged upstream around Craighead Point, they could not know that after leaving Fort Pillow they would spend many months guarding bridges "and doing very irksome garrison duty" around Columbus, until April 9, 1864, three days before Forrest attacked the garrison at Fort Pillow, when the 32nd Iowa Infantry would lose almost half its men in a battle at Pleasant Hill, Louisiana. "The 32nd, which had hitherto been confined to garrison duty, until all connected with it were impatient and indignant at such treatment," one of them wrote, "has at last been tried in the severest shock of battle, and the long list of killed and wounded demonstrates what Iowa men do when their blood is up."[34]

Wolfe's men sulked on for the rest of the year, and at one point drunkenly threatened to mutiny. His garrison was down to 580 men, of whom 112 were on the sick list or otherwise out of commission. When a small squad of his mounted infantry returned from Brownsville to report that Colonels Jacob Biffle and Jesse Forrest had trotted into the area with about a thousand Confederate cavalry, Wolfe pleaded that he had "not sufficient force to operate against them" and asked Asboth for "two full companies of Cavalry immediately." At last, on July 27, 1863, Hurlbut announced to Colonel Wolfe that he was no longer commandant and that Fort Pillow itself was no longer to be considered a Union post. Nevertheless, Wolfe and his Hoosiers were left to rot at Fort Pillow for another six months.[35]

"The time is now for the execution of a design long contemplated," wrote William Tecumseh Sherman on January 11, 1864. He was discreetly referring to the first of his so-called Hard War campaigns: a mass march on Meridian to destroy the railroad and thus make it "impossible for the enemy to maintain any considerable force in Mississippi." "At the same time," he added in his memoirs, "I wanted to destroy General Forrest."[36]

For this enormous expedition he would no longer countenance Hurlbut's excuses, nor accept that all he could spare was the 52nd Indiana. Sherman therefore ordered that Paducah's garrison be reduced to three companies, Cairo's to seven, Columbus's to one white and one black company, and Memphis's to two black and two white regiments; the remainder—most of Hurlbut's command—was to fall into step with the rest of Sherman's expedition.

A South Carolina lawyer who had fled Charleston to escape his debtors, Stephen Augustus Hurlbut had settled in Illinois in 1845 and immersed himself in politics. He had been the tall, dark beau ideal of a Southern gentleman, but decades of dissipation and defeats at the polls had fattened his midriff, dimmed his eyes, blemished his face with erysipelas, and thinned his hair sufficiently to betray a large and distracting pair of ears. A spendthrift, a climber, and a drunk, he had been a loyal supporter of the president, swelling Lincoln's cheering sections at the Lincoln-Douglas debates with his Illinois militia. The president had sent him down to Charleston to assess the situation at Fort Sumter, and after spending most of his time dodging his creditors, Hurlbut returned to report that secession was inevitable. Considering his political connections, his commission as brigadier general was no less inevitable. Though Hurlbut was a notorious inebriate whose binges would shame his adopted state, the president apparently took his drinking no more seriously than he took Grant's. But in Hurlbut's case, Lincoln was mistaken.

As Union commander at Memphis, Hurlbut oversaw perhaps the most blatantly corrupt regime of the many that disgraced Northern occupation throughout the West. His subordinates would trade in rebel cotton, assist smugglers in exchange for bribes, and collect ransom from wealthy families whose homes they ransacked and whose sons they held hostage in the verminous dungeons of Fort Pickering.[37]

When, in April 1864, he was ordered to explain why he had again garrisoned Fort Pillow, Hurlbut would plead that he "never had any orders to evacuate" Fort Pillow. "My orders from General Sherman," he said, "were to hold certain fortified points on the river. I never had any instructions with regard to Fort Pillow one way or the other that I recollect. I considered it necessary to hold it, and never intended to abandon it." He believed that Fort Pillow "should be held always, and there is nothing in my instructions that requires it to be abandoned."[38]

Hurlbut was mistaken, or lying. He did receive such instructions, and Sherman could not have been more explicit. "Abandon Corinth and Fort Pillow absolutely," he commanded on January 11, "removing all public property to Cairo or Memphis; also leave all black troops and such of the local Tennessee regiments as can be employed, with minute instructions to the commanders of posts at Paducah, Columbus, Cairo, Memphis, and such others as you judge best to have fixed to organize and arm the loyal citizens for self-defense"—thereby replacing the Northern troops Sherman was scooping up with Southern blacks and whites.[39]

Though Hurlbut hated to see the lower Mississippi's Union defenses reduced to such a remnant, he did as he was told. The very day he received Sherman's order, he commanded Wolfe to "send forward to Memphis the two best of his three batteries of light artillery," send "all public property" to Cairo or Memphis, completely abandon Fort Pillow, and transport his garrison to Memphis.[40]

Wolfe was delighted to comply with Hurlbut's order. To prevent Hurlbut's entertaining any second thoughts about evacuating the garrison, the colonel continued to report little rebel activity in the area. "The surrounding country is at present unusually quiet," he wrote, "free from marauding bands with the exception of a very few guerrillas that still infest Tipton County."[41]

Abandoning Fort Pillow was no small matter. The heavy guns had to be dismounted and loaded on steamers. To accomplish this, twenty-five black artillerists of the 1st Tennessee Heavy Artillery were shipped up from Memphis. All of the contrabands who had moved into Fort Pillow since Wolfe's last purge had to be transported up to Island No. 10, which Hurlbut had urged General Andrew Jackson Smith to garrison with "Negro soldiers" to guard against Confederate attacks. On January 24, 1864, on an island two miles north of Helena, Arkansas, 250 rebel cavalry had "fired upon a party of black woodchoppers, stolen some two dozen mules and oxen, and set fire to their shanties."[42]

Fifteen months' worth of the garrison's supplies and equipage, "horses, Mules, Bridles, Saddles, and Wagons," and surplus tents and clothing had to be collected and inventoried and turned over to the quartermaster. Soldiers' families posed an even more complicated problem. "Twelve or thirteen Tennessee boys had enlisted in our Company," recalled Addison Sleeth. "Some of these were married. Then some of our old Yankee boys had married Dixie girls, and it was now a question what to do with their wives. Most of them sent their wives to Northern homes and soon all was ready to go." On Tuesday, January 19, the 52nd "left the keeping of Ft. Pillow to others" and crowded aboard the steamer *Thistle,* which would take three days to make its way to Memphis, plowing down a river clogged with ice.[43]

"WE SOLDIERS ARE MEN"

BLACK TROOPS

1863–1864

In March 1863, Secretary of War Edwin Stanton sent Adjutant General Lorenzo Thomas to the lower Mississippi Valley to recruit black regiments. *Harper's Weekly* characterized him as a belated convert to the recruitment of black troops, but he entered upon his new assignment with vigor. Traveling down the Mississippi, Thomas paused at post after Union post to broadcast Lincoln's policy. It was the president's wish and the government's policy, he declared, that "all officers and enlisted men were required to treat the blacks kindly, and encourage their seeking the protection of the troops, to be fed and clothed as far as possible until they could be able to provide for themselves; the able-bodied men to be organized into regiments." Thomas warned that he "would not hesitate to dismiss from the service" any officer who stood in the way.[1]

Long before the Emancipation Proclamation, African Americans had fought for the country that had enslaved them. Early in the Civil War, many free blacks stepped forward to serve as laborers and officers' servants, and some light-skinned African Americans had already "passed" into white regiments as full-fledged soldiers. Many of the latter were apparently never discovered, while others were caught out by their color-conscious comrades.[2]

When it came to recruiting contrabands, Secretary of the Navy Gideon Welles got a considerable jump on the army. In April 1862, as the "hot and sickly season" approached, Welles had ordered Admiral Charles Davis to employ what he called "acclimated labor" to assist his overburdened white crews. Davis was to enlist contrabands "freely," and pay them "as boys at $8,

$9, or $10 per month and one ration." In May and June 1862, Charles Webb of Nashville and James Hennessy of Columbia County accordingly enlisted above Fort Pillow as first-class boys and served for the duration of the war.[3]

The black artillery regiments that would fight at Fort Pillow had their origins in the navy's experience with contrabands, for it was in the navy that they first demonstrated their proficiency with big guns. "The able-bodied negro," wrote Lieutenant Commander R. B. Lowry, "makes a good artillery-man." For the "working of the great guns, for coolness, quickness in handling the rammers, sponges, powder, shot, and shell, I found that they were exceedingly apt, and fond of it." The contrabands' "docility and aptness for military subordination would make them excellent garrison soldiers."[4]

Whatever the truth about their "docility," or, for that matter, their immunity to "remittent fever" (one Union doctor determined that blacks were only 15 percent less likely than whites to contract malaria), the idea of turning blacks into garrison soldiers appealed to the Union command for several reasons. First, as Sherman prepared to march on Georgia, black troops would free up regiments like the the 32nd Iowa Infantry for field duty. Second, as artillerists they could be confined to their posts, thus minimizing their contact with local whites. Third, a lot of the work that went into operating guns involved heavy labor—heaving shells and cannonballs, hauling cannon into place, pulling caissons, driving mules—which the Union army regarded as especially suitable employment for strong-backed former slaves accustomed to manual toil and Dixie heat. And finally, if contrabands did not work out as artillerists, the army could always blame the navy for giving it a bum steer.[5]

Organizing black regiments required officers of quality. Union general Augustus Louis Chetlain forbade any man "of known intemperate habits" from applying to become an officer in a black regiment and warned that any "incompetent or bad men" who found their way "accidentally into one of these regiments" would be "weeded out summarily." He likewise refused to accept any white man who believed he was "making a sacrifice in accepting a position in a colored regiment" or did so only in order to obtain higher rank and pay. Chetlain's aim was "to make colored troops equal if not superior to the best white troops in Drill and Discipline & officers" because colored troops were likely to form "no inconsiderable portion" of the country's permanent armed forces. "It can be no 'sacrifice,' to any man," he concluded, to command in "a service which gives Liberty to slaves and manhood to chattels, as well as soldiers to the Union."[6]

Among the commanders who enthusiastically endorsed the recruitment of black artillerists was General Hurlbut. "He says his corps will give it their support," wrote Thomas, "especially those regiments which have been in battle. He desires 600 as artillerists, to man the heavy guns in position, which he says can readily be raised from the contrabands within his lines. I have authorized him to raise six companies, and select the officers. He knows intelligent sergeants," wrote Thomas, "who will make good captains."[7]

Hurlbut found one of these "intelligent sergeants" serving in the 1st Missouri Light Artillery: Quartermaster Sergeant Lionel F. Booth. Born in Philadelphia in 1838, Booth had worked as a clerk in a law office until his twentieth birthday, when, with his brother John, he went west to Missouri and joined the frontier army. By 1862, he had risen to quartermaster sergeant in Company F of the 1st Missouri Light Artillery.[8]

At first his company served in central and southwest Missouri. In August 1862 it backed fourteen companies of Federal cavalry in the Battle of Lone Jack, exchanging fire with an outnumbering Confederate force before retreating with heavy losses. During this period Booth had been absent with what the regimental surgeon called "debilitas." But he returned to active duty in time to join General John Schofield's Southwest Missouri campaign and take part in the Battle of Prairie Grove, Arkansas, when the 1st Missouri crossed the icy Illinois River and after engaging Confederate major general Tom Hindman's batteries in an artillery duel, drove back a rebel counterattack with rounds of cannister in a battle that secured northwestern Arkansas for the Union.

It was during his service in the siege of Vicksburg, however, that Booth first caught his superiors' attention as a "steady, intelligent & worthy young man." On Hurlbut's recommendation, Lorenzo Thomas selected him to recruit Company A of what was dubbed the 1st Alabama Siege Artillery. Five feet nine inches tall, fair skinned, blue eyed, with a tousle of light brown hair, Booth was a man of "experience, tried courage," and, it was said, "irreproachable character." Presumably he had also developed some considerable sympathy for contrabands, for, as lieutenant and then captain, he proved an effective recruiter and a conscientious commander of the first battalion of what eventually came to be known as the 6th United States Colored Heavy Artillery (USCHA).

Many of the contrabands who were now poised to enlist as soldiers in the Union army knew exactly what they were getting into. The slaves of John J. Williams and William Harrell Cherry of Savannah, Tennessee, got their introduction to the horrors of war after the Battle of Shiloh. "A quiet, sober looking old town," as one visitor described it, Savannah was the Hardin County seat and home to 1,000 of the county's 11,000 inhabitants, of whom 1,600 were slaves. Though the town itself lined a single street along a bluff overlooking the Tennessee River, it was from the large plantations along its outskirts that the Union's 16th Army Corps would recruit a large number of its black soldiers, including at least five of the artillerists who would defend Fort Pillow.

Williams and Cherry were partners in a thriving mercantile concern that had enabled each of them to obtain large plantations. Cherry's spread, bounded picturesquely by a canebrake and worked by forty slaves, lay in the sandy bottoms of the Tennessee River. Williams was a secessionist, Cherry a vocal Unionist, and when the majority of Hardin's menfolk flocked to the Confederate standard, Cherry "narrowly escaped hanging two or three times" and holed up in his mansion as his partner organized a company of Confederate cavalry.

On February 16, 1862, Savannah's brown-jeaned Home Guards, armed with shotguns and squirrel rifles, were patrolling the town bluff when a man swam to shore from a passing steamboat and gasped the news that Fort Donelson had fallen, and the Yankees were on their way. At this the Home Guards melted into the countryside—some to join the Confederate army at Murfreesboro, the rest to protect their farms—but not before they had burned forty bales of William Cherry's cotton.

The next day, Cherry emerged from his house to welcome the Yankee marines who landed at Savannah to search the town for weapons. He offered his mansion to the injured and ailing Charles Ferguson Smith, the hardest-fighting Union general in the siege of Fort Donelson, a mustachioed Philadelphian who had been put in command of the Western army while Grant shadow-boxed with Henry Halleck over charges of drunkenness and insubordination. Smith had been felled not by bullets or shrapnel but by an infected abrasion he had received by scraping his shin on a gunwale while stepping from one boat to another. Now he held court in an upstairs bedroom, his bandaged shin hanging from the frame of Cherry's four-poster as he barked commands to his subordinates.[9]

A few Union flatboats and gunboats began to turn up along Savannah's riverfront, their decks crowded with soldiers. When they took sick, Cherry urged them to bivouac on abandoned secessionist property, including his father-in-law's house, while, deeper inland, rebel press gangs rode from farm to farm, rounding up every man of military age they could catch, whatever his views on secession. At Cherry's behest, the Yankees sent a gunboat with a regiment and a half of infantry to protect the county's homegrown Yankees, forty-five of whom promptly enlisted in the Ohio infantry.

On the sunny morning of March 11, slaves and soldiers gathered along the bluff to cheer as a flotilla of steamers and gunboats turned the little town of Savannah into a mere suburb of a vast floating city: "unexpected, grand, and indeed terrible, it was," wrote an observer. Over a hundred boats occupied an entire mile along both sides of the river, bristling with guns and bustling with soldiers.[10]

Within a few days, Cherry's mansion became the headquarters of none other than Major General Ulysses S. Grant himself, come to take command from Smith. Reinstated by Halleck, he arrived on crutches after a fall from his horse, and thus the Cherry mansion became host and clinic to two crippled commanders. No sooner had Grant settled into the Cherry mansion than he began to receive complaints from local planters that his soldiers were spiriting their slaves aboard steamers and whisking them off to labor at Pittsburg Landing. Grant at least made a show of trying to stop this practice. But it was not high on his list of priorities, and on Sunday, April 6, it shrank to insignificance. Grant had just hobbled down the stairs to join the Cherry family at breakfast when one of his staff rushed in to report heavy firing from the direction of Pittsburg Landing. Bidding the Cherrys a hasty good-bye, he climbed aboard the gunboat *Tigress* and steamed into the Tennessee's tawny stream, bound for "Bloody Shiloh."[11]

Whatever their masters' differences, the slaves of William Cherry; his partner, Jack Williams; and Cherry's father-in-law, James Irwin, were members of a large extended family. James Irwin's slave Eli was born in Savannah in about 1836, the son of a slave named Julius. Tall and dark, even as a boy Eli walked with a peculiar hitch in his gait. His playmates included William Cherry's slave Jack, and Jack Williams's slave Peter. Up to the age of about seven they cavorted with Eli's brothers Gideon and West, under the supervision of older slave boys, like Newton Campbell, Eli Falls, James Kerr, and Dick Kendall, all of whom would join the Union army.

On April 8, 1862, they witnessed one of the signal horrors of the Civil War: the aftermath of the Battle of Shiloh, in which over forty thousand Confederates collided with over sixty-two thousand Yankees, resulting in some twenty-three thousand casualties. The battle was the wedge that would ultimately split the Confederacy along the fissure of the Mississippi, and effectively drive its army out of Tennessee. Thus posterity would judge it a Union victory. But it could hardly have seemed so to the citizens and slaves of Savannah as the Union dead and wounded were dumped along the town's riverfront in bloody heaps and rows.

"All the buildings in the little straggling village had been taken possession of for hospital purposes," wrote a witness. "Here and there, on porches and in yards, lay the bodies of those who had died during the night. In almost every house surgeons were at work dressing wounds and amputating shattered limbs." To the slaves of Savannah it was a monstrous mutation of the violence they had come to expect of white people. They knew how brutal whites could be to blacks, but now even that seemed to pale beside the treatment they were meting out to one another. Touring a Yankee hospital, one slave wondered sadly why whites "couldn't settle their disputes without killing."[12]

After getting an eyeful of "this ghastliest picture of war," Eli Irwin and his boyhood playmates were swept along by the Union army on its march on Corinth. John J. Williams's slaves had no choice, for their secessionist master's "house was burned & the Negros drove off." But others, like William Cherry's slave Jack, apparently volunteered with their masters' consent, if not their blessing.[13]

By 1863, many of the black recruits from Savannah were married, and some now brought their wives and children along with them on their journey to Corinth, Mississippi. Jack Cherry, who preferred, in honor of his Savior, to be called "J.C.," had officiated at their betrothals as a slave preacher, conducting Eli Irwin's wedding to a slave girl from the neighborhood named Danie Masters. Jack Williams's prized Virginia slave Peter was permitted to marry a fellow slave named Alsie, a widowed mother whom Williams had recently purchased from New Orleans. By the spring of 1862, Danie had given birth to a son named Daniel, and Alsie had borne four children, only one of whom would survive the hardships of slavery and the pestilence of Union contraband camps.[14]

At Corinth, Dick Kendall and "J.C." Cherry joined the 55th United States Colored Infantry (USCI), but the rest enlisted in a company of 16th Army Corps artillerists that would eventually be divided between the 2nd U.S. Colored Light Artillery and the 6th U.S. Colored Heavy Artillery. Eli barely qualified. According to Peter Williams, the army examiner told him "that if he gave out while in the army, it would be on account of his breast weakening." Booth's recruiting examiner was not particularly selective. For instance, he passed a black enlistee named Willis Ligon even though his comrades claimed he was so deaf "he had to be hollered at." "The doctor did not have me take off my clothes," Ligon recalled. "He just took hold of my arms and bent them and examined me to see if I was afflicted in any way."[15]

Evidence of abuse—from whipping and branding scars to cropped ears—packed the examiners' reports, beating "all the antislavery sermons ever preached." Most recruits spoke of their punishments casually, as if recounting "a tooth ache, an accident to existence unpleasant enough—but to be endured as best they may." One examiner reported that half of the recruits he examined were scarred on their backs, some so badly that the flesh had grown back in ridges and ropes "as large as my little finger."[16]

Once a recruit passed his physical, barbers shaved off his braided hair, after which he was ordered to scour himself with lye soap and water. His old clothes were either burned, returned to his family, or distributed among refugees by the local superintendent of contrabands. The army furnished each recruit with a blanket, a blouse, a pair of infantry pants, a pair of boots, two pairs of socks, two white flannel shirts, and a cap, and each company with fifty tin plates, cups, knives, forks, spoons, "and the usual number of mess pans and camp kettles." For many recruits these were their first possessions.[17]

"A clean new suit of army blue was now put on him," wrote an officer of black infantry, "together with a full suit of military accouterments, and a gun was placed in his hands, and, lo! he was completely metamorphosed." The former slave's "plantation manners of tucking his hat under their arms and averting his gaze" was replaced by "the upright form, the open face, the gentlemanly address and soldierly salute."[18]

"Where the Negro had been kicked around before," wrote James Thomas, "he was now lifted to the highest gift, or elevation: his government's protector. Should a foot be lifted to give him a kick, he would reply, 'dont touch these clothes,'" and "at the same time show the Eagles on his coat." "Put a United States uniform on his back," wrote an officer, "and the *chattel* is a *man*."[19]

Nothing was likelier to inspire slaves to enlist than the sight of black troops marching by. "You ought to seen them big black bucks," recalled a former slave named Mingo White. "Their suits was so fine trimmed with them eagle buttons, and they was gold too. And their shoes shined so they hurt your eyes." "I was in the field shucking corn on the Murfreesboro Pike," recalled a Williamson County slave. "All at once I heard a band playing. Everybody in the field broke and ran. Not a man was left on the place. We all went and joined the army."[20]

"Now we soldiers are men," said a black volunteer, "—men the first time in our lives. Now we can look our old master in the face. They used to sell and ship us, and we did not say a word. Now we ain't afraid, if they meet us, to run the bayonet through them."[21]

According to the abolitionist *Liberator,* Emanuel Nichols of Company B, 6th USCHA, was a Michigan freedman who had come south to enlist in the Union army. If so, he was probably the only Northern freedman to serve at Fort Pillow. The rest were slaves.[22]

Some feigned ignorance when asked their occupations and birthplaces so their owners would not find them. But a few listed "farmer," "waggoner," "carpenter." Those who gave their birthplaces were from all over the slaveholding United States: Tennessee, Kentucky, Alabama, Virginia, Mississippi, South Carolina, Arkansas, and Missouri.

Most black enlistees arrived at recruiting stations with first names only. Masters used to amuse themselves by giving their slaves mock-grandiose names like Caesar, Napoleon, and Emperor or Victoria, Ruth, and Diana. Others took the low road. "My master's name was Simms," recalled Bill Simms, "and I was known as Simms's Bill, just like horses." A slave named Jack Sawyer tended hogs, so his master called him Jack Swine until he accidentally lost a leg, whereupon he renamed him Doctor Jack.[23]

"The government seemed to be in a almighty hurry to have us get names," recalled Martin Jackson, and many recruits had to invent them on the spot. Some chose the names of their former masters, not out of devotion but because they feared that unless they employed their masters' names, the relatives from whom they had been separated by slavery and now military service would never be able to find them. Some retained the names parents gave them and the names their masters gave them. Some chose the names of heroes like Lincoln and John Brown, and biblical patriarchs, prophets, and kings. Others chose names like Donkey, Coffee, Hominy—anglicizations of Dongko, Kofi, Kwame. Martin Jackson decided not to take his master's name but, recalling that his African grandfather's name was Jeaceo, called himself Jackson.[24]

Captain Deloz Carson of Company D of the 6th USCHA (6/D) did not allow Private Sherry Blain to choose his name. Blain had been sold as a boy after his parents, Mary and Willis Thornton, died in the mid-1850s. His new master was a transplanted middle-aged Virginian named Nathan Blain whose plantation lay near Fayette Depot, Tennessee, a few miles north of Wolf River. Master Blain was a terror to his slaves. Sherry recalled how Blain employed a fellow slave named Bob to teach his bloodhounds to catch runaways. "They used to run him to train their dogs," he recalled. "I've seen as many as fifteen dogs after him at one time. In these chases he was bitten— several times, to my knowledge—through the veins in his legs." For seven years Bob limped around as a field hand, until the fall of 1863, when he and Sherry and his brother Aaron were among the four or five Blain slaves out of the approximately thirty-four local black males who eluded their master's bloodhounds and fled to a Union recruiting station at Fayette Depot to join the 6th USCHA.[25]

Intending to free himself of any association with Nathan Blain, he gave Captain Carson his birth name—Sherry Finette Thornton. But Carson demanded to know who his master was, and on being told, put down "Blain" for his surname. His brother Aaron gave his name as "Finette." But Carson wrote it down as "Fentis." And so it went for the rest of Carson's recruits at Fayette Depot. As a consequence there was "a heap of mixing up of names of our regiment."[26]

Captain Booth, on the other hand, refused to employ a slave's master's name. Allen James Walker was born in 1845 "in the family of and a slave to Mrs. Sallie Walker near Germantown, Shelby County, Tennessee. My mother, Cleary Walker, belonged to Mrs. Walker also," he recalled. "My father was a white man whom I never knew, and my mother never told me who he was," although a comrade later identified Sallie Walker's husband as his father. Walker was eighteen years old and stood a little under five feet nine, with brown eyes and a "yellow" complexion, when he was "made up with the original organization under Major Booth." When Walker enlisted, "I gave them my name as Allen James and added that I belonged to the widow Walker. They said they wanted my name, not my owner's, and so enrolled me as Allen James, the name my mother gave me." Among the men who served at Fort Pillow were Lincolns and Washingtons and Jeffersons, and others that resonate like characters in a folktale: Moses Wiseman, Fate Sledge, Amdead Burgess, Shackleford, Destiny, Gallow.[27]

Each black artillerist was given "a gun and blue clothes" and the run of a row of barracks at Fort Pickering that white troops had left behind, near which their families were at first allowed to camp. Soon after arriving in Corinth, Eli Cothel came down with the smallpox that had plagued the 6th USCHA's white predecessors and now spread through the camp, killing one of his children. After the 16th Army Corps moved most of its black recruits from Corinth to Memphis, the army separated them from their families and banned their wives from camp. Reduced to drinking river water fouled by sewage, relegated to mildewed, leaking tents, many recruits died of pneumonia compounded by rheumatism and diarrhea. "The men have been sleeping on damp ground," wrote Booth, "with nothing to protect them from the earth," and such exposure was putting a high percentage of his men on the sick list. He applied for a regimental surgeon and almost eight thousand board feet of lumber to floor his men's tents in the rainy weather.[28]

Brigadier General John Dunlap Stevenson complained that he had to contend with at least six hundred "wives & children of Federal Soldiers that require to be cared for and also about the same number or more contrabands." To ease the congestion, U.S. agents seized a five-thousand-acre isle across from Memphis's riverfront called President's Island, which had been deserted by its rebel owners. The east end of the island was heavily timbered, but the west end was cultivated, and it was here that the army systematically "corralled" the families of its black recruits, as the contrabands themselves put it.[29]

As slave dealer, Confederate cavalry commander, and eventual Klansman, Nathan Bedford Forrest would prove an agency of fate throughout the lives of the men who served at Fort Pillow. In about 1859, Rosa Spearman Hooper had been sold to Forrest by her Lexington, Kentucky, master and transported in one of Forrest's droves to Yalabusha County, where he sold her to a man named Spearman. Shortly thereafter she moved with Spearman's three other slaves to his plantation outside Coffeeville, Tennessee, where, as Spearman's "house girl," she fell in love with Thomas Hooper, an enslaved field hand who worked on the plantation down the road.[30]

Apparently Spearman and Hooper were perfectly happy to allow Rosa and Thomas to sleep together, for they produced for the Spearman estate two children in quick succession, though one would die as a small child early in the war. They were never married, however. "They may have considered themselves morally husband and wife," sneered Spearman's son, W. Young, "but that relation was not recognized by our family." As the white Spearmans saw it, "they just copulated together." Rosa explained, however, that "colored people had nothing to do but stand up and get married. They never had no hurrah like they do now." They could not have "a home to themselves, but the woman lived at her master's home and the man was allowed to go to see her over a week, on Saturday nights, and if the white folks were good they would let him come twice a week."[31]

Sometime in early 1864, Thomas and Rosa gathered up their toddling daughter Josephine and ran away from their masters. "One night they were missing," recalled Spearman's son, "together with their child, or *her* child, and it was learned that they had joined the Federal Army." "Josephine was a little bit of a thing," Rosa remembered, "just big enough to walk when we left home. We had to carry her. I believe it was sorter cold weather when we come off from home. We went to Corinth, Mississippi and got there after a day and a night's travel." "I recollect seeing them come in walking," said Thomas's comrade, Alexander Nason, "and Tom carrying the child in his arms."[32]

Hooper immediately enlisted in Company C of the 6th USCHA and proved such "a good, steady soldier" that on March 1, 1864, after the regiment was transferred to Memphis, he was promoted to corporal. "Tom and I lived in a soldier's tent," recalled Rosa. "A good many of the soldiers had their wives with them. I lived with Tom and done his washing but not cooking—they had a man do that."[33]

Long before they would fatally converge at Fort Pillow, Private Willis Ligon and Nathan Bedford Forrest had become well acquainted with each other. Willis's last master was Clark Bobo, a wealthy planter with eighty-two slaves who served as one of Forrest's agents in the slave trade, alerting him to the availability of stock when a slaveholder died or fell into debt. "A stout, hardy boy," Ligon worked as Bobo's table servant, perhaps because he could not readily overhear his master's conversation: a series of boyhood ear infections had impaired his hearing in his right ear. In any case, he used to wait on the future Wizard of the Saddle when Forrest and his brothers dropped in at the Bobo house near Moon Lake on their slave-buying rounds.[34]

Ligon never knew his father's name, "as I was taken away from my mother when I was quite small." After Clark Bobo's death, Willis was sold to Bobo's sister in Coahoma County, Mississippi. But the change apparently did not sit well with him, and in 1862, while still in his teens, he ran away from his new mistress's house, crossed the Mississippi to join the Union army's Pioneer Corps in Arkansas, and enlisted eventually in the 6th USCHA.

"I fought to free my mammy and her little children," a veteran recalled. But the contrabands who joined the Union army knew they were risking not only their own lives but the lives of loved ones who remained in slavery. One recruit trembled for his sister back in the slave South, afraid her defiant pride in his service in the Union army would get her killed. He was right to worry. A black private named Glover received word from his wife that her overseer had "most cruelly" whipped her with a buggy harness. After a Woodford County, Kentucky, slave master named Warren Wiley found out that the runaway husband of his slave Patsey had joined the Union army, "he treated me more cruelly than ever: whipping me frequently without any cause and insulting me on every occasion." Even after Patsey's husband was killed, her master "whipped me severely, saying my husband had gone into the army to fight against white folks, and he—my master—would let me know that I was foolish to let my husband go" and would "take it out of my back." He would "kill me by piecemeal," he said, and hoped "that the last one of the nigger soldiers would be Killed." For the last whipping he gave her, "he took me into the Kitchen, tied my hands, tore all my clothes off until I was entirely naked, bent me down, placed my head between his Knees, then whipped me most unmercifully."[35]

Some masters tried to induce their former slaves to desert the army. Giles Johnson, a private in Company L of the 2nd USCLA, was the former slave of John Campbell, a farmer living near Wall Hill in Marshall County, Mississippi. Johnson frequently visited the Campbell farm to see his enslaved wife. One of his master's relatives, a widow named Sally Price, lived near the contraband hospital in Memphis, and "very frequently urged Giles to desert," promising him that the family would furnish him "with a first rate suit of citizen's clothes" if he would obtain a pass and drive himself and Mrs. Price back to Mississippi. A local family named Caldwell also worked on Johnson to persuade one of their former slaves, Private Colin Campbell of the 55th U.S. Colored Infantry, to desert as well. But they all remained with their regiments.[36]

After a Williamson County slave ran off and joined the army, his mistress exclaimed, "Don't you remember how I nursed you when you were sick? And now you are fighting against me!"

"No, ma'am," he replied, "I am not fighting against you. I am fighting for my freedom.'"[37]

In June, Lieutenant Colonel W. R. Roberts had assigned First Lieutenant David C. Mooney of the 1st Tennessee Heavy Artillery (African Descent) to recruit contrabands at Fort Pillow. "All Officers will render him there assistance in Obtaining Recruits," wrote Colonel Wolfe. "It is desired that these Regiments be filled as speedily as possible and all Able Bodied Colored men that are now employed in the Regiment as Cooks must be allowed to enlist without hindrance. There places can be filled by those who may hereafter come within our lines."[38]

Lieutenant B. K. Logan was ordered to deliver to Island No. 10 all of the contrabands who had gathered at Fort Pillow since the last evacuation and hand over fourteen new recruits to the 2nd Regiment Heavy Artillery. But apparently the contrabands kept pouring in, for within the month thirty-eight more men had been recruited at Fort Pillow and transported down to Island No. 10. Lieutenant Colonel W. R. Roberts picked up more recruits— Addison, John, William, Willis, Robin—from among the slaves of a local secessionist named W. R. Carr, and another twenty at Tiptonville, while Wolfe continued to relay their kith and kin to Island No. 10.[39]

Camp life freed former slaves to worship as they pleased and to discover, as they mingled with their comrades from different counties and different states, that African Americans had evolved, in their secret meetings and brush arbor churches, their own liturgy. Though officers sometimes felt compelled to break up their recruits' midnight camp meetings, even at bayonet point, many were moved by their troops' "Cromwellian fervor." After a sermon by a black reverend, soldiers of the 12th USCI fell to their knees in prayer or lay on the ground all night as if in a trance. "Surely," one of their officers said, walking among them, "God is with these people."[40]

The men and boys the army recruited for black regiments could be rough company, however. Cora Gillam used to ascribe her uncle Tom's ferocity to his Cherokee blood. One day a white mob in Little Rock, Arkansas, jailed him for reading a newspaper to his fellow slaves. "Twenty of them say they would beat him, each man, 'til they was so tired they can't lay on one more lick." But Tom leaped on the first man to enter his cell "and laid him out. No white man could stand against him in that Indian fighting spirit. They was scared of him. He almost tore that jailhouse down." Tom escaped, and was recaptured and imprisoned, but before they could hang him the Yankees turned up, set him free, and enrolled him in the army.[41]

Sarah Fitzpatrick's father was a slave driver, one of the black slave overseers commonly employed on large plantations. "He didn't have to do no hard work like the others. He carried his strop just like the white overseers, and had power to whup 'Niggers' just like they did. 'Course he always tried to make it easy for them so he wouldn't have to beat them." When the Yankees came "and seed my daddy with a big strap on his belt, driving 'Niggers' just like white folks, they made him 'hit the grit,' and then they caught him and took him with the Union Army."[42]

"I was surrounded by men whose daily habit was to brag, bully, and brow-beat," recalled Elijah Marrs of his first week in a black regiment, "and it illy fared with anyone who was too timid to stand up for himself." His comrades spent most of their leisure hours in jumping, wrestling, and playing marbles. Marrs remembered his horror when, his first night in the barracks, a man in the lower of the two bunks beneath him accidentally fired off his gun, killing the man in the middle bunk, and how "in less than two hours afterwards the body of the man shot was robbed of three hundred dollars that he had received that day as a substitute."[43]

In August a band of nine contrabands at Island No. 10, led by a white man, confirmed the worst fears of both Northern and Southern whites by murdering a local family named Beckam. "Nine of the murderers were arrested," wrote Colonel Roberts, "with the bloody arms and plunder on their persons." Perhaps because they were hunted down and captured by black soldiers of the 2nd Heavy Artillery, the crime failed to cause the kind of scandal that might have crippled efforts at black recruitment. In October 1863, a group of black troops was ordered to repay a local man for the lumber they had stripped off his barn, and any soldier found guilty of committing further depredations was to be summarily mustered out of the army.[44]

Men from Colonel Frank A. Kendrick's West Tennessee Infantry (African Descent) were reported to have "conducted midnight raids and robberies" around Moscow, Tennessee, and "deliberately fired upon peaceable citizens in their own houses and committed thefts and outrages that are a disgrace to the service." Kendrick issued a special order reminding officers that they would be held responsible for their men's malfeasance. But in the end an investigation exonerated his men, who were nowhere near the area where the outrages occurred. He suggested that the culprits were in fact from a company of colored heavy artillery recruits who were being recruited at Lafayette by Captain Deloz Carson.[45]

Afraid Carson's men might commit further outrages that would bring disgrace upon the Union cause, General Grenville Dodge ordered his company to Corinth. "My associates & self have raised this Co. by considerable hard labor, and the expenditure of nearly $100 in money," Carson protested. "I therefore earnestly & respectfully request that if compatible with the interest of the service, your order be countermanded." After several of his men were arrested, Carson was allowed to keep the remainder of his company, which he would command at Fort Pillow the following spring.[46]

The army began to receive complaints not only from slaveholders but from Federal officers that recruiting agents were deceiving blacks into joining with vaunting promises of high pay and luxurious living conditions. A man from Corinth who claimed he was a former Iowa cavalryman authorized to raise a regiment of his own scouted the country west of the Tennessee River, "seizing the property of peacable and unoffending citizens" in the company of "a lot of thieves and negro recruiting officers." Colonel Reuben Delaney Mussey prepared "Instructions for Agents Recruiting Colored Men for the U.S. Service" that he hoped would address some of the complaints that had been lodged against his own agents.[47]

At Paducah, a recruiter named Samuel Walker found thirty to forty men fit for service, and enlisted them in the 2nd Tennessee Heavy Artillery. But he met with resistance from Colonel James Martin and his superintendent of contrabands, who prevented about one hundred contrabands from enlisting. "This is an enigma to me," said Asboth. "Explain at once." Asboth ordered Martin to "send all colored men who have been recruited for the 2nd Tenn. Heavy Artillery to Columbus, in charge of an officer," and to allow army agents to recruit in his contraband camp. But Martin apparently dragged his feet, for a month later Asboth had to repeat his command.[48]

It was to men like Martin that Lincoln addressed one of his most forceful defenses of black recruitment. "You say you will not fight beside negroes," he said. "Some of them seem willing to fight for you." He predicted that when the war was over, there would be black veterans who would be able to say that "with silent tongue, and clenched teeth, and steady eye, and well-poised bayonet, they have helped mankind on to this great consummation; while, I fear, there will be some white ones, unable to forget that, with malignant heart, and deceitful speech, they have strove to hinder it." "The Government should arm the colored men of the Free States as well as the slaves of the south," wrote Second Lieutenant Thomas O. Howard of the 32nd Iowa, months after his regiment had departed from Fort Pillow, "and thereby give effect to the Emancipation proclamation of freedom" for a people who had "no rights under the Constitution or by the laws of war except the right to die."[49]

Most white proponents of black recruitment were not so lofty. "Every negro received saves a white man," declared a Missouri paper, "and we must confess that our sympathies are decidedly for the white man." "I believe," agreed the commander of a Kansas regiment of black volunteers, "the Negro may just as well become food for powder as my son."[50]

Abolitionist officers tended to be prigs and kept a tight rein on their men's behavior. "I do not allow a bit of profane language in my command," wrote C. P. Lyman of the 100th USCI. "I would reduce an N.C.O. to the ranks as soon as for profanity as for any other offence. I am glad to say that there is not a hundredth part as much profanity in our Regt. than there is in the white Regts with which I am acquainted."[51]

Some commanders put black troops to questionable use. On October 13, 1863, a recruiting agent reported from Gallatin that General Eleazor Paine had assigned some raw black recruits, unarmed and ill-clad, to escort a Union wagon train. "I understood General Paine to say that the advantage of sending them was to awe opposition," but the ploy did not work; the rebels attacked the train, killing one recruit. "It is slaughter to send out men in the condition our troops went."[52]

Acting on complaints from headquarters, on February 17 Booth had to scold his regiment for providing an insufficient number of men to labor on Union fortifications. He ordered that every morning first sergeants report the number of men they sent out on fatigue duty, including the "wood train." Elijah Marrs bridled when he and his men were ordered to clear ground for new barracks. He would ask himself, "Is my condition any better now than before I entered the army? But the idea would come to me that I was a soldier fighting for my freedom," and that the time would come "when no man can say to me, 'Come,' and 'Go,' and I be forced to obey." The thought, he said, "filled me with joy."[53]

In November 1863, Lorenzo Thomas ordered that officers could no longer require black soldiers "to perform any labor which is not shared by the white troops, but will receive, in all respects, the same treatment and be allowed the same opportunities for drill and instructions." Trained infantry recruits were deployed along the railways, where Stephen D. Lee, on a feint thirty-eight miles east of Memphis, ordered his men to open up with sniper fire. But the black troops stood their ground, returned fire, and proudly returned with a rebel prisoner.[54]

Ten days later, at Moscow, in the first major engagement between black troops and West Tennessee rebels, what was now called the 2nd West Tennessee Light Battery demonstrated an "accuracy in throwing shells right into the midst of the Confederate ranks and causing the rebels to retreat" that "surprised even their officers." Three blacks were killed and twelve were wounded, and as Hurlbut reported to Sherman, "the Negro regiment behaved splendidly." "After they fight their first battle," said a former slave named Cornelius Garner, "every general want them. They won the war for the white man. Yessir."[55]

The Union army's practice of arming runaways so inflamed the South that the Confederacy declared that all runaway slaves would be returned to their owners and any captured white officer or noncommissioned officer of a black regiment would be put to death for "inciting servile insurrection."

"Uneasiness is felt in some quarters lest the rebels should execute their brutal threats of hanging the officers of black regiments and selling the privates into slavery. But no apprehension need be entertained on this score," wrote *Harper's Weekly,* for even Jefferson Davis would have to realize that any "indignities offered to them would at once be followed by retaliation upon rebel prisoners in our hands. The 8400 prisoners taken by General Grant at Vicksburg," it concluded, "are a pretty fair security for our negro troops."[56]

They proved little or no security at all, however. In May 1863 the Confederates at Port Hudson prevented Union soldiers from burying black soldiers under the usual flag of truce. On June 16, 1863, the citizens of Jackson, Tennessee, from which the Yankees had withdrawn their forces, almost lynched a black scout and his white comrades whom the rebels had captured in an engagement with Union cavalry. The Confederacy's trans-Mississippi commander, Lieutenant General Kirby Smith, had a policy of taking no black prisoners, and if that could not be managed, to hang the few he captured alive. Joe Wheeler's men were notorious for disguising themselves in Yankee uniforms, tricking slaves into confiding that they wanted to be free, and then shooting them.[57]

On August 3, 1863, the 4th Mississippi Cavalry (CSA) took part in the capture of a detachment composed mostly of a "Corps d'Afrique" that had been trotting around East Feliciana Parish, Louisiana, collecting black recruits. "What disposition shall I make of negroes captured in arms?" their colonel wired Major General William Joseph Hardee. There is no record of his reply, but subsequently the Confederate command investigated rumors that the captive black soldiers and their lieutenant had been executed. Most rebel officers, however, sold their black prisoners, returned them to their masters, or put them to work. If they survived their capture, Northern freedmen were sold on the auction block. Other commands ran a profitable slave-trading racket, kidnapping slaves, selling them, and pocketing the proceeds.[58]

Whatever their officers' preferences, many Confederate soldiers vowed to show black soldiers no mercy. Seventeen-year-old Isaac Dunbar "Dunnie" Affleck joined Company B of B. F. Terry's Texas Rangers in Shiloh's wake. "They are raising negro regiments every where," Dunnie reported from the field in March 1863. "If we ever come in contack with any of them," he said, "we intend to hoist the black flag and give no quarter, and I think we can soon stop them fighting against us here. But I don't think there is much fight in a negro, at least they have not stood up before us yet." But they would stand up to Affleck, and Terry's Texas Rangers, and Nathan Bedford Forrest himself.[59]

In response to Confederate threats to enslave black troops and show no mercy to their white officers, Lincoln declared that "to sell or enslave any captured person, on account of his color, and for no offense against the laws of war, is a relapse into barbarism, and a crime against the civilization of the age." He therefore ordered that "for every soldier of the United States killed in violation of the laws of war, a Rebel soldier shall be executed; and for every one enslaved by the enemy or sold into slavery, a Rebel soldier shall be placed at hard labor on public works, and continued at such labor until the other shall be released and receive the treatment due to a prisoner of war." But in the end Lincoln never carried out such threats.[60]

The Confederacy's policy failed to slow the recruitment of blacks, and white applicants were encouraged by Stanton's directive that discharged whites who joined black regiments as officers and sergeants could regard their service as a continuation of their service in their former regiments and thus receive "the bounties now allowed to Veteran Volunteers." Within a week, General Chetlain had received so many applications for positions in regiments of African descent that he refused to accept any more.[61]

On March 17, Lieutenant Colonel Thomas J. Jackson was put in command of what was now called the 1st Alabama Siege Artillery, but was about to be redubbed the 6th USCHA. "It takes a Gentleman to make a good soldier," he told his men, "and it is to be expected that you all will act as becomes Gentlemen in the discharge of your duties. You must be and act as men. You must behave as men, for you are striving for that which is dearer to man than life and that is Liberty. You must drop all your childish games."[62]

The next day, however, Jackson turned the command of the 6th USCHA over to a newly promoted Major Lionel Booth.[63]

HOMEGROWN YANKS
BRADFORD'S BATTALION

1863–1864

THE MAN TO WHOM COMMAND OF THE UNION GARRISON WOULD FALL during the rebel attack on Fort Pillow was one of a number of marginal amateur warriors and local Unionists who emerged in West Tennessee after Sherman began to strip his Western commands of their veteran white regiments. Faced with the task of replacing seasoned troops with Unionist partisans of doubtful loyalty and lax discipline, in the summer of 1863 Military Governor Andrew Johnson granted permission to a young Obion County lawyer and vociferous Unionist named William H. Bradford to recruit and organize a cavalry regiment in West Tennessee. Having already enlisted "quite a number of men at or in the vicinity of Union City," Bradford was "anxious to have them mustered into the service and supplied with rations, blankets, camp & garrison equipage, also arms & accoutrements when mustered into service."[1]

The Bradfords of Tennessee had a history of swimming upriver. William's father, Theodorick Fowke Bradford Sr., had been an East Tennessee state legislator and publisher of the *Shelbyville Herald*, Bedford County's first newspaper. Denouncing Andrew Jackson's Union Bank as a despotic scheme to benefit big land speculators at the expense of poor settlers, he ran unsuccessfully for Congress against James Knox Polk, and joined forces with the contrarian Davy Crockett in his virulent attacks on Old Hickory.[2]

Theodorick raised six daughters and three sons on the Duck River's Wartrace Fork, less than a mile from Nathan Bedford Forrest's birthplace. His sons Barkley and Ted were about Forrest's age, and it is reasonable to imagine the Bradford and Forrest boys encountering each other on their gambols along the Duck. The eldest boy, Barkley, followed Crockett to his doom in Texas. But Ted junior and his little brother William, who was born a year before the Forrests emigrated to Mississippi, joined the bar and moved to West Tennessee after their father's death, bringing their East Tennessee Unionism with them.

Neither of them prospered. Ted hung his shingle in Dyersburg. By 1860 and the age of thirty-five, he had married a New England girl and sired three children, but listed assets of only about two thousand dollars, including his horse. William set up his practice in neighboring Obion County. At the age of twenty-eight, William was the more prominent, or in any case conspicuous, of the Bradford boys: trumpeting his Unionist sympathies, spying on his secessionist neighbors, and eventually reporting their plots and machinations to Military Governor Andrew Johnson. In November 1862, he denounced a local judge named Samuel T. Williams for convening his court without legal authority and delivering secessionist diatribes from the bench, whereupon General Hurlbut closed his court and threatened to bar Williams from running for office.

According to Colonel Thomas Harris of the 54th Illinois, Troy, Tennessee, in wartime was "a hot-bed of traitors." In the fall of 1862, Bradford was apparently kidnapped by a band of rebel guerrillas who haunted a nearby swamp, "carrying off Union citizens and robbing them of their property, especially horses." Federal authorities regarded Bradford as such a Unionist "main stand-by" that Harris threatened to burn Troy to the ground if he was not returned. The threat apparently worked, for Bradford reemerged from the bottoms more vehemently Unionist than ever. But during his captivity Judge Williams, who claimed to support the Union but nonetheless felt that local Yankee officers had "exceedingly wrong notions on the subject of slavery," was exonerated after Union colonel Isaac Hawkins of Tennessee, later the victim of an ingenious rebel bluff at Union City, intervened with a plea and, according to local lore, a gift to Governor Johnson.

Enraged, Bradford gave up on law and politics and, fashioning himself a colonel, raised a company of Home Guards. "Under the pretense of scouring the country for arms and rebel soldiers," wrote Forrest's authorized biographers, Bradford "traversed the surrounding country with detachments, robbing the people of their horses, mules, beef cattle, beds, plates, wearing apparel, money, and every possible movable article of value, besides venting upon the wives and daughters of Southern soldiers the most opprobrious and obscene epithets, with more than one extreme outrage upon the persons of these victims of their hate and lust." Such, in any case, would be the rebels' postmortem case against William Bradford.[3]

Bradford raised his recruitment banners at Paducah, Union City, and amid the twice-abandoned ruins of Fort Pillow, collecting a motley assortment of men from the surrounding countryside for what was dubbed Bradford's Battalion but would later be incorrectly but indelibly called the 13th (it was officially the 14th) Tennessee Cavalry.

Many of Bradford's enlistees were Unionist refugees who, like the contrabands, had fled with their families to the Yankee lines. They were small farmers, for the most part, and many were family men. Daniel Stamps of Coffee County, Tennessee, was married with one daughter and a small farm within a few miles of Fort Pillow when he and his brother Jack joined the latecomers to the Union standard who enlisted in Company E. Some of them were long in the tooth. The oldest enlisted man at Fort Pillow was apparently Leander C. Vaught of Company C, a comparative codger at forty-seven years of age. Forty-year-old Al Middleton of Weakley County had a wife and daughter when he enlisted at Union City in Company C.[4]

Their median age was about twenty-three, two years older than Forrest's men. Twenty-seven percent of Bradford's troopers were over thirty, and about half claimed to be in their twenties, although so many boys lied about their age that some of them were probably considerably younger. Over a fifth gave their ages as nineteen and under.[5]

At least 10 percent had deserted from the rebel army. Afraid for their families in Union-occupied West Tennessee, convinced the secessionist cause was already lost, or simply sick to death of war, they had shucked their butternut uniforms in disgust and returned home to protect their families from rebel guerrillas and Yankee foragers. By early 1864, many of them had fled to the Union lines for safety and, like some of their black counterparts, joined up out of sheer necessity.[6]

Posted to Union City in the fall of 1863, Bradford tried to bring some order to his motley companies of aspiring cavalry. He banned "promiscuous and straggling firing" of weapons, "pleasure riding," horse races, and raiding the fortification's abatis for firewood. "Not fewer than three persons will be permitted to leave camp together, and these must be armed, and must not go more than *two miles* from camp." Each officer was required "to attend 'water call' to see personally that all the horses of his company are properly taken to water." Horses were to be kept "well groomed morning and evening, and at noon need only be fed." But commanding a regiment required more than do's and don'ts and timetables. It required earning men's trust, something Bradford would find elusive.[7]

Early in his recruitment drive, Bradford reckoned he had found a shortcut to the formation of his first company in a Kentuckian named Jonathan F. Gregory whom he had encountered recruiting men for Hurst's 6th Tennessee Cavalry. Bradford promised Gregory a captaincy if he brought his recruits into the 13th instead. Gregory agreed, and his men took Bradford's promise so seriously that they immediately and proudly took to calling their enterprising commander Captain Gregory as they gathered at Paducah to be mustered in.[8]

On February 2, 1864, William Sooy Smith, the Department of the Mississippi's chief of cavalry, ordered Bradford to Fort Pillow to establish a "recruiting rendezvous" for his 13th Tennessee Cavalry. Approved by General Hurlbut, the order reached Bradford at Union City, and two days later, as Sherman set forth from Vicksburg to take Meridian, the 13th Tennessee Cavalry proceeded via Columbus to Fort Pillow.[9]

Thomas H. Harris insisted that Smith had merely acceded to Bradford's own request to leave Kentucky, where he had been "finding recruiting very difficult," and search for enlistees in Fort Pillow's vicinity. It is possible that Sherman himself had had second thoughts about abandoning Fort Pillow "completely," and directed Smith to station the 13th there. But there is no documentary evidence to support this conjecture, and though Sherman did at one point expansively declare that he would leave the garrisoning of the Mississippi to Hurlbut's "discretion," he meant the garrisoning of only those posts he intended Hurlbut to continue to occupy. After the fall of Fort Pillow, Sherman would maintain that he had assumed all along that, as per his original orders, Fort Pillow had remained abandoned. "I think General Sherman did not purpose to withdraw a heavy force to pursue Forrest," testified General Mason Brayman, at Cairo, for Sherman believed "we had force enough to hold the important points on the river." But Brayman and Hurlbut second-guessed Sherman because they felt that "the strength of the enemy and the scattered condition of our small detachments was not fully understood."[10]

Contradicting Harris and the documentary evidence of Bradford's original orders, Hurlbut claimed that his intention was not just to establish a recruiting station but to occupy Fort Pillow and thus prevent the rebels from planting artillery on the bluff. But the deployment would seem so inexplicable and the explanations so contradictory that some retrospectively suspected Hurlbut of sending troops to protect his interest in the illegal cotton trade. But it seems unlikely that Booth would have acceded without protest to sending his black troops into harm's way merely to patrol West Tennessee cotton crops.[11]

On February 8, three days after Forrest reported to Jefferson Davis that both Fort Pillow and Columbus had been evacuated and West Tennessee was "almost entirely clear of Federal troops," the 13th Tennessee Cavalry, Major William H. Bradford commanding, began to reoccupy the post.[12]

"You will take a good defensible position for your camp," Smith instructed Bradford,

> taking advantage of any intrenchments that may already exist, and constructing any that may be necessary. You will scout the surrounding country thoroughly as far to the rear as you may deem it safe to take your command, making every effort in your power to hunt up and destroy guerrilla parties. You will subsist your command upon the country as far as possible, and take the stock necessary to keep it well mounted, giving vouchers to loyal men only. Keep your command in condition for active service at all times, drawing arms, ammunition, and equipments from the ordnance department at this city. Use all diligence to recruit your regiment rapidly, and apply to the chief commissary of musters, stationed here, to muster your men promptly.[13]

A commissioned officer and forty men from Company A of what was about to be dubbed the 2nd U.S. Colored Light Artillery (USCLA) arrived from Memphis about a week later to place field guns at the fort. On March 7, Lorenzo Thomas announced that he intended "to find competent garrisons" for black troops along the Mississippi, and it may have been at his urging that Hurlbut deployed black artillery to Fort Pillow.[14]

Though Bradford himself had supported the enlistment of black troops, many of his West Tennesseean white recruits, some of whom had fought for the Confederacy until Donelson and Shiloh, were hostile to blacks and doubted their ability to fight, let alone man artillery. To keep the two groups separated, Bradford assigned the 2nd USCLA to an abandoned camp behind the northernmost breastworks of the fort and kept them at their guns while his white troopers scoured the countryside for forage.

Contemptuous of neutrals, Bradford immediately began to round up local men. A North Carolina native named Jim Alsobrook had been farming ninety acres about thirty-five miles from Fort Pillow for some thirty years. Alsobrook had been conscripted into the 15th Consolidated Tennessee Cavalry (CSA) but deserted soon afterward and returned to his farm. On February 15, a squad of foragers from the 13th trotted up to his gate and handed Alsobrook a note for $250 in exchange for a horse and a quantity of salt. As the soldiers were leaving, a slave Alsobrook had hired from his mother-in-law suddenly bolted. The soldiers chased him down and asked him why he had run. The slave replied that he had been told that the Yankees were rounding up blacks and taking them to Dyersburg. The soldiers arrested Alsobrook for spreading rumors and brought him to Fort Pillow, where he claimed he had been set up by an old enemy named Miles A. Goforth, "who was mad with me and told Maj Bradford that he knew me and that I was a guerilla." Nonetheless, he was incarcerated at Fort Pillow for several weeks, and spent two more in Memphis before a friend could finally arrange his release.[15]

Bradford had little respect for the locals' professions of loyalty. "Some of the worst rebels have been captured here with oaths of allegiance in their pockets," recalled Captain James Marshall of the Union gunboat *New Era*. "Major Bradford captured some whom he knew personally to be the worst rebels." Sixty-five-year-old Lemuel Curlin of Obion County was born in North Carolina and served briefly in the War of 1812. "It was hard for that kind of Men to turn against the US Government," his physician explained. "I was a soldier in the Mexican War. That made my devotion so great to the Old Flag I could not turn against it." His three sons felt differently, however, and joined James J. Neely's 4th Tennessee Infantry CSA. Curlin "done my best to keep them from going. I tried to get the two oldest to go to Canada," he said, "because I could not keep them from going into the southern army. They went contrary to my voice." Curlin voted twice against secession and often fed the Union soldiers who passed his farm, but this did not prevent Captain Joseph F. Peck of Bradford's Battalion from relieving this illiterate old Unionist veteran of two mules and a sack of bacon.[16]

In early 1864 Fielding Hurst's 6th Tennessee Cavalry brought Bradford a most unlikely captive: the Reverend George Washington Harris. Known as the "unmitred or unordained bishop of West Tennessee," G. W. was the sixty-seven-year-old big brother of rebel governor Isham Harris, who was

then riding with Forrest in Mississippi. The Bradfords were acquainted with
the reverend, for he and William had been neighbors in Dyersburg. Bradford duly took him into custody for sedition, but, lacking a chaplain of his
own, prevailed upon Harris to preach to the 13th. The old man thereupon
launched into a blistering secessionist harangue studded with biblical defenses of slavery plucked from the pages of Leviticus. Though Bradford decided to let it pass, and Harris was apparently treated with deference,
Forrest demanded that the old man immediately be given "a fair trial before
a competent tribunal," threatening that if "the Bishop of West Tennessee"
died in Yankee custody, Forrest would execute five of his Yankee prisoners.
The reverend was eventually set free.[17]

Bradford's boys were ordered to grub up the countryside for provisions.
Compared even to the 52nd Indiana Infantry, they proved voracious foragers. A farmer named Embry complained that Bradford's men took all nine
of his horses, "depriveing me of the means of makeing a crop." In early
March, a former state legislator from Lauderdale County reported that West
Tennessee whites flocking to the Union standard at Fort Pillow had
"stripped the people of provisions."[18]

Bradford eventually broke his promise to Jon Gregory and gave the captaincy of Gregory's Company A to his brother Ted after he and his wife were
chased out of Dyersburg for their Unionist views. Ted's appointment was
not sanctioned by Memphis until January, by which time Bradford had assembled four full companies and was rapidly recruiting a fifth. Hurlbut's examining board was so doubtful of William's military aptitude, however, that
it declined to make him even a lieutenant colonel. Eventually describing
Bradford as "very young" and "entirely inexperienced," Hurlbut made him a
major instead, thus stalling the rise of the ambitious young men who had
signed up to serve under him.[19]

Bradford's broken promises and bald nepotism so enraged Gregory and
his men that they began to desert from Fort Pillow in droves. By February 20, disaffection compounded by lack of pay, freezing weather, and rampant disease had spread to the rest of Bradford's companies.[20]

On paper, at least, his battalion numbered 419 men by the end of
March, but only 292, or about 70 percent of his command, including 65
unassigned recruits, were at Fort Pillow. Of these, only 266, or a little less
than two-thirds, were fit for duty. One hundred twenty-seven men were absent or sick: 112 of them (more than a quarter of Bradford's total force) were
absent without leave, and four were under arrest. Five had died of disease,

26 were sick, and though 12 deserters had returned in the previous month, 24 more men had deserted, half of them from Company D. The regiment had collected only 107 horses, 3 of which were unserviceable, and the highest proportion of horses to men (54 percent) was among the "unassigned recruits" of Company E, indicating that they had probably brought their own. The lowest proportion (23 percent) was in Theodorick Bradford's Company A, whose deserters had apparently taken their horses with them.[21]

Recruitment had stalled; the only gains Bradford could report were the twelve deserters who had returned and one invalid who had recuperated, but they were outnumbered more than two to one by his losses. By the eve of the attack on Fort Pillow, the number of men on the sick roll would decline somewhat to twenty-three, but on the night of April 10 alone, twenty of Bradford's men would desert en masse.[22]

Young Read Johnson had been a clerk in his father's grocery store in Hickman County, but sometime early in the war the store went under, and in November 1863, Johnson enlisted in the 13th Tennessee Cavalry. After his regiment was posted to Fort Pillow, Johnson was detached to serve as a mail clerk in the provost marshal's office. On February 20, he wrote one of the few letters that survive from the last Union garrison at Fort Pillow. "I am well and as fat as a Bear," he said, and doing "a good deal better than I was doing at Union City," where he had been assigned "to stand picketts." At Fort Pillow he didn't "have Eney thing to do but rite passes and tend to the mail."

In a previous letter he had told his mother that his company had found comfortable lodgings at Fort Pillow in what he described as good "slave houses." But by the first of March they were to move into some winter quarters the regiment was constructing. In any case, Johnson did not imagine the regiment would remain at Fort Pillow very long, "for all our boys is leaving here and runing [off] and going home. Since we came here we have lost 15 men. Our company lost 8 men last night, and I think that we will be moved to Memphis soon." In fact, Bradford had just left to persuade Hurlbut to assign his regiment to Memphis. "Yuo can come on a visett," Johnson told his mother, who hoped to join her only son at Fort Pillow if she could "only get a house," "but yuo cant get a house here but store houses and hotels."[23]

Bradford's mission to Memphis was unavailing. Inexplicably, Hurlbut refused to allow Bradford to evacuate a post Sherman had ordered abandoned, and the young major returned to his regiment in a funk. On February 23, in the presence of several other officers, Bradford accused the embittered Lieutenant Jon Gregory of encouraging his men to desert and ordered his staff to arrest him. Cursing Bradford, Gregory reportedly reached for his pistol, but Bradford somehow beat him to the draw and felled him with a single shot to the stomach that took five days to kill him. Though Gregory's mother decried the shooting as an "unprovoked murder," Bradford was never charged.[24]

Gregory's death did not cool Bradford's temper nor slow the 13th's desertions. With his "captain" dead, an earnest young volunteer named James Park left Bradford's regiment and made his way to Paducah to join the 15th Tennessee Cavalry. But the 15th's Major Wiley Waller told him that "he had done wrong to leave his company, and that he could not join another command without first obtaining a transfer." So Park returned to Fort Pillow, where Bradford denied his request and refused to remove a charge of desertion. Only his death at Fort Pillow would save him from a court-martial. "It is a burning shame for such a patriot to be Branded with the dishonor of desertion," wrote Major Waller after the war. "The boy had no notion of desertion, and his father and family are true and tried patriots."[25]

Perhaps the best gauge of what a poor commander Bradford proved to be was the eagerness with which his men tried to join Fielding Hurst's ill-managed 6th instead. An impoverished Kentuckian named James M. Moore shuttled haplessly between the two regiments. Captured by Forrest while on patrol with the 6th, he was paroled at Trenton, Tennessee, in December 1862. Moore was disgusted by the way Hurst and his officers treated their men. A comrade recalled that for six months the men of his company "could see other soldiers around us who were treated as soldiers, drawing their pay &c. and everything going along smoothly when with us we got no pay and could see no prospect for it."

So in November 1863, Moore left the 6th and signed up with the 13th, only to find that things were no better under Bradford than they had been under Hurst. Caught between a rock and a hard place, Moore was among those who deserted from Fort Pillow in February to join—or in his case, rejoin—the 6th. But no sooner had he reached Hurst's command than he was arrested for desertion. Released on a technicality after his captain conceded that he had never actually been mustered in, the ill-used James M. Moore resignedly returned to the 13th, only to fall into the hands of the rebels after the assault on Fort Pillow, languish in Andersonville, and die in September of scurvy, dysentery, and starvation.[26]

A firm number of actual as opposed to alleged desertions from so decimated, irregular, and undocumented a regiment as the 13th is impossible to pin down. Among the men of the 13th who almost certainly deserted was

Bill Henry of Weakley County. A member of Company E, he would claim that his captain had permitted him to leave his regiment at Union City sometime in late March so that he could escort his mother to safety in Illinois. He said he then tried to return to his regiment at Union City only to find that the garrison had surrendered. Some twelve miles from Union City, he had the bad luck to be captured himself.[27]

Anderson Jones claimed that five days after he enlisted in the 13th, Bradford granted him a sixty-day furlough, "and the very day my furlough expired my said regiment was attacked and cut to pieces by Forrests men and were all killed or captured or scattered so that I never rejoined my said company." Nothing, however, could be unlikelier than Bradford's granting furloughs at a time when desertions were so rife and Forrest was at large. In fact, his returns for March show only one man absent with leave.[28]

By the spring of 1864, in a hollow perpendicular to the river, a veritable town arose. The station included stores, groceries, a hotel, even a photographic portrait studio. In fact, to one observer the post appeared to be nothing but a military town boasting an "extra large supply of sutlers goods" which merchants hoped to barter for whatever cotton they could find that was still "in the hands of planters."[29]

Among the merchants was the aspiring New England barrel maker Edward B. Benton. He must have been especially pleased that Hurlbut had seen fit to regarrison Fort Pillow, for by now he had employed "government darkeys," as he called them, to begin to prepare one hundred nearby acres for cotton cultivation. The contrabands had been provided courtesy of their superintendent at Memphis, and lived in their predecessors' camp.[30]

By the authority of the adjutant general's office, Fort Pillow was one of the few places along the Mississippi where civilians were allowed to go ashore, and thus proved a magnet for smugglers and entrepreneurs. Another of the garrison's merchants was Eugene Bestor Van Camp. Born in Kentucky in 1838, he had moved with his father, Aaron, to Washington, where Van Camp senior opened a practice as a dentist. Dr. Van Camp was "one of the most bitter and uncompromising secessionists in the city," and when war broke out his house in D.C. became a kind of rebel post office, funneling correspondence to secessionists throughout the South. Leaving his studies at Georgetown University, Eugene joined the Confederacy, enlisting in the 6th Virginia Cavalry in April 1861. Wounded at the Battle of Strasburg, he either deserted or was captured; either way, the Yankees transported him to Baltimore, where, upon reciting the Oath of Allegiance, he was eventually paroled and returned to D.C. Accused of rebel sympathies, he was banished from the capital by the provost marshal and warned not to return to the South. Nevertheless, January 1864 found him in Vicksburg, Mississippi, assisting his father in his cotton speculations. A Memphian named B. D. Hyam described Eugene as "very erratic, going backwards and forward between Vicksburg and [Memphis] pretty often," and suspected both father and son of spying on behalf of the Confederacy. Nevertheless, Dr. Van Camp managed to wangle a trading permit from Hurlbut, and in early April sent Eugene to Fort Pillow to establish a store. Only three days before Forrest attacked Fort Pillow, the unfortunate Eugene Bestor Van Camp opened for business.[31]

"UNEQUAL STRIFE"
FORREST'S CAVALRY

1861–1864

Hurrah for the saddle! and ho for the Colt!
Here's to our sweethearts at home!
We are off on a raid, but are never afraid,
*   In whatever land we may roam. . . .*
Old Forrest, sitting on his good black horse,
Is waving his saber on high;
. . . Let the sunbeams flash or the thunder crash,
We will follow it, or we'll die!

—CAPTAIN JAMES M. M'CANN
"The Song of Forrest's Men"[1]

IN A THEATER OF WAR THAT PITTED SOUTHERNER AGAINST SOUTHERNER, each side dismissed the other as riffraff: thugs, drunkards, drifters, slackers, and assorted detrimentals who haunted the periphery of the great plantations or the back alleys and riverfronts of Southern towns; the "poor white trash" of antebellum lore. But they were wrong. Each side looked ragtag to the other, and it often was, but where each regarded its own raggedness as a badge of sacrifice and honor and its own savagery as proof of its courage, it dismissed the other side's raggedness and savagery as evidence of ignorance and backwoods barbarity.

Though West Tennessee's slaveholders were generally wealthier than nonslaveholders, and a higher proportion fought for the Confederacy, all classes were about equally represented on both sides. As John Milton Hubbard would discover after his 7th Tennessee Cavalry (CSA) captured the 7th Tennessee Cavalry (USA), the bluecoats "turned out to be jolly good fellows, molded much after the pattern of our own Seventh Tennessee, Confederate."[2]

The ancestry of the men who rode with Forrest was about evenly divided among English, Scottish, and Irish, with a scattering of French, German, Dutch, and Swiss. According to a survey of Tennessee's Confederate veterans that was conducted in the early 1900s, the vast majority of Forrest's Tennessee cavalrymen were first- or second-generation Tennesseans, but their ancestors were no strangers to slavery. The preponderance of the Mississippians who served under Forrest had emigrated from the Carolinas, and, like the ancestors of the Wizard's Missouri Cavalry, most of his Tennesseeans' forebears had pressed westward from "slavery's cradle" in Virginia, bringing their slaves along with them. Of the 137 veterans of Forrest's regiments who listed their ancestry, only two had families that had emigrated from free states: New Jersey and Massachusetts.[3]

Three-quarters of Forrest's Tennesseeans were living in the western half of the state when they enlisted.[4] Though four of them were in their thirties in 1864, cavalry service was a young man's game. The average trooper was a little over twenty-one years of age, and almost a quarter were eighteen and under. Though their fathers' acreage ranged from none to 3,200, the average soldier came from a farm of some 450 acres. The median value of their property was around $13,000 ($20,000 if you include the families that claimed a net worth of over $100,000). Over 80 percent of those who rode with Forrest at Fort Pillow were the sons of farmers of one description or another, including men who also described themselves as carpenters, stock raisers, millers, overseers, a clerk, a mechanic, a trader, a tobacconist, and a justice of the peace. The nonfarmers included a preacher, a clerk, a doctor, a stagecoach driver, a lawyer, a mail carrier, and a newspaper publisher.

Newt Cannon of the 11th Tennessee Cavalry maintained that "a large percent of the Confederate army owned no slaves and were among the first to volunteer," the implication being that they therefore could not have been fighting for slavery's perpetuation. This is commonly claimed about the Confederate army as a whole, but it is not known how many stood to inherit slaves if the South won the war, or came from families that worked or owned slaves. Most rebels were too young to own anything, let alone slaves, and like Forrest himself, many a poor Southern boy saw slaveholding as the surest path to prosperity.[5]

Two-thirds of Forrest's men—and almost three-quarters of those who served at Fort Pillow—came from slave-owning families averaging about 18 slaves apiece. This number is skewed somewhat by the large slaveholders scattered among their number—Jack Shaw of the 14th, for instance, claimed his family owned 300 slaves; the Witherspoon brothers of the 7th claimed 175; their comrade Billy Anthony owned 200. But even when the calculation is extended to all 201 respondents, including those whose families did not own slaves, the average number of slaves per trooper's family came to about a dozen. Not all of the big slave owners were officers, either. Though the family of the 20th's Lieutenant John Russell Dance owned 75 slaves, Private Willy Wade's owned 35, Private W. T. Sutton's owned 60, and Private Jim Monroe's parents owned 110.[6]

The vast majority recalled that slave owners related positively to non–slave owners, and vice versa. Some large slaveholders insisted that the slave owners did all they could to help their less propertied neighbors. "There were many acts of charity," Lieutenant Dance insisted, that "passed unknown to the world" because "the southern gentleman who helped a friend or needy young man never let it be known to the public." Though only six disagreed to some degree, among their number were a banker, a miller, and a doctor—members of less vested professions who probably observed more such interactions than most.[7]

In the opinion of Meriwether Donaldson of the 12th Kentucky Cavalry, "the rich slave owners did little work of a usual character" and sustained "quite an arristocratic spirit." In any case, to some men there did seem to be a correlation between slavery and the poor white's prospects. Hamp Cheney of the 2nd Tennessee Cavalry believed that a poor white's chances were poorest "where the work on the plantations was done by negroes," but since Tennessee had fewer slaves per capita than the Deep South, and its climate "permitted white men to do a greater variety of labor, there were probably many more opportunities for a man to make and save money." The implication was nonetheless clear: the more slaves in a county, the worse for the whites who owned none.[8]

That some of Forrest's men did not own or stand to inherit slaves did not make them kindlier disposed to black people. Those poor whites who were materially worse off than the house slaves of wealthy masters harbored deep resentments compounded by their growing conviction that the entire war was being waged on behalf of the planter class. This at least suggests the complexity and range of the relationships between slaveholding officers and their men. Many a poor young soldier might well have envied or resented the wealth and idleness and vaunting pretensions of old-line planters whose families had owned slaves for generations. But they admired a man like Forrest as the embodiment of the promise of the slave society they were fighting for: the poor boy who had made good by the sweat of his brow and the sharpness of his wits; the canny, hardscrabble speculator who saw slavery's road to wealth laid out before him and boldly took it, as they themselves hoped to take it if only the goddamn Yankees would get out of their way.

The cavalrymen's education was rudimentary. There was no publicly funded education in Tennessee before the war, so it was left to communities and congregations to hire teachers and establish schools. Some teachers barely qualified. W. H. "Billy" Matthews of Maury County recalled that his first teacher was a woman who "couldent spell to Baker." Most boys who went to country schools attended only part time. Higher education was a province of the rich, for not only could their families afford to send them to school, but their slaves' labor freed up time to study. "Men that owned," recalled Private J. P. Walker of Bedford County, "was in a better condition to educate there children than poor people."[9]

Long before they joined the army, Forrest's boys lived by a warrior's code. When John Wyeth failed to retaliate after a playmate slapped him, his mother, a Scot from "Clan Allan," threatened to whip him if he did not defend himself. An obstreperous patriotic strain coursed through their lineage. Johnny McMurtry of the 15th claimed that his grandfather had been drafted into the British army in Belfast and shipped over to fight Americans, whereupon he had deserted and fought alongside the rebels for seven years. John W. Carroll of the 21st recalled how his hard-drinking Irish grandfather used to thrill him with his account of the Battle of New Orleans.[10]

When the South issued its summons, they were eager for the fray. Forrest's recruiters rode under gaudy versions of company banners and treated large crowds to pit barbecues of cattle, sheep, and pigs. At a single rally in the little town of Eagleville, Tennessee, Forrest collected a company of 104 men. John Weatherred was only fifteen years old when he "heard the fife and drums and speeches urging all people of the South to defend their rights, their homes and firesides from the designing Northern Yankees who wish to take our property and destroy the Constitution of the United States." Repeatedly rejected as too young, Weatherred "imbibed the war spirit immediately," and enlisted in the 9th shortly before his sixteenth birthday.[11]

Many more believed themselves to have been forced into fighting by Yankee depredations. "In the spring of 1864," recalled Bill Hight of Bedford County, "the Yankees worried us so much as my father was a full blooded Rebel" that Hight left home and joined Forrest's cavalry. After his hometown, Columbia, Tennessee, was occupied by Yankees, Edward Perry Davis "ran away at night and went to Perry Co. and enlisted in 9th Tenn. Cav." At Eagleville a recruit declared to Forrest that whipping the Yankees would be a "breakfast job." "I left home," wrote Jesse Green of the 19th, "and entered the war for three weeks, and was gone for nearly three years." Though there was honor in being among the first to join, it took even greater courage to enlist after it became apparent that the war would drag on for years, and at tremendous cost.[12]

Forrest's men were not all secessionists. "Some of us, though young men," wrote John Hubbard, "had been thinking over the grave questions for some time, particularly during the exciting political canvass of the previous year. Many who admitted the abstract right of Secession but had voted against it as wrong under the circumstances, if not impracticable, were yet hoping that a wicked war would somehow be averted." All his life, Robert Florence Street of the 10th would wonder "why men will pick up arms and shoot the life out of each other that did not aught against each other."[13]

"I could not wholly believe with either extreme," Henry Watterson recalled. He figured the war "could not last very long" because "the odds against the South were too great." But on "reaching home I found myself alone. The boys were all gone to the front. The girls were—well, they were all crazy. My native country was about to be invaded. Propinquity. Sympathy. So, casting opinions to the winds, in I went on feeling. And that is how I became a rebel," he said, "a case of 'first endure and then embrace,' because I soon got to be a pretty good rebel and went the limit, changing my coat as it were," though even "with a gray jacket on my back and ready to do or die, I retained my belief that Secession was treason, that disunion was the height of folly and that the South was bound to go down in the unequal strife."[14]

"I was not in favor of seccession," recalled George Washington Brown of the 3rd, "but I wished to go with my State." "My sympathies naturally went out to the Southern people," wrote John Carroll, "not that I owned any property in slaves [though in fact he stood to inherit a few], but I naturally loved the Sunny South together with all her institutions, then as now; whether right or wrong, was no question with me."[15]

Some of Forrest's boys opposed slavery. Bill Mays of Dyer County had grown up with slavery. But he "had not studied the subject of one man owning another" until he drove his father's hogs down to Mississippi, where slave owners "would bring out their negroes to [do the] killing," he said. "That was a big day with the negroes eating the scraps. I remember one day while they were killing hogs, a big gate fell on one of the little negroes about five or six, and killed it. The overseer told two of the negro men to go and bury it. They picked it up and went off somewhere, was not gone but a little while." That night the overseer declared that "in a short time the negroes would all be free," and told Mays that "he did not think from what he had seen that God would suffer it much longer."[16]

Many of Forrest's men had originally served in Confederate infantry regiments. After Billy Johnston was crippled by a wound at Shiloh, he went out and bought a horse and rode with the 7th for the rest of the war.[17]

Badly wounded at Perryville, John Carroll of the 27th Tennessee Infantry limped home to Henderson County on a crutch to raise a new company of mounted volunteers. "We had many difficulties," he recalled. "We had no arms except occasionally a flint-lock shotgun that we could pick up. We went along, enrolled whom we could and let them remain at home. This enrollment was secretly carried on until such a time as we could get men enough to organize a company." By the summer of 1863, Carroll had formed a company of the 21st with "men enough to start South but no arms or ammunition."[18]

After the Confederate army's reorganization in 1862, about a thousand infantrymen joined Forrest's command. At one point 654 deserting foot soldiers were found on his rolls. Forrest was promptly ordered to arrest them all and have them sent back to their commands "under proper guard." But in the end only 97 returned, and Forrest's recruiters continued to range far and wide, to the outrage of the Confederacy's high command. Officers as well as men bristled at the inequities of the conscription law. "There is dissatisfaction in camps to some extent about the conscription, the way it is carried on," wrote John Crutchfield of the 20th. "I do not know what I will do. I can tell you one thing. I am under military arrest for not bringing in Conscripts. I will not march any man before me on foot unless they will make all go: that is, take the rich as well as the poor."[19]

Slogging along the roadsides, splashed with the mud or choking in the dust kicked up by cavalry horses as they trotted past, rebel foot soldiers might have envied Forrest's troopers their mode of transportation. But the men of Forrest's cavalry experienced the worst of both services, fighting on foot and employing their mounts only to race from one battle to another or pursue a retreating foe. Forrest conceived of his fighters not as dragoons "who fought indifferently on foot or horseback," nor as cavalry who fought only mounted and with sabers. "We was mounted infantry," recalled J. P. Wilson, "armed with long guns."[20]

They sure looked tough. Most of them were "slender-built men" and, since many were former infantrymen, not as short as professional cavalry tended to be. From weeks without bathing, hunkered around campfires, especially in the winter months, they became "smoked": so blackened by soot and dust that from a distance they appeared to some Union soldiers like black troops in rebel uniforms. "I look like a border ruffian now," wrote a rebel trooper, "with a black hat & a black plume in it—a red shirt, military pants & horseman's boots—with large Spanish spurs and a beard all over my face."[21]

Some cavalrymen received a full allotment of clothing when they joined up. Others brought clothes from home. "My wife and mother made all the clothes I wore," wrote John Brownlow of the 19th. "For winter wear they would mix white and black wool to geather, card, spin, and weave them a long overcoat. They were very comfortable and looked real well. I was verry proud of them." But for the rest, recalled S. P. Driver of the 7th, "clothing was our greatest want."[22]

Many of Forrest's men wore captured Yankee uniforms. "We had the Yank prisoners out on the field burying some of there dead," John Rabb wrote after a battle. "The hogs got a holt of some of the Yankey dead before the fight was over." Nevertheless, he managed to strip the corpses of "a big Yank over coat and a sack Yank cote" plus "two pare of wollen pants and pleanty of drawers" and a "good pare of boots and pleanty of mony."[23]

Taylor's comrade John Brownlow recalled that by the time of the Battle of Nashville nearly all of Forrest's men would wear "yanky over coates or oil cloth." The result was that "we got considerably mixed up." But before long, recalled George Baskerville of the 12th, "the blue was changed but definitely to brown." And not just from wear and tear, either, for they usually dyed their captured Union uniforms "at the first stop."[24]

They were marvelous horsemen. "War suits them," said Sherman of the gray riders. "The rascals are brave, fine riders and dangerous subjects in every sense." In fact, in his judgment, they were "the best cavalry in the world." "The boy of the old South learned to ride and to shoot almost as soon as he learned to walk," wrote John Wyeth. "I began to ride when I was only four years old, and at ten was the possessor of my own horse and gun." Often slaves taught children how to ride.[25]

Wyeth recalled that he and his men were trained to swing "head downward" on either side of their horses at a full gallop "to pick up any object from the ground." They were equally adept at mounting their horses, "and from either side I could mount or leap entirely over my horse, and vault into the saddle from behind, with my pistol buckled around the waist, by placing my two hands on the horse's rump."[26]

Forrest's own feats of horsemanship were legendary. At the Battle of Thompson's Station, Forrest's horse Roderick, which used to follow the general around like a hound, was struck three times. At last Forrest switched mounts, but hearing the roar of battle, Roderick charged back to rejoin the general, jumping three fences before a fourth wound finally brought him down. When, near Rossville, Georgia, a minié ball severed an artery in his horse's neck, Forrest plugged the hole with his index finger and continued galloping after the Federals. After his enemy had fled, he finally removed his finger, whereupon the horse collapsed and died. In an engagement at Pontotoc, Mississippi, two horses were killed under him, one by a spray of bullets that shattered the general's saddle but left him miraculously unharmed. That same day another round wounded his third mount, King Phillip, who, with his ears back and his teeth bared, charged anything clad in blue.[27]

At Vicksburg, Forrest's men had to feed their horses "on mulberry leaves and the long moss which hangs from the trees in that section of the country." "In times of stress, when food was scarce and Fanny was hungry," wrote Wyeth, "I have often shared with her the roasting-ears of corn issued to me as my rations." Horses often took more lead than their riders. "My poor horse," wrote L. B. Giles of the 8th Texas Cavalry, "who received some of the lead intended for his master, and yet had no personal interest in the row, had five bullet wounds." All their lives Forrest's men would be haunted by the cries of wounded horses stranded on the field of battle.[28]

The troopers' first weapons were whatever rifles, pistols, knives and swords their families could provide. "We were armed with such shot guns and pistols as we could get at home," wrote Newt Cannon of the 11th. All of J. D. Hughes's comrades in Company A of the 2nd provided their own horses, uniforms, and weapons: muzzle loaders and double-barreled shotguns. "Alas! the god of war never beheld such a wonderful collection of antique weapons," wrote a Mississippian. "There were guns with only a vent, to be fired with a live coal, guns without ramrods, barrels without stocks, stocks without barrels, guns without cocks, cocks without pans": what he called a "beggarly array of trash."[29]

Forrest's handpicked escort, perhaps alone among the Wizard's troopers, carried sabers, and would employ them most notably in hand-to-hand fighting at Memphis. Forrest himself appropriated a Yankee sword of Damascus steel and sharpened both edges so he could slash at his foe with every sweep of his arm. It proved a formidable weapon. In the heat of battle at Okolona, Mississippi, he almost entirely severed the head of a Federal officer with a single stroke. But it did not take Forrest long to figure out that though flashing sabers made an impressive display, for men on horseback, pistols were far more effective.[30]

"At the beginning," wrote Giles, "the possession of a good pistol was a requisite for enlistment. If a man died or was killed his comrades kept his pistol. When a prisoner of the enemy's cavalry was taken this part of his outfit was added to the general stock, so that after a few months most, if not all, had two weapons of this kind, and some even tried to carry three or four."[31]

Forrest's men captured Yankee arms with the same alacrity with which they seized horses and uniforms. "Our necessities," wrote H. C. Coles of the 4th Tennessee, "were principally supplied by our foes." "Sometimes, on the eve of a battle," wrote Dabney Maury, Forrest would turn and address the convalescents and liberated prisoners he accumulated on his raids. "I have no arms for you yet," he would tell them, "but fall in here behind, and you shall have plenty of good Yankee arms presently."[32]

They performed almost every kind of military duty. "In the cavalry we are always actively engaged in some kind of an enterprise," wrote Given Campbell, "burning trains, obtaining army supplies, capturing boats, tearing up rail roads, fighting Yankees on land & gunboats on water." When asked for his observations during the war, Bob McCalister of the 11th replied, "The experance of a cavalry man is some what complicated: hear today, gone tomorrow, most always on the go, either running too or from the foe, and having to hustle. There was but little time for observations." Besides, a cavalryman was not much interested in observations anyway, "as he had more serious matters to contemplate."[33]

"By his captures," wrote Forrest's commander of artillery, "the Federal Government supplied him with guns and artillery and more ordnance, commissary, and quartermaster's stores than he could use." But his men would have begged to differ, for theirs was a war of extreme privation. "We were exposed to all the hardships possible under Bedford Forest," recalled M. B. Dinwiddie of the 20th: "scant clothing, and most of time half rashings." For J. W. Shankle of the 16th, it was a "life of hardships: poorly clad and oftimes went 3 and 4 days without anything to eat."[34]

"Camp life was unpleasant," remembered William James Sutton, who served with the 16th. In the camp of the 7th Tennessee Cavalry "the men and horses all camped together and the odor and filth were not agreeable."

There were often "no ditches around our tents," recalled Lieutenant William Frazier of the 10th, "so the rain run all over the ground under our tents. So we could stand or sit up all the night, or lie down in mud as we choose."[35]

"I want to say that when I was with Forrest that I never slept in a tent," declared Archie Hughes of the 9th. "His command had no tents, as they had no use for them" because "they were in the saddle all the time." George Baskerville of the 12th could recall only a single month when he and his comrades stayed in camp long enough to put up tents. Usually the best they could do was erect "sleeping places out of little poles" and cover them with oilcloths.[36]

They did not "mind so much the rains of summer-time," Wyeth recalled, "but the winter rains, the sleet, the snow, and the biting wind made us think of home and wish 'the cruel war was over.'" Jack Dunavant of the 1st remembered going to sleep on the ground one night and awaking next morning "covered up in snow." They improvised elaborate systems for keeping warm. "For want of bedding in bitter coald weather wee would build a big fire," recalled Bob Bowden of the 3rd, "sit around telling yarns until fire burn down. Then we would throw the hot ashes over the ground, then dig it up, and I spread one blanket on the ground." All but one of them lay down, and then the last man would throw a blanket over them. "He would pile some tops over them, then they would let him root up" in the middle of the others.[37]

Another enemy of sleep was lice. "The bite is like that of no other insect that live on human flesh or blood," Jack Claiborne of the 8th Texas recalled; "it sets the body on fire." Many nights Claiborne noticed that sleeping men were "continually in motion and are kept warm by these body lice companions." Their hardships made them especially vulnerable to disease. Bad water was usually the culprit. One soldier stationed in Mississippi described having to drink water that was "thick enough to bear the weight of an ordinary hat and warmer than milk just milked from a cow." "We drink Cistern water which is said to be the healthiest, though it is a well-defined case 'of animal nature' [being] literally alive with wiggle tails and various tribes of smaller animalculae, which gambol about under your nose quite lively whilst you take a drink."[38]

Forrest's men probably got less sleep and under worse conditions than just about any other soldiers in the war. Before electricity, Americans averaged ten hours of sleep per day, but Forrest's men slept in fitful stages of four or five hours at the most, and though some learned how to doze in the saddle, the long-term effects on their bodies and psyches were severe, not only impairing their coordination and judgment, but inducing everything from chronic irritability and depression to paranoia and other psychoses.[39]

Though the 8th Texas Rangers were "eager to get into a fight, going through wet and cold, marching day & night," measles and pneumonia "thinned the companys down so that each company could not send more than fifty or sixty on a scout." Three weeks after joining the 21st, Jim Pearce came down with typhoid while on a "recruiting raid," as he called it. Some illnesses were not the direct result of conditions in camp. "There is a good deal of sickness in our company," wrote Lieutenant Hugh Black of the 6th Regiment of Florida Volunteers from Knoxville, Tennessee, "but nothing serious. The most of the diseases is caused from our boys visiting the women to much."[40]

"Our ambulance facilities were so poor," recalled Newt Cannon of the 11th, "that many were left when they were shot down." The 4th often had to leave an ailing Jack Vaughan behind, but he proudly told his grandchildren that "as soon as he would get better he began to make his way back to his command and stayed to the last."[41]

They lived for the most part on what they called "hard eats." "I have eaten raw corn—green pumpkins and most anything else on these raids," recalled Lee Billingsley of the 2nd. "Our rations were poor," wrote John Bell of the 21st; "musty corn meal, and bacon and beef when we could get it." "At one time," wrote Jesse Green of the 19th, "I went two nights and one day with out a bite to eat. At the Chickamauga fight Billie Ham and I were brought a piece of old cornpone, and our stomachs were so weak we couldn't eat it." "Some of the boys indulged in the rare dish of a rodent, well cooked in a hollow log and that without taking off his epidermis or taking out his internal viscera," recalled Charlie Rice of the 7th. Though he himself "did not indulge in the above," he did enjoy a "bucket full of steak" cut from a mule that had been killed in battle. Bad food inflicted bouts of severe diarrhea—a particular misery for men in the saddle.[42]

They slaughtered so many animals along their way that it haunted some of them long after the war. Returning home from the war, Sam Martin of the 12th would plunge into a delirium in which he was convinced that "the house top was covered with men dressed in cowhides literally covering me with cow hair." At last he fled the house and doused himself in his father's cow pond, and later ascribed his nightmarish vision to the beef bones he had gnawed while campaigning with Forrest.[43]

Some men took to the life. "As to camp life sleeping, eating etc.," recalled Marc Crump of the 2nd, " I enjoyed it all except prison life and battle." "We were a jolly set," Andy McCleary declared, "and would sometimes joke or play pranks on each other while the fight was going on." "We lived pretty hard," wrote R. W. Michie of the 19th, "but the boys of my age enjoyed it." "Forrest's Command," bragged Solomon Brantley of the 7th Tennessee Cavalry, "was a fighting Piece of Machinery."[44]

Bobby Rogers of the 7th boasted that Forrest "was hunting yanks all the time and was capturing and killing yanks all the time, and I was in every little fight that Forest [got] up." "A man who can show that he was with Forrest the last year and a half of the war is no ordinary man," wrote Lieutenant James Dinkins of Chalmers's staff. "You can depend on that."[45]

Considering the peculiar hardships and perils of serving under Forrest, however, it is no wonder that desertions from his command were legion. But there were other dynamics at work. First among them was the nature of the Western rebels themselves and the cavalry in particular. It was the Southerner's individualism and autonomy to which secessionist agitators and rebel recruiters had appealed. Like their ancestors in the Continental army, they saw themselves as citizen soldiers, and many of them never entirely comprehended what regular military service required. Fighting for their independence, many refused to accept that the Confederacy had any more right to order them around than the Yankees had. L. B. Giles's description of Terry's Texas Rangers could apply in varying degrees to all of Forrest's regiments. "From the standpoint of the martinet," he wrote, "our organization could hardly be called a regiment." One general called it a "damned armed mob." "Volunteers we began," wrote a comrade, "volunteers we remained to the end."[46]

Punishments for desertion were meted out haphazardly and at times indulgently by officers who dared not risk alienating men who were often more loyal to each other than they were to the cause. Officers rarely imposed capital punishment until after the fall of Vicksburg, when rebel volunteers learned in battle the necessity of loyalty and steadfastness. Thereafter, squads were sent out to round up deserters, many with orders to execute them on the spot. In 1863 authorities throughout the Confederacy were directed to cooperate in the capture and arrest of shirkers, stragglers, and deserters. Though the Confederacy offered to pay their captors five dollars per deserter, what passed for West Tennessee's civil authorities often extended their protection to shirkers and their families.[47]

During the war, Forrest was often seen "with a pack of hounds following him," and there is substantial evidence that he and his men employed them to hunt down deserters. When deserters were rounded up, many merely took the first opportunity that presented itself to desert again. "Unless one were inherently loyal," wrote a Mississippian, "no amount of persuasion, intimidation, and punishment meted out by the loyal against him contained any lasting efficacy."[48]

Part of the problem was the anomalous status of Tennessee and Kentucky. "The people of Tennessee were very greatly dissatisfied at the loss of their capitol city," Nashville, in 1862, "and the destruction of the property and supplies," wrote Jack Claiborne of Terry's Texas Rangers. "Many of the army were Tennesseans, and they were hard to handle." During the retreat to Corinth "not a few quit the ranks when their homes, families and kindred were left behind." Forrest complained that his Kentuckians kept slipping through his fingers, "for, though they would flock to General Johnson's standard upon his appearance in the State, as soon as he turned southward, they would scatter to attach themselves to roving bands of guerillas, jayhawkers, and plunderers who preyed upon the people." Texans fled across the Rio Grande to Mexico. Some Mississippians complained of what they called "Haystack Secessionists": men who professed rebel sympathies but did whatever they could to stay close to home. "There are men enough at home today, who belong to the army," wrote Frank Montgomery of the 1st Mississippi Cavalry, "to drive the Yankees from the south, and gain our independence, without help from any quarter. But they will not come out and cannot be driven out. They basely prefer to dodge about the swamps like runaway negroes, and try to save their miserable lives."[49]

Not all of them were "skulkers," however; many were "true soldiers, debilitated from disease or wounds." "I was never discharged," recalled Jim Hinson of the 10th. Sent home on furlough to recruit horses, he "got cut off from my command and could not get back without being in danger of capture." Others made it a practice to desert the Confederate units that had conscripted them, join the Union army, and, after obtaining transportation to a particular theater of the war, slip off to join the Confederate units of their choice. One hundred out of 130 Mississippians the Union army conscripted escaped to join Forrest's command.[50]

On January 3, 1863, Brigadier General James Madison Tuttle would report that "large numbers of Forrest's unarmed conscripts are escaping. Most of them work their way Home, But some of them come in & say they want to go Home on any terms. Say they were forced &c." "I am sorry to say a great many have deserted," wrote a trooper of the 1st Mississippi. "I saw a poor fellow shot for desertion a short time ago. He belonged to the brigade, and was shot in presence of it, but I fear it has failed to check the evil."[51]

M. B. Dinwiddie of the 20th recalled that "quite a number" of his company deserted: "so much so that Forest had to have two shot, laid them by

the road side, labeled in large letters, 'The fate of a deserter.'" "Forrest had a
standing order to shoot any man who ran," wrote Wyeth, "and himself set
the example on more than one occasion." At Pulaski, Forrest had three of his
soldiers shot for spending the night in their nearby homes. A member of the
8th Texas Cavalry deplored Forrest's summary executions. "On two or three
occasions the Rangers were the observers of the shooting of men for of-
fenses, and they failed to see the justice of the proceedings from their idea
of the matter, and while little was said or heard from them, it was notorious
that they did not have that respect for a general who shot his men to death,
that they did for men who obtained more and better fighting by some other
system."[52]

Forrest once ordered his men to execute nineteen West Tennessee levies
caught in the act of deserting. "Their coffins were made, their graves dug
and the culprits advised to make their peace with their Maker and the
world," recalled R. R. Hancock of the 22nd Tennessee Cavalry. "Bell's
Brigade, mounting and moving out into a large field, was formed in line on
three sides of a square, while the culprits, blindfolded and seated on their
coffins, occupied the center of the other side of the square." But just as the
firing squad was about to shoot, a staff officer came rushing up to address
the culprits.

"General Forrest," he said, "has requested me to say to you that it was
unpleasant to him to shed blood in this manner, and that, through the peti-
tions of the clergy, the prominent citizens and ladies of Oxford and your officers, if you will now promise to make good and faithful soldiers he would
pardon you."

"We will!" they shouted. "WE WILL!" to the cheers of the entire brigade.[53]

"He bitterly hated a coward," wrote Tully Brown, who served with Forrest as an artillerist, "and I tell you, a man had to be a most dastardly coward to play the coward act in Bedford Forrest's command. He might escape
the Federal musketry by his cowardice, but he ran into something very much
worse": the Wizard himself. "He would shoot him down in a minute. I saw
him whip a soldier like a dog at West Point for running from his line, and I
have never heard such talk as he gave; it blistered worse than the cane he
was using."[54]

Captain F. G. Terry of the 8th Kentucky Cavalry recalled the grief of his
comrade Captain James Powell over the fate of his only son, a seventeen-
year-old civilian named Gee Powell, whom Forrest executed. The killing had
its origin in a collision between Forrest and the 3rd Kentucky Cavalry, members of which had recently attacked Forrest's guardhouse at West Point,
Mississippi, to release some comrades the general had imprisoned "for some

misdemeanor." The killing "was an outrage," Terry declared, "without law or excuse, and done in a frenzy." J. F. Rickman of the 28th Mississippi put it plainly. "Forrest was cruel," he said.[55]

From the first, Bill Sutton of the 16th "had fears of defeat. I served with Gen. Bedford Forrest Cavalry command and was under fire twenty-six times. We were usually outnumbered, hence we suffered defeat more often than victory." As early as 1862, Captain Given Campbell of the 2nd Kentucky Cavalry had seen so much combat that he believed he had been "born to die by the hand of the country's enemies." He wrote that his fiancée and his family were "the only bonds which tie me to life, and if they should end un-happily broken," he would carry his life "on my sword point, for I am be-coming reckless & I had almost said desperate. I have been deeply stung by thorns through my family," for the Unionists had "insulted my mother & sis-ters & murdered my friends."[56]

The few comforts Forrest's men could rely upon were provided by the slaves who accompanied them into the war. "My father sent with me as body guard a negro boy of my age who had been considered my servant since my birth," recalled John Russell Dance of the 8th. "He was eager to go and stayed with me where possible" and remained "very faithful in all my hardship during the war."[57]

Other blacks made their way into Confederate camps to hire them-selves out to officers. Chalmers fretted about the number of blacks who fol-lowed his men, and in September 1863 directed that "no negroes will be permitted to remain with this command" except for "one servant for each of-ficer, one teamster for each wagon or ambulance, & four cooks & four wash-ermen for each company. Each negro will be furnished with a pass to be approved by the Regimental or Battalion commander," and all others were "sent out of camp at once."[58]

In looking back, wrote Mercer Otey, "it seems strange that officers in the army, at a time when they were barely existing on a third of a pound of bacon a day and a little corn meal, should have decreased their slender store by sharing it with servants." But their store would have been a good deal more slender if they had not had slaves to steal for them. They served as for-agers, cooks, body servants, launderers, grooms, horse holders in battle, team-sters, orderlies. Otey was "amazed at the fidelity of our slaves during the trying times of those days, surrounded as they were by temptations and in-ducements to abandon us."[59]

"I had with me a favorite servant, whose name was Jake Jones," recalled

Frank Montgomery of the 1st Mississippi. "I had purchased Jake Jones a year or two before the war, for a house-servant and carriage-driver, and he was a very bright boy, though without education of any kind." Montgomery kept Jones with him for many months, "but so many of my negroes had gone to the federals before the end of that year, leaving only a few old men and boys and women and children, that I determined to send him home and take a younger boy." Montgomery told Jones "that if the south was conquered in the war he would be free; if the south was successful and he was faithful to his trust I would give him his freedom." Jones was "faithful to the end," but after the war "he fell into bad habits, drinking and using that horrible drug, morphine, and one night murdered a negro woman."[60]

Some servants actually fought alongside their masters. At the Battle of Brandy Station two body servants picked up some discarded weapons and joined in the rebel charge, capturing a "Yankee Negro" and bringing him back to the Confederate camp to act as their servant. An armed slave belonging to Captain Thomas Buchanan of Stewart's 15th Tennessee Cavalry reportedly fought alongside his master in a number of engagements. After the war, ninety-one black Tennesseeans and their families applied for pensions for service in the Confederate cavalry; at least one of them, Thornton Forrest, was Forrest's slave.[61]

A slave named Luke, who had served through the war as John Andrew Wilson's slave, asked for a parole when his former master, the colonel of the 24th, surrendered to a Yankee officer in Columbia, Mississippi. "Luke, you don't need one," said Wilson. "You never been a soldier."

"Yes, I has been a soldier—for four years," Luke replied. "Now you and that man don't want to do me that way."

The Yankee officer declared that Luke "made more sense" than Wilson did, and gave him his parole.[62]

At least seventeen black applicants for Confederate pensions were present at the Battle of Fort Pillow. A good many joined Confederate units because eventually they might lead them to the Yankees, to whom they intended to escape. Others who expected to be treated with at least a measure of gratitude and respect for sticking by their masters soon ran off in disgust. At one rebel encampment near Milton, Tennessee, George L. Knox noticed that by the middle of 1863 the whites "were very rough, swearing and cursing at every Negro they thought would be glad to leave them to go to the Yankees," he wrote. "If a rebel soldier saw a colored man have on a good hat, and he had an old one, he would drive up and take it off his head, throw his old hat at him, and gallop away. After one month's experience in the rebel army I left it."[63]

When someone questioned the righteousness of the Confederate cause, however, Forrest and his men could point to their loyal servants. If slavery was so cruel, they asked, what about old Dan over there, shining Lieutenant Humphrey's boots? Or Isaac, laying out Lieutenant Blake's bedroll? What about the Reverend Cox's man Allen, setting up for evening prayer? Or good old Thornton ladling out stew to his master (and half brother), Lieutenant Felen? Remember how Henry Love, that "most intelligent" Negro, led Captain Alexander's horses hundreds of miles home after his master was captured? Remember how, at Shiloh, the mighty slave Fielding carried young Rennolds off the battlefield on his back? And that same day, didn't Elias, a boy but seventeen years old, carry Sergeant Daniel off the field when he was wounded and subsequently nurse him back to health? Recalled William Witherspoon of the 7th Tennessee Cavalry, "In the four years of conflict, all over the South the Negro—then a slave—although Lincoln's emancipation proclamation made him free, was loyal to his master and family. The fact being so universal we can not honor and love too much our old time, before-the-war negroes, and that we certainly do."[64]

Of course, almost 179,000 "old time, before-the-war negroes" joined the Union army, 20,133 of them credited to Tennessee and almost 24,000 to Kentucky. But the rebels refused to believe that these taunting, arrogant Negroes the Yankees had contaminated with their lies and promises were the same stock as their own loyal servants. It wouldn't be the good Negroes standing up there along the ramparts at Fort Pillow, mooning the rebels, cursing them, threatening them with rifles and cannon. The good Negroes rode with Forrest. The blue-clad blacks had to be the castoffs: the troublous bucks that always took a whipping before they would settle down to work, the dregs their fathers sold downriver.

DUCKWORTH'S BLUFF

UNION CITY

Spring 1864

DURING THE WEEKS LEADING UP TO THE ATTACK ON FORT PILLOW, two precursory battles at Union City, Tennessee, and Paducah, Kentucky, would combine to seal the fate of the Federal garrison at Fort Pillow. By New Year's Day 1864, the Union was beginning to doubt whether West Tennessee was still worth occupying. In the stasis of a cold winter, Yankee officers took to granting furloughs to hundreds, if not thousands, of their men. An old friend of Lincoln's on a tour of the Western theater argued that the continued Yankee occupation of West Tennessee would merely serve to harden rebel sentiment. He urged "the withdrawal of all the forces now in the west from their inland operations, and after securely fortifying all important towns, or at least one every fifty or sixty miles, on the Ohio below Evansville, and on the lower Mississippi, also Nashville," the transfer of all the troops at Paducah, Columbus, Fort Pillow, and even Memphis "to the taking of Mobile, Pensacola, Charleston, Savannah &c. on the Coast, and Montgomery, Augusta and other cities on rivers which can be visited and held by our gun boats."[1]

But whether or not the Yankees thought West Tennessee worth occupying, Nathan Bedford Forrest judged it well worth raiding. He needed supplies and recruits, hoped to hector Sherman's supply lines, and was itching to go after Fielding Hurst and his 6th Tennessee Cavalry (USA), who, for sheer savagery and cunning, had thus far proven a match for the secessionist guerrillas they harassed. According to rebel dispatches, his men "wantonly murdered" a "deformed and almost helpless" sixteen-year-old named Lee Dougherty and, after killing a cavalryman from the 16th Tennessee Cavalry, refused to permit his family the "rights of sepulture."[2]

A citizen named S. M. Winkler appealed for relief to Hurlbut as a Union man and fellow Mason. He and his neighbors had been persecuted by Union soldiers who had

> foraged upon us until we are left without any thing whatever. These troops, not content to snatch the little meat and bread—of which we always gave them a share—from our tables, took the small stock we had out of the smoke-house, plundering it of all it contained. They also took the corn and fodder which we had bought, and to crown the whole, they took the condemned stock which I had a short time before bought to replace that which the men under the command of Col. [Hurst] had stolen.

Winkler asked, "General & Companion Hurlbut, What are we to do?"[3]

In the first week of February, Hurst galloped into Jackson with his cavalry to demand that its citizens repay him the $5,139.20 he had been required by the Union authorities at Memphis to return to a local woman named Newman whose farm his men had looted. If the people of Jackson did not come up with the money "in greenbacks or Kentucky money," Hurst threatened, he would burn the town to the ground. Seven days later, they paid up. Around the middle of the month, Hurst's boys captured a lieutenant and two privates from Forrest's 19th Tennessee Cavalry in McNairy County, Tennessee, ran them into Haywood County, and apparently shot them down in cold blood.[4]

Hurst might have pleaded that he was only following orders. Ben Grierson, Hurlbut's cavalry commander, had ordered Hurst to "scour the country well on your route and reach Memphis as soon as possible after the 1st of February. You will gather all serviceable stock on your route as heretofore directed, and subsist your command upon the country." On January 17, General William Sooy Smith, the chief of cavalry of the Department of the Mississippi, reported to Grant that he had given Hurst "a roving commission" and directed him "to 'grub up' West Tennessee. I think," he assured Grant, "he will reduce that district to order."[5]

Hurst's men, however, exceeded their instructions. They left one of Forrest's men to die "after cutting off his tongue, punching out his eyes, splitting his mouth on each side to his ears, and inflicting other mutilations." After arresting Lieutenant Willis Dodds of Colonel Newsom's regiment at his father's home in Henderson County, they apparently put him to death "by the most inhuman process of torture." According to a rebel infantryman who saw his body afterward, "it was most horribly mutilated, the face having been skinned, the nose cut off, the under jaw disjointed, the privates cut off, and the body otherwise barbarously lacerated and most wantonly injured."[6]

Outraged, Forrest demanded that Hurst and his officers give themselves up and stand trial before a Confederate tribunal for extortion and murder. When the Union command at Memphis predictably refused his demand, Forrest issued a decree denouncing Fielding Hurst and his command as outlaws "not entitled to be treated as prisoners of war falling into the hands of the forces of the Confederate States."[7]

Promoted to lieutenant general, Forrest now commanded the Northern Cavalry Department, consisting of "all cavalry commands in West Tennessee and northern Mississippi." His previous command had been depleted by desertions, injuries, deaths, and illnesses, but he believed that "the strength of the enemy in our front, and their merciless ravages on this portion of the Country during the past two years should furnish a sufficient appeal to men to rally at once for the defense of their homes."[8]

Operating on home turf, Forrest's agents assembled as many of the Western Confederacy's disparate cavalry commands and companies and bands of guerrillas as they could round up. But Forrest's attempts to reorganize his men were arduous. John Carroll of the 21st recalled a rumor that the Confederate army intended to arrest and return to their former regiments men who joined Forrest's command after deserting from the infantry. The story precipitated "a regular stampede; men left in dozens until within a short time there were only 150 men present out of the 300 taken out." Forrest was reduced to turning what had been a battalion "into one company." After the Wizard replaced the commander of his Old Regiment with a supernumerary, its officers objected, whereupon, in Forrest's absence, they were all arrested for mutiny. "We felt it our duty to contend for the rights of our wounded brother officer; hence the arrest for mutiny. But when Forrest returned he gave us what we asked for."[9]

"The difficulties attending organizing regiments by consolidating the odds and ends of paper commands into full regiments," he wrote Jefferson Davis, "have caused quite a number of disaffected officers and men to run away." By mid-February 1864, however, Forrest had at last cobbled his command together. His First Brigade—five regiments and two battalions of West Tennesseeans—was placed under the command of Brigadier General Robert Richardson, who, as a heedless and freewheeling partisan, swung in and out of Forrest's favor. Colonel Black Bob McCulloch commanded the

Second Brigade, consisting of his own 2nd Missouri Cavalry, Texas and Tennessee battalions, W. W. Faulkner's Kentuckians, Alexander H. Chalmers's Mississippi Battalion, and a detachment from the 2nd Arkansas Cavalry. Colonel Tyree H. Bell commanded Forrest's Third Brigade, consisting of the Tennessee regiments of Colonels Russell, Wilson, and Barteau. And finally, Bedford's brother, Colonel Jeffrey E. Forrest, commanded the Fourth Brigade, including Forrest's Old Regiment, Duckworth's Tennesseeans, and Duff's, George's, and McGuirk's Mississippi regiments.[10]

Early in March, General Abraham Buford had joined Forrest's command, bringing with him the remnants of three decimated Kentucky infantry regiments—some 700 veterans—who had applied to serve as mounted infantry. Richmond refused, however, to supply them with horses—two-thirds of them were still on foot—and now Buford turned to Forrest to find them mounts. Convinced that as natives of western Kentucky they would come in handy as recruiters and scouts, Forrest welcomed them into his fold.[11]

On March 9, riding at the head of some 2,800 men, Forrest trotted forth, his "unmounted Kentuckians trudging along on foot, happy at the thought," wrote one of Forrest's biographers, "of having their faces turned once more to their homes, whither they were now going to replenish their wardrobes" and secure fresh mounts "to carry them henceforth with the Wizard of the Saddle." Other brigades rode in relays; General Chalmers crossed with McCulloch's brigade into West Tennessee near LaGrange, reaching Bolivar just as Neely's brigade rode on from Bolivar to Sommerville.[12]

"Away we clattered for West Tennessee and Kentucky," wrote Mercer Otey. "Ah! but those were glorious spring days, and as fine a lot of fellows," he recalled, "as ever flashed a saber. Every man sat his steed as if he was part and parcel of the beast he strode, and it mattered little how mettlesome the nag, the rider was the master, and fit to fight mounted or dismounted."[13]

In a region "of the most scanty and unfulfilled promise," the little town of Union City had "struggled into an amphibious subsistence; but it had never thriven." The town rested on land "just so much raised above the broad swamp of Northwestern Tennessee" that only "whisky, with men to drink it, and a Methodist Church South with men to people it, were possible. For many a mile around," wrote local Union commandant Colonel George Waring, "the forest and swamps were well nigh impenetrable," and the only roads "were wood trails leading to nowhere in particular." The town lay at the crossing, or "union," of two railroads, "one pointing towards Mobile and one towards Memphis." Though neither actually reached its ostensible destination, they looked sufficiently strategic on the Union army's maps to justify garrisoning the place with bluecoats.

Among these were the troopers of William Bradford's 13th Tennessee Cavalry, which was busily absorbing the majority of Dyer County Unionists, most of whom hailed from an isolated northern portion of the county so loyal to the Federal government that it was known as "Blue America." The 13th spent that fall joining the rest of the garrison in "a happy round of drills, inspections, horse-races, cockfights and poker." Waring was so contemptuous of West Tennesseeans in general and the citizens of Union City in particular that at one point he allowed his men to confiscate all the blankets in what was left of the town and lay them across its muddy streets so they could parade in full dress without spoiling their boots and uniforms. Union City, sneered Waring, was "not a city at all" and "'Disunion' would have been its fairer description."[14]

Like every Federal post along the Mississippi that March, Union City was in a state of understandable alarm. As Forrest's various detachments, numbering some 6,000 men, zigzagged north out of Mississippi and up into West Tennessee, the Union command tallied up all the troops in the stripped-down garrisons along the Mississippi and determined, to its horror, that they amounted to only 2,600 men.[15]

"Three-fourths of the men were colored," Brigadier General Mason Brayman would testify,

> a portion of them not mustered into service and commanded by officers temporarily assigned, awaiting commission. Of the white troops about one-half at the posts on the river were on duty as provost marshals' guards and similar detached duties, leaving but a small number in condition for movement. The fortifications were in an unfinished condition, that at Cairo rendered almost useless by long neglect. Many of the guns were dismounted, or otherwise unfit for service, and the supply of ammunition deficient and defective. A body of cavalry at Paducah were not mounted, and only part of those at Union City. I had not enough mounted men within my reach for orderlies.[16]

After Bradford's doomed battalion decamped for Fort Pillow, it was replaced by the troublous 7th Tennessee Cavalry (USA) under the command of the luckless forty-six-year-old Colonel Isaac Roberts Hawkins. Back in December 1862, Hawkins and his ill-trained and ill-equipped conscripts had been driven back at Trenton, Tennessee, by Forrest's Colonel George G. Dibrell, and within three days found themselves under siege by Forrest himself. After rebel gunners prepared to fire a fourth round at Trenton's well-fortified stockade, Hawkins and 300 of his men surrendered while the rest of his regiment, having evaded capture, fought the rebels with varying degrees of success. Eventually released and restored to command, in October 1863 Hawkins was ordered to take his veterans and his conscripts to Union City.

A month later they were sent down to LaGrange with Hurst's 6th Tennessee Cavalry to guard the railway while Sherman consolidated his troops for the Meridian expedition. But they "behaved badly," and Hurlbut ordered Hawkins and his men back to Memphis, where he intended to "make something of them or break them." Hurlbut must have believed either that he had succeeded or that he could not afford to break anybody now that Sherman was siphoning off his corps, for within a few weeks he sent Hawkins and 175 troopers upriver, where they careened from post to post, recruiting another 300 Kentuckians and West Tennesseeans. Some of these men were deserters from the rebel army, but most were untested boys convinced by months of Yankee occupation that the Southern cause was lost.[17]

By March 20, every packet and telegraph brought fresh rumors of Forrest's movements. He was reported at Jackson, he was at Tupelo, he was crossing by steamboat at Eastport; he was here, he was there, he was everywhere at once. Though Forrest apparently intended to attack Columbus and Paducah, and his rebel cavalry was still some sixty miles off, Hawkins feared that his undermanned and oversupplied Yankee outpost at Union City might prove an irresistible target. He sent a plea for reinforcements to Columbus twenty-six miles away, and to Cairo another twenty miles upriver, and on March 23 received a dispatch from General Mason Brayman at Cairo that on the orders of General Hurlbut, who happened at the time to be visiting from Memphis, he was on his way with some two thousand reinforcements.[18]

Then the telegraph went dead.[19]

Hawkins had read Forrest right for a change. Union City did look to the Wizard of the Saddle like a sitting duck, and the sheer symmetry of sending his own 7th Tennessee Cavalry against his former captive's 7th Tennessee Cavalry was too delicious to resist.

The 7th Tennessee Cavalry (CSA) was commanded by Colonel William

Lafayette Duckworth, an oddly whittled-down fellow with a sparse cap of brilliantined hair plastered over the top of his skull, and long, overcompensating chin whiskers that reached down to the second row of brass buttons on his shad-bellied coat. Though a Tennessee Unionist would characterize him as "a notorious scoundrel" who "never had any reputation, either before the war or afterward," Duckworth had been a country doctor and a popular Methodist preacher, professions that "had not been without value in turning him out a diplomatist." He commanded more or less by default, for by the time he took up the reins, the 7th had passed through the hands of a string of contentious commanders.[20]

Duckworth knew the territory. Two years earlier he and the 7th had actually defended Union City against a Yankee attack, and soon afterward covered the rebel garrison's evacuation of Fort Pillow. Whatever his reputation or training, he was about to pull off the biggest coup of Forrest's second West Tennessee campaign and one of the war's most audacious bluffs. The Wizard sent Duckworth and his cavalry off to Union City with a taunt. "You damn boys have been bragging you could whip half a dozen Yankees," he declared, standing in his stirrups. "You are the 7th Tennessee Rebs," he said. "The 7th Tennessee Yanks are at Union City. I am going to send you there to clean them up. If you don't," he snarled over his shoulder, reining his horse around, "never come back here."[21]

As Duckworth led his force of about four hundred men out of camp, some of his men began to have second thoughts. "Maybe we've been talking too strong," William Witherspoon remembered one of Duckworth's troopers saying. "But Forrest has called our hands. If they fight, we have a job on our shoulders. We are in for it, and with any showing will clean them up." So on they rode, their ranks swelled slightly by men from Forrest's Old Regiment and seventy-five of Faulkner's men whom they encountered en route, though Unionist guerrillas apparently somewhat reduced their numbers by taking potshots from the surrounding woods.[22]

Convinced that Forrest was on his way, by four in the afternoon of March 23 Hawkins had sent scouts out to watch for him. Captain James H. Odlin, Brayman's chief of staff, arrived from Columbus to confer with Hawkins, rescue an idle locomotive and nine freight cars loaded with government and railroad property, and bring back some 150 contraband railway workers who had recently completed the line to Columbus.

Hawkins told him "that the ferries on the Obion had been destroyed," Odlin testified, "and that scouts whom he had expected in the day before had not returned; that he supposed that they were captured, or that it was impossible for them to get across the Obion." But after encountering Duckworth's advance column near Jacksonville, his scouts did manage to gallop back late that night and alert Colonel Hawkins. Doubling his pickets and keeping several of his companies saddled all night, Hawkins braced for an attack by what he now believed to be Forrest's entire force.[23]

At three in the morning, a courier rode in to report that Hawkins's pickets had been surrounded on the road to Dresden by a rebel force equipped with artillery. Captain Odlin told Hawkins "that I must leave," for his orders were to save the contrabands and the trainload of Federal and railway property lying idle at the junction. Hawkins asked him how many reinforcements he could send up, for though "he thought he could hold the place with his regiment if he had some artillery," he could not "contend against artillery without he had some himself."

Odlin replied that though he would "immediately push forward reenforcements," they would have to come all the way from Cairo, because the garrison at Columbus comprised "only 1,100 men in all"—the returns show 998 regulars—all but 100 of them black troops "who had never been in a fight." Odlin later claimed that he cautioned Hawkins not to disgrace the command by retreating "without having seen the enemy." Before falling back to Columbus, Hawkins "must have a skirmish with them," Odlin said, "and feel their strength" lest the alarm prove false "or he found that he had fallen back before a small number of men."[24]

Odlin chugged out of Union City with his trainload of stores and contrabands, racing across a trestle minutes after Duckworth's men had put it to the torch. Hawkins apparently ordered his men to put several of the town's buildings to the torch to deny the rebels cover. Duckworth and his men had expected to find Union City unfortified, but by the light from the ensuing conflagration they found to their dismay that not only was Union City surrounded by an abatis of fallen trees; the garrison was entrenched in a new seventy-square-yard redoubt surrounded by ten-foot walls topped with logs perforated every few yards by portholes.[25]

After some intense skirmishing, Hawkins's skirmishers fled into the fort, leaving behind two dead and several wounded. Captain Thomas Gray took up a position at a breastwork his men had erected on the eastern side of the redoubt. "As soon as it was light enough to see," recalled Captain John W. Beattie, "we found the rebels were all around our camp." Captain P. K. Parsons, most of whose men were on picket duty, ventured out to try to find them, only to discover that Duckworth had the garrison surrounded.[26]

At about 5:30 a.m. the rebels, mounted on horseback, charged on all sides, shrieking and firing away with their carbines. But as Duckworth quickly learned, it does not pay to attack an entrenched fortification on horseback. Before his men got very far, the "Galvanized Yankees" of Hawkins's command opened fire through their portholes, hurling them back "with but little difficulty." Duckworth's men dismounted and had somewhat better luck on foot; Faulkner's Kentuckians, for example, managed to scramble to within twenty-five yards of the work. But Hawkins's sharpshooters inflicted "considerable loss," severely wounding the Kentuckians' lieutenant colonel, W. D. Lannom, and bringing the assault to a halt. "After that," recalled Captain Gray, the Union garrison was "very exultant, and ready to meet the rebels anywhere."[27]

The frustrated Confederates sullenly hunkered down. Private William Witherspoon reported that he and his comrades crawled on all fours among the fallen timbers of Union City's abatis, trying to get a bead on Hawkins's men as they popped their heads above the breastworks out of "curiosity or something else." When a head did appear, recalled Witherspoon, "a dozen or more rifles would bang away and the owner of that head be put out of service." But in fact they managed to kill only one of Hawkins's men—a sergeant—and wounded no others, and in two subsequent assaults—one from the northwest, the other from the northeast—Duckworth suffered considerable losses and gained no ground.[28]

A jubilant Captain Gray declared to Hawkins that the rebels were defeated and would "either leave the field or assemble and make a consolidated charge." As Captain Beattie's sharpshooters continued to fire on Duckworth's battered cavalry, "a great many of our men lay down inside of our works and went to sleep, as they felt altogether easy about the matter."[29]

Another attacker might have given up the battle as lost. But not William Lafayette Duckworth. The old buzzard was one of Forrest's most attentive students and had learned from the Wizard that backwoods cunning could be as effective a weapon as artillery. Though war meant fighting, as Forrest was supposed to have said, and fighting meant killing, he had taught his subordinates that it was better still if you could win without fighting, and that took tricks.

———————————

After Duckworth's fourth futile assault on Union City's bulwark, the two sides spent an hour and a half exchanging potshots. The Federals "were all in good spirits," recalled Captain Gray, and were firing from their portholes when a delegation of rebel officers abruptly rode into view, bearing a flag of truce. Gray alerted Hawkins and rode out to meet the rebels, calling the delegation to a halt a couple of hundred yards from the breastworks.

"They said they wished to see the commander of the forces there," Gray testified. "I told them I had notified him, and he would be there in a moment." As they waited, the rebels did not like the way Gray was peering around at the rebels in the abatis and ordered him placed under arrest. "I demanded their right to order me under arrest under a flag of truce, and told them I had as much right to look around as they had." Just then Hawkins turned up and accepted a piece of paper from the rebel couriers and rode back to the breastworks with Captain Gray.

"As soon as I got back," Gray recalled, "I made it my business to go around inside the breastworks to get a view of the rebel troops. They were there upon stumps and logs, and every place where they could see"; nevertheless, Gray and his men "were satisfied they were whipped." The Union men "were just as cool and quiet as you ever saw men," recalled Parsons: "not a bit excited, but talking and laughing."

Hawkins called a council of his officers and read them the rebels' demand.

I have your garrison completely surrounded, and demand an unconditional surrender of your forces. If you comply with the demand, you are promised the treatment due to prisoners of war, according to usages in civilized warfare. If you persist in a defense, you must take the consequences.
By order of
N. B. Forrest, Major General.

This implication that Forrest himself was in command of the assault on Union City was intended by Duckworth to rattle Hawkins. But the root of the demand's wording would echo in Forrest's subsequent demands at Paducah and Fort Pillow, and as such provide some of the most damning evidence of premeditation in the carnage at Fort Pillow three weeks later. Treatment according to the rules of "civilized warfare" is not a negotiating point but should obtain whether or not a garrison puts up resistance. But unless the note was intended merely as a bluff, it betrayed the belief of Forrest and his officers—Abraham Buford was about to make a similar threat at Columbus, Kentucky, though solely against the garrison's blacks—that fair treatment could be conditioned upon a foe's surrender and withheld if an enemy refused.[30]

The wording at Union City, however, was Duckworth's, not Forrest's.

The general was nowhere near; his signature was a forgery. But to spare himself and his men the ignominy of returning to Forrest in defeat, Duckworth had invoked the Wizard's ghost. The only artillery pieces Duckworth could muster were the dummy guns his black servants and laborers were erecting from logs and wagon wheels just within range of Hawkins's telescope. His only reinforcements were the phantom regiments Duckworth had instructed his buglers and black horse holders to greet out of the garrison's view with blaring tattoos and loud, celebratory shouts.

Hawkins asked his officers "what they thought best to be done." "When he asked me about it," recalled Beattie, "I told him that if they had artillery they could whip us; but if they had no artillery we could fight them till hell froze over." After all, if the rebels had guns, why had they not fired them by now? The battle so far had been "a rebel defeat," and if Captain Odlin's word could be counted on, reinforcements were due to arrive from Cairo at any moment.[31]

The garrison's resolve was shaken, however, when Hawkins's telegraph operator rushed in to report that he had climbed atop a shanty with a telescope and spotted rebel artillery in the distance.

Poor Hawkins was no poker player. "If they have artillery, and we renew the fight," he groaned, "like enough they will kill every man of us they got." Believing "it would save a great many lives if we would surrender," he rode out to negotiate the garrison's capitulation. Captain Beattie rode by his side, still trying to talk Hawkins out of surrendering even as they approached the rebel flag of truce. "We have the rebels whipped," he insisted.[32]

Unpersuaded, Hawkins demanded to meet with Forrest himself, but Duckworth coolly replied with another forgery. "I am not in the habit of meeting officers inferior to myself in rank," it said, "but I will send Col. Duckworth, who is your equal in rank, and who is authorized to arrange terms and conditions with you."

When Duckworth trotted up to deliver the note, Hawkins pleaded for more time to confer with his officers, whereupon Duckworth granted him fifteen minutes more but added grimly that his gunners were itching to blow up the Yankees and leave not even "a greasy spot."[33]

By now more of his officers claimed to have spotted rebel artillery aimed in the garrison's direction. "We agreed then he should make the surrender," Beattie testified, "on condition that we should be paroled there, without being taken away from the place, and each one allowed to keep his private property, and the officers allowed to keep their fire-arms." Beattie insisted that Hawkins's officers understood that the colonel would only "surrender on those conditions; and if they did not accept them, then we were to fight them as long as a man was left." But Duckworth had thoroughly rattled Hawkins, and at 11:00 a.m., Hawkins fell for his bluff, riding back out and agreeing to surrender.[34]

No immediate announcement was made to the men watching from the breastworks, but they knew what it meant when Hawkins returned from his parley in the company of a rebel officer. Stunned, outraged, Gray himself hastily "hid a couple of revolvers and some other things I had; I did not know whether I should ever find them again or not." Every one of his men "tried to hide his stuff. Some broke their guns, and all were denouncing Colonel Hawkins as a coward, in surrendering them without cause."

"Some said that the colonel was half rebel, anyway," recalled Gray; "others said that he was a little cowardly, and surrendered to an imaginary foe."[35]

"The next thing I knew," recalled Beattie, "there was an order came there for us to march our men out and lay down their arms." "Curses loud and deep," recalled Gray, "came from every squad of our boys, whose coolness & bravery had fairly won a victory." As they marched, many of them weeping, out of the fort, Hawkins's men stacked their busted rifles before the colonel's headquarters and watched as Duckworth's men "piled into our camp and cleaned out everything"; and "what they could not carry off they burned." Though Duckworth agreed to permit Hawkins's men to keep their personal property, only Hawkins's officers were allowed to ride their horses as their men marched past a gloating Colonel Duckworth and his staff.[36]

Duckworth's black laborers and horse holders, who had had a hand in constructing the phony artillery, were "jubilant over this ruse and were yelling, 'Here's your artillery! Toot! Toot! Toot!' with all their thumbs stuck over their ears, working the hand like a mule's ear." Thus the 7th Tennessee Cavalry (USA) began to comprehend the totality of its disgrace. Hawkins had surrendered a well-fortified, well-armed, and defiant garrison to a vastly outnumbered foe whose only cannon were logs and whose commander was not the great Forrest but a scraggly nonentity named Duckworth.[37]

Nor was that all, for at the very hour of Hawkins's surrender, General Mason Brayman and his reinforcements were riding to their rescue. Brayman would claim to have brought 2,000 troops with him, though how he managed to scrounge up so many soldiers is a mystery, for in his testimony he claimed that as of March 20 he could muster only 231 men. In any case, after disembarking at Columbus, they had ridden the newly laid rails to the northern end of the charred trestle, only to be informed that the garrison had surrendered, whereupon, instead of attempting a rescue, Brayman ordered the locomotive to reverse direction and returned to Cairo.[38]

Six miles away at Union City, Hawkins's men tore at their blankets and clothing with knives to prevent the rebels from using them, and hastily buried their regimental flag. But a rebel dug it up and claimed it as a trophy. When a captive officer tried to buy it back, pleading that his sister had sewn it, the trooper refused.[39]

"If your sister's good looking," he said, "she and I can probably make a trade. But you and I? Never. Say to her it is in the hands of men who know how to defend such emblems."[40]

Not all the rebels were so scornful. One of Duckworth's troopers called Colonel Hawkins "a God damned coward," but conceded that "he had good men." "These men of the Seventh Tennessee, Federal, bore up manfully," recalled John Milton Hubbard, and after "talking with many of the officers and men I concluded that their chagrin would have been amusing, if it had not been pathetic," for Hawkins had given them up when there was not "an effective Confederate cannon in West Tennessee, and Forrest was well on his way to Paducah."[41]

The rebels did not provide their prisoners with anything to eat "until the second night, when they gave them about an ounce of fat bacon each," and a few men received a little bread. The rebels carried away "300 horses, a few mules, 500 pistols and sabres, and some $60,000 in cash." The prisoners "were marched two days in muddy, rainy weather without a mouthful of food," and all the "money, watches & pocket knives which could be found on the persons of the prisoners were officially taken on the 26th while at Trenton," though several had been robbed "privately by their guards" a day or two before, and all along the way they were divested of "blankets, overcoats & other clothing." At Trenton the rebels "marched the men up in front of the court-house, passed them in one at a time and searched them, taking boots, hats, coats, blankets, and money from them. There were a great many of our men who had new boots, and the rebels would take the new boots and give them their old ones, and so they exchanged hats and blankets."[42]

Several dozen managed to escape before the rebels counted their prisoners, including Gray, Beattie, and Hawkins's son, as they "were not guarded very closely." Furious, Forrest would order his men to shoot all the prisoners if another escaped, and in the meantime the rebels made Colonel Hawkins and the other officers walk in ankle-deep mud while his men confiscated their clothes, blankets, and saddlebags. Hawkins protested repeatedly, reminding Duckworth that he had agreed to allow his prisoners to keep their

personal property. Though Duckworth solemnly promised that he was keeping strict accounts, the captive regiment's possessions were never returned.
By the time the captives staggered four by four into Humboldt, Hawkins's
condition was so pathetic that a citizen handed him two pairs of socks and
a handkerchief.[43]

"Some five hundred Tennesseans, who had been captured by Forrest,
arrived among us," an Andersonville inmate wrote of the 7th's influx on the
morning of April 22, 1864. Most of them were "hatless, bootless, and shoe-
less, without coats, pants and blankets," he said, and

> wholly destitute of cups, plates, spoons, and dishes of every kind as
> well as of all means of purchasing them; they having been stripped of
> these things by their captors. In their destitute condition they were
> turned into the stockade and left to shift for themselves in the best
> manner they could. To borrow cups of the fellow-prisoners was an
> impossibility, for no one could be expected to lend what, if it were not
> returned, would insure his own destruction, particularly when the
> borrower was an utter stranger. There was nothing left for them but
> to bake their raw meal and bacon upon stones and chips, eat it with-
> out moisture, and afterward to go to the brook like beasts to quench
> their thirst.

Hawkins's surrender cost his regiment many more lives than it saved.
The 7th Tennessee Cavalry would suffer the fourth highest number of prison
fatalities of any Union regiment. Two out of three of its troopers never returned home. According to the historian Peggy Scott Holley, "Two hundred
and seven died at Andersonville, sixteen at Millen, twelve at Savannah, ten
at Mobile, seven at Florence," eight in the postwar explosion of the steamboat *Sultana*, "four at Charleston, seventeen in northern hospitals, seven en
route to and from various prisons or hospitals, two on furlough, and one at
an unknown place." And that accounts for only those soldiers whose records
survive. Some would die of the aftereffects of their imprisonment, while
others lived the rest of their lives disabled by their months of unspeakable
incarceration in the pestilential prisons of the South.[44]

PADUCAH

FORT ANDERSON

September 6, 1861–March 26, 1864

BACK IN SEPTEMBER 1861, ULYSSES S. GRANT OCCUPIED THE PROSPER-
ous Ohio River town of Paducah, Kentucky, and just northwest of down-
town began to erect a bastion he dubbed Fort Anderson. Though he
characterized his occupation as protecting the community from Confederate invasion, to the residents of Paducah he and his troops were the in-
vaders. Local people, like most of the surrounding Jackson Purchase area of
southwestern Kentucky and northwestern Tennessee, were strongly secessionist and deeply resented Yankee occupation. "As near as I am able to get
the mind of the people in this place," wrote a Yankee visitor, "I think the inhabitants of the town would as leave have a regiment of Confederates quartered here as the Union forces who are now garrisoned near the city."[1]

Grant's real interest in Paducah was strictly strategic. The town commanded the Ohio River, and profited from a convergence of railroad lines
that ran to Memphis, Nashville, and points south. Fort Anderson consisted
of a large earthwork flanked (as at Union City and Fort Pillow) by an abatis
of fallen timber along its landward boundaries. Grant set aside a large building nearby for a marine hospital to house the invalid sailors and marines
whose gunboats docked along the riverfront.[2]

Though Paducah sat on low ground and suffered from poor drainage,
there had been "quite an effort on the part of the people to have a city,"
wrote a visitor in 1864. "Several streets are well macadamized and bordered
with curb stones. There are several good buildings for dwellings and stores,
but it has a good deal the air of a southern town." Out on the town's levee he
counted over fifty cotton bales and a dozen tobacco casks: an indication that
there was still "a little business going on in this part of the country."[3]

Posts all along the lower Mississippi had entered a scoundrel time of informers, smugglers, saboteurs, and spies, but Paducah was especially corrupt. Merchants eager to prove their loyalty squeezed out their competitors by providing Union commandants with lists of the loyal and disloyal. One roster, titled "Dangerous and Unreliable Men," included the mayor, the city marshal, and his deputy, as well as several judges, doctors, preachers, and most of the town's merchants. After Hurlbut replaced a pliant Colonel Henry Dougherty with the by-the-book Colonel James S. Martin, Paducah's loyalists begged the army to remove their town from Grant's jurisdiction and bring back Dougherty.[4]

Dougherty, however, had despised Paducah. "Southern rights men are greatly in the majority," he complained, and under the terms of their state's neutrality Kentuckians were able to elect their own officials. The county judge they had returned to office had "headed a vigilance committee here at the beginning of the Rebellion and banished loyal men from the state" by every "conceivable manner," including "setting them adrift in the Ohio River in skiffs without care," robbing them, "and committing violence on their persons in broad daylight in the streets of Paducah. They captured a steamboat at the landing, ran it up the Tennessee River, and finally burnt her to keep her from falling into the hands of our forces." The only ambition of "these sharp nosed, sandy headed, gander legged Kentuckyans," wrote an Ohio soldier, was "a log house; dirty young ones, 6 to 15 in number; a whife as motly as a pot pie that even makes all their pies to sell; and own one she-nigger."[5]

On the question of how to handle refugee slaves, Colonel Martin tried to cut a middle path. The contrabands' situation in Kentucky was even more perilous than in Tennessee because officially the state was not Union occupied but loyal—or, in effect, neutral—despite the fact that the army did in fact occupy such key positions as Columbus and Paducah. Nowhere did the Emancipation Proclamation's caveats have a more tragic effect than in Kentucky, where contrabands escaping from Confederate states thought they could find safe haven at Union-occupied posts, only to discover, too late, that the state's slave laws still remained in effect, including a provision that even legally emancipated freedmen emigrating to Kentucky from other states were to be immediately enslaved.[6]

In April 1863, Colonel Martin issued a pass to a couple named Curd to come into his lines at Paducah "for the purpose of looking after some contrabands." If blacks were "willing to accompany them," he wrote a subordinate, "you will allow them to do so." But this hardly satisfied slave owners, who saw in such a stipulation the effective end of slavery itself. "To say that I may take my negroes home if they *wish* to go," wrote a slaveholder, or control them if they "are *willing* I should, is to say that slavery ceases to exist except at the will of the slave."[7]

Martin was buffaloed. Like Wolfe at Fort Pillow, he kept asking headquarters to clarify the regulations regarding contrabands, which he now interpreted to hold that any loyal master could reclaim his escaped slaves. He gave his protection only to "such persons of African descent within the lines of this Post, who are or have been emancipated from slavery by the treason of their former masters and by the Proclamation of the President of the United States."[8]

Martin's superintendent of contrabands, Samuel Walker, oversaw 188 refugees, including forty-five children, most of whom had already settled around the fort when Walker established a camp for them. The remainder, he said, had "come within our lines voluntarily. Ten or twelve arrived last night," he wrote on June 19, "bringing with them Wagons, horses, &c." As far as he could determine, none of them were "negroes who have been freed by the 'President's' Proclamation" unless, of course, their masters were disloyal, but how was he supposed to determine that? Martin concluded that "citizens of Kentucky having slaves within my lines can recover them by Civil Authority, and that I have no right to interfere and must not aid or abet in their escape."[9]

Far from interfering, his officers actively aided and abetted in their capture. Martin's policy, vigorously enforced by his subordinates, resulted in the betrayal of scores of contrabands whose ultimate fate is unknown. Apparently at the behest and possibly in the paid employ of local slaveholders, Quartermaster Quincy J. Drake, a lieutenant in the 12th Illinois Infantry, rounded up as many of Paducah's contrabands as he could find and led them to his own laborers' camp at a nearby rolling mill "to prevent them," he said, from "scattering." But when they reached the camp, they were greeted by a police officer and a band of former masters who, brandishing manacles, whips, and warrants obligingly endorsed by Drake, began to lay claim to their runaway slaves. Accused of colluding with rebels and slave masters, Drake insisted that he did not learn about the abduction until he had returned from dinner to find the camp deserted. Nevertheless, the abductions continued. In the end, Martin decided that his only recourse was to send his contrabands to Columbus and let Asboth try to figure out what to do with them.[10]

On December 30, 1863, the *Louisville Journal* protested rather disingenuously that the citizens of Paducah, "who have never drawn a breath that was tainted with the noxious vapor of treason," were being "subjected to such severe restrictions as to debar them from the necessaries of life." The paper conceded that the Jackson's Purchase region of Kentucky might not be "the most loyal section of the state," but many of its inhabitants who had never been "seduced into the support of the Confederacy" were now "beset on one side by thieving and merciless guerillas and on the other by the unrelaxing rigor of Federal military rule" which turned "a deaf ear to all their complaints of hunger and nakedness."

For this the *Journal* did not blame the newly appointed commander at Paducah, Colonel Stephen G. Hicks, who, despite his "kindness of heart," had been compelled by the real culprit, General Hurlbut, to impose the same harsh rule at Paducah that Hurlbut found "necessary in the midst of treason at Memphis." The result of the military's stringent restrictions on trade was that women and children living beyond Federal lines were not only starving but could not even "get shoes nor a yard of material to make a garment."[11]

A veteran of the Mexican War, Colonel Stephen G. Hicks had been "partially disabled by wounds received at Pittsburg Landing."[12] But Hicks was a vigorous, vigilant officer. With his burly frame, close-cut beard, and narrow eyes, he resembled an even flintier Ulysses S. Grant. His garrison numbered 665 officers and men: 274 of them were black soldiers from the 1st Kentucky Heavy Artillery; the rest, white troops from the 122nd Illinois Infantry and 16th Kentucky Cavalry.

In the early-morning drizzle of March 25, 1864, Union scouts galloped into town to report that a muddy mass of rebel horsemen was roaring up the road from Mayfield. As the alarm spread, a motley fleet of small boats began to ferry hastily dressed and shivering women, children, and frightened Unionist civilians across to the Illinois side of the Ohio River.

Hicks summoned his men into Fort Anderson, and there they hunkered down along the breastworks, awaiting an attack from a rebel force almost ten times their number and under the personal command of the war's most formidable cavalryman. In one of the hardest rides of their career, Forrest's troopers had raced almost nonstop for twenty-six miles. At the head of the column rode Forrest's Kentucky brigade under the command of Colonel Albert P. "Sam" Thompson, a Paducah attorney determined to rescue his hometown from Yankee tyranny. New to Forrest's service, Thompson set such a "lively" pace, recalled Sergeant R. R. Hancock of the 22nd (formerly the 2nd) Tennessee, that his artillery battery "had to move very rapidly down grade and on level road in order to make up time lost in going up grade." The 22nd rode "at a gallop the greater portion of that twenty-six miles," and with only a few gentle showers to cool their horses.[13]

As Forrest and his men reached Paducah's outskirts, rebel sympathizers stood in the rain to cheer him. By now, word had reached Forrest of Duckworth's almost comical victory at Union City, and the Wizard was determined to repeat it. The difference this time was that Forrest's command, unlike Duckworth's, actually did vastly outnumber the Yankee garrison. Since some of Hicks's men were former slaves whom their own white comrades dismissed as mere impersonators of elite artillerymen, Forrest and his men expected another easy victory as they swarmed through town and invested the fort in a half-moon formation.

As a few stranded civilians sought shelter in the fort and drainage ditches, it appeared to the captains of two gunboats that "the rebels took advantage" by firing at the boats from behind the women. Captain James H. Odlin reported that the straggling "women, children, and other noncombatants" were ordered "to run down to the river bank to the left of our fort" and board "a little ferry-boat." But as the civilians scrambled for the riverbank, "rebel sharpshooters got in among them, so that we could not fire upon them without killing the women and children." As rebel marksmen "fired on our troops in the fort and on the gunboats, wounding one officer on a gunboat and two men," six women—nurses from the marine hospital—were made "to stand up in front of their sharpshooters, where it was impossible for us to return the fire without killing the women."[14]

After his troops spent several hours raiding the commissariat and nicking away at the breastworks with sniper fire, Forrest raised a flag of truce and confidently dispatched a courier to the gates of Fort Anderson bearing a note that offered essentially the same terms that had worked so well for Duckworth at Union City:

> Having a force amply sufficient to carry your works and reduce the place, and in order to avoid the unnecessary effusion of blood, I demand the surrender of the fort and troops, with all public property. If you surrender, you shall be treated as prisoners of war; but if I have to storm your works, you may expect no quarter.[15]

By now, however, Hicks had also been apprised of Duckworth's trickery at Union City. Angered to see that Forrest's men were meanwhile taking advantage of the truce by dispersing along the levee and planting a battery in town, Hicks decided not to follow Isaac Hawkins into ignominy but to call Forrest's bluff.[16]

"I have been placed here by my government to defend this post," he replied, "and in this, as well as all other orders from my superior, I feel it to be my duty as an honorable officer to obey. I must, therefore, respectfully decline surrendering as you may require."[17]

As Forrest's disappointed delegates rode back, they reportedly shot down "in the streets some citizens and some men straggling from the hospital." Some of Forrest's biographers maintain that Colonel Sam Thompson thereupon took it upon himself to storm Fort Anderson on his own initiative. It is certainly possible that Thompson, new to Forrest's command, could have managed one charge contrary to Forrest's wishes, but not the three separate charges he would make with two Kentucky regiments, all while Forrest's sharpshooters and a ragtag band of local secessionists sniped at the Union gunboats from the upper-story windows of the homes and "heavy warehouses" that lined the riverfront.[18]

The gunboat *Peosta* was badly perforated but managed, with the *Captain Smith*, *Captain O'Neil* and *Paw Paw*, to return a fire so destructive that, to the cheering of the garrison, it toppled and ignited almost a quarter of the town. ("Most of the inhabitants being still rebel sympathizers," explained General Brayman, the Union navy gun crews experienced "less than the usual regret in performing the duty.") The gunboats' barrage scattered "shingles, brick chimneys and window glass in wild profusion upon our heads," wrote one of Forrest's officers. "One building in particular seemed to have attracted a well directed and concentrated fire, by the annoyance our men gave the gunners of a siege gun."[19]

"The negro troops, with the heavy artillery, were compelled to stand up on the platforms to man the guns," reported Captain Odlin, "their only protection there being a little bank or ridge of earth about knee high. Our loss in killed resulted from this exposure." Forrest's men "got up on the tops of houses, and also in the hospital, and fired down into the fort upon our gunners. But the troops fought bravely, without flinching. As soon as a man fell at the guns, one of his comrades would drag him out of the way and take his place." A black sergeant proved "conspicuous for his gallantry. He did not always use military terms, but his words answered as well. 'Hurry, boys! Load afore the smoke clears,'—and before the advancing column of the enemy had gained many steps, a terrific discharge of spherical case or other shot staggered them back."[20]

The black troops, "having muskets as well as serving the artillery, would load and fire their muskets while the artillery was being fired," reported Odlin. The white troops "fought as well as any men could be expected to fight," but they were "better covered and had more protection" than their black comrades. The result was that eleven of the fourteen Union soldiers killed at Paducah were black.[21]

As the Union gunboats retaliated by pumping round after round into the sharpshooters' roost, the roof was "first carried away by a shell; next disappears an adjoining shed, which a moment before exhibited first, a head, then a rifle, afterwards a blue wreath of smoke; and other shot tore the building asunder, capsized several men, wounded many, and killed one." Among Forrest's casualties was Captain McKnight of the 22nd Tennessee Cavalry, whose head was "fearfully crushed" by flying bricks.[22]

As Thompson prepared a third assault, "canister, grape and minnie balls were poured incessantly from the besieged garrison," reported one of Forrest's officers, while the "bursting shells, and the crashing of the solid shot from the gunboats, thunder[ed] through the buildings above and around us," killing several civilians, including a woman and child. Steaming past Paducah during the barrage, a local woman named Frances Wallace watched from a steamboat with her friend Mally as their world went up in flames. "I see one of my houses burnt to ashes. Mally fears hers is hurt also. But what is the fate of our friends in the town?" She was to learn that another of her sisters was at home during the battle when "a ball entered the house & exploded near the children's bed. What an escape! All very much frightened. All the houses near the spot struck. Much suffering."[23]

During the third charge, as the ever ardent Sam Thompson galloped past the door to his old law office, a shot either from the gunboats or, according to some accounts, from one of Fort Anderson's black artillerymen knocked his head from his shoulders. His stunned Kentuckians retreated into the ruins of the town, and the rest of Forrest's men "took shelter behind houses, in rooms, and hollows," from which they "kept up a scattering fire" until, wrote an officer, "the thickening shades of night began to obscure the outline of the fort, swallowing up guns, Yankees and earthworks in one dark ominous picture."[24]

After looting the town of horses and medical and military stores, Forrest departed, declaring to a local rebel sympathizer that "in no engagement during the war had he been so badly cut up and crippled as at this place." It was a good thing for the Union garrison too, for, unbeknownst to Forrest, Hicks was down to only two more rounds of ammunition. "Fully determined never to surrender while I had a man alive," Hicks had ordered that the remaining ammunition "be equally distributed; the men to fix their bayonets; to make good use of the ammunition they had, and, when that was exhausted, to receive the enemy on the point of the bayonet," an order that was greeted by his men "with loud shouts and cheers."[25]

Forrest would boast that he had "held the town for ten hours, capturing a large amount of clothing, several hundred horses, a large lot of medical stores for the command, burning a steamer, the dock, and all cotton on the landing." But Hicks reported that his "loss in government stores was inconsiderable. The quartermaster's depot, a temporary wooden building, was burned, and in consequence thereof a small lot of quartermaster's property was lost," but the "commissary stores, and most of our government horses, mules, wagons, &c., were saved," including 140 army horses that Hicks had hidden outside town.[26]

Though no one has satisfactorily tallied the number of Forrest's casualties, the Wizard had met with far less success than Duckworth had achieved at Union City, and at far greater cost. Indeed, it would be Duckworth and his victorious 7th Tennessee Cavalry's turn to taunt Forrest and his officers for failing to achieve their objective. Forrest later contended that he withdrew his forces from Paducah "on account of the prevalence of small-pox in the place," but his men knew better; you do not collect heaps of clothing and blankets, let alone the scores of hospital patients Forrest captured, from a post infested with smallpox. "We took Paduca and many prisoners," wrote Lieutenant Lauchlan Donaldson of the 12th Kentucky, "but could not hold it on acct. of the fort near the river and the gun boats."[27]

And the garrison's black artillerists. "I have been one of those men who never had much confidence in colored troops fighting," Colonel Hicks confessed, "but those doubts are now all removed, for they fought as bravely as any troops in the fort." "I cannot refrain," General Brayman wrote to Sherman, "from special reference to the fidelity and courage of the black soldiers, who, though not mustered nor paid, and without regular organization or officers, fought bravely and patiently to the end."[28]

According to Chalmers, Forrest's men led sixty-four prisoners away from Paducah, but since by all accounts nearly the entire Federal force had retired into the fort, they were, with the exception of a handful of prisoners scooped up during a recent skirmish at Benton, patients stranded in the marine hospital. As Forrest retreated to Mayfield, pausing only to set fire to Yankee tents and a train of cars, a third of his men doubled back into Paducah's eastern blocks, where, "freed from official restrictions, they entered sutler stores" and dressing themselves "handsomely, filled their pockets with de-

sirable articles of diminutive size" until their horses groaned "under a burden of every conceivable variety of goods such as are found in a Yankee
shop." The town was enveloped in "a pale, lurid light" that gave "a ghostly
appearance to man and beast as they dashed, more like spectres than human beings, up and down the stony streets, some with plunder, others without plunder, some entirely hidden under the weight of clothing—horse and
rider almost imperceptibly drowned in the abundance of dry goods."[29]

The next morning, as Hicks and his men set fire to the surviving structures from which the rebels had poured their fire, rebel couriers from the
22nd trotted into town under a flag of truce, bearing a message from Forrest.
"I understand," it began, that "you hold in your possession in the guardhouse at Paducah a number of confederate soldiers as prisoners of war. I
have in my possession about thirty-five or forty federal soldiers who were
captured here yesterday, and about five hundred who were captured at
Union City. I propose to exchange man for man, according to rank, so far as
you may hold confederate soldiers."[30]

As Hicks's delegation carried Forrest's note back to their commander,
"citizens, soldiers and negroes began to collect from all quarters," one of the
couriers recalled, "and soon upwards of five hundred beings moved in one
resistless body towards the flag of truce." Hicks and his staff demanded and
received a list of Forrest's prisoners, and an hour later, with a soldier's cold
logic, he categorically refused to exchange healthy rebels for his own wounded
and sickly men.

"The main body of the rebels," wrote Odlin, "Forrest with them, retreated on the Mayfield road, while about 300 of his men remained in the
town making movements and feints on the fort, to prevent our sending out
and ascertaining his movements." Forrest's cavalry marched his sickly prisoners "ten miles, and then camped them down in a swampy piece of ground
at night." Despite the stores of clothing Forrest's men had plundered, the
prisoners' clothes were "nearly all taken from them. Some of them were left
bareheaded and barefooted, with nothing on but their pants and shirts,
compelled to stay in that swampy ravine all night long, with nothing to eat,
and not permitted to have fires."[31]

Finally, after one more barrage from the gunboats, the last of Forrest's
men retired, though, at least according to the Yankee press, not until they
had killed "as many negroes as they could." As they rode out of sight, a silence descended on the garrison and the riverfront and the smoking ruins of
the town. Chalmers would later congratulate the Kentucky regiments that
assaulted Fort Anderson for rescuing Kentucky from "the iron heels of abolition, despotism, and the rule of the Negro." But they had accomplished no

such thing. Not only had Forrest exhausted his gambits of bluff and bluster that had served him so well in the past, he had himself been bluffed into withdrawing by a garrison that had all but exhausted its ammunition.[32]

As much harm as Forrest's defeat would do to his reputation for invincibility, however, the Paducah affair would have even more disastrous consequences for the Union garrison at Fort Pillow. Not only would it incense and embolden Forrest's men and force the Wizard to make good on one of his threats of no quarter if his terms were refused; it convinced William Bradford that Forrest was all bluff: that as soon as he declined Forrest's invitation to surrender, the Wizard would withdraw as he had withdrawn from Paducah, burning a few outbuildings and firing a few last desultory shots, perhaps, but otherwise retreating in chagrin and frustration.[33]

Unable to find fit housing for his wife and twin babies at Fort Pillow, an Alabaman orderly sergeant in Bradford's Company A named George Craig had sent his family up to Paducah. After Forrest's assault on Fort Anderson, Craig had heard nothing from his wife. He would later claim that on April 10 he volunteered to ride to Paducah and track down a number of the late Captain Gregory's loyalists who had deserted from Craig's company, "carrying with them the Arms and Ammunition and &c. and &c. belonging to the company." But it is just as likely that after news reached him of Forrest's attack, he simply deserted the 13th to find his family.

In any case, when Craig reached Paducah he was horrified to learn that his wife and twin boys had not survived Forrest's attack three weeks before. Having missed the barges that carried the town's noncombatants across the river, Craig's wife had sought refuge from the Union gunboats' incessant cannonade in a canal filled with mud and water. There she had died of exposure, and the twins with her, and someone in Hicks's garrison did not spare Craig the details: that their bodies "lay unattended for 48 hours after death," during which rats had eaten one of his wife's breasts "and the head off of one of my little babes."[34]

"ALL IS QUIET"
BOOTH AT FORT PILLOW
March 28–April 12, 1864

IN LATE MARCH, FIFTY-NINE-YEAR-OLD BRIGADIER GENERAL MASON Brayman took the reins at Cairo.[1] A former colleague of Lincoln's in Springfield, Illinois, Brayman was lean and mercurial, with a grizzled, close-cropped Sherman beard but none of Sherman's instinct for the jugular. Sherman ordered his commanders along the Mississippi to go after Forrest and, if not destroy him, at least chase him back to Mississippi. Convinced, however, that southern Illinois was "infested with domestic traitors, and rebels from the south," and that Forrest intended to cross the Ohio and make common cause with Illinois copperheads, Brayman defied Sherman's order. He destroyed all the skiffs and ferries along the lower Ohio, suspended all commerce in his district, arrested all disloyal or badly disposed locals, closed all taverns and brothels, and ordered his pickets to shoot on sight anyone they suspected of being up to no good. "Our posts and towns are crowded with dangerous persons," he declared. "They intend us mischief. I am satisfied that concerted rebel activity exists across the river"—a claim that Sherman would dismiss as "ridiculous nonsense."[2]

Brayman shared an instinct for the capillaries with his old Illinois crony Stephen Augustus Hurlbut, who was driving Sherman to distraction with his relentless pleas and excuses. Writing from Memphis on March 30, Hurlbut complained that he had only 2,250 cavalry and could muster only 2,500 white and 2,600 black infantry, whereas he had received reports that Black Bob McCulloch alone had trotted through La Grange just the day before with 1,500 men while Forrest himself rode with a force of 4,500.[3]

It is curious that in arguing against an offensive, Hurlbut should have considerably overestimated the force at his disposal, unless it was to disguise from Sherman the extent to which he had allowed Memphis's defenses to deteriorate. On April 24, his cavalry commander, Brigadier General Benjamin Henry Grierson, would report that he had only 1,700 effective cavalry, while Ralph Buckland, his infantry commander, could summon less than a quarter the number of foot soldiers Hurlbut had counted only three weeks before.

Sherman gave Buckland a direct order to attack Forrest at once, but apparently Hurlbut's timidity was viral, for Buckland thereupon raised Hurlbut's estimate of Forrest's force to seven thousand, and claimed that another six thousand rebels under Stephen D. Lee were hovering within striking distance of Memphis itself. According to Grierson, Buckland had therefore "considered it hazardous to weaken the garrison at Memphis by sending any portion of the Infantry force in search of the enemy," and Hurlbut would commit himself to engaging Forrest only in the unlikely event he came "within reach of infantry." In the meantime, he would keep Grierson and his cavalry close to home, patrolling the Memphis fairgrounds "so as to meet any sudden dash." Within ten days of his original calculation, Hurlbut would raise Buckland's estimate of Forrest's force to eight thousand effectives and four three-inch rifled guns; however, he claimed that Forrest's aim was not to attack any more of the river forts but to zigzag up into Kentucky, turn eastward, and then descend into middle Tennessee, which was fortunately well beyond Hurlbut's jurisdiction.[4]

On March 28, 1864, Hurlbut ordered Major Lionel Booth to proceed to Fort Pillow with his 6th USCHA. While stationed in St. Louis, Major Booth had married an Ohio girl named Lizzie Wayt, the daughter of an English father and a Northern Irish mother. She was about twenty-four years old, a native of Martinsburg, West Virginia, and apparently good-looking enough to elicit at least one indecent proposal from a member of Hurlbut's staff. With Forrest on the loose, however, and his men forbidden to bring along their wives, Booth deemed it prudent to leave Lizzie behind at Memphis. At 4:00 p.m. on March 28, within hours of receiving Hurlbut's orders, he bade his bride farewell and, with his regiment of black artillerists and white officers, boarded the steamer *Gladiator* and chugged up from Memphis through the rain.[5]

"As you will be, if I am correct in my memory, the senior officer at that post," wrote Hurlbut, "you will take command, conferring, however, freely and fully with Major Bradford, 13th Tennessee cavalry, whom you will find a good officer, though not of much experience." He described Fort Pillow as boasting "commanding" positions that could be "held by a great force against almost any odds." He told Booth he was sending along two twelve-pound howitzers, "as I hope it will not be necessary to mount heavy guns. You will, however, immediately examine the ground and the works, and if, in your opinion, 20-pound Parrotts"—rifled artillery—"can be advantageously used, I will order them to you."

Hurlbut described Bradford as "well acquainted with the country," and Booth was to see to it that Bradford kept his scouts "well out and forward." Hurlbut believed that after Forrest's "check at Paducah," the Wizard was not disposed to attack any more river forts, and promised that as soon as Forrest had crossed the Tennessee River, Hurlbut would evacuate the entire garrison. "Nevertheless," he said, "act promptly in putting the works into perfect order, and the post into its strongest defense." Hurlbut urged Booth to "allow as little intercourse as possible" between his black troops and the local population, "and cause all supplies which go out to be examined with great strictness. No man whose loyalty is questionable should be allowed to come in or go out while the enemy is in West Tennessee."[6]

Hurlbut assured Bradford in turn that Booth's four companies of black artillerists were "good troops, well tried and commanded by a good officer," who had also drilled them as infantry. "I think these troops had better hold the forts," Hurlbut wrote to Bradford, "while yours are held for exterior garrison," but "in case of an attack, you will of course seek refuge in the fortifications." With a garrison of seven hundred good men, Hurlbut concluded, "your post can be held until assistance arrives."[7]

The garrison would number considerably fewer effective defenders than that, however. Out of a potential force of 410 men and officers (414 minus the 4 men listed as "lost") only 246 officers and men, or 60 percent of Booth's command, proceeded to Fort Pillow on March 29. One hundred eleven (27 percent) were knocked out of commission by sickness and 48 were on detached duty elsewhere. Since Company E of the 6th USCHA fielded only 1 man, it would be proper to say that Booth joined the 24 men and one officer of Company D of the 2nd USCLA (of the 32 men sent from Memphis, 6 were sick and 2 were on special duty) with only Companies A through D of the 6th USCHA. Thus to Bradford's 266 effectives and the 2nd USCLA's 24, Booth was adding only 246 combatants, for a total garrison of 536 combat-ready officers and men.[8]

Although several men had deserted and then returned to duty by the time the command departed from Memphis, on the day of their arrival at Fort Pillow, only 6 men were listed as AWOL, and just 1 as a deserter. It is true that these black troops had not yet been in battle and that the option of returning home did not appeal to escaped slaves the way it might to white soldiers. Nevertheless, the 2nd and the 6th experienced an unusually low rate of AWOLs and desertions, especially compared to the hemorrhaging 13th Tennessee Cavalry's 112 AWOLs and 24 deserters in the month of March alone; unusually small, in fact, compared to any of Forrest's regiments. Nevertheless, illness had depleted the garrison's ranks of black artillerists in the same proportion (27 percent) in which desertion had depleted the ranks of Bradford's Battalion.

In addition to Bradford's cavalry and Booth's artillery, the garrison could call upon the services of the Union gunboat *New Era,* which her captain, James Marshall, kept tied up at the wharf. Weighed down by a sloping skirt of heavy timbers across its deck and two batteries of three twenty-four-pound howitzers each, the wooden-hulled and wood-burning *New Era* had a four-foot draft and could attain upriver speeds of almost seven knots.[9]

The picked men of the 2nd USCLA boasted seventeen horses and two 3.6-pound guns, but in Booth's report dated March 29, Companies A through D of the 6th arrived with neither guns nor horses. The two guns that Hurlbut promised turned up eventually, but the two Parrott guns that arrived sometime in early April raise one of the mysteries of the Fort Pillow record. Hurlbut indicated that he would send Booth two additional guns if Booth requested them. But there is no record of such a request, nor, in fact, of any correspondence from Booth during the ten days leading up to the day of the battle.[10]

After the battle, Booth's former colonel, Thomas Jackson, would make and then hastily retract an allegation that Booth had begged Hurlbut for reinforcements. It may be that the letter requesting the additional guns contained some such appeal, for it is odd that there was such a dearth of correspondence—not even a telegram—during the last week of Booth's life, especially since Hurlbut had instructed this conscientious officer to keep him posted. It is possible, if improbable, that as the army's inspectors and then congressional investigators closed in on Hurlbut, he destroyed any subsequent correspondence that might have laid the blame for the massacre at his door. There is no evidence that Booth wired Cairo for assistance, nor is it likely he would have been tempted, as Brayman had a reputation for refusing to provide black artillery regiments with horses and threatening to appropriate their guns.

One possible reason Hurlbut chose to send Booth's battery to Fort Pillow was to spare them the epidemic of smallpox that was raging through

Memphis. But another reason was that Bradford was a sincere proponent of the recruitment of black troops. The Bradfords had owned no slaves and regarded the peculiar institution as a "dead care" on the "body politic of the state." In November 1863, while still actively recruiting men for the 13th, Bradford had heartily endorsed a local doctor's plan to raise a battery of colored light artillery. "I think the requisite number of blacks can be obtained," he assured Andrew Johnson, from "the slave owners of this section of the state," who were "mostly disloyal and earnest sympathizers with the rebellion, however earnestly some of them strive to disguise it." Besides, Bradford concluded, forming black regiments would prevent the slaves from being "used many and various ways by our enemies."[11]

He was in the minority in this respect. Among the men of the 13th least likely to approve of serving with black troops was Neal Clark, a thirty-one-year-old former overseer who, for an average wage of two hundred dollars a year, had enforced the servitude of slaves in Heywood and Madison counties. In any case, Bradford had kept his white troopers separated from the forty black artillerists of the 2nd USCLA after they joined the garrison in February.[12]

Arriving at Fort Pillow on March 29, Major Booth immediately set about trying to improve the fortifications. Deeming the garrison much too spread out, he decided to concentrate his defenses on the thirty-acre promontory atop which his artillerists were encamped. He replaced the horseshoe wall that defined this innermost bastion with a zigzag of three redans—walls set at salient angles—and poked his battalion's two twelve-pounders and two ten-pound Parrott guns through its portholes. "Working his command day and night," he ordered his men to excavate a series of oblong rifle pits on the bluff's eastern slope. It is likely that several of the black artillerists digging pits and trenches that week had been among the impressed slaves who had built Fort Pillow in the first place, for the Confederates had recruited their laborers from many of the same plantations from which the Union army had recruited black troops.[13]

After his men finished shoring up Fort Pillow's defenses, Booth reported to Hurlbut that he believed he could hold the post against any foe for at least forty-eight hours. But his own men were not so sure. Sergeant Henry Weaver of the 6th USCHA feared that in the event of an attack, Booth's rifle pits, platforms, and embrasures would eventually prove "of more use to [the rebels] than to us."[14]

———————————

Perhaps the murkiest personage to turn up at Fort Pillow in those early April days was a sturdy, black-haired young woman of about twenty-six years of age named Mollie Pittman. She was born Mary Ann Pittman, the sole child of a poor Kentucky laborer who moved the family to Dyer County before the war to work for Thomas Buchanan, a future captain in the 15th Tennessee Cavalry. She grew into a quick-witted, dauntless woman with a "deep, dark, penetrating eye," and when war broke out she assisted W. H. Craig in raising an infantry company known as the Bell Greys. Pittman appears to have passed herself off as Thomas Phillips, serving as a substitute for the real Tom Phillips, a Dyer County carpenter. As Phillips she rose to company commander until her discharge in May 1862, after which she and some of her men joined Forrest's cavalry, where she took the name Rawley and again served briefly as a lieutenant. Perhaps it was after her gender was discovered that Forrest, impressed by her pluck and gift for impersonation, enlisted her to act as a spy and smuggler under the name Mary Hays.

Her chief assignment was to purchase supplies—mostly small arms and ammunition—from the secessionist Beauvais family of St. Louis and convey them to Forrest. Joining a secret copperhead society known as the Southern League, she made three trips before her capture, and it was after her third run, as she was pausing at Randolph, that she received orders from Forrest to meet him at his camp some ten miles from Fort Pillow to pick up a rebel uniform and resume her masquerade as Lieutenant Rawley. "He said he would rather detail ten of his best officers for this business," she bragged, "than lose my services at that time."

Pittman immediately set off on her mule. Some half dozen miles from Fort Pillow, she was stopped by suspicious Union scouts who searched her baggage and brought her back to Fort Pillow. "I resolved, be the result with me personally what it might," she would rather grandly testify, "never to return to the Confederate service and continue my former career." Pittman claimed that upon reaching Fort Pillow she tried to demonstrate her good faith by telling them everything she knew and everything she had done on behalf of the Confederacy. She even offered to lead Major Booth to the Wizard's camp, where she "would be able to place him in possession of General Forrest as a prisoner in a short time." Major Booth "seemed to believe me," she recalled, "and was anxious to carry my proposition out; yet he feared and hesitated, and after a considerable consultation with other officers, finally resolved not to venture on it."

Pittman would claim that while she was at Fort Pillow a local man she only dimly recognized took her aside, addressed her as Lieutenant Rawley, and told her that Forrest intended to descend on the garrison with four thousand men. The Wizard, he said, was determined to take the fort "if it took every man he had," and teach them a lesson "for arresting a woman."

Her informant proceeded to Booth's headquarters and asked for a pass out of the fort. When Booth asked about his loyalty, one of Bradford's Tennessee soldiers testified that he was a Union man.

"Must I grant this pass, Mollie," Booth asked, "or must I not?"

"Use your own judgment," Pittman replied. "You know your own business best."

Booth gave the man his pass, but after he departed, Pittman told Booth what the man had told her. "My advice was to evacuate the fort or re-enforce it at once, for if Forrest did get possession, the Federal forces, and especially the officers, would be badly used."

"Mollie," Booth was said to have replied, "now make your preparation to go to Memphis this evening, for I be damned if he shall have you."

Ordering Captain Marshall of the *New Era* to put Mollie aboard the first boat that came downriver, Booth sent her off to Memphis, perhaps hoping she could convince Hurlbut that he required reinforcements.[15]

That was Mollie's story, anyway, none of which could be proven or refuted after Forrest's attack on Fort Pillow. Pittman was placed in isolation at Irving Block prison, and remained at Memphis telling the authorities her tales, and impressing them with a knowledge of military affairs that few civilians, or officers, for that matter, could match. She said she had learned from an encounter with Forrest that Lincoln's secretary of the treasury Salmon Chase was a copperhead who had exchanged twenty thousand dollars in Federal greenbacks for nine hundred dollars' worth of Confederate gold. She claimed that members of the Southern League put on blackface to pose as colored troops and went around St. Louis killing Union pickets. She informed on her fellow prisoners for giving secret signals to passersby.[16]

At last the authorities proposed, supposedly with the blessing of Secretary of War Edwin Stanton, that she prove her fidelity to the Union by visiting the Beauvais family in St. Louis, to see if they would continue to do business with her, ostensibly on behalf of the Confederacy. Apparently she did as she was told, for she was present when the Yankees arrested the senior Beauvais in his store. But it is no surprise that after the war Mary Ann "Mollie" Pittman—aka Thomas Phillips, aka Lieutenant Rawley, aka Mary Simpson, Timms, or Hays—would entirely vanish.[17]

On March 30, an exhausted and famished young white man cantered into Fort Pillow on a lathered horse and identified himself as Captain Thomas P. Gray of the 7th Tennessee Cavalry (USA). Captured with Hawkins's command at Union City, Gray had tried to convince his fellow officers to attack their guards and flee, but had "met the opposition of the officers, because it was the general opinion that if we were caught, one in every ten would be killed."

So he slipped away on his own, shinning it for

twenty-five hours without stopping, through the brush, dodging the rebels and guerillas. I was then directed by a negro to a farm where there were no whites, and where, he said, I could get a horse. When I got there I found I was so tired and sleepy that I dared not risk myself on a horse, and I secreted myself and rested there until early the next morning. . . . I told the negroes, as I laid down, that if any strangers came on the place, or any one inquiring for Yankees, to tell them that one had been there and pressed a horse and gone on. They did so; and more than that, they told the guerillas that I had been gone but a few minutes, and if they hurried they would catch me. They dashed on five miles further, and then gave up the chase and turned back.

After a five-hour, forty-mile bareback ride, Gray reported to Booth "that I did not think there was any danger of an attack, because I thought I should have seen or heard something more to indicate it." Nevertheless, he had heard a few vagrant rumors to the contrary and urged Booth "to be on the lookout" in any case. Alarmed, Booth immediately ordered Major Bradford to send several squads of his men on a scout.

They rode to within five miles of Brownsville, where Bob Richardson's men tried to cut them off, but they escaped by making a sudden rush on Richardson's left flank and managed to get away without losing any men or prisoners. Richardson's men chased after them, only to be turned back at Ripley by a single volley that apparently emptied several rebel saddles. The Union scouts heard rumors that Fielding Hurst had been defeated "somewhere near or on the Hatchie, south of Brownsville," though "there seemed to be a prevailing opinion" that Hurst was on his way to Brownsville. They could find "no organized bands of Guerrillas Between Ripley and Fort Pillow," but they did pass "a great many stragglers on the roads, and at the houses along the Road the other side of Ripley" who, at the first sight of Bradford's scouts, "immediately took to the Woods and Bush."

Before daylight on March 31, the apparently tireless Captain Thomas Gray galloped into Memphis and demanded to see Hurlbut at once. Rising from bed, Hurlbut listened as Gray relayed the rumors he had heard about Forrest's intentions to attack Fort Pillow.[18]

Hurlbut immediately ordered Grierson to "take all the available Cavalry force at or near Memphis, and move as rapidly as possible to attack the force under Genl Forrest," but the key words here were "available" and "possible," for the rest of his orders stuttered with anxiety. "The march must be active," Grierson was told, "and at the same time cautious." Hurlbut warned Grierson that Forrest had tapped the telegraph lines near Paducah, intercepting Sherman's orders to General James Veatch to land at Savannah on the Tennessee River and move toward the Hatchie. "Large discretion must be given you," Hurlbut concluded, "but a Cavalry officer is rarely found fault with for dash." Forrest would "either push his leading force boldly across the Tennessee or return upon his tracks, picking up his rear guard at Jackson or La-Grange."[19]

Meanwhile, Hurlbut tried to assure Sherman that Forrest had been "severely crippled in the Paducah affair, and suffered very heavy loss." Forrest's "whole movement and the state of the country," he added, "indicate retreat." Nevertheless, Hurlbut reported that he was making "every effort" to speed up reenlistments of veterans, "and every Regiment of Cavalry or Infantry entitled to re-enlist in the corps has done so. The result is that fragments of non-veterans of the several regiments are left," which limited "the efficiency of the cavalry."[20]

Hurlbut's constant plea, however, was for more horses. Grierson had only 2,200 in his command, despite Hurlbut's urgent requests during the past winter for 5,000 more. Hurlbut deemed it "utterly useless" to pursue Forrest with infantry, especially when the people of West Tennessee remained "overwhelmingly disloyal" and "readily report all movements of our troops, and rarely furnish any news of the enemy." Kentuckians were no better, and Hurlbut considered "the damage done to Paducah as a proper lesson to that place and its vicinity." Hurlbut believed that if not for Forrest's defeat at Paducah he would have attacked Cairo and Mound City. Even as he sent Grierson off to chase after Forrest, he broadly interpreted his instructions from Sherman to be "not to interrupt anything further than to hold the points on the River until the return of the veterans and of the detached forces now in the field" and to maintain "a moveable force near Memphis."[21]

Sherman was fed up. Trying to get Hurlbut to move was like pushing a string. But it probably did not matter to Hurlbut's career that he would disgrace himself over the next couple of weeks, for his days at Memphis were already numbered. Sherman had decided to send Brigadier General John W.

Corse down the Mississippi "to give life to Hurlbut's movements against Forrest." Corse boarded the dispatch steamer *Silver Wave* at Nashville and, with stops at Paducah, Cairo, Columbus, and Memphis, set out to coordinate a "grand roundup" of Forrest's command. Sherman thereupon ordered A. J. Smith to rush ten thousand men cross-country to cut Forrest off at Grenada, Mississippi, in the hope that Smith's advance would prove "a big bomb-shell in Forrest's camp" and make the Wizard "pay dear for his foolish dash at Paducah."[22]

Sherman shot off another order predicated on the assumption that after licking his wounds at Jackson, Forrest was preparing to flee south. "No matter what strength," he commanded Hurlbut, hoping to forestall another of Hurlbut's pleas for more troops and horses, "you should move toward the Hatchie and prevent his escape, more especially with any train or plunder." Forrest, he said, "has had all he wants of attacking fortified places, and the more he attempts it the better we should be satisfied." But Hurlbut wired back that on April 3 Grierson had come upon a portion of Forrest's command near Somerville "and found them too strong." Ignoring Sherman's "no matter what strength," Hurlbut declined "to do more than keep him North until proper force comes."[23]

On April 4, a detachment from Chalmers's division escorted Forrest's prisoners south via Pocahontas, Tennessee, leading Grierson to believe that, thus disencumbered, the Wizard intended to descend on Memphis. "The enemy, in very considerable force, are near Rising Sun," Hurlbut wired Buckland. "It would be very like their tactics" to cross Wolf River suddenly somewhere near Moscow or Germantown, "and move upon the city." Hurlbut urged "great vigilance" and demanded "that all officers and men be held to strict attention to their duties." Though he admitted it was "purely guess work" because he could obtain "no information from the country," by April 5 Hurlbut had convinced himself that Forrest was merely distracting Grierson with his best men while he and the rest of his command escaped south with their plunder.[24]

On April 6, cavalry major Ira Gifford noted at Memphis "the unusual number of enlisted men now present in this command" who rode their own privately owned horses and were "unable to do the duties of a Cavalryman for various reasons, thereby preventing the Government of the United States from the use of their horses & horse equipments for which they receive full pay & allowance." Gifford urged that no cavalrymen be permitted to keep any private stock and that all such serviceable stock be purchased by the government. Some of those men Gifford complained about were members of Bradford's Battalion who lay sick in various post hospitals.[25]

"We are just resting from the severe mental and bodily duty consequent in keeping vigil" over General Forrest, wrote a Minnesota infantryman stationed at Memphis. "He has threatened us since the 23rd of March with an attack until two days since when he probably thought it best to pay some attention to what our General Grierson was doing by way of cutting off his retreat. It is not justly known where either of the forces are at present, but I am inclined to think they are somewhere in the interior trying to see each other without getting hurt."[26]

On April 7, Hurlbut reported to Buckland that Forrest was back in the neighborhood. Hurlbut ordered Grierson's cavalry "to be at the Fair ground by day light. If the attack be made in force dismounted, the Regiments and Batteries should have instructions, if they cannot hold their ground, to retire concentrically on the line of the Bayou." If it proved necessary "to abandon any buildings containing public stores," Hurlbut ordered, they were to be incinerated.[27]

Three days later, General McPherson proposed combining two divisions of Hurlbut's 16th Army Corps with two divisions from the 17th, leaving only the remaining divisions along the river under Hurlbut's command. Since this would greatly reduce his command, Hurlbut demanded in vain that he be permitted to supersede General Lorenzo Thomas in commanding black troops, complaining that the current "system by which Brigadier-General Thomas is authorized to issue independent orders direct to them, without passing through my headquarters, is injurious in every respect." He asked to be allowed to occupy Yazoo City, Mississippi, with one regiment of white troops, two of colored infantry, and a regiment of colored cavalry, though the black troopers lacked seven hundred carbines, "which I have not to give them." Hurlbut reiterated that the success so far of Forrest's raid was the consequence not of timidity on his part but of his own lack of veteran troops and an inadequate supply of horses.[28]

Sherman was fit to be tied. "Hurlbut has at Memphis Buckland's brigade, 2,000; Grierson's cavalry, mounted, 2,400; dismounted, 3,000; in the fort 1,200 blacks, and outside of the fort full 2,000 blacks; in all 10,600," he wrote McPherson, "which are amply sufficient, besides three full regiments of armed citizens. [Fort Pickering] has sixty heavy guns mounted. I feel no apprehension whatever for the safety of Memphis, but only that Hurlbut may exhibit timidity and alarm."[29]

The next day he urged McPherson to send any troops he could spare up the Tennessee and march them west toward Jackson "or Paris even," for "it would disturb Forrest more than anything Hurlbut will do from Memphis." In any case, Sherman was convinced that "the more of the enemy's cavalry that keep over toward the Mississippi," the better it was for the Union, "as our object is to disperse them. They cannot make a lodgment on the river, anyhow," he said, "and only wander about consuming the resources of their own people."[30]

Bradford's scouts returned on April 3 with six rebel prisoners, including one of Duckworth's furloughed lieutenants and two guerrillas described to Booth by local people as "very desperate men." They reported that Dyersburg, Chestnut Bluff, and Brownsville were "hot beds of Secession." But Booth assured Hurlbut that "if these places were cleaned out," and loyal citizens received "assistance from the Government, they would immediately form themselves into organized bands to protect life and property, and assist in Enforcing law and order in the different Districts, and to the upholding of the supremacy of the United States Government, both Civil and Military." Though Booth also relayed a rumor that several local guerrilla bands were converging on Jackson to join Forrest, the Wizard was "opposed to this Guerrilla Warfare, and is endeavoring by force and strategy to bring these bands of Guerrillas into the regular Army." For now, wrote Booth, "everything seems to be very quiet within a radius of from thirty to forty miles around, and I do not think any apprehensions need be felt, or fears entertained in reference to this place being attacked, or even threatened. I think," he concluded, "it is perfectly safe."[31]

Though these last lines are often quoted to show that Booth was either oblivious of or at least unaware of any rebel movements in the vicinity of Fort Pillow, the rest of his report demonstrates that his scouts were scouring the area thoroughly. In fact, at the time Booth wrote his dispatch, Forrest was indeed camped at Jackson recruiting partisans, and had not yet decided to attack Fort Pillow.

"A BITTERNESS OF FEELING"

FORREST

March 28–April 12, 1864

THE SCOUTS' REPORT THAT COLONEL FIELDING HURST AND HIS 6TH Tennessee Cavalry (USA) had met with a stunning defeat was entirely accurate. The day Booth arrived at Fort Pillow, as Mississippi general James Ronald Chalmers crossed into Tennessee near La Grange, and Colonel James J. Neely, riding with three of Forrest's regiments near his hometown of Bolivar, Tennessee, encountered Hurst and his men posted in a field outside of town. "As we plunged down through the woods toward them, firing and shouting," recalled John Johnston of Neely's command, "they broke and fled."[1]

"We fought till we were nearly surrounded," wrote a private in Hurst's 6th Tennessee Cavalry, "& Then we had to run like young Devils just from the Lower regions of hell." Neely's outnumbering cavalry killed a score of Hurst's men and took some fifty prisoners, plus hundreds of rounds of ammunition, all of Hurst's wagons, ambulances, and papers, as well as his "mistresses, black and white," and drove him "hatless into Memphis." Assigned to guard duty, Hurst and his men were ridiculed as "Conquered Rebels" by Yankee regulars who insinuated "that they had just as leave have us on the other Side as not."[2]

Guarding Memphis would "not at all Suit" Fielding Hurst. "I don't like to be compelled to keep my Regiment where a Rebel has more influence over the authorities than a loyal man," he fumed to Andrew Johnson, "neither do I like the idea of guarding Rebel Property, whilst the owners of Said Property are living luxuriently under the protection of my Government, and at the Same time plotting treason against that Government." But like it or not, Hurst's boys would never again be allowed to venture far from Memphis, and by the end of the war, Major General Edward Hatch would accuse Fielding Hurst's brother-in-law of extorting fifty thousand dollars from the people of McNairy County, and Hurst himself of taking home one hundred thousand dollars in extortion and bribes.[3]

Abraham Buford's division of Confederate cavalry started south via Mayfield, where it encamped with the 22nd Tennessee and the 8th Kentucky, enabling the men of the 3rd and 7th Kentucky regiments to proceed in detachments to their homes to scare up recruits and "visit their kindred, from whom they had been long separated."[4]

During the recent reorganization, Forrest had placed Tyree Bell in command of one of his brigades. Unlike Chalmers, Bell was Forrest's kind of man. Few dared to cross him. Over the course of the war he had developed a special hatred for the "Haystack Secessionists" and "Homegrown Yankees" who obstructed his recruiting drives at every turn. Commissioned a captain in the 12th Infantry in the summer of 1861, he was soon elected lieutenant colonel by his men, whom he led so deep into the thick of battle at Belmont and Shiloh that at Shiloh alone the Yankees shot two horses out from under him. After bridling under Braxton Bragg's petulant and inept command, he was delighted to attach himself to Bedford Forrest, a man after his own bold heart.[5]

Bell's brigade was allowed to remain at Trenton, from whose environs most of his men had come, in order to recruit and obtain summer uniforms from their families, while McCulloch's brigade hovered around Bolivar, trotting to and fro to give Unionist informers the impression of vast numbers. Forrest meanwhile ordered the remainder of his force to fan out by regiments and scour the country between the Tennessee and Obion rivers, hunting deserters and rounding up horses and arms.[6]

After Union City's surrender, McDonald's battalion had been assigned the task of tracking any Yankee movement out of Memphis. But when no such movement materialized, he was allowed to take his men back to their native Fayette County "to visit their friends and refit, especially clothing." The battalion's Lieutenant Colonel James M. Crews kept twenty men from each of three companies in camp, and on the night of April 2 heard that a large Yankee force was approaching on the Somerville Road. Part of this force consisted of the vestiges of Fielding Hurst's command, sent out from Memphis with a day's rations on orders from Grierson. Crews raised his colors on high ground and did everything he could to conceal from the Yankees that they far outnumbered his sixty men.[7]

As the Yankees lined up in a long battle formation with detachments covering their flanks, Crews sent twelve men through the woods to attack the right and ten to attack the left. As they opened fire, he charged down the middle of the road with the rest of his men, and so panicked the center of the Yankee line that the Federals fell back hundreds of yards. Darting back and forth, barking commands at imaginary units, Crews employed his commander's wizardry to convince the Federals that they were outnumbered and outclassed. Thus as Grierson retreated all the way to Memphis, sixty Confederate cavalrymen, at the cost of only two men wounded, sent four Yankee regiments—perhaps as many as 2,200 men—fleeing back to Raleigh with a loss of six killed, at least fifteen wounded, and three captured. Delighted by yet another of his officers' victorious bluffs, Forrest granted six-day furloughs to the men of the 13th, 14th, and 15th so they could go home and "secure clothing, horses, and supplies." They would not return to service until a day after the attack on Fort Pillow.[8]

By April 3, Buford's loyal Kentuckians had returned from their furloughs and ridden down to Trenton, where Buford established his division headquarters. There they were joined by Tyree Bell's brigade, Faulkner's regiment, and a contingent of aspiring but unmounted Kentucky cavalry, all with orders to keep their men ready to move at a moment's notice "with ten days' subsistence constantly on hand."[9]

Forrest and his men returned to·Jackson, where he received a hero's welcome. Until Grant moved his army south into Mississippi, Jackson had been the center of Union military operations in West Tennessee, and its neighborhood had been "well combed for supplies for the army" ever since. It was Jackson that Fielding Hurst had held for ransom, and now its citizens greeted Forrest and his men as liberators. "'Twere useless to dilate upon the cordial reception with which we were greeted by the citizens," wrote Dewitt Clinton Fort, "especially the beautiful ladies of the place." Even the most aristocratic women "engaged in familiar conversations with the common soldier." Fort and his comrades "were glad to see the beautiful Jackson ladies, and they seemed glad to see 'we' soldiers." Confederate governor Isham Harris, who had apparently remained in Jackson during the assault on Fort Pillow, was pleased to inform Lieutenant General Leonidas Polk that he had come away from Forrest's raid "highly gratified with the state of feeling among the people" of West Tennessee.[10]

Forrest settled into his headquarters and dictated a report on his progress. "In all engagements so far in west Tennessee," he said, "my loss in the aggregate is fifteen killed and forty-two wounded" while the loss of the enemy was "79 killed, 102 wounded, and 612 captured." Forrest felt "confident of my ability to whip any cavalry they can send against me," and asserted he could, "if need be, avoid their infantry. If permitted to remain in west Tennessee," Forrest said, he "would be glad to have my artillery with me, and will send for it, as I could operate effectively with my rifle battery on the rivers." In the meantime, he was "clearly of opinion that with a brigade of infantry at Corinth, as a force upon which I could fall back if too hard pressed, that I can hold west Tennessee against three times my numbers, and could send rapidly out from here all conscripts and deserters for service in infantry." Though he was finding "corn scarcer than I had thought," he had collected "plenty of meal, flour, and bacon for troops. If supplied with the right kind of money or cotton," he could "furnish my command with all small-arm ammunition required, and I think with small arms also," for he had encountered a smuggler who claimed he could provide Forrest with ten thousand pounds of lead from the Union armories at Corinth.[11]

He concluded his report by announcing his next target. "There is a Federal force of 500 or 600 at Fort Pillow," he said, "which I shall attend to in a day or two, as they have horses and supplies which we need."[12]

In this first declaration of his intention to attack Fort Pillow, the Wizard made no mention of the garrison's wickedness, or depredations by the 13th, or rape and pillage on the part of Booth's black troops. Only later, after allegations of a massacre began to circulate, would Forrest and his officers assert that he had never intended to attack Fort Pillow until implored to do so by delegations of Jackson's leading citizens, male and female, who claimed to have been cruelly victimized by the garrison.[13]

"For days before the capture of Fort Pillow," Colonel Clarke Russell Barteau of the 22nd would write twenty years later, "citizens fleeing to us from its vicinity brought doleful tales of outrages committed by the Federal forces in that stronghold. The helpless families of some of our soldiers had been victims of their raiding parties. A strong feeling prevailed in favor of capturing the fort, but it was not expected to be done without fighting and loss of life."[14]

"The families of many of Forrest's men had been grievously wronged, despoiled and insulted by detachments of Bradford's men," wrote R. R. Hancock of Barteau's regiment. "Forrest determined to break up their lair, and capture or destroy them before leaving that section of the country for other operations." Another local story had it that Bradford's men had hanged a man named Erasmus Thurmond who refused "to divulge where he had hidden his gold," though it is likelier that this was the work of a Union guer-

rilla leader named Tom Mays. One of the chief complaints was that Bradford
had been "negro stealing"—he would have called it emancipating and
recruiting—among the local farms.[15]

According to John Johnston, when a delegation of men and women
came to Forrest and begged him "to capture and break up the garrison" at
Fort Pillow, "he replied that he did not have men enough to take the place
(as they were strongly entrenched and had six pieces of artillery) and could
not do so without a great sacrifice of his men. But the women tearfully
begged him to deliver them from the ravages and insults of these wretches,
at which Gen. Forrest was so affected that he said to the ladies, 'You may go
home and rest assured that I will take the fort if it costs me my life.'" "General Forrest was a man of great sympathy," wrote Ted Brewer of the 20th
Tennessee, "and when he heard the pathetic stories told by the ladies, he
changed his plans and decided to attack Fort Pillow." Despite the fact that
"attacking the fort would take him fifty miles out of his way, Forrest felt that
if he ignored the citizens' complaints he would lose many new recruits to desertion before he could reach northern Mississippi." But John Wyeth gave
less credence to the claim that Forrest's principal intent was avenging Yankee depredations and believed, as Forrest's own declaration stated, that the
attack arose out of his "determination to appropriate the much needed
horses and supplies of the garrison."[16]

Perhaps it is fitting that the Battle of Fort Pillow should have been preceded
by a lynching. On April 4, as the Wizard rested at Jackson, Dewitt Clinton
Fort obtained permission to ride twelve miles north to Spring Creek to shoe
his horse. "Arriving there early on Monday morning," Fort was told that the
local blacksmith was two miles off assisting in the investigation of the murder of a local white girl named Margaret Hennings. Proceeding to her family's farm, Fort found

> the neighbors for miles around assembled to ferret out the villainy of
> one of the most atrocious, cruel and bloody murders ever committed
> by brutal man. Miss Margaret Henning, a beautiful, accomplished
> and lovely young lady about the age of twenty, had on the evening be-
> fore been murdered near the house by having her head almost sev-
> ered from the body with a sharp instrument in the hands of some
> unknown person or persons. A full day's investigation established the
> fact that certain negroes in the neighborhood deserved punishment
> for the offense.

Whether or not the three blacks were actually guilty of killing Margaret Henning, they apparently had long been suspected of cooperating with the Yankees, and "the condition of the country," wrote Fort, "rendered it dangerous for the people and impractical for the courts to do justice in this matter," for Fort Pillow had afforded an "asylum to which the offenders could flee and forever escape the punishment merited by the grossest violation of human, natural, and divine laws."

So that evening the three men were dragged out and hanged in a proceeding that was "irregular and summary." Fort explained that because the ordinary "institutions of society were so broken down by the law and its ministers having been swept from the land," lynchings were all that prevented "the weak and defenseless" from living at "the mercy of the strong, cruel and unrelenting."[17]

"So far," Forrest bragged to Joe Johnston on April 6, "I have been successful in every engagement with the enemy and have accomplished all that could be reasonably expected of me." He claimed "entire possession of West Tennessee and Kentucky south and west of Tennessee River, except the posts on the river of Memphis, Fort Pillow, Columbus, and Paducah."[18]

To capture Fort Pillow, Forrest decided first to arrange an elaborate diversionary feint on Memphis. On the Wizard's behalf, Chalmers ordered Duckworth of the 7th to "assume command of all the troops near Brownsville" and assemble all but three companies of the 7th "as rapidly as possible. Scouts will be kept out in the direction of Fort Pillow," Chalmers continued, "and a picket at the railroad bridge who will prevent all crossing without proper authority & will keep the water well pumped out of the boat in the pontoon bridge." Forrest instructed Neely to take his entire brigade, minus the furloughed companies of the 7th Cavalry, back to the scene of his recent triumph at Raleigh, "and make every preparation as if to build a bridge across Wolf River," while part of his command ranged conspicuously along "the Big Creek and Moscow road as if intending to cross the river at those places, the object being to impress the enemy with the belief that General Forrest was about to descend on Memphis." Colonel John McGuirk and his Mississippians were ordered to ride out of their native state and spread the word that General Stephen D. Lee was about to join Forrest in a pincer movement on Memphis. It would later please Chalmers to report that both Neely and McGuirk "executed these orders with promptness and success."[19]

Abraham Buford proposed that he be sent on a separate errand. During a sojourn at Trenton, the hulking Kentuckian had picked up a Yankee paper and read a report that ridiculed Forrest's men for capturing only citizens' horses at Paducah, and neglecting to seize the garrison's 140 mounts, which Colonel Hicks had kept hidden at a rolling mill on the outskirts of town. Affronted by the ridicule but grateful for the tip, Buford received permission to march on Paducah with eight hundred Kentuckians and correct Forrest's oversight with a raid on the garrison's secret stable of "very much needed" horses.[20]

In the meantime, Forrest had moved Tyree Bell's brigade to Eaton in nearby Gibson County, almost forty miles northeast of Ripley, where they were joined by Colonels Russell and Greer. McCulloch's brigade encamped on the Forked Deer River, some nine miles from Brownsville, where they were to remain on the alert. On April 8, Forrest issued both brigades "five days' Cooked ration" and ordered them to "be ready to move" at a moment's notice.[21]

The moment came on April 10. Forrest commanded Tyree Bell's brigade from Buford's division, McCulloch's brigade from Chalmers's division, and Captain Edwin S. Walton and his battery of three mountain howitzers to ride hard for Fort Pillow. Chalmers's orders were to reach Fort Pillow before daybreak on April 12, by forced march if necessary.

It certainly was necessary. Chalmers set off at once from Jackson and collected McCulloch's 1,500 troopers outside Brownsville. Together they would get a formidable head start on Tyree Bell, who had to be notified by sending a courier thirty miles to his encampment at Eaton, Tennessee, some fifty miles from Fort Pillow. Bell and his 1,700 men spent the afternoon cooking their five-day rations and did not mount up until 9:00 p.m. Even then they had to wait until midnight for Walton's battery to catch up after an arduous slog through the bottoms, during which Walton himself, badly shot up at Vicksburg, may have slowed his battery's progress. Bell's brigade made only ten miles through the rain that night, and then just before daybreak rested for one soggy hour. Otherwise, from the time they left Eaton to the time they trotted up to within a mile and a half of Fort Pillow, they were in the saddle for almost sixty hours straight.[22]

After returning from Paducah, Forrest's consumptive adjutant general, Major John P. Strange, had begun to cough up blood. As Forrest prepared to move on Fort Pillow, he decided to leave him in the care of Willie Forrest, the Wizard's son and aide-de-camp. This made Captain Charles W. Anderson the only officer from Forrest's staff to accompany the Wizard on his expedition against Fort Pillow.[23]

Anderson had originally joined the Confederacy's transportation department, but was so outraged by Yankee depredations in his hometown that he applied to join up with Forrest. "Soon after applying to Forrest," recalled a comrade, "he wrote an official paper so concisely that the General determined to make him his secretary." Anderson looked the part: an unprepossessing but vigorous little man with a large head, a prominent nose, and a shrewd squint. To him had fallen the task of translating his commander's terse, profane backwoods patois into the kind of erudite rhetoric that Richmond required of its officers' dispatches.[24]

"I move to-morrow on Fort Pillow with two brigades," Forrest wrote Stephen Lee on the night of April 10, "the force at that point being 300 whites and 600 negroes": an enlargement on his original and more accurate estimate of a total Union garrison of from 500 to 600 men. Be it 500, 600, or 900 men, Forrest was taking no chances. The Yankees would estimate his force at anywhere from 2,500 to 10,000 men; Forrest himself would put it at 1,500. But almost certainly his combined force, including his escort of 80 elite troops, could not have been less than 2,300 strong, or about four times the size of the Union garrison at Fort Pillow.[25]

On the morning of the eleventh, Forrest followed Chalmers's trail with his escort and a detachment from the 19th Tennessee Cavalry. Their saddlebags were stuffed with four days' rations and sixty rounds of ammunition, and their blood was boiling over news of the summary execution of five of their comrades by Hurst's Homemade Yankees. Duckworth's 7th Tennessee Cavalry ranged around Randolph, on the watch for a Yankee advance up the Mississippi. Buford sent a portion of his division to demand the surrender of the Union garrison at Columbus as Union gunboats desperately steamed west along the Cumberland to lend the garrison support, while Buford himself moved on Paducah to rustle the last of the garrison's horses.[26]

At about two in the afternoon, Forrest caught up to Chalmers at Brownsville and ordered him and McCulloch to march at whatever pace would be necessary to reach Fort Pillow before dawn the next morning: a distance of thirty-eight miles. They set off at 3:30 in the afternoon and rode through the rain and into a night so dark that McCulloch's men could barely make out the rumps of the horses in front of them, let alone the muddy parameters of the road. But except for an occasional pause to examine the condition of a doubtful, slip-slapped country bridge, they rode all night without stopping.[27]

"Travailed west," one of Forrest's Escort wrote in his diary: an inadvertently apt description of the march that night, for it fell to Forrest and his Escort to follow some miles behind the rest of the expedition, their horses slipping and sinking in the mud churned up by McCulloch's brigade.[28]

Also known as Jackson's Company of Tennessee Cavalry, Forrest's Escort had been raised at least in part by a grandnephew of Daniel Boone named Montgomery Little, and included a Lieutenant Nathaniel Boone. "A splendid company, of seventy five young men," wrote Chalmers, "who each seemed inspired with the reckless courage of their leader," the Escort was composed of picked men from middle Tennessee, whom Forrest had provided with "the best horses." After the Battle of Somerville in late December 1863, they had acquired "a complete outfit of Sharps Rifles, Colts, Repeaters & accoutrements." It was their "use of these arms in future engagements that aided so materially to make the Escort a terror to the Enemy." Though they were the finest marksmen in Forrest's command, the men of his Escort, perhaps alone among Forrest's enlisted men, apparently carried sabers, and would employ them most notably in hand-to-hand fighting with Federal cavalry at Memphis.[29]

Some of Forrest's regiments despised the Escort because one of its primary duties was to ride in the rear of a column, rounding up stragglers and shooting deserters. But it was a favorite of Colonel Bob McCulloch, who at the Battle of Okolona two months before had "asked as a special favor that his regiment and the Escort be permitted to fight together." Mustered into service in October 1862, the Escort suffered heavy casualties and would lose at least two-thirds of its men by the end of the war.[30]

Forrest's entourage included the shot-up Colonel Drew Moore Wisdom of the 19th, a lifelong West Tennesseean who had been badly wounded serving as an infantry captain in Missouri. After Shiloh, he joined the cavalry, and fighting under Forrest was wounded again at Harrisburg, Mississippi. He would take a leading part at Brice's Crossroads, and was about to have the honor of leading Forrest's Tennesseeans in their assault on Fort Pillow.[31]

Riding with Forrest that day was Samuel Hughes, one of a large contingent of black servants and teamsters who accompanied his command throughout the war, cooking, washing, holding their masters' horses as they advanced on foot. Born the property of Reinold Long of Alabama in about 1839, he was taken as a boy to Carroll County, Mississippi, by Reinold's son-in-law, Andrew Hughes. Sam's relatives, including a nephew named Charles Koon, joined the 6th USCHA. But Sam went to war as a cook for two local Confederate boys, Private F. C. Gardiner and Second Lieutenant Richard T. Gardiner of the 15th Tennessee Cavalry, and would encounter his nephew in the bloody aftermath of the battle that was about to commence.[32]

Another of the slaves riding with Forrest that day was thirty-two-year-old Nick Hamer. Hamer was born in North Carolina and hired out at the age of twenty-five to a Choctaw County, Mississippi, farmer. But when the war broke out four years later, his owner, William F. Hamer of the 5th Mississippi Cavalry, fetched his slave along "to wait on him and finally to cook for his mess." Hamer served his master faithfully, and remained with his master throughout the war.

"I was a witness of the fight at Fort Pillow," Hamer later testified.

> We left the camp and trodded all day, and just at night we came to our camping place, and then we found a farmer's house. When we went out to him and asked him for corn and fodder to feed our horses, he said that he did not have any. We knew this was not true, and so we hunted around and finally found his corn hid in a double log house. There was a great lot of it and, as we got the corn out and had just commenced to feed our horses, an order came for us to mount and march.[33]

Also riding with Forrest was Paul Anderson, his chief of scouts, an old Texas Ranger who "affected all the vagaries of the cowboy costume, mingled with that of the Mexican greaser, as shown in the white sombrero, leather-fringed breeches, and jangling spurs. His voice had a peculiar nasal twang," recalled Mercer Otey, "and his slowness of speech caused him great difficulty in spinning his yarns." As they rode into Lauderdale County, however, Anderson appears to have been temporarily superseded by a local man named W. J. Shaw who had just escaped from Bradford's custody and was thus "entirely familiar with the topography of the enclosure, as well as the number of troops defending the works."[34]

They may well have been further enlightened by a Tipton County man named Inman (his first name was not recorded) who had ostensibly enlisted in Company E of the 13th Tennessee Cavalry (USA) on the eve of the massacre. He then disappears from the record, but he may well have been one of the Inmans who rode with Barteau's 22nd Tennessee Cavalry and had recently joined the 13th only in order to spy on the garrison.[35]

In fact, any number of recent deserters from Bradford's garrison could have provided Forrest with intelligence; Surgeon Charles Fitch "learned that there were some twenty of the Tenn. Cav. Deserted during the night of the 11th." Perhaps tipped off by a rebel spy, Private Fred Kelso of Company C of the 13th (13/C) deserted Fort Pillow the day before the massacre and went home to Dyer County. At the time of his enlistment, Johnny Walters was a struggling young Obion County farmer reduced to renting his "poor and worn out land" to his neighbors just so he could afford to buy corn for his wife and three children. A private in 13/D, Walters deserted his regiment on the eve of the massacre, probably to see to his impoverished family; his ailing wife would die within the year. He did not return to service until September, but perhaps because of his family's desperate straits, he was neither shot nor imprisoned but forfeited "all pay and privileges."[36]

The ostensible field commander in the assault on Fort Pillow was the diminutive, ferocious James Ronald Chalmers. While serving as a lackluster infantry officer, he had briefly and ineffectively commanded Forrest at Shiloh. After switching over to the cavalry, however, he spent the fall of 1863 in Mississippi harassing Yankee patrols and earning the affectionate sobriquet "Little 'Un" from his troopers. The son of the De Soto County senator who had approved Forrest's appointment as Hernando's coroner, peacemaker, and slave catcher, Chalmers graduated from South Carolina College and joined his father's law practice in Marshall County. Following the senator's death in 1853, Chalmers labored hard to establish himself as his father's political heir, eventually winning election as one of the youngest district attorneys in the country.[37]

In 1861, as a delegate to Mississippi's secession convention, Chalmers had chaired the committee on military affairs. The roots of his commitment to the secessionist cause were entangled in his family's heavy investment in the peculiar institution. By 1860, slightly over 50 percent of Mississippi's population were slaves, but the ratio in De Soto County had risen to almost 60 percent. The Chalmers family housed its forty-four slaves in six slave cabins. Twenty-six of their slaves were male, thirty-one were over the age of twelve (including a nonagenarian and a centenarian), and ten were of mixed race: an unusually high proportion for the area.

A decade younger and about a foot shorter than the Wizard of the Saddle, Chalmers nonetheless had an aristocratic self-regard that was positively Virginian. In breeding, education, politesse, and sheer refinement of character, he deemed himself the semiliterate Forrest's superior. (One young gentleman-soldier groaned at the prospect of being commanded by a "vulgarian" like Forrest, "a man having no pretension to gentility—a negro trader, gambler,—an ambitious man, careless of the lives of his men so long as preferment be *en prospectu*."[38])

Forrest did not like Chalmers much either, and seemed to go out of his way to discomfit him. They began to exchange chilly little notes about trifling slights and inconveniences: Forrest requisitioned Chalmers's tent for his brother's use, took a wagon from him to haul his cook's stove. On March 9, Forrest replaced Chalmers as commander of his First Division with McCulloch, whom he now recommended for a brigadier generalship. Reporting to Polk that Chalmers had "never been satisfied since I came here, and being satisfied that I have not had and will not receive his support and cooperation," Forrest "deemed it necessary that we should separate. I must have the cordial support of my subordinate officers in order to succeed and make my command effective."[39]

As McCulloch led his division to Panola, Mississippi, destroying stills and collecting deserters and stragglers along his way, Chalmers demanded a court of inquiry. Polk ruled that Forrest had exceeded his authority, and restored the badly ruffled little Mississippian to command, whereupon Forrest ordered Chalmers to meet him in West Tennessee, "and bring with him all the scattered remnants of his command."[40]

Now, in the wee hours of April 12, Chalmers paused one ridge east of Fort Pillow to deploy his command for a three-pronged attack. "McCulloch's brigade moved down the Fulton road to Gaines's farm," he wrote, "thence north to the fort on a road running parallel with the Mississippi River." A large detachment of the 16th Tennessee moved along the Ripley Road under the command of Colonel A. N. Wilson, whose brother J. Cardwell Wilson—one of four Wilson brothers who served under Forrest—would be mortally wounded in the attack that followed. And an officer was posted to direct Tyree Bell's brigade, with Barteau's 22nd (previously the 2nd) Tennessee Cavalry and the 21st under Colonel Robert Milton Russell, a West Point graduate from Trenton, Tennessee, to move down Coal Creek and attack the fort from the north.[41]

"Forrest will carry his men further than any other man I know of," Hurlbut would testify. "He is desperate." His men would have agreed. Of all of Forrest's troops, Bell's brigade was the most exhausted. "McCulloch's men had decidedly the advantage of Bell's," wrote Sergeant Hancock, "from the fact that by getting well on their way Sunday they got to rest Sunday night, while, as we have seen, Bell's men were in the saddle nearly all night, and then also Monday and Monday night, resulting in many of Bell's men being made sick."[42]

By this time Forrest's veterans were already "contemplating not only the possibility but the probability" of the Confederacy's ultimate defeat, wrote John Milton Hubbard, "and were therefore mentally prepared for almost anything which fate could decree."[43] Frustrated by their failure to capture and hang the elusive Hurst, humiliated by their failure to take Paducah after Duckworth's ingenious triumph at Union City, provoked by the unex-

pectedly lethal skill of Fort Anderson's black gunners, they had been encouraged by their officers to lump Booth's black artillerists with Bradford's
men and Bradford's men not only with Hurst's atrocious cavalry but the vagrant bands of Unionist guerrillas that still ranged along the river. "Tho' hungry, tired and sleepy," wrote Dewitt Clinton Fort, "we went cheerfully into
the fight."[44]

"Those within the fort knew that they deserved condign punishment,"
wrote Hubbard, "because of the outrages committed on innocent people."
"The rebel Tennesseans," wrote a Confederate paper, "have about the same
bitterness against Tennesseans in the Federal army, as against the negroes."
Bell had a special hatred of the deserters from the 47th Tennessee Infantry
who had served in his brigade earlier in the war and had now given their
allegiance to Bradford. As Forrest himself declared, "The fort was filled
with niggers and deserters from our army—men who lived side by side with
my men."[45]

"It is difficult for those who did not live through this unhappy period,
and in this immediate section," explained John Wyeth, who served with the
4th Alabama Cavalry during the war, "to appreciate the bitterness of feeling
which then prevailed." Three years of civil war had had

> a deplorable effect upon the morals of the rank and file of either army.
> War does not bring out the noblest traits in the majority of those who
> from choice or necessity follow its bloodstained paths. Too often the
> better qualities hide away, and those that are harsh and cruel prevail.
> Some of Forrest's men treasured a deep resentment against some of
> the officers and soldiers of this garrison. They had been neighbors in
> times of peace, and had taken opposite sides when the war came on.
> These men had suffered violence to person and property, and their
> wives and children, in the enforced absence of their natural protec-
> tors, had suffered various indignities at the hands of the "Tennessee
> Tories," as the loyal Tennesseeans were called by their neighbors who
> sided with the South. When they met in single combat, or in scout-
> ing parties, or in battle, as far as these individuals were concerned, it
> was too often a duel to the death. Between the parties to these neigh-
> borhood feuds the laws of war did not prevail.[46]

Though Forrest deplored the anarchy of guerrilla warfare, he did not
hesitate when it suited him, as now, to exploit the "bitterness of feeling" that
existed between his regulars and their homegrown foe.

Black troops had already distinguished themselves at Milliken's Bend, among other battles, and then at Paducah, and the Southern white nightmare of a servile war, and the prospect of a Northern victory setting blacks above their former masters, meant that it was not just militarily but psychologically essential to the Confederates to nip black recruitment in the bud. The recent murder of Margaret Henning outraged the troopers who had camped at nearby Jackson and listened with relish to Dewitt Clinton Fort's account of her alleged black murderers' lynching.

Some Southern accounts would blame Yankee depredations on Booth's black artillerists. "Many of the citizens of West Tennessee, principally ladies," wrote Ted Brewer of the 20th, had begged Forrest "not to fail to take Fort Pillow before he left the State," because "the troops at Fort Pillow were principally negroes who formerly belonged to people that lived in West Tennessee. They had terrorized their old masters' families until they did not know what to expect next." A. J. Grantham of Lieutenant Colonel Reid's 5th Mississippi Cavalry recalled as a nonagenarian that he and his men had been told that the black troops stationed at Fort Pillow had robbed and plundered Lauderdale County. By another account, Forrest told his men that "many of the Colored troops at the fort were runaway slaves from the area, and were now engaged in a campaign of terror against their former owners."[47]

Lieutenant James Dinkins of Chalmers's command recalled that Forrest was

> told by citizens living in the direction of Fort Pillow, that bands of Federal and negro soldiers made frequent raids through the country, robbing people of any thing they could find, and insulting in the grossest manner any lady who protested against their action. The negro soldiers were especially insulting to the wives and families of Confederate soldiers. In some cases, they committed an unpardonable, brutish and fiendish crime on ladies. Numbers of our men lived in that country, and they joined in the appeal to Forrest to give them protection. He decided to do so.[48]

The charges against the black troops were almost certainly false. After the war not a single one of the many claims against the garrison made by local citizens for compensation involved any of the black regiments. One reason the Union Army formed black artillery companies, especially heavy artillery, was in order to keep them fixed at Union posts. Booth was under orders to keep his men holed up in the innermost bastion and away from the locals, and every evidence suggests he did. Not one of the men of the 6th USCHA had a horse, and the forty members of the 2nd USCLA had only seventeen mounts, all of which were required to haul artillery. The 13th itself had many fewer horses than men, and would not have spared any of them for a black foraging expedition.

The very presence of black troops at Fort Pillow, however, and the attitude of the freedmen toward their former owners, were enough to outrage local whites. It is possible, though unlikely, that contrabands from Fort Pillow committed depredations, but any rapes would almost certainly have been reported to the Union authorities by local Unionist slaveholders eager to prove that blacks were unworthy of freedom. It is far likelier that this charge was invented either beforehand by local secessionists to whip up Forrest and his men, or afterward by soldiers seeking to explain and excuse the slaughter of black troops that was to follow, for it was a reflex in that time and place to counter allegations of white barbarity with perfervid accusations of black men assaulting white women.

Many of Forrest's men had already declared an eagerness to "kill niggers." Before his escape, Captain Thomas Gray of the 7th recalled hearing Duckworth's lieutenants

> say repeatedly that they intended to kill negro troops wherever they could find them; that they had heard that there were negro troops at Union City, and that they had intended to kill them if they had found any there. They also said they had understood there were negro troops at Paducah and Mayfield, and that they intended to kill them if they got them. And they said that they did not consider officers who commanded negro troops to be any better than the negroes themselves.[49]

Only a few of Duckworth's men would fight at Fort Pillow, but their sentiments were shared by the men of other regiments, many of whom would soon have an opportunity to act on them.

———————————

Stopping about a mile and a half from Fort Pillow, Chalmers's cavalry dismounted in the dark and, "leaving every fourth man to hold horses," crept up to within sight of the fortifications. As Wilson and his men approached the mouth of Coal Creek, McCulloch's "Missouri Mongols" made their wary way past the unmanned watchtower on the Fulton Road and then along "the ravines and short hills which encompassed the place," with Captain Frank J. Smith and his advance guard leading the way.[50]

McCulloch's men crept up on the Union garrison's drowsy pickets from Bradford's 13th, capturing or killing them as they dozed, stoked fires, played cards. But at least one of their number escaped, and as Captain Smith led his skirmishers through the gloom, the rattle of musket fire rose out of the snarl of the abatis, skittering up the slopes to where Booth and Bradford were stirring.[51]

McCulloch's boys were a fiery lot. Black Bob and his cousin and second-in-command, Lieutenant Colonel Robert A. McCulloch, had grown up together in Cooper County, Missouri, in the densely slaveholding portion of the state known as "Little Dixie" that ranged along the western bank of the Mississippi and both banks of the Missouri as it traversed the state from St. Louis west to Kansas City. But by Cooper County standards, the McCullochs were small-time slaveholders: five of them owned fourteen slaves, of which Robert McCulloch apparently owned but two. Colonel McCulloch, nicknamed Bob, was born in Virginia in 1820, five years before his cousin, Robert A. But they were so inseparable that some historians have mistaken them for brothers, or even father and son.[52]

Though their early martial training was negligible, almost every man in Cooper County, excluding slaves, carried a gun, for it fell to each man to protect his family and property from brigands, Indians, and the "whisky traders, grog-shop keepers and their bloated customers, blacklegs, and infidels" who served as sheriffs and deputies. It is hard to imagine anyone likelier to start a fight or less likely to take orders than a Cooper County white man.[53]

Robert A. McCulloch intended to become a brick mason, while his older cousin Bob prepared to take over the management of his family's farm. But in 1849, they caught the gold fever that was then raging through Missouri, emptying farms of menfolk. In April, they ventured forth with half a hundred of their kith and kin, bound for California on the Santa Fe Trail, which in those days originated in Boonville and led young men, so it was said, "from Civilization to Sundown." It took them four months to reach California, and along the way Robert A. tried to lift his fellow forty-niners' spirits with his fiddle. They staked a claim on the Sacramento River, but two years' panning did not yield even enough gold to pay their way home. Robert A. limped back to Cooper County as a mule train captain; Bob returned a year later with nothing to show for his pains but an experience transporting a body of men over great distances that, unbeknownst to him, would one day serve him as well in preparing him for cavalry command as slave trading had prepared Forrest.[54]

Upon their shamefaced return, the McCulloch cousins found their proslavery kith and kin girding their loins to prevent Kansas from voting itself a free state, thereby joining Illinois to the east and Iowa to the north to isolate Missouri as a vulnerable peninsular outpost of American slavery. Disappointed in their dreams of riches, the two McCullochs apparently jumped into the fray with both feet, joining proslavery vigilantes in taking potshots at the steamboats that carried Kansas-bound abolitionist settlers up the Missouri River. Bob was appointed a delegate to the proslavery convention of 1855, traveling to Lexington to rub elbows with secessionist movers and shakers. In 1856, one of the cousins (they are sometimes difficult to distinguish on contemporary rolls) attended a meeting in Boonville "for the purpose of raising men and money to aid the law and order men in Kansas. Let every pro-slavery man attend," trumpeted a broadside. "Bring your guns and horses. Let us sustain the Government, and drive back the abolitionists who are murdering our citizens."[55]

Perhaps nowhere and at no previous period in American history did white American kill white American with such impunity as in Kansas and Missouri in the 1850s. The atrocities committed by both sides stank in the nostrils of North and South. Bob would raise a rebel company in Missouri, go on to command a number of brigades, fight with almost superhuman bravery, and at different times rescue James Chalmers and Nathan Bedford Forrest himself from annihilation. In October 1863 Chalmers reminded his superiors that McCulloch had been "recommended for promotion several times before, and was informed recently that as soon as a brigade could be organized for him, he would be promoted." But there was something sufficiently malodorous about him to prevent his promotion to brigadier general until the Confederacy's eleventh hour. In fact, his commission would not reach him until after the cause was lost.[56]

The inseparable McCullochs commanded together, of course: Bob as colonel and Robert A. as lieutenant colonel of the 2nd Missouri Cavalry. To distinguish between the two, their men took to referring to Bob as "Black-haired Bob" and to Robert A., whose hair was turning gray, as "White-haired Bob." "A man of strong personality and a strict disciplinarian," Colonel Bob could be as "gentle and tender as a woman," recalled one of his men. "He knew personally every man in his regiment, and when in camp made their comfort his first consideration." He was a square-built, ham-handed man with a full beard that emphasized a high forehead and a rather empty gaze.

Robert A. was a ganglier, more approachable man with a reputation for fair-mindedness and a penchant for entertaining his men with his fiddle.[57]

Whatever their differences, they sure could fight. General Sterling Price, William Jackson, Stephen Lee, Earl Van Dorn, and William N. R. Beall all selected the McCulloch boys and their Missouri Mongols to serve "on the point of danger." Like Forrest, the McCullochs subscribed to the notion that war meant fighting and fighting meant killing. By the end of the war their flesh would bear proof of their fearlessness. Colonel Bob was shot in the shoulder at Tupelo, the ball piercing his lung, and another ball shattered his hand at Harrisburg, Mississippi; in fact he spent much of the latter part of the war traveling in an ambulance. At Wilson's Creek in August 1864, Robert A. would be shot in the stomach by a Yankee firing from such close range that he powder-burned the lieutenant colonel's butternut coat.[58]

It is possible that what stuck in Richmond's craw was simply Colonel Bob's gambling, which was so prodigious that when his command bivouacked in a church during the Battle of Holly Springs, his men changed its name from Antioch to "Ante-Up." Or perhaps it was his regiment's habit of "stealing cotton, horses, mules, waggons and slaves, and keeping the spoils for themselves." Judging from the regiment's records, Bob McCulloch's officers were a restive lot: always noisily protesting promotions and demotions; demanding elections; resigning or deserting, and in one case taking most of a company with them.[59]

Such shenanigans, however, were hardly unique to the 2nd Missouri Cavalry. More likely what offended Richmond's olfaction was the regiment's whiff of the bushwhacker. The 2nd Missouri Cavalry consisted in significant part of men who had disgraced the proslavery cause with their depredations in Kansas. Its core companies were initially mustered into service at the same place and on the same day as William Quantrill's cutthroat band. Slavery had been so baldly and undeniably the cause of the border wars that they were an embarrassment to those Confederate statesmen who, to ennoble their cause and reassure their British sympathizers, contended and, in many cases, convinced themselves that they were fighting not for slavery but for human freedom. But Colonel McCulloch's nickname was soon shortened to "Black Bob," and carried with it the snap of the black flag.[60]

FIRST FIRE
FORT PILLOW

5:30 a.m.–3:00 p.m., April 12, 1864

ONE OF THE FIRST PEOPLE IN THE FORT PILLOW GARRISON TO HEAR THE pickets' cry of "The rebels are coming" was an Iowa doctor named Charles Fitch, who sprang out of bed, hurried into his clothes, and ran down to the river to rouse the provost marshal, thirty-five-year-old Captain John T. Young of the 24th Missouri Infantry.

At the beginning of the war, Young seemed to be a man on the rise. A schoolteacher from Randolph County, Missouri, he was one of the Western army's most literate young officers. Tall and fair, he cut a commanding figure and had trusted that as soon as Bradford became colonel of the 13th Tennessee Cavalry, he would be promoted to major. But Bradford repeatedly proved himself unworthy of a colonelcy, and Young now found himself stalled in the contumacious garrison at Fort Pillow, nursing a chronic case of bronchitis and passing judgment on the shirkers, inebriates, deserters, whores, spies, slavenappers, black marketeers, outright thieves and murderers, and assorted scoundrels who freely passed in and out of its works. Wakened by Fitch, Young now fumbled out of his bed and, grabbing his revolver, raced up to Booth's zigzag bastion.[1]

Sounding the alarm "to the hotel and stores as I passed," Fitch returned immediately to the hospital to evacuate his patients. Panicked black women and children were already rushing past him, racing for the river. Gazing up beyond the log and wattle dispensary, Fitch saw smoke and flames begin to rise as the rebels set the contraband camp ablaze.

"In an instant I started for Major Booth's Quarters," wrote Fitch, "and found him at or near the Earth work, making preparations to give the Rebs a warm reception." Buttoning his coat, Booth hustled Companies D and E of the 13th into the outermost rifle pits to hold the rebels back and "ascertain the position and number of the enemy" as his artillerists trained their guns on the roads to Ripley and Fulton.[2]

Bradford's crony, attorney James McCoy of Obion County, had attached himself to the major's entourage and was lying in bed in Bradford's quarters recovering from a recent injury to his hands when he first heard the alarm. "Major Bradford was up immediately the alarm was given," McCoy recalled, and after Booth sent orders to Captain James Marshall of the *New Era* to evacuate the noncombatants fleeing down the ravine to the river, Bradford urged McCoy to join them because with his "mashed" hands he would only get in the way.[3]

At the first alarm, Captain Marshall had "immediately got the ship cleared for action" and pulled her out into the stream. But he still "had no idea that there would be a fight" and, thinking "it would merely be a little skirmish," served his men their breakfasts. Booth and Marshall "had previously established signals," Marshall testified, "by which Booth could indicate certain points where he would want me to use my guns." As the crackle of musket fire skittered across the water, and a glow rose above the bluff from the flames consuming the tents and shacks in the contraband camp, Booth signaled Marshall "to commence firing up what we call No. 1 ravine," the defile that ran from the junction of the Ripley and Fulton roads down to the river. "Then he signaled me to fire up Coal Creek ravine No. 3, and I then moved up there. Before I left down here at ravine No. 1, the rebel sharpshooters were firing at me rapidly."[4]

At yet another signal from the bluff, Marshall brought the *New Era* up to the bank, where "women and children, some sick negroes, and boys" had gathered around the largest of the three coal barges moored along the bank. A loyalist "refugee in the Federal lines," Rosa Johnson, testified that she was at Fort Pillow looking after her son William of Bradford's Battalion when the rebels attacked. Accompanying Rosa was Anna Ruffin, who had been tending her husband, Thomas, who had recently ruptured himself on the horn of his saddle chasing after a detachment of Texas Rangers. She and Rosa would return the next morning to search for their menfolk.[5]

Rosa Spearman Hooper, the wife of Tom Hooper of 6/C, was one of the hundreds, perhaps thousands, of slaves Forrest had bought and sold. In about 1859, Rosa was sold to Forrest by her Lexington, Kentucky, master and transported in one of Forrest's droves to Yalobusha County, Mississippi. She and Tom escaped together, and together they had remained, until now: though Major Booth had officially forbidden the regiment's wives and womenfolk to accompany them, Rosa had defied Booth's ban and "went anyhow."[6]

Crouching with her in the barge was Rachel Parks, wife of another family man: Ransom Parks of 2/A. In 1859, a white minister named Enloe, whose cousin Abraham Enloe was once rumored to have been Abraham Lincoln's natural father, had officiated at her wedding to Ransom Parks. After the war broke out, they picked up their two children and fled from the William Buford plantation in Lafayette County, Mississippi, to Jackson, Tennessee, where Ransom worked as a cook for Fielding Hurst's 6th Tennessee Cavalry. After the fall of Corinth, however, he enlisted in Company A of the 2nd USCLA. A low, heavyset man with a pockmarked gingerbread complexion, Parks was always sickly, recalled Rachel, "and was never able to do much duty as a soldier and was in consequence of his health detailed as a nurse."[7]

Marshall shouted to them over the din "to get into the barge if they wished to save themselves, and I would take them out of danger." After the panicked exodus of sutlers, clerks, contrabands, and cavalry wives had scrambled aboard, Marshall yanked the barge away from the riverbank and towed it above Coal Creek as rebel sharpshooters continued to fire at them, reportedly killing one woman. None of the wives would learn their husbands' fate until the next morning. Reaching the bar, Marshall urged the refugees to seek shelter among "the trees and bushes around them there"; then he steamed back downstream to resume firing on the rebels.[8]

A second doctor, Chapman Underwood, had just returned from detached duty at Memphis and was rooming with another of Bradford's old Obion County cronies, First Lieutenant Nicholas Logan of 13/C. "About the time I got up and washed," wrote Underwood, "the pickets ran in and said Forrest was coming." As Underwood started for the fort, Logan advised him to escape on the New Era, for he "knew the feeling the rebels had towards me," recalled Underwood, who described himself as "a notorious character with them" who always had to flee "whenever they came around," for they had been hunting him for months, and shot at him "frequently." Underwood rushed aboard the coal barge, but, unlike McCoy, he remained aboard the New Era to serve as a volunteer sharpshooter.[9]

Chugging back up toward Coal Creek ravine, Marshall saw that the refugees on the bar were still being "fired at much." He bullhorned to them to find shelter in a nearby house. At a little after 8:00 a.m., Marshall would resume his fire along the river, "keeping underway, running a head, and dropping as required," while "firing as signaled from the fort." Because of the strong wind and the swift, rain-swollen current, however, "our firing was from our starboard battery," whose guns soon became "quite hot and very foul."[10]

Other civilians, including at least two contraband women and a number of black boys, either refused to flee aboard the barge or were too late to join the exodus. Some of the boys, still in their teens, ran into the fort as stranded women and children sought refuge in the snarl of driftwood along the river-bank. Jacob Thompson was a former slave from Brown's Mills in the new state of West Virginia, whose Unionists had seceded, in effect, from seces-sionist Virginia in 1863. His master, however, was Lieutenant Colonel Tazewell Lee Hargrove of the 44th North Carolina Infantry (CSA), but while the 44th was on the march, Thompson had run off and ingratiated himself with officers of the 11th Illinois Cavalry, for whom he cooked for two years. He returned briefly to his master, "but he got to cutting up," Thompson re-called, "and I came away again." The morning of April 12 found Thompson cooking at John Nelson's shabby little hotel. Though Thompson had never received any military training, when Forrest attacked he "went up in the fort and fought with the rest."[11]

Several white civilians joined in the defense as well. The hotelier John Nelson, Thompson's boss, "entered the works and tendered my services to Major Booth." The newly arrived merchant Eugene Van Camp joined the garrison's riflemen along the parapets, where a minié ball would all but sever his left hand. A clerk from upstate New York named James Brigham inserted himself behind a parapet "and was engaged with a musket in defending the fort." The merchant Hardy Revelle also took his place behind the breast-works, while the Minnesota photographer Charley Robinson and his partner George Washington Crafts "put on our blouses and went up to the fort & got our guns & amunition. George took his station in the Fort while I took my place in 'Co C' 13th Tenn who were outside skirmishing." Elvis Bevel, who had crossed from Arkansas to find refuge from rebel guerrillas, now slid into one of the rifle pits, from which he was soon evicted by rebel sharpshooters, forcing him to withdraw "behind a large stump near the fort."[12]

In his house in town, Edward Benton, the entrepreneurial owner of the bluff, was awakened by a contraband in his employ. "Oh, Mr. Benton," he said, jarring his boss awake, "all of Forrest's men have come, and they are just going into the fort. What will I do?"

Benton rushed out of his bed and "looked out of the window towards the fort, and saw about three or four hundred of Forrest's men drawn up in a line, and some one was making a speech to them, which was answered by cheering."

Packing his valise, Benton "started for the fort in a roundabout way." He tried to bring along three of the many contrabands he had hired from the camp in Memphis to put in a cotton crop, but they ran off, while the rest, including "one yellow woman," shut themselves up in his house. "By running the pickets," Benton proceeded "immediately to Major Booth and asked for a gun, and took my stand with the soldiers inside the breastworks, where I remained and shot at every person of Forrest's men that I could get a chance at, firing forty-eight shots in all."[13]

First Sergeant Henry Weaver of 6/C had just called the roll and gone down to the river to converse with Lieutenant Thomas W. McClure when the two men "heard an uncommon noise and commotion around headquarters, and soon the cry that the rebels were coming." A husband and father, and the semiliterate son of a pioneer, McClure and his old friend John D. Hill had worked together as cabinetmakers in Wabash, Indiana. They were about to be separated by Hill's admission to law school when the war reunited them in the ranks of the 14th Indiana Light Artillery. After the Battle of Parker Crossroads, they had both applied for commissions in the 6th USCHA, in which Hill and McClure were appointed Company C's first and second lieutenants respectively. Described by his commander as a "sober, reliable and trustworthy officer," McClure was a "healthy, active" thirty-year-old who had never been "excused from duty a day on account of disease or sickness."

After McClure and Weaver commanded Company C to fall in, Booth ordered them to take possession of two ten-pounder Parrott guns and haul them into the fort. McClure's artillerists installed the guns in the south end of the works, with McClure taking charge of the cannon on the right and Weaver on the left.[14]

Awakened by the rebel fire, post adjutant Mack J. Leaming hastily ascended the ravine road and scrambled into the fort. Formerly a private in the 72nd Illinois Infantry, Lieutenant Leaming of La Porte, Indiana, was a veteran of the siege of Vicksburg and numerous expeditions against guerrillas in Tennessee, Kentucky, and Missouri. Rushing into the fort, he found everyone in a state of "so much hurry and confusion that our flag was not raised." Leaming ordered it flown immediately, and at the sight of it "our troops set up vociferous cheers, especially the colored troops, who entered into the fight with great energy and spirit." Many of his men, "particularly the colored soldiers, had never before been under fire; yet every man did his duty with a courage and determined resolution, seldom if ever surpassed in similar engagements." And yet it must have rattled Bradford's officers to learn that some twenty more of their men had deserted since roll call the night before.[15]

Though the 13th occupied a superior position southeast of the black troops' camp, they soon abandoned it for the safety of Booth's battery. Thus the garrison was a victim, in part, of its own bigotry. Because of the bad feeling between the black artillerists and the Southern whites of the 13th, the two groups had been kept separated. Had they been able to camp together, or had some of Booth's artillerists been stationed with their guns in the 13th's camp, Bradford's boys might have held the knoll and denied the rebel sharpshooters their advantage. But now, perhaps dismayed to find that another twenty of their comrades had slipped off in the night, they rushed "back in disorder, leaving their horses and all their camp equipage behind. The rebels soon commenced running off the horses" despite the garrison's "brisk fire of musketry," as well as a cannonade from the 2nd USCLA's battery.[16]

Booth reinforced the skirmishers from the 13th with a detachment from 6/B under twenty-six-year-old Sergeant Wilbur Gaylord, a white nurseryman from Geneva, Ohio, who, as member of the 14th Independent Battery of the Ohio Light Artillery, had seen action at Shiloh. In November 1863, he had been detailed to assist in the training of black gunners, and he had only recently risen from his sickbed after a bout with the measles. Booth deployed Gaylord and twenty of his best men to a position more than a hundred yards southeast of the fort with orders "to hold the position as long as possible without being captured."[17]

At first the rebel advance seemed inexorable. Wilson's regiment had been deployed by now "to occupy the close attention of the garrison by an immediate, vigorous skirmish." "They kept up a steady fire by sharpshooters behind trees, and logs, and high knolls," recalled Leaming, and at one point Booth thought he saw them "planting some artillery, or looking for places to plant it. They began to draw nearer and nearer." By 8:00 a.m. most of the garrison had been driven into the fort, and the rebels, "realizing their advantage, pushed up near." They advanced "so close, in fact," wrote an officer of the 22nd Tennessee Cavalry, "that it became decidedly hazardous" for a Federal to show his head "to our marksmen, to say nothing of their features which they managed to keep pretty much below the battlements."[18]

"The Rebel sharp shooters must have fired at the Breast works over one hour without doing any harm," countered Dr. Fitch. "I was the first one wounded, which was merely a flesh wound in my left Thigh." Booth commanded him "to take his instruments and his medicines down under the bluff and stick up flags there and have the wounded taken down to him." So Fitch limped down the ravine road to the riverbank, where he tore his red flannel shirt into flags that he tied to "every bush around the bottom of the hill."[19]

Wounded while firing at the rebels, the civilian James Brigham soon tumbled after Fitch and spent the rest of the battle assisting with the wounded by the river. Dr. Fitch was impressed by the wounded men's resilience. "There was little or no straggling of our Forces," he reported. "They all fought like Braves. The wounded were all brought down to the Bluff as fast as they were wounded, and their wounds dressed."[20]

Approaching from the east, some nine miles from the fort, Forrest and his entourage could begin to hear the distant thrum of Union artillery. Spurring their horses, they trotted for another five miles, the sound of battle crackling now in the morning air, until they were met by a local man named Laney with a message from Chalmers reporting that he had driven the enemy into the works and rifle pits, but that the fort itself could not be taken "without heavy cost."[21]

On the western outskirts of Ripley, Forrest turned left onto a small road that ran through the tiny settlements of Mack, Glimp, Cherry, and finally Price, where he and his men turned right onto a muddy little road running toward the low hills between Price and the river. He arrived at the outer fortifications midmorning, and as his Escort dismounted to fill their canteens from a nearby spring, Laney directed him to where Chalmers's officers were conferring under a giant oak tree that Fort Pillow's successive garrisons had spared.[22]

"From ten a.m. until General Forrest came, there was but little change in our position," wrote Anderson French of the 22nd Tennessee Cavalry. "We had taken shelter behind trees and logs, and would occasionally jet a shot at some venturesome Federal who would expose his head above the fort." Otherwise the assault had stalled. "The enemy felt perfectly secure," recalled one of Chalmers's Mississippians, "and had no idea that any force could successfully storm their position. They waved their hats, telling our men: 'Come on, you dirty rebels.'" In fact, "the negro soldiers were perfectly offensive in offering banters."[23]

According to Nick Hamer, the slave who had accompanied Forrest on his ride to Fort Pillow, by the time Forrest arrived, Chalmers's men had begun to fall "back toward their horses." Forrest demanded "to know why they were going back, and our men said they had got out of ammunition. He asked where their wagons were, and they said they did not know, as the wagons could not keep up. He then ordered them to stop" and commanded his Escort "to donate their cartridges."[24]

Chalmers deemed the fort impregnable, but Forrest, who tended to trust "no other eyes than his own," decided to see for himself. "No matter how much confidence he had in his officers," explained Wyeth, "he never entrusted to anyone the task of making him acquainted with the strength of a point to be assailed, the topography of the ground to be traversed, or the various obstacles to be overcome."[25]

Spurring his horse westward with Captain Charles Anderson at his side, Forrest began to gallop to and fro, well within the garrison's range, examining firsthand every knoll and ravine and devising "a final plan of operations." "Almost immediately a rifle ball fired from the fort struck and mortally wounded his horse," wrote Robert Selph Henry. "Frantic with pain, the animal reared and fell over backward, carrying his rider with him and inflicting upon the General bruises and injuries which were painful and even serious." But Forrest wiped away the mud from his bruised limbs and mounted a second horse, which, after cantering a few yards, was also shot and killed. An alarmed Captain Anderson begged him to proceed on foot, but Forrest mounted yet a third horse, declaring that he was "just as apt to be hit one way as another," and, besides, could see better and scout faster from horseback.[26]

All the while the Wizard kept exhorting his men forward "through the underbrush and stumps toward the fort in short rushes, each advance being covered by the fire of sharpshooters converging from both sides upon the defenders behind the parapet." As he ranged around the field he deployed sharpshooters "on every commanding position" with instructions "to shoot at anything which showed itself from the fort."[27]

Forrest was especially eager to keep the New Era at bay, for he had seen what these lethal turtles had done to Floyd's command at Fort Donelson and to his own men two weeks earlier at Paducah. Though the gunboat's fire had been ineffectual so far, Forrest knew it was only a matter of time before more Yankee gunboats joined the fray.[28]

Before his hour's scout was over, his third mount was slightly wounded, but by now the Wizard had determined that if his men could occupy a portion of the trench to the south of the fort, they would be protected from Fort Pillow's fire. In addition, Forrest surveyed two ridges "four to five hundred yards distant, eastward and north-eastward from the enemy's position," which would give his men "excellent cover, from which they completely commanded the interior of the Federal works, and might effectually silence their fire."[29]

To Forrest the assault looked far from hopeless, and it must have been satisfying to return from his perilous ride to tell the vaunting little aristocrat so. Pointing westward, he turned to his old warhorse Black Bob McCulloch and asked if he would consider "capturing the barracks and houses which were near the fort and between it and my position."

"If I can get possession of the houses," McCulloch replied, "I can silence the enemy's artillery."

Forrest nodded. "Go ahead," he said, "and take them."[30]

He ordered a no doubt chagrined General Chalmers "to advance his lines and gain position on the slope, where our men would be perfectly protected from the heavy fire of artillery and musketry" because the garrison "could not depress their pieces so as to rake the slopes, nor could they fire on them with small-arms except by mounting the breastworks and exposing themselves to the fire of our sharpshooters, who, under cover of stumps and logs, forced them to keep down inside the works."[31]

"The accurate and persistent work" of Forrest's sharpshooters, wrote Wyeth, "either kept the heads of the garrison below the parapet or, when they rose to fire, made the discharge of their pieces premature and their aim too uncertain to be effective."[32]

At Forrest's "move up," McCulloch "made the charge in short order, and very soon," he recalled, "had my men in and behind the houses, from which the artillery on that side was silenced by sharpshooters," while other portions of his brigade occupied the rifle pits Bradford had evacuated, southeast of the fort. Forrest ordered Russell's and Wilson's forces forward to Barteau's left, "to a position in which their men were well sheltered by the conformation of the ground." The fire was intense. "I was one of a squad placed out on the old confederate trenches as sharpshooters to keep them down in the fort," recalled J. J. White of Russell's 20th. "I was sent by officers with [a] message to General Bell and had to go down a long hill in plain view of the fort, which was very risky business. But," concluded White, "I made it through."[33]

Though Sergeant Weaver and his crew had to improvise a platform under their gun before it "could be used to any effect," they managed to lay it down in time to fire "at the advancing enemy as they came in sight," though to his dismay "not more than one in five of the shells burst, owing to poor fuses."

Suddenly, Weaver recalled, "some one called out that Lt. McClure was wounded, and I saw him going toward and over the bluff, holding one arm in the hand of the other," headed for Fitch's riverbank hospital. His wound must have been excruciating: the ball had passed just above McClure's elbow, carrying a wad of his uniform with it and hacking through his humerus before passing out of his arm and lodging in his side.[34]

His friend and immediate superior John D. Hill fared worse. From the moment the alarm spread, many of Booth's artillerists had urged the major to burn down the four rows of barracks the 32nd Iowa had erected to the south of the inner works. But Booth had refused at first. Had Major Booth permitted his sappers to destroy the barracks, insisted burly Thomas Addison—at forty years of age the grand old man of 6/C—"the rebels never would have got the advantage of us"; but the barracks would soon afford the rebels "better breastworks for them than *we* had."[35]

Watching now as the rebels swarmed toward the barracks, however, Booth changed his mind and deployed Lieutenant Hill to put the barracks to the torch. But Booth's order came too late; Lieutenant Hill and a civilian were able to put only the first row to the torch before Hill was shot and killed by one of the rebel sharpshooters who were already creeping in among the adjacent rows. Within an hour and a half of the outbreak of hostilities, Captain Smith's absence, Lieutenant Hill's death, and Second Lieutenant McClure's wound had left 6/C under the sole command of Sergeant Henry Weaver.

Booth had been right to worry about the approach of rebel artillery. Though Captain Walton's two rifled howitzers were still several miles away, his advance scouts were indeed searching the terrain for the most advantageous emplacement. Booth darted from gun to gun, directing his crews to fire shrapnel at the snipers gathering like hornets on the surrounding knolls. As the rebels moved closer, he must have wished he had been equipped with mortars, for the angle of fire was proving too steep for his artillery. But Lionel Booth would not live long enough to see his worst fears realized. At nine o'clock, as he stepped over the trail of Sergeant Weaver's gun and exhorted his men never to give up their colors, a rebel sharpshooter's minié ball came buzzing through porthole number 2 and slammed into his chest.[36]

Hardy Revelle, the dry-goods clerk, was "standing not more than 10 paces from Major Booth when he fell, struck in the heart by a musket-bullet." "He expired instantly," recalled Sergeant Wilbur Gaylord, who picked up Booth's body and skidded down the hill with it, depositing it on the riverbank for the gunboat to retrieve.[37]

Command now fell to the brave but erratic and woefully inexperienced William Bradford. Though rebel sharpshooters had infiltrated the three remaining rows of barracks and snipers nested in superior positions on two knolls had "commenced a brisk fire on the fort," the garrison's skirmishers had been holding their own. But Bradford was in a state of considerable shock. As the rebels drew nearer, some white skirmishers began to abandon the rifle pits. "The rebels came within thirty rods" and stole two horses, recalled Sergeant Gaylord of 6/B, and "at the same time stuck a rebel flag on the fortifications." While he and his artillerists held their rifle pits, "the white men on my right retreated to the fort," and rather than order them back, Bradford decided to heed their alarm.[38]

As rebel minié balls continued to hack away at the parapet, Bradford's first act as Booth's heir to Fort Pillow's command was to order his skirmishers out of the rifle pits and back into the fort. It was the first in a series of fatal mistakes Bradford would make that day. Private John Kennedy and his comrades in 6/D believed that had Bradford allowed his sharpshooters to remain in their rifle pits, from which they could fire far more effectively than the men behind the enfiladed parapet, they could have held off the enemy indefinitely. In any case, the skirmishers' retreat proved costly. Leading his squad out of the rifle pits, Second Lieutenant John C. Barr of 13/D had climbed to within six feet of the inner works when a rebel sharpshooter sent a ball through his head, sending his lifeless body rolling down the slope.[39]

The rebels seemed intent on beheading the 6th by increments. With Booth dead, Captain Charles J. Epeneter of Company A became the 6th USCHA's senior officer, but his tenure was brief. His men had always had a hard time pronouncing his last name; it came out "Ebony" or "Ebeneezer." An Iowa brewer and vinegar maker, he had joined Lionel Booth in the 1st Missouri Light Artillery as a sergeant. After participating in a hard-won Union victory at Hill's Plantation in Arkansas, however, he was demoted to private for insubordination, which must have made him all the more receptive to Lorenzo Thomas's call for white officers for black regiments. In the fall of 1863, Epeneter and his messmate, Peter Bischoff of St. Louis, had traded their dwindling prospects in the 1st Missouri Light Artillery for lieutenancies in the 6th USCHA, in which Epeneter had risen to captain upon Booth's promotion to major. Now, just as Gaylord returned from depositing Booth's body by the river, Epeneter and Bischoff were manning the gun at portal number 4, up the line from Lieutenant Alexander M. Hunter of the 2nd USCLA, when a sniper's bullet sideswiped Epeneter, shattering the right side of his forehead all the way up to his hairline, just as Lieutenant John H. Porter of 13/B fell to the ground with a wound to the head.[40]

Standing at their portholes, Booth's black artillerists were especially exposed to the rebels' lethal fire. Early in the fight, Rachel Anderson's ailing husband, Ransom, of 6/B was severely wounded in the shoulder and chest. Alfred Isbell suffered gunshot wounds to his left arm, wrist and hand. The slave of two masters in East Tennessee, Eli Cothel had fled from the plantation of a Major Fleming in July 1863, made his fitful way to Corinth, and joined Company B of what was to become the 6th USCHA. Over the course of his brief military career he had been promoted to corporal and then sergeant, reduced to ranks for "conduct unbecoming," and in February 1864 promoted back to corporal. Now Cothel was shot in the leg and littered down to Dr. Fitch's "little hospital under the hill."[41]

Eli Falls of 6/A had followed the Union army to Corinth, cooked for Major Booth and Captain Epencter, and messed with Elias and West Erwin, fellow slaves of Jack Williams and William Cherry of Savannah, Tennessee. Shot during the battle, he nonetheless remained on the bluff with the garrison. Henry Gibson of the 2nd USCLA was struck so hard in the shoulder that his comrades Frank Hogan and Sandy Addison, who had run away from neighboring plantations with him, guessed he'd been hit by grapeshot. Whatever it was, it ripped his arm from his body, and within fifteen minutes he had bled to death. Fighting alongside the artillerists of the 2nd USCLA, a "poor but honest" fifty-year-old Memphis sutler named Alexander was killed during the fight and was "afterwards seen dead, still holding in his hands the musket he used so well." He left a widow and two small children.[42]

While standing between comrades Rufus McKissick and Benjamin Collier of 2/A, twenty-six-year-old Charles Jackson of Hardeman County was fatally shot in the head. At forty-two, Jacob Jones was one of the regiment's oldest soldiers. The slave of a Madison County, Tennessee, farmer named David Jones, he had married a fellow slave named Adaline in 1845 and by the outbreak of the war had fathered two children. He and his brother Benjamin had joined 6/A in June 1863, and were fighting side by side at Fort Pillow when Jacob was struck by a bullet "in the breast. He was killed instantly," recalled Benjamin, who pulled his brother's body "back out of the way."[43]

At the commencement of the fight, artillerist Sam Green had taken his place at the northernmost gun with Sergeant Mullins of 6/B. Green had been run off by his master to Jackson, Mississippi, where he was captured by the Union army and taken to Vicksburg. Eventually transported to Corinth, he was recruited by a French lieutenant named Henry Lippett. "And a good one he was," recalled Green, as vouched for by the fact that not one of his recruits deserted. After "both infantry drill and also artillery drill upon the siege guns at Corinth," Green was proud of his skill as an artilleryman, and his "artilleryman's jacket with the red trimmings."

His eyes chronically inflamed by gun smoke, Green was assigned the task of installing cartridges and fuses and thus "acting as springer and primer to one of the heavy siege guns early in the action." The gun was among the most exposed to enemy fire, for the embankment came up to only "about our waists." During the battle, Sergeant Mullins was severely wounded but managed somehow to make his way to safety after Green's lieutenant, Epeneter, was shot in the head.[44]

Nor did Green emerge unscathed. "While I was serving my gun, I was first struck upon the left foot by a rifle ball that cut off my big toe." He was subsequently shot through the back of his right hand, and suffered a severe contusion when his gun recoiled and "the butt end of the cannon" struck him in the hip, knocking him to the ground. His comrades carried him to a tent, but remarkably, Green soon shrugged off his injuries and "returned to my duty."

Green's valor was by no means unique. Though shot in the forearm, Private Willis Ligon, the former house slave who had waited on Forrest and his brothers during the Wizard's slave-trading days, now stood by his gun at Fort Pillow. "I had nobody to relieve me," he recalled, so he "just stood in one place until the fight was over." Already deaf in his left ear from boyhood infections, he was now nearly deafened in his right by the battery's pounding roar.[45]

"There were a great many of the negroes wounded," recalled Sergeant Weaver of 6/C, "because they would keep getting up to shoot, and were where they could be hit." "Never did men fight better," wrote Second Lieutenant Daniel Van Horn of 6/D, "and when the odds against us are considered it is truly miraculous that we should have held the fort an hour. To the colored troops is due the successful holding out until 4 p.m.," for they "were constantly at their posts, and in fact through the whole engagement showed a valor not, under the circumstances, to have been expected from troops less than veterans, either white or black." According to "the uniform and voluntary testimony of the rebel officers as well as the survivors of the fight," a correspondent for the *Missouri Democrat* would write after interviewing various participants the following day, "the negro artillery regiments fought with the bravery and coolness of veterans and served the guns with skill and precision." When a reporter for the *Cairo News* asked the survivors from the 13th Tennessee Cavalry "about the conduct of the negroes, they gave them great praise, saying they fought as only brave men can fight."[46]

James Brigham of New York declared that every man, "both black and white, fought manfully. I saw several negroes wounded, with blood running from their bodies, still engaged loading and firing cannon and muskets cheerfully." Five or six hundred men "successfully" defended Fort Pillow for eight hours "against 3,500 to 4,000 barbarians." Brigham would later overhear Confederate officers declare the assault on Fort Pillow "the hardest contested engagement that Forrest had ever been engaged in."[47]

"Although our garrison was almost completely surrounded," wrote Lieutenant Leaming, "all attempts of the enemy to carry our works by assault were successfully repulsed, notwithstanding his great superiority in numbers." Late in the morning, the rebels made a second concerted attempt to take the inner works, but "were again successfully repulsed with severe loss." Every time Forrest's men attacked, the black troops "would put their hats on the bayonets of their guns and hold them up for the confederates to shoot at, and also would make insulting remarks to their former owners who were in the attacking forces."[48]

Nevertheless, the mass of Forrest's command did not retreat all the way back from whence they came, but advanced incrementally, shooting and scurrying from stump to hillock to ditch. Firing from high knolls east of the fort, rebel sharpshooters kept the garrison's riflemen pinned down as a large contingent of McCulloch's men, obscured by the smoke from the incinerated row of barracks, slipped in among the three remaining rows that stood a mere sixty yards down the southwestern slope, where the angle of fire was so steep that the garrison's cannon could not dip their muzzles far enough to reach them.[49]

A white teamster named David Harrison had brought his rifle into the inner works and joined in the defense. But late in the morning Bradford asked him to organize a wagon train to haul ammunition and provisions into the fort. "The rebels were throwing balls around there," he said, "but I kept hauling." Though the rest of the wagons refused to go back after delivering their first load, Harrison returned four times before he "concluded I would not haul any more."[50]

Walton's battery, the rebel artillery the late Major Booth had been dreading, arrived before noon and began to fire upon the *New Era* from a section of high bluff south of the ravine, "where a plunging fire would necessarily drive her from her position," wrote Captain Anderson. But "of this movement she was doubtless advised by a signal from the fort," for the *New Era* immediately "steamed up the river and out of range before we could open fire on her." Had Marshall piloted his gunboat downriver instead, the battle might have turned out differently, for he could have fired directly upon McCulloch's men, smashing the barracks and driving Forrest's sharpshooters back from knoll and bluff.[51]

Barteau and his 22nd Tennessee Cavalry moved along the bottom of the bluff, which effectively shielded them from the garrison's fire. It should have rendered them vulnerable to gunfire from the *New Era* except that Marshall had shut his ports to protect his men from Anderson's sharpshooters as they fired from below the steamboat landing. Dodging fire from Walton's field pieces, the *New Era* could only maneuver "around for a while, as though she was trying to scare us off of that bluff without firing a gun," and finally, to Barteau's enormous relief, came to a "halt several hundred yards above the fort," where the *New Era* would remain a "silent spectator" for the rest of the fight, "and as useless to the enemy," added Dewitt Clinton Fort, "as it was harmless to us."[52]

After Anderson returned from helping Walton position his two guns at the southernmost reach of the bluff, he found "our whole force, under a terrific fire from the artillery and small arms of the garrison, was closing rapidly around the works. Bell's brigade was on the right, extending from the mouth of Coal Creek southward. Raising the standard of Chalmers's 18th Mississippi Battalion within view of the garrison, McCulloch's brigade occupied the left, extending from the ravine below the Fort north to where it met Bell's line abreast of the fort."[53]

"Our men pushed forward across the gullies and over the rough ground under a heavy fire from the fort," wrote Lieutenant James Dinkins of Mississippi. The bluecoats "exposed themselves above the works, firing at our line, and cursing and daring us to come on." After several hours' combat and "considerable loss," wrote Forrest, "the desired position was gained," and his main line "was now within an average distance of 100 yards from the fort," extending in an almost unbroken arc from Coal Creek in the north to the bluff south of the ravine.[54]

"These positions thus secured were fatal to the defense," wrote Hancock, "for the Confederates were now so placed that artillery could not be brought to bear upon them with much effect, except at a mortal exposure of the gunners, while rearward of the advance line were numerous sharp-shooters, favorably posted on several commanding ridges, ready to pick off any of the garrison showing their heads above, or, indeed, any men moving about within the circuit of, the parapets." By now, insisted Anderson, "it was perfectly apparent to any man endowed with the smallest amount of common sense that to all intents and purposes the fort was ours." Nevertheless the firing eased off somewhat as Forrest's men began to run out of ammunition and had to wait for the command's ordnance wagons to drag their way "through the April mud of the road from Brownsville."[55]

The news that Forrest had marched out of Jackson and, contrary to expectations, had not headed directly south but east, toward Fort Pillow, snapped Hurlbut out of his torpor. At 7:00 a.m. he had telegraphed Buckland to "send with all possible dispatch a good regiment, with four days' rations" and "forty rounds of ammunition," to rescue Fort Pillow's garrison from Forrest's clutches. "Promptness," he concluded, "is all important."[56]

Buckland promptly ordered Colonel Ignatz G. Kappner and his 55th U.S. Colored Infantry, many of whom—including the slaves of Williams and Cherry of Savannah—had lived in bondage with Booth's men, to embark immediately on the steamer *Glendal.* With these reinforcements, Hurlbut assured Kappner,

> and the great natural strength of the place, you should be able to hold it. Immediately upon landing, ascertain as nearly as you can from Major Booth the precise state of affairs, and send report to Cairo and here. If you find on approaching Fort Pillow that it has unfortunately been taken, you will request the officer of the gunboat to reconnoiter as closely as possible, and develop some accurate idea of the strength of the enemy, and return. If you succeed in re-enforcing the fort, in time it must be held at all hazards and to the last man. Report immediately and by every boat that passes.[57]

After deploying the 55th, Hurlbut hit the bottle. That afternoon he sat in on a court-martial, where Colonel Thomas Worthington of the 46th Ohio Infantry, describing Hurlbut as "a General scarcely ever clear of liquor," watched him as he "staggered into his court room to decide on the cases of men better and abler than himself."[58]

Writing from Nashville on the day of the attack on Fort Pillow, Sherman told Hurlbut that even if he could find Forrest he did not intend to move against him for fear such a diversion would weaken his campaign against Johnston. "Until McPherson's Veteran Volunteers assemble at Cairo," Sherman wrote, "I cannot make any plans to attack Forrest where he is." In fact, weary of Hurlbut's cries of wolf, and ignorant of Forrest's attack on Fort Pillow, Sherman was still convinced that the Wizard was on his way back down to Mississippi.[59]

Observing the battle from "an eminence included in the old Confederate lines, from which Forrest commanded a full view of the interior of the Federal works, and of their whole defensive resources," the Wizard saw that though even Wilson, positioned at the bottom of the deep ravine on the northern end of the line, was as protected from the garrison's fire as McCulloch's men to the southeast, nevertheless "to make a rush for this point for two or three hundred yards would expose him to great loss, for although there were numerous depressions intervening, there were just as many hilltops which could be swept by the artillery and small arms from the east and north faces of the parapet." Forrest therefore concluded that though "the place was practically in his possession," actually storming the fort would cost him more men, and to little purpose.[60]

The Wizard proceeded on foot to the far northern end of the skirmish line where Barteau's men, at considerable loss, had occupied the ravine that ran down to Coal Creek. As they lay huddled some seventy-five yards from the parapet, Forrest demanded to know who was in charge. Company A's twenty-three-year-old Second Lieutenant Anderson H. French of Barteau's 22nd identified himself with a crisp salute.[61]

"Never did men behave more bravely and nobly than did those under me," French wrote of his company's actions at Fort Pillow. "Over half of them were killed or wounded before the fort was stormed." By the time Forrest came around, they had "advanced to within about one hundred yards of the fort," where they were subjected to "a galling fire from the fort and the gunboat in the river." They had taken cover behind trees and logs and could only occasionally "jet a shot at some venturesome Federal who would expose his head above the fort."[62]

That was not good enough for Forrest, however, who immediately ordered French to advance.

"General," French replied, "that is death."

Forrest nonetheless repeated his order.

French turned to his men, gave the order to advance, "and at the same time started forward." But none of his men would follow, "and well it was that they did not, for they could not have lived one moment." The garrison's sharpshooters immediately opened fire, peppering the ground with minié balls. French dashed "some ten steps from where I started" and dropped down behind a log, where, as minié balls hacked and chipped at its bark, he decided to await further orders.[63]

"YES OR NO"
TRUCE

3:00 p.m.–4:00 p.m., April 12, 1864

BY 3:00 P.M. THE TWO SIDES HAD REACHED A KIND OF STALEMATE. Occupying the ravine had already proved more arduous than Forrest had anticipated, and threatened to result in the "heavy cost" about which Chalmers had warned him. The rebels would later tell Dr. Fitch that they had lost seventy-five killed and wounded, though what documentation survives suggests it was fifty-two. Bell's men had been forced to move with great caution, coordinating their advance with sharpshooters "who, as Bell's troops would rush over the exposed places, would open in lively fashion at any men of the garrison who would show their heads and shoulders in the endeavor to fire upon the advancing line."[1]

"Strange to say after five hours constant firing," wrote Sergeant Achilles Clark of the 20th Tennessee, "the Yankees had not killed a single one" of Russell's men, "and wounded only a very few," though one of them was the popular Captain J. Cardwell Wilson of Henry County, who had fallen within sixty yards of the fort, shot through the lungs "while charging at the head of his company." Carried eighteen miles to a farm and guarded by two of his men, Clark would die six days later.[2]

Rather than try to break through the garrison's defenses or risk the landing of Union reinforcements, Forrest finally turned to Chalmers and said, "We'd better give them a chance to surrender." "It was the plain duty of the Federal commander," wrote Barteau, "in view of the situation, to yield to the demand and thus save human life."[3]

Once the ordnance wagons arrived after their slow, muddy progress from Brownsville, and his men had at last refilled their cartridge boxes, Forrest commanded his bugler to signal a truce. As Bradford ordered his garrison to cease firing and his brother Ted signaled the *New Era* to stay put, Chalmers assigned the task of carrying his surrender demand to his adjutant general, Captain Walter A. Goodman, whom the little Mississippian described as "a man of brilliant intellect, cool in battle and untiring in his devotion to the cause and the discharge of his duty."[4]

Forrest's note read:

Headquarters Confederate Cavalry,
Near Fort Pillow, April 12, 1864.
The conduct of the officers and men garrisoning Fort Pillow has been such as to entitle them to being treated as prisoners of war. I demand the unconditional surrender of this garrison, promising you that you shall be treated as prisoners of war. My men have received a fresh supply of ammunition, and from their present position can easily assault and capture the fort. Should my demand be refused, I cannot be responsible for the fate of your command.
(Signed)
N. B. Forrest to Major L. F. Booth, Commanding U. S. Forces.[5]

"When the note was handed to me," Goodman recalled, "there was some discussion about it" among Forrest's officers, "and it was asked whether it was intended to include the negro soldiers as well as the white; to which both General Forrest and General Chalmers replied that it was so intended; and that if the fort was surrendered, the whole garrison, white and black, would be treated as prisoners of war." This, at least, is the message Forrest wanted Goodman to convey. But it is doubtful whether the Wizard was sincere, for later, in defending the reenslavement of his black prisoners, he would insist that he was merely following a Confederate policy that he had neither the power nor the right to defy.[6]

"Tie your handkerchief on a stick," Chalmers instructed Goodman, "and we will put you over the wall. Tell Major Booth that General Forrest desires to avoid any sacrifice of life, and therefore will give him an opportunity to surrender." But if Booth refused, "say to him, 'The men are in no humor to be brought face-to-face with the negro soldiers who have insulted their families.'"[7]

Goodman did not have to go far to deliver Forrest's surrender demand. Flanked by his bodyguards—Captain Tom Henderson of the scouts and Lieutenant Frank Rodgers of Forrest's Old Regiment—Goodman drew to a halt just to the left of McCulloch's position on the most elevated stretch of the entrenchment, where he was met by Lieutenant Mack J. Leaming, Captain John T. Young, Captain Theodorick Bradford, and four troopers.[8]

Forrest proceeded to an eminence four hundred yards from the fort to await Bradford's reply. The garrison's delegation took the surrender demand back to Bradford, who replied within a few minutes with a note of his own, "almost illegibly written with a pencil, on a soiled scrap of paper, transmitted without envelope."

"Your demand," it said, "does not produce the desired effect." Bradford slyly ordered it signed, "Major Lionel F. Booth."[9]

"Desiring to conceal from the enemy the fact of the death of Major Booth" and convince Forrest that Booth "was still in command," explained his adjutant, Lieutenant Leaming, "it was deemed not only proper but advisable that I append his name to the communication."[10]

It was certainly improper, and no less inadvisable. By sustaining this fiction, Bradford may merely have intended to mislead Forrest about the garrison's losses. Possibly he hoped to obtain better terms than he could hope for in his own name, although it is a tossup whether Forrest would have been more contemptuous of Bradford or an officer of black artillery. Bradford may have seen some indefinable advantage in pretending, as Duckworth had done at Union City, that a superior officer was present. But Bradford was also thinking of the cautionary example of Colonel Hawkins falling for the rebels' bluff at Union City and the inspiring example set by the defiant Colonel Hicks at Paducah. "Brave to a fault" and not fully cognizant of his peril, Bradford refused to be intimidated by Forrest's threat.[11]

Bradford's coy reply rankled Forrest, and he immediately sent Goodman back with a demand that Bradford (or Booth, as he believed him to be) answer "Yes" or "No" in "plain English."

Goodman cantered back to deliver Forrest's response as Forrest himself and several other officers watched from a distance. "If I am compelled to butt my men against their works," Forrest grumbled to his officers, "it will be bad for them."[12]

By now the garrison had spied rebels sneaking forward under the flag of truce, and Bradford's officers mentioned to Goodman "that this and other movements excited our suspicion, that they were moving their troops."[13]

Goodman mildly replied that his fellow officers "had noticed it themselves, and had it stopped; that it was unintentional on their part, and that it should not be repeated." The garrison's officers apparently did not demand that the rebels withdraw from the positions they had obtained during the truce, and it is almost inconceivable that Forrest would have acceded to such a demand if they had. The damage was done.[14]

As the two delegations awaited Booth's reply, one of the Union officers "who had remained with the flag expressed the belief that Forrest was not present," and that like Duckworth at Union City, one of his subordinate officers was posing as the Wizard himself. Another Federal stated that he was acquainted with General Forrest by sight, and demanded that the general show himself. Captain Young himself would recall that "a majority of the officers of the garrison doubted whether General Forrest was present, and had the impression that it was a ruse to induce the surrender of the fort." No doubt with a sigh of annoyance, Goodman commanded one of his subordinates, Captain Tom Henderson, to ride back to Forrest and suggest to the general "that the enemy might surrender sooner if he were to go forward and satisfy them of his presence."[15]

Forrest impatiently spurred his horse "to the spot where the flag stood and was presented to Captain Young of the 24th Missouri Infantry and also the party who claimed to know the General." As Forrest galloped out into plain view, "exposing himself to the fort," he was greeted by a cacophony of "insults and physical gestures from its occupants."[16]

The Union officers "both remarked that they had no longer any doubt" of Forrest's presence, and yet according to Young many of Bradford's men would remain convinced "that General Forrest was not in the vicinity of the fort." They should have consulted some of their artillerists, like the former table servant Willis Ligon, who recognized Forrest from his slave-trading rounds.[17]

As Forrest returned to his position on the knoll, Captain Charles Anderson rode up from his station at the mouth of the ravine to report that he had spotted smoke from Union boats downriver and, peering through his telescope, had seen that one was "crowded from forecastle to hurricane deck with Federal soldiers." Forrest ordered Anderson to position two companies of McCulloch's brigade on a bluff overlooking the river "within sixty yards of the south entrance of the fort." Anderson's sharpshooters descended one of the paths that crisscrossed the face of the bluff and stationed themselves in rifle pits, some of which were washed out, others aswamp with mud and clay clods from the bluff above, as the Yankee steamboats puffed upriver.[18]

The garrison's next reply confirmed the Wizard's growing suspicion that its officers were merely stalling for time. Still posing as Booth, Bradford asked for an hour more in which to consider Forrest's terms and to confer with Captain Marshall about surrendering the *New Era*. Forrest suspected that any consultation with the captain of the *New Era* would merely be a ploy to arrange the garrison's rescue or reinforcement. "The gunboat had ceased firing," according to Forrest's official account, "and the smoke of three other boats ascending the river was in view, the foremost boat apparently crowded with troops; and believing the request for an hour was to gain time for reinforcements to arrive, and that the desire to consult the officers of the gunboat was a pretext by which they desired improperly to communicate with her, I at once sent a reply by Captain Goodman, who bore the flag, directing him to remain until he received a reply, or until the expiration of the time proposed."[19]

Bradford was no longer counting on the *New Era*, trapped as she was upstream, but on two Yankee vessels—the steamer *Liberty* and the gunboat *Olive Branch*—with their cargoes of infantry and artillery. "After our men had been fighting about four hours, and were pretty well tired out," wrote Charley Robinson, "the smoke of a steamboat was seen down the river."[20]

"You have done well, my boys," declared Bradford. "Hold out a little longer for there is a boat coming with reinforcements, and if we can hold the place a little longer, we'll have plenty of help, as there is a thousand soldiers on the boat."

Robinson would "never forget the glad shout that went up from the little Fort on this announcement nor will I forget how sad we all felt when the boat passed by & never offered to land." The boat in question was the steamer *Liberty* carrying a cargo of hundreds (not a thousand) troops, and though it paused by the bar to evacuate the few refugees still huddled inside the coal barge, after a volley from the rebels it continued downstream.[21]

Here Brigadier General George Foster Shepley of Maine, recently dismissed military governor of Louisiana, makes a gratuitous appearance. A small man with a receding hairline and a long but sparse Vandyke, he was probably responsible for much of the corruption in New Orleans for which Ben Butler had been blamed; at one point, either out of frustration or in exchange for a bribe, he issued a blanket pardon that emptied Louisiana's prisons of its most dangerous criminals. With Hurlbut's extortionist command at Memphis and Brayman's scandal-ridden regime at Cairo, Shepley's inept and corrupt administration was an integral part of the Union army's squalid continuum along the Mississippi.[22]

Ordered to leave New Orleans and report to Grant, on April 6 Shepley had journeyed up the Mississippi aboard the steamer *Olive Branch* with 150 women and children. "The steamer was unarmed," Shepley testified, "and had no troops and no muskets for protection against guerillas when landing at wood yards and other places." After a pause at Vicksburg, Shepley returned to the *Olive Branch* to find that one Ohio and one Missouri battery with 120 men plus "horses, guns, caissons, wagons, tents, and baggage" had boarded "with orders, as I afterwards learned on inquiring, to report to General Brayman, at Cairo."

Shepley was discomfited. "The horses occupied all the available space, fore and aft, on the sides of the boilers and machinery, which were on deck. The guns, caissons, baggage wagons, tents, garrison and camp equipage, were piled up together on the bows, leaving only space for the gang plank," and yet none of the artillerists had small arms, "so that when the boat landed, as happened in one instance at a wood yard where guerillas had just passed, the pickets thrown out to prevent surprise were necessarily unarmed."[23]

Two and a half miles from Fort Pillow, a party of women had hailed the *Olive Branch* from the shore to report that "the rebels had attacked Fort Pillow and captured two boats on the river, and would take us if we went on." Captain B. Rushmore Pegram of the *Olive Branch* tried to heed their warning and head back down to Memphis. But Shepley, ignoring the boat owner's pleas for the safety of his craft and the welfare of the women and children among his passengers, countermanded Pegram's order. Spotting the small Ohio steamer *Hope* approaching without passengers, the general ordered her captain "to cast off the coal barges he had in tow," Shepley testified, "and take me on board with a section of a battery to go to Fort Pillow." But just as the captain began to "disencumber his boat of the coal barges," Shepley flagged down a larger steamboat called the *M. R. Cheek*, "and went aboard myself with Captain Thornton, of my staff, and Captain Williams the ranking officer of the batteries," some of which they began to transfer from the *Olive Branch* to the *Cheek*.

Suddenly yet another boat steamed into view from upriver, this one crowded with infantry. Shepley and his officers "could not distinguish at first whether they were Union or rebel soldiers." Suspecting that the steamer might be one of the boats that the women had claimed that Forrest had captured, Shepley ordered Pegram to swing the *Olive Branch* out into the river and overtake the boat. But when the mystery boat drew nearer, they saw it was the Union steamer *Liberty* with "United States infantry soldiers on board."

Her skipper, Captain John Booth, called out that she had just passed Fort Pillow, but kept the *Liberty* "going rapidly down with the current," Shepley testified.

"All right up there!" Booth shouted as the *Liberty* hurried past. "You can go by. The gunboat is lying off the fort."[24]

Shepley's staff urged the general to remain behind on the *Cheek* while they scouted Fort Pillow on the *Olive Branch*.

"No," Shepley claimed he replied. "I will go myself, and personally ascertain the condition of affairs."

So Shepley and his staff reboarded the *Olive Branch* and continued upstream with the two steamers following in her wake. As they neared Fort Pillow, "some stragglers or guerrillas fired from the shore with musketry," apparently prompting one of the steamers to fall back.

In fact, these were Anderson's sharpshooters, sent up the riverbank to fire two or three "admonitory" rounds at the *Olive Branch's* pilothouse. From their position on the bluff, well south of the parapet, they had spotted the steamers approaching. "The channel of the Mississippi River at Fort Pillow runs close under the bluff," and as the foremost steamer, the *Olive Branch*, drew near, Anderson ordered two of his men to fire at her pilothouse. The second shot "secured attention at once," Anderson recalled, and the *Olive Branch* veered off toward the bar across the river, followed by the *Hope* and the *M. R. Cheek*.[25]

As they reached the *New Era*, whose engines balked and groaned midcurrent more than a mile from Fort Pillow, Shepley could see that the Union flag was still flying from the parapet. An officer from the *New Era* rowed up to the *Olive Branch* in a skiff and urged Shepley to continue to Cairo and tell Brayman to send Captain Marshall more ordnance.

As they conferred, "no signal of any kind was made to the boat from the fort," Shepley insisted, "or from the shore," though as they began to head upstream to Cairo, they could see a flag of truce flying "outside the fortifications."

Shepley concluded "that the captain of the *Olive Branch* was not only justified in going on, but bound to proceed" because he would have been "incapable of rendering any assistance, being entirely defenseless. If any guns could have been placed in position on the boat, they could not have been elevated to reach sharpshooters on the high steep bluff outside the fort." None of which explains why Shepley did not at least stop the *Liberty* either to confer or to order artillery positioned on the sandbar, thus affording his gunners a more effective angle of fire.[26]

On the other hand, his timidity and the evasive action of his impotent armada contradict rebel reports that at the time of the truce Yankee boats crowded with troops and artillery were "steaming toward the fort, intent on going to the rescue of the beleaguered garrison," for the *Liberty* had already passed out of sight with its cargo of infantry, the *New Era* never budged, and a couple of rounds from Anderson's sharpshooters had convinced the remaining Union boats to veer away from the fort and flee.[27]

The rebels justified Anderson's violation of the truce by accusing the garrison of not signaling the truce to Shepley, when in fact Shepley saw the flag flying from the river. "The Confederate detachments which went to the riverbank, moreover," wrote Henry, "did not put themselves in better position for the assault. They put themselves entirely out of that part of the action." But this is sophistry. The reason they scuttled down to the river was to keep the gunboats and reinforcements at bay and thus facilitate the assault, a movement as vital to the success of the attack as any other.[28]

Shepley had a general's aptitude for shifting blame, and certainly there was enough to go around. "Coming from New Orleans, and having no knowledge of affairs in that military district," he testified, "we had no means of knowing or suspecting that so strong a position," with "uninterrupted water communication above and below," had not been adequately garrisoned, "when it was in Constant communication with General Hurlbut at Memphis." And yet as military governor of Louisiana, Shepley must have or certainly should have known about Forrest's raids along the Mississippi and the weakness of the Union's river forts.

Though he told Brayman that he had seen the Union flag go down, Shepley would not venture to guess whether it had been lowered by the garrison or shot from its halyard. "We supposed the object of the rebels was rather to seize a boat to effect a crossing into Arkansas, than to capture the fort." Had it not been "for the appearance of the *Liberty*," Shepley insisted, "I should have attempted a landing at Fort Pillow in the small steamer. If any intimation had been given from the gunboat, or the shore, I should have landed personally from the *Olive Branch*." But, he said, "the order given to the contrary prevented it," though Shepley could have overruled Marshall just as he had overruled Pegram an hour before, or acted independently from the bar, or, for that matter, at least sent one of his steamers downstream to retrieve the *Liberty*'s infantrymen, land them upriver, and try to reinforce the garrison.[29]

Instead he ordered the *Olive Branch* to continue upriver, and as it steamed toward Craighead Point, skipper Charles C. G. Thornton "went to the stern of our boat" and saw that the *New Era* had "steamed up a little ways, as I supposed for the purpose of firing upon the right flank of the rebels." Thornton "could see a line of fire or smoke in the woods, which we supposed to be from the musketry of the rebels. We then saw a flag raised up on a pole at the fort, I should think ten or twelve feet high. I supposed that our flag had been shot away, and they were raising it again," for the garrison's gunfire was "pretty heavy, while the fire of the enemy appeared to be from musketry." But by the time he testified a week later, he had "no doubt" that it was the rebel flag he had seen raised, "after the fort was taken." However, the rebel flag was not raised until perhaps half an hour after the attack, by which time the *Olive Branch* had turned around Craighead Point.[30]

Second Lieutenant John C. Akerstrom of 13/A served as the post's quartermaster general. But he was a murky figure, his name given in some records as John G. and in others as Charles J. He was apparently from New York, but in trying to account for his particularly horrible fate at Fort Pillow, some said he had been recognized by Forrest's men as a deserter from the rebel army, or in any case as a native of West Tennessee. "Mr. Akerstrom was in his office down under the hill after the flag of truce was in," observed James McCoy from the deck of the *New Era*. Akerstrom "made some signs for us to come to him." Other accounts maintain that it was Ted Bradford and not Akerstrom who had signaled; perhaps they both did: Akerstrom from below, trying to get the *New Era*'s attention; Ted Bradford from above, trying to beckon back the *Liberty*.[31]

"After their commander, Major Bradford, had given General Forrest the double cross," goes one rebel account, "and had carried on peace negotiations with him while making arrangements with the gunboats for assistance, every man in our command felt that the Federals had put themselves outside the pale of consideration—yet Forrest's men were considerate." But if Shepley and Thornton told the truth—though it is by no means certain that they did—and the garrison did not signal to the *Olive Branch,* and the *Olive Branch,* in turn, saw the flag of truce flying, it would debunk one of Forrest's counterclaims of Union truce violations that he later made in response to the overwhelming Yankee testimony about Confederate truce violations.[32]

By now the rebels assumed that the garrison would surrender. "Fort Pillow, at least after the Confederates secured possession of the rifle-pits and huts near the parapet, was untenable," wrote Forrest's authorized biographers, "and consequently its defense unjustifiable. Indeed, we know of no instance of such manifest indefensibility." Not only were the Yankees outnumbered; "every foot" of the fort "was completely enfiladed and swept by Confederate sharp-shooters." In addition, the inner fort was so small and densely crowded "that a sharp-shooter's bullet could scarcely miss an object, and the jeopardy of the men was the more fearfully augmented." In fact, according to Jordan and Pryor, Forrest could have established his men under cover at good rifle range and made the work untenable without attempting to storm it. Which begs the question of why Forrest stormed it in the end, especially if it meant losing many more of his men.[33]

Nor do these contentions jibe with the garrison's relatively few dead and wounded. Had the defenders been able to continue firing—rather than holding off during the hour-long truce that enabled Forrest's men to consolidate, reload their cartridge boxes, rest, consume the garrison's comestibles, and advance toward the parapets without risking fire from the garrison—they might have held out at least until nightfall, which, had they been better served by the gunboats, may have been long enough to receive reinforcements or arrange an evacuation. Nathan Fulks of the 13th believed "we would have whipped them if the flag of truce had not come in," and if "we had not let them get the dead-wood on us."[34]

Nothing in the story of Fort Pillow is more fraught with confusion and casuistry than the question of whether Forrest's men violated the truce by crawling forward and improving their positions. A large number of Union witnesses would maintain that they did, but various Southern historians and Confederate veterans of the battle dismissed the charge, citing as proof the fact that by the time of the truce the rebels had already occupied the positions they were accused of subsequently obtaining by deception.[35]

These accounts refer to ravines, ditches, rifle pits, and entrenchments, and some sources use these terms almost interchangeably. There were two primary ravines involved: the one that led from the junction of the Ripley and Fulton roads down to the river, and another just north of the parapet that ran down to the mouth of Coal Creek; and there is no question that by the time of the truce, some Confederate cavalry had occupied both positions. There is also no doubt that by then other rebel troopers had advanced into the second entrenchment that had been excavated during rebel occupation. But between this entrenchment and the fort lay a series of rifle pits—elongated foxholes, most of them—recently dug by Booth; and finally, along the base of the parapet itself, separated from the wall by a narrow ledge, ran a ditch six to eight feet deep and twelve to fourteen feet wide.

Daniel Rankin has been criticized for first testifying that during the siege the rebels took possession "of our rifle-pits" and then accusing Forrest's men of sneaking into the "ditch" during the truce. But by "rifle-pits" he meant the positions the garrison's sharpshooters occupied after the pickets were driven in, and by "ditch" he meant the trench that ran along the base of the Yankee bastion's exterior.

A number of rebels did indeed infiltrate some of the rifle pits that morning. French and his men occupied a position in the northern ravine, and a detachment of McCulloch's sharpshooters had taken positions among the three rows of barracks south of the breastwork. But a denial based solely on the fact that some of the rebels already held some of the positions in question cannot preclude the possibility that more men scuttled up the slope and crowded into such positions when the flag of truce was flying, especially when the rebel officers who bore the flag of truce blandly admitted to having observed their men doing just that.

The evidence that while the white flag was still flying Forrest's men fitfully continued to advance, and were joined in this transgression by more and more of their comrades, is overwhelming. Among the most credible Federal witnesses was Commissary Sergeant Daniel Stamps of 13/E. A crack shot, he had led a squad of sharpshooters outside the works to prevent the rebels from taking positions in the abandoned picket posts around the fort. "We fired very deliberately while we were outside of the fort," Stamps testified, "and I saw a great many fall dead from the effects of our guns." Nevertheless, after two hours of effective fire, Bradford had ordered them back into the works. "I staid within the fort perhaps about one hour," Stamps said, when Bradford ordered his little squad of sharpshooters to "go down under the bluff to repulse the enemy," who were "reported as coming down Coal Creek." About halfway down the bluff, Stamps and his men "attained a good position where we could see the enemy very plainly, being ourselves secreted behind some logs. I kept up a steady fire all the time I was in this place," striking "one of the enemy at nearly every shot."

After the flag of truce was raised and "all firing had ceased," Stamps and his men were outraged to see that the rebels Stamps and his squad had been keeping at bay were now rather casually advancing up Coal Creek. "When the rebels had got a good position, where they could pick our men off as they came out of the fort," he recalled, "I saw them break ranks and get water out of the river and make every preparation for a fight."[36]

Accompanying Stamps, James Taylor of 13/E also denounced the rebels for blatantly "disposing their troops, plundering our camp, and stealing goods from the quartermaster's and other stores. They formed at the same time on two sides of our garrison, and placed their sharpshooters in our deserted barracks."[37]

As the rebels moved "up all around in large force," even unto "the ditch beyond which our cannon were placed," Jack Ray of 13/B poked his head up over the works and asked some of the rebels "why they came so close while the flag of truce was being canvassed." But the rebels "only replied that they knew their business there." When Ray and his comrades "threatened to fire if they came any nearer," the rebels "jumped into the ditches outside of our fort." Ray heard some of his officers say "that the white flag was a bad thing," and the rebels "were slipping on us." Ray recalled overhearing Lieutenant Akerstrom protesting that "it was against the rules of war for them to come up in that way."[38]

The Federal case that Forrest violated the truce would be buttressed by the autobiography of one of his own men: John W. Carroll of Wilson's 21st, a close associate of Forrest's and, in later years, a fellow Klansman. "While the flag of truce was up," he wrote, Carroll and Captain James Stinnett of Company F "with some picked men crawled up close under the guns to be ready in case they refused to surrender" and "to prevent them from discharging their cannon into our ranks."[39]

Forrest argued with some justice that during the truce he was forced to move Anderson's sharpshooters downriver because the Union gunboats appeared to be taking advantage of the truce. But if his men's other, more substantial (and advantageous) violations along the horseshoe line and down Coal Creek were sanctioned by Forrest and his officers, their only conceivable defense is that they were so confident the garrison would surrender that they believed that moving their men a few yards closer during the truce would simply hasten the garrison's inevitable capitulation. But Forrest's cavalry had been accused most recently of committing the same violations at Union City and Paducah, and it is at least reasonable to conclude either that at these moments Forrest lost a significant measure of control over his men or that strictly observing a truce was simply another of those military niceties with which the brutally pragmatic Wizard had no patience.

Determined one way or another to take the fort before the Federal gunships could deploy reinforcements, Forrest replied in writing to Bradford's ambiguous response:

> Maj. L. F. Booth,
> Commanding U.S. Forces at Fort Pillow:
> Sir: I have the honor to acknowledge the receipt of your note, asking one hour to consider my demand for your surrender. Your request cannot be granted. I will allow you twenty minutes from the receipt of this note for consideration: if at the expiration of that time the fort

is not surrendered, I shall assault it. I do not demand the surrender of the gun-boat.

Very respectfully, your obedient servant,

N. B. Forrest,

Major-General, C. S. Army.[40]

According to Jordan and Pryor, Forrest instructed Goodman to add verbally that "so great was the animosity existing between the Tennesseeans of the two commands" that Forrest would not take responsibility "for the consequences if obliged to storm the Place."[41]

"It was said," Chalmers would write fifteen years later, "that Forrest's demand for a surrender at Paducah, coupled with an implied threat that he would not be responsible for the consequences if compelled to take the place by assault, showed a predetermination to cold blooded murder. This was the form of his first demand for surrender made at Murfreesboro, and he practiced it afterwards just as he practiced his flank attack, and for the same purpose, and with the same effect, to intimidate his adversary."[42]

Chalmers only begged the question. After all, Colonel Hicks at Paducah had just refused to be intimidated by a nearly identical threat, and Forrest must have understood that his do-or-die boilerplate demands would lose their potency if it got around that the Wizard did not follow through on his threats. The threat he made to Bradford may have been "another form of the same threat which Forrest had so often and so successfully used ever since his first capture of Murfreesboro by stratagem and bluff." But in every previous case, Forrest's foe had either surrendered on such terms or, as at Paducah, proved too formidable for Forrest to defeat and thus carry out—or refrain from carrying out—his threat. Whether the threat was a matter of strategy, animosity, or pique, the Wizard's warnings and Bradford's refusal freed Forrest's men to show a defiant foe no mercy.[43]

Soon after Goodman had returned to the flag of truce with Forrest's final demand, the Wizard himself rode up.

"That gives you twenty minutes to surrender," he shouted. "I am General Forrest."

Forrest may not have demanded a more immediate reply in order to give his own men more time to advance. But he had apparently also received reports that the garrison's defenders were getting drunk, whereupon he replied, "I will give them time to get drunk."[44]

The rebels' assertions that the Union garrison was inebriated would be leveled well after the political storm over the battle was blowing. They were made with the intention of deprecating the black artillerists' reckless bravery in defense of Fort Pillow and the garrison's obstinate refusal to surrender. Many Southern accounts would similarly dismiss Fort Pillow's defense as "lamentable fatuity," "foolhardiness," "credulity," or the consequence of drunkenness and inexperience.

"To those familiar with the two classes, black and white, which composed the bulk of the private soldiers in the garrison at Fort Pillow," sniffed Wyeth, with their "fondness for intoxicating drinks, especially so with the Negroes just free from slavery, it will readily be accepted that they did not fail to take advantage of the opportunities here offered to drink to excess." Wyeth ascribed their insulting conduct during the truce and their "insane resistance" to inebriation, though of course they need not have been drunk to hurl insults if they believed, as Bradford promised, that they were about to be rescued by a Union gunboat, nor to fight desperately against a foe that had refused to "be responsible" for their fate and intended, at the very least, to force them back into slavery.[45]

Nevertheless, enough Confederates made this claim—almost fifty, by Robert Selph Henry's count—that it was probably true. Fortifying troops with alcohol was common enough in both armies, and would have been especially welcome on a day as wet and windy as April 12, 1864. In fact, it may have been doled out during the truce as the garrison's reward for holding Forrest's men at bay. Among the relics dug up at Fort Pillow over a century later was a bottle of Dr. J. Hostetter's Stomach Bitters, a 94-proof "invigorant" that the Union army itself doled out to brace its men for battle.[46]

On the other hand, there was plenty of drinking on both sides that day. Forrest's men were no strangers to liquor. According to Captain Charles Anderson, the Wizard himself "didn't know whisky from brandy," and Tully Brown "never knew him to touch it but two or three times during the war, and that was when he was wounded." But when it came to his men consuming liquor, he was not always as severe as some have portrayed him. Whiskey was freely consumed in the card games he enjoyed, and the orders he gave to destroy distilleries had more to do with conserving corn for men and horses than preventing the production of moonshine. As for his men, J. D. McKlin of the 2nd waxed ironic about the regiment's fondness for drink. "We never got drunk," he said, "but always remained animated and sufficiently patriotic to express ourselves freely as to the certain success of the Confederacy, and our unbounded love for and confidence in our friends, the Jews," who sold them their wine. During a skirmish in December 1864, Captain Jim Barbour of Forrest's Old Regiment and his company would get so drunk that they were unable to prevent a small Yankee force from retrieving a group of Union boats their colonel David Kelley had captured.[47]

While the negotiations were stuttering along southeast of the parapet, Forrest's own men took the opportunity to rummage around among the supplies that the 13th had abandoned when it fled its camp. They soon came upon "any amount of whiskey," wrote Dewitt Clinton Fort. Meanwhile, McCulloch's men "broke into the quartermaster's stores which had been captured at this time, and before they could be compelled to quit the building had had access to a supply of whisky which they discovered there." Wyeth claimed that "the moment Forrest learned that his men were pillaging the captured stores, he rode there rapidly and put a stop to it in person," but he may not have found out in time to prevent his empty-stomached men from getting drunk, and it is likely that McCulloch's men, lurking in the warren of barracks and quartermaster's stores, managed a furtive swig or two even after Forrest barked at them. "The enemy inside the fort had plenty" as well, Fort recalled, and "the consequence was, that after the usual ceremonies of demand and refusal to surrender the garrison, a fight commenced with renewed vigor (all having imbibed)." But then nothing sobered men more quickly than battle.[48]

At the northern arc of the rebels' half-moon formation, Anderson French took advantage of the truce to come out from behind the log that had protected him after Forrest's peremptory order to advance. Taking a seat, the young lieutenant began to engage the black artillerists in conversation. "One of them asked me if I did not get hit before I reached the log," French remembered, "and when I informed him that I was not hurt, he said that he would get me as soon as that flag left the fort. I therefore kept one eye on it, and as soon as it started out I again took my position behind the log."[49]

Meanwhile a white Union bugler—a straggler, perhaps, from the scattered picket—decided he would take the opportunity to creep out of hiding and make his way down one of the riverside paths to retrieve a horse he had left tethered in a gulch. Riding up to the head of the ravine, Major Anderson watched awhile as the unsuspecting bugler untied his horse and prepared to ride off. But when he turned around, he encountered Anderson's six-shooter leveled at his head. "Ordering him to hand me his carbine end-butt foremost," Anderson recalled, "and then to untie his horse and lead him out ahead of me, I rode down and around" to rejoin Forrest, who by now had entirely run out of patience.[50]

After the battle, some rebels would speculate that Major Bradford must have refused to surrender because he could not assure himself that Forrest would keep his promise and treat the black troops as prisoners of war. "Forrest sent a flag of truce to the white general asking him to surrender," recalled Andrew Jackson Grantham of the 5th Mississippi, "after which his nigger troops would be treated as prisoners of war." But as a matter of fact, some rank-and-file rebels intimated to Leaming "that they would not be; and said it was bad enough to give to the 'home-made Yankees'—meaning the Tennessee soldiers—treatment as soldiers without treating the negroes so, too."[51]

By prearrangement with Captain Marshall, Bradford may still have counted on falling back to the river for a rescue. If so, argued Anderson, he was a fool.

> The movement of two howitzers to the low bluff had driven the *New Era* from the only position in which her promised aid could have been at all available. Marshall did know, and Maj. Bradford ought to have known, that with the channel of the river right under the bluff, and a broad bar with shallow water right opposite the fort, the *New Era* could not get sufficient "offing" to elevate her guns and do any damage to parties on top of a bluff at least eighty feet above the water line.[52]

In any case, Bradford "stood a while," contemplating Forrest's ultimatum. No doubt the few surviving officers of the black artillery regiments were loath to surrender, if only because it was Confederate policy to execute such officers for inciting a servile insurrection. If Forrest could not be trusted to keep his men in place during a truce, how could he be trusted to keep his promise to treat the artillerists and their officers as prisoners of war? Soon word began to circulate through the garrison that Bradford and his officers had voted unanimously to turn Forrest down. "Major Bradford refused to accept any such terms," recalled Lieutenants Smith and Cleary, and declared to his officers that if the rebels intended to take the fort "they could try it on."[53]

Apparently Bradford's defiance met with his garrison's approval, for by all accounts they were generally in good spirits and confident that they "would be able to hold the Fort against the overwhelming forces against them." "Up to this time," recalled Sergeant Weaver, "but few had been killed but a good many wounded." Edward Benton believed that up to the time of the truce fewer than twenty had been killed; Sergeant Gaylord put the number at ten. Dr. Fitch estimated twenty to twenty-five killed or wounded—perhaps half the number of rebel casualties.[54]

Among the dead was Elam Cashion of 13/D. "Tell My Dier sister and Dier little bothers Houdy for me And tell theme To Do the bst they can," he had recently written his family. "When I think A bout them my heart Fills with greef so that I can't hardly wright." Apologizing for his poor spelling, he signed off, "Yours Most truly until Deth, E. V. Cashion." Tom Cartwright of 13/A had been struck by a bullet whose trajectory into his shoulder and down his spinal cord suggests he may have been shot by a sniper from the 13th's abandoned camp. Over six feet tall and weighing 190 pounds, the illiterate twenty-one-year-old Irish recruit Thomas Loftis had proved too easy a target to avoid getting shot in the arm.[55]

Along the northern stretch of the parapet, black troops responded to Forrest's demand with "defiance and insult," wrote Barteau, "for the same reply that was given to General Forrest seemed to be the one heralded from the negroes on the works to our men on the outside." The artillerists "called to us with opprobrious names and dared us to the attempt," indulging "in the most provoking, impudent jeers," all the more infuriating coming from the lips of former slaves.[56]

"If you want the fort," they shouted, "come and take it!"[57]

"Come on, you dirty Rebels!"[58]

"Damn you, what are you here for?"[59]

Barteau, alone among the rebel officers, claimed that during this time the garrison even fired "several shots" at his men, but that he did not allow his men to return fire. At the southern end of the parapet the artillerists "shouted to McCulloch's men," wrote Wyeth, "many of whom had come out from behind the barracks and houses which concealed and protected them, daring them to try to take the fort, and hurling epithets at them couched in most obscene and abusive terms and accompanied by gestures and actions not to be described": mooning them and shaking their genitals. "If their officers made any effort to put a stop to this unusual exhibition, it was without effect."[60]

Just as Bradford's twenty minutes wound down, Lieutenant Leaming returned to hand Forrest Bradford's reply.

"I took it out in a sealed envelope, and gave it to him," Leaming testified. "The General opened it and read it."

"General," it said, "I will not surrender. Very respectfully, your obedient servant, L. F. Booth, Commanding U.S. Forces, Fort Pillow."[61]

"Nothing was said," Leaming testified. "We simply saluted, and they went their way, and I returned back into the fort."[62]

"BLOODY WORK"
THE FINAL ASSAULT
4:00 p.m., April 12, 1864

ACCORDING TO ANDREW JACKSON GRANTHAM OF THE 5TH MISSISSIPPI, when Bradford's reply was relayed along Forrest's line, it mutated from "I will not surrender" to "Go to hell, and turn your dogs loose." As the word spread among Forrest's ranks that they would have to storm the parapets, a trooper remarked to Dewitt Clinton Fort that "there was to be bloody work" that day.[1]

Forrest would not—could not—simply withdraw as he had done at Paducah. Indeed, the immediacy with which his attack followed the withdrawal of the flag of truce indicates that he had already made extensive preparations to follow through on his threats. "Bell's brigade occupied the right," he wrote, "with his extreme right resting on Cold Creek. McCulloch's brigade occupied the left, extending from the centre to the river. Three companies of his own regiment were placed in an old rifle-pit on the left and almost in the rear of the fort. On the right a portion of Barteau's regiment was also under the bluff, and in [the] rear of the fort." "The commanding ridges eastward and north-eastward of the work were studded with sharp-shooters," wrote Jordan and Pryor, and one squad had "completely enfiladed" the southern side of the Federal works, "the face most strongly garnished with artillery."[2]

Major Charles Anderson warned Forrest that two barges lay moored by the river, awaiting the garrison and ready to be towed away by the *New Era*. "I was equally particular in impressing upon him the hazardous position of the detachment on the face of the bluff, out of sight of and entirely separated from, the balance of the command." If Forrest's assault failed, Anderson pointed out, his men could be wiped out by a combined sortie from the fort and a barrage from the gunboat.

Forrest instructed Anderson to return to his detachment and keep out of the assault on the fort in order to "pour fire into the open ports of the *New Era*" if she tried to return to the fray. As soon as the garrison fled to the river, Anderson was "to fight everything *blue* between wind and water," Forrest commanded, "until yonder flag comes down." Anderson rode off and relayed these instructions to his men, then took a position on horseback only fifty yards from the parapet but out of sight of the garrison. "From this position I had a full view of the entire waterline in rear of the fort, and much of the slope above it."[3]

One of Forrest's biographers tried to guess Forrest's thoughts at this moment. By now the Wizard may have concluded that an all-out assault was "all for the best," wrote Eric William Sheppard. If Forrest had to send his men over the ramparts and into the fort, "better this than any other" fort, for inside its walls "were the two breeds of men they hated most in life—the Tennessee Tories" and the "nigger dressed up as a soldier—the nigger fit for nothing but slavery—the nigger that had set white men all over America for four years at each other's throats." It was high time the "Tories and niggers should realize once and for all that they couldn't stand up to Southerners in fair fight," and that Forrest made good on his threats. "There'd be hell to pay all right," Sheppard imagined Forrest thinking, but the time had come to let loose the dogs of war.[4]

Whatever else was preying on his mind, Forrest also realized that from a purely military point of view he had reached the point of no return. "My dispositions had all been made," he would write President Davis, "and my force was in a position that would enable me to take the fort with less loss than to have withdrawn under fire."[5]

"His orders to the troops were explicit," wrote Wyeth. "They were told that they must storm the fort; every gun and pistol was to be loaded; not a shot was to be fired by the assaulting line until they were inside the works and hand to hand; they must make it quick work. The men were informed that the sharpshooters would keep the heads of the Federals behind the parapet until they could cross the ditch and climb the embankment. He would be where he could watch the entire field, and would note which command would be first over the walls." When the bugle sounded the charge, "they were to go."[6]

"With a few energetic words," wrote Hancock, Forrest "stimulated the pride of his men to do their duty." But there is some debate about what those words were. "General Chalmers," said Forrest, "tell your men to plant their flags on that cursed fort, and take what they find." According to one participant Forrest told them to be "merciful to the negroes," but added that they were not to forget Captain Bob Perry of the 18th Mississippi, who, Forrest's men had been led to believe, "had been captured and murdered by negro soldiers." To Captain James Dinkins of Chalmers's consolidated regiment, Forrest looked like "the incarnation of all the destructive powers of earth" and seemed "to battle what a cyclone is to an April shower" as he trotted slowly back to his observation point, exhorting his men with, "At 'em! At 'em!" "His voice could be heard by the Yankees," Dinkins recalled, though what the Yankees heard the general chant was not "At 'em" but "No quarter!"[7]

That in any case was the cry his subordinates Bell and Chalmers took up as their men prepared to storm the fort. After French's men had refused his order to advance earlier that afternoon, Forrest probably concluded that if his men were to vault the parapet, he first had to whip his troopers into a rage. Incensed, and probably inebriated, they hardly needed stirring. "Our men," wrote Clarke Barteau, "as by one impulse, seem to have determined they would take the fort, and that, too, independently of officers or orders, and had no command been given to 'charge,' I verily believe that after the insults given them during the truce they would have taken the fort by storm any way."[8]

In any case, neither Forrest nor his subordinates took any "effective steps," wrote Sheppard, to "forestall or guard against the manifestations of the very natural feelings of personal hatred and desire for vengeance which animated many of their men," and would allow them "for a space prolonged beyond necessity or reason, free license to gratify these feelings at the expense of an enemy for the most part disarmed and helpless." Despite all the extenuating circumstances, Sheppard concluded that Forrest would "stand convicted at the bar of history."[9]

The Wizard, recalled Grantham, had "turned us loose."[10]

The guns on the fort looked so savage, recalled Dinkins, that Chalmers ordered McCulloch to hold back one regiment to sustain a covering fire while the remaining troopers clambered over the works. Even so, to the rebels huddled in the ditches, climbing into the fort looked like "defying death itself."[11]

With the withdrawal of the flag of truce, the garrison, including every able-bodied contraband, sutler, and refugee, readied their rifles. The 13th was apparently armed with the carbines that had by then become standard issue for cavalry; the artillerists carried muskets. All but a couple of Sergeant Henry's and Lieutenant Hunter's cannoneers had been killed or wounded, and their ammunition was almost gone; nevertheless, they filled their cannon with grapeshot and prayed that their fuses were dry enough to ignite. "All along the inner aspect of the embankment," the garrison "crouched beneath the parapet, their guns resting on the crest, and all ready for the onslaught" as Major Bradford, with his saber drawn, strode from gun to gun.[12]

The Confederates, for their part, were armed with carbines, shotguns, and muskets, the latter loaded with a lethal close-quarter combination of what they called "three bucks and a ball"—three buckshot and a minié—which was capable of inflicting a ragged wound that "sometimes looked as though it had been done with a hatchet." Most of them carried six-shooters as well. "Being a courier," wrote Robert Burfford, "I did not carry a gun, but I had two six-shooters and a horse pistol."[13] Only a few officers carried swords.

It was almost 4:00 p.m., and "the two hostile banners were flouting the breeze in disagreeable proximity." Perhaps five minutes had passed since Forrest received Bradford's reply, and the eyes of both garrison and attacker alike followed the general as he spurred his horse up to the distant knoll in the company of his German bugler, Joe Gaus. Reaching the summit, he turned and paused a moment to observe Bell pressing more of his men into the northern ditch, and McCulloch's troopers advancing among the barracks. All was ready.[14]

"Blow the charge, Gaus," said Forrest without taking his eyes from the field. "Blow the charge."[15]

Gaus raised his battle-battered bugle to his lips, and at "the first blare," wrote Dinkins, "the Confederates opened a galling fire on the parapet as they advanced, which was replied to by the garrison for a few moments with great spirit." The echoes of the bugle's first blast, wrote Fort, "broke the spell which bound the garrison, and the firing from artillery and musketry which was now poured upon us was the severest" they had experienced all day. "It made an awful din," wrote Wyeth. "The wild, defiant yell of the assailants, mingled with the crackle and roar of musketry and the thundering cannon" as they harmlessly swept the surrounding hills with grapeshot. But the fire from the rebels' sharpshooters was so deadly that the garrison still "could not rise high enough from their cover to fire," Dinkins recalled, nor reload their artillery "without being shot." "As the blue caps of the garrison rose above the horseshoe line of the parapet to deliver their volley," wrote Wyeth, "a shower of missiles whizzed by and into them, while bits of pulverized earth flew in their faces as the bullets from the unerring aim of 250 sharpshooters sped through the air and plowed miniature furrows along the floorlike top of the embankment."[16]

A large force of dismounted troopers "came upon us from the ravine toward the east of where I stood," recalled Hardy Revelle. "It seemed to come down Cold Creek. They charged upon our ranks. Another large force of rebel cavalry charged from the south of east, and another force from the northward."[17]

While bugler Gaus continued to sound the charge, "the main Confederate force, as with a single impulse, surged onward, like a tawny wave." "The sight of negro soldiers," wrote a rebel participant, had "stirred the bosoms of our soldiers with courageous madness." "The outside of the fort was in ridges," recalled Dinkins, "caused by heavy rains washing out gullies," and these "afforded hand holds to the men in climbing up." But the deep ditch that Booth had excavated along the outer wall of the parapet was too wide to leap and too deep and slick for a man to climb out of unassisted. Encumbered by their arms and cartridge boxes, unable to obtain footholds upon "the slanting bank of earth where ditch and embankment met," Forrest's men skidded straight down to the muddy bottom, some fourteen feet below the breastwork's crest.[18]

An experienced artillerist, the late Major Booth would have rolled grenades and short-fused shells into the ditch and "exterminated these reckless horsemen." But it did not occur to Bradford, and the rebels paused in relative safety in the bottom of the ditch, cocking their "guns and navy sixes" and making ready for their final lunge.[19]

Some three hundred of Forrest's men hunched down in the ditch to give an equal number of their comrades purchase, lending their backs and shoulders and intertwined hands to boost them to the narrow ledge that separated the ditch from the parapet. From here, in turn, this first rank reached back to haul their comrades up beside them. Peppered by sharpshooters, the defenders could not fire on the men who were now pressed against the opposite side of the breastwork, but they could and did fire at the wave of men rising out of the rifle pits.

Placed in command of the 5th Mississippi after his heroism at Paducah, Lieutenant Colonel Wyly Martin Reed was standing with Lieutenant N. B. Burton some eighty yards from the parapet, exhorting his men to charge, when they were both struck by bullets. Burton fell dead, and Reed, one of Forrest's preacher-colonels, teetered back, mortally wounded. ("He was a good man," Forrest would mourn after his death weeks later, "brave and patriotic.") Charging at the parapets from the 13th's camp, Private Samuel Allen was also struck dead, and elsewhere men fell wounded.[20]

When all but the most diminutive rebel skirmisher had managed to clear the ditch, they climbed in one long wave to the crest of the parapet "as nimbly and as swiftly as squirrels. The impetuosity of the attack was re-markable," wrote Dinkins. "The men had stood by and heard and saw what was going on. Their friends and families had been insulted and outraged. They were ready and eager to avenge those wrongs."[21]

"When Bell saw his men fired upon," reported Thomas Berry of the 9th Texas Cavalry, "he mounted his horse and led his command over the em-bankment," saying, "No quarter to wretches like these!"[22]

As Bell's men broke through the center, Barteau's 22nd Tennessee had rushed in from the north and McCulloch's brigade from the south almost simultaneously. Among the first to mount the crest was Second Lieutenant Anderson French of the 22nd, determined to redeem himself and his men after their refusal to advance only a couple of hours before.[23]

To the stunned garrison desperately reloading their muskets, their at-tackers seemed to rise "from out of the very earth." "They had been told," wrote Dinkins, "that the rebels could not get over the works and into the fort, and did not believe they could, but the sight of the 'Johnnies' was a flat contradiction of the blustering lie." For the rebels as well, "it was like a ter-rible shock," wrote Fort, to be confronted with their foe at such close quar-ters. There was an awestruck instant of silence as the rebels found their balance and glared down at the thunderstruck garrison. Some of the de-fenders managed to get off a volley or two, killing Privates John Beard of the 20th and Reuben Burrows of the 15th and wounding several others. Then, with a yell, the rebels fired down upon them.[24]

Recounting an earlier skirmish, J. K. P. Blackburn described the horri-fying damage the cavalry's carbines and shotguns could inflict on a line of bluecoats. "In a twinkling of an eye almost," he wrote, "both barrels of every shotgun in our line loaded with fifteen to twenty buckshot in each barrel was turned into that blue line and lo! what destruction and confusion fol-lowed. It reminded me then of a large covey of quail bunched on the ground, shot into with a load of bird shot," leaving them "squirming and fluttering around on the ground."[25]

No sooner had the first wave of rebels fired and jumped into the fortifi-cation than a second wave popped up onto the parapet and opened fire.[26]

"The charge was simultaneous and well sustained from every point," wrote Fort, and the assault "an instantaneous success." As the rebels leaped through the gun smoke and into the fort itself, some of them pressed the muzzles of their guns against the defenders' blue blouses and fired, inflict-ing "wounds almost of necessity instantly fatal." Almost, but a lot of their fire was wild. "I was wounded with a musket ball through the right ankle," wrote Sergeant Gaylord of 6/B. Two hundred rebels passed by him as he lay bleeding, "when one rebel noticed that I was alive" and shot at him again and missed. Daniel Rankin was shot in the leg at the rim of the bluff, and as his assailant reloaded he threw himself over the edge, stopping his fall by "catching hold of a little locust." James Taylor and his brother Frank were wounded as they scrambled down the bluff. John Haskins of 6/B was shot in the arm.[27]

"The sight was terrific," wrote a rebel witness,

> the slaughter sickening. Wearied with the slow process of shooting with guns, our troops commenced with their repeaters, and every fire brought down a foe, and so close was the fight, that the dead would frequently fall upon the soldier that killed. Still the enemy would not or knew not how to surrender. The Federal flag, that hated emblem of tyranny, was still proudly waving over the scene.[28]

By now "nearly all the officers had been killed," testified Lieutenant Mack Leaming of the 13th, "especially of the colored troops, and there was no one hardly to guide the men." The garrison had "fought bravely, indeed," until the rebels leaped into their midst.[29]

"In the shortest time after the charge was ordered," wrote Fort, "we had the indisputed possession of the Fort. It was so incredible a fact that those who had actually performed it could hardly realize its accomplishment. We could scarcely trust our own eyes: so quickly was the face of affairs changed under great excitement." Within five minutes of the bugle's call, the rebels had possession of the fort.[30]

"As we charged over the ramparts," wrote Fort, "the enemy's garrison of mixed complexion retreated over the bluff down to the water's edge." The black artillerists and their officers would claim that the whites broke first; Bradford's whites insisted it was the blacks. "The rebels charged after the flag of truce," wrote Sergeant Weaver, "the Tennessee cavalry broke, and was followed down the hill by the colored soldiers."[31]

After a wounded Captain Epeneter staggered down to the river, his messmate, First Lieutenant Peter Bischoff, had taken command of the gun crew at portal 4. A sergeant from the 1st Missouri Light Artillery, Bischoff had transferred to become first lieutenant of 6/A. "During the last attack," testified Private John Kennedy of 2/D, "when the rebels entered the works, I heard Major Bradford give the command, 'Boys, save your lives.'"

Bischoff was outraged. "Do not let the men leave their pieces," he protested. "Let us fight yet."

But Bradford looked around at the swarm of rebels overrunning the fort and shook his head.

"It is of no use anymore," he declared, whereupon "the men left their pieces and tried to escape in different directions and manners."[32]

"The Major started and told us to take care of ourselves," Nathan Fulks of the 13th testified, "and I and twenty more men broke for the hollow."[33]

"The niggers first ran out of the fort," asserted W. P. Walker of the 13th, and it was only when the rebels "commenced shooting us" that Bradford's men "ran down under the hill." The disparity was a mere matter of a few seconds. For all intents and purposes they fled at once. In the ensuing chaos, amid the flash of muzzles, the buzz of minié balls, the roil of gun smoke, the war cry of the rebels and the howls of the wounded, it must have been hard to tell. Civilians less invested in the reputation of any particular regiment could not tell the difference. "A large number of the soldiers," recalled the hotelier John Nelson, "black and white, and also a few citizens, myself among the number, rushed down the bluff towards the river." Dr. Chapman Underwood, observing from the *New Era,* would also testify that "white and black all rushed out of the fort together, threw down their arms, and ran down the hill."[34]

The black troops stationed in the center of the Federal line bore the brunt of the initial attack as Bell's troops burst in. "What was called brigade or battalion attacked the centre of the fort where several companies of colored troops were stationed. They finally gave way," Leaming reported, "and, before we could fill up the breach, the enemy got inside the fort, and then they came in on the other two sides, and had complete possession of the fort." Private William F. Mays testified that "the negroes gave way upon the left and ran down the bluff, leaving an opening through which the rebels entered."[35]

If the blacks were the first to flee, it is no wonder. Not only were the artillerists the special targets of Bell's most concerted attack, for the rebels' first order of business was putting the garrison's guns out of commission; they were armed with muskets and, unlike the men of the 13th with their repeating rifles, could get off only one round before the rebels were upon them.

"There were some tents erected within the fort nearest the river," wrote Jordan and Pryor, "and these blocked the way to rapid egress. As the retreating mass crowded the narrow paths between the tents, they were pelted by the shower of lead which slaughtered them by scores. They fell in piles three or four deep: heaps of bleeding, mangled bodies." Several artillerists, too sick to join in the defense, had spent the battle on their backs in a row of hospital tents near the rim of the bluff, where, as the battle progressed, they had been joined by wounded men like the civilian John Penwell of Michigan.[36]

Penwell had just fired his musket and was "feeling for a cartridge" when he "heard a shot behind me" and saw the rebels "come running right up to us." When they were within ten feet of him, Penwell threw down his musket.

"Do you surrender?" a rebel asked.

Penwell hastily replied that he did.

"Die, then, you damned Yankee son of a bitch," the rebel snapped back, and shot him.

"More passed by me," Penwell testified, "and commenced hallooing." Three or four "stopped where I was and jumped on me and stripped me, taking my boots and coat and hat, and $45 or $50 in greenbacks."

One of them said, "He ain't dead," as he jerked Penwell up "and took off my coat. It hurt me pretty bad."

Penwell begged them to "kill me, out and out."

"Hit him a crack on the head," said one of the rebels.

"Let the poor fellow be and get well, if he can," another said. "He has nothing more left now."[37]

William Mays of the 13th "saw four white men and 25 negroes" shot in the fort, and heard the rebels on "all sides" crying, "Give them no quarter; kill them; kill them; it is General Forrest's orders."[38]

"If there was a single negro soldier there who was not killed," boasted Robert Bufferd, who emptied all three of his pistols into the garrison, "I never knew it." "Their fort turned out to be a great slaughter pen," wrote Achilles Clark of the 20th. "Blood—human blood—stood about in pools, and brains could have been gathered up in any quantity."[39]

Some rebel participants reported that there was liquor on the black artillerists' breath. Barteau testified that he and his staff "found barrels of whisky and ale and bottles of brandy open, and tin cups in the barrels out of which they had been drinking. We also found water-buckets sitting around in the fort with whisky and dippers in them, which showed very clearly that the whisky had been thus passed around to the Federal troops." Chalmers would swear that "those of the garrison who were sober enough to realize the hopelessness of their situation after the fort was stormed, surrendered, and thus escaped being killed or wounded."[40]

Watching and listening from the sandbar, the civilian James McCoy could see "a cloud" of rebels—Dr. Chapman Underwood likened them to bees—swarming into the fort "and our men in the fort running out," and make out on the river wind "a great deal of screaming and praying for mercy." The men fell back in no order, but in groups of a dozen or more, dripping from the parapet like wax melting from the rim of a candle. According to Henry Weaver, "Lieutenant Van Horn begged and ordered them to stop, but each one sought safety in flight."[41]

"They ran with all their speed," wrote Dinkins. "Our men called on them to halt, firing at them as they ran. Not one, however, would halt, unless a bullet caught him. They ran to the high bluff and jumped over. Those who did never knew what the end was. They were too flat to bury." The artillerists "went over the bluff like sheep through a gate. They would jump as high as they could. They would not surrender."[42]

From their sharpshooters' nests along the earthworks "down by the river under the fort," Daniel Stamps of 13/E and his sharpshooters had resumed firing at the rebels advancing from upriver. Stamps claimed he dropped a rebel "at every shot," but then the garrison began to run out of the fort and "down the bluff, close to my vicinity." Skidding past him, they warned Stamps that the rebels were showing no mercy to white or black, whereupon he dropped his gun as well "and ran down with them, closely pursued by the enemy."[43]

Southern sources insist that even as the Union soldiers fled down the bluff, most of them remained armed. "The garrison did not yield," wrote Dinkins, "did not lay down their arms, nor take down their flag, but fled with guns in their hands to another position in which they were promised relief, and while on their way returned the fire." As proof they cited the six cartridge boxes Anderson would find "piled against the upturned roots of an old tree," and the 269 to 275 muskets they claimed they retrieved between the edge of the bluff and the river. Some cartridge boxes and muskets were undoubtedly left over from Stamps and his sharpshooters, but several Federal survivors testified that upon surrendering they did indeed drop their muskets and cartridge boxes by the river. Others may have been carried down the slope during the morning by skirmishers, wounded men, and their escorts. Descending a steep eighty-foot bluff would have been hard enough without toting muskets and cartridge boxes. If most of the guns were found at the base of the slope, that could just as easily confirm what many Union witnesses like John Nelson asserted: that all but a very few of the defenders whom the rebels "hemmed in" had thrown down their weapons as they leaped off the bluff, and that by the time they reached the bottom most of the Federals were "without arms."[44]

No doubt several Federals did turn and fire up the slope, since the rebels seemed intent on shooting all those who "turned back and surrendered." "Negroes," wrote Wyeth, "some few of whom, either insanely intoxicated or convinced from the slaughter that had transpired that no quarter would be shown them, and determined to sell their lives as dearly as possible, still offered resistance and continued to fire at the Confederates," though he conceded that there were "not many who were guilty of this insanity."[45]

Though their fire apparently did the rebels no harm, nevertheless it was "enough to justify their assailants to close in upon them from the bluff above and from either side of the riverbank and continue to shoot them down." In the process, admitted Wyeth, "there were a number of men, both white and black, shot down who were trying to surrender and should have been spared," though he agreed with Anderson that "the heavy loss in killed and wounded during their retreat was alone due to the incapacity of their commander, the drunken condition of the men, and the fatal agreement with and promise of Captain Marshall of the *New Era* to protect and succor them when driven from the works." An officer of Barteau's 22nd reported that the rebels, "maddened by excitement, shot down the retreating Yankees, and not until they had attained the water's edge and turned to beg for mercy, did any prisoners fall into our hands. Thus the whites received quarter, but the negroes were shown no mercy."[46]

Some of Forrest's defenders deprecate Union testimony that several men were bayoneted to death, on the grounds that neither rebel nor Union cavalry carried bayonets. But the black artillerists were armed with muskets equipped with bayonets, and it does not take much imagination to see how it would have been perfectly possible, and may have struck some rebels as perfectly fitting, to finish off their foes with their own weapons.[47]

Three vagrant accounts assert that the garrison tricked the rebels by raising a flag of truce and then opening fire when the rebels entered the fort to accept its surrender. "The negroes ran out down to the river," Forrest was quoted as telling the *Philadelphia Weekly Times* after the war, "and although the [white] flag was flying, they kept on turning back and shooting at my men, who consequently continued to fire into them crowded on the brink of the river, and they killed a good many of them in spite of my efforts and those of their officers to stop them"; but it must be asked why Forrest would have tried to stop his men if they were indeed returning Yankee fire.[48]

"It is true," wrote Confederate governor Isham Harris, "that a few, black and white, threw down their arms and made signs of surrender—but at the same time the men on each side of them still retained their arms and kept up a constant fire and show of resistance. In the heat, din and confusion of a fire at such close quarters there was no chance for discrimination." "No one was to blame" for the massacre "but those blind misguided creatures, those poor negroes," wrote Thomas Berry. "They were officered by a Northern fanatic"—Bradford was actually a Tennesseean—"who urged them to do this dastardly deed," namely to open fire on the Confederates after the garrison had ostensibly surrendered, thus giving Forrest's men no choice "but to defend themselves, which they did, and they always did."[49]

Barteau was especially adamant about the garrison returning fire as they fled. "They made a wild, crazy, scattering fight. They acted like a crowd of drunken men. They would at one moment yield and throw down their guns," he wrote, "and then would rush again to arms, seize their guns and renew the fire. If one squad was left as prisoners," Barteau recalled twenty years later, "it was soon discovered that they could not be trusted as having surrendered, for taking the first opportunity they would break loose again and engage in the contest." "Many of them had thrown down their arms while running and seemed desirous to surrender," wrote Fort, "while many others had carried their guns with them and were loading and firing back up the bluff at us with a desperation which seemed worse than senseless. We could only stand there and fire until the last man of them was ready to surrender." And yet, "no one has found a good way to surrender," wrote one of Forrest's defenders, "while your fellow soldiers are shooting at the men from whom you are begging for mercy."[50]

Citing an interview with Forrest, Mercer Otey would claim that as the rebels "unsuspectingly entered the works, they were met by a galling fire poured into them by the fleeing Federals, who were protecting themselves in the shelter afforded by the river bank, while the gunboat opened a brisk broadside on our troops. They were maddened by such perfidy. Many of the enemy were plainly visible trying to pack their boxes of ammunition to the river bank, hoping there to continue the fight. It so exasperated our men that they drove the enemy into the river, and shot them as they tried to gain the gunboat." Forrest would give a similar account to an adoring interviewer, claiming that "the negroes brought it all upon themselves; that after the white flag had been raised, and while it was flying, they continued to shoot his men, who, much infuriated, shot the negroes." He boasted that it had "created a great terror of him ever after among the negro troops," and that for the rest of his war he employed the example of Fort Pillow "as a caution against resistance, and an incentive to prompt surrender when dealing with the commanders of negro troops."[51]

Chalmers claimed that the retreating Federals who returned fire were "the only men shot after the flag was hauled down." But the preponderance of the evidence suggests a furious, prolonged, and indiscriminate fire that Chalmers himself may have encouraged. As the garrison skidded down the bluff "the detachment from Barteau on the right and the three companies on the left poured into them an enfilading and deadly fire, at a distance of 40 to 100 yards," recalled Anderson, "while the line of attackers reached the brow and mowed down their rear."[52]

From Barteau's position on the slope of the bluff north of the bastion, "the yells of our troops as they mounted the parapets could be plainly heard above the din and rattle of musketry, and in a moment more the whole force of the garrison came rushing down the bluff toward the water with arms in hand, but only to fall thick and fast from the short range fire of the detachment temporarily under my command, which threw them into unutterable dismay and confusion." According to Brigham, however, the garrison threw down its arms "as soon as the Confederates got into the fort," many of them exclaiming, "We surrender." "We were followed closely and fiercely by the advancing rebel forces," Revelle recalled, "their fire never ceasing at all. Our men had given signals themselves that they surrendered, many of them throwing up their hands to show they were unarmed and submitted to overwhelming odds."[53]

South of the ravine, Anderson's sharpshooters swung their sights from the closed portholes of the *New Era* up the riverfront to the Federals fleeing down the bluff, becoming, in effect, an execution squad. "Upon them," wrote Anderson, "we opened a destructive fire." "Thus being exposed to a fire from both flanks, as well as rear," wrote Hancock, "their ranks were fearfully thinned as they fled down that bluff toward the river."[54]

"The bigger portion of the darkeys," Benton testified, "jumped down the bank towards the Mississippi river, without any arms at all." Bradford apparently expected that once his men had cleared the fort, the *New Era* would open fire on the rebels with canister and advance to the riverfront to tow the survivors away in the two coal barges cabled by the wharf. "They had been promised," wrote Wyeth, "aid from the gunboat and safety from pursuit when once below the crest of the riverbank." But contrary to what Forrest would later tell Mercer Otey, Marshall, apparently afraid he would hit his own men, never opened fire, leaving the major and his men trapped along the river's edge like ducks in a shooting gallery. "Finding that the succor which they had been promised from the gunboat was not rendered nor at hand," wrote Hancock, "they were greatly bewildered."[55]

Anderson boasted that his command "did the most destructive as well as the very last firing done at Fort Pillow," but excused his men's excesses because from their position they could not see which flag was flying over the parapet. However, they could see the white makeshift flags of truce—from torn white shirts to handkerchiefs—that the garrison desperately waved along the riverbank, and the red hospital flags tied all around Fitch's field hospital, which should have protected the morning's wounded from further harm.[56]

"Hundreds were killed in the water endeavoring to escape," wrote a rebel witness. "Others rushed to the passage between the fort and the river for the purpose of passing down the river towards Memphis." But Anderson's men "opened fire upon them, and the enemy rushed upon a coal barge and endeavored to push it off; but a concentrated fire from our whole column, soon put an end to this experiment." After running down the bluff, Sergeant Henry Weaver of 6/C jumped into the water "and hid myself between the bank and the coal barge. They were shooting the negroes over my head all the time, and they were falling off into the water." One rebel estimated that "several hundred were shot in this boat" and along Coal Creek "while endeavoring to escape." The number of Federals in the water "was so great," he wrote, "that they resembled a drove of hogs swimming across the stream. But not a man escaped in this way. The head above the water was a beautiful mark for the trusty rifle of our unerring marksmen," and "the Mississippi River was crimsoned with the red blood of the flying foe."[57]

Anderson's "furious and fatal" volleys sent the panic-stricken garrison rushing "wildly along the face of the bluff up the river, thinking that way was open for escape." But as they reached "the upper limit of the fort, the detachment from Barteau's regiment stationed opposite the mouth of Cold Creek ravine opened upon the fugitives another volley which stopped their flight in this direction, and turned them like frightened sheep once more back in the direction they had first taken when they sought safety beneath the bank." Together Anderson and Barteau "cut off all effective retreat." Anderson's men "employed themselves," wrote two Union lieutenants, "in shooting down the negro troops as fast as they made their appearance."[58]

RIVER RUN RED
MASSACRE

4:30 p.m., April 12, 1864

SETTING ASIDE THE REBELS' TRUCE VIOLATIONS, THE ASSAULT ON FORT Pillow thus far had been marked by extraordinary courage on both sides. The horrors of the engagement had for the most part been the horrors attendant on armed combat. But as the surrendering Federals threw down their weapons, waved their white flags, and begged the rebels for mercy, the attack on Fort Pillow mutated into murder.

After several volleys from Anderson's men to the south, Bell's from the bluff, and Barteau's from the north, the rebels rampaged along the river, Daniel Stamps testified, shouting to one another that "it was General Forrest's orders to them to shoot us and give us no quarter at all." As they closed in around the bottom of the bluff, Stamps tried to flee up the hill, but "just as I started, I was shot in the thigh."[1]

Hiding behind a log by the river, James Walls of 13/E heard a cacophony of rebel yells over the roar and crackle of gunfire.

"Shoot him, shoot him!"

"Yonder goes one!"

"Kill him, kill him!"

"The bullets were flying so thick" that Walls threw down his arms and surrendered. One of the rebels held his fire, at least at first, "but as I turned around he or some other one shot me," the ball striking his buttock and passing upward to emerge from under his rib cage.

Walls turned to a rebel officer and "begged him not to let them shoot me again, and he said they would not. One man, after he was shot down, was shot again. After I was shot down, the man I surrendered to went around the tree I was against" and shot a horse that was either too worn out or badly wounded to be of any use to the rebels.[2]

One of the Federals who admitted to carrying his gun and cartridge box down the bluff was Corporal William Dickey of the 13th, who hid with a buddy behind a stump. Too terrified to fire his musket, he watched a single rebel "shoot as many as four negroes just as fast as he could load his gun and shoot." When the rebel trooper turned in his direction, "I begged him not to shoot me" and "gave him my gun."

The trooper took Dickey's caps as well. "I want them to kill niggers," he said.[3]

"I begged him to let me go with him, as I would be exposed there."

"No," replied the rebel, "stay there."

A second rebel agreed to spare Dickey's life, but refused to take him into his protective custody. Instead, he "ordered me to stay with my wounded partner, who was lying in some brush. I crawled in the brush to him. He was suffering very much." Dickey loosened his partner's belt and placed his cartridge box under his head, but a group of rebels "under the hill spied us moving in the brush and ordered us to come out. My partner could not come out," but Dickey cautiously emerged. "They ordered me to come to them," and Dickey fell behind one of them, begging him not to shoot him. But he had gone no more than ten steps when the rebel he was following turned about and shot him in the stomach.[4]

Saber in hand—some said he had affixed a white handkerchief to his sword point—Major William Bradford had fled down the bluff and across the riverbank in his shirtsleeves. Stopping at the water's edge, he threw up both hands, "crying at the top of his voice that he surrendered."[5]

But the rebels replied that he "could not surrender" and "kept firing volley after volley at him." Still calling out that he surrendered, he kept backing into the water until it was up to his chin. He swam "some five or six Rods into the River," wrote Dr. Fitch, "and then turned and swam back to the shore. During this time there were thousands of shots fired at him"—others said fifty rounds—but somehow Bradford emerged from the water unscathed. Raising his hands high again, he ran up the ravine, again shouting, "I surrender! I surrender!" The rebels kept firing at him, but he seemed at least temporarily charmed, for not a single shot so much as grazed him.[6]

Several Confederate officers looked on, but "none of them ordered the firing to cease." It was only "when they found they could not hit him" that Forrest's men "allowed him to give himself up as a prisoner, and paroled him to the limits of the camp."[7]

A significant number of disarmed men were apparently shot down after capture as they obeyed rebel orders to climb the bluff and return to the fort.
The teamster Davy Harrison of 13/D had run down under the bluff and huddled with two other men "close under a log."

The rebels began to fire at everyone, black and white, killing one of Harrison's companions. Harrison threw up his hands and cried, "Don't shoot
me! I surrender!"

"Go on up the hill," a rebel commanded.

According to a reporter who interviewed him the next day, Harrison asked
the rebel to walk in front of him for fear "he would be shot by others." The
rebel told him to go along, but he had not proceeded more than a few steps
before he met another trooper who raised his pistol and aimed it at him.
Harrison begged the rebel not to fire, but, "paying no attention to his request," the trooper shot him first through the shoulder and a second time
through his leg.

"I fell," Harrison testified, "and, while I was undertaking to get up again,
I was hit in the body; and this arm that was hit fell over behind me." In fact,
the shot had shattered the head of his humerus, nearly amputating his arm.

As he lay bleeding, Harrison asked a passing rebel to share some water
from his canteen.

"Damn you," the rebel replied. "I have nothing for you fellows. You Tennesseeans pretend to be men, and you fight side by side with niggers. I have
nothing for you."

Another rebel approached with his pistol drawn "and asked if I had any
money. I told him I had a little, and he told me to give it to him," but Harrison "told him my shoulder was hurt, and he must take it himself. He turned
me over and took about $90 and my watch."[8]

Born in Arkansas, raised in Tennessee, Jack Shelton of 13/E was another
of the men who were shot while obeying their captors' command to march
back up the hill. Shot in the leg, he asked his assailants "if they did not respect prisoners of war."

"No," one of them answered, "we do not," then he raised his revolver
and "popped three or four caps in my face."[9]

Hardy Revelle was about halfway up the hill, "partially secreted in a
kind of ravine with Dr. Fitch," when he saw two white soldiers of the 13th
"standing behind a stump on which they had fixed a white handkerchief,
their hands thrown up. They asked for quarter. When they stood on their

feet they were exposed, and I saw them shot down by rebel soldiers and killed."

A rebel captain "then came where we were" and, threatening to "shoot their goddamn brains out" if they disobeyed, ordered "all the Federals—white and black—to move up the hill." Revelle and a number of surrendered men immediately began the steep climb. But as they ascended, Revelle saw about four "white men fall on both sides of me, who were shot down by rebel soldiers who were stationed upon the brow of the hill. We were at the time marching directly toward the men who fired upon us."

Nor were whites the only victims at this time. "I also saw negroes shot down with pistols in the hands of rebels. One was killed at my side. I saw another negro struck on the head with a saber by a rebel soldier. I suppose he was also killed. One more just in front of me was knocked down with the butt of a musket." Continuing to make his way up the hill, Revelle "expected each moment to meet my fate with the rest."[10]

One of the rest was Eli Falls of the 6th. As he and his comrades made their way up the trail, rebel soldiers apparently sprayed them with bullets. "I was the second man shot while in the hands of the rebel officers," Falls recalled, "obeying their commands while marching up the hill." But he was by no means the last. Duncan Harding of 2/A was first shot in the arm and then ordered up the bluff, "and while they were marching me up the hill, they shot me again through the thigh" as an officer shouted, "Kill the goddamn nigger!"[11]

Daniel Tyler of the 2nd had managed to avoid injury during the battle, but after he surrendered, a rebel private struck him down with the butt of his carbine and, as he lay on the muddy ground, jabbed him in the eye with the tip of the barrel.

Tyler was soon ordered to get to his feet and join his fellow prisoners as they marched back up the hill to the fort. As he trudged along with the others, another rebel private approached with his musket raised as if to fire.

Tyler instinctively reached out to push the muzzle aside.[12]

"Whose gun are you holding?" the rebel demanded to know.

"Nobody's," Tyler replied.

The rebel apparently took his reply as an insult. "Goddamn you," he declared. "I will shoot you."

He pulled the trigger, striking Tyler in the shoulder, and as Tyler recoiled, releasing the rifle barrel, a second rebel shot him as well. Stunned, blinded, Tyler tumbled back down the bluff to where his comrades' corpses lay "all round like hogs."[13]

"The officers all being killed or wounded," Sandy Addison of 6/A testified, "the white flag was raised by one of the colored men, but they kept firing upon us. I do not know how many, but a great many were killed under the white flag." Corporal Jerry Stewart of the 6th and Sergeant Manuel Underwood of the 2nd had raised a white flag together as they fled to the riverbank, "but the enemy paid no attention. A rebel officer rode up to the bank," a comrade testified, "and said that General Forrest ordered every damned nigger to be shot down. So the enemy kept on firing on our defenseless men."[14]

The photographer Charley Robinson was luckier in his ascension. From his hiding place behind a large log he "could see our poor fellows bleeding" and hear them cry, "I surrender." But they surrendered in vain, for the rebels "now ran down the bank and, putting their revolvers to their heads, would blow out their brains or lift them up on bayonets and throw them headlong into the river below." One of Chalmers's men discovered Robinson and his companion, a soldier from 13/C. "He pulled out his revolver and shot the soldier right in the head," Robinson wrote, "scattering the blood & brains [on] my face."

Pressing his revolver against Robinson's chest, he said, "You'll fight with the niggers again will you, you damned Yankee?" and pulled the trigger. But in shooting Robinson's companion, he had used up his last round, and the revolver did not fire.

"Come up the hill," he commanded, and Robinson "went up with him in front of me. When I got near the top, the soldiers wanted to shoot the damned Yankee, but the fellow who took me told them no, that I was his property."[15]

At first "the fire seemed to slacken," Lieutenant Leaming testified, but the scene that soon followed "beggars all description." From 4:00 p.m. "until dark, and at intervals throughout the night, our men were shot down without mercy." The black troops suffered most. "The negroes ran down the hill towards the river, but the rebels kept shooting them as they were running" and

> shot some again after they had fallen; robbed and plundered them. After everything was all gone, after we had given up the fort entirely, the guns thrown away and the firing on our part stopped, they still kept up their murderous fire, more especially on the colored troops, I thought, although the white troops suffered a great deal. I know the colored troops had a great deal the worst of it.

Leaming testified that Forrest's officers, a few of whom had followed their men to the river, "seemed to hold themselves back" from restraining their men.[16]

―――――――

"Many of the white men," wrote Wyeth, "more intelligent than their colored comrades, threw themselves behind the logs, stumps, brush heaps, or into the gullies which they encountered in their flight, and thus saved themselves from the frightful mortality which befell the terror-stricken." But intelligence had nothing to do with it. Blacks tried to find refuge in the hollows under the bluff and the trenches along its slope, but some of the men of the 13th refused to share their hiding places with their black comrades. After Daniel Rankin of 13/C and two of his white comrades found a hiding place behind a stump, "some darkeys came there," Rankin recalled, but seeing that the rebels were singling out black troops and reckoning that "if they were not with us, we might get clear," he and his pals told the black soldiers "to go away."[17]

The artillerists' only hope, it seemed, was to swim across Coal Creek or the Mississippi itself, scramble across the sandbar, and squatter their way to the *New Era*. But such was the strength of the current and the ferocity of the gunfire that apparently not one soldier made it across. "The Mississippi's current, swollen by the spring rain, was strong enough along the riverfront to carry away weak or wounded swimmers, and even the wide mouth of Coal Creek was running fast and deep." Fleeing up Coal Creek, hoping to lose themselves in the woods on Craighead Point, some black artillerists were apparently sucked into the stream's muddy bed or drowned in the backwater. Joseph Ray ran "with a whole lot of the others into the Mississippi River and was drowned." Charles Key of 2/D "saw one man start up the bank after he was shot in the arm, and then a fellow knocked him back into the river with his carbine, and then shot him."[18]

"They shot them down like beeves, in every direction," observed Dr. Underwood from the *New Era*. "I think I saw about 200 run down next to the water, and some of them into the water, and they shot them until I did not see a man standing." "I don't suppose one of them got more than 30 yards into the river before they were shot," recalled James McCoy, who watched with Underwood from the gunboat. "The bullets rained as thick in the water as you ever saw a hail-storm."[19]

On this point both sides agreed. Thomas Berry of the 9th Texas Cavalry recalled that Forrest's men fired so many shots into the river that the water "seemed to seethe and boil with bullets." "Numbers of the garrison were drowned," wrote James Dinkins. "Those who reached the river never stopped, but plunged in. They were frightened out of all reason." Wyeth would describe them as "wild with fright or frenzied by liquor or the wounds they had received." "The actual loss of life will perhaps never be known," Forrest himself reported. "There was in the fort a large number of citizens who had fled there to escape the conscript law. Most of these ran into the river and were drowned."[20]

"We surrender!" the civilian James Brigham heard many of the men exclaim. He said he could not "recount but a small part of the barbarities I saw on that fatal day, when hundreds of loyal soldiers were murdered in cold blood." The black troops "were shot as fast as they were seen," wrote Corporal William Dickey of 13/D. "One poor fellow was shot as he reached the bank of the river. They ran down and hauled him out. He got on his hands and knees, and was crawling along, when a secesh soldier put his revolver to his head, and blew his brains out."[21]

John Haskins of 6/B was shot in the flesh of his left arm as he threw down his musket, ran southward along the bank of the Mississippi, and flung himself into the stream. Six or seven more men, apparently unable to swim, hesitated to follow him into the water and were picked off by the sharpshooters on the bluff above. His wound was minor but bled profusely, and he was able to convince the rebel soldier who dragged him back onto the bank to rifle his pockets that he was dead or dying. But when it seemed safe to move about, Haskins climbed into a coal boat and hid there until nightfall.[22]

"KILL THE LAST DAMN ONE"
BRADFORD'S BATTALION

4:00 p.m.–7:00 p.m., April 12, 1864

PALE, DARK-HAIRED, BLUE-EYED JACK SIMMONS AND HIS PAL JIM Meador were both in their twenties when they enlisted in 13/A. In August 1863, they had ridden together out of Paris, Tennessee, with Simmons's brother-in-law, Bill Albritton, evading the bands of rebel guerrillas that haunted the route to Paducah. It must have fallen to Meador to fill in his pals about life in the army; early in the war he had deserted from Barteau's 2nd Tennessee Cavalry, a Confederate unit from his native Henry County that, as the recently reorganized 22nd, was wreaking such havoc along the upper reaches of the riverbank. Lying wounded in the sand, Meador could hear a rebel officer give a command to his men. "Don't show the white men any more quarter than the negroes," he shouted, "because they are no better, and not so good, or they would not fight with the negroes."[1]

Meador watched as one rebel trooper forced a Union sergeant to "kneel down and ask for quarter," while another came up and snapped his pistol at him twice. In the end, the others "told him not to shoot him." Nevertheless, Meador "saw them shoot others when they were kneeling down."[2]

"Here in this melee," wrote Wyeth, "in the fire and excitement of the assault," the rebels "found opportunity and made excuse for bloody vengeance. No official surrender; the flag still flying; some of the Federals, no matter how few, still firing back; and they shot them down regardless of the cry for quarter."[3]

After the Battle of Shiloh, the survivors from the 47th Tennessee Infantry had been inducted into the 12th Tennessee Cavalry under the same Tyree H. Bell who now commanded the center of the attack on Fort Pillow. But ten of them had deserted and eventually enlisted in Bradford's Battalion, where Bell's officers recognized them among the Homemade Yankees at Fort Pillow. Twenty-two-year-old John Scoby of Company B would be the only one of the ten to survive Bell's wrath that day, only to die of dysentery at Andersonville the following September.[4]

Bryant Johnson of 13/D had served in the Confederate army as a trooper in the 2nd Kentucky Mounted Infantry, another of the rebel regiments that had been captured at Fort Donelson and then paroled, only to wade into the carnage at Shiloh. Johnson deserted and returned to his farm in Gibson County. But in late 1863, rebel depredations had compelled him to borrow a horse from a neighbor, bid his wife and two children good-bye, and ride off to Union City to join the 13th. An old friend, Orderly Sergeant A. C. Foster of Forrest's Old Regiment, kept him out of harm's way. But neither Foster nor the ministrations of his comrade and fellow prisoner Doc Alexander could save his life at Andersonville, where he died that summer of scurvy and fever.[5]

Woody Cooksey of 13/A was in his thirties and the father of four children when his wife died in Paducah in June 1863. Placing his children in his brother's care, he was about to ride off to join Bradford's Battalion when his oldest daughter, Mary Jane, "called his attention to the fact, that he might never return, and that the ages of his children had never been set down." So Cooksey "got her bible & gave instruction to her" to write down their ages. Now, in the midst of the mayhem, he threw down his gun just outside the fort when a rebel shot him in the left thigh bone with three buckshot and a minié ball.

"Hand me up your money, you damned son of a bitch," his assailant commanded as Cooksey lay sprawled on the ground.

Cooksey outraged his attacker by replying that he had only four bits on him.

"I have a damned nigh notion," the rebel snarled, "to hit you in the head on account of staying here and fighting with the niggers."

Before he could make good on his threat, however, his attacker "heard a rally about the bank and went down" where the rebels were shooting Union soldiers "and throwing them in the river." Cooksey could not explain why he was shot, except that it appeared to him that the rebels intended to shoot "the balance" of the survivors.[6]

Jason Loudon of 13/B was "shot after I had surrendered, and while I had my hands up and was imploring them to show me mercy." He must have instinctively dropped his hand to protect his leg when the rebel shot him, because the bullet passed through his hand and into his thigh. As he crumpled over, another rebel struck him down with the butt of his carbine.

Loudon saw the rebels shoot six men after they had surrendered, including Virginia-born thirty-eight-year-old Commissary Sergeant Leonidas Gwaltney of 13/B, who had just handed his pistol over to the rebels and was throwing up his hands and begging for mercy when "they took his own revolver and shot him with its contents twice through the head, killing him instantly."[7]

Unanimously elected 13/E's first lieutenant and quartermaster, Cordy Revelle had nevertheless worked as a clerk for a local cotton trader while his brother Hardy clerked for one of the post's dry goods merchants. In this capacity Cordy had probably acted as a bagman for the various Union officers who profited from the cotton trade at Fort Pillow. "I knew him well," recalled Eli Cothel of 6/B. "I worked with him. He was a small fellow, weak and puny." From his refuge by the river, Cothel watched as the rebels disarmed Revelle, cursed him, and shot him through the head.[8]

The next morning a white man would report that the rebels had burned Revelle to death, but according to his comrades he was shot. A somewhat likelier victim of burning was Captain John Akerstrom of 13/A, whose fate was the subject of persistent rumors and speculation. Jack Ray of 13/B, who was beside Akerstrom when he was shot in the forehead, saw him fall on his face "about two minutes after the flag of truce went back." Ray thought he had been killed, "but later heard he was only wounded." Eli Carlton testified that he saw Akerstrom walking in rebel custody, and his captors declaring, "Here is one of our men. Let's take him up and fix him."[9]

As the rebels began to finish off the white soldiers who had remained in the fort, twenty-year-old Sergeant Billy Walker of 13/D and his comrades "ran down under the hill." But the rebels " followed us up" and "just shot us down without showing us any quarter at all."

He heard one soldier declare that a general whose name Walker could not quite make out (he guessed it was Chalmers) had commanded them to "shoot every one of us, and take no prisoners," whereupon "they shot us down." Walker handed his money over to a rebel private and begged for his life, but his captor raised his pistol and fired at least three times, hitting Walker's arm and neck, grazing his face, and slicing open his eye, while shouting, "Take that, you 'negro equality.'"

Walker testified that he watched as the rebels began to shoot everyone around him: blacks first, he said, then whites. He saw "some knock them over the heads with muskets, and some stick sabers into them."

"They were shooting continually," testified the sharpshooting Daniel Stamps of 13/E, whose bugler brother would be captured that day. "I saw them shooting the white men there who were on their knees, holding up their hands to them." He saw them spare one man whom they forced to "get down on his knees and beg of them."[10]

Over the din, Stamps could just make out the voice of a rebel officer shouting a command from the rim of the bluff. Turning to one of the rebels guarding him, Stamps asked what the officer was saying.

"Kill the last damn one of them," replied the soldier, who shouted back up to the officer that Stamps and his comrades had surrendered and therefore "must not be shot."

"Crazy with rage that he had not been obeyed," the officer called back, "I tell you to kill the last God damned one of them," and galloped off.

Shot in the hip, James Taylor heard the same officer shouting from the bluff. "Kill them, God damn them," he bellowed. "It is General Forrest's orders."[11]

Wiley Robinson of 13/A was not quite eighteen years old at the time of the attack, but had already served, however briefly, in two other Union regiments. He probably received more wounds that day than any other survivor from Bradford's Battalion: once in the hand during the battle, and then five or six more times in various parts of his body after he had run down to the river and thrown down his gun. Bullets passed through his thigh and his ankle and one lodged in his left lung. Considering the extent of his injuries, his testimony two weeks later would be understandably brief. The rebels "swore at us," he said, "and then shot us." He saw more than one rebel officer ride past, commanding their men "to kill us all," and was shot the last time in the leg while he lay on the ground."[12]

Nineteen-year-old Ike Ledbetter of Lauderdale County, Tennessee, had enlisted at Bradford's Fort Pillow recruiting station. He must have been a young man of considerable promise if doubtful allegiance, for he had already served as a second lieutenant in the 3rd (Lillard's) Tennessee Mounted Infantry (CSA). He resigned early in the war, ostensibly to join the East Tennesseean 5th Tennessee Cavalry (CSA), but he deserted instead, returning home to his farm to get married. Either to protect himself from his former comrades or escape his new bride, he had joined Company E of Bradford's Battalion in February.

Private Ledbetter claimed he saw about twenty of his comrades "hold up their hands and cry to them not to shoot, but they shot them just the same." Ledbetter himself was shot twice: the first ball "slightly grazed my head," apparently just before he dislocated his elbow by flinging himself off the rim of the bluff. But as he lay by the river, gripping his arm, a second shot struck him in the right side, exiting his left hip.

His assailant skidded after him down the bluff "and finding I was not dead, he cursed me," and "was fixing to shoot me again" with his revolver when another rebel "told him not to," whereupon "they took everything I had, even to my pocket-knife."[13]

Among the men of the 13th killed that afternoon were the former slave overseer Neal Clark; the already badly injured Andrew Glass, an apparently hapless father of twin boys who in 1863 had been run over by a rolling log, accidentally shot by a comrade, and infected with syphilis; Daniel Fields of 13/B, who was in his thirties and the father of four children; and nineteen-year-old Robert McKenzie of Coffee County, Tennessee, who would take two agonizing days to die from a shot in the bowels.[14]

"Goddamn 'em," Nathan Fulks of 13/D heard the rebels shout. "Kill 'em! Kill 'em!"

Fulks threw down his gun. "I have surrendered," he declared, handing them his cartridge box. "Don't shoot me!"

They did shoot Fulks, however, "and hit just about where the shoe comes up on my leg."

Hopping on his good foot, Fulks begged them not to shoot him again, but one of them raised his gun and took aim at his other leg.

"God damn you," he declared, "you fight with the niggers, and we will kill the last one of you!"

The rebel fired, fracturing both of the bones in his thigh, and Fulks crumpled to the ground. Another of the rebels immediately "set out to shoot me again," but one of his Confederate comrades interceded, saying, "Don't shoot the white fellows anymore."[15]

BLACK FLAG
6TH USCHA AND 2ND USCLA
4:00 p.m.–6:00 p.m., April 12, 1864

THE FEW SURVIVING WHITE OFFICERS OF THE BLACK ARTILLERY REGI-
ments told much the same story. Though the rebels killed a number of
wounded black artillerists at Dr. Fitch's makeshift hospital and had threatened to kill any white officer of black troops they came upon, they spared
Captain Charles Epeneter and his lieutenant, Peter Bischoff of 6/A, as
Epeneter lay with his shattered forehead bound in a bloody rag, and Second
Lieutenant Tom McClure of 6/C, whose gun-shot arm was encased in a roll
of bark his men had peeled for him from a nearby stump. Though First
Lieutenant Alexander Hunter (2/F) tried to escape up Coal Creek, he too
was captured, not killed. Second Lieutenant Daniel Van Horn of 6/D was
only slightly wounded and, though captured, slipped away by donning civilian clothes and ducking into the woods.[1]

Captain Deloz Carson of 6/D, who had spent one hundred dollars of his
own money to recruit his company, was not so fortunate. "I heard some of
the enemy ask him if he belonged to a nigger regiment," recalled Frank
Hogan. "He told them he did. They asked him how he came here. He told
them he was detailed there. Then they told him *they* would give him a detail," whereupon a rebel first lieutenant shot him dead: "a prisoner without
arms."[2]

Emerging from the river, Sergeant Henry Weaver of 6/C surrendered to
a rebel, begging him not to shoot. "We don't shoot white men," the rebel
replied. "But what in hell are you here fighting with the damned nigger for?"[3]

"I soon got away from him," Weaver testified, "for he was too intent on
murder to mind me." But Weaver had gone only a few steps "when another
rebel met me and demanded my greenbacks, and after robbing me of every-

thing but my clothes," left Weaver "as not worthy of his further notice." Some men were "shot down so close to me," recalled Weaver, "that they would nearly fall on me."[4]

A portion of his ankle carried off by a minié ball after the rebels stormed the parapet, Sergeant Wilbur Gaylord of 6/B had tumbled down the bluff and lay on the sandy bank. "One rebel noticed that I was alive, shot at me again and missed me," Gaylord testified. "I told him I was wounded, and that I would surrender, when a Texas ranger stepped up and took me prisoner." Led back to the fort, Gaylord saw the rebels "shoot down three black men, who were begging for their life, and who had surrendered."[5]

The slaughter of black troops continued long after the rebels had begun to spare the whites. "After I surrendered I did not go down the hill," testified Private Emanuel Nichols of 6/B; nevertheless, a rebel shot him under the ear, knocking him to the ground. "If he don't shoot me any more," Nichols remembered thinking, "this won't hurt me."

"One of their officers came along and hallooed, 'Forrest says, no quarter! no quarter!' and the next one hallooed, 'Black flag! Black flag!'"

His comrade Alfred Coleman recalled hearing the soldiers of the 2nd Missouri Cavalry say they had sworn to "show no quarter to colored troops, nor to any of the officers with them, but would kill them all." Coleman lay near the fort "under a white-oak log" and therefore "could not see a great way." Nevertheless, he did see two men force one wounded white cavalryman—probably Nathan Fulks—"to stand up on one leg," and then shoot him down. He claimed that he saw a single Missouri captain shoot "six colored men himself, with a revolver."[6]

A rebel private found Alexander Nason of 6/C hiding by a log, ordered him to his feet, and as he stood before him, shot him in the head.[7]

The rebels gave "but little" quarter, wrote Achilles Clark of Forrest's 20th Tennessee. "The slaughter was awful. Words cannot describe the scene. The poor deluded negros would run up to our men, fall upon their knees, and, with uplifted hands, scream for mercy. But they were ordered to their feet and then shot down."[8]

Two rebels spotted Arthur Edmonds of 6/C hiding behind a log near the fort. "I asked them not to shoot me," Edmonds recalled. But one of them squatted down beside him with his pistol drawn.

"God damn you," he snarled. "You are fighting against your master."

The two rebels shot him three times, and a half hour later, as Edmonds lay bleeding, a lieutenant rode up to him and reined his horse to a halt. "You goddamn nigger," he exclaimed, raising his pistol. A rebel captain standing nearby commanded him not to shoot, but the lieutenant fired anyway, grazing Edmonds's right temple before spurring his horse away.[9]

George Shaw may have run into the same rebel. When he got within ten feet of the river he heard a trooper curse him. "Damn you," he said, "what are you doing here?"

"Please," Shaw begged, "don't shoot me."

"Damn you," he said, "you are fighting against your master."

"He raised his gun and fired, and the bullet went into my mouth and out the back part of my head. They threw me into the river," he testified, where he somehow "swam around and hung on there in the water until night."

As he squattered through the shallows, Shaw came within ten feet of three teenage contraband boys struggling "in the water, with their heads out. They could not swim." The boys begged for mercy, but the rebels shot each of them in the forehead. "They were not soldiers," he said, "but contraband boys, helping us on the breast works."

"Boys, I will have you arrested," a rebel officer snapped, "if you don't quit killing them boys."

"Damn it," replied another, "let them go on; it isn't our law to take any niggers prisoner. Kill every one of them."[10]

As John F. Ray of 13/B ran down the bluff, he saw "12 white soldiers and perhaps 30 negroes shot down after surrender and while begging for mercy." Ray himself was shot in the back of the knee after he had thrown down his weapon. Crumpling to the ground, he "saw a small negro boy" of about eight years of age seated on a horse behind a rebel lieutenant.

Suddenly an officer with a star on his "long gray coat" trotted up to the lieutenant in a rage. "Take that God-damned nigger down and shoot him," he commanded.

The lieutenant protested that the boy was "nothing more than a child."

"Damn the difference," replied the officer. "Take him down and shoot him, or I'll shoot you instead."

Whereupon the lieutenant duly dropped the boy to the ground and shot him dead.[11]

Joe Key of 6/A sometimes called himself Joseph Jarrett, after his original owners, the Barrett family of Virginia. Before the war, he had been transported to Lauderdale County, Alabama, where he became one of the 130 slaves of William Henry Keys, a spectacularly wealthy planter and gun maker whose plantation occupied a fertile tract known as the Reserve. Joe had married a stout and resourceful slave named Clara who, under circumstances she would not discuss, had already borne a child by another man.[12]

Married by an elderly slave minister named Jerry Key, Key and Clara lived happily as man and wife. Clara bore three sons and two daughters and was pregnant with a sixth child when a Yankee detachment passed by their owner's plantation in August 1862. Camping by the Tennessee River, opposite the Key place, the Yankees began to ferry across to gather up "all the colored men they could." "All of us children stood around and hollered and cried," recalled his son Taylor. "I don't know whether they were compelled to go or not, but I know that all the able-bodied negroes on the place did go with the Yankees that day." "The Union soldiers came through and told us we 'had to go,'" recalled a fellow slave named Jesse Smith, "and we all saddled up and went together."

"A good many of the men had their wives with them," recalled Key's comrade, Henry Garner, "and some married after they joined the regiment." When Joe's regiment left for Corinth, he begged Clara to join him, but she had to remain behind to care for their newborn daughter, Alice Virginia. For the rest of what little life remained to him, Joe Key pined for his family. "I saw Joe nearly every day while he was at Corinth," Jesse Smith recalled. "He did not marry or take up with any woman. He never noticed a woman at all, but was concerned about his wife and children." Now he lay dead upon the riverbank.[13]

To the charge that African American women and children were killed after the surrender, Forrest's defenders answered that all of the contrabands had been evacuated by the *New Era* that morning. But the impromptu evacuation was carried out while the battle was already under way, and it is certain that, as at Paducah, not every woman and child made it to the gunboat in time to steam to safety on the bar. After the battle, Forrest's officers would themselves report taking black women and children captive at Fort Pillow, and since the rebels never reached the refugees stranded on the bar, they must have been captured around the fort.[14]

Several straggling and terrified women and children could have sought refuge behind the parapets, under the bluff, or, like Benton's "Yellow woman," in one of the shelters in town. Some soldiers' wives may have decided to stay by their husbands, or to nurse their ailing menfolk in the hospital tents. Edward Benton would assert that the rebels captured his servant woman and executed two or three of the hands who had followed him into Booth's bastion, including the "boy" who had awakened him that morning and alerted him to the attack.[15]

White and black survivors testified to the killing of women and children. William F. Mays of 13/B recalled watching a rebel walk up to "two negro women and three little children."

"Yes," he said, "God damn you. You thought you were free, did you?" He shot them all with his carbine, and all of them fell but "one little fellow" whom he knocked "in the head with the breech of his gun." James Lewis of 6/C claimed he also saw "two women shot by the river bank and their bodies thrown into the river after the place was taken." And his comrade Thomas Addison knew the names of two officers' errand boys—Dave and Anderson—who had stuck by their employers during the battle. Though he heard but did not see the rebels shoot them down, he later watched them tote the boys' corpses up the bluff for burial "because they were small."[16]

After the rebels captured Sergeant Jerry Stewart of 6/A, First Lieutenant J. J. Eubanks of McCulloch's 2nd Missouri Cavalry "told me to tell him if there were any nigger officers taken prisoners, and to point them out to him." Knowing what would befall them if he did, however, Stewart claimed he "did not know any." In their frustration, the rebels confronted a civilian named Alexander and asked him where he belonged. "He told them he was a sutler," Stewart remembered. "They then told him he was no better than the rest, and they shot him." At one point Stewart heard one of Forrest's lieutenants brag that he had just put five balls into the body of a Federal who was trying to escape.[17]

At forty years of age, burly Tom Addison of South Carolina was apparently the oldest man in Company C of the 6th USCHA. Born in South Carolina, he had been taken to Mississippi in 1843 when he was nineteen years old, but more than twenty years of hard use had given him the grizzled, hangdog appearance of an old man. During the siege that morning, a minié ball grazed his face, but he received his most terrible wound after he ran to the river, when a rebel fired his pistol from four or five paces, sending a ball smashing through his nose, destroying his right eye, and shattering every bone in the right side of his face. Addison collapsed to the ground in shock, blinded by blood, whereupon a rebel "came along and turned me over."[18]

"God damn his old soul," the rebel remarked to a comrade as he snatched money from Addison's pockets. "He is sure dead now. He is a big, old, fat fellow," the soldier declared, and proceeded to the next victim. For two hours,

Addison played possum, listening as the rebels shot down wounded soldiers and young officers' servants all around him. "They shot a great many that evening," he testified. "I heard them say, 'Turn around so that I can shoot you good,' and then I heard them fire."[19]

Sherry Blain and George Houston of 6/D were two "of the few who escaped by hiding under a washed-out stump." According to Houston, as the slaughter began, the two comrades had "just schemed around and got away." Their buddy Wesley McDowell tried to squeeze under the stump with them, but the rebels "spied him and killed him." From their hiding place, Blain and Houston heard a rebel officer ride up and declare that General Forrest had "ordered every damned nigger to be shot down." Among the wounded was Blain's brother Aaron. After throwing down his arms and surrendering, Aaron was shot through both legs by a rebel with a carbine who declared, as Aaron fell, that "they were going to kill us all." Though he somehow managed to avoid further injury, Aaron saw the rebels shoot two men as they attempted to swim away, and kill a wounded man that evening while holding him up by the arms.[20]

Sandy Cole of 6/D testified that a rebel private shot him twice as he retreated down the bluff, first in the arm and then in the thigh. But he managed to scramble out into the shallows and hide behind some brush, from which vantage point he saw about seven of his comrades shot "right through the head." Left by the rebels for dead, Cole's comrade Nathan Hunter lay under the bluff. The rebels rifled his pockets, pulled his boots from his feet, rolled him over, and finally pronounced him "killed." The rebels "shot down a whole parcel along with me," Hunter testified. "Their bodies were lying there along the river bank the next morning. They kicked some of them into the river after they were shot dead."[21]

Alexander Nason was a twenty-year-old Mississippi slave who had adopted the last name of his master, R. M. Nason of Grenada, Mississippi, when he joined the Union army. Born in South Carolina, he had been taken as a boy to Carroll County, Mississippi, by an aspiring planter named Nathan Koon, from whom he ran away with at least two fellow slaves to join Company C of the 2nd USCLA.

After running under the bluff, Nason tried to hide behind a log with a number of his comrades, but the rebels found him "and told me to get up, and as I got up they shot me" along with "several other black men with me." Nason claimed to have seen the rebels throw several of his comrades into the river after they were "about dead." They declared that they were "allowed to kill every damned nigger in the fort—not spare one." The rebels shot Nason in the back of his head and neck and left him for dead.[22]

Benjamin Robinson of 6/D was one of only a few black soldiers who, by the time of the battle, had attained the rank of sergeant. He saw his friend and comrade Sandy Sherman "murdered in cold blood, while a prisoner." He saw the rebels "shoot two white men right by the side of me after they had laid their guns down," and a black man "clear over into the river." The rebels then "hallooed to me to come up the hill, and I came up."

"Give me your money, you damned nigger," one of them demanded.

Robinson told them he did not have any.

"Give me your money," the rebel repeated, "or I will blow your brains out."

"Then they told me to lie down, and I laid down." After they had "stripped everything off me," they dragged Robinson up the hill "a little piece, and laid me down flat on my stomach," where he lay "till night."[23]

After Jacob Thompson of Nelson's hotel surrendered, a rebel private raised a pistol to his head. "God damn you," he exclaimed, "I will shoot you, old friend," and fired. Thompson was holding his hand to his head, and the bullet shattered his thumb and lodged in his skull. "After they shot me through the hand and head," Thompson testified, "they beat up all this part of my head"—indicating one side of his head—"with the breech of their guns." The rebels "shot about fifty, white and black, right there," he said. Forrest's troopers "called them out like dogs" from their hiding places under the bluff "and shot them down. They would call out a white man and shoot him down, and call out a colored man and shoot him down: do it just as fast as they could make their guns go off."[24]

Struck over the head by a rebel musket, Armstrong Burgess of 6/B regained consciousness only to find himself in rebel custody, from which he would not escape until the following spring. Burgess would bear a deep dent in his skull from his wound at Fort Pillow. Oliver Scott of 6/D was remembered by his comrades as having been the "blackest complected man" in the regiment. The slave of Nathaniel Scott of Yalobusha County, Mississippi, he was about nineteen when he joined the Union army. He quickly fell ill, and was not able to return to active duty until January 1864. Perhaps because of his complexion, he was singled out for especially brutal treatment at Fort Pillow: "beaten and trampled in the action of that day by the rebel troops under Forrest." He was struck on the back of the head, near the base of his neck, with a carbine, and after receiving injuries to his left wrist and right elbow, "besides blows and bruises in other parts of the body," was left senseless on the ground.[25]

Rebels continued to skid down from the fort to fire short range into the

Federals dashing up and down the riverfront, jumping into the river, or cowering among the detritus of stumps and logs and brambles that bristled along the base of the bluff. But others contented themselves with standing along the rim of the bluff and sharpshooting, and Charley Robinson "heard them laugh & cheer when they were shooting our boys who had jumped into the river to keep from being cut to pieces."[26]

It apparently amused some of Forrest's men to shoot their victims in the leg, force them to stand, and then shoot them dead. "In many instances," testified Lieutenants Smith and Cleary, who interviewed the wounded the next day, "the men begged for life at the hands of the enemy, even on their knees. They were only made to stand upon their feet and then summarily shot down." James Walls of 13/E saw rebels "make lots of niggers stand up, and then they shot them down like hogs." Alfred Coleman of 6/B "saw them take one of the Tennessee cavalry, who was wounded in one leg, so that he could not stand on it. Two men took him, and made him stand up on one leg, and then shot him down."[27]

Dr. Fitch's hospital became the target of some of the rebels' most craven attacks. "A short distance from me," wrote John Shelton of 13/E, "and within view, a number of our wounded had been placed in an area marked off by red flags," near where "Major Booth's body lay." But as they passed these wounded men, the rebels "fired right into them and struck them with the butts of their muskets. The cries for mercy and groans which arose from the poor fellows were heartrending." According to Edward Benton, not only was "the hospital flag flying," but the wounded were "holding white handkerchiefs over their heads. I saw at least ten soldiers shot individually with white handkerchiefs over their heads. They tore off pieces of their shirts— anything they could get—for flags of truce and to denote surrender."[28]

Fitch and his steward, Thomas C. George of the 7th Kansas Cavalry (USA), stood together among the wounded soldiers. "They were assembled, as it were, with red flags stationed around them," Fitch recalled; nevertheless, he thought, the rebels killed all but two: Epeneter and Bischoff of 6/A. "The most of them were chopped to pieces with sabers."[29]

While lying in Fitch's hospital with a leg wound he had received that morning, Eli Carlton of 6/B was shot in the left shoulder and fell back, feigning death. "Do you fight with these God damned niggers?" a rebel asked one of the wounded whites lying nearby.

He replied that he did.

"I would not kill you," the rebel exclaimed, "but, God damn you, you fight with these damned niggers, and we will kill you," and he "blew his brains out of his head." Carlton counted eighteen men attacked in the hospital, and six more below him, by the river.[30]

Nor was Fitch's station under the bluff the only hospital the rebels attacked. There were three more: the artillerists' tents in the fort, the permanent hospital east of the parapet, and a row of four or five barracks south of the breastwork. Coming to after having been shot and cracked on the head, the civilian John Penwell joined a wounded artillery captain in one of several plank-floored "hospital tents" that the garrison's wounded would occupy. But they too became targets. Corporal Frank Hogan of 6/A watched a squad of rebels "kill three sick men that were lying helpless in their tents." John Kennedy of 2/D saw some rebels "go in a tent where Sergeant Miles and Private Lewis Ingraham, Peter Lake, and Andrew Smith—all of my Battery— were lying on their beds wounded, and kill them, shooting them through their heads and bodies—notwithstanding their cries for mercy."[31]

One of Wiley Robinson's comrades from 13/A was killed when the rebels "fired into the hospital," presumably meaning the original log and wattle hospital building southeast of the parapet. Survivors would tell Surgeon Horace Wardner of Mound City that "nearly all who were in the hospital were killed." Wardner himself treated "a young negro boy, probably sixteen years old, who was in the hospital there sick with fever, and unable to get away. The rebels entered the hospital, and with a saber hacked his head, no doubt with the intention of splitting it open. The boy put up his hand to protect his head, and they cut off one or two of his fingers." Unconscious when he reached Mound City, the boy would die of his wounds a week later.[32]

"I THOUGHT MY HEART WOULD BURST"
FORREST

4:00 p.m.–8:00 p.m., April 12, 1864

THE CONTINUING DEBATE OVER WHETHER THERE WAS A MASSACRE AT Fort Pillow is usually conducted piecemeal. Both sides seem to subscribe to the notion that it qualified as a massacre only if it can be proven that Forrest and his officers *intended* a massacre. Immediately after the battle, the North contrived to show that Forrest and his officers explicitly ordered their men to slaughter the garrison, while the South tried to demonstrate that any excesses were the inevitable consequences of the drunkenness, incompetence, and foolhardiness of the garrison itself.

"When the Confederates swarmed over the trenches that had been held defiantly for some eight hours in the face of numbers so manifestly superior," wrote Forrest's authorized biographers, "the garrison did not yield; did not lay down their arms, nor draw down their flag; but with a lamentable fatuity, the mass of them, with arms still in their hands, fled toward another position in which they were promised relief, and while on the way thither, returned the fire of their pursuers," though "not as a mass, but in instances so numerous as to render inevitable a fire upon their whole body, even had it not been the necessary consequence of their efforts to escape capture, whether with arms in their hands or not."[1]

Whether the massacre was premeditated or spontaneous does not address the more fundamental question of whether a massacre took place, which, going solely by the disproportion of Union to Confederate casualties after the fort was overrun, it certainly did, in every dictionary sense of the word. Forrest's defenders have argued that Bradford should have surrendered and thus spared his garrison what followed. But many rebels insisted that they would have slaughtered the garrison whether or not it surrendered.

Be that as it may, blaming the victims of the massacre for not taking Forrest's threat seriously cannot excuse the threat itself nor its protracted and anarchic execution.[2]

—————————

Forrest had watched proudly from the knoll as his men teemed over the breastworks and overwhelmed the garrison. One officer of the 22nd described how he "calmly surveyed his success, regarding it as a natural result of an encounter with the vandals." Bruised from his earlier fall, his horse limping along under him, it took the Wizard ten minutes to cover the broken ground that lay between his overlook and Fort Pillow's breastworks. After two horses had been shot out from under him and one wounded, his uniform must have been a bloody mess, which probably accounts for the rumor that he had been wounded during the siege.[3]

There was still firing going on when he reached the parapet: scattered fire within the fort itself, and a more intense barrage down by the river as the garrison's survivors ran and hid and begged for mercy. Barteau ordered the Union flag cut down, and Private John Doak Carr of the 22nd sliced the halyards. After the Stars and Stripes dropped to the ground, Carr presented the flag to Forrest. But according to John Nelson, "After I entered the fort, and after the United States flag had been taken down, the rebels held it up in their hands in the presence of their officers, and thus gave the rebels outside a chance to still continue their slaughter, and I did not notice that any rebel officer" forbade it.[4]

The strong river wind would have blown the gun smoke away almost as quickly as it issued from the barrels of his troopers' carbines and pistols, so Forrest would have been able to see what was transpiring below. But if he paid any attention it was fleeting, for his first concern was to prevent the *New Era* from firing on his men or moving in to retrieve the garrison's survivors. Captain Theodorick Bradford had just wigwagged, "We are hard pressed, and shall be overpowered" to the *New Era* when Forrest spotted him and ordered his men to "shoot that man with the black flag" (it was actually blue), whereupon the major's brother "was literally shot to pieces." The correspondent for the *Cairo News* painted a more heroic picture of Ted Bradford's death. "After he had surrendered," he wrote, "he was basely shot, but, having his revolver still at his side, he emptied it among a crowd of rebels, bringing three of the scoundrels to the ground." Be that as it may, Captain Bradford "was instantly riddled with bullets," Smith and Cleary were told, "nearly a full regiment having fired their pieces upon him."[5]

As several survivors climbed back up to the fort, the firing continued.

"When I re-entered the fort there was still some shooting going on," recalled the hotelier John Nelson, though he "heard a rebel officer tell a soldier not to kill any more of those negroes. He said that they would all be killed, anyway, when they were tried," presumably for servile insurrection.[6]

A week after the massacre, one of Forrest's own men, Sergeant Achilles Clark of the 20th Tennessee Cavalry, wrote home that he "with several others tried to stop the butchery and at one time had partially succeeded," but that "Gen. Forrest ordered them shot down like dogs, and the carnage continued" until "finally our men became sick of blood and the firing ceased." The Henry County native's account, written not for public consumption but for his sisters, both of them the wives of slaveholding Confederate soldiers, was one of two known accounts provided by a rebel participant who ranked lower than lieutenant. For all these reasons, and because it parallels so many of the Yankee accounts of Forrest's orders to "kill them all," his letter provides perhaps the most damaging evidence of Forrest's initial role as a proponent of massacre. The other account came from the scout Dewitt Clinton Fort, who wrote that "neither General Forrest nor any other general living could have checked the assault sooner than it was done, after having carried the works. So loud was the noise that General Forrest could not have been heard could he have given orders," which suggests that he didn't. "Gabriel's trumpet would not have been listened to had it sounded; for at least thirty minutes after we were in possession of the fort."[7]

Dr. Charles Fitch's encounter with Forrest provides some clues to Forrest's mood that evening. After most of his patients had been killed, Fitch "formed lock step with a Rebel Soldier who was leading a horse up the Bluff." As he reentered the fort, Fitch asked who was in command.

"General Forrest," another soldier replied.

"Where is he?" Fitch asked.

The soldier pointed some forty feet off. "That's him," he said, "sighting the Parrott gun on the gunboat."

Fitch scrambled up the bluff to where Forrest was assisting his artillerists as they prepared to fire the gun upriver.

"Are you General Forrest?" asked Fitch.

"Yes, sir," he replied. "What do you want?"

Fitch identified himself "as the surgeon of the Post, and asked protection from him that was due a prisoner."

"You are a surgeon of a damn Nigger Regiment," Forrest snarled back at him.

Fitch protested that he was the surgeon for the 13th.

Forrest glared at him. "You are a damn Tennessee Yankee, then."

Fitch replied that he was actually born in Massachusetts and lived in Iowa.

"What in hell are you down *here* for?" Forrest demanded to know. "I have a great mind to have you killed for being down here." Declaring that if only "the North West had staid at home, the war would have been over long ago," the Wizard finally ordered one of his men to take charge of Fitch "and see that I was not harmed, for which I thanked him."[8]

Thus Forrest extended his protection to a Union surgeon, but on the narrow grounds that he was not an officer of a colored regiment, a West Tennesseean, or a combatant, but an Iowa surgeon of a white regiment, and even then he expressed his "great mind" to kill him. But the real significance of this encounter lies in the fact that it occurred while the massacre was still going on, for though some Southern accounts claim that Forrest's first order of business was to stop the slaughter and lower the garrison's flag, he was obviously more concerned about the threat posed by the *New Era,* to whose fire his men were now dangerously exposed.

"'Twas but the work of an instant to turn the guns, so lately used for our destruction, upon the boat," an officer from the 22nd Tennessee reported. "Two shots were fired, and she headed off up the stream." This might suggest that Forrest did not linger long at the guns, but the anonymous officer was wrong on both counts. Lee H. Russ of Forrest's Escort, who had followed the general into the fort, recalled how he and two of his comrades had to grab the wheels of the Parrott gun, back it out of the embrasure, roll it to the rim of the bluff, and aim it at the gunboat. As one of his buddies loaded the charge, Russ rammed it home, only to discover that when the artillerists fled down the bluff they had taken their lanyards with them. So one of Russ's buddies, Sergeant Billy Matthews, unbreeched his carbine, "drew a cartridge and forced it, inverted, into the magazine and closed up the breech, thus cutting off the ball and furnishing him a blank charge." Stepping to one side, Matthews "deliberately fired his carbine into the touchhole of the cannon." It worked.[9]

It is possible that as Forrest headed for the Parrott gun he may have issued an order to halt the slaughter within the fort itself. But if so, it was ignored, and as he and his Escort fired at the *New Era,* Forrest did nothing to stop the slaughter below, much of which was being carried out in his name and well within his view. Fifteen years after the massacre, Dr. Fitch wrote a defense of Forrest, contending that the general had been so preoccupied with his captured artillery that Fitch "did not think" Forrest was aware of "what was going on under the bluffs." But his encounter with Forrest was brief and occurred well after the slaughter had begun, and the mercy he was shown by both Forrest and Chalmers, and for which he was deeply grateful, has little bearing on the fates of the black soldiers and Homegrown Yankees of the garrison.[10]

It took only five shots from the Parrott gun to dissuade James Marshall from attempting a rescue. He did not even fire back. As the shells fell "over and around us," Marshall ordered his men to get the New Era under way and move her upstream. At the sound of the guns, the rebels briefly paused in their "bloody work" to let out "a proud, exultant shout of victory" that skittered across the Mississippi's surface and echoed through the surrounding woods.[11]

"I had to leave," Marshall would plead, "because, if I came down here, the channel would force me to go around the point, and then, with the guns in the fort, they would sink me. Had I been below here at the time, I think I could have routed them out." But this begs the question of why he had not taken "the favorable position" in the first place. Marshall also explained that he refused to fire because "part of our own men were in the fort at the same time, and I should have killed them as well as the rebels." Once the New Era was out of range, Marshall reported, he at last "came to" beside the bar "and took on board women and children that had been driven from the fort," plus the Arkansas civilian Elvis Bevel, apparently the only man who had managed that afternoon to beat his way to the New Era.[12]

By this time Marshall's crew had expended most of the New Era's ammunition: 191 rounds of shell, 85 of shrapnel, and 6 of canister, plus 375 rifle and 96 revolver cartridges. Nevertheless, the rebels would denounce Marshall for having been "recreant at this critical moment" by failing to give the beleaguered garrison any support whatsoever. "No timely shower of canister came from its ports to drive back the Confederates, who swiftly and hotly followed after the escaping negroes and Tennesseans." "The naval commander," wrote Dinkins, "evidently was more concerned for the safety of himself and his craft" than the garrison's survival. "It would have been far better for his name and fame," concluded Anderson, "had he moved his vessel promptly into action, and perished in attempting to do as he promised," for Marshall's "abandonment of the garrison, first led and then left hundreds of his countrymen and comrades to a swift and sweeping destruction." As Sergeant William Winn, a passenger on the New Era, would testify, the gunboat "steamed up the river, out of range, leaving behind us a scene of cold-blooded murder too cruel and barbarous for the human mind to express."[13]

By now many of Forrest's men were in a frenzy. Down by the river they began to line up the survivors and the wounded and then shoot them down one after another. "Every man seemed to be crying for quarter," wrote Fitch, "the rebs paying no attention to their cries except to reply, 'If you Damn scoundrels surrender, fall into line!'" "There were over 20 who fell into the line, near the edge of the River, when there was a volley fired into them, bringing them all down but two. These men were all holding up their hands, pleading for quarter."[14]

Several witnesses testified that to this point only a few rebel officers had joined their men down by the river, where rebels stalked among the shallows, firing at men they suspected of playing possum, and beating the bushes for survivors. William Mays watched as two rebels dragged a black soldier from behind a hollow log. "One rebel held him by the foot," Mays wrote, "while another shot him."[15]

Aaron Fentis of 6/D saw the rebels shoot two whites and two blacks as they swam out into the river. "They took another man by the arm, and held him up, and shot him in the breast," after which another rebel held his carbine up against Fentis after he surrendered, and fired a bullet through both his legs.[16]

"At the river," wrote Tennessee's secessionist governor, Isham Harris, the rebels "kept up the fire, until the number was fearfully reduced, and until, as General Forrest states himself, he absolutely sickened to witness the slaughter. He ordered the firing to cease, and dispersed his staff along the lines with orders to that effect. It was next to impossible to effect an immediate cessation of the firing; the enemy themselves still fighting." Of far greater consequence—for by now just about every Federal had dropped his weapon—was the continual roar of pistols and carbines, the war cries of the rebels, and the screams and pleas of the garrison's survivors.[17]

"War means fighting," Forrest was said to have remarked, "and fighting means killing." Whether or not he ever put it that way exactly, he believed it, and in his battle furies never shrank from shedding blood. What he could not abide, however, was losing control. His authoritarian temperament—reinforced by his experience in Mississippi law enforcement, the slave trade, and now the military—could not tolerate disobedience. Nothing could incite his wrath like a soldier who defied his orders.

Once the *New Era* had steamed off and the shooting in the fort and along the river had subsided into sporadic gunfire, he left the Parrott gun and mounted his horse, declaring that it was time to gather the survivors together, bury the dead, collect whatever he could carry off—"six pieces of artillery and about three hundred and fifty stand of small arms," plus large stores of blankets, clothes, "crackers, cheese, lager beer and wines"—and burn whatever was left over. Jacob Thompson, the black cook from Nelson's hotel, apparently mistook Chalmers for Forrest as he rode along the riverbank, doing nothing to stop the massacre as his men called the Federals "out like dogs, and shot them down." But after Forrest ordered the firing to stop, wrote Wyeth, "Generals Chalmers and Bell, and Colonels McCulloch, Barteau, Wisdom, and Captain Anderson, who were immediately with their troops, enforced the order."[18]

Or tried to. Up to now Chalmers had been determined to teach "the mongrel garrison of blacks and renegades a lesson long to be remembered." But now he found it necessary to reverse engines and order a "strong guard" into the fort, "mounted in double file," to form a hollow square around the prisoners, "after which," wrote Dr. Fitch, "we were not molested." Chalmers was compelled to arrest one of his men for killing a Federal after Forrest ordered a cease-fire. But even this did not entirely stop the slaughter down below.[19]

"Both Generals Forrest and Chalmers," wrote Dinkins, "made every effort to stop the firing, and so energetic were their efforts that the firing ceased within fifteen minutes from the time of the termination of the truce, and all allegations to the contrary are malicious inventions." But there is much testimony to the contrary from other rebel participants who admired Forrest. A story would circulate that he actually shot one of his men for disobeying his command to cease firing.[20]

According to Thomas Berry of the 9th Texas Cavalry, Forrest had to employ "the flat of his sword on the back and shoulders of many of his own men before he finally put a stop to it." Berry claimed that two of Forrest's regiments turned on him "and threatened him with loaded guns if he should strike another man." Forrest had to send his aides to fetch his Escort and Old Regiment, "and threatened to shoot the first man that dared to fire another gun." A rebel officer told a correspondent for the *Cairo News* "that Gen. Forrest shot one of his men and cut another with his saber who were shooting down prisoners": a story Union captain John Young would confirm for a correspondent for the *Memphis Argus*.[21]

Three days after the battle, Surgeon Sam Caldwell of the 21st Tennessee Cavalry wrote home that "if General Forrest had not run between our men & the Yanks with his pistol and saber drawn, not a man would have been spared." But it was too little too late. By the time the Wizard intervened,

Caldwell reckoned that only about 170 of over 535 Federals, contrabands, and Unionist citizens had survived the slaughter. "The rest," he said, were "numbered with the dead."[22]

The Wizard's reasons for saving the remaining black troops were practical. Alfred Coleman of 6/B heard one of McCulloch's captains say that Forrest put a stop to the slaughter because he needed negroes "to help to haul the artillery." According to Coleman, about a dozen artillerists were put to work pulling the garrison's guns out from behind the breastworks, and "the secesh whip them as they were going out, just like they were horses." According to Private Major Williams of 6/B, after one of Forrest's officers said, "Kill all the niggers," a second officer replied, "No. Forrest says take them and carry them with him to wait upon him and cook for him, and put them in jail and send them to their masters."[23]

Forrest apparently stepped in to save several individual black soldiers whom he recognized from his slave-trading days. "General Forrest rode his horse over me three or four times," Manuel Nichols of 6/B testified. Nichols did not recognize Forrest "until I heard his men call his name. He said to some negro men that he knew them; that they had been in his nigger yard in Memphis." Forrest bragged to them that he had not been "worth five dollars when he started" but had "got rich trading in negroes."[24]

Nichols's comrade Sam Green testified that it was General Chalmers who had come in "with his Confederate troops" and begun

> to kill everybody: the well ones and the wounded. Someone struck me on the back of my head and knocked me senseless when I was in line with the prisoners. I finally came to myself and got up again, and I tell you, Boss, if it had not been for General Forrest coming up and ordering the Confederates to stop killing the prisoners, there would not one of us been alive today to claim a pension.[25]

His ears ringing and his arm bleeding, Willis Ligon of 6/C had almost made good his escape. "I was off to myself, trying to run away," when he was shot in the head "after the firing had ceased." The ball hit him in the back of his skull and exited his face. Willis guessed that of the twenty survivors from his regiment whom the rebels rounded up by the river, ten were wounded, and nearly all of those who had been killed had thrown down their arms.

"I would have been killed also," he recalled, but for Forrest, whom he had often served at his master's table and who now recognized him among the prisoners and gave him protection.[26]

Dinkins would go so far as to suggest that

any other people, under similar circumstances, would have killed every Negro in the fort. The feeling which a Southern man has for a negro is difficult for others to understand. He was regarded then as a piece of property, and when he did wrong was treated in the same way that a refractory horse or child would be. He was brought into subjection, after which there was no feeling of bitterness. Our men felt outraged, and killed every rascal as long as they resisted or ran. But, when they had been captured, they were as safe as they could have been anywhere.[27]

This was antebellum claptrap. But Forrest did describe black troops as "that ignorant, deluded, but unfortunate people" who had been tricked by the treacherous Yankees into fighting against their former masters, whereas he condemned the garrison's whites as deserters, traitors, rapists, and thieves. Despite Northern accusations to the contrary, Forrest may have been more inclined to save blacks than whites. He was certainly determined to teach them the terrible consequences of joining the Union army. But masters flogged their errant slaves; they rarely killed them. Besides, as a former slave trader he understood the value of black captives and would have regarded the artillerists' utter annihilation as a terrible waste of manpower.

Forrest was not the only Confederate to recognize former slaves among Fort Pillow's dead and wounded. The brothers Adam, Simon, and Essex Middleton, all of them privates in 6/C, had run away together from their secessionist master, Holland Middleton of Panola County, Mississippi. On the afternoon of April 12, Holland's oldest son, Captain William Green Middleton of the 18th Mississippi Cavalry, encountered Essex in the fort. Recognizing his master, Essex "threw down his gun" and surrendered. But by then Simon and Adam had already been killed; Middleton would come upon their corpses by the river. Their little brother reckoned that Captain Middleton himself had "helped kill them"; in any case, only a few months before he himself would be killed at Harrisburg, the captain returned Essex to slavery.[28]

Charles Macklin stood out among his comrades in 6/C. Over six feet tall and of a gingerbread complexion, from birth he sported a small patch of white hair near his temple. When Macklin was "very young," a man named Koon sold him away from his parents to a Carroll County, Mississippi, planter named Macklin whose name Charles adopted after he ran off in August 1863 and joined the Union army. Charles's uncle, Samuel Hughes, had gone off to war to cook for two Confederate brothers who rode with Forrest on this his second West Tennessee raid. Hughes had last seen his nephew on the the night he ran away from their master. By Forrest's order, "the negroes belonging with or attached to the various commands" were not to be permitted to remain with the wagon train, "nor at the front," but were "sent to the rear in charge of led horses." Consequently, they did not witness the slaughter by the river, only its aftermath. But that evening, Hughes was permitted to pick his way along the riverbank, where he was grieved to recognize his nephew's corpse by the patch of white hair above his ear.[29]

In 1844, a planter named John Meeks of McNairy County had celebrated his brother Orval's majority by purchasing a family of slaves from their grandparents and dividing them up between them. Though separated by ten arduous miles of hilly terrain, Frank Meeks and his parents, Lucinda and Lewis, would often visit. Their strong bond of "love and affection," wrote Frank's master John, "common from parent to child, and from child to parent, was plain to be seen," though John claimed to know "as much about Frank as I knew about my children," and recalled that "Frank lived with me like one of my children."

When asked whether Frank had ever contributed to his parents' support, his former owner took umbrage. "I don't suppose he did," he snapped. "And they didn't need it, for they were slaves themselves." Lucinda needed no support "further than she received from her owner" Orval, whom his brother described as a "good man."

Frank apparently did not share Master John's regard for his brother, for according to Frank's sister, while the Yankees were encamped at Corinth, he used to black the boots of Union officers every Sunday and bring his tips and snatches of dress goods and cooking utensils home to his mother. "I never saw him afterwards," wrote John Meeks, "but was frequently informed sometime afterwards that he belonged to the Federal army." Ever since joining the 6th USCHA, he had sent portions of his pay to his mother via his sister, who also worked for the Yankees, cooking and washing. Meeks was told that Frank was killed at Fort Pillow, where he was seen "lying among the Slain by one of my neighbor soldier boys who knew him well." According to James Lewis of 6/C, he was shot well after he had surrendered.[30]

However horrified Forrest was said to have been by his command's excesses, the Wizard's first pronouncement to his men that evening was not reproachful but proud, fond, boastful. "Just after the firing had ceased," wrote

Hancock, Forrest pointed back to the knoll from which he had issued his command to charge.

"When from my position on that hill I saw my men pouring over these breastworks," he declared, placing his hand over his chest, "it seemed that my heart would burst within me. Men," he continued over their shouts and cheers, "if you'll do as I say, I'll always lead you to victory. I've taken every place that the Federals occupied in West Tennessee and North Mississippi except Memphis," he boasted, "and, if they don't mind, I'll have that place too in less than six weeks. They killed two horses from under me today—a third was wounded—and knocked me to my knees a time or two." The Federals had "thought, by damn, they were going to get me, anyway." But he had gotten them instead.[31]

PLUNDER
FORT PILLOW

5:00 p.m. to Midnight, April 12, 1864

DURING THE MASSACRE, "SOME FEW OF THE REBEL OFFICERS AND MEN objected to these cruelties and outrages," John Kennedy of 2/D told his captain, "but could not prevent it." Shot in the ankle, and fired at as he lay bleeding by the parapet, Sergeant Wilbur Gaylord was saved from further injury by a Texas Ranger. The teamster David Harrison had been denied water by two passing rebels, but "another man, who *was* a man, came along and brought me some water."[1]

"One line officer," the *Cairo News* was told, "exerted himself to stop the slaughter. To this man's noble exertions are due most of the lives that were saved. Several of the wounded said, 'He saved my life, God bless him!' His name, if ever known, will be honored by all loyal men, while they execrate the memory of Chalmers and those who carried out his fiendish orders."[2]

Lieutenant Mack Leaming was fortunate to run into a fellow Mason among the rebel officers. "He got two of our colored soldiers to assist me up the hill, and he brought me some water." (This may well have been Chalmers himself, for long afterward, Leaming would greet Chalmers in the halls of Congress and otherwise inexplicably thank him for his kindness.) Leaming testified that around dusk he heard some gunfire and someone called out, "They're shooting the darky soldiers!" Whereupon a rebel officer rode up and shouted, "Stop that firing! Arrest that man!"[3]

The survivors seemed to single out the Texans as decent men who protected the wounded and fetched them water. Tom Burney of the 8th Texas Rangers once tried to explain his views on the shooting of prisoners. While being led to prison during the Atlanta campaign, one of the ten Yankees that his company had captured "began to be very boisterous and just wouldn't be quiet at all," wrote Burney. One of Burney's comrades "told him if he didn't stop his racket he would kill him and he got worse than ever and cursed the fellow and dared him to shoot. Well, he shot and Mr. Yank fell dead, shot in the eye and through the head. That was the first prisoner I ever saw killed, and the man who did the shooting killed himself in this county." Burney declared that he "never did anything of that kind in the four years I served in the army, and if I should serve as long again I could not shoot a prisoner."[4]

Less fastidious rebels continued to pick their way among the wounded, finishing them off with the butts of their carbines. Others employed sabers and the garrison's discarded bayonets. They may have intended these blows as coups de grâce, or reverted to more silent means of killing the Federals to avoid alerting officers to the protracted slaughter. In any case, rebel claims that all firing had ceased within fifteen to thirty minutes of their taking the fort do not address these more furtive means of killing prisoners or the sporadic gunfire that according to most witnesses continued well into the evening and would resume before dawn.[5]

"I had as yet had no guard over me," wrote the daguerreotypist Charley Robinson, "and as I had a grey suit on except the blouse" and because after the rebels "killed our boys they would take off their coats & put them on," he was "dressed as they were," and was able to walk "right amongst them" to the rim of the bluff. As the firing ceased in the fort, he stood and watched the mayhem below. "I saw them shoot & bayonet our poor fellows after they surrendered," he said. "I saw them take off their clothes after they were dead. I saw them pick the pockets of the dead, & heard them laugh & cheer when they were shooting our boys who had jumped into the river to keep from being cut to pieces." And he continued to stand there "after the firing was over," and, thinking the rebels had done "all they could do," looked down at the dead and wounded Federals littering the riverbank below. "It was truly a hard sight," he said.[6]

"When the fight was over and the smoke cleared," wrote John W. Carroll of Wilson's 21st, "there was not many of them left." Billy Mays of 13/B testified that after the principal firing had stopped, the rebels returned, "shooting and robbing the dead of their money and clothes." "They robbed every citizen," Benton testified, "taking off most of their clothing." Benton himself was relieved of seventy dollars and his pocketbook by a rebel captain.[7]

Thinking Nathan Hunter of 6/D was dead, they pulled off his boots.[8] "They thought they had killed me," recalled Sergeant William Walker of 13/D. "They searched my pockets half a dozen times or more and took my pocket-book from me." Some rebels offered their protection only after their captives handed over their money, knives, coins, pocket books, watches. "Soon after I was shot I was robbed," Leaming testified. "A secesh soldier came along, and wanted to know if I had any greenbacks. I gave him my pocket-book. I had about a hundred dollars, I think, more or less, and a gold watch and gold chain. They took everything in the way of valuables that I had. I saw them robbing others. That seemed to be the general way they served the wounded."[9]

Fleeing to within two feet of the water, John Kennedy of 2/D had been shot through both of his legs and was lying in the mud when "he was taken by the rebels, who searched him, turning his pockets inside out, requesting him to give up his greenbacks, &c." As Manuel Nichols played possum, a rebel dug around in his uniform and stole his pocketwatch and pocket-book. "I had some of these brass things that looked like cents," he remembered. "They said, 'Here's some money; here's some money.' I said to myself, 'You got fooled *that* time.'"[10]

"After the fight," wrote Sam Caldwell of the 16th Tennessee, his comrades "commenced the plunder of the town" and set it ablaze. "I got nothin except what the boys gave me which was a new hat—a pair of the finest boots you ever saw—a pair of pants—two shirts—2 ladies collars & 2 pair of shoes too large for anybody & 2 bolts of Sea Island domestic," though he expected he would have to dispose of the bolts, "for my horse can't possibly pack them." Forrest assessed the plunder at over one hundred thousand dollars, not including the garrison's six guns and 350 small arms.[11]

"The plundering of the encampment," exulted an officer of the 22nd, "afforded no small feature of interest; the sacking of the stores no little excitement, and the brave band of soldiers, after becoming undisputed masters of the fort, with prisoners properly secured, devoted energies and attention to the well filled stores of the commissary and quartermaster's department, and the encampment, which abounded with crackers, cheese, lager beer and wines, to the hearty delight of our troops, who had ridden all night and fought all day without eating."[12]

Edward Benton, the owner of Fort Pillow's site, sought protection from the rebel captain who had robbed him. Benton told him that since "he had taken all my money, he must keep me from being shot like a dog, as I was a citizen," he added disingenuously, "and had nothing to do with the fight." Cursing Benton and the rest of the garrison for fighting "like devils" and trying "to kill all of Forrest's men," the captain nevertheless allowed Benton to follow him down the southern slope of the knoll to the rear of the row of improvised hotels and stores that his comrades were already looting. "He gave me a soldier's coat and told me to wait a moment until he could step in and steal his share." But as soon as the captain ducked off to claim his plunder, Benton grabbed some clothing, a saddle blanket, and a halter. Posing as a rebel, he headed eastward, toward the abatis. Along the way, near the smoking ruins of the contraband camp, he saw "three persons shot—mulattoes and blacks—shot down singly in cold blood." Considering himself lucky to be alive, Benton worked his way among the abatis's maze of fallen timbers, where he hid himself until nightfall.[13]

Sergeant Henry Weaver of 6/C was captured by a rebel "and taken into the town." Weaver entered a store, where his rebel captor "went to pillaging." Weaver found some civilian clothing and slipped it on, and after ducking out of the store soon realized that no one knew he was a Federal. Being a white man, he decided not to run but to mingle with the rebels until nightfall, when he "walked off just as if I had a right to go." Hardy Revelle, whose lieutenant brother Cordy was by now among the slain, had a similar experience. "At the top of the hill I met a man named Cutler, a citizen of Fort Pillow," who spoke to a rebel captain on Revelle's behalf. The captain ordered them down to Revelle's store to help him filch a pair of boots. Mission accomplished, the captain led the two civilians to Colonel McCulloch's field headquarters, where "the captain introduced me to a lieutenant and to a surgeon of the rebel army." After the surgeon compelled Revelle to show him "where goods could be found, the lieutenant got a saddle and bridle and some bits, and then we helped them to carry them to where their horses were outside of the fortifications." Their party was soon joined by another civilian named Medlin, who "helped the lieutenant to mount and pack his goods," in return for which he gave them all permission to depart "and instructed us as to the best means of escape."[14]

During the assault, the daguerreotypist Charley Robinson got separated from his partner, George Washington Craft, but soon spotted him among the rebels' drove of prisoners. "I can tell you, we were glad to see each other. He said that he was all right & not hurt," Robinson wrote. "They wouldn't let us talk much so I had to leave him & go on to the Fort" with McCulloch's adjutant, John T. Chandler, "who had ridden back to see where I was. I had a little dispute here with the guard who had George in charge & he pulled out his revolver & said he would shoot me. But Chandler came back & took me with him," after which Robinson did not see Craft again. Apparently on Chandler's recommendation, McCulloch granted Robinson's release and wrote out a pass. But "now I had no place to stay," he wrote home, "for they had burnt my house & in fact every house in town & the country people were about all Secesh." After being arrested repeatedly, Robinson "concluded to go to the swamps & stay until the rebels left the country," so he "staid in the swamp in day time & slept at one of the citizens' houses at night."[15]

James Brigham was another of those taken prisoner and marched to McCulloch's headquarters. Along the way he "saw the Confederates shoot and kill and wound both white and black Federal prisoners." He saw "officers as well as privates kill and wound prisoners," and heard them threaten to take the "prisoners still further into the country, and make an example of them." McCulloch released Brigham also on the grounds that he was a private citizen.[16]

———————————

Squads of rebels continued to make their way along the riverbank, searching among the tangle of logs and brush for fugitive Union soldiers. Two months later, after the Battle of Brice's Crossroads, rebel patrols would bluff black soldiers hiding in the bushes into giving themselves up by employing an old slave catcher's trick: randomly calling out, "Come out of there, you grand rascals, or I will kill you," whereupon two or three, "thinking they had been discovered, would come crawling out and surrender."[17]

Forrest's defenders dismiss as outlandish Edward Benton's assertion that the rebels used bloodhounds to flush out the survivors of the massacre. But not only was it said that Forrest sometimes kept dogs among his equipage; there is also testimony that his recruiters employed bloodhounds to track down skulkers and deserters. In any case, they would not have been required to bring their own hounds, since there were a number of substantial plantations with a full complement of slaves, and among large slaveholders hounds were a necessity. According to Elvis Bevel, for at least two days squads of Forrest's men ranged through the woods at Plum Run, six miles above Fort Pillow, "hunting for negroes." It hardly strains credulity to imagine that men serving under Forrest, himself an ex–slave catcher and slave trader, some of them professional slave catchers themselves and many of them veterans of recruitment campaigns, could at least have borrowed hounds from local secessionists and employed them in time-honored antebellum fashion to catch men they regarded, after all, as runaway slaves.[18]

Sometime before 7:00 p.m., Forrest returned the command of the two brigades to Chalmers, ordering his men "to complete the burial of the dead," to collect all "arms and other portable property, and, if possible, to transfer the Federal wounded to the first steamer that might be passing; and, finally, to follow with the division and the unwounded prisoners, as soon as practicable, to Brownsville." Chalmers commanded Bell and his brigade to take charge of "all the unwounded prisoners and those whose injuries were not serious enough to prevent them from marching" and follow Forrest back to Jackson.[19]

Bell and his brigade camped about a mile farther east, while Forrest and his Escort would spend the night six or seven miles up the road to Brownsville. By seven o'clock, wrote Chalmers's adjutant, "the prisoners and artillery had been removed, and the troops were moved back from the river and put into camp." McCulloch's Missourians camped less than a mile from the breastworks, leaving only a small guard to look after the wounded prisoners, while McCulloch himself found shelter in a nearby farmhouse. Frank Hogan of 6/A reported that as a captive he overheard the colonel ask his adjutant, Lieutenant Lucius Gaines, how many Federals had been killed. Three hundred so far, Gaines replied, but not all of the returns were in.[20]

Black Bob McCulloch's Missouri Mongols were an odd choice to entrust with the safety of the survivors. They had declared within Alfred Coleman's hearing that "they would show no quarter to colored troops, nor to any of the officers with them, but would kill them all," and that "they had been talking about fighting under the black flag," and had "come as nigh fulfilling that here as if they had a black flag."[21]

Colonel Clarke Barteau would recall that after the battle, Black Bob had been "earnest in his expressions of the good conduct, forbearance, and obedience of his men after the foolhardy and strange manner in which the Federals had acted, causing unnecessary sacrifice of life." In later years McCulloch himself would flatly deny that anyone was shot after the garrison surrendered, and swear that "not a gun was fired, nor a prisoner or noncombatant shot, to my knowledge or belief, after the surrender was made," a claim to which nobody gives credence. Barteau himself hedged a little on McCulloch's mea non culpa. He maintained that "the best fighting men" in Bell's and McCulloch's brigades "had no hand in the barbarities. Only one hundred and fifty men out of the two brigades had any hand in it," he wrote, and "their atrocities disgraced them in the eyes of the better soldiery." Be that as it may, 150 men would have been capable of extensive mayhem, and the "better soldiery" never brought a single charge against them.[22]

After the prisoners had been collected and herded back up the slope to the breastworks, "the unwounded of the garrison were detailed, under the supervision of their own officers, to bury the dead and remove the wounded to the hospitals, tents and buildings." But several survivors testified to seeing rebel burial details at work as well, as they would have been required to do after the most able-bodied prisoners were marched off. "As fast as possible," wrote Hancock, "the wounded of both sides were gleaned from the bloody field and placed under shelter and the professional care of Confederate surgeons of the several regiments present." "The most of our Wounded," wrote Dr. Fitch, "were gathered up by the Rebels and placed in a building which Major Booth used for his Head Quarters."[23]

As it became apparent that many of his prisoners were too grievously wounded to travel, Forrest ordered his adjutant, Charles Anderson, to "procure a skiff, and take with him Captain Young," the provost marshal of the decimated garrison, with whom the rebels had become acquainted during the truce negotiations, and deliver a message signed by Forrest and addressed to Captain Marshall of the *New Era*. "Sir," it said, "My aide-de-camp, Captain Charles W. Anderson, is fully authorized to negotiate with you for the delivery of the wounded of the garrison at this place on board your vessel."[24]

"The object was to deliver into his hands as soon as possible all the Federal wounded," wrote Jordan and Pryor. But Anderson discovered that all the boats and skiffs had been "taken off by citizens escaping from the fort during the engagement." So he and Young trotted up and down the riverbank, trying to summon the *New Era* with a white flag.[25]

After what Marshall had just witnessed, however, he was not about to trust another of Forrest's flags of truce. He presently repaired upriver, around Craighead Point, where he would remain through the night, all the while "fearful," as he testified, that the rebels might "hail in a steamboat from below, capture her, put on four or five hundred men, and come after me."[26]

"When Major Anderson returned and reported his failure to communicate with the *New Era*," recalled Robert Burfford of Forrest's Old Regiment, "the General at once caused details to be made of all the unwounded Federals under their own officers to first bring into the fort and houses on the hill all their wounded comrades," and then to bury their dead. Once the wounded and their comrades' denuded corpses "had been removed from the face of the bluff, a detail of our own men was sent down to gather up all the small arms thrown down by the garrison."[27]

The rebels had already thrown some of the wounded into the river to drown; others who had fled into the Mississippi—many of them undocumented contrabands and civilians—disappeared under the turbid current; and after the firing ceased, some rebels saved themselves the trouble of toting bodies uphill by simply rolling them into the stream.[28]

At the captive Major Bradford's own request, Forrest ordered his burial parties to inter the garrison's dead in the ditch outside the southernmost breastworks: the remains of the whites at the upper end, those of the blacks at the
bottom. The officers' corpses were to be buried separately, including the riddled body of Bradford's brother Ted, for whose interment Bradford had been
temporarily paroled. Most, but apparently not all, of the officers were buried
by the rebels. Some were buried in the ditch with their men. Major Booth
"was buried on the bank," Sergeant Benjamin Robinson testified, "right side
of me," where a rebel trooper had stripped Major Booth's corpse of its
bloody uniform and was amusing his comrades by parading around in it.[29]

As the rebels imprisoned most of the wounded whites in Bradford's old
headquarters south of the parapet, "the unwounded of the garrison were detailed," wrote Anderson, "under the supervision of their own officers, to bury
the dead and remove the wounded to the hospitals, tents and buildings" under the overall command of Captain O. B. Farriss of 22/K.[30]

Farriss must have been in a hurry to return to camp, for the burials were
hasty and unceremonious. "They were all pitched in in any way—some on
their faces, some on their sides, some on their backs." "Some had just been
thrown in the trench at the end of the fort," Eli Bangs testified after viewing
the graves the next day, "white and black together." Some of the bodies "had
their hands or feet or face out. I should judge there were probably 100 bodies there. They had apparently thrown them in miscellaneously, and thrown
a little dirt over them, not covering them up completely."[31]

Black prisoners buried their comrades, brothers, cousins, former fellow
slaves of the same master. Corporal Reason Barker and Private Henry Miller
buried their comrade Harry Hunter of 6/D. Charles Williams helped to bury
Robert Green of 6/A; they had escaped together from neighboring plantations. Granville Hill buried Corporal Tom Davis of 2/D; the two had been
slaves of the same master. Davis's slave name had been Warren, but he had
changed it to Davis upon enlisting. His newly widowed mother, Martha, had
lived in Jackson, Tennessee, until she followed Thomas's regiment to Memphis in January 1863, whereupon he rented her a house in the city and gave
her fifteen dollars a month out of his soldier's wages.[32]

Severely wounded in the side, Lieutenant Leaming of the 13th was carried up to the edge of the fort and laid down where "there seemed to be
quite a number of dead collected" that the rebels were throwing "into the
outside trench." "There's a man who's not quite dead yet," Leaming over-

heard a rebel declare, and Frank Hogan of 6/A testified that he "saw them bury one of our men alive, being only wounded." Sergeant Benjamin Robinson of 6/D spied one black man "working his hand after he was buried."[33]

By the next day stories would circulate that several blacks had been buried alive. "One negro was made to assist in digging a pit to bury the dead in, and was himself cast in among others and buried," the *Cairo News* reported from interviews conducted at Fort Pillow the next morning. "Five are known to have been buried alive; of these two dug themselves out and are now alive in the hospital. Daniel Tyler of Company B was shot three times, and struck on the head, knocking out his eye. After this he was buried, but, not liking his quarters, dug out."[34]

Forrest's defenders protested that if any men were buried alive that night it must have been the fault of the burial details, which, they maintained, were composed exclusively of Federal prisoners. Though a few Federal survivors testified that they assisted in the burial, others who witnessed the interments testified that their dead comrades were buried either by the rebels or under strict rebel supervision. The burials apparently proceeded in two stages: the first performed by the "unwounded prisoners" under rebel supervision, who labored until late evening when Bell, as per Chalmers's command, collected them all and marched them off as prisoners; the second undertaken by the rebels themselves, whose burial parties continued to work well into the night.[35]

Captain James Dinkins of the 18th Mississippi hinted at what may have resulted in the burying alive of several of the wounded. He recalled that as the rebel burial parties worked their way along the bank, some of the artillerists lay "flat on their faces, pretending to be dead. When one of them was reached, the men began to dig his grave near where he lay. He raised his head just a little, and said, 'Marster, for God's sake, spare me; I didn't want to leave home; dey 'scripted me. Spare me, marster, and take me home. Dey 'scripted me.' He was spared, and many others in the same way." It may be that some men, among them Daniel Tyler, were either too badly wounded to protest their interment or chose to let the rebels bury them under a thin layer of sand rather than risk being shot outright.[36]

For over four hours the burial crews labored, while most of the wounded—especially the black captives—would be "left unattended for the night and most of the dead unburied." "After securing all desirable articles," wrote an officer of the 22nd, "we ignited stores, tents and stables, and as in the affair at Paducah, withdrew by its light."[37]

In disputing the claim that as the rebels put the fort to the torch, some men were burned alive, Forrest's defenders conceded "that burned bodies were found by the burial parties from the *Silver Cloud,* the *Platte Valley* and the *New Era,*" but Jordan and Pryor, with Forrest's authorization, maintained that "these were the bodies of some negroes who had been killed in the tents."

The burning to death of invalid blacks was not without precedent. On June 29, 1863, Alfred Ellet of the Mississippi Marine Brigade docked with his command at Goodrich Landing to find the surrounding plantations— mansion houses, cotton gins, and slave quarters—in flames. After an engagement with rebel cavalry, Ellet "found the road strewn with abandoned booty stolen from the houses they had burned; among other articles, a very fine piano." But the rebels'"main object" had been "to secure the negroes stolen from the plantations along the river, some hundreds of whom they had captured." At three plantations Ellet came upon "the charred remains of human beings who had been burned in the general conflagration. No doubt they were the sick negroes whom the unscrupulous enemy were too indifferent to remove." He believed that "there were many others on the 20 or more other plantations that I did not visit which were burned in like manner."[38]

In defending Forrest against this one charge, the Wizard's champions unconsciously conceded another, which was that the rebels shot sick and wounded men as they lay helpless in the hospital tents. Wyeth conceded that the rebels set fire to buildings that night, but rather disingenuously cited the hotelier John Penwell's testimony that before the tent he shared with a wounded artillery officer was torched, the rebels carried the two of them out, as if this somehow negated the possibility that other rebel squads set fire to tents and cabins with wounded men inside, or that in the gloaming the rebels could have mistaken some of the more severely wounded men for corpses.[39]

In any case, Wyeth failed to add that the rest of Penwell's testimony actually supported the claim that wounded men were burned alive. Shot through the breast, tromped on, and robbed, Penwell lay among the wounded in a tent near one of the four or five huts the rebels set aside for prisoners south of the breastworks. "In the night," a rebel officer appeared with a squad of arsonists and "roused us up."

"Get out," he barked, "if you don't want to get burned to death."

Penwell appealed to the officer in charge to allow some of the less seriously injured prisoners to remove their comrades from the huts nearby, "as there were some eight or nine wounded men in there, and a negro who had his hip broken."

"The white men can help themselves out," replied the officer. "The damned nigger shan't come out of that."

Though it was "very painful," Penwell staggered out of the tent, reckoning that he "could bear the pain better than run the risk of being burned up." But he never knew "whether they got the wounded out or not."[40]

James Walls of 13/E heard the rebels tell each other "to stick torches all around." "They came with a chunk of fire to burn the building where I was in with the dead," recalled Billy Mays of 13/B. A rebel poked his head through the door and gave the interior a hasty look.

"These damned sons of bitches are all dead," he declared, and moved on.[41]

"While I was in the major's headquarters," said Nathan Fulks of 13/D, "they commenced burning the buildings, and I begged one of them to take me out and not let us burn there."

"I am hunting up a piece of yellow flag for you," the rebel sneered.[42]

The most vivid, and the only purportedly eyewitness, testimony came from Ransom Anderson of 6/B. He claimed that the rebels escorted some of the most badly wounded men into a hut. "They were wounded," he said, "and could not walk." Their captors "told them they were going to have the doctor see them," he said, and then they bolted the door from the outside. "I saw a rebel soldier take some grass and lay it by the door," Anderson testified, "and set it on fire. The door was pine plank, and it caught easy." Asked how he knew his comrades were trapped inside, Anderson replied that he had previously looked in on them and that now, as the flames rose, he "heard them hallooing there when the houses were burning."[43]

Robert Selph Henry dismissed Anderson's testimony by claiming that "all other evidence is that the tents and huts were burned on the following day." Whatever the merits of Anderson's story, however, in fact there is ample testimony from both sides that the rebels burned most of the station on the night of April 12 but spared Bradford's former headquarters and its adjacent outbuildings, to which some white prisoners had been taken, and outside of which many of the wounded blacks had been collected.[44]

"WALK OR DIE"
PRISONERS

From April 12, 1864

THE OFFICIAL TALLY OF THE PRISONERS WHOM THE REBELS DEEMED FIT enough to march to Jackson numbered 158: 141 from the 13th Tennessee Cavalry; Lieutenant Hunter and a Private Abraham Baker of the 2nd USCLA; Captain Epeneter, Lieutenant Bischoff, Sergeant Hennessy, and Privates A. G. Hatfield and J. Thompson of the 6th USCHA; 6 men from assorted other regiments (including one from Wolfe's 52nd Indiana); and 4 civilians.[1]

For some reason the tally included three black privates, men the Confederacy did not recognize and would not ordinarily have listed as prisoners of war. In fact, the total number of prisoners from black regiments was at least sixty-two, of whom thirteen would escape en route. "The prisoners were placed in my charge," wrote Barteau, "to be taken to Tupelo. Almost without exception they blamed their officers for the great loss of life. They told me that they had been led to believe that if they surrendered they would be killed by Forrest, and they were surprised and gratified at their humane treatment," though under the circumstances, and after what they had witnessed and survived, it is unlikely any of them would have dared to complain. "On the route south, to relieve their fatigue," Barteau reported, "I had my men dismount at times and let the prisoners ride."[2]

McCulloch's men, however, retained a number of black captives "for their personal convenience," for which Chalmers would chide the colonel a week later. "These negroes must be called in & returned as prisoners at once," he said. Chalmers had also heard that McCulloch's men had absconded with a considerable amount of the cash they had looted from stores and plucked from the pockets of the dead and wounded. "This money must be turned over at once to the Quarter Master of your brigade," Chalmers insisted, "for the use of the Government in compliance with the requirements of orders heretofore issued."[3]

The rebels described their prisoners as "unwounded," but they were probably referring to the 147 whites they led away, of whom only 3 can be documented as having been seriously injured. Of the 62 black captives, however, at least 32 were wounded, most of them seriously: shot in the hip, through both legs, in the shoulder; struck in the head with rifle butts.[4]

Among these was short, "chunky-built" Sam Green of 6/B, who had stuck by his gun with such tenacity. His big toe shot away, his hand plowed up by a minié ball, his hip badly bruised by his cannon's recoil, his skull cracked from a musket blow to the head after he had surrendered, this hero of the defense of Fort Pillow was nevertheless forced to march "nearly all that night."

When, years later, a pension examiner asked Green how he could have marched with such injuries, Green replied, "Well, Boss, to tell you the God's truth, from the sights I saw then that day after we were captured, it just meant walk on that leg or die. And I walked and made no complaint, as it was not healthy for 'niggers' to complain in my condition."[5]

James Brigham "saw officers as well as privates kill and wound prisoners," and would hear them say "that they intended taking the prisoners still farther into the country and making an example of them." Some black prisoners, he testified, "were severely beaten" along the way. Among them was John Kennedy of 2/D, who claimed some rebels tied him to a tree and lashed him "with a gun sling." Bob Winston of 2/B was shot down the next morning because "he would not go fast." Among the prisoners shuffling along in Bell's coffle were black women and children the rebels had flushed out of the woods.[6]

The rebels did not release every white civilian captive. Suspected of profiteering or committing outrages or deserting from the rebel army, five of them joined Bell's coffle. By about 10:00 p.m., the prisoners had marched three miles east of the Mississippi. As the prisoners "were passing by us with some of our wounded," wrote Dr. Fitch, "the Officer of the Guard ordered me to go with them, and dress their wounds. I started but had not gone but a few Rods before I was ordered to return. On returning, the officer of the guard informed me that Forrest had given orders for me to be held as a Prisoner." He said that the general ordinarily would not take a surgeon prisoner, but the Yankees were holding one of his surgeons captive "in close confinement." ("The Federals didn't recognize surgeons and took them prisoner," explained Surgeon R. E. Howlett of McCulloch's 2nd Missouri Cavalry.

"This cartel was changed two or three times during the war," but whenever it was Union policy to take surgeons prisoner, Howlet made sure he "always carried a pistol.")[7]

His ankle shattered, Sergeant Wilbur Gaylord of 6/B was taken to one of the garrison's abandoned picket posts and loaded onto a rebel ambulance with the mortally wounded Lieutenant Colonel Wyly Martin Reed of the 5th Mississippi, who would die at Jackson after nineteen days of excruciating pain. They were taken to a farmhouse, where Gaylord spent the night under guard in the out-of-doors "on account of the houses being filled with their wounded. I bandaged my own wound with my drawers," he said, "and a colored man brought water and sat by me so that I could keep my foot wet."[8]

Wounded in the left side during the engagement and shot twice—once in the head—after surrendering, Manuel Nichols of 6/B lay on the bluff near a shack filled with wounded black and white soldiers. After one of his comrades entered the house for a drink of water, Nichols "took a stick and tried to get to the house," but before he could reach it, some of the rebels came along "and saw a little boy belonging to company D. One of them had his musket on his shoulder, and shot the boy down."

"All you damned niggers come out of the house," he shouted. "I am going to shoot you."

"Boys," advised the frightened whites inside, "it is only death anyhow. If you don't go out, they will come in and carry you out."

At that moment, Nichols's "strength seemed to come to me as if I had never been shot," and he ran down to the river, never pausing even after a rebel, firing from a distance, shot him through the flesh of his right arm.[9]

Dangerously wounded in the armpit and the side, Billy Mays of 13/B was ordered to his feet by an officer wielding a saber. "I succeeded in getting up," Mays testified, "and got among a small squad he had already gathered up." But Mays lagged behind and slipped down to the river during the night, concluding that "it was best to lie still." He did not move again until late that night, when he "crawled in with some of the dead and laid there until the next morning."[10]

Shot "in the arm, and the shoulder, and the neck, and in the eye," Sergeant William Walker of 13/D had also played possum, even as the rebels rifled his pockets. Like John Haskins, Jacob Wilson of 6/B played dead in the shallows, gradually working his way downriver until he reached a flatboat drawn up on the riverbank. When all was quiet, Wilson crawled in, hauled three more wounded comrades aboard, and cut it loose. Feigning death, they floated downriver until they ground up against the bank, where they would be discovered next day by a squad of Federals.[11]

A rebel private warned Jerry Stewart of 6/A that "all the colored boys that could escape had best to do so by all means, for General Forrest was going to burn or whip them to death after they got farther south." Shot after he had surrendered, Sergeant Benjamin Robinson of 6/D was told that the rebels intended to kill him the next morning. Unable to walk, he "crawled down the hill." Philip Young of 6/A repeatedly heard rebel officers declare that "they intended to kill the last one of the negroes after they got as far down south as they wanted to. A captain in the Confederate army swore he would shoot me after I had been prisoner thirteen days."[12]

Nearly blinded by a shot to the face, Thomas Addison of 6/C was making his way down to the little rivulet that emptied into the mouth of Coal Creek when he encountered a rebel soldier.

"Old man, if you stay here they will kill you," he said, "but if you get into the water till the boat comes along, they may save you."

Addison fled into the woods.[13]

That night a rebel laid claim to George Shaw of 6/B and ordered him "to wait on him a little, and sent me back to a house about two hundred yards, and told me to stay all night." At five the next morning, "another man came along."

"If you will go home with me," he said, "I will take good care of you," but if Shaw stayed he would "never leave."

Shaw was "so outdone" that he did not know what to do. "If you will take care of me," he replied, "I will go."

The man took him to a nearby farm, but no sooner had he left Shaw alone than two more rebels turned up.

"Damn you," one of them cursed Shaw, "we will kill you, and not be fooling about any longer."

"Don't shoot me," Shaw begged.

"Go out and hold my horse," one of them abruptly commanded.

Shaw took a couple of steps toward the horse.

"Turn around," said the rebel. "I'll hold my horse, and shoot you, too."

As soon as Shaw turned around, the rebel shot him in the face.

"I fell down as if I was dead. He shot me again, and hit my arm, not my head. I laid there until I could hear him no more."

His face caked with blood, Shaw somehow got to his feet, made his way back to Fort Pillow, and "wandered about there until a gunboat came along."[14]

PAROLED
FORT PILLOW

April 12–13, 1864

IN THE NIGHT, THE RAIN CLOUDS ROLLED AWAY, ONLY TO BE REPLACED by the smoke billowing from the station's ruins.[1]

Two weeks before he would die of his wounds, Woody Cooksey of 13/A would testify that "late into the night" the rebels were "burning houses and burying the dead and stealing goods," but in the morning "they commenced on the negroes again, and killed all they came across, as far as I could see." Lying near the fort, he saw them kill about seven blacks that morning. "I saw one of them shoot a black fellow in the head with three buck shot and a musket ball." But the soldier still lived, so the rebel "took his pistol and fired that at his head. The black man still moved, and then the fellow took his saber and stuck it in the hole in the negro's head and jammed it way down, and said, 'Now, God damn you, die!'

"The negro did not say anything, but he moved, and the fellow took his carbine and beat his head soft."[2]

After nightfall, Daniel Stamps of 13/E had managed to drag himself up to the fort and spent the night tending to the deep bullet wound to his thigh. Before the sun rose at 5:30 a.m., a squad of McCulloch's men returned to the fort on a mission. Though "they did not attempt to hurt us white men," Stamps saw them execute "some 20 or 25" wounded negroes who had made their way back up the hill.[3]

That morning James Walls of 13/E was lying by the river when the rebels came "prying around there, and would come to a nigger and say, 'You ain't dead are you?'" The black soldier "would not say anything, and then the se-cesh would get down off their horses, prick them in their sides, and say,

'Damn you, you ain't dead. Get up.' Then they would make them get up on their knees, when they would shoot them down like hogs."[4]

By one account, possibly apocryphal, undoubtedly embellished, the rebels came upon an artillerist's biracial wife who had ventured out before dawn to search among the dead and wounded for her husband.

"She was the daughter of a wealthy and influential rebel residing at Columbus," wrote the abolitionist ex-slave William Wells Brown.

> Going from body to body with all the earnestness with which love could inspire an affectionate heart, she at last found the object of her search. He was not dead; but both legs were broken. The wife had succeeded in getting him out from among the piles of dead, and was bathing his face, and giving him water to drink from a pool near by, which had been replenished by the rain that fell a few hours before. At this moment she was seen by the murderous band; and the cry was at once raised, "Kill the wench, kill her!" The next moment the sharp crack of a musket was heard, and the angel of mercy fell a corpse on the body of her wounded husband, who was soon after knocked in the head by the butt-end of the same weapon.[5]

Acting Master's Mate Eli Bangs of the *New Era* testified that among the seventy to eighty bodies his detail would bury was the corpse of "one white woman" who may have been the mulatto wife Brown memorialized. Additionally or perhaps alternatively, Chapman Underwood did claim that he heard "a gun or a pistol fired up the bank" that morning, "and soon afterwards a negro woman came in, who was shot through the knee, and said it was done about that time."[6]

Well after daybreak, Lieutenant Mack Leaming began to make out the muffled report of "cannon down the river." The rebels immediately set the remaining buildings ablaze, including the two cabins in which Leaming and several other white Union survivors lay wounded.

Someone called out that there were wounded men inside, but the rebels set fire to them anyway. Shot through the side, the bullet having ranged down through one lung and lodged in his hip, Leaming was "entirely helpless," and as the fire engulfed the building he had "almost given up every hope of being saved" when one of his own men, "who was less severely wounded than myself, succeeded in drawing me out of the building, which the flames were then rapidly consuming." The rebels "drew us down a little way, in a sort of gulley, and we lay there in the hot sun without water or anything."

A squad of rebels now approached, apparently "for the purpose of murdering what negroes they could find. They began to shoot the wounded negroes all around there, interspersed with the whites. I was lying a little way from a wounded negro, when a secesh soldier came up to him."

"What in hell are you doing here?" the rebel demanded to know.

Trying to get on the gunboat, the soldier replied.

"You want to fight us again, do you?" the rebel replied, raising his gun. "Damn you, I'll teach you," and shot him dead.

Another black soldier who did not seem badly wounded stood nearby and begged the same rebel not to shoot him. But the Confederate reloaded his gun and "drew up his gun and took deliberate aim at his head." At first the gun would not fire, but he pulled the trigger again and the gun went off, killing him instantly.[7]

One rebel soldier threatened to kill Daniel Stamps "because I would not tell him where a poor negro soldier was who had been wounded badly, but who had crawled off on his hands and knees and hidden behind a log."[8]

———————————

The cause of the rebels' frantic activity was the approach of the Union gunboat *Silver Cloud.* On the night of April 12, the news of Fort Pillow's fall had reached Admiral David Porter via the steamer *Ike Hammett,* whose captain reported that for the first time since the Battle of Memphis, the rebels had blockaded the Mississippi.[9]

Porter's command had immediately dispatched the *General Lyon* to confirm the report, while Captain William Ferguson of the *Silver Cloud* hitched his gunboat to the swift steamer *Platte Valley* and headed for Fort Pillow.[10]

As they passed the little settlement of Fulton in the predawn light, the *Platte Valley's* crew spotted a file of rebel cavalry trotting along the river road. Ferguson ordered his gunners to open fire, and the horsemen spurred their mounts across the swampy fields that flanked the town, galloping out of sight and range. It was then, as the boom of the *Silver Cloud's* artillery rolled up the Mississippi (her guns could be heard as far away as Memphis), that McCulloch's men began to burn what was left of the station.[11]

Unhitching itself from the *Platte Valley* and proceeding on its own steam, the *Silver Cloud* had begun heaving its way up against the Mississippi current the two and a half miles to Fort Pillow when somebody signaled from a flatboat on the Arkansas shore. It turned out to be Jacob Wilson and the three wounded comrades he had pulled aboard the night before. Hoisted onto the *Silver Cloud*'s deck, he and his men gave Ferguson their first account of the massacre.[12]

Pulling back into the stream, the *Silver Cloud* resumed its journey, coming within view of Fort Pillow at about 7:00 a.m. Seeing that the rebels had carried off the garrison's guns, Ferguson fired a few volleys and made a landing to bring aboard "some twenty of our troops, some of them badly wounded, who had concealed themselves along the bank, and came out when they saw my vessel. Whilst doing so I was fired upon by rebel sharpshooters posted on the hills, and one wounded man limping down to the vessel was shot." Heaving the *Silver Cloud* back into the river, Ferguson transferred his rescued passengers to the steamer *Lady Pike* (which had just rounded Craighead Point, ahead of the *New Era*) and resumed his cannonade.[13]

"The commissary and other public buildings, together with some 12 stores, private property, were in flames," wrote a passenger. "The rebels could be seen moving about, applying torches to the barracks, huts, and stables." Captain Ferguson ordered his pilot to move up within range for his five-second shells, which, for some thirty minutes or more, he continued firing at the detached squads they spied moving along the riverbank.[14]

Back at the fort, Daniel Stamps had seen only one rebel officer that morning riding "along while they were shooting the negroes, and said nothing to them." The officer sported "a feather in his cap," he said, "and looked like he might have been a captain." In any case, he "was the only man I saw pass that looked like an officer while they were shooting the negroes."

"Captain," Stamps called out, "what are you going to do with us wounded fellows?"

"Put you in the gunboats," he replied.[15]

Aboard the *Silver Cloud* that morning were Captain William T. Smith of 6/C, First Lieutenant Frank Smith of 13/D, and Second Lieutenant William Cleary of 13/B returning from their mission to Memphis. Watching from the deck as the gunship came within view of Fort Pillow, Cleary saw the rebels "shoot one man just before we landed," and watched as "an escort of about twenty men rode up to a livery stable and set it on fire. The gunboat fired at them but did not hit them, and they got on their horses and rode off at a trot. There were some paths down the hill, and a man came along down one of them." As the escort paused, Cleary saw a soldier he took for an officer pull out a revolver and "very deliberately" shoot at the man before galloping off "in quick time."[16]

At Forrest's temporary camp at Durhamville, a few miles south of Ripley, the Wizard and his Escort were preparing to proceed to Jackson when their horses twitched and balked at the thump of the *Silver Cloud*'s cannonade. Fearing that the *New Era* had pinned McCulloch's men in the fort, Forrest ordered Captain Charles Anderson and an escort of three men back to the river to see how McCulloch was faring and to try once again to persuade the *New Era* to pick up the wounded under a flag of truce. That Forrest felt the need to send Anderson back as his emissary suggests that after the slaughter of the day before, he did not trust Chalmers to honor a truce and properly oversee the transfer of prisoners.[17]

Pausing to announce his presence to Chalmers, Anderson encountered Captain Young among the Mississippian's prisoners and received Chalmers's permission to take the captured station's provost marshal with him to flag down the *New Era,* as they had attempted to do the evening before. Chalmers contributed seven of his men to Anderson's escort, and Anderson and Young departed.[18]

When Anderson reached Fort Pillow, he found McCulloch's men huddled in the ravines as Union shells arced up from the river and burst around them. Acting under Forrest's authority, Anderson ordered McCulloch's men to withdraw to the woods beyond the abatis as he trotted up to the rim of the bluff.[19]

Below, on the river, he saw that the barrage was coming not from the battered and depleted *New Era,* which was still hanging back behind Craighead Point, but a fresh Federal gunboat with an abundance of ordnance.

Anderson immediately led Captain Young down to the riverbank, waving a flag of truce. "The *Silver Cloud* ceased firing and steamed warily forward," he recalled, "shutting her engines within hailing distance of the fort."

"What do you want?" Captain Ferguson shouted through his bullhorn.

Anderson called back that he had come to negotiate a truce and asked Ferguson to send an officer ashore so he could relay a written communication from Forrest's command.

Ferguson cast around for an army officer willing to parley with Anderson. Captain William Smith was the senior army officer on board, but as he surveyed the horrific scene along the riverbank, he told Ferguson that "he did not like to go on shore" for fear the rebels would make good on Richmond's policy of summarily executing white officers of black troops. First Lieutenant Frank Smith, perhaps because he was heartily despised by Lauderdale County's secessionists, also recused himself. So Ferguson as-

signed the task to Second Lieutenant Cleary of the 13th and one of his own
naval officers.

As the *Silver Cloud*'s crew lowered a launch, Anderson turned away to
write down his terms. But when he turned back around, he was alarmed to
see that the launch was manned by six armed marines rowing a pair of officers toward him under not a white but a Union flag.

"Waving him back, and calling his attention to our white flag," Anderson
told Cleary that he would not parley "until he returned to his vessel, hoisted
a white flag, and returned in his launch with his oarsmen unarmed."

Cleary realized his mistake, and after returning to the *Silver Cloud*,
drew up to the landing, unarmed and flying a flag of truce. Stepping out of
the launch, Cleary greeted Anderson and retrieved his note. Anderson proposed that "if we would recognize the parole of Forrest, we might take our
wounded on the gunboat." He offered the Yankees a nine-to-five truce during which he would guarantee the safety of the *Silver Cloud* and the *Platte
Valley* and their crews as they littered the garrison's wounded aboard.[20]

"I am authorized," Anderson wrote, "to say by Major-General Forrest"
that he intended "to place the badly wounded of your Army on board of your
boats, provided you will acknowledge their parole. I shall send all (white or
black) who desire to go."[21]

After a brief conference with Cleary and his comrades, Ferguson accepted Anderson's terms. Ferguson wigwagged to the *Platte Valley,* poised
about a mile upriver, to meet him at the landing. After the two great boats
steamed up to the wharf, Ferguson welcomed Anderson aboard and offered
him pen and paper to draw up a formal agreement in duplicate.

> It is agreed that until 5 o'clock p.m. this evening details from United
> States forces or others interested in the burial of the dead or the re-
> covery of the wounded, shall have free access to the fort and the
> grounds around it until 5 o'clock p.m. this evening.[22]

Anderson signed both copies and, leaving a sergeant to guard Captain
Young, hastened back to Chalmers's headquarters to notify his staff that he
had promised Ferguson his protection.[23]

Anderson delicately explained to the bantam Mississippian and his staff
that they were of course entirely free to come down to the riverside at any
time, but "for fear of a collision," none of Chalmers's enlisted men would be
"allowed to come within the old Confederate intrenchments." Chalmers
agreed and Anderson sent his escort to clear the fort of rebel stragglers, allowing only surgeons and their assistants to remain.[24]

Anderson was joined at the landing by a clerk from the *Platte Valley* and an ensign from the *Silver Cloud* to record the names of the parolees. All night long, Captain James Marshall had kept his *New Era* anchored around Craig-head Point, well out of range of Forrest's captured artillery, to await orders, ammunition, reinforcements, or some other dispensation. Marshall warily steered his pockmarked gunboat around the bend to discover that the *Silver Cloud* and the *Platte Valley* were now moored at the landing while a line of rebel onlookers—Anderson's escort—watched from the rim of the bluff. "We acted pretty cautiously," wrote Dr. Underwood, "and held out a signal, and the gunboat answered it, and then we went in."[25]

The *New Era*'s arrival agitated Anderson, whose sharpshooters had driven her off the day before. He insisted that all of the wounded be loaded onto the *Platte Valley,* which had the capacity to transport six hundred men, and posted guards at both of the gunboats' gangways to prevent any of the garrison's wounded from sneaking aboard and taking part in a counterattack once the truce was over.[26]

Still under the watchful eye of a rebel sergeant, Captain Young learned that his wife was aboard one of the steamers "in great stress of mind as to his fate." He begged Anderson to permit him to visit her and "assure her of his safety, give some instructions as to his private affairs, and bid her farewell." Anderson granted his request, stipulating that on his honor he must return by 2:00 p.m. This special favor made Young's comrades suspicious. "It was a subject of considerable remark," read an insinuating report in the *Missouri Democrat,* "that Captain Young was treated by the rebels with so much favor, and it is said that his brother, who has been in the rebel army, kept a grog shop at the fort, and was a rebel sympathizer."[27]

Once his men had herded the rebel stragglers out of the fort, Anderson signaled to Ferguson to "run out his stagings," as "the fort and all its surroundings were now in his possession." Anderson himself stood on the gangway of the *Platte Valley,* recording the names of the garrison's broken, bleeding survivors as the sailors and marines escorted and littered them onto the deck.[28]

A reporter traveling aboard the *Silver Cloud* wrote that "those wounded who could walk were generally brought down the bluffs, supported on either side by a rebel soldier." With the assistance of rebel surgeons, Anderson's squad sorted the prisoners into two groups: badly injured parolees and captives fit to march. About fourteen blacks and thirty-four whites were granted paroles. Some stood, some knelt, some lay flat on their backs. All of them were badly wounded, soaked in gore, and streaked with mud and ashes. Several lay unconscious from loss of blood and blows and shots to the head, and a few of them would not survive their voyage to Mound City. The rebels had stripped them of their jackets, belts, boots, and personal effects, and though some of the whites had been bandaged by rebel surgeons, the rest had improvised their own bindings, slings, tourniquets, and splints from torn shirts, drawers and stockings, belts, bark, and driftwood.[29]

The parolees proceeded one by one, whites first. Some teetered aboard unassisted, some leaned on a marine's shoulder, others had to be littered up on stretchers. The sight of them, as they paused before Anderson at the foot of the gangway to croak their names, ranks, regiments, and companies, filled the passengers of the *Platte Valley* with rage.

"Thomas Loftis, Company A, 13th Tennessee Cavalry," declared a burly survivor in a thick Irish brogue as he marched up the gangway, his arm shattered the morning before. After recuperating at Overton Hospital in Memphis, Loftis would return to his regiment at Columbus, Kentucky, and suffer saber wounds and a gunshot in his side in the defeat and capture of Jim Kess's rebel guerrillas. Deemed "unable to perform any manual labor," he would be discharged in August, and spend the rest of his working life in Martin, Tennessee, "ditching for the farmers" and coughing up blood. In 1904, his employer would describe Loftis as "a poor ignorant Irishman" who had lived "a hard life" from "hand to mouth" without "home or friends." Loftis was "good natured and harmless," he concluded, "and is a pal with our children and grand children." But he was also a drunk. Eventually admitted to the Western Kentucky Asylum for the Insane, he died in 1908.[30]

A marine assisted John C. Simmons of 13/A up the gangway. A native of Henry County, Simmons had received an "ugly wound at time of capture," a ball striking his back and doing "great violence" to the muscles of his shoulder. He would be treated at Memphis and Mound City, and finally at Jefferson Barracks in Missouri, from which he was eventually discharged on a surgeon's certificate. Unable to raise his hands above his head, subject to fits of nervous irritability, he would spend the rest of his life farming first in his native Henry County and then New Concord, Kentucky, where he moved in 1884 and struggled to make ends meet for himself and his five children.[31]

Simmons's comrade James Meador was shot clear through one lung during the battle. A second wound, striking near his left collarbone and passing out his back, would not be discovered until he had been taken to Mound City, where Simmons feared it would be "impossible for him to recover." But he did, in part, and was discharged in November. No doubt fearing reprisals if he returned to Henry County, Meador moved immediately to Illinois, studied in public school for a few months, clerked for a grocer in Indiana a few years, and then moved down to Kentucky to manage a tenant farm. Described by an examiner as "totally incapacitated" and unable to "stoop or exorsise without pain," Meador died in 1887 at the age of forty-two.[32]

Simmons's brother-in-law, Sergeant Bill Albritton, had been shot after surrendering. The shot had injured his left elbow so severely that the day after he was brought to Memphis on the hospital boat Red Rover, the surgeons at Overton Hospital would elect to amputate two-thirds of his arm. Nevertheless he returned briefly to service in June. His wife died without issue in 1876, and though he was incapable of performing manual labor and relied on the charity of his neighbors, he remarried in Christian County, Kentucky, and fathered five children. The pension office sent him fifteen dollars a month for his pains, but refused to fit him with an artificial arm.[33]

After suffering six serious wounds, seventeen-year-old Wiley Robinson of 13/A had to be littered aboard the Platte Valley but he eventually recovered. Jim McMichael of 13/C had been shot no fewer than four times after he had surrendered: the first shot glancing across his skull, the second plowing up his forearm, the third lodging irretrievably in his stomach, the fourth penetrating his side.[34]

Shot four times after surrendering, a final shot plowing across his left eye, Sergeant William Walker of 13/D would live the rest of his life crippled and half blind. Discharged on a surgeon's certificate, he left his native Tennessee for Illinois and died in Metropolis in 1922. Wounded in the side, the ball plunging downward into his vitals, Isaac Ledbetter of 13/E would almost succumb to "bowel trouble." Discharged in July, he became a Methodist minister and postal clerk and sired six children. Probably the longest-lived of the survivors of the Fort Pillow massacre, Ledbetter died in Morrilton, Arkansas, in 1935.[35]

Shot as he fled over the bluff, unable to walk, Daniel Rankin of 13/C had been carried about two miles from the parapet and given a parole. The next morning three rebels put him on a horse and led him to the house of an elderly farmer, who began to escort him down to the gunboats in the company of a couple of rebel surgeons. He almost did not make it. When they reached the river, "a rebel lieutenant colonel took my parole from me, said it was forged, and that he was going to take me back." But the surgeons vouched for him, and at last Rankin was allowed to board the Silver Cloud.[36]

Rankin would eventually move to the president's old hometown of Salem, Illinois, but it did not prove to be the stepping-stone it had been for young Abe Lincoln. Rankin complained that as a result of his wound "my knee is enlarged, and I can cary nothing more than my own wait, or the cap of my knee will fly out of place and render me unfit for labour for several weeks at a time." He declared that his experience at Fort Pillow had deranged him, and for the rest of his life he suffered from "melancholy and a demented mind."[37]

After lying all night with a deep gunshot to his thigh, Daniel Stamps of 13/E was transferred to a boat bound for Memphis, where the surgeons deemed his wound "severe." No sooner had he recovered sufficiently to rejoin his regiment than he came down with measles and then developed, perhaps as a consequence, a case of night blindness. "He could not see any after sunset," his friend John Copher testified. "He would hafte be led abut by some of his comrades." In fact his brother John found it necessary to "lead him on the car when we was mustered out of serves." Stamps's first wife bore him two more children, but apparently left him, for she died in 1877, two years after he married a Texas girl named Sally Hill. He died in Kaufman County, Texas, in 1907.[38]

Edward Benton, whose property was now strewn with Union dead, spent the night lost in a tangle of fallen timber. "About two o'clock," he said, "the dogs were getting so close to me that I knew they were on my track." Stumbling out of the abatis and down Coal Creek ravine, he swam across to the bar and climbed aboard the *Lady Pike*. By now he had had enough of West Tennessee, and moved to St. Louis to open a store. Eventually he migrated down the Mississippi to Shreveport, Louisiana, where he prospered as a businessman, and then moved to New Orleans, where he became the president of something called the Accommodation Bank.[39]

At ten in the morning, Dr. Fitch was escorted to the river with his hard-won parole in hand. "As I came in," he said, "I passed by the Hospitals. They were burned down." Joe Turpin of 13/E "was lying on a Cot some five Rods from where the log cabin Hospital stood," too sick with typhoid fever to "give me any reliable information of what became of the rest of them." Fitch and Acting Assistant Surgeon William N. McCoy treated twelve of the parolees from Fort Pillow, all of whom had been wounded after surrender. Fitch continued to serve until August, when he allowed his contract with the army to lapse and returned home to Chariton, Iowa. He died in 1890.[40]

Billy Bancom of Obion County, the father of two children, was brought on board the *Platte Valley* with a compound fracture of the right forearm and died two months later at Overton Hospital in Memphis of chronic diarrhea. Frank Key of Henry County was the father of five when he enlisted in 13/D.

A full-page advertisement for Forrest's slave-trading business from a prewar edition of the Memphis city directory. TENNESSEE STATE LIBRARY AND ARCHIVES

Before the war, Nathan Bedford Forrest rose from hardscrabble farmer to lawman, slave catcher, wealthy slave trader, planter, and Memphis alderman. PRIVATE COLLECTION

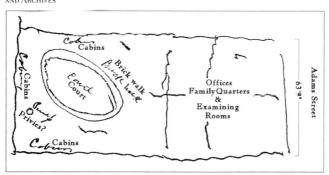

This map of General Forrest's trading camp on Adams Street in Memphis was based on the memories of a former slave named Horatio Eden, who, with his mother, was sold by Forrest. Slaves awaited sale in the cabins that formed a "U" around the circular brick court, where they were paraded on sales days. A complex to the right included Forrest's residence, office, and examining rooms where female slaves were inspected. TENNESSEE STATE LIBRARY AND ARCHIVES

A brick-chimneyed slave cabin similar to those on Forrest's plantation. His slaves lived in two parallel rows of such cabins on his plantation in Hernando, Mississippi. AUTHOR'S COLLECTION

Contraband laborers en route to working on Union fortifications. AUTHOR'S COLLECTION

Examination of black recruits. AUTHOR'S COLLECTION

This popular sequence of images depicts the transformation of a boy from escaped slave to soldier, or, in this case, to drummer boy. The black artillerists who defended Fort Pillow were, with one or two possible exceptions, fugitive slaves primarily from farms and plantations in Mississippi and Tennessee. AUTHOR'S COLLECTION

Of the thirty-nine men of the 2nd USCLA who served at Fort Pillow, ten were confirmed killed, fourteen were reported missing and presumed killed, nine were re-enslaved by Forrest, four escaped and/or deserted on the day of the battle, and two were paroled to Mound City. CHICAGO HISTORICAL SOCIETY

Black troops hauling captured rebel artillery. AUTHOR'S COLLECTION

William Ellis of Company C, 6th USCHA, was taken prisoner at Fort Pillow and taken to Mobile to work on rebel fortifications. After the fall of Mobile, he returned to his regiment, now the 11th USCI, and was kept in a hospital to recover from his captivity. Captain William Smith recalled that Ellis had "a care-worn, anxious expression which we attributed to the experiences and hardships attendant upon his efforts to get into our lines." Here he poses after the war in his Masonic apron. NATIONAL ARCHIVES AND RECORDS ADMINISTRATION

"Passing Glimpse of Fort Pillow" drawn late in the war by Elijah Evan Edwards, chaplain of the 7th Minnesota Infantry. ARCHIVES OF DEPAUW UNIVERSITY AND INDIANA UNITED METHODISM

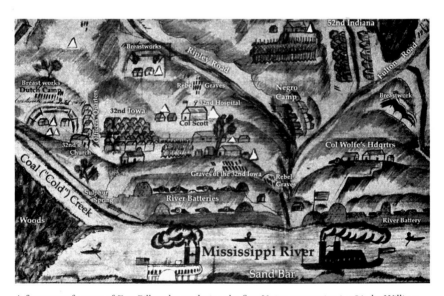

A fragment of a map of Fort Pillow drawn during the first Union occupation in 1863 by William D. Power of the 32nd Iowa. The area immediately above Coal Creek labeled "Dutch Camp" became the focus of the rebel assault a year later, during which the rows of barracks to its right provided Forrest's men with cover from the garrison's fire. When the garrison was evacuated by the 52nd Indiana, the river batteries pictured along the face of the bluff were removed.
COLLECTION OF ROBERT MAINFORT

Major General Stephen Augustus Hurlbut, who, as commander in Memphis of the 16th Army Corps, garrisoned Fort Pillow in contravention of Sherman's explicit instructions. PRIVATE COLLECTION

William Tecumseh Sherman removed most of the veteran troops of the Union's western army from the Mississippi to marshal his forces for his Atlanta Campaign, leaving orders with General Hurlbut to abandon Fort Pillow. Enraged by Hurlbut's disobedience and frustrated by his timidity in pursuing Forrest, Sherman removed Hurlbut from command of the 16th Army Corps after the attack. AUTHOR'S COLLECTION

Confederate cavalry returning from a successful raid in pursuit of fresh horses and provisions. AUTHOR'S COLLECTION

Five of Terry's Texas Rangers, aka the 8th Tennessee Cavalry, which participated in the attack on Fort Pillow, but whose members were singled out by the Yankee witnesses for the mercy they showed the defenders. PRIVATE COLLECTION

Brigadier General James Ronald Chalmers was field commander during the battle. AUTHOR'S COLLECTION

Major Charles W. Anderson of Forrest's staff commanded a squad of snipers on the bluff.
AUTHOR'S COLLECTION

Colonel William L. Duckworth and his 7th Tennessee Cavalry bluffed Union City's federal garrison into surrendering at almost the same time Forrest failed to take Paducah. AUTHOR'S COLLECTION

General Nathan Bedford Forrest. LIBRARY OF CONGRESS

Colonel Robert "Black Bob" McCulloch and his Missourians attacked Fort Pillow from the south.
AUTHOR'S COLLECTION

Brigadier General Tyree Bell, whose brigade, with Colonel A. N. Wilson's, formed the center of the assault. AUTHOR'S COLLECTION

Colonel Clarke R. Barteau and his 22nd (formerly 2nd) Tennessee Cavalry attacked Fort Pillow from the north.
AUTHOR'S COLLECTION

In this very accurate illustration, Forrest's men in their motley uniforms help each other climb out of the trench at the base of the works in preparation for their final assault. PRIVATE COLLECTION

The garrison flees as the rebels fire down from the top of the works. PRIVATE COLLECTION

A widely circulated depiction of the massacre by the river. The illustrator probably intended the figure in the upper right corner to represent Forrest, and the Union officer holding up a sword with a white flag attached to represent Major William Bradford. AUTHOR'S COLLECTION

Radical Republican Benjamin "Bluff Ben" Wade, who brandished his Joint Committee on the Conduct of the War to prod Lincoln into total war. His investigation into the Fort Pillow affair and subsequent report caused a sensation. LIBRARY OF CONGRESS

The inebriate Thomas Jefferson Jackson, 24-hour colonel of the 6th USCHA, whose tales of being a survivor of the battle were as extravagant as his whiskers. COLLECTION OF ROBERT MAINFORT

A white-haired Forrest photographed after the war. A born-again experience softened him, just as chronic diarrhea reduced him to a husk of himself. His wife noticed that toward the end of his life he was always hungry and thirsty, an indication that what killed the indefatigable Wizard may have been diabetes mellitus. AUTHOR'S COLLECTION

This panel from an 1868 broadside by Thomas Nast portrays a demonic Forrest leading the slaughter at Fort Pillow. The cartoon was accompanied by an excerpt from Wade and Gooch's report quoting Forrest as crying, "No quarter!" and a portion of his own report on the battle commending Chalmers for his conduct. COLLECTION OF JEFF COOPERSMITH

He survived the night, but died of his wounds before he could be littered aboard. Shot in the back and arms after surrender, the gallant teamster Davy Harrison would survive only three more weeks and die of his wounds in May.[41]

After the last of the thirty-four white parolees had been helped aboard, it was the black artillerists' turn to proceed up the gangway. All day long they would rise like ghosts from the clusters of dead, the river, the piles of drift-wood, even from the shallow graves in which they had been buried the night before. "Old man" Thomas Addison of 6/C emerged from the river where, at a rebel soldier's kindly suggestion, he had been hiding all night. With one eye shot out and his nose blown away, he was a ghastly apparition, and though the surgeons at Mound City would give him little chance of surviv-ing, survive he did, and spent the rest of his life in Mound City as a laborer.[42]

Still shaking with rage after seeing his wounded comrades shot and burned, Ransom Anderson of 6/B stumbled up, blood caked around the saber wounds to his head and hands. After throwing down his arms and sur-rendering, Aaron Blain of 6/D had been shot through both legs by a rebel with a carbine who declared that "they were going to kill us all." But he somehow managed to avoid further injury. After Anderson raised his flag of truce and the *Platte Valley* began taking on prisoners, Aaron heard a rebel soldier declare that "they would have shot us all if the gunboat had not come along."[43]

That morning Aaron was reunited with his brother Sherry, who emerged from his hiding place with their comrade, George Houston. Sherry Blain would return to his regiment and serve for the rest of the war with what little was left of his company. After his discharge in January 1866, Blain reclaimed his father's name—Thornton—and he and his sergeant, Frank Thompson, moved to Vincent, Arkansas, where they boarded with Thompson's half sis-ter Ellen, whose husband, Samuel Evans, was another former Fayette County slave and Union veteran. There they would all labor for a couple of years, but the presence of black Union veterans riled the local whites, and one day in 1868 masked Klansmen shot Evans down as he was walking home along the Bay Ferry Road. Evans managed to stagger home but died in Sherry's arms, leaving Ellen a widow. Though about a dozen years Sherry's senior, she married Blain, and they lived out their lives in poverty, working as field hands for local white farmers.

Praising God for his deliverance from Forrest's men, Blain's friend

George Houston became a minister of the gospel. Perhaps recalling his place of refuge at Fort Pillow, he would live out his days in Memphis "at the foot of Alabama Street, under the bluff, Fort Pickering region," in a place a pension examiner described as "almost inaccessible," which was probably how Houston wanted it.[44]

His arm shattered, his right leg mangled, Corporal Eli Cothel of 6/B would be discharged in November on a medical certificate with his comrade Arthur Edmonds, who had somehow survived a pistol shot to the head. After the war, Edmonds became an itinerant preacher, but his slave wife, Fannie, refused to travel with him, and they were divorced in 1870. Preaching may have been about all he was fit for. The wounds to his head gave him a "swimming so that I cannot stoop," his right wrist was shattered, and his shoulder was so mangled by a burst of rebel buckshot that his arm merely hung by his side. He lived the rest of his life in a declension of communities: first Memphis, then Tupelo, and finally Delta Bottoms, Mississippi.[45]

Wounded in the arm and thigh, Sandy Cole of 6/D had to be helped up the gangway and would be discharged at Mound City on a surgeon's certificate. Hardin Capers of 6/A had suffered wounds severe enough to secure his parole and to prevent his testifying in detail. But on April 23 he managed to dictate a statement naming all the men he had seen murdered that morning.[46]

Shot in the back of his head and neck and left for dead, Alexander Nason of 2/C picked his way out from among a tangle of driftwood and gave his name to Anderson. A Mound City surgeon would judge his wound "not serious," and three months later, Nason would return to his regiment. By the time of his discharge in October 1865, Nason had risen to orderly sergeant. His wound would leave a deep depression just behind his left ear, and he spent the rest of his life as a Memphis teamster and "chore boy," collecting a pension of eight dollars a month. Dizzy, half deaf, he would complain in old age that "most all the time I has a deadly pain on [the right] side of my head. It works down the leader of my back," he said, "and hurts me powerful."[47]

Manuel Nichols of 6/B, the putative freedman from Michigan, crawled out of his hiding place with wounds to his head, hands, and arm. His surgeon was convinced that he would not survive his wounds, and William Lloyd Garrison's *Liberator* would print his eulogy. "Manuel's blood is crying to me from the ground," his comrade Daniel Tyler was represented as declaring, "and I want to be able, sometime, to say to Manuel Nichols' wife, up there in Michigan, that his fall has had a compensation. And may God speed the day when this whole slaveholders' rebellion—what remains of it—shall be 'Buried Alive!'" But the eulogy was premature. Ten days after the massacre, Nichols was well enough to give a brief, if somewhat conflicting, affidavit, and he would live to join the 11th U.S. Colored Infantry, into which the remnants of the two black artillery regiments that served at Fort Pillow were eventually merged.[48]

AFTERMATH
TOURING THE FORT
April 13, 1864

As THE LAST OF THE WOUNDED CROWDED ABOARD THE *PLATTE VALLEY*, Lieutenants Frank Smith and William Cleary asked Anderson a question that would be repeated all morning: How could the rebels justify massacring black troops? Anderson explained "that they did not consider colored men as soldiers, but as property, and as such, being used by our people, they had destroyed them," in a manner "concurred by Forrest, Chalmers, and McCullough, and other officers."[1]

The Yankees would soon get the chance to ask the same question of Chalmers himself. Around midday, the little general and his staff trotted down the ravine road to notify Anderson that he was prepared to move his division to Brownsville. But before he departed, he wanted to offer Anderson a detachment to escort his little squad back to Forrest's headquarters at Jackson. Convinced he would be able to catch up to Chalmers, encumbered as they were by wagons and artillery, Anderson politely declined the offer. But Chalmers and his staff lingered for about an hour, introducing themselves to the Federal officers gathered at the landing.[2]

The general remarked that he guessed his men had taken about twenty-five negroes prisoner.

A gunboat officer asked him if most of the negroes were killed after the rebels had taken possession of the fort.

"Chalmers replied that he thought they had been, and that the men of General Forrest's command had such a hatred toward the armed negro that they could not be restrained from killing the negroes after they had captured them."

Contrary to what Anderson had blurted to Smith and Cleary, Chalmers claimed that neither he nor Forrest ordered a massacre and had stopped it "as soon as they were able to do so." Nevertheless, Chalmers said that the black troops' treatment "was nothing better than we could expect so long as we persisted in arming the negro."

Chalmers told the assembled officers "that all of his forces would be out of the place by 3 o'clock of that day, and that the main body was already moving," and promised the Yankees "that Forrest's command would never fire on transport steamers."[3]

In the meantime, Cleary accepted Chalmers's invitation to tour the battlefield "to find out if any of our men were left alive." He was accompanied by Captain Ferguson, Captain John G. Woodruff of the 113th Illinois Infantry, N. D. Wetmore of the *Memphis Argus,* a reporter for the *Virginia Repository,* and a rebel escort under the "Little 'Un's" brother, Colonel Alexander Chalmers of the 18th Mississippi Cavalry. Dr. Chapman Underwood, who had ridden out the battle aboard the *New Era,* declined to join them, for though "there were some sick men in the hospital," he was "afraid to go on shore after the rebels got there."[4]

Though Cleary was relieved to find that the man he had earlier seen fired upon was able to walk, what he was about to witness would turn his stomach. Riding up to the top of the bluff, he came upon "some of our dead half buried," he said, and the corpses of five negroes "lying upon the boards and straw in the tents which had been set on fire. It seemed to me as if the fire could not have been set more than half an hour before," he testified, because "their flesh was frying off them, and their clothes were burning."

Cleary could not tell from his inspection whether the rebels had moved the sick out of the post hospital before they set it ablaze, but "understood the rebels went in where there were some twenty or thirty negroes sick, and hacked them over their heads with sabers and shot them. The negroes," and not the white survivors from the 13th, "had been moved from the heights up on the hill into two large tents" until they were "full of colored troops." For his part, Captain Woodruff counted "the dead bodies of 15 negroes," including two burning corpses. Most of them had been shot in the head at close range, he guessed, for they "were burned as if by powder around the holes in their heads."[5]

Captain Ferguson found what he called "unmistakable evidences of a massacre carried on long after any resistance could have been offered, with a cold-blooded barbarity and perseverance which nothing can palliate." The corpses "with gaping wounds, some bayoneted through the eyes, some with

268 RIVER RUN RED

skulls beaten through, others with hideous wounds as if their bowels had been ripped open with bowie-knives, plainly told that but little quarter was shown to our troops." They were "strewn from the fort to the river bank, in the ravines and hollows, behind logs and under the brush where they had crept for protection from the assassins who pursued them." He saw bodies of men that had been "bayoneted, beaten, and shot to death, showing how cold-blooded and persistent was the slaughter of our unfortunate troops."[6]

"I passed up the bank of the river and counted fifty dead strewed along," wrote a reporter. One of the victims "had crawled into a hollow log and was killed in it; another had got over the bank into the river, and got to a board that ran out into the water." The reporter found him lying on it "stark and still" and facedown, "with his feet in the water." Other men "had tried to hide in crevices made by the falling bank, and could not be seen without difficulty, but they were singled out and killed. From the best information I could get the white soldiers were, to a very considerable extent, treated in the same way."[7]

Wetmore of the *Argus* counted "200 or more dead bodies mangled, dying as they did, pleading for quarter, many with faces distorted with pain, eyes bayoneted, skulls broken, and some with bowels torn from the human casements, some so besmeared with blood and the flesh of comrades as to render them incognito to even their own fathers and mothers." In the storming of a fort "where such desperate resistance is offered," Wetmore conceded that "many, very many, must fall. But at Fort Pillow I have every evidence that instead of honorable warfare," the rebels had "pursued that of indiscriminate butchery."[8]

Recoiling from all this horror, Cleary demanded of Colonel Chalmers that he tell him if this "was the way he allowed his men to do."

Described by a female admirer as "a handsome young fellow, as gallant as he looked, and full of humor," the colonel replied that "he could not control his men very well," and in any case regarded the treatment his men had meted out as "justifiable in regard to negroes," for they "did not recognize negroes as soldiers." Cleary also heard "a great many rebel soldiers say they did not intend to recognize those black devils as soldiers." If Cleary's comrades in Bradford's Battalion "had not been fighting with black troops," they said, "they would not have hurt us at all, but they did not intend to give any quarter to negroes."[9]

By now local people had begun to emerge from the surrounding woods to inspect the field and scavenge for supplies and keepsakes. Anderson would contend that he "cheerfully and pleasantly" permitted a number of the *New Era's* refugee passengers to search for their loved ones and inspect the fort, though by the terms of the truce the fort was now in Ferguson's control anyway. "All of them did so, many of them bringing back in their hands buckles, belts, balls, buttons, etc., picked up on the grounds, which they requested permission to carry with them as relics and mementoes."[10]

Ferried across from her refuge on the sandbar, the former slave Rachel Parks sought her husband, Ransom, of 2/A, only to be told by a survivor as she returned to the *New Era* that he had died of his wounds in the night. Nancy Hopper looked in vain for her brother Danny of 13/D, who was already on a long march to Andersonville, "black scurvy," and death. Rosa Johnson climbed up into the fort, expecting to find her son Bill of 13/B, who had written her in February advising her not to come to Fort Pillow until proper shelter was available. "I went around," she testified, "where I saw some half buried, some with feet out, or hands out, or heads out; but I could not find him." She came upon a pile of earth with "a crack in it, which looked like a wounded man had been buried there, and had tried to get out, and had jammed the dirt, for they buried the wounded and the dead altogether there." Elsewhere she "saw a man lying there burned, they said; but I did not go close to him. I was looking all around the fort for my child, and did not pay attention to anything else." But he too was marching to Andersonville and his doom. Anne Jane Ruffin was more fortunate. She spotted her husband, Tom, of 13/C painfully making his way up the gangway, and would join him on the *Platte Valley* for the journey upriver to Mound City.[11]

Three women testified that while searching along the river for their loved ones, they came across the charred body of Lieutenant John C. Akerstrom, which appeared to them to have been nailed to the side of his quarters and set on fire. Anne Jane Ruffin described Akerstrom's body "lying upon the back, its arms outstretched, with some planks under it." Cleary testified that when someone asked the rebels why Akerstrom's body had not been properly buried, "some of the rebels said he was a damned conscript that had run away from Forrest."[12]

Cleary had "never heard Lieutenant Akerstrom say any such thing." In fact, Akerstrom was a New Yorker, and there is no record of his having served in the rebel army. Nevertheless, congressional investigators would accept this probably groundless claim as fact. In the unlikely event that James McCoy identified him correctly from his vantage point on the *New Era,* four hundred yards from the bluff, Akerstrom, like his comrade Ted

Bradford, may have earned the special enmity of the rebels by having tried during the truce to wigwag a signal to the gunboat.[13]

Jacob Thompson, the cook from Fort Pillow's lone hotel, claimed that as he made his way down to the river that morning with a bullet lodged in his skull, he saw a man nailed through his wrist "to the side of a house," and the smoldering bodies, "burned almost in two," of white sergeants from black regiments who had been nailed to logs and set on fire. As outrageous and singular as this seems, it was a common practice in McCulloch's Missouri to execute errant slaves by burning them to death. Nevertheless, what these witnesses probably saw were the bodies of men who, either pre- or post-mortem, had been burned in the barracks in a conflagration that had incinerated the plank floor, leaving only charred log joists studded with nails.[14]

The crew of the *New Era*, with the assistance of several of the more ambulatory survivors Ferguson had picked up, "buried 64 men before the flag of truce was withdrawn," reported James Marshall, who estimated that the rebels had already buried "between 300 and 400." An unknown number of these had been buried where they lay, in the soft flats along the riverbank, only to be washed away by the rising Mississippi.[15]

Among the missing was James Ricks of 6/A. When his slave father, Alfred, died in early cotton-picking season in 1857, Ricks had been the one child old enough to support his widowed mother, Louisa, and his siblings. He proved a diligent and industrious provider. His fellow slaves and future comrades-in-arms recalled that James was "very thrifty," and worked "outside of his regularly required duty as a slave" cultivating his own cotton, corn, and vegetable patches and selling charcoal to his master's blacksmith shop. "In this way he procured considerable" and gave his mother "all he made," including the fifteen dollars he earned annually from his cotton patch. After joining the 6th USCHA under the name James Ricks, he continued to support his family with his soldier's wages, including a ten-dollar greenback he relayed to Louisa a few days before the Battle of Fort Pillow.[16]

Some artillerists sought out the bodies of their brothers and comrades and messmates: fellow slaves of the same master who had joined up with them ten months before. Henry Richardson came upon his fellow slave Daniel Ray of 6/D. Sandy Addison and Charles Williams buried the body of their comrade Robert Green of 6/A. In 1856, repeating the vows recited to him by a black minister named James Bosworth, Green had married Elizabeth, the slave of a Dr. Crump of Hardin County, Tennessee. By the time he joined the 6th, Elizabeth had borne him several children, now rendered fatherless in the slaughter by the river.[17]

As the truce deadline approached, the Federal burial parties made their way back up the gangway, leaving many bodies still unburied. The white parolees were shown to the *Platte Valley*'s staterooms. "Too much praise cannot be bestowed upon Captain Riley, as well as all other officers of the *Platte Valley*," reported Wetmore of the *Argus*, "for the manner in which they provided for the wounded, requiring the passengers to give up their staterooms, furnishing at once proper sustenance of food, and nourishing drinks to those who were unable to eat. There were a great many ladies on board who, God bless them, true to their nature, went at once to work alleviating as far as possible their sufferings."[18]

Fitch reported that eight parolees died en route to Mound City, all but one of them white. Eighteen more would die at Mound City that spring and summer, among them Lieutenant John H. Porter of 13/D. Married for ten years, the father of two sons and two daughters, he had been shot in the head during the siege and died of infection on June 21. Another was a black officer's servant named Bill Jordan who was picked up by the *Platte Valley* with his arm shot up and his ankle so badly shattered that his foot would have to be amputated. Jordan died in Mound City of shock and loss of blood.[19]

While the wounded whites were attended to indoors, the blacks were placed upon the gunwales. "I was in Cairo when the *Platte Valley* came up, and it was an awful scene," a correspondent for the *Mound City Dispatch* would write the next day. "There were quite a number of colored soldiers on board, who had been wounded, and were not as well cared for as the whites: they were lying on the guards and on the deck, and some of them were suffering from cold; others were wet by the water that sloshed over the guards, while they were suffering from their wounds."[20]

Almost as disgraceful was the welcome accorded Chalmers and his staff by "two or three Federal band-box officers on board the *Platte Valley*" who, according to the *Missouri Democrat*, "made themselves conspicuous in fawning around the rebel officers. They brought Gen. Chalmers and several subordinate cut-throat looking officers on board the *Platte Valley*, drank with them, introduced them to their wives, and invited them to dinner." It seemed to parolee Bill Johnson of 13/B that the Union officers made "very free with them." Astonishingly enough, one of the Union officers who cordially fraternized with Chalmers and his staff was Captain John G. Woodruff of the

113th Illinois Infantry, who had just toured the battlefield and counted fifteen corpses of black troops, several of them still smoldering.[21]

Anderson accepted the two officers' invitation to share a drink at the *Platte Valley*'s bar, "little thinking," he wrote, that it would "cost them their commissions. For this courtesy and kindness, one officer was cashiered and the other reduced to the ranks."[22]

"I went on board the boat," recalled John Penwell, "and took my seat right in front of the saloon," for he was acquainted with the bartender "and wanted to get a chance to get some wine, as I was very weak." But just as he stepped up to the rail, "one of our officers—a lieutenant or a captain, I don't know which—stepped in front of me and almost shoved me away, and called up one of the rebel officers and took a drink with him; and I saw our officers drinking with the rebel officers several times." "I thought our officers," Lieutenant Mack Leaming bitterly remarked, "might have been in better business."[23]

Chalmers and his men "were generally well clad," the *Democrat* reported, "but had very little to distinguish them from the privates. Gen. Chalmers had simply a black feather in his hat, and the other officers stripes on their collars." The Union officers on board made room for Chalmers and his men "at the ladies' table." As they sat down to await their luncheon, the little general and former DA soliloquized that though he did not "countenance" nor "encourage his soldiers in killing captive negro soldiers," he believed "it was right and justifiable." Some of the rebel officers declared that "they had only about twenty-five colored prisoners, and they were old servants of white officers, and that all colored soldiers were killed."[24]

Several of the little Mississippian's officers "bragged a great deal about their victory," Chapman Underwood testified, "and said it was a matter of no consequence. They hated to have such a fight as that," and not kill or capture more Federals. One of the officers from the *New Era* "got into a squabble" with the rebels, "and said they did not treat the flag of truce right."

"Damn you," an Illinois officer snarled at the rebels. "I've had eighteen fights with you." But after what the rebels had done at Fort Pillow, he declared he would no longer treat them as prisoners of war.

Chalmers politely replied that he would treat *him* as a prisoner of war, but never the "'home-made Yankees."[25]

James McCoy testified that the Union officers greeted Chalmers and his men cordially, "just as though there had been no fight." In high dudgeon, McCoy stomped over to the *New Era* and asked Captain Marshall's permission to shoot Chalmers then and there. But Marshall reminded the irate civilian that while "the flag of truce was up," killing the Little 'Un would violate "the rules of war."[26]

Nevertheless, "either by accident or from a just idea of the fitness of things," a "high-spirited" James Marshall peremptorily rang the signal to move out, whereupon the rebel officers rushed up from the table and "skedaddled, leaving their soup untouched."[27]

A little before 5:00 p.m., Anderson disembarked from the *Platte Valley* and urged Chalmers to order the steamers to shove off, for he intended to burn what little remained of the post. Anderson assured Ferguson that Forrest's command was miles off and that he could "depart at his leisure, and without fear of molestation." Letting go their lines and lowering their white flags, the steamers chuffed and heaved back into the current.[28]

In the meantime, the Union hospital boat *Red Rover* had arrived on the scene. After the *Platte Valley* pulled away from the landing, Anderson signaled that he had discovered over a dozen more wounded Federals in the smoking ruins of the fort. So the *Red Rover* came in and brought them aboard, where "fleet Surgeon Ninian Pinkney, with his usual promptness, provided comfortable quarters for them," the *Argus* reported, "and with his little army of assistant surgeons soon had their wounds dressed."[29]

The *New Era* headed downriver to recover a coal barge that had broken loose during the fight and tow it to Flour Island, opposite Fulton. The *Red Rover*, with its cargo of "refugees, women and children," headed south for Memphis under the *Silver Cloud*'s protection while the *Platte Valley* and the *Lady Pike* proceeded upriver to Cairo. Despite Anderson's assurance of safe passage, the *Platte Valley*'s artillerists kept her nine guns primed all night.[30]

Saluting Ferguson, Anderson and his detachment of ten troopers slowly made their way back up to the fort, where he ordered his men to dismount and begin distributing tinder among the remaining buildings. As the *Silver Cloud* swung back into the stream, Anderson's men piled hospital beds, bunks, and mattresses into teetering heaps and, kindling them with straw, put what remained of the ruined fort to the torch.

"We then mounted our horses," recalled Anderson, "and bade Fort Pillow a lasting adieu." Spurring their horses, Anderson and his escort, with Young still in their custody, hustled up the Ripley Road in hopes of catching up to their comrades.[31]

Major William Bradford had emerged from the massacre without so much as a scratch. Though Wyeth took it as "proof of the control that Forrest had over his men that he was not shot, even after the surrender," it was not for want of trying. Whether he was unusually fleet or momentarily charmed, none of the hundreds of shots that were fired at him had so much as grazed him as he ran into and then out of the river, back up to the parapet, and into Forrest's grudging custody. Bradford had given "his parole of honor that he would report again to the Confederates in their camp that night as soon as his brother was interred." But here the story gets blurred.[32]

Some say he simply slipped away at this point, others that he did indeed return to rebel custody, only to escape that night. Dr. Fitch encountered him around 7:00 p.m. and remembered asking him why he had not surrendered the garrison.

"Because," Bradford replied, "my name is not Hawkins," meaning, of course, the hornswoggled Union commander at Union City.

The captured trader W. R. McLagan testified that he also encountered Major Bradford that evening. "He told me himself that he was Major Bradford," he claimed, but wanted his identity kept from the guards "as he had enemies there; and it never would have been known," McLagan continued, "but for a detective in the confederate army from Obion county, Tennessee, named Willis Wright, who recognized him as Major Bradford, and told them of it."[33]

Apparently McLagan had a personal beef with Wright, whom he called "a notorious spy and smuggler," and the rebels had already established Bradford's identity. But it is possible that what McLagan meant was that after dressing himself in civilian clothes, Bradford tried to lose himself in McCulloch's drove before slipping off toward the Hatchie. "The Rebel soldiers were frequently making the remark that Major Bradford ought to be killed," Dr. Fitch recalled. "The Major must have heard such remarks often during the night." The last Frank Hogan of 6/A saw of Bradford was his hunched form lying under a blanket among the other prisoners. But the next morning, when McCulloch came by to order the prisoners to light a campfire, Bradford was nowhere to be found.[34]

As the prisoners were driven south, they asked "why Major Bradford was not with us." Some of the rebels told Fitch "that he had been paroled for twenty-four hours, others that Forrest had taken Bradford with him." But Fitch found it hard to believe that Bradford "would take a parole for 24 hours, knowing, as he did, that his life would not be safe." Captains Poston and Young predicted to Fitch "that the Rebs would kill Major Bradford," and tell their prisoners the next morning "that Major Bradford had violated his parole."[35]

When a search party from the 7th caught up with Bradford, he was dressed in civilian clothes and preparing to cross the Hatchie. He claimed to be a rebel conscript, but he had no papers to prove it. Duckworth's men brought him before their colonel, who recognized him as Bradford and placed him in the 7th's custody, bound for Forrest's headquarters in Jackson. But as they set forth, five of Bradford's guards were ordered back to Duckworth's headquarters, where "those five guards," including one of the 7th's lieutenants, "seemed to have received special instructions about something," McLagan testified. "I don't know what. After marching about five miles from Brownsville, we halted" and five guards prodded Bradford "about fifty yards from the road. He seemed to understand what they were going to do with him. He asked for mercy, and said that he had fought them manfully, and wished to be treated as a prisoner of war."

At 2:00 a.m. on April 15, McLagan escaped, and as he fitfully wended his way back to Fort Pillow, he passed by Bradford's "yet unburied" corpse. "The moon was shining brightly," McLagan testified, "and it seemed to me that the buzzards had eaten his face considerably." McLagan surmised after inspecting Bradford's corpse that three of the five guards had shot him down. "One shot struck him about in the temple, a second in the left breast, and the third shot went through the thick part of the thigh. He was killed instantly. They left his body lying there."[36]

Two months later, when Forrest protested Northern charges that his men had perpetrated an atrocity, Union general Cadwallader Colder Washburn replied that Bradford's murder "hardly justifies your remark that your operations have been conducted on civilized principles, and, until you take some steps to bring the perpetrators of this outrage to justice, the world will not fail to believe that it had your sanction."[37]

Forrest replied in high dudgeon that he had not known anything about Bradford's death until about nine days after the fact, when Duckworth's men reported that Bradford had been shot while trying to escape. "It was an act," wrote Forrest's authorized biographers, "in which no officer was concerned, mainly due, we are satisfied, after the most rigid inquiry, to private vengeance for well authenticated outrages committed by Bradford and his band upon the defenseless families of the men of Forrest's Cavalry." "If he was improperly killed," Forrest told Washburn, "nothing would afford me more pleasure than to punish the perpetrators to the full extent of the law." But "there is nothing in the records," concluded Wyeth, "to show that the

men who murdered Major Bradford were ever brought to trial for this un-
warrantable act."[38]

In the late afternoon of April 13, Captain Young had duly returned to Anderson's custody, pausing for a moment on the riverbank to wave to his tearful
bride. Despite Young's services as a truce bearer, or any secessionist sympathies his fellow prisoners suspected him of harboring, the rebels prized their
young captive too much to let him go. He and Bischoff "were conveyed or
taken on foot by forced marches," during which they "had to sleep on the
ground entirely without beding or any Covering," the rebels having taken
their "Over coats, blankets and all heavy clothing."[39]

At Somerville on April 15 they were all placed in the custody of Colonel
Barteau and his 22nd Tennessee Cavalry. The weather "was very inclement"
and Young came down with a "violent cold, resulting in pleurisy and a Cough
which Settled on his lungs, which disability soon prostrated his system to
such an extent" as to render him incapable of walking, so that he had to be
"conveyed the last few days of said march in an open wagon." They all proceeded from Okolona to Meridian, Mississippi, and from there to Demopo-
lis, Alabama, where for two days they were locked up in a "very open" old
cotton shed that exposed them "to greater suffering."[40]

The rebels transported them next to Selma, Alabama, from which they
"marched by foot to Cahaba, Alabama, at which place they were kept in
prison about five weeks," during which time Young was treated in a rebel
hospital. They were then taken to Montgomery and shortly thereafter "conveyed to Andersonville prison where they remained a few days" before proceeding to Macon, Georgia, "where they were confined in prison several
weeks," before shuttling back to Cahaba, where the rebels separated Bischoff
and Young.[41]

In the meantime, to counter Northern accusations that he and his men
had perpetrated a massacre, Forrest urged General Leonidas Polk to take
special care of Young in hopes of persuading the young captain to corroborate Forrest's version of the battle. Eventually a letter signed by Young
emerged stating that "when the final assault was made, I was captured at my
post inside the works, and have been treated as a prisoner of war." On June 23,
in a letter to Union general Cadwallader Washburn, Forrest enclosed a second purported missive as proof that no atrocities were committed at Fort
Pillow, that the garrison never surrendered, and that he had treated his prisoners with decency and consideration.[42]

The letter was predated April 19 and addressed to Forrest. "Your request, made through Judge Scruggs, that I should make a statement as to the treatment of Federal dead and wounded at Fort Pillow, has been made known to me," it began. "Details from Federal prisoners were made to collect the dead and wounded. The dead were buried by their surviving comrades. I saw no ill-treatment of the wounded on the evening of the battle, or next morning." Among the wounded "were some colored troops," the note continued, though it did not say how many. It went on to endorse the brief portion of Anderson's report that Young was permitted to see: an account of Young's waving down the *Silver Cloud* and the subsequent evacuation of the wounded.

General Washburn was not impressed. "How far a statement of a person under duress," he wrote Forrest's superior, Major General Stephen Dill Lee, "and in the position of Captain Young, should go to disprove the sworn testimony of the hundred eye-witnesses who had ample opportunity of seeing and knowing," Washburn would leave others to judge. But what really struck Washburn was what Young did not say. "Does he say that our soldiers were *not* inhumanly treated? No. Does he say that he was in a position to *see* in case they *had* been mistreated? No. He simply says that he 'saw no ill-treatment' of their wounded."[43]

If Young is to be believed, Washburn's suspicions were well founded. In a letter written after his release from rebel prison in September, Young reported to Washburn that he had signed these letters "under protest." When General Stephen D. Lee ordered Young removed from Andersonville, returned to Cahaba, and separated from Bischoff, Young "appealed to the officer in command to know why I was taken from the other officers, but received no explanation. Many of my friends among the Federal officers who had been prisoners longer than myself felt uneasy at the proceeding, and advised me to make my escape going back," for fear the rebels intended to retaliate against him. "Consequently I felt considerable uneasiness of mind."

Young was placed under guard in the Cahaba prison hospital, with still no explanation from the military authorities.

On the day following, I was informed by a sick Federal officer, also in hospital, that he had learned that I had been recognized by some Confederate as a deserter from the Confederate army, and that I was to be court-martialed and shot. The colored waiters about the hospital told me the same thing, and although I knew that the muster-rolls of my country would show that I had been in the volunteer service since 1st of May, 1861, I still felt uneasy, having fresh in my mind Fort

Pillow, and the summary manner the Confederate officers have of disposing of men on some occasions.

After several days of gnawing suspense, the rebel provost marshal summoned Young to his office and handed him a sheaf of papers "made out by General Forrest, for my signature. Looking over the papers I found that signing them would be an indorsement of General Forrest's official report of the Fort Pillow affair. I, of course, returned the papers, positively refusing to have anything to do with them." Later the same day, Young was shown a modified version of Forrest's draft. Young again refused to sign, and sent a note to Forrest saying that although he dismissed as "exaggerated" some of the Northern versions of the Fort Pillow affair that he had seen reprinted in Southern papers, "I also thought that his own official report was equally so in some particulars."

Forrest now asked Polk to delegate his old friend Judge Phineas Thomas Scruggs of Shelby County to interview Young and extract from him a letter that toed the rebel line. A week later, the commander of the Cahaba prison introduced Young to Scruggs to "have a talk with me about the Fort Pillow fight," as Young recalled. "I found the judge very affable and rather disposed to flatter me." Conveying General Forrest's high estimation of Young as "a gentleman and a soldier," Scruggs "went on to [talk] over a great many things that were testified to before the military commission which I was perfectly ignorant of, never having seen the testimony. He then produced papers which General Forrest wished me to sign.[44]

"Upon examination I found them about the same as those previously shown me, and refused again to sign them; but the judge was very importunate and finally prevailed on me to sign the papers," promising Young "that if I wished it, they should only be seen by General Forrest himself; that they were not intended to be used by him as testimony, but merely for his own satisfaction." Indeed, even in the letter in which he had transcribed the notes that had been exchanged during the truce at Fort Pillow, Young had added a caveat. "My present condition," he had written, "would preclude the idea of this being an official statement."

Captain John T. Young wanly hoped "that these papers signed by me, or rather extorted from me while under duress, will not be used by my Government to my disparagement, for my only wish now is, after over three years' service, to recruit my health, which has suffered badly by imprisonment, and go in for the war."

After Young's release, he was found to be suffering from "the effects of general debility with his whole system breaking down & laboring from the

effects of a weakness & disease of the lungs resulting from disease contracted while a prisoner which rendered him unable to perform further duty
as a soldier. But being anxious to perform some kind of service & being a
very valuable officer, he was placed on duty as Assistant Provost Marshall at
St. Louis, Missouri, where he remained until discharged." In 1869 he became a schoolteacher in Randolph County, Missouri. Suffering from a dis-
eased spleen and weak lungs, he died in 1915 in Los Angeles at the Pacific
branch of the National Home for Disabled Volunteer Soldiers.[45]

As the *Platte Valley* proceeded upstream, officers and correspondents flitted
from survivor to survivor, pumping them for information about the battle.
"The wounded negroes we have aboard," reported the *Cairo News,* had
"feigned themselves dead until we came along," and all told the same story
about truce violations, attack, surrender, and massacre.[46]

At Cairo the *Platte Valley* turned up the Ohio, and it reached nearby
Mound City at 9:00 p.m. on April 14. Cairo sat on a small panhandle of Illinois that the Union army considered a "geographical wedge piercing the
South." But Cairo was one of the Union's strangest posts: a floating city pop-
ulated by contrabands, engineers, carpenters, soldiers, shipwrights, steve-
dores: all barracked on barges whose hulls bumped and grated against
steamboats, tugboats, hospital ships, and floating machine shops. The army's
presence was insignificant; it was to the Mississippi fleet's rotation of gunboats that Mound City owed its security. Cairo's garrison was even smaller
than Fort Pillow's: 358 officers and men, of which 35 were troopers from
Hawkins's otherwise surrendered 7th Tennessee Cavalry (USA). This small
guard tediously patroled parapets "very much injured by the rains." Only one
of Cairo's six guns was serviceable, and that was aimed upriver at the city.
The post's magazine was nearly empty, and what ammunition there was had
been soaked by rain leaking in through the roof.[47]

So it was not exactly safe harbor. Convinced that Forrest's (or Buford's)
next move would be "to destroy the large amount of ordnance stores we have
at Mound City, and other Government property at that place," Fleet Captain Alexander M. Pennock ordered his gunboats to destroy all the ferries
and skiffs between Mound City and Paducah. "We have taken every pre-
caution in our power to guard against it," reported Pennock, whose sailors
kept "a constant lookout for rebel arsonists." But on the night of April 15, a
hundred Confederate guerrillas from Kentucky crept into Mound City, fired
upon a Union gunboat, and merrily galloped away.[48]

"Thousands of our brave soldiers are frequently landed here," wrote

General Mason Brayman, "often at night and during storms; and it must continue to be so, for this must remain the great point of reshipment, yet no proper barracks are provided." That spring, Union regiments had "spent the nights in the open air, deep in the mud, and assailed by storms. The Soldiers' Home, under the benevolent care of the Sanitary Commission, provides temporary food and shelter, but is inadequate to the demand." Men who arrived without officers were often left to fend for themselves in the street, "to become the prey of sharpers and victims of the many temptations which beset them."[49]

The Mound City hospital had been notoriously filthy until the arrival of a stout, no-nonsense nurse named Mary Bickerdyke. Like some frontier Florence Nightingale, Bickerdyke had bullied a staff of indolent quacks and orderlies into allowing her to dress wounds, scrub floors, and boil all the linens every week. Bickerdyke had long since moved on to other battlefields, but her legacy was a staff that, by the dismal standards of the day, kept the hospital clean and orderly.[50]

Head Surgeon Horace Wardner met the Fort Pillow parolees at the landing with a corps of navy litter-bearers and ushered them into his hospital. He counted thirty-four whites on the *Platte Valley,* "twenty-seven colored men, and one colored woman, and seven corpses of those who died on their way here." They were "the worst butchered men I have ever seen," he said. "I have been in several hard battles, but I have never seen men so mangled as they were."[51]

Their wounds were filthy, and fearing that if they were kept together they would spread infection to one another, Surgeon Wardner distributed them throughout the hospital. "Dr. Wardner says the negroes exhibit wonderful tenacity of life," wrote the *Cairo News,* "and of the desperately wounded at Fort Pillow nearly all will recover." But before the week was out, Wardner would become less sanguine, predicting that about a third of them would not survive their wounds. When an officer was sent to collect the survivors of the 6th USCHA from Cairo, Mound City, and New Madrid, Missouri, and return them for duty at Memphis, few of them were able to make the journey. On April 19, Colonel William D. Turner would begin to assign men from various white regiments to replace the sergeants of the 6th USCHA who had been killed or disabled at Fort Pillow.[52]

Her ordnance replenished by the gunboat *Volunteer,* the *New Era* hauled anchor off Barfield Point on the morning of the fourteenth and headed back

up to Fort Pillow under a white flag to see "if there were any wounded or unburied bodies" left over.[53]

Coming within sight of Fulton, Captain Marshall brought aboard a
cluster of civilians who had been "captured by the enemy and released." As
he pulled back into the stream, however, he spied a band of fifty rebels who
had made their way out to Flour Island and set fire to the runaway coal barge
he had towed there the night before. "I put the refugees on the shore," Marshall testified, "took down the white flag, and started after them." The rebels
dashed out of sight, leaving burning piles of wood, "and we followed them
clear round and drove them off." The Union gunboats *Moose* and *Hastings*
joined in the fray, the former blocking a rebel attempt to capture the steamboats that had paused by the bar, the latter shelling the woods all the way up
to Plum Point. In all, Marshall fired thirty-four rounds of shrapnel "to scatter the rebels swarming along Coal Creek, setting fire to shacks and coal
barges."[54]

Marshall was about to find out that the dead were not the only Unionists the *Platte Valley* had left behind. After returning to Fort Pillow that
morning, the daguerreotypist Charley Robinson had been horrified to find
that he had not yet seen all of the rebels' "cruel actions, for there were the
charred remains of some of the wounded soldiers, who we had left in their
houses, thinking that as they were wounded, they would be treated kindly."
Now he ran up and down the riverbank, shouting to the *New Era* to pick
him up.[55]

All through the night of April 13, Private Major Williams of 6/B had remained in hiding from the rebels' dogs and search parties, and did not dare
return to the fort until the next day. Williams encountered a comrade and
half a dozen local whites "who were walking over the place." During the *Silver Cloud*'s barrage the previous morning, Duncan Harding of 6/A had
slipped away from his captors and spent the night of the thirteenth in a pile
of brush and logs.[56]

Sergeant Wilbur H. Gaylord testified that on the afternoon of April 14,
the rebels took "a young man whose father lived near here, and who had
been wounded in the fight, to the woods," and shot him three times in his
back "and into his head," and left him where he fell. On the morning of the
fifteenth, a group of local men brought the half-dead boy to the house where
Gaylord was being cared for, "and then carried us both to Fort Pillow in an
old cart that they fixed up for the occasion, in hopes of getting us on board
of a gunboat. Upon our arrival there a gunboat lay on the opposite bank, but
we could not hail her." The locals carted the boy away, said Gaylord, "but I

would not go back." The following afternoon, he was picked up by the gun-boat *Silver Cloud*.[57]

On April 14, after working his way up along the Mississippi's Tennessee bank, the Unionist refugee Elvis Bevel of Arkansas encountered Captain Oliver B. Farriss of Barteau's 22nd Tennessee Cavalry (CSA). "His soldiers said they were hunting for negroes," Bevel testified, but a day later the gun-boat *Moose* would shell them out of the woods. Charley Robinson added that until the *New Era* chased them off, the rebels scoured the swamp south of the fort with hounds. As late as the fifteenth, vestiges of Forrest's com-mand still lurking in the surrounding woods continued to take potshots at the Union gunboats that drew up to Fort Pillow to collect survivors and bury the dead.[58]

The *Cairo News* reported that "about four miles above the fort, lodged against the trunk of a tree, were seen by passengers on the *Platte Valley*, six dead bodies. In another place three bodies were seen. A number of other bodies were seen singly on the banks." But corpses don't float upriver; these were probably the remains of soldiers and contrabands who had fled up the Tennessee shore, only to be hunted down by squads of rebels and packs of hounds.[59]

On the afternoon of April 13, as the survivors of the massacre were still limp-ing up the *Platte Valley*'s gangway, the Wizard had arrived at Brownsville, where "citizens of all classes, old men and women, received General Forrest with tokens of gratitude. The ladies assembled at the courthouse," recalled Dinkins, "received him publicly, and testified their profound appreciation for delivery from further insult and outrage."[60]

According to Thomas Berry of the 9th Texas Cavalry, Forrest had com-manded eleven thousand men during his West Tennessee campaign: "effec-tives equipped without a dollar's cost" to the Confederacy. "This unlettered modern Ajax," as Berry called him, "had not met with a single reverse in his belligerent career since October 1, when he became his own master. He had fought 46 battles, captured 31,000 prisoners, and destroyed over $10,000,000 worth of property."[61]

"With this affair at Fort Pillow," wrote John Johnson, "ended the story of robberies and murders by such irresponsible and lawless bands" as Hurst's Unionists. "Their time of retribution had come, and Forrest was now a ter-rible factor to be counted on in all future operations in this part of the coun-try, and such men as these had no stomach for encountering this kind of an enemy." "West Tennessee," trumpeted Chalmers, "is redeemed."[62]

On April 15, Forrest and his scribes would report from Jackson that his victory at Fort Pillow had been "complete." He guessed that the garrison's loss was "upward of 500 killed" with "but few of the officers escaping" and expressed the hope "that these facts will demonstrate to the Northern people that negro soldiers cannot cope with Southerners." Though the Union's loss would never be known because "large numbers ran into the river and were shot and drowned," the Mississippi, he bragged, "was dyed with the blood of the slaughtered for 200 yards."[63]

It was "unfortunate" that Forrest had "repeated this boast that had probably been made by some of his men," wrote a cavalryman of the 14th who was not present at Fort Pillow. "As he did not go down the slope to the river, this had to be hearsay evidence. With the current of the river as it was, a herd of a hundred cattle could have been slaughtered there and not give enough blood to dye the river for fifty yards." But however inconvenient Forrest's boast was to his defenders, the Wizard had actually enjoyed a splendid view from the bluff of both the river and the shallower and slower-moving Coal Creek. In any case, whether or not this description was exaggerated hearsay, it was, after all, a boast: proof that Forrest at least initially took great satisfaction and even pride in the extent of the sanguinary slaughter his troopers had perpetrated.[64]

The Southern press loudly broadcast Forrest's triumph. "The invincible and unconquered Forrest never wearies in his accustomed vocation," raved the itinerant *Memphis Daily Appeal,* which was reduced to hauling around its press and publishing from the road. "Each victory, although great, seems to be eclipsed by another still greater. The capture of Fort Pillow is one of the most brilliant achievements of the war. It has been regarded as Gibraltar. Our own people spent much money and labor in fortifying it," and the Yankees had "added much to its strength. Nature has made it almost impregnable. But General Forrest, strong as it was known to be, conceived the idea of storming and taking it."[65]

"We have an account from the West," wrote a Confederate War Department clerk in Richmond, "to the effect that Forrest stormed Fort Pillow, putting all the garrison, but one hundred, to the sword." At a time when the Confederate government was seriously considering abandoning Richmond to free itself of extortionate prices, Forrest's victory was welcome news. "The bloody work has commenced in earnest."[66]

"Hear today some items from Forrest," wrote the Reverend Sam Agnew of Mississippi. "It is said he has recently captured Fort Pillow. This place was garrisoned by negroes mostly—the garrison numbered about 500. They felt secure and at the outset hoisted the black flag and consequently no quarter [was] given them and many were slaughtered. Forrest is said to have been slightly wounded three times in the fight. Forrest I hear had only 7 killed."[67]

"Out of 700 men composing the garrison," reported the *Charleston Mercury,* "500 were killed, these last including all the officers of the fort." "I write with pleasure," wrote an anonymous officer of the 22nd, "that another brilliant and decided victory has attended our operations in Western Tennessee and Kentucky, and that Gen. Forrest has added immeasurably to the imperishableness of his acquired laurels, as one of the greatest military chieftains of this age by his splendid success in the capture of Fort Pillow on the 12th inst." "Your brilliant campaign in West Tennessee has given me great satisfaction," Leonidas Polk wrote Forrest, "and entitles you to the thanks of your countrymen."[68]

As the Northern press began to publish its denunciatory coverage of the fall of Fort Pillow, however, the Wizard began to suppress the note of triumphant glee with which he first reported his attack on Fort Pillow and to prepare a more sober account. But for the Southern public's consumption he was not so circumspect. Seven months later, in a speech in Florence, Alabama, where several Fort Pillow captives still languished in prison, an obdurate Forrest would employ the same imagery before a crowd that had come to serenade him, boasting that he had "seen the Mississippi run with blood for 200 hundred yards, and I'm gwine to see it again." The crowd responded with cheers.[69]

After Forrest returned to Jackson, Colonel James Neely led a diversionary expedition to Wolf River, where, as conspicuously as possible, he built pontoon bridges as if preparing to cross with a large cavalry force and attack Memphis. Colonel John McGuirk of the 3rd Mississippi Cavalry meanwhile scampered around the city's southern suburbs, firing at Union pickets. These feints had the desired effect on General Stephen Hurlbut, who, instead of attempting to cut off Forrest's imminent escape south, hunkered down at Fort Pickering and called on Vicksburg to send him four regiments' worth of reinforcements "that I may have some moveable troops."[70]

Forrest's troops were eminently movable, of course. As the sun rose on the carnage at Fort Pillow, a detachment from General Abraham Buford's brigade rode up to the parapets at Columbus, Kentucky, to demand that garrison's surrender. The terms were boilerplate Forrest.

Fully capable of taking Columbus and its garrison by force, I desire to avoid the shedding of blood and therefore demand the unconditional surrender of the forces under your command. Should you surrender, the negroes now in arms will be returned to their masters. Should I, however, be compelled to take the place, no quarter will be shown to the negro troops whatever; the white troops will be treated as prisoners of war.[71]

The note bore the absent Buford's name, and the rebels did what they could to give an impression of a large force, riding their horses in and out of the garrison's sight. But Colonel William Hudson Lawrence, commander of the post, was no Hawkins.

Among doses of Dr. Shallenbergers Fever & Ague Pills, Benjamin Densmore of the 3rd Minnesota Infantry reported that the "inhuman treatment which the union forces received" at Fort Pillow had prompted the Fort Halleck garrison at Columbus

to exercise unusual precautions & to strengthen our position much as may be. For several days every man, not otherwise on stated detail, has been in the trenches, widening and deepening the ditches—also constructing works to protect the commissary. Buildings outside of & near the fort have been either taken down or burned so that the enemy can not employ them for a lodgment.[72]

After serving the rebel truce delegation a hearty breakfast, Lawrence conferred with his officers and composed the following reply: "Being placed by my Government with adequate force to hold and repel all enemies from my post," he declared, "surrender is out of the question."[73]

The rebels—some estimated the size of the detachment at merely 80 to 150 men—decided against an attack and soon retired, consoling themselves with the capture of about 150 horses and mules. Though the garrison's surrender would have been nice, Buford's detachment had accomplished its primary purpose, which was to prevent the Columbus garrison from sending reinforcements to Fort Anderson while Buford himself bore down on Paducah.[74]

After driving Colonel Stephen Hicks's pickets into the fort and dodging fire from four Yankee gunboats, Buford and his men rounded up the horses the Paducah garrison had hidden from Forrest at a rolling mill nearby. "As a part of his movement," wrote Wyeth, "as soon as he had driven the pickets in, he sent a flag of truce to the Federal commander, with a note, to which the name of General Forrest was signed, demanding the surrender of the garrison and fort," and again "threatening to give no quarter if he were compelled to carry the place by assault."[75]

Long since reinforced, reequipped, and resupplied, Hicks accepted Buford's offer of an hour's truce in which to evacuate women and children to the gunboats. "After that time," he replied, "come ahead. I am ready for you." But Buford was by no means ready for him. Leaving a detachment under Faulkner to "keep up the scare," the hulking general departed that night with some 140 Union army horses.[76]

In late April, while Forrest was packing his kit at Jackson for his escape south, the Union army sent two infantry regiments fanning out across Lauderdale County. Remarking that his attempt to lure Sherman into chasing him into West Tennessee "was about played out," Forrest cantered out of Jackson on May 1. Refusing an order to campaign alongside "Fighting Joe" Wheeler, in whom his men "had no confidence," Forrest took a lot of men with him out of Tennessee, though "not as many," claimed Union general Granville Moody, "as had been widely reported."[77]

Before departing, Forrest and his staff prepared a second, more complete account of the Fort Pillow affair, free of the gloating tone of the first. He had demanded the garrison's surrender "to prevent further loss of life," he said, and believed the garrison's "capture without further bloodshed a certainty." He still made no mention of the garrison being intoxicated, claimed that among his captives were "about forty negro women and children," and praised Chalmers and his men for their "gallantry and courage."[78]

Dinkins remembered that the women of Jackson fawned upon Forrest and his officers and "served the men with nice things to eat and welcomed them heartedly." As his detachments kept Memphis wondering where he would strike next, Forrest slipped back down to Mississippi virtually undetected, just as he had done after his first West Tennessee raid. "The command had been actively engaged for some time," wrote Dinkins, "and the beautiful prairies of East Mississippi, with plenty of corn and fodder, were just what the men and horses needed."[79]

HELLHOLES
ANDERSONVILLE AND FLORENCE
From April 13, 1864

AROUND 5:30 A.M. ON APRIL 13, COLONEL BELL HAD ORDERED THAT breakfast be served to his ambulatory prisoners, after which, wrote Dr. Fitch, "we were formed into a line and our names taken. There were 101 prisoners," over twenty of them wounded. As Forrest and his generals decided their fates, all the prisoners "had to sleep on the ground entirely without beding or any Covering," the rebels having taken their "Over coats, blankets and all heavy clothing" to warm their own wounded. McCulloch had "pressed all the conveyances he could find to take away his own wounded," Sergeant Wilbur Gaylord of 6/B testified. "Not finding sufficient, nor having negroes enough," the rebels had to fashion "stretchers from blankets."[1]

It took the prisoners from Fort Pillow seven days to march to Jackson and then south to Okolona, Mississippi, where Brigadier General Samuel Jameson Gholson of Mississippi requested that Forrest's black prisoners be separated out and put to work on the railway.[2]

Toward the end of their dismal journey south, many of Forrest's white prisoners were too weak to walk and had to be transported in open wagons to Andersonville Prison, where they were to join Hawkins's disgraced 7th Tennessee Cavalry (USA), fresh from its fiasco at Union City. But some white captives did not live long enough to enter Andersonville's stockade.[3]

Billy Nail of 13/E had the misfortune of falling into the hands of the very Confederate unit from which he had deserted earlier in the war: Forrest's 16th Tennessee Cavalry. His family back in Crockett County believed he was killed during the battle, but he appears on Forrest's list of captives. Since there is no record of his reaching a rebel prison, either he died of his wounds during the march, or his former comrades executed him as a deserter. His second wife, Sally, was pregnant with his sixth child when he died, and in August gave birth to a boy.[4]

In one of the cruelest ironies of the war, the white Fort Pillow survivors would, with the rest of Andersonville's prisoners, fall victim to the North's indignation over the Fort Pillow massacre, for by the time they arrived at Andersonville an outraged Stanton had declared that after Fort Pillow the Union would no longer exchange prisoners with the Confederacy until Richmond agreed to recognize black soldiers as prisoners of war. The rebels refused, and the impasse contributed to the horrendous overcrowding of rebel prisons.[5]

Built to accommodate a maximum of ten thousand, Camp Sumter, as Andersonville's prison was called, would contain as many as thirty-three thousand Federals at a time. Apparently the rebels barely deigned to recognize homegrown Yankees either, for though almost 30 percent of Andersonville's aggregate forty-five thousand inmates would die by the end of the war, Andersonville would claim the lives of 107, or 77 percent, of its 139 documented Fort Pillow prisoners.

After the Union captured Vicksburg, the army discovered a great many rebel combatants who turned out to have previously signed paroles pledging not to take up arms again. Grant was therefore in no hurry to resolve the impasse, for the termination of exchanges benefited the side that could afford to lose the most men. If such was the Federals' calculation, the Union itself must share some of the blame for Andersonville's subsequent horrors. But there was plenty of blame to go around. The camp was located in a malarial swamp with nothing but an open trough for human waste and an inadequate and contaminated water supply. Richmond's callous inattention, sadistic guards, inadequate medical care, Georgia's swelter, the camp's incompetent administration, and the Confederacy's own shrinking resources combined to make Camp Sumter the Civil War's ultimate hellhole.

An Ohioan's description of the arrival of the 7th at Andersonville could have applied to the survivors of the 13th, except that far fewer of Hawkins's men were wounded.

> Some five hundred Tennesseans, who had been captured by Forrest—
> arrived among us; the most of who were hatless, bootless, and shoeless,
> without coats, pants and blankets. . . . They were wholly destitute of
> cups, plates, spoons, and dishes of every kind as well as of all means
> of purchasing them; they having been stripped of these things by
> their captors. In their destitute condition they were turned into the
> stockade and left to shift for themselves in the best manner they

could. To borrow cups of the fellow-prisoners was an impossibility, for no one could be expected to lend what, if it were not returned, would insure his own destruction, particularly when the borrower was an utter stranger. There was nothing left for them but to bake their raw meal and bacon upon stones and chips, eat it without moisture, and afterward to go to the brook like beasts to quench their thirst.[6]

The first of the Fort Pillow survivors to die at Andersonville was apparently nineteen-year-old Bill Lovett of 13/A, who succumbed on May 19, only a few days after he and his comrades reached the prison. He was one of six who died that May, but the fatalities accelerated as the weather turned tropical. Eleven would die in June, seventeen in July, twenty-eight in August, twenty-seven in September.

These deaths reverberated throughout West Tennessee. One of the casualties that June was George W. Babb Jr. From the age of eleven, Babb had been his family's mainstay. His father had kidney trouble and could not farm, so every spring his diligent son would work for his grandmother for twelve dollars a month and, except for what little he spent on clothes, hand over everything else to his parents. A Union sympathizer, Babb had fled from the Confederate press gangs that plagued Obion County and moved to Illinois in 1862 to live with his older brother Jasper. But on November 25, 1863, he had returned to Tennessee to serve in Bradford's regiment, and ten days later he was mustered into Company A. While out on a scout his feet froze, and on February 12 he was admitted to the hospital at Paducah, about twenty miles from his home, and became one of the many Marine Hospital patients Forrest captured and offered to exchange. His mother was informed of his capture by Colonel Edward Crossland of Forrest's command, who, returning home wounded, promised to try to get him released. But by the time Crossland was well enough to keep his promise, Babb had died at Andersonville.[7]

Paton Alexander of Obion County was in his forties when he enrolled: a married man with five children, the oldest of whom, William, was thirteen years old. He had already seen combat in the Mexican War, serving with Haynes's Company of Tennessee Mexican War Volunteers, and as one of the few veterans in Bradford's Battalion had been mustered in as a corporal in Company D. He died of scurvy in July. Another casualty that month, eighteen-year-old Henry Clay Carter, had been working as a farm hand for his widowed mother in Crockett County when he and his big brother

William joined 13/E in January 1864. The two brothers were able to escape death at Fort Pillow but not at Andersonville, where Henry died of scurvy and "dysenteria."[8]

Andrew McKee of Dyer County was thirty-eight years old when he joined 13/C. Having borne him three sons and two daughters, his first wife died in 1857, but a few months later he married Nancy Landry Russell, who in 1858 added another daughter to his brood. Captured at Fort Pillow and imprisoned at Andersonville, in September he died of scurvy with his comrades looking on. Two of McKee's sons lived for about three years with their stepmother, after which they were "turned loose to drift for themselves and never got any education of any consequence."[9]

Danny Hopper of Madison County was just a kid when he enlisted in 13/D in December 1863. Captured at Fort Pillow, Hopper died at Andersonville in September of "black scurvy." Described as an honest, robust Obion County man who always took "a deep interest in the comity of his family," Benjamin W. King was mustered into Company D in January 1864, captured at Fort Pillow, and died at Andersonville of chronic diarrhea.[10]

Private Ephraim L. Churchwell of Decatur County, Tennessee, was a blacksmith for Company A and the father of five children. Captured at Fort Pillow, he died on October 11, 1864, of scurvy. Jim Clark of Obion County appears to have deserted from the 13th "before Pay Rolls were made out." His neighbor John Fields filed a claim with the quartermaster general's office in which he maintained that he used to hide Clark and his friend Chapman Underwood from the rebels when they were home. By April 12, Clark was back with his comrades at Fort Pillow, just in time to be captured and taken to Andersonville, where he died of scurvy in October.[11]

A few survived, but barely. Trained as a wagonmaker and carpenter, George Ellis was working as a dry goods clerk at Columbus when he enlisted as a sergeant in Company C. In the snows and freezing rains of February 1863 rheumatism sank so deeply into his joints and bones that he was unable to serve in the field. By the time of his capture at Fort Pillow, he was reduced to shuffling papers for Bradford and his staff. Despite starvation and exposure and a case of the mumps, he somehow survived captivity in the Confederacy's "outrageous prisons" at Andersonville and Florence, South Carolina. Nevertheless, he returned to his regiment a fragile husk of himself, and by 1879 was forced to give up his craft and take up preaching in the woods and fields around Gardner Station, Tennessee.[12]

Jim Christenberg of Company A was a prodigious bounder when he joined the 13th. As a brakeman on the Memphis and Ohio Railroad, he had taken full advantage of his mobility by marrying at least two women: one as a Mr. Medicus, the other as a Mr. James. By the time he joined the 13th, he had already gotten a taste of army life foraging for the 19th and 26th Illinois Infantries. Arrested by the rebels and imprisoned at Trenton, Tennessee, he finagled his release with the help of a friend, and at the age of thirty joined Bradford's Battalion in the summer of 1863. Prison, however, seems to have been Christenberg's destiny. Not long after his regiment was moved to Fort Pillow, he was incarcerated again for abandoning his post and committing depredations against local citizens, and then imprisoned yet again by the rebels after his capture at Fort Pillow. He adapted well enough to his captivity to survive both Richmond's notorious Libby Prison and Andersonville, but perhaps freedom did not agree with him so well, for shortly after his release in March 1865, he died in Nashville of an unspecified disease, leaving at least two wives and an unknown number of children.[13]

Doctor Z. Alexander was no doctor, though by the end of the war he might have wished he were. A farmer from Obion County, Tennessee, he enrolled at Union City in December 1863, and at the time of the battle at Fort Pillow was recuperating from an illness at home in Troy, when his house "was surrounded by confederate soldiers," and he was captured as well. An old friend and fellow prisoner named James Welch of the 7th Tennessee Cavalry testified that Alexander "was A sound man untell he was taken prisner at fort piller and placed in that prison Hell at Antersonville georga." "While in prison," Alexander himself recalled, "I lay upon the bare ground, and had only one blanket to protect me from the sun and weather. Had very rough, unpalatable food, and but litle of that. I was weak, emaciated, and broken down in health generally." Suffering from scurvy, lumbago, and a case of chronic diarrhea that resulted in hemorrhoids "quite as large as an English walnut," Alexander complained that he left Andersonville chronically "ill in body and mind." Perhaps to divert attention from the rather dubious circumstances of his capture, Alexander accused the pension office of discriminating against Homegrown Yankees like himself. "Don't doo like Jenral Farest," he told them, "when he masecred forte piller after surrender becose we wer tenn solgers. There was not but few of bradfords battalion ever returned from prison and not but three was able to doo eny duty, but if you think it is rong" to count him and his comrades as legitimate Union soldiers, then the United States might as well "nock us in the hed as old forist did and let us go."[14]

Tom McMurry of 13/E emerged from Andersonville with aches in his joints and jaws, loose teeth, and chest pains, and eventually drank himself to death. Incarceration reduced Anderson Bailey of Company B to a shell. He suffered from tuberculosis, scurvy, diarrhea, and ulcers on his legs that ran all the way to the bone and reerupted every year for the rest of his life.[15]

Hard luck followed even the escapees. Bugler Miles Deason of 13/B slipped away from the carnage at Fort Pillow and eventually returned to what was left of Bradford's 13th. By July 1864, the 13th Tennessee Cavalry showed only two officers and forty men, and on August 22, 1864, Military Governor Andrew Johnson changed the decimated regiment's designation from the 13th to the 14th Tennessee Cavalry, and then consolidated it into Company E of Hurst's 6th Tennessee Cavalry. Deason's comrade George H. Dunn judged him "a good and faithful soldier whilst in the service," but Deason was declared a deserter after disappearing near Johnsonville during a skirmish with a detachment of Forrest's cavalry. A day or so later, his comrades found his bugle hanging from a tree and his horse grazing not far from where Deason had last been sighted. He never returned home, and his parents struggled to accept the army's claim that their boy had deserted. But thirteen years later, a number of Confederate cavalry veterans came forward to testify that they had seen Deason executed by a squad of guerrillas. "Deason was in arms when captured," one of them recalled, "and said he belonged to the United States Cavalry." Nevertheless, a motley squad commanded by Captain Bruce L. Phillips of the 14th Tennessee Infantry shot Deason to death. If the story is true, Miles M. Deason was apparently the only captive from the 13th to be subsequently killed in action.[16]

Perhaps the unluckiest member of that unfortunate garrison was a white farmer from Sevier County, Tennessee, named John W. Long. Caught up in three of the Civil War's worst horrors, he was probably merely passing through Fort Pillow at the time of the massacre, for he belonged not to the 13th but to the 3rd East Tennessee Cavalry, having enlisted at Murfreesboro the previous December. It is a mystery why Long was at Fort Pillow in the first place, for by March the rest of his regiment had returned to Nashville to escort convoys and guard railroads. Nevertheless, there he was, and he managed to survive the battle in fair enough shape to add his name to the Wizard's list of prisoners. Nathan Bedford Forrest was the last man on earth a member of the 3rd would have chosen as his captor, however, for just two months before the Battle of Fort Pillow, the 3rd had killed Forrest's dashing young brother Jeffrey at Okolona, Mississippi. Long managed, however, to survive the forced march south and nearly a year's imprisonment at Andersonville. Then, in late April 1865, he boarded a steamship with some 2,300 others, most of them fellow parolees from rebel prison camps. Possibly by accident, possibly as the result of sabotage by a former St. Louis fireman and unrepentant rebel arsonist named Robert Louden, the steamship *Sultana* blew up near Memphis on April 27, 1865. Among the 1,800 men, women, and children who were burned to death or drowned was poor, luckless John W. Long, survivor of the most notorious massacre and most miserable prison in the Civil War only to die in the most devastating marine catastrophe in American history. He was twenty-three years old.[17]

None of the Fort Pillow prisoners at Andersonville escaped, but the few who were incarcerated elsewhere in the South made several attempts. Imprisoned in an old cotton house at Hamburg, across the river from Augusta, Georgia, Martin V. Day of 13/C was "half starved, sometimes more than half naked and often quite sick." Almost a year to the day after the massacre, he and a Michigan cavalryman escaped by jumping out a window. They spent a little over a week together "hiding and traveling toward Charleston, when one night as they were crossing a stream on a Rail Road bridge in South Carolina they were captured by a squad of Home Guards" and taken to a prison in Midway. Two weeks later, news reached them that General Joe Johnson had surrendered to Sherman. Day's guards told him that they had orders to release all prisoners of war but because the roads were full of rebel soldiers "they would keep them a while for fear they would be killed." Two days later, Day was finally "turned out of prison." "Sick, weak, nearly naked," and flat broke, he walked for about three days to the nearest Union encampment at Summerville, where his countrymen gave him "an old suit of clothes and something to eat," and put him on a train to Charleston. After several weeks, he finally found what remained of his regiment reorganized into Company E of the 6th Tennessee Cavalry and stationed at Pulaski.[18]

After the war, Anderson Jones of 13/C made the unlikely claim that only five days after his enlistment, Bradford had granted him a sixty-day furlough, "and the very day my furlough expired, my said regiment was attacked and cut to pieces by Forrest's men and were all killed or captured or scattered." Captured a few days later at his home "by the troops of Bell and Buford," Jones was conveyed to Mobile and then to Andersonville, and was finally "sent out to the front to dig pits and build breastworks." Jones said he was "closely guarded as a prisoner of war," but on July 3 he managed to escape by jumping from a railroad bridge and into a creek as his train rounded the foot of Georgia's Kennesaw Mountain. Jones "slowly made my way back by a circuitous route to Columbus, Kentucky," where he encountered First Lieutenant Frank Smith and joined his comrades in 6/E.[19]

Six out of the approximately fourteen Fort Pillow survivors imprisoned at Florence, South Carolina, did not survive their incarceration. Though Colonel John F. Iverson, the prison commandant, was unusually kind to Northern prisoners, he regarded Homegrown Yankees as "damned traitors" and treated them harshly. Humphrey Jones and John Burrus died in the fall of 1864. Turner Lunceford of Haywood County died of scurvy and starvation, and his comrade James W. Antwine, a past deserter from the Confederate army, died of exposure. Lunceford and Antwine each left a widow and four children; their comrade Michael Cleek left five.[20]

First Lieutenant Nicholas Logan of 13/C was imprisoned at Macon, Georgia. According to Leaming, the guards singled Logan out for "mistreatment" as a "home-made Yankee," and he died within weeks of his capture, leaving a widow and four children. G. W. Kirk of 13/A had deserted from the 11th Texas Cavalry (CSA) earlier in the war, and subsequently deserted from the 13th in February. He returned to Fort Pillow, however, in time for the massacre, and was captured and shipped off to Richmond, Virginia. He survived his imprisonment, but just barely. Headed home aboard the paroled prison ship *Gen*, he would die off Cape Hatteras on March 30, 1865.[21]

In the 1890s, Carroll County's Bethel Baptist Church proposed hiring one of Forrest's ex-officers as its minister. When Alfred D. Bennett, one of the few members of the 7th (USA) to have survived Andersonville, objected, his fellow elders urged him "to forgive as Jesus did." But Bennett was unimpressed.

"The Lord was just crucified," he replied. "He never had to go to Andersonville Prison."[22]

SLAVES AGAIN
BLACK PRISONERS

April 12, 1864–January 1865

LIEUTENANTS FRANK SMITH AND WILLIAM CLEARY CLAIMED THAT THE rebels "hung and shot the negroes" they had captured "as they passed along toward Brownsville, until they were rid of them all." But they were mistaken. A Confederacy short on labor prized them as recaptured slaves, and cither sold them, returned them to their masters, or put them to work on rebel fortifications.[1]

Long before Fort Pillow's fall, Forrest's men had become experienced at disposing of black captives. All through the war his command had intercepted slaves the Union army had emancipated, impressing them as laborers and officers' servants, or returning them to their masters. The following Union pass was found on a contraband named Wally Carns who, with his family, was captured by General Chalmers while trying to make his way north:

> Head Quarters Army of The South West
> <u>Helena Ark Aug 15"</u> 186[illegible]
> Special Orders No. <u>1250</u>
> <u>Wally Carns & family,</u> a colored____ formerly a slave<u>s,</u> having by direction of <u>their</u> owner been engaged in the rebel service are hereby confiscated as being contraband of war, and not being in the Public Service <u>are</u> permitted to pass the pickets of this command northward, and <u>are</u> forever emancipated from a master who permitted them to assist in an attempt to break up the Government and Laws of our Country.
> By Command Of Major General Curtis.[2]

Chalmers sold the Carns family back into bondage.

Forrest now ordered Chalmers to see to it that "no negroes will be delivered to their owners on the march. They must all go to Jackson." Though Sandy Addison testified to seeing four black captives shot down after marching a mile or so from Fort Pillow, the black soldiers who were taken prisoner after the massacre fared far better than their white counterparts. Of Forrest's approximately sixty-two black prisoners, thirteen escaped, and forty-three eventually returned to their regiments, and all this despite the fact that more than half of them were wounded, many of them seriously.[3]

The reason their mortality rate was comparatively low was because the artillerists, unlike their white comrades, "were considered as private property by the Confederates, who did not recognize Mr. Lincoln's proclamation as giving their slaves legitimate freedom." Acclimatized to the South, accustomed to hardship, well trained in the art of survival, they also had monetary value to the South, and, once the rebels' rage was expended, received far better treatment than Andersonville's inmates.[4]

Badly wounded, exhausted, convinced in some cases that their execution was imminent, some of them endeavored to elicit their former masters' sympathy. Colonel Barteau reported that along the march his black prisoners "freely expressed themselves as to the conduct of many of their white officers, and many of them admitted with expressions of condemnation the great error into which they had been led as to the defense of the fort, their drunkenness and folly of conduct, putting the blame upon their officers."[5]

As their battle rage receded, the rebels spared a few prisoners they deemed too weak to continue their journey south. Henry Parker of 6/D was so badly wounded in the hip that three days after the massacre the rebels pronounced him worthless as a slave and left him by the side of the road to die. He did not die, however, and somehow made his way back to Memphis, where the Union army pronounced him worthless as a soldier and discharged him. Shot in the groin, John Cowan of 2/C was also left by the wayside; he would live another thirteen years until his chronically infected wound finally killed him.[6]

Over the days following the massacre, escapees trickled into Memphis and Cairo, picked up from the riverbank by a variety of vessels. By one exaggerated account, seventy-one men of the 6th USCHA had turned up by the first of May "after being prisoners several days." On the night of April 16 a gunboat had turned up at Mound City with ten more wounded men and twenty other escapees and refugees. Over the next month more men would stagger into Fort Pickering, one by one.[7]

More blacks than whites escaped from Forrest as they made their way south, in part because the rebels, trusting that the artillerists were reluctant conscripts and so sentimental about their bondage that they were eager to return to their masters, sent them off on errands. Alfred Coleman of 6/B, for example, was assigned the task of feeding the rebels' horses, but once he "got the horses between me and them," he escaped into a "dark and drizzling rain."[8]

Sent down to a creek to fetch water for McCulloch, Frank Hogan of 6/A escaped from Forrest about two hours before daylight on April 13 and, zigzagging back and forth along the river road after the manner of runaway slaves, made his way to within a few miles of Fort Pickering, where he was brought in by a Union patrol.[9]

Philip Young of 6/A was held captive for thirteen days and brought to Holly Springs, Mississippi, with over a hundred white and about thirty black prisoners. Along the way, he repeatedly heard rebel officers declare "that they intended to kill the last one of the negroes after they got as far down south as they wanted to," and a rebel captain "swore he would shoot me after I had been prisoner thirteen days." Taking him at his word, Young slipped away on the morning of the thirteenth day and found his way back up to Memphis.[10]

Armstrong Burgess, who had fled his master in Franklin County, Alabama, to join 6/B, was among those who, though presumed to have been killed at Fort Pillow, limped back to their regiment a year or so after the massacre. Struck over the head by a rebel musket, he regained consciousness only to find himself in rebel custody, from which he did not escape until the following spring. Burgess bore a deep dent in his skull from his wound at Fort Pillow, an injury that may have contributed to the fistfights that led to his eventual incarceration in Irving Block prison. Burgess apparently ascribed his mood swings to a case of syphilis he claimed to have contracted during the war, but his doctor could never find any evidence of it. Burgess's first wife, by whom he had eight children, died in 1906, whereupon this luckless old veteran married a woman named Lewisa who, within a few months of their wedding, was killed in Brinkley, Arkansas, by a tornado.[11]

Fifteen-year-old Joe Boyd Jr. and his mother, Caroline, had toiled as slaves on the Boyd plantation in Somerville, Tennessee, while his father, Joe senior, labored on the Bright place nearby. Boyd was among the host of runaway slaves who flocked to the Union lines after the fall of Corinth on May 30, 1862. For some months he lived in the sprawl of Corinth's contraband camp and apparently worked as a servant, accompanying his Yankee employer on scouts around Meridian and Coldwater, Mississippi, until finally, in November 1863, he joined Company D of the 6th USCHA. Though shot through the right knee, Boyd was one of those badly wounded black soldiers whom Forrest's command nonetheless deemed fit to march. Marched and transported to Chickasaw, Mississippi, "and held for about a year," he escaped "and returned to my regiment at Memphis, Tennessee" on July 18, 1865.[12]

After his capture, Henry Dix of 6/D cooked for a sergeant of the 15th Mississippi Cavalry, which spent most of its time with no fixed camp, scouting in Mississippi and Alabama. He was recaptured every time he tried to escape, but finally released with a number of other prisoners after the Battle of Selma "by Gen. Forrest of the Confederate Army who informed them that they were *free*," whereupon Dix immediately reported to his regiment in Memphis.[13]

Another of those who staggered back to Memphis that first year was Thomas Grier of Madison County, Tennessee, who had found himself a few days after the battle languishing in rebel custody in La Grange, Tennessee, the scene of his enrollment in the Union army. Separated from the other prisoners, he was taken to De Soto County, Mississippi, where he slaved for a planter named Arthur McKracken. But in March 1865, he made his escape and found his way back to his regiment.[14]

According to a comrade, Elias Irwin was "subjected to such ill treatment" at Fort Pillow that he was nearly "buried alive." He was taken with Samuel Green and Charles Fox to Mobile and eventually to the salt works at Clarksville, Alabama. The following spring he managed to slip away from his guards and make his way to the Union lines near Selma. General James Harrison Wilson and his officers offered to employ him as a servant until, they said, they could find a safe way to transport him back to his regiment. But either Wilson's command grew so attached to Irwin's services that they would not let him go or Wilson was far more cautious than his counterparts about obtaining transport for the survivors of the Fort Pillow massacre, for Elias cooked and washed and guarded rebel prisoners for them for almost a year, and was not allowed to return to Memphis until September 1865.[15]

———

At the time of Fort Pillow's fall, General Leonidas Polk complained that he was having "great difficulty" procuring slaves from local planters "to complete the works for the defense of Mobile." He eagerly requisitioned Forrest's black captives and on May 20 delivered them to Mobile's commander, General Dabney H. Maury. "Put them to work on fortifications," Maury instructed his chief engineer, and "keep records of the time in order to remunerate their owners."[16]

Georgia-born Anthony Flowers, who had had the bad luck to enroll in Company C of the 6th USCHA less than a week before the massacre, was put to work building Confederate fortifications, despite a right leg so severely damaged by gunshot wounds that his broken shin had practically formed a second knee, and a left foot so shattered that it merely flopped alongside him when he walked.[17]

Saved from death by Forrest himself, the gallant gunner Willis Ligon of 6/C "did not sign any papers with the Confederates or enlist with them," but they "made me promise to stay with them." At the end of August, however, he escaped during the rebel retreat from Holly Springs. "The confederates kept passing me and saying, 'trot up or the Yankees will get you,' so I just kept dropping back, and at last I just got out into the wood and waited until night and traveled two or three days before I reached the Union soldiers."[18]

A rebel struck Roach Turner of Madison County, Tennessee, in the lower abdomen with a rifle butt before taking him into captivity. A boyhood friend who, as a private in the 61st USCI, was aboard the *Silver Cloud* the morning after the battle, recognized him sitting among Forrest's prisoners. Turner was taken down to Pontotoc, Mississippi, and put to work on the plantation of John E. Steel. But that May his owner, a Confederate major named Turner, found out where the Confederates were keeping him and brought him home to Tennessee. Escaping from Turner's plantation in October, he returned to his regiment and was mustered out the following January.[19]

"I was not treated like the other prisoners," recalled Allen James Walker. After his capture, Corporal John C. Peevey of Willis's Texas Battalion made Walker "change my U.S. uniform for Confederate clothes and kept me with them for nearly a year" as his servant. "I went with them all over Tennessee, Alabama, and Mississippi," until around New Year's 1865, when "Peevey sent me with his brother" to their small farm near Gonzales, the "Cradle of Texas Independence," where they made him "practically their slave, and I put in a crop that Spring for them."[20]

Like many another Texas slave, Walker was not informed that the war was over until mid-July 1865. "Hearing of some U.S. soldiers coming through there, I ran off and got with a wagon train" that took him to Columbus, Texas, sixty-five miles west of Houston, "where I was turned over to headquarters and given transportation to Galveston. Here I was sent to New Orleans by ship," and from there to New York, where he fell in with a crowd of veterans from the "many regiments scattered about." The army "sent us all round in Virginia and North Carolina, dropping each man off as he reached his command," until they reached Baltimore, where Walker "was given transportation by rail to Cairo, Illinois, and from there by boat to Memphis,

Tennessee, where I arrived about November 14, 1865, and found my regiment camped on Vance Street." Now known as "the 11th U.S. Colored Volunteer Infantry" and commanded by Colonel Turner, "the regiment was filled up with strangers, recruits and substitutes," though he was relieved to find that "several of the old company boys were still there." After being discharged, Walker lived in Germantown, Tennessee, until he moved back to Memphis in 1894.[21]

One of the few black captives to survive the battle uninjured was a former slave from Grenada, Mississippi, named Charles Fox. After Forrest's drove reached Ripley, he was separated from the others, taken to Oxford, Mississippi, and briefly returned to his master in Grenada. What befell him at his master's hands he does not tell, but after only a week he was sent away to a military prison in Mobile, Alabama, from which he would be taken in irons and under guard to work the town wharf as a stevedore. After four months of loading and unloading cargo for the Confederates, he was taken up the Tom Bigbee River to labor for five more months in Clarksville, Alabama, on one of the Confederacy's few remaining sources of the saltpeter required for the manufacture of gunpowder. He was then taken to Huntsville, where, to impede Sherman's progress, the rebels put him to work burning bridges and destroying railroads. When the Federals closed in on Alabama, he was taken to Jackson, Mississippi; from there, General Chalmers, whom he had last seen riding along the riverbank, exhorting his soldiers to wipe out black troops, sent him to work on a plantation near Shreveport, Louisiana. There he remained until the Federals ventured into the parish, whereupon he and perhaps a dozen other slaves and prisoners ran to the Union lines. The Federals transported him to Little Rock and finally back to his regiment in Memphis, where he reappeared, a ghost of himself, in mid-July 1865. After the war Fox would become an accomplished cook at a distinguished Memphis hotel called the Carlton House.[22]

Badly wounded in the hip, the sole survivor of his gun crew, the heroic Sam Green of 6/B had a tale to tell. After the rebels separated out the black prisoners, they eventually loaded them into boats bound for Fort Gaines, an island stronghold at the head of Mobile Bay. There they were imprisoned on a barge, to which "sand was brought by other boats, and we took wheelbarrows and carried this sand and dumped it in the bay and built up the land inside of the spiles until we could plant siege guns upon the fort we built."

Green remained on Mobile Bay for about six months, "when I was taken across to Mobile and put to work in Hitchock's Press," a large ironsmith shop that specialized in forging iron for rebel pontoons. Here he ran into Henry Dix of his old regiment, who had also been captured at Fort Pillow but had proceeded to Mobile by a roundabout route, via Horton County, Mississippi, where he had worked under guard on an officer's plantation.

At Hitchock's Press, Green labored as "a striker for a white blacksmith" and in his spare time split firewood for an Irish woman who lived next door. Green remained in Mobile until the city was attacked by the Federals in late July 1864. "While the fight was going on at Fort [Blakely]," he recalled, "the forges and iron work at Hitchock's Press were all loaded on a steamboat to be taken to Selma, Alabama. It was intended that all the workmen should go on the boat and go to some place. But after the iron was loaded, I just stepped around the corner" and ducked into the house of the Irish woman for whom he had split wood and who now hid him from the rebels until the Union army landed on Sunday, April 9, 1865, just three days shy of the anniversary of his capture at Fort Pillow.

At ten that morning, Green bade farewell to his Irish hostess and made for the Yankee camp, where Green informed the Union commander that there were black Union prisoners in Mobile, and the Yankee general immediately sent squads fanning out through the city to gather them up. The general told him and his comrade Armstrong Burgess that their regiment was back in Memphis. Even though it had been "made up new," he said, they still belonged to it "and must go back."

The general wrote out "transportation papers to go to New Orleans" and then up the river to Fort Pickering on the *Belle of Memphis,* the same boat that had transported Green's company to Fort Pillow over a year before. At Memphis, Green "found my old company at Dunn Green at the foot of Poplar Street." But he and Burgess hardly knew their own company, "as we had all new officers and many new men. The men who recognized us— there was mighty few of them left—said, 'The dead had come to life.'"

During the year following the attack on Fort Pillow, recalled Green's sergeant, Wilbur Gaylord, "the old men of company B came straggling back one at a time." According to his comrade Benjamin Jones, who had himself survived wounds received at Fort Pillow, Green had returned to Memphis "a generally used-up man" who "didn't do much duty" after his return but hung "round the camp pretty much." After his discharge in January 1866, Green worked on the levee at Memphis and lived with his wife, Jane, "in a little hut on the Pigeon Roost Road" until a white man named Peck "claimed the ground we lived on" and ran him off. For a while he worked for a Memphis reaper, packing grain and stacking hay, for which, because of his injuries, he was paid about half the standard wage. He subsequently tenant-farmed for Bev Davis of Horn Lake, Mississippi, but by now his nagging wounds and his ever dimmer prospects had embittered him. His fellow tenant farmers found him a "not entirely peaceable person." A black neighbor named Morning Clay recalled how Green had "tried to Boss me, and I wouldn't have it. Sam had a quarrel with me: two or three of 'em. He hit me, and I have the marks of it now. Sam was quarrelsome," Clay concluded, "a kind of bigoted fellow." Deeming him "a good worker, but a bad man," Green's employer dismissed him after he had planted a single crop.

Green returned to Memphis and worked nights manning the casting ladle in Randall and Heath's Foundry, where he did what he could to hide his disability so that his employers would not cut his wages. He finally emigrated by steamer to Helena, Arkansas, where he took on a series of jobs, harvesting a crop on what had been none other than Gideon Pillow's plantation, and hauling seed for Bennett's Cotton Seed Factory. But by the time he reached the age of sixty his old wounds and a life of crushing poverty had turned him into what a white benefactor described as "an almost helpless cripple" who would "doubtless have died of starvation but for the contributions of his neighbors."

"I have no home or any means of support," he wrote the Pension Office in an apparently futile effort to receive support. "I have no family except one small boy called Jessy who is my child and is seven years old. He is all the help I have about the house. He brings my wood and water." In fact, at the time of Green's writing, Jessy was "away asking for food for both of us to eat."

"Few, it appears," concluded his pension examiner, "escaped the vortex of blood."[23]

ALARMS AND FLIGHT
THE NORTH
From April 13, 1864

NEWS OF THE MASSACRE PULSED ERRATICALLY ALONG THE TELEGRAPH lines that connected the Mississippi River outposts to the Union command. A day after the massacre, Hurlbut had reported to Major General McPherson that "after resistance had ceased, the enemy, in gross violation of all honorable warfare, butchered in cold blood the prisoners and wounded." He reported that "the Colored Troops fought desperately, and nearly all of them were killed or wounded, but few held as prisoners." He said he had received notice of the attack at 7:00 p.m. on April 12, and "immediately ordered the 55th United States Infantry (colored) to embark on the steamer 'Glendale,' but within an hour after issuing the order, authentic intelligence of the capture of the fort and garrison and of the force of the enemy was received, and the order countermanded."

Hurlbut urged the War Department to make every effort to ensure that black prisoners of war received the same treatment as their white comrades. "Not only is it due our good name, but it will be necessary to preserve discipline among them. In case of an action in which they shall be successfully engaged, it will be nearly impracticable to restrain them from retaliation." In closing, Hurlbut mourned Major Lionel Booth as "a good soldier and a brave officer."[1]

Meanwhile, General Mason Brayman telegraphed Sherman from his headquarters at Cairo that he feared that Fort Pillow had fallen. "General Shepley passed yesterday and saw the flag go down and thinks it a Surrender," he said. "I have enough troops now from below, and will go down if necessary to that point. Captain Pennock will send gunboats. If lost, [Fort Pillow] will be retaken immediately."[2]

Sherman, however, dismissed Brayman's fear for the simple reason that four months earlier, as per his order, Hurlbut had evacuated Fort Pillow. "Fort Pillow has no guns or garrison," he wired back confidently. "It was evacuated before I went out to Meridian." But on April 14, Brayman confirmed Shepley's report. "Fort Pillow was taken by storm at 3 p.m. on the 12th," he told Sherman, "with six guns." Approximately one hundred were taken prisoner, "and the rest killed. The whole affair was a scene of murder."[3]

Sherman was thunderstruck. Not only had Hurlbut proved too timid to chase Forrest out of West Tennessee, he had garrisoned, inadequately and in violation of Sherman's orders, one of the most demonstrably indefensible forts on the entire Mississippi. "We have lost 250 killed and wounded," Hurlbut wrote Sherman. "The rebels butchered the negro troops after resistance ceased. Our garrison was four companies U.S. Heavy Artillery (Colored), and 250 recruits [of the] 13th Tennessee Cavalry, in all about 550 men," which he insisted should have been "a sufficient force" for a fort originally designed to garrison ten thousand. Though Hurlbut tried to put the best face on it by guessing that "the enemy will not remain long," he had no intention of finding out for himself. He told a lieutenant commander of the Mississippi fleet that he would "be much obliged if you will direct such movements on the part of the gun-boats as will ascertain the fact of occupation or abandonment."[4]

On April 15, Secretary of War Edwin Stanton wrote Grant to confirm that Forrest had indeed captured Fort Pillow, and to report that the rebels had "sacked Paducah again, and have demanded surrender of Columbus, which has not yet been given up. The slaughter at Fort Pillow is great." "The Sioux Indians after this," Washburn wired Sherman, "will be regarded as models of humanity." "I don't understand it, as the place was long since abandoned by my order," Sherman wired McPherson. "I don't know what these men were doing at Fort Pillow," he wrote Grant. "I ordered it to be abandoned before I went to Meridian, and it was so abandoned. General Hurlbut must have sent this garrison up recently from Memphis." So many men were on furlough, he said, that Grierson and Hurlbut were afraid to go after Forrest. "I don't know what to do with Hurlbut," Sherman groaned. He had "full 10,000 men at Memphis, but if he had a million he would be on the defensive." Sherman saw the disaster at Fort Pillow as the "first fruits of the system of trading posts designed to assist the loyal people of the interior. All these stations are a weakness," he declared, "and offer tempting chances for plunder." It seemed to Sherman that Forrest "has our men down there in cow, but I will try new leaders, for I believe our men will fight if led."[5]

Realizing the full extent of the catastrophe, Grant finally overcame his understandable reluctance to demote one of Lincoln's most loyal political allies. A few days after the massacre, Sherman wired Hurlbut, accusing him of "marked timidity in the management of affairs since Forrest passed north of Memphis. General Grant orders me to relieve you. You will proceed to Cairo and take command there."[6]

Hurlbut demanded a court of inquiry, a request Lincoln gently—and Grant not so gently—would deny.[7] In a pioneering nondenial denial, Hurlbut would answer the charge of drunkenness by dismissing it as "a very old story," and address the charge of timidity by asserting that during the time he had "held the City of Memphis for two weeks, cut off by Van Dorn's raid from Genl Grant's army, with four regiments of untried Infantry and a squadron of Cavalry," at every sunrise he could be found "on horseback and on the lines."

His dismissal opened a floodgate of accusations that he was not just a drunkard but a crook and an extortionist whose underlings had imprisoned the sons of Memphis's wealthiest families and held them for ransom. One of the worst allegations centered around Hurlbut's favoring an Illinois pal named McCarty, who, it was claimed, had used his influence in Washington to obtain Hurlbut's appointment as a major general and shared the profits of his nefarious speculations in exchange for permits to trade in illegal goods, including a shipment he made to De Soto County, Mississippi, in December 1862. Hurlbut denied any knowledge of McCarty's machinations and characterized his two accusers as traitors, smugglers, and even adulterers. When Provost Marshal C. M. Willard of Chicago accused the general of dismissing him for interfering in his profiteering, Hurlbut denounced him as a "perfect 'Copperhead.'" He summed up his defense by inviting his superiors' "scrutinizing investigation," but in effect conceding his utter failure as a district commander. For despite his "almost arbitrary power" over the citizens of Memphis, the "atmosphere [reeked] with corruption in a city where all the quick witted rascals from all quarters have accumulated, where honesty is the exception and vice the rule, where trade runs riot in speculation, and speculation grows into gambling," a pursuit Hurlbut knew something about.[8]

Grant shrewdly replaced Hurlbut with his own close friend and tireless promoter, General Cadwallader Washburn: the brother of Illinois Republican congressman Elihu Benjamin Washburne (the added *e* was Elihu's touch) and, like Hurlbut, one of Lincoln's staunchest political allies. But Sherman's choice of General Samuel Davis Sturgis to replace the once-lionized Benjamin Grierson was peculiar. Sturgis had been severely criticized for prematurely withdrawing his forces at Wilson's Creek in 1861, and within a couple of months would so disgrace himself at Brice's Crossroads that he would spend the rest of the war "awaiting orders."[9]

"I have sent Sturgis down to whip Forrest," Sherman declared. General James Birdseye McPherson, now in command of the Army of the Tennessee, ordered every Union regiment in West Tennessee to hunt down and destroy Forrest or, failing that, to prevent him from hauling his plunder back to Mississippi. Though "Paducah, Cairo, Columbus, Memphis, Vicksburg and Natchez must be held at all hazards," McPherson took a dim view of defending small river forts like Fort Pillow and Columbus, and proposed a system of larger garrisons, cavalry scouts, gunboats, and marines to keep the Mississippi open to Union traffic. "All troops along the Miss. and Ohio Rivers," McPherson ordered, "must strike at the Enemy wherever he is in reach and strike hard."[10]

Hurlbut's belated and well-deserved demotion did nothing to humble the righteousness of the North's indignation. General McPherson deemed Fort Pillow "a deplorable affair"—the annihilation of a force that should not even have been there in the first place—but believed that in the end its propaganda value would make it "most damaging to the rebels." "This is the most infernal outrage that has been committed since the war began," wrote General Augustus Chetlain, who had answered Hurlbut's call for artillery at Fort Pillow by sending Booth and his 6th USCHA to Bradford's aid. "There is a great deal of excitement in town in consequence of this affair, especially among our colored troops. If this is to be the game of the enemy they will soon learn that it is one at which two can play."[11]

———————————

As details of the massacre sifted in, Northern editorialists and politicians vied with one another to issue the most vehement expressions of outrage. A delegate to Union-occupied Louisiana's constitutional convention condemned the "Slaveholding chivalry" that had induced "the enemies of this country" to wage "a war of extermination" and "provoke the United States government to a bloody retaliation." The *New York Herald* reported how "insatiate as fiends, bloodthirsty as devils incarnate, the rebels commenced an indiscriminate butchery of the whites and blacks, including those of both colors who had been previously wounded." "The whole civilized world will be shocked by the great atrocity at Fort Pillow," the *Chicago Tribune* predicted, "but in no respect does the act misrepresent the nature and precedents of Slavery." Such was the theme of many Northern editorials that week: that the butchery at Fort Pillow could only have been committed by the soldiers of a slaveholding society.[12]

"I want no peace with Fort Pillow murderers," declared a delegate to Maryland's constitutional convention. "I want no peace with men who will destroy and torture our prisoners in the way they have done, until they will lay down their arms," he said, "and submit to the authority of the Government, and acknowledge and yield to the civilization of the age."[13]

The massacre had put the fear of God in West Tennessee's Union occupiers. "Possibly, ere this leaves my tent," wrote a white lieutenant in the 66th USCI, "we will have suffered the fate of the troops at Fort Pillow. It is currently reported that the fort was taken by the rebels, and the garrison massacred. If I must lose my life thus, I will not die begging; and if this report be true, I look for the time when they will be rewarded." But because there were so few white officers of colored regiments they were in "much more danger."[14]

Belle Edmondson of Shelby County was delighted to observe that after the fall of Fort Pillow, "the Yanks are frightened to death in Memphis. How I wish we could get possession of our City once more!" she exclaimed. "Navigation of the Mississippi above blockaded for the present, and I hope, forever to the Yankees."[15]

Hurlbut wanted to move five thousand men to the Tennessee River but felt he was not "at liberty to deviate from Genl Sherman's orders" to turn his command over to Brigadier General Ralph Pomeroy Buckland until Washburn reached Memphis. The city was "full of all kinds of flying reports," he said. Many civilians believed that Leonidas Polk with his infantry was descending on Corinth, while others said he was moving on La Grange.

"Memphis itself, if attacked by a competent force, is not a defensible point," Hurlbut reminded McPherson. But in the event of an assault, he declared, he would draw in his pickets, burn all the bridges, and hold on "as long as it may be tenable." However he had "no expectation" of such an attack, "as it is very generally & properly understood that as a last resort I will destroy the city before it shall be held by the enemy." Though the Union army had managed to repair all the damage Forrest had wrought along the railway between Mobile and Okolona, Hurlbut still considered "the situation in West Tennessee very precarious and one that calls for the early concentration of troops to drive the enemy from their location."[16]

In Gallatin, Tennessee, a diarist wrote that the Yankees were "scared to death; they are looking for Forrest. No passes given. All the stores are closed." "The Yankees have a great dread of Forrest," wrote a Southern correspondent. "The first question asked by nearly every prisoner we capture is 'Where is Forrest?'" The Yankees "believe the extravagant stories of the Yankee papers in reference to the massacre at Fort Pillow, and they expect no quarter if they should unfortunately fall into his hands."[17]

Frederick Douglass hoped that "contrary to the expectations" of those Northern whites who saw the slaughter as the inevitable consequence of black recruitment, "this horrible massacre at Fort Pillow" would instill in African Americans not terror but "an eagerness for the chance to avenge their slaughtered brethren." Congressman William Darrah Kelley of Pennsylvania also defended black recruitment, but not by appealing to the better angels of white Americans. "I ask you, mother, was it not better that we should take the rebel's slave and put him in the ranks of our army to fight, than that we should take your son and put him there?" And did "you, father, regret that it was not your son who was put to death at Fort Pillow?"[18]

Some black soldiers, however, had grown weary of being told by whites that it was up to them to avenge Fort Pillow and free their people. "I want to know," asked a black soldier stationed in South Carolina, "if it was not the white man that put them in bondage. How can they hold us responsible for their evils? And how can they expect that we should do more to blot it out than they are willing to do themselves?" He did not wonder "at the conduct and disaster that transpired at Fort Pillow. I wonder that we have not had more New York riots and Fort Pillow massacres."[19]

The African American press begged its readers, however, to rededicate themselves to the Confederacy's defeat. "The southern breezes bring a wail of horror from the devoted Fort Pillow," the *Christian Recorder* editorialized. "Yet, through this bloody sea lies the land of liberty; and although we may have to pour out rivers of blood, liberty is not attainable without it." For ex-slaves, the massacre was merely butchery "on a grander scale, than those thousands of similar ones performed daily by the lords of the lash, before this rebellion—and, instead of daunting our courage, should only nerve us to do and dare more in this struggle for human rights and universal liberty."[20]

Despite such hopes, black recruitment in the West stalled and desertions from black regiments multiplied as it became clear that Lincoln was reluctant to order reprisals against the rebels who had decimated their brethren at Fort Pillow. In Texas, three days after Fort Pillow's fall, a regiment of black Rhode Island artillery had to be subdued with cannon after declaring themselves "out of the service." In late June, Chetlain reported that "the crime of Desertion" among black troops was "prevailing to an alarming extent," and warned that all deserters, "when apprehended, will immediately be placed in close confinement, proceedings instituted against them, and vigorously prosecuted with a view to making examples of flagrant cases." By October, the remaining companies of the 2nd USCLA were reporting that eighty-one men had died of disease, and forty-one men, twenty of them unmustered recruits, had deserted.[21]

"We supposed that the late horrible massacre at Fort Pillow," wrote a Philadelphia recruiter,

> if noticed, as the people generally anticipate it will be, by a vigorous proclamation from the Government, directing severe retaliation on the enemy for any similar outrages in the future, will impart a fresh momentum to recruiting. The colored people are excited. They now need to be encouraged. If the Government will give emphatic expression to the general desire on the subject . . . and Congress should speedily place black troops on the same footing as other troops, we could raise, in my judgment, two, three, or more regiments here. At present recruiting is dull in spite of the liberal bounties offered.[22]

The number of whites volunteering to officer black regiments also sharply declined, and a great number of applicants withdrew their names. General Chetlain blamed their reluctance to join on "the tardiness of the Government to retaliate for the outrages committed at Fort Pillow." So few whites were coming forward to command black troops that Chetlain asked whether Lorenzo Thomas would consider promoting blacks to serve as officers.[23]

When it came to assigning blame for the massacre, some editorialists did not limit themselves to the Confederates. The *Anglo African* blamed the Federals as well. What could anyone expect when colored troops were being offered inferior pay and Union soldiers abused black people "right under the windows" of the White House? "Villains dressed in the garb of Union soldiers were permitted to insult colored people," and it was not until whites complained that the soldiers were removed to a camp outside the city.[24]

"We cannot pass over the Fort Pillow massacre in silence," wrote a Connecticut woman to the *New York Independent*. She proposed that the best retaliation would be to give black men "the right of suffrage" and make them citizens. "Such a response would be a greater protection to the black soldier," she wrote. "He would be recognized as a man. It would do infinitely greater damage to the rebel cause; for it would be a blow aimed at its very corner-stone. We must remember that, while we deny to these blacks the rights of men, we share in the guilt of those who slaughter them like cattle."[25]

The sixty-seven-year-old New York abolitionist Gerritt Smith, who had helped to bankroll John Brown's raid on Harpers Ferry, extended the blame for Fort Pillow all the way to England "because it was she who planted slavery in America, and because it is slavery out which this crime has come. Our nation however is the far guiltier one. The guilt of this crime is upon all her people who have contributed to that public sentiment which releases white men from respecting the rights of black men." Smith believed that even President Lincoln was "not entirely innocent" of the massacre because he had been so slow to extend protection to black troops and refused to recognize the right of African Americans to vote.[26]

WADE AND GOOCH
THE JOINT SUBCOMMITTEE ON THE CONDUCT OF THE WAR

April 15–May 5, 1864

FOUR DAYS AFTER THE MASSACRE, STANTON ORDERED SHERMAN TO "direct a competent officer to investigate and report minutely, and as early as possible, the facts in relation to the alleged butchery of our troops at Fort Pillow." Sherman promptly passed the task on to Brayman, who began collecting affidavits from the patients at Mound City. But no doubt to Grant and Sherman's enormous relief, the investigation was soon turned over to the Joint Subcommittee on the Conduct of the War, whose recommendations they would not be obliged to follow.[1]

One of the arguments Forrest's defenders would make to prove that even the Union command did not believe reports of a massacre at Fort Pillow was the fact that even such harsh and remorseless generals as Grant and Sherman never ordered reprisals. But by April 23, Sherman had concluded that Northern threats and condemnations would prove entirely useless and so proposed that the question of reprisals be quietly left up to "the negroes themselves." The Confederate army "cares no more for our clamor than the idle wind," he wrote Stanton, "but they will heed the slaughter that will follow as the natural consequence of their own inhuman acts." The truth, he said, was that the rebels' savage hatred of black troops "cannot be restrained." Thus far black troops had been "comparatively well behaved, and have not committed the horrid excesses and barbarities which the Southern papers so much dreaded." But eventually "the effect will be of course to make the negroes desperate, and when in turn they commit horrid acts of retaliation," he wrote with characteristically brutal pragmatism, "we will be relieved of the responsibility." He doubted the wisdom "of any fixed rule by our Government, but let soldiers affected make their rules as we progress. We will use their own logic against them, as we have from the beginning of the war."[2]

In Washington, moral outrage and Radical Republican opportunism combined to keep the Fort Pillow affair from receding into the horrific generality of the war. The massacre must have seemed like an Old Testament godsend to sixty-four-year-old Senator Benjamin Franklin Wade of Massachusetts, a staunch abolitionist who, from the moment of Lincoln's election, had pressed for total war against the secessionist slave masters of the South. His mighty jaw, downturned bulldog mouth, and undisguised extremism had earned him the nickname "Bluff Ben."

Wade had loudly deplored Lincoln's initial attempts to find a peaceful resolution to the crisis of secession, and, once the war began, criticized his generals for lacking an instinct for the jugular. Now, as the 1864 election loomed, he worked behind the scenes to deny Lincoln a second term, and with an unseemly ardor set out to convince war-weary Northerners that the South was a land of barbarians. "Mercy to traitors," he declared, "is cruelty to loyal men." One of his staunchest allies was Massachusetts representative Daniel Wheelwright Gooch. Gooch had a homely, fretful countenance not improved by spectacles and a sparse beard. Though he was twenty years Wade's junior, the two men understood each other; one of Gooch's most famous speeches was titled "Any Compromise a Defeat."[3]

Their weapon of choice was the Joint Committee on the Conduct of the War that Wade had established in 1861 to goad the army, navy, and indeed, his countrymen into fighting an all-out war. Lincoln blandly ignored its early calls for the firing of McClellan; the reinstatement of Frémont, Burnside, and Butler; and various other measures it deemed critical to the emancipation of the slaves, the utter defeat of the South, and the advancement of Wade's fellow Radicals. Nevertheless, the joint committee proved a persistent thorn in the president's side.

In early 1864, Lincoln and the committee had differed most strenuously on how to treat the South after the war. Two months before the massacre, Wade had introduced a vindictive Reconstruction bill that would refuse amnesty to all Confederate officers, civil and military, and forever disenfranchise any rebels who retained their offices after the bill's passage. However eager Wade was to abolish slavery, he was a colonization man, and to gain enough votes to pass his bill, traded away Negro suffrage. The bill would indeed pass both houses, and by comfortable margins. But Lincoln refused to be hemmed in by such draconian constraints and saw in the bill's patent mean-spiritedness the seeds of a postwar Democratic resurgence. Knowing a power play when he saw one, Lincoln pocket-vetoed Wade-Davis after the close of the congressional session. Wade bitterly and publicly protested Lincoln's "dictatorial usurpation," but after he threatened to retaliate by sinking Lincoln's chances for reelection, his fellow Republicans would eventually join their Democratic colleagues in denouncing him as a demagogue.

In April 1864, however, Wade was still proceeding from strength to strength. Convinced that the residual sympathy for the South in some Northern quarters—especially the Union's West Point–dominated officer corps—was crippling the war effort, the committee had blamed Yankee defeats on the fact that Union soldiers and especially their officers did not "adequately hate" the enemy. Wade's agenda was to force the army to take bolder, more drastic measures by cultivating in Northern hearts and minds a deep loathing for the South.

To that end, the committee used its investigatory mandate to dig up doubtful but lurid stories of Confederate atrocities. After the First Battle of Bull Run, it had delectatiously reported that inexperienced rebel surgeons had delighted in hacking into the limbs of wounded Yankee prisoners, that Confederate officers had refused to bury the Union dead, and that some bodies had been decapitated, emasculated, and even boiled down to extract shinbones and skulls to serve as drumsticks and serving bowls. To punish these and the other alleged crimes, the Radicals constantly urged the president to retaliate, and at one point even proposed that Lincoln enlist large numbers of Native Americans and give them license to visit the barbarities of Indian warfare on the rebels.

In the aftermath of the fall of Fort Pillow, they denounced Lincoln for hesitating to avenge the massacre with reprisals. Speaking at the opening of a sanitary fair in Baltimore, Lincoln felt called upon to address the subject. "He declared that if the statements, as now reported, should be officially substantiated, he would retaliate amply upon the rebels, but that he had not yet decided in what manner he would execute the *lex talionis*." "I am glad," wrote Wade's son, "that the President has decided to retaliate for the wrongs committed by the rebels on our soldiers." But Lincoln's large heart was not in it.[4]

Despairing of the president and his generals, Wade's allies in Congress passed a resolution appointing a Joint *Sub*committee on the Conduct of the

War "to inquire into the truth of the rumored slaughter of the Union troops after their surrender at the recent attack of rebel forces upon Fort Pillow, Tennessee; and also whether Fort Pillow could have been evacuated or sufficiently re-enforced; and if so, why it was not done."[5]

Supplied with Stanton's letters of introduction, Wade and Gooch departed from Washington a week after the massacre, determined to gather the kind of evidence Lincoln said he required before he would consider ordering his troops to engage in acts of reprisal. At 8:00 a.m. on April 22, after three days of nonstop travel, Wade and Gooch reached Cairo and lost no time interrogating General Brayman, who had collected a sheaf of affidavits from various witnesses and was completing his own report on the massacre. They then proceeded a short distance up the Ohio to the Mound City hospital to question the wounded.[6]

Gathering at the bedsides of blacks and whites alike, "some of them pierced and cut in the face and eyes with bayonets and swords, while other parts of their bodies were smashed and disfigured either by steel or lead," Wade and Gooch began to question men encased in bloody bandages and laboring for every breath. Some were too weak to answer more than a few questions, some were too far gone to testify at all. After reading the affidavits Brayman had been collecting since the fifteenth and interviewing twenty-four witnesses over the course of the first day alone, they accepted the hospitality of Fleet Captain A. M. Pennock on his flagship, from which Gooch excitedly wrote to Stanton that he and Wade had already heard enough to conclude that "the atrocities at Fort Pillow" had "exceeded the representations in the papers."[7]

After three days of gathering testimony at Cairo and Mound City, Wade and Gooch boarded the *Hastings* for the journey to Fort Pillow itself. Pulling up to the landing, they interviewed James Marshall and the crew of the *New Era,* as well as the civilian members of the burial detail the gunboat was guarding, three of whom testified to finding a body with its clothes nailed to the plank floor of an incinerated tent.[8]

Wade and Gooch climbed up the ravine road and toured the ruined fort. Some 150 yards from the parapet, they spied three decomposed corpses lying on the ground in hospital garb: perhaps the three who had been shot down while making their way to the river on April 13 under a rebel surgeon's escort. Among the ten they interviewed at Fort Pillow were Sergeant Henry Weaver of 6/C, who was recuperating aboard the *New Era;* Alfred Coleman of 6/B; and Hurlbut's adjutant, Lieutenant Colonel Thomas Harris of the 16th Army Corps.[9]

General Hurlbut testified in Memphis that "the black troops will hereafter be uncontrollable, unless the government take some prompt and energetic action upon the subject. I know very well that my colored regiments at Memphis, officers and men, will never give quarter."

"They never ought to," Wade interjected.

To which Hurlbut replied, "They never will."[10]

That Wade and Gooch were predisposed to pronounce the Fort Pillow affair a massacre is unquestionable, for nothing could better serve their agenda than what they hoped to portray as an enormous, concerted slaughter of a helpless garrison. For this reason, the conclusions reached in Wade and Gooch's summary, with their partisan exclusions and emphases, are of little use in reconstructing what happened, especially the context of what happened.

Their most glaring omission was a thorough investigation into exactly why, against Sherman's orders, Hurlbut had stationed Bradford and his 13th Cavalry at Fort Pillow in the first place. If it was to prevent the rebels from stationing artillery on the bluff and firing on river traffic, why did it take him so long to assign a battery, and why only two light guns at first? If it was to recruit black troops, why did he wait so long before stationing a black regiment at Fort Pillow?

When Wade gently pressed Hurlbut on the subject, the general grew peevish. "I considered Fort Pillow as a place which ought to be held with a small garrison," he snapped, "and I think so yet, and any navy officer or river man will tell you that the situation of the channel there requires it."

"I am not questioning that at all," Wade hastened to say. "I merely inquired as to the fact."

Hurlbut said he continued to think that "500 ready troops, properly supplied with artillery, and properly covered with works, could hold the place until re-enforced," which was "all that is necessary," though Forrest had just demonstrated that with a small detachment of sharpshooters an enemy could not only keep gunboats out of range but prevent reinforcements from landing.

Or did Hurlbut mean that Booth's command was not "ready," that there was not enough artillery, that the works were not properly "covered"? Apparently not, for he described Booth approvingly as "an old soldier" from the regular army and "the best man I had for that purpose. I received a report from him 'that he could hold that post against any force for forty-eight hours,' which was all I expected him to do, and if he had not been killed I think he would have held it. I have no doubt," Hurlbut concluded, "that his death was the immediate cause of the capture of the place," for though William Bradford was "a very good gentleman," he was a "very young officer, entirely inexperienced in these matters." The subcommittee apparently did not think to ask why, then, Hurlbut had appointed him commander of the 13th and, initially, of the Fort Pillow garrison.

Hurlbut claimed that the station had never been evacuated, and insisted that Sherman had never commanded him to abandon it. The one piece of evidence that Hurlbut had been given free rein was a March 29 letter from Sherman saying that Hurlbut was "so thoroughly familiar with matters along the Mississippi river that I do not deem it necessary to give any specific instructions but shall rely largely upon your judgement and discretion." But by then Hurlbut had not only stationed Bradford's Battalion and a battery of the 2nd USCLA at Fort Pillow but sent Booth and his 6th USCHA to the bluff just the day before.[11]

"*Some* discretion, I suppose," Hurlbut huffed to Wade, "belongs to an officer in charge of as much range as I have had to hold; and I certainly should not abandon that place, if I had troops to hold it."

Rather than press Hurlbut to account for his timidity and outright defiance of Sherman's explicit orders, Wade asked the general for hearsay: "Did you hear anything about their setting fire to hospitals, while the wounded were in there?" "Did you hear, recently after that capture, of anybody being nailed to a building and burned?" "Did you learn that from a source that you could give credit to?" And so on.

When Wade asked if Hurlbut had anything else to add, he more or less pleaded the Fifth. "I do not know that I can state anything more than my opinion in regard to certain things that might have been done," he said. "I do not know that it is worthwhile to do that. As I am under censure myself, at present I prefer not to."[12]

Hurlbut's interview proved to be his swan song.[13] On May 2, he received a telegram from General Henry Halleck relieving him "of all military command."[14] Blaming Hurlbut for Forrest's victories along the Mississippi, Sherman transferred him from Cairo to New Orleans, where he continued his pattern of inebriation and corruption in the Department of the Gulf. In November Lincoln would admonish Hurlbut for his "gratuitous hostility" to a new Louisiana constitution that the president deemed "better for the black man than we have in Illinois." Hurlbut characteristically both denied the accusation and pleaded the burdens of command. It took until June 1865 for the army to decide that prosecuting Hurlbut would serve no useful purpose.

Though he claimed he had entered the service of his country "very comfortably poor" and had not saved a dime of his army pay, Hurlbut would return to Belvidere, Illinois, after the war rich in cash and political chips. Despite continuing charges of corruption and drunkenness, in later years he realized his prewar ambitions of being elected to Congress and serving as an ambassador in South America. Impressing his hosts with his fluent Spanish, he was appointed the American ambassador to Colombia and then Peru, where, after disgracing himself and his country in a drunken altercation with the vacationing American ambassador to Chile, he died in 1882.[15]

Some of Wade and Gooch's questions were undeniably leading, but only when judged without reference to the affidavits many witnesses had already provided. In those cases, they merely asked questions to elicit in oral testimony what the witnesses had already testified to in their depositions. In many cases they sought specific corroboration or repudiation of another witness's testimony. Here, as an example, are the questions they posed to Frank Hogan of 6/A.

> Were you at Fort Pillow on the day of the fight? In what company and regiment? . . . What did you see there that day, especially after the fort was taken? . . . After they had given up? . . . Did they say anything more at the time they shot him? . . . What was the rank of the secesh officer? . . . Do you know the name of the officer he shot? . . . Why did they not shoot you? . . . How long did you stay with them? Where did you go then? . . . Do you know anything of the rebels burning any of the tents that had wounded men in them? . . . About what time of the day was that? . . . Did you hear the men in there after they set the building on fire? . . . How long had they been sick? . . . Did you see them bury any of our men? . . . Were they all really dead or not? . . . Did you see the man? . . . How came they to bury him when he was alive? . . . Have you seen the three bodies that are now lying over beyond? . . . Did you know them?

Some of these questions would not have been permitted in criminal court, and of course there was no cross-examination from the rebel point of view. But they are typical of the sort of questions posed in civil proceedings and congressional hearings. What lends credence to most of the answers such questions elicited are the many instances in which, despite numerous opportunities to ingratiate themselves with Wade and Gooch by telling them what they wanted to hear, many witnesses—especially the enlisted men—declined to corroborate some of the other witnesses' most lurid testimony.

Critics of the testimony collected in the subcommittee's report suggest that most of the affidavits the army collected within days of the massacre, and the oral testimony the subcommittee itself collected within two weeks of the massacre, had been fatally contaminated by Wade and Gooch's scorched-earth agenda. They maintain that the witnesses were bullied into making up stories about rebel atrocities by senior officers deeply humiliated and appalled by the Union's defeat at Fort Pillow. But at the same time they condemn the witnesses for contradicting one another. What is most striking about the testimony, however, is its consistency. Once it is broken down chronologically, and the individual accounts compared one to another, almost every supposed disparity proves immaterial, inconsequential, or entirely explicable.

Some critics regard the testimony's very consistency, however, as evidence of a conspiracy to falsify the evidence. If there was a conspiracy to agree upon concocted tales of rebel atrocity, however, it is difficult to imagine how the conspirators, within days of the massacre, could have managed to get all of the witnesses' stories straight, spread out as they were from Mound City and Cairo to Fort Pillow and Memphis. Nor can it account for the corroborative testimony of the naval personnel who submitted affidavits while patrolling the Mississippi, the civilians who wrote home, the rebel participants who reported the horrors to their families, and the survivors who would submit statements to the army's pension and ration commutation boards years later.

One of the most sweeping critics of the survivors' testimony was an Arizona lawyer named Abraham Davis, who, in addition to attacking the testimony's supposed contradictions, pointed out that though all of the enlisted men who testified—black and white—signed their names with an X, the transcription of their testimony was in correct English "without a misspelled word or grammatical error." This is not entirely true. Misspelled words would not have been employed in a conscientious transcription of oral testimony, and there are plenty of grammatical errors among the transcripts and affidavits. More important, illiteracy in mid-nineteenth-century America precluded neither intelligence nor sound, coherent speech.[16]

The Southern bias against black testimony was deep and long-standing. Antebellum laws had effectively prohibited slaves from testifying, and a reflexive disinclination to take a black man's word over a white's colors many critiques of the Union testimony. Some critics suspected that the transcriptions themselves were frauds because they represented African American speech without resorting to the dialect form that was de rigueur in the American press, North and South. But it was to the transcribers' credit that they did not garnish their transcriptions of black speech with quaint spellings and contractions. Instead, they did what many historians have done since when quoting from contrived black dialect transcribed by whites, which is to spell everything—except for idioms like "marse" and "whupping"—correctly and completely but retain its grammatical structure. This approach does better justice to the interviewee and shortens some of the distance between the speaker and the reader. But then it was the shortening of that distance that disturbed so many of Forrest's defenders, whose tone suggests that they were fundamentally affronted that any one, even a Yankee, should take the word of former slaves and white turncoats over the word of Southern officers and gentlemen. "You might not think it worth while," Edward Benton of Fort Pillow insisted to the subcommittee, "to take the evidence" of people even he called "Darkies," but it was "a great deal more to be relied upon than the Southern evidence there."[17]

Finally, there may be disparities and promptings and a not-so-well-hidden agenda running through Wade's distillation of the evidence in the subcommittee's final report. But compared to what? The most glaring weakness in the continuing critique of the testimony compiled first by Brayman and then by Wade and Gooch is that the Confederacy never countered with testimony from its own enlisted men. Perhaps this was merely a case of Southern feudalism: a belief that gentlemen should not have to turn to the poor whites they commanded for corroboration. But if the private letters of the rebels Achilles Clark and Samuel H. Caldwell are any indication, it is likelier that their officers knew that their own men would not back them up. And so Forrest would try to elicit corroboration from the captive Captain Young, which, under duress, he only partially provided and ultimately renounced; and from subordinate officers invested in defending their reputations against not only Northern condemnation but Richmond's disdain for its Western army.

Wade and Gooch obtained so much corroborated testimony that a massacre took place that in the end they hardly needed to embellish it. Wade and Gooch may have been fanatical and untrustworthy, and their summary of the testimony they collected perfervid. But there is little evidence that their agenda affected the actual testimony of the survivors of the Fort Pillow massacre. Even the most inveterate liars will tell the truth when the facts are on their side.

Tennessee's Confederate governor Isham Harris wrote a rebuttal to Wade and Gooch's report based, he said, on an interview with Forrest himself, which, under such headlines as "The Fort Pillow Affair: Refutation of Yankee Slanders," was reprinted in papers all over the South.

"In the heat, din and confusion of a fire at such close quarters," wrote Harris, "there was no chance for discrimination." He blamed Bradford's mule-headed refusal to surrender for the slaughter of what he said was five hundred out of eight hundred Federals, and the garrison itself for continuing to fire as they fled to the river; and he depicted a "sickened" Forrest riding up and down his lines, desperately trying to halt the killing.

"There is not the semblance of a shadow of truth," wrote Harris, "in the Federal exaggerations of wholesale slaughter." But His Excellency should have checked his dictionary for the definition of "wholesale"—"done on a large scale and indiscriminately"—which fits the engagement even as the governor himself described it.[18]

Southern papers that had once celebrated the extent of the Union's casualties at Fort Pillow now published blanket denials that there ever was a massacre. On May 13, the itinerant secessionist *Memphis Appeal* printed the first rebel claim that the Federal garrison at Fort Pillow had been drunk, and it was at this point, a little more than a month after the massacre, that Forrest sent Judge Scruggs down to elicit from Captain Young corroboration of Forrest's own account of the battle. The Wizard claimed that Young would be only one of several captive Union officers he intended to interview, but if he did, none of the others cooperated, and the letter Young eventually signed was not exactly a ringing endorsement of the rebel version of the battle.[19]

Richmond nevertheless circled its wagons around Forrest. On May 23, in defiance of Wade and Gooch's charges, the Confederate Congress voted its thanks to Forrest and his men "for their late brilliant and successful campaign in Mississippi, West Tennessee, and Kentucky—a campaign which has conferred upon its authors fame as enduring as the records of the struggle which they have so brilliantly illustrated."[20]

"A CHOICE OF EVILS"
RETALIATION

May 1–25, 1864

WADE AND GOOCH LOST NO TIME IN DISSEMINATING THEIR FINDINGS to the press. A day after they returned to Washington, the *New York Herald* reported that they had taken "fifty-seven depositions, all of which more than confirm the newspaper accounts of the massacre. They say that it would be impossible to exaggerate the cruelties committed." The subcommittee's final report was written by Wade. It accused Forrest of violating the truce and ascribed the slaughter not to the passions of the moment but to a deliberate attempt to wipe out Tennessee Unionists and discourage blacks from enlisting.[1]

On May 5, Wade and Gooch submitted their *Report of the Joint Subcommittee on the Conduct of the War* to Congress, which ordered forty thousand copies printed and bound. One of "the most expert propaganda productions of the war," the report galvanized the North, muffled calls to negotiate with the Confederacy, and aided Lincoln, Grant, and Sherman in their determination to wage total war. One Northerner suggested that Lincoln should send a copy "to every home," for it was a more effective recruitment tool "than the draft or his greenbacks."[2]

In anticipation of the report's publication, Lincoln asked his cabinet members to advise him on the proper response to the carnage at Fort Pillow. Secretary of State William Seward urged the president to give the rebels an opportunity to defend themselves against the accusation of wholesale massacre. If the charges proved true, they would be obliged "to disavow them and give satisfactory pledges that they shall not be repeated hereafter" or take responsibility for the fates of a number of "vigorously confined" Confederate prisoners equal in rank and number to the men massacred at Fort Pillow.[3]

Secretary of War Edwin Stanton was not so circumspect. A Radical himself, he urged Lincoln to hold hostage a number of imprisoned Confederate officers equal to the number of Union soldiers killed at Fort Pillow, releasing them only after Forrest and his officers were given over to Federal authorities to stand trial. He also demanded that Forrest and Chalmers be exempted from any amnesty or exchange. Should Richmond refuse to give up Forrest and his officers, "such measures will be taken," he wrote, "by way of retributary justice for the massacre of Fort Pillow, as are justified by the laws of civilized warfare." He specified officers instead of enlisted men because "the rebels have selected white officers of colored regiments and excluded them from the benefit of the laws of war for no other reason than that they command special troops." In addition, according to Stanton, the Confederate army was, in effect, a feudal horde, many of whose privates were conscripted and "held in arms by terror and rigorous punishment from their own officers." Only the feelings of members of the officer class were "at all regarded in the rebel States," or had any "interest or influence in bringing about more humane conduct on the part of the rebel authorities." Stanton ordered the rations doled out to rebel prisoners cut by a fifth, and when he received a report that a rebel deserter claiming to have taken part in the battle had offered to take the Oath of Allegiance at Covington, Kentucky, he ordered the provost marshal to "arrest him and send him under guard to Washington," though by then the deserter in question had fled.[4]

Secretary of the Navy Gideon Welles sent the president an admittedly "crude and immature" letter warning Lincoln that "vindictive warfare" of the kind practiced by the rebels on black troops "will unavoidably provoke retaliation by the race proscribed. The persecuted will become equally unrelenting towards their persecutors and if not checked a war of extermination will be the consequence." Welles urged that "the officer in command and such others as are known to have participated with him should be held accountable for the murders and punished accordingly." If the Confederate government refused to punish Forrest and his officers, Welles agreed with Seward that captive rebel officers should be taken into "close custody and held accountable for the conduct of the war by the rebels on humane and civilized principles."[5]

Attorney General Edward Bates, the first American cabinet officer to hail from west of the Mississippi, took the opportunity to remind Lincoln of Bates's opposition to the recruitment of black troops in the first place. The

Missourian said he knew "something of the cherished passions and the educated prejudices of the Southern people," and had feared from the beginning that "the employment of negro troops would add fuel to the flame already fiercely burning and thus excite their evil passions to deeds of horror, shocking to humanity and to Christian civilization." Recoiling from the prospect of the Union and the Confederacy being pulled into an endless cycle of retribution, Bates proposed demanding that the Confederates surrender Forrest and Chalmers, and, if they refused, commanding Union forces to execute any captives from Forrest's command who had taken part in the assault on Fort Pillow. He urged this not on the basis of law or morality but purely as a matter of sound policy, though he realized that Lincoln had, "at best, a choice of evils."[6]

Secretary of the Interior John Palmer Usher wrote that until the Union enjoyed another signal victory it would be unwise to take any extreme action, and even then the Union should retaliate only "as far as the laws of war and humanity will permit." The Indianan proposed executing an equal number of men from Forrest's command, "designating in every instance, as far as practicable, officers instead of privates." In the meantime, "the colored troops should be satisfied that it is the unalterable purpose of this government to protect them in good faith and to its utmost ability."[7]

The president, as usual, kept his own counsel. As his ministers' memoranda piled up on his desk, he agreed to meet Frederick Douglass to discuss the massacre and the unequal pay and promotions accorded black troops by the Union army. Impressing Douglass as "an honest man" whom he could "love, honor, and trust without reserve or doubt," Lincoln agreed about the justice of equal pay and promotion for black soldiers, but disagreed "entirely" with Douglass's call for reprisals. "I shall never forget the benignant expression of his face," Douglass recalled, "the tearful look of his eye, and the quiver in his voice, when he deprecated a resort to retaliatory measures."

"Once begun," Lincoln groaned, "I do not know where such a measure would stop."

"He said he could not take men out and kill them in cold blood for what was done by others," Douglass wrote. "If he could get hold of the persons who were guilty of killing the colored prisoners in cold blood, the case would be different. But he could not kill the innocent for the guilty."[8]

Other black leaders were not so moved by Lincoln's reluctance to avenge Fort Pillow and saw it as a manifestation of the president's latent bigotry. An outraged Thomas Hinton of the *Christian Recorder* proposed three resolutions: that the Union "execute as many traitors as will correspond with the number of our citizens and soldiers who have been thus wantonly massacred at Fort Pillow," that the "greatest traitors are such Governors and such Legislators as would recognize the so-called Confederacy" and perpetuate "an institution that has fostered all this strife, carnage, bloodshed and butchery that now pervades our borders, and that has given development to the latent and destructive propensities of an ignorant and benighted people, ruled over and governed by a bigoted, selfish, egotistical, cruel and bloodthirsty slave-holding oligarchy"; and "as it is eminently necessary to get rid of a few of the big fish first"—and here the editorial broke into verse:

> That we hang home-traitors up to dry,
> While we look after the smaller fry:
> That he who would for traitors make apology,
> We'll allow to dance the old Doxology,
> Of unmeasured step to time,
> By the pathos of a trap and the jerk of a line.[9]

Lincoln did draft a lawyerly letter to Stanton outlining a possible policy on retaliation. "Please notify the insurgents," the president began,

> through the proper military channels and forms, that the government of the United States has satisfactory proof of the massacre by insurgent forces, at Fort-Pillow, on the 12th and 13th days of April last, of fully _____ white and colored officers and soldiers of the United States, after the latter had ceased resistance, and asked quarter of the former.
>
> That with reference to said massacre, the government of the United States has assigned and set apart by name _____ insurgent officers, theretofore, and up to that time, held by said government as prisoners of war.
>
> That, as blood can not restore blood, and government should not act for revenge, any assurance, as nearly perfect as the case admits, given on or before the first day of July next, that there shall be no similar massacre, nor any officer or soldier of the United States, whether white or colored, now held, or hereafter captured by the insurgents, shall be treated other than according to the laws of war, will insure the replacing of said insurgent officers in the simple condition of prisoners of war.
>
> That the insurgents having refused to exchange, or to give any account or explanation in regard to colored soldiers of the United States

captured by them, a number of insurgent prisoners equal to the number of such colored soldiers supposed to have been captured by said insurgents will, from time to time, be assigned and set aside, with reference to such captured colored soldiers, and will, if the insurgents assent, be exchanged for such colored soldiers; but that if no satisfactory attention shall be given to this notice, by said insurgents, on or before the first day of July next, it will be assumed by the government of the United States, that said captured colored troops shall have been murdered, or subjected to Slavery, and that said government will, upon said assumption, take such action as may then appear expedient and just.[10]

But Lincoln never signed the letter, and Stanton never received it. According to the president's secretaries, Fort Pillow was soon "crowded out of the President's view by Grant's Wilderness Campaign." On September 5, 1864, Lincoln wanly ordered one Nathan Bedford Forrest to appear in U.S. circuit court by March 6, 1865, to answer the charge of treason.[11] But Lincoln's idea of retaliation was winning the war.[12]

Every major Northern paper and a good many minor dailies reprinted the joint subcommittee's report in its entirety, raising an outcry that exceeded Wade and Gooch's fondest hopes. "We have but one grade of soldiers," declared the *Philadelphia Press,* "and if, by the slaughter of those of color, the rebels attempt to force upon us a difference we repudiate, we must teach them that in murdering our troops, they earn the death sentence for themselves." "The annals of savage warfare nowhere record a more inhuman, fiendish butchery than this," said *Harper's Weekly,* "perpetrated by the representatives of the 'superior civilization' of the States in rebellion." No wonder "our officers and soldiers in the West are determined to avenge, at all opportunities, the cold-blooded murder of their comrades; and yet we can but contemplate with pain the savage practices which rebel inhumanity thus forces upon the service."[13]

"Will our Government," asked a citizen of Buffalo, "allow the rebels to do as they please, to have their own way, Massacre here and there, our hero soldiers, and yet not visit *swift justice* and *sure vengence* upon them?" Loyalists demanded of Lincoln "*retaliation* for the horrible crimes of the 'Fort Pillow affair' and not that only but *all others & similar cases.*" "Rebel Savagery" read the headline in the Unionist Franklin (Virginia) *Repository.*[14]

"I shall not issue any orders," warned Cad Washburn as he took the reins at Memphis, "requiring the troops of this command to spare the monsters engaging in a transaction that renders the Sepoy a humane being and Nana-Sahib a clever gentleman," by which he referred to the recent rebellion of native troops in India and the Maratha prince the British had blamed for the worst of the rebel atrocities. "It was in vain," wrote Horace Greeley, "that Forrest and his superior, Lt. Gen S. D. Lee, undertook to palliate this infernal atrocity, in defiance of their own record," because the testimony gathered by the subcommittee "proves that the murderers a hundred times declared that they shot the Blacks because they were 'niggers,' and the Whites for 'fighting with niggers.' If human testimony ever did or can establish any thing," concluded Greeley, "then this is proved a case of deliberate, wholesale massacre of prisoners of war after they had surrendered."[15]

Though Wade and Gooch had managed with their report to radicalize some moderates, the subcommittee was unable to translate its findings into legislation. For two weeks Congress debated what to do about the awful conditions in Confederate prisons that the subcommittee had described in the second portion of its report. "Retaliation has in all ages of the world been a means of bringing inhuman and savage foes to a sense of their duty," Wade boomed in the chamber of the Senate. Anyone who hesitated to subject captive rebels to the same treatment to which imprisoned Yankee were being subjected he accused of indulging in a "mawkish idea of humanity."[16]

Though he was a zealous abolitionist, Charles Sumner of Massachusetts joined an unusual alliance of Democrats and Radical Republicans to block Wade's way, denouncing his proposals as an imitation of Confederate savagery that their consciences would not permit. In the end a resolution was passed, but stripped of the retributive measures Wade and Gooch had championed.[17]

In the weeks that followed the fall of Fort Pillow, some rebel officers did not hesitate to follow Forrest's example whenever they encountered African American troops. On April 18, a Confederate force massacred wounded black troops at Poison Springs, Arkansas.[18]

"Out of 438 officers and men in the battle, the 1st Kansas Colored Infantry lost 182 men, 117 listed as killed." Three days later, a burial detail came upon the corpses of six white officers and eighty black infantrymen. "The white dead were all scalped and stripped of clothing which was carried off by the rebels. To add insult to the dead officers, they were laid on their faces and a circle of their colored soldiers made around them. Some wounded soldiers were bitten by rattlesnakes. Confederate losses number 16 killed, 88 wounded and 10 missing."[19]

Only eight days after the fall of Fort Pillow, a force under Confederate general R. F. Hoke had massacred black prisoners at Plymouth, North Carolina, in a manner eerily reminiscent of Fort Pillow. "All the negroes found in blue uniform or with any outward marks of a Union soldier upon him was killed," Orderly Sergeant Sam Johnson testified.

> I saw some taken into the woods and hung. Others I saw stripped of all their clothing, and they stood upon the bank of the river with their faces riverwards, and then they were shot. Still others were killed by having their brains beaten out by the butt end of the muskets in the hands of the Rebels. All were not killed the day of the capture. Those that were not, were placed in a room with their officers, [who] . . . having previously been dragged through the town with ropes around their necks, . . . were kept confined until the following morning when the remainder of the black soldiers were killed.[20]

At Saltville, Virginia, in October, black regiments in the front rank of a Federal force faced "Dibrell's & Robertson's Brigades in line of battle" and "were almost annihilated." The next day, Confederate general Felix Robertson told an approving Kentucky cavalry officer named Edward Guerrant that "he had killed nearly all the negroes." Robertson sent scouts out onto the field, "and the continued ring of the rifle sung the death knell of many a poor negro who was unfortunate enough not to be killed yesterday. Our men took no negro prisoners." According to another officer, the Union whites had failed to alert their black comrades to the rebels' advance as they "folded their tents and silently stole away. The poor unfortunate negroes had over-slept themselves and found that they had been deserted by their comrades and left to be massacred." A detachment of the 5th United States Colored Cavalry lost seventy-five killed and missing and thirty-seven wounded. A local farmer killed one of the missing whom he found lying wounded in the woods. "Poor negro!" Guerrant sneered. "Farewell."[21]

On October 13, at Dalton, Georgia, Confederate general John Bell Hood would present the 44th USCI with an evocative note: "I demand the immediate and unconditional surrender of the post and garrison under your command," it read, "and should this be acceded to, all white officers and soldiers will be paroled in a few days. If the place is carried by assault, no prisoners will be taken."

As Colonel Lewis Johnson considered this demand, Hood violated the flag of truce by "getting everything in position," including twenty guns and thousands of men "anxious to move upon the 'niggers.'" When Johnson "protested against the barbarous measures which he threatened in his summons," Hood replied "that he could not restrain his men, and would not if he could; that I could choose between surrender and death." Johnson chose surrender "under conditions that the men were to be treated humanely, officers and white soldiers to be paroled, officers to retain their swords and such private property as they could carry." As for the captive black troops, Hood informed Johnson that he intended to "return all slaves belonging to persons in the Confederacy to their masters." When Johnson protested that he had surrendered black as well as white soldiers as prisoners of war, Hood replied contemptuously that Johnson "might surrender them as whatever I pleased," but he would return them to slavery. "The colored soldiers displayed the greatest anxiety to fight," Johnson said, and it grieved him "to be compelled to surrender men who showed so much spirit and bravery."

After the surrender, "my men, especially the colored soldiers, were immediately robbed and abused in a terrible manner. The treatment of the officers of my regiment exceeded anything in brutality I have ever witnessed." Confederate general William Brimage Bate

> distinguished himself especially by meanness and beastly conduct. He had my colored soldiers robbed of their shoes (this was done systematically and by his order), and sent them down to the railroad and made them tear up the track for a distance of nearly two miles. One of my soldiers, who refused to injure the track, was shot on the spot, as were also five others shortly after the surrender, who, having been sick, were unable to keep up with the rest on the march.[22]

"I am in for the doctrine of extermination of all Rebels," a Union officer confided to his sister. "This may seem hard to you," he wrote, "but This is God's own doctrine. All rebels against Him will be punished eternally, and accordingly all Rebs against the Govt. should be exterminated, so far as it is in the power of man to exterminate. They are nothing more nor less than Devils incarnate, Big and Little, Male and Female."[23]

W. B. Allen of North Carolina recalled that after his imprisonment at the notorious Union Fort Pulaski, his Yankee captors retaliated against him and his comrades for the Fort Pillow massacre with "low diet and brutal treatment." He claimed that 150 out of 600 died within six months. According to another prisoner, George Albright of North Carolina, they suffered "all kinds of indignities at the hands of negro guards." A preacher reported that the rebel prisoners he encountered in a guardhouse "were actually in mortal dread of their colored guard, lest, remembering Fort Pillow, they might lay violent hands on them. There is no doubt that a salutary fear of our colored soldiers is pervading the rebel camps."[24] In July, a black sentinel was charged with overstepping his authority by bayoneting a Georgian prisoner who had ventured onto an off-limits gallery on his way to the privy. "One rebel said to me: 'You have killed him dead,'" recalled the sentinel, who was eventually let off. "And I said: 'Yes, by God! They buried us alive at Fort Pillow.'"[25]

For many of the Homegrown Yankees in the West, however, it was not the massacre of black troops that they vowed to avenge, but the slaughter of their white comrades in Bradford's Battalion. In a Union camp in Pike County, Tennessee, Ezra Stearns of the 1st Michigan Engineers, some of whose officers had volunteered to command the 1st U.S. Colored Infantry, wrote to his sister, "I heard an account of the massacre at Fort Pillow, and I hope that they will yet bag Forest and all of his men and string them up to the nearest tree that they come to. There are a lot of Tenn Cavalry guarding the road here, and they all swear that if they get their eyes upon Forest, they will show him no mercy."[26]

"REMEMBER FORT PILLOW"

BLACK FEDERALS AND WHITE CONFEDERATES

From June 10, 1864

ON JUNE 10, 1864, AT A BATTLE IN MISSISSIPPI KNOWN TO THE CON-federates as Tishomingo Creek and to the Federals as Brice's Crossroads, Forrest encountered an outnumbering black and white Union force sent down from Memphis under General Samuel Davis Sturgis. Informed by scouts and spies that black troops had sworn revenge on Forrest's men for the massacre at Fort Pillow, "we boys knew there were negroes somewhere" in the vicinity of Tishomingo Creek, wrote Second Lieutenant William Witherspoon of Duckworth's 7th Tennessee Cavalry, "but up to that time they were not 'come-at-able.' We kept asking each other, 'Where were the damn negroes?'"[1]

Forrest ordered his men to charge across an open field, recalled Sol Brantley of Duckworth's 7th, but "we kept on going, and the enemy was so excited that they was shooting too high and cannon balls and bombs was flying over our heads, singing like bumble bees." After the rebels broke their lines, the Federals, black and white, rallied two miles from the crossroads "and again made stout battle for about half an hour," recalled Hancock of Barteau's 22nd Tennessee Cavalry. At last they countercharged their pursuers, only to run into range of double charges of rebel canister. "As the negro soldiery broke, after their last stand, they were seen generally to tear something from their uniform and throw it away, which subsequently proved to have been a badge on which was printed, 'REMEMBER FORT PILLOW,'" while at the same time their white officers "threw off their shoulder straps, or insignia of rank."[2]

Convinced they would be massacred like their comrades at Fort Pillow, "many of them were shot down while thus wildly persisting in seeking safety in flight," and "some of them even went so far as to cut off the legs of their pants at the knees" so they could pass themselves off as slaves. Forrest's weary men pursued them for five or six miles, not giving up the chase until dark. Some black troops were betrayed by civilians as they cut through the brush. "We were more humane to them," Hancock declared, "than they had sworn to be to us. We did not kill them on the spot," he said, "as the poor, misguided wretches had been made to believe" would happen, but treated them "kindly" by arranging to have them "put up for sale, assigned as laborers to Confederate forces, or returned to their masters as slaves."[3]

The rebel Sol Brantley remembered it differently. "We run them all the way from the field of battle to Ripley, Miss.," he wrote, "a distance of 60 miles. We capture white prisoners all along, but no negro prisoners were taken. The negroes throwed their guns down and then their coats and last of all their shoes and run back towards Memphis much faster than when they come out to meet us, and I venture to say," Brantley concluded, "that if any of those negroes are living today they will tell you that they dident even have time to start a crap game in Miss."[4]

Exhausted after a day's fighting, the rebels were nonetheless rejuvenated by the repeated cry, "Here are the damn negroes!" According to Union accounts, as their white officers fled into the woods, the black troops covered Sturgis's retreat, pausing to fire every two hundred yards and thus preventing the rebels from cutting up the Yankee rear, even countercharging at one point with fixed bayonets and at great cost. John A. Crutchfield of Russell's 20th Tennessee Cavalry called Tishomingo Creek "one of the hardest fought battles since the war began."[5]

Wounded stragglers hid as best they could in the underbrush, and the road in both directions was lined with abandoned Union wagons "as far as could be seen," recalled a resident. "Several dead negroes in blue uniform were lying by the roadside not far from our dwelling." It was "certain that a great many negroes were killed. They wore the badge, 'Remember Fort Pillow,' and it was said that they carried a black flag. This incensed the Southern soldiers, and they relentlessly shot them down." In fact, wrote Samuel Agnew, "most of the negroes were shot, our men being so much incensed that they shoot them wherever they see them." Agnew conceded that "we have in our army some as vile men as the Yankees can have."[6]

A local farmer and his slaves helped to inter the Union dead. The whites were "buried shallow, the negroes especially so." On their march into battle, the black troops had struck Agnew as "specially insolent." They had shaken "their fists at the ladies" and boasted that "they were going to show Forrest that they were his rulers." But now, "as they returned, their tune was changed.

With tears in their eyes, some of them came to my mother and asked her what they must do. Would Mr. Forrest kill them?" But not all the black survivors of the Battle of Brice's Crossroads were so meek. After the battle, in the hills above Tishomingo Creek, a large black soldier attacked a Mississippi lieutenant, "throwing a large hickory stick at him, which came very near striking him."[7]

Sherman deplored Sturgis's dismal loss against so inferior a Confederate force. The debacle would haunt the remainder of Sturgis's army career, which would include sending George Armstrong Custer and his 7th Cavalry to their doom at Little Bighorn in 1876. Sherman ordered General A. J. Smith to turn back from Mobile and "go out from Memphis and defeat Forrest at all costs."[8]

There seemed a good chance he might succeed. "Forrest's horses are much jaded and need rest," wrote Samuel Agnew, "and if the Yankees would come out now he would not be prepared to meet them." The Yankees managed to capture a number of Forrest's officers, including his ailing adjutant general John P. Strange. "After moving us to several places," wrote a fellow captive, "we eventually reached Cairo, Illinois," where a Federal detachment "with fixed bayonets came into camp and called out five of us." They had read in the papers about Union threats to retaliate against Forrest's command "for something he was charged with having done." Incarcerated in "a horrid dungeon, or jail, in the town of Cairo, and locked in a loathsome, filthy cell," the captive rebels concluded that their "end was near, and resolved to meet it as soldiers." But to their great relief they were treated like all the other prisoners and put on a boat bound for the prison camp at Alton.[9]

Forrest's subsequent letter to Union general Washburn demanding to know what treatment rebel prisoners were going to receive after Fort Pillow triggered some of the war's most acrimonious correspondence. "The recent battle of Tishomingo Creek was far more bloody than it would otherwise have been," he wrote, "but for the fact that your men evidently expected to be slaughtered when captured, and both sides acted as though neither felt safe in surrendering, even when further resistance was useless." Forrest declared that he had "conducted the war on civilized principles, and desire still to do so," but that he owed it to his command to "know the position they occupy and the policy you intend to pursue."[10]

At first, Washburn replied not to Forrest but to his superior, S. D. Lee. "From statements that have been made to me by colored soldiers who were eye-witnesses," he wrote, "it would seem that the massacre of Fort Pillow had been reproduced at the late affair at Brice's Cross-Roads. If true and not disavowed they must lead to consequences hereafter fearful to contemplate." If Lee and his subordinates "intended to raise the black flag against that unfortunate race, they will cheerfully accept the issue," he continued. "No troops have fought more gallantly and none have conducted themselves with greater propriety. They have fully vindicated their right (so long denied) to be treated as men."[11]

Two days later, Washburn addressed a letter directly to Forrest. "Your declaration that you have conducted the war on all occasions on civilized principles cannot be accepted," he said, "but I receive with satisfaction the intimation in your letter that the recent slaughter of colored troops at the battle of Tishomingo Creek resulted rather from the desperation with which they fought than a predetermined intention to give them no quarter. You must have learned by this time that the attempt to intimidate the colored troops by indiscriminate slaughter has signally failed, and that, instead of a feeling of terror, you have aroused a spirit of courage and desperation that will not drown at your bidding."[12]

Forrest and his staff were outraged. "I regard your letter as discourteous to the commanding officer of this department," he fumed, "and grossly insulting to myself." That Washburn's troops "expected to be slaughtered," he wrote, "appears to me, after the oath they took, to be a very reasonable and natural expectation. Yet you, who sent them out, knowing and now admitting that they had sworn to such a policy, are complaining of atrocities, and demanding acknowledgments and disavowals on the part of the very men you sent forth sworn to 'slay whenever in your power." Washburn's rank forbade "doubt as to the fact that you and every officer and man of your department is identified with this policy and responsible for it," and Forrest would "not permit" Washburn "to limit the operations of your unholy scheme and visit its terrible consequences alone upon that ignorant, deluded, but unfortunate people, the negro, whose destruction you are planning in order to accomplish ours. The negroes have our sympathy," he said, "and so far as consistent with safety," Forrest would "spare them at the expense of those who are alone responsible for the inauguration of a worse than savage warfare."

The Confederacy regarded captured black troops as recovered property, Forrest said, and if Washburn wanted to challenge that policy, he should take it up with Richmond. Forrest informed Washburn that he had in his custody "over 2,000 of Sturgis' command prisoners, and will hold every officer and private as hostage until I receive your declarations and am satisfied that you carry out in good faith the answers you make, and until I am assured that no Confederate soldier has been foully dealt with from the day of the battle at Tishomingo Creek to this time."[13]

"The character and tenor" of Washburn's letter was "so outrageously insulting," Forrest wrote S. D. Lee, "that but for its importance to my men—not myself—I should not have replied to it at all." Up to then he had resisted defending his actions at Fort Pillow against Wade and Gooch's charges, but now he submitted Anderson's account to the assistant adjutant general, along with Young's ambiguous letter. As for himself, Forrest was "entirely conscious of right" and had "no explanations, apologies, or disavowals to make to General Washburn, nor to any one else but my Government, through my superior officers."[14]

"We have counted the cost," S. D. Lee wrote Washburn, "and are prepared to go to any extremes, and although it is far from our wish to fight under the black flag, still if you drive us to it we will accept the issue." Nor would white Union soldiers be exempt, for "the unfortunate people whom you pretend to be aiding are not considered entirely responsible for their acts, influenced as they are by the superior intellect of their white brothers."

Lee closed his missive by reporting that the black troops who had survived Fort Pillow and Tishomingo were "wandering over the countryside, attempting to return to their masters."[15] "If this remark is intended as a joke," Washburn snorted, "it is acknowledged as a good one, but if stated as a fact, permit me to correct your misapprehensions by informing you that most of them have rejoined their respective commands, their search for their late 'masters' having proved bootless." The Federal government was "lenient and forbearing," Washburn told Forrest, "and it is not yet too late for you to secure for yourself and soldiers a continuance of the treatment due to honorable warriors, by a public disclaimer of barbarities already committed, and a vigorous effort to punish the wretches who committed them." Enclosing with his compliments a copy of Wade and Gooch's *Report,* Washburn declared it was "useless to prolong the discussion. But I say to you now, clearly and unequivocally, that such measure of treatment as you mete out to Federal soldiers will be measured to you again. If you give no quarter," he growled, "you must expect none."[16]

Thus, just as Lincoln had feared, threats and reprisals had bred nothing but more threats and reprisals, and not only cost the North casualties but a measure of its moral hegemony. "The implied admissions of the Federal generals are infamous," Confederate secretary of war James Alexander Seddon wrote his president, "and are properly exposed, especially in General Forrest's second letter, which, though neither elegant nor strictly grammatical, is better, being very much to the point and in the true spirit."[17]

"The tone of the correspondence on the part of our officers is approved," Jefferson Davis replied. "Much misrepresentation of events connected with the capture of Fort Pillow has been thrown upon the world," and it was "due to our Government that the truth should be sent out to correct the false impression extensively created." But Forrest's own account of the battle had been lost with the effects of Leonidas Polk on June 14, when he was killed by a Yankee cannonball at Pine Mountain, Georgia.

To counter Wade and Gooch's extensive interviews and the affidavits that Brayman had collected from Union survivors, Davis now urged Seddon and Forrest to obtain more testimony to corroborate their account. But aside from eliciting a second ambiguous note from the captive Captain Young, they never did.[18]

On an expedition along the Rappahannock River, Private George W. Reed of the 36th USCI "had the pleasure of conversing with some of the colored soldiers who were wounded in the late battles. I am told by them that their officers could not manage them, they were so eager to fight. Whenever they caught a rebel they cried out, 'No quarter! Remember Fort Pillow! No quarter for rebs!' &c. They distinguished themselves highly," and were "all eager to go back to retaliate for the Fort Pillow massacre."[19]

Addressing his soldiers at Chicago, Colonel John A. Bross of the 27th USCI vowed that "when I lead these men into battle, we shall remember Fort Pillow, and shall not ask for quarter. I leave a home and friends as dear as can be found on earth, but if it is the will of Providence that I do not return, I ask no nobler epitaph than that I fell for my country at the head of this black and blue regiment."[20]

Just before allegedly executing twenty-three rebels they had captured during an engagement in Georgia, Yankee soldiers first demanded to know whether their captives remembered Fort Pillow. "We want revenge," one of the Yankees declared, "and we are bound to have it one way or another. They must pay for these deeds of cruelty. We want revenge for our brother soldiers and will have it." George Templeton Strong, cofounder of the Sanitary Commission, claimed that black troops never reported any prisoners. "I suppose they have to kill their prisoners before they can take them," he commented. "When they go into action, they yell 'Fort Pillow!'" An officer in the Army of the Potomac remarked that when black soldiers went into battle yelling "Fort Pillow," Confederate troops "did not normally hold up very well."[21]

"You heard of the rebs murdering our prisoners at Fort Pillow," wrote Charles Boardman of the 145th Pennsylvania Infantry. "Shot & burned them alive. Makes a man's blood cold to think they will come with a flag of truce

& kill so many after they surrendered & set bloodhounds on them that tried to escape." A Union cavalryman encountered a detachment from Forrest's command at Bolivar. "They stood us a little fight," he said, "but we just gave the yell" and leaped over their bulwark "without much opposition on the part of the Fort Pillow [murderers]. Some of our cavalry did not take them prisoners. They just killed them where they found them," he wrote, "that is to pay for their unmercifully murdering our men" at Fort Pillow.[22]

After Forrest's victory at Tishomingo Creek, Charles Anderson addressed the Wizard's troops on the general's behalf. At Fort Pillow, he said, they had exhibited "conspicuous gallantry. In the face of a murderous fire from two gunboats and six pieces of artillery on the fort, you stormed the works and either killed or captured the entire garrison, a motley herd of negroes, traitors, and Yankees." Then, after Sturgis and Grierson and the "best appointed forces ever equipped by the Yankee nation" marched out of Memphis "with threats of vengeance toward you and your commander for the bloody victory of Fort Pillow, made a massacre only by dastardly Yankee reporters," Forrest's troopers had again "met the enemy and defeated him. Victory was never more glorious, disaster never more crushing and signal. From a proud and defiant foe, en route to the heart of your country, with declarations both by negro and white troops of 'no quarter to Forrest or his men,' Sturgis had become an enemy beaten, defeated, routed, destroyed."

And yet, Anderson warned his men, the Yankees were "again preparing to break through the living wall erected by your noble bosoms and big hearts," and here he resorted to the same kind of peroration that had preceded the Battle of Fort Pillow.

> In the name and recollection of ruined homes, desolated fields, and the bleaching bones of your martyred comrades, you are appealed to again. The smoke of your burning homesteads, the screams of your insulted women, and the cries of starving children will again nerve your strong arms with strength. Your fathers of '76 had much to fight for, but how little and unimportant was their cause compared with yours. They fought not against annihilation, but simply to be independent of a foreign yet a constitutional and free Government. You are struggling against the most odious of all tyranny, for existence itself, for your property, your homes, your wives, and children, against your own enslavement, against emancipation, confiscation, and subjugation, with all their attendant horrors.[23]

The United States Colored Infantry did itself proud in the siege of Peters-burg, Virginia, bravely charging a series of well-fortified positions with the same reckless daring (and some of the same mercilessness) that the rebels had shown at Fort Pillow. "Away went Uncle Sam's sable sons across an old field nearly three-quarters of a mile wide," reported Chaplain Henry Turner of the 1st USCI,

> in the face of rebel grape and canister and the unbroken clatter of thousands of muskets. Nothing less than the pen of horror could be-gin to describe the terrific roar and dying yells of that awful yet mas-terly charge and daring feat. The rebel balls would tear up the ground at times, and create such a heavy dust in front of our charging army, that they could scarcely see the forts for which they were making. But onward they went, through dust and every impediment, while they and the rebels were both crying out "Fort Pillow!" This seems to be the battle-cry on both sides. But onward they went, waxing stronger and mightier every time Fort Pillow was mentioned. Soon the boys were at the base of the Fort, climbing over [the] abatis, and jumping the deep ditches, ravines, &c. The last load fired by the rebel battery was a cartridge of powder, not having time to put the ball in, which flashed and did no injury.[24]

A white Pennsylvanian fighting before Petersburg wrote home that "the Johnnies are not as much afraid of us as they are of the Mokes [black troops]. When they charge they will not take any prisoners, if they can help it. Their cry is, 'Remember Fort Pillow!'" Although "sometimes, in their ex-citement, when they catch a man they say: 'Remember what you done to us, way back, down there!'"[25]

In the siege of Richmond, the 29th USCI, consisting primarily of free blacks from Connecticut, would brave heavy rifle fire to charge the rebel breastworks, and as Confederate artillery began to sweep their ranks, they not only held their ground but wiped out the rebel gunners. Replenishing their exhausted ammunition from their own dead and wounded, "they vied with each other in deeds of daring."

During lulls in the battle they would taunt the rebels, challenging them to show themselves. "How about Fort Pillow today?" one of them shouted.

"Look over here, Johnny," another called out, "and see how niggers can shoot!"

They exposed themselves with such "recklessness and indifference" that their officers were obliged "to restrain them from useless exhibitions of their courage."[26]

"The Colored Troops do exceedingly well," wrote C. P. Lyman of the 100th USCI; "everybody speaks well of them. They have raised themselves and all mankind in the scale of manhood by their bold achievements—for I hold that, as water seeks a common level, so the raising of a certain class of the people *must* of necessity raise the whole community!" This may have been true of the infantry, but not everyone spoke so well of the gunners of the 2nd USCLA, which had lost a company at Fort Pillow two months before. One of their captains wrote to complain that during the attack on Petersburg his men proved incapable of calculating distances or fuse lengths properly, thus forcing their officers to operate the guns.[27]

Perhaps the army's faltering belief in black artillery and its commanders' repeated refusals to arm and supply them properly were why the survivors of the 6th USCHA, most of whose best-trained gunners had been killed at Fort Pillow, were reorganized into the 11th United States Colored Infantry. Despite the continuing high rate of mortality among the black soldiers' families on President's Island, just off Memphis in the Mississippi's stream, Colonel William Turner enforced the prohibition against women in camp, with the exception of hospital cooks and nurses. This meant that black troops had to make their way from Fort Pickering to President's Island to see their loved ones, and risk capture by the squads of rebels that lurked around Shelby County, capturing stragglers and picking off black pickets. On July 22, 1864, the rebels captured Private Wilson Wood of the 6th USCHA and held him in a prison camp, with the declared intention of handing him over to his owner or putting him to work for the Confederate army. "When the United States made negroes soldiers," protested Brayman, "it assured towards them the same obligations as were due to any others who might wear its uniform and bear its flag." But the rebels, of course, had never given any such assurances.[28]

In mid-November, members of the 2nd USCLA and a detachment of the 13th USCI acquitted themselves well in a skirmish at Johnsonville, Tennessee, standing their ground against a furious barrage and with their well-aimed shells forcing the rebel batteries across the river to withdraw. Soon afterward the 3rd U.S. Colored Cavalry encountered an outnumbering force near Yazoo City and holed up in a small earthen fort. Confident of victory, dismissing colored troops as "outside the pale of civilized warfare," the rebels "refused to treat on terms usually accorded to a defeated foe," and charged them again and again. But the black troopers "responded with yells of defiance as they met the onslaught of the enemy, hurling them back. Again and again the enemy returned to the attack, only to suffer repulse from the well directed volleys of the black." The rebels learned, "alas, too late," wrote the regiment's chronicler, "that they had a foe before them worthy of their steel" and that "the scenes of Fort Pillow could not be reenacted here."[29]

"Remember Fort Pillow" would become a postwar rebel cry as well, and sometimes a man's former master was all that stood between him and white vigilantes.

Henry F. Pyles recalled a day after Reconstruction when a group of whites tied a rope around a veteran of the 6th USCA named Jordan, and, en route to his lynching, paraded him past Addison Pyles, his former master.

"Where you taking my nigger!" Pyles demanded to know, running out into the road.

"He ain't your nigger no more; you know that," the ringleader shot back. "Your nigger Jordan been in the Yankee army, and he was in the battle at Fort Piller and help kill our white folks, and you know it!"

"That boy maybe didn't kill Confederates," declared Pyles, "but you and him both know my two boys killed plenty Yankees, and you forgot I lost one of my boys in the War. Ain't that enough to pay for letting my nigger alone?"

Chastised, the vigilantes let Jordan go.[30]

ICONS
FORT PILLOW MYTHS
April 25, 1864–January 1865

Two black survivors of the Fort Pillow massacre achieved at least a temporary fame. Daniel Tyler of 6/B had survived a night of particular horror. Badly wounded, he had been thrown into the sepulchral ditch on the night of April 12th "with a great many others, white and, black, several of whom were alive. They were all buried up together." But Tyler had not protested his interment, for "I knew if I said anything they would kill me."[1]

Fortunately, he was able to creep to the outer edge of the ditch, where his head would be nearer the surface. "With his one good hand he was able to dig his head out," but the wounded men buried under him "were buried so deep that they could not get out, and died." Before dawn on the thirteenth, after Tyler had completely worked his way out of his grave, a rebel informed him that Chalmers intended to take all the blacks away before the gunboat came and kill them on the road. But just then the *Silver Cloud* opened fire, and the rebels "commenced moving off. They wanted me to go with them," Tyler said, "but I would not go," so he "turned around, and came down to the river bank and got on the gunboat."[2]

The *Cairo News* described Tyler as joking that he had dug out of his grave because he had not liked "his quarters. He laughs over his adventures, and says he is one of the best 'dug-outs' in the world." *Harper's Weekly* depicted a more sober and stentorian Tyler in an ostensible first-person narrative that has all the markings of abolitionist propaganda. "My name is Daniel Taylor [*sic*]," it begins, "and my skin is dark, as my mother's was before me. I have heard that my father had a white face, but I think his heart and life were blacker than my mother's skin. I was born a slave, and remained a slave until last April, when I found deliverance and shelter under the flag that my master was fighting to dishonor." Freedom had come to him when "I was working in the fields down in Alabama, my heart full of bitterness and unutterable longings," and so on, whereas in fact he was a Mississippi slave who was probably scooped up by a squad of Yankee recruiters. Filched from newspaper reports and embellished by the escaped slave and abolitionist author and orator William Wells Brown, the account turned Tyler into a kind of icon.[3]

His champions apparently lost track of him, however, or chose not to report on his ultimate fate. Though badly wounded and nearly blind, Tyler returned to his regiment in May. But the following November he apparently went off somewhere to recuperate from his wounds. When Tyler returned to his regiment in March, the army charged him with being absent without leave and ordered him incarcerated in the Irving Block military prison in Memphis.[4]

Conditions at Irving Block prison were a scandal. "Nearly all of the partitions" in the prison had been "torn down by the prisoners" for ventilation. Because the gas fixtures had been "wantonly torn out and destroyed," candles provided the only illumination. The kitchens were filthy, and the dispensary was of "limited scale and in terrible condition," with no records, stores, or "comforts." Medical attendance was "very poor indeed" and the assistant surgeon, G. W. Johnson, was "not to be relied upon at all."[5]

Tyler must have felt as though he had been buried alive all over again. In a sense, he had, for it was in this Union hellhole that Daniel Tyler, abolitionist icon and gravely wounded survivor of the very worst the rebels could dish out, would be left to waste away for four months without charges ever being brought against him. Abandoned and forgotten by his officers, he died a prisoner on July 12, 1865.[6]

———————

The garrison's other icon was Eli Cothel of 6/B. "As an evidence that the fort never did surrender," wrote Lieutenant Colonel Thomas J. Jackson four days after the battle,

> we have the flag of the battalion preserved to us in the following manner: Private Eli Cothel Company (B) 6 U.S. Heavy Artillery (colored), being wounded some three different times and scarcely able to move, saw the flag proudly waving from the staff, crawled to the same, and hauled it down. While the rebels were not noticing what he was doing, he tied the same around him, using it as a bandage to his wounds.[7]

In his testimony, Cothel himself made no mention of this spectacular act of heroism, nor did the subcommittee see fit to ask him about it. In fact, his testimony demonstrates that if a black soldier did heroically rescue the flag, it could not have been Cothel, for he was shot in the morning and littered down to Fitch's makeshift surgery, where he was shot a second time, and from which he escaped by crawling into a stand of brush by the river. It is curious, therefore, that Jackson should have selected as the beneficiary of his extravagant fiction former sergeant Cothel, who had been demoted to corporal in 1863 for "conduct unbecoming a commissioned officer."[8]

In his report, Jackson further gilded Cothel's lily by portraying him rather than Tyler digging his way out of a grave, when Cothel himself stated that he hid in the brush until the next morning and then climbed aboard the gunboat. One can only guess at the reaction of men like Tyler, who had indeed crawled out of his grave, and whose thunder Jackson and Cothel had stolen; or courageous artillerists like Willis Ligon and Samuel Green, who had fought the rebels so manfully.[9]

The flag was probably obtained by less dramatic means. Jackson's subsequent denials and demonstrable falsehoods cast enormous doubt on his integrity, not to mention his sobriety. Briefly appointed commander of the 6th, he probably kept a regimental flag in his possession, pulled it out of his trunk, invented the story for the benefit of the reporters who crowded the bar at the Gayoso Hotel, and staged Mrs. Booth's ceremonial return of the colors to her martyred husband's regiment to answer the Northern editorialists who saw the massacre as proof of the folly of arming blacks.

For reasons that would emerge later, Wade and Gooch never called on Jackson to testify. From the joint subcommittee's point of view the problem with Jackson's story was not merely evidentiary but political, because any hint that the garrison never entirely surrendered would have muddied their claim that the rebels had committed a massacre from first to last. This may also explain why the only slightly wounded Second Lieutenant Daniel Van Horn of 6/D was not called upon to testify, either, for in his first report he had proudly asserted that the garrison continued to fire back all the way down to the river. This was all very admirable, but rather inconvenient to the subcommittee's scenario, for in the name of establishing the rebels' craven barbarity, Wade and Gooch sought to portray the Federals as having all immediately thrown down their arms. Thus would they do a number of Fort Pillow's most die-hard defenders a considerable disservice.

Twenty-four-year-old Lizzie Wayt Booth, the widow of the martyred major of the 6th USCHA, also proved to be one of the less durable icons of the Fort Pillow affair. She was born in Martinsburg, Ohio, to an English father and a Northern Irish mother, and four of her brothers would serve in the Union army. Where and when she met and married Booth is not known, but it must have been when she was no older than eighteen; the blue-eyed Philadelphia clerk joined the 1st Missouri Infantry in 1858, and in 1864 Lizzie Booth would allude to her prewar "frontier service," which suggests that she had followed her husband west.[10]

She did not follow her husband to Fort Pillow, however, and when word reached Memphis of the garrison's decimation, a solicitous Hurlbut ordered a steamboat to take her upriver to learn her husband's fate. After a pause at Mound City to visit the survivors of the major's regiment, and a subsequent stopover at Fort Pillow to locate Lionel's grave, she returned to Fort Pickering in her widow's weeds to take center stage in a flag ceremony that her friend Tom Jackson had arranged.

Within view of the Mississippi, "whose waters a few days before had been reddened with the blood of their comrades," about a dozen survivors of the 6th, some of them badly wounded, stood in a row along Fort Pickering's bluff as Mrs. Booth presented the flag—"torn with balls, stained with smoke, and clotted with human blood"—that Eli Cothel had ostensibly rescued to what little remained of his regiment.

"Boys," she said, her voice low,

I have just come from a visit to the hospital at Mound City. There I saw your comrades wounded at the bloody struggle at Fort Pillow. There I found this flag; you recognize it. One of your comrades saved it from the insulting touch of traitors at Fort Pillow. I have given to my country all I had to give: my husband. Such a gift! Yet I have freely given him for freedom and my country. Next [to] my husband's cold remains, the dearest object left me in the world is this flag—the flag that once waved in proud defiance over the works of Fort Pillow. Soldiers, this flag I give you, knowing that you will ever remember the last words of my noble husband: "Never surrender the flag to traitors."

Accepting the flag, Jackson had her husband's men kneel down before her and vow to avenge "their brave and fallen comrades," whereupon she was presented with "something over $500" which various officers had raised among themselves.[11]

After playing her part in Jackson's pageant, the widow Booth met with the widows of the major's fallen men. They asked her what would become of them now, for though their husbands were eligible for pensions, the government refused to recognize slave marriages. Mrs. Booth promised to do something about it, and, with a portion of the money she had been given, boarded a train for Washington to take up the matter with the president himself.

No doubt relieved that Mrs. Booth had not come to the White House to demand reprisals, Lincoln heard her out on the subject of black widows' pensions and wrote her the following letter of introduction to Senator Charles Sumner:

The bearer of this is the widow of Major Booth, who fell at Fort Pillow. She makes a point, which I think very worthy of consideration which is, widows and children *in fact,* of colored soldiers who fall in our service be placed in law, the same as if their marriages were legal so they can have the benefit of the provisions [for] the widows & orphans of white soldiers. Please see & hear Mrs. Booth.[12]

At least in part because of her advocacy, Congress eventually passed a bill "to provide suitable relief for the widows and children of the colored soldiers in the service of the United States, who were lately massacred at Fort Pillow." The pension office did eventually recognize marriages entered upon "according to the customs of slavery," so long as the widow could produce witnesses to their betrothal. And on June 15, a month after the publication of Wade and Gooch's report, black troops finally won their fight for parity.[13]

Upon Mrs. Booth's return to Memphis, General Washburn offered her a position as an inspector in the provost guard. Her job was to search for contraband on the persons of the Southern women who passed in and out of Memphis. The Provost Guard's reluctance to search females had made women especially effective smugglers. "The ladies in this neighborhood," wrote a Mississippian, "take extensive advantage of the extensive domain of crinoline to do an extensive smuggling business." Suspicious of a woman who seemed to struggle as she climbed out of her carriage, inspectors found that she had tied a dozen boots around an enormous girdle, each filled with "whiskey, military lace, and other supplies greatly in demand in the Confederacy." A black woman was found with an entire demijohn of brandy under her capacious skirts.

On August 13, it fell to Mrs. Booth to search the person of one Mrs. Mary Noel. For the sake of her subjects' modesty, she must have conducted these inspections in private, and perhaps hearing a peculiar clinking as she rifled through Mrs. Noel's skirts and petticoats, she found $280 worth of $20 gold pieces. Conveying gold out of Union lines was strictly forbidden, and would have been enough to land Mrs. Noel in Irving Block prison. But in exchange for a bribe of five $20 gold pieces, Mrs. Booth pronounced her clean of contraband and let her go.[14] As Mrs. Noel proceeded into Mississippi, however, a suspicious guard ordered her to halt and discovered the remaining nine gold pieces. Out of a failure of nerve, or in hopes of ingratiating herself with her captors, she accused Mrs. Booth of taking the rest, whereupon the widow of the martyr of Fort Pillow was taken into custody.

A court of inquiry believed Mrs. Noel, and in drumhead fashion sentenced the major's wife to a year in prison at Alton, Illinois. "I am a friendless penniless woman," she protested to Washburn on August 25, "who has ever been devoted [and] patriotic and have suffered much, oh how much! for the national cause." She described herself as "the needy hapless widow of a gallant officer who fell so nobly at his post of duty," and yet at her hearing she had not been allowed "*one* friend or *counselor,* nor was I allowed to make a statement to you."

She also claimed that after the hearing, Judge Advocate R. W. Pike followed her home to her "wretched apartment" and suggested "there was *one* way to be free." But Mrs. Booth "resented the insult" and spurned his advances, whereupon he sent her to Irving Block prison, where Daniel Tyler of her husband's regiment lay dying.[15]

A back room on the second floor of the middle tier of Irving Block was reserved for white female prisoners, primarily prostitutes the provost guard rounded up periodically and halfheartedly and then released into the dismal stream of Memphis's back alleys. In June, an investigating committee found the women's cells unventilated, filthy, and poorly guarded.[16]

"You know my loyalty is *above suspicion,*" Mrs. Booth insisted, though it was her integrity, not her loyalty, that was in question. "Considering the fearful oath I administered to my regiment," she continued, "and many acts which evince my intense hatred of rebels and my desire to go with the expedition for personal revenge," how could Washburn think she would "assist the enemy for a few paltry dollars?" Could he "not commute my sentence to requiring me to live any where north? I ask this in the name of common humanity and of Justice and because it will be no *honor* to the country when it is said that the widow of a Fort Pillow martyr—moneyless, friendless—was charged with official misconduct and sentenced to *state prison* for one year unless released by welcome death."[17]

It is unlikely that the army was eager to pursue the case and thereby besmirch the memory of a fallen hero. But Mrs. Booth demanded "an *imme-diate thorough investigation* which I am *confident* will not only reflect credit upon my abillity in the position I have filled (not through *Service* but *Poverty*) but establish my innocence." Though she must have retained at least a portion of the five hundred dollars her husband's officers had collected for her, she said she was "penniless and have no means of support but my own labor, and the injustice done me will prevent my accepting or holding any position under Government, and I cannot seek employment with this invented disgrace hanging over me." The military reluctantly obliged, and on September 16, officially charged her with bribery.[18]

While languishing in prison, Mrs. Booth heard that a recently captured veteran of the Fort Pillow battle, Captain G. P. M. Turner of the 5th Mississippi Cavalry, occupied a cell in the Confederate wing of Irving Block. She asked the provost marshal's permission to interview Turner to confirm her husband's burial site. Though she actually already knew where the major was buried, her inquiry may have been part of her effort to remind the authorities of who she was: the grieving, loyal widow of a brave young officer.[19]

On September 20, Mrs. Booth was found guilty in an "informal" hearing that Washburn deemed so flawed that he finally let her walk. A week later, the allegedly lecherous R. W. Pike wrote that he was "done with Mrs. Booth." Weary of her protests and machinations, the authorities asked her— and later commanded her—to leave town on the next boat north. But she had no intention of leaving and, however penniless she had portrayed herself to Washburn, rented a house in the city next to a French restaurant, where she conducted an unspecified business and sublet several rooms. After she went east to visit her sister in Trenton, New Jersey, a tenant laid claim to the entire house and threw out her belongings. "In consequence," she declared, "my business was broken up, and I am now at great loss." But Lizzie Wayt Booth was never at a loss for long. In December 1865, she would be asked by a solicitous Major General Montgomery Meigs to assist in the identification of bodies disinterred at Fort Pillow. She eventually married a prosperous German stockbroker named Herman Hill and moved to Salt Lake City.[20]

Though Lieutenant Colonel Thomas Jackson of the 6th USCHA was another casualty of the massacre, his wounds were self-inflicted. He did not inspire much confidence. A skinny man with extravagant burnside whiskers, he had a slightly cockeyed gaze that alcohol accentuated. Neither Wade and Gooch nor any of Jackson's superiors read his secondhand account of the battle, which never proceeded beyond a rough draft. Emphasizing the fort's vulnerability and the last-ditch firing of the retreating garrison, it would not have been welcome.

After Mrs. Booth returned from Mound City, she informed Jackson that several of her husband's men had told her that during the days preceding the massacre, Major Booth had repeatedly pleaded with Hurlbut to send reinforcements. According to Mrs. Booth, Jackson replied at the time that he was not aware of any requests from her husband, but within a few hours of their encounter, three of his fellow officers heard him loudly contradict himself over drinks at a sutler's establishment in the lines of the 2nd USCLA.

"I know that Major Booth wrote three times to Major General Hurlbut for reinforcements," Jackson told them, "the last time about five days before the battle. I have his private letters," he said.

"Tom," he quoted Booth as writing, "if I had you and your men here under your command, I would feel safe. But as it is, I have no hopes."

Jackson reportedly claimed that Booth had actually sent two special messengers down to Memphis to press Hurlbut for reinforcements, but to no avail. Nor would General Chetlain allow Jackson himself to join Booth at Fort Pillow with the remainder of the regiment. "The affair at Fort Pillow," Jackson concluded, "rests on some Generals' shoulders."[21]

The three officers waited almost two weeks before reporting Jackson's remarks to Colonel Ignatz Kappner. Kappner brought the matter before Hurlbut, who promptly demanded an explanation. Jackson denied ever saying any such thing. "I have never reported that Maj. L. F. Booth made application for reinforcements," he wrote. "I think the way the report gained currency was through Mrs. Booth," who said she had heard the story from wounded men at Mound City, "but now believes that it is not so." Mrs. Booth vouched for this, and assured investigators that she did not "entertain any other sentiment toward Genl Hulburt but the warmest gratitude." The whole thing, she suspected, had been "gotten up by a person to whom Col Jackson has been a kind friend." Be that as it may, the following February, a military board judged Jackson "unfitted for the position which he now occupies" and honorably discharged him for "past services."[22]

Though Thomas Jefferson Jackson's military career is difficult to piece together, one thing is certain: he was not present at the Battle of Fort Pillow. A veteran of Stone River and Chickamauga, he had joined the 6th USCHA from the 42nd Indiana Volunteer Infantry in March 1864. Jackson's brother, the Reverend John Walker Jackson, had made "the first speech in Philadelphia, on behalf of arming colored men during the late civil war," and may have persuaded Jackson to make the switch.[23]

"I desire authority to raise a regiment of blacks," Jackson had written Lorenzo Thomas, "to be armed and equipped as soldiers." He offered to provide "references as to my standing in society, and ability to command and drill a regiment. I have been in the service nineteen months, thirteen of which I have commanded a company." Jackson had been wounded in the jaw and taken prisoner at Waterford, Mississippi, escaping after almost three months' incarceration by wading through a cesspool to the Mississippi River and slogging his way back to Memphis.[24]

That, in any case, is what he told an interviewer while serving as a member of the Kansas state legislature. But he apparently told his friends and colleagues a good deal more. He claimed that he had "a silver jawbone, which was put in by the surgeons when they got through operating on him" after he had been found among "the piles of dead" at Fort Pillow. "In the particular bunch of men which was surrounded in this fight," wrote the *Hutchinson* (KS) *News,* "he and one of the negro privates were all that were left alive."

The story got better.

> Col. Jackson was found, 48 hours after he had been kicked into the river, by a federal gunboat, lying in the stream, his arms clinched around a log, and in a dying condition. He was brought back to life and went to a hospital for a long time. Here a silver, or metal brace, was placed in the side of his head where the rebel musket had beaten in a hole. This metal plate, or others that were substituted, was worn up to the time of his death. He had a huge depression in his side, caused by wounds received, and one arm had been practically useless for a good many years.[25]

Declaring to President Johnson, "I love the military service," Jackson applied in vain for reappointment to the army's officer corps. He moved to Kansas in 1885, served in the legislature as a clerk and then as an elected representative, and twenty years later, while attempting to board a moving train, fell under a Pullman's wheels. "His right arm was severed near the shoulder," grieved a colleague, "and both his legs below the knees, thereby crushing and dissevering his limbs, that the armed savage rebel, General Forrest, at Fort Pillow in 1864, tried but failed to do. Although thus horribly and fatally dismembered, he retained consciousness, and was taken to 'Agnew Hospital,' where he received every possible attention, and assistance, of skilled Surgeons. He succumbed to the inevitable, and yielded his heroic life there, to the Eternal Hospital of Salvation."[26]

"BRAVE TO RECKLESSNESS"
THE MEMPHIS RAID

August 20–December 3, 1864

AFTER WHAT WAS PERHAPS HIS MOST IMPRESSIVE VICTORY, AT Tishomingo Creek, the tide seemed about to turn against Forrest at Harrisburg, Mississippi. Puffed up by the praise he had received for his foray into West Tennessee, he refused to invest fresh troops in a charge on a Union position at Harrisburg that he might well have taken in another temper but now deemed "impregnable." In the middle of the battle he rejected General Stephen D. Lee's battle plan entirely and began to issue contradictory commands that sent officers careening around the battlefield in confusion. In the end, the rebels charged the Federals as a disorganized mob, losing 1,310 men, almost half their active force, as against 674 Union casualties.

Forrest was nonetheless unbowed. "If I knew as much about West Point tactics as you," he told a stunned General Lee, who had granted the Wizard wide latitude, "the Yankees would whip hell out of me every day."[1] But both Lee and the impromptu frontier tactician had lost the day. "Our brigade was considerably damaged and forced to retire," wrote John Carroll, and "many of our men shed tears, this being the first repulse we had met with."[2]

Over the course of the war it had become an article of faith among the Federals that though the rebels could have taken Memphis on a couple of occasions, they were "too deeply interested" in the city's trade "to do anything that would interrupt it."[3] The city on the bluff had become the Western Confederacy's most reliable source of contraband goods: especially medicine, liquor, and gold. The cracks in the cordon Washburn tried to maintain around Memphis were wide enough for a group of disguised rebel officers to squeeze through on one occasion, attend the theater, and leave the names of their commands on their playbills. Though exhausted, emaciated, and jaundiced from a coalescence of injuries, ailments, and privations, and so badly crippled by a wound to his big toe that he had to be carted around in a buggy, Forrest nonetheless contrived a bold raid. On August 20, near Oxford, Mississippi, as his men formed a broken line before a Yankee force of twenty-five thousand men under Major General Andrew Jackson Smith, Forrest sent out a call "for volunteers to go on a heavy detached service and none but good horses allowed to go." Chagrined by his defeat at Harrisburg, still bristling from Washburn's high-handed lectures on civilized warfare, the Wizard did not inform his "very formidable" volunteer force where they were headed, but as they circled around Smith's command and crossed into Tennessee, they guessed that Forrest intended to raid Memphis itself.[4]

Forrest's purposes were various. After his recent reverses, his troopers' morale was at an all-time low, and it was crucial to his own very useful legend that he demonstrate to both friend and foe that he could still strike whenever and wherever he pleased. He was determined to force the Yankees who patrolled northern Mississippi to hole up in Memphis. But more specifically, and personally, he was incensed by reports that Yankee occupiers had abused his crippled brother John, and determined to capture General Cad Washburn, whose acid reproaches for the massacre at Fort Pillow had penetrated Forrest to the bone.

Heavily patrolled, a hundred miles distant, Memphis seemed an almost impossible goal. But Forrest had just the men to achieve it. His advance would be led by his younger but stronger brother Captain William Forrest: the only man, it was said, of whom the Wizard was afraid. "Brave to recklessness," wrote James Dinkins, Bill Forrest "did not fear one man, nor did he fear a hundred men, and yet he was as sympathetic as a woman. He never provoked a quarrel, but when disturbed, would shoot a man at the slightest provocation." A slender, dashing version of the Wizard, Lieutenant Jesse A. Forrest of Wilson's 16th also came along to avenge his brother John. Though not as imposing as either Bedford or Bill, Jesse had the requisite Forrest Vandyke, the family pugnacity, and a glint of bully-boy humor in his restless hazel eyes.[5]

Though still dinged up from a host of battlefield injuries and suffering from a bad case of boils, Bedford himself accompanied the expedition, pitching in as his men hitched together a pontoon bridge over Coldwater River. Leading their mounts across this "considerable stream," Forrest and his troopers remounted and rode through the night, driving their horses so hard that some dropped dead along the way.[6]

Arriving within sight of Memphis before daybreak, Forrest dismounted from his lathered warhorse King Phillip and gave his orders to his field officers, who relayed them to their men in hushed voices. The expedition would proceed in three separate detachments to different sections of the city. Speed was of the essence; they were to stop for nothing.[7]

"While we believed that General Forrest was acting upon reliable information from spies and scouts as to the situation of affairs in Memphis," wrote John Milton Hubbard, "we knew that there was always a chance for an enemy to be fully informed. In that case, we did not know but that deadly ambuscades would be set for us." But all of the men riding at the head of the 14th Tennessee, wrote Hubbard, "understood that Captain Bill Forrest and his company would surprise and capture the vidette and outpost." "A shot from Captain Bill Forrest's pistol," recalled John Carroll of Bell's brigade, "notified us that the Federal outpost had been encountered." Riding well ahead of the others, Bill had killed a picket with one shot, and captured the rest.[8]

Forrest and Black Bob McCulloch led the 2nd Missouri toward the State Female College, which the Union army had converted into a military facility. King Phillip carried him over and through row upon row of garden fencing. Forrest swept through "like a scythe over a wheat field," his "long cavalry saber raised in his right hand," and looking "more like a devil incarnate than anything those Yankees ever saw." But a few of them had seen him before, at Fort Pillow, for among the camps Forrest traversed was the 2nd USCLA's, whose records his Missouri Mongols destroyed with firebrands as they galloped among the regiment's tents.

Riding by fours, the other two detachments proceeded into the city at a rapid pace. But as the 14th turned off Kerr Street and onto Mississippi Avenue, the front ranks plunged into a mudhole "which, in the dim light, looked interminable." Their squealing mounts fell over each other, hurling their riders into the mud, and as the cursing troopers struggled to climb back into their saddles, a Federal battery opened fire on Captain Bill Forrest's detachment from the direction of Trigg Avenue, where Sergeant Benjamin Thacker of the 2nd USCLA had teamed up with a white lieutenant from the 61st USCI to fire a round that knocked one of Forrest's troopers off his saddle. At one point, Forrest himself, with the Second Missouri, attacked an advancing Federal detachment of cavalry, and "with his own hands" killed a Yankee colonel.[9]

The black troops defended the college "with credit," wrote Dinkins, and as dawn broke, Forrest abandoned his hope of capturing the place; "in disorganized squads," his unit began to beat its way out of the city, leaving it to his brothers to give the Memphis Raid its mythic touches.

Captain Bill's men had meanwhile "charged into the city through the enemy's encampment," reported a member of Forrest's Escort, shooting and riding down Yankees "as they leaped from their bunks in their night clothes, frightened out of there wits and endeavoring to make their escape." The Yankees "looked like ghosts, but to them we paid no attention save to give them a passing shot." The Yankee fire had been hesitant and scattered, for a thick fog hung in the gloom, "making it impossible to distinguish a gray from a blue uniform." But as Captain Bill and his boys rode up to Washburn's headquarters in the Gayoso Hotel and labored to break down the door, they were greeted with heavy firing from rooftops, cellars, and upper-story windows. Crashing through at last, Bill Forrest rode his horse into the lobby, and in hand-to-hand fighting that more resembled a lethal Old West barroom brawl than a military engagement, his men battled their way upstairs. By now, Washburn had escaped out the back and galloped the half mile to Fort Pickering in his pajamas. But Jesse Forrest managed to carry off the general's dress uniform as Bill and his men rounded up most of Washburn's staff and herded them out into the street in their bare feet and nightclothes.[10]

Perhaps the only Union general to draw solace from Forrest's raid was Hurlbut. "They removed me from command because I couldn't keep Forrest out of West Tennessee," he remarked, "but apparently Washburn can't keep him out of his bedroom."[11]

Somewhat reinvigorated by his Memphis raid, Forrest attacked a Federal stronghold at Athens, Alabama, that was not unlike Fort Pillow except that almost the entire garrison was black. After a brief bombardment he demanded its surrender, threatening another massacre if the commander refused. The commander demanded to see the size of Forrest's force, to which Forrest cheerfully agreed, personally leading the Union officer around his camp as his troops furtively positioned and repositioned themselves to convey an impression of great numbers. The commander returned to his blockhouse and tried to stall. When one of his officers threatened Forrest's emissary, the general ordered his batteries to open fire, and they continued firing even after a white flag was spotted fluttering outside a porthole. Forrest captured an enormous store of equipment and supplies and 1,300 officers and men, whom he ordered transported south.[12]

Over the next four days he persuaded three more Federal blockhouses to surrender, and on September 26 he captured two thousand contrabands the retreating Yankees had left behind in a commissary yard. Finding the blacks in rags, he ordered them all to strip and burned their clothes and two hundred of their houses. But as usual Forrest had a hard time keeping hold of his prisoners. "There being only a few men left as a guard," the rebels were "not able to cope with the federal forces," and the Yankees regained the contrabands "over which we had a skirmish."[13]

Bell's brigade returned to the Mississippi to take Columbus, Kentucky, the stronghold that Buford's detachment had been unable to bluff into surrendering. This time no bluff was required, for Bell was well supplied with artillery, and as his batteries opened fire, black and white Federals retreated into the fort's outbuildings. "But shot and shell crashing and tearing through these feeble barriers either set them on fire or leveled them to the ground," wrote R. R. Hancock of Barteau's 22nd Tennessee Cavalry, "killing and wounding their inmates and adding to the wild helplessness and confusion of the enemy, who though making, meanwhile, no proffer to surrender, had, nevertheless, become utterly impotent for defense."

After the surrender, Hancock viewed the carnage, "a sanguinary, sickening spectacle," he said, "another shocking illustration of the little capacity for command and deficiency of military knowledge of those appointed to the Federal Government over their negro troops, rather than an example of a stout, loyal maintenance of a soldier's post." Two hundred corpses gave the scene "the aspect of a slaughter-pen," he said, for the "bursting shells had done their work effectively among this poor, misofficered force."[14]

———

As summer turned to fall, scanty supplies and the sheer number of Federal soldiers pouring into Tennessee reduced Forrest to conducting guerrilla warfare, flitting about the outskirts of Union-held towns, capturing stragglers, disrupting railways, harassing supply lines. West Tennesseeans began to turn their backs on the sinking Confederacy, hiding their livestock from rebel foragers and refusing their currency.[15]

Forrest's demoralized officers began to fall out among themselves. At Pam Landing, Tennessee, Chalmers brought charges against Abraham Buford for conduct prejudicial to military order and discipline. On October 16, Forrest's command found Colonels Duckworth, Neely, and Stewart and three subordinate officers guilty of disobedience, "conduct prejudicial to good order & military discipline," and inciting and joining in a mutiny. Of Forrest's senior officers, only a few—like Tyree Bell (who would be commissioned a brigadier general in February) and Colonel David Kelley—would make it through the war with records unblemished by charges of mutiny, disobedience, thievery, or drunkenness.[16]

By early November, Forrest seemed worn out. "I have been constantly in the field since 1861," he told his superiors, "and have spent half the entire time in the saddle." His strength was failing, and it was "absolutely necessary that I should have some rest." But they could not afford to let him rest, and after they ordered him back to West Tennessee, he seemed to get his second wind. At Paris Landing in Henry County, his officers burned or captured four Federal boats and two barges loaded with supplies. On November 3, Forrest opened fire on the Union supply depot at Johnsonville with ten guns, disabling several gunboats moored at the town's wharf. Apparently invigorated by combat, Forrest gleefully commanded one of the guns with amateurish commands, chanting, "A rickety-shay! A rickety-shay! I'll hit her next time!" By dark he had burned down the entire waterfront, including warehouses of whiskey that caught fire and sent torrents of flame through Sherman's supplies, "filling the air with the blended yet distinct fumes of burning spirits, sugar, coffee, and meat." When Forrest returned the next morning to inspect the devastation, a regiment of blacks across the river shook their fists and hurled curses at him. Forrest ordered his gunners to open fire, killing a few and scattering the rest. Forrest captured Fort Heiman next, and Washburn began to worry that he might return to Fort Pillow and place a battery on the bluff. Forrest's reputation grew to such an extent that a minister in Newark, New Jersey, compared his men to the ancient Amalekites, a marauding tribe sent by Yahweh to punish the early Israelites for their idolatry.[17]

That fall, what remained of Forrest's troopers serenaded him in Florence, Alabama, where such Fort Pillow prisoners as Captain Young were languishing. "Well, soldiers," Forrest declared, "I come here to jine you. I'm gwine to show you the way into Tennessee. My conscripts are going, and I know Hood's veterans can go. I came down here with 350 men. I got 3500 conscripts. Since May I have fought in every county in West Tennessee. I fought in the streets of Memphis, and the women run out in their night clothes to see us, and they will do it again in Nashville. I have fought a battle every twenty-five days." It was in this speech that he boasted of having "seen the Mississippi run with blood for two hundred yards," and promised that he was "gwine to see it again." "It is needless to say," wrote an observer, "that every sentence of this characteristic speech elicited a shout."[18]

But most of the blood being shed was Confederate. Some regard the collision between Hood's Army of Tennessee and General George Henry Thomas's Army of the Cumberland at Franklin, Tennessee, as the most dramatic engagement of the war, exceeding even Pickett's Charge at Gettysburg in the gallantry and desperation with which the rebels attacked the Yankee line. Hood's men advanced in their thousands without artillery preparation across two miles of open ground, only to be mowed down in an assault that John Brownlow of Forrest's 19th Tennessee Cavalry deemed "the greatest mistake that was made during the war."[19]

Though the Yankees withdrew to Nashville with 2,326 casualties, Franklin cost the Confederates 6,252 men and officers, and five of their generals. The battle was a catastrophe for Hood's Army of the Tennessee and sealed the doom of the Confederate West. In the ensuing Battle of Nashville, Hood was outnumbered three to one, and attacks by General Thomas, "the Rock of Chickamauga," twice broke Hood's line and sent what was left of his army fleeing southward under a frigid downpour, saved from total annihilation by Forrest's rearguard. Conspicuous in this action were the Union army's black infantry, whose bodies Thomas found mingled with dead rebels in a trench: conclusive proof, the Virginian admitted, that black men would fight.[20]

"I never felt mutch like fighting after that," wrote Brownlow. Knowing the war was lost, Forrest's cavalry tended not to hurl themselves at the enemy any longer. Bell's recruiters in Dyer County met with open defiance from veterans of rebel catastrophes and Yankee prisons.[21]

The fall of Atlanta and the inevitability of Union victory emboldened the Yankees. At Murfreesboro, they attacked Forrest while he was still in the middle of issuing orders, and in the ensuing confusion his men retreated. Forrest rode after them, trying in vain to turn them back. At one point—so goes the story—he actually shot a rebel color bearer who refused his order to halt, then began to strike at fleeing infantrymen with the recovered colors. Forrest's temper became so dangerously frayed that he even drew a pistol on an infantry general for having the audacity to ask him to clear his men and horses out of his foot soldiers' way.[22]

———————————

The war was going so badly that Richmond revived a proposal it had once dismissed as against its interests and beneath its dignity: enlisting slaves in the Confederate army and emancipating them in return for their service. The news was greeted with mordant laughter in the North. "The so-called Confederates promise the slaves their freedom, if they will assist them in gaining their independence," wrote Thomas Webster of the 43rd USCI. "How magnanimous and free-hearted they are!" But, he added, "one thing is settled, and that is, the poor, suffering slaves at the south will be free; but no thanks to the Southern chivalry!" The rebels "ask those, who, in days gone by, and, indeed, at the present time, are not considered as human beings by them," to do "what they themselves have not been able to do." Forrest's rank and file were no more positive about the idea. "The 'bill' putting negroes in the army," George Walthall of the 18th Mississippi Cavalry would write home, "is a bad law" that would compel "a great many" whites to run away, "and carry their arms."[23]

Forrest tried to greet 1865 with a stirring address to his troops. In words that, in exhaustion and defeat, he would soon be forced to swallow, he told them not to be

> allured by the siren song of peace, for there can be no peace save upon your separate independent nationality. You can never again unite with those who have murdered your sons, outraged your helpless families, and with demoniac malice wantonly destroyed your property, and now seek to make slaves of you. A proposition of reunion with a people who have avowed their purpose to appropriate the property and to subjugate or annihilate the freemen of the South would stamp with infamy the names of your gallant dead and the living heroes of this war.

He and his probable ghostwriter, Major Charles Anderson, went on to total up their loot and itemize their triumphs, among which they included their thwarted assault on Paducah. But these were not the same men Forrest had addressed the year before. Two thousand of what he gave as an original force of five thousand men had been killed or wounded, two hundred captured and imprisoned. The Army of the Tennessee was shattered, and an emaciated, dinged-up, and short-tempered Forrest had tasted defeat as well as victory. By now his hair had turned so white it reminded one observer of a founding father's wig.[24]

As he marched them eastward in a desultory effort to harass Sherman's supply lines, many of his veteran troopers looked back over their shoulders at their unprotected farms and families and, slipping past Forrest's vigilant Escort, peeled away from the line of march and headed home. Forrest threatened to exterminate them all, and to stem the hemorrhaging in his ranks, resorted to the firing squad.[25]

John Milton Hubbard rode past the dead bodies of a man and a boy Forrest had ordered executed for desertion. "Their hats had been placed over their faces," he wrote, "but labels written in large letters told the story: *Shot for Desertion."* The man and boy were actually Kentucky farmers walking home from work, but they carried no identifying papers, and despite the fact that "there was no proof adduced to show that they belonged to our cavalry," Forrest had ordered them shot anyway. Hubbard saw the executions as evidence of the bankruptcy of the rebel cause. "The power of all Confederate courtsmartial was flitting fast," he wrote, "and the bloody hand, under all the circumstances in this case, might well have been stayed." "Everybody in low spirits," wrote Ben Bondurant of the 20th Tennessee Cavalry. "All talking about going home and quitting the War, for it is a failure."[26]

On March 6, 1865, the date by which Lincoln had commanded the marshal of the District of West Tennessee to arrest Forrest on a charge of treason, the Wizard was still very much at large. Overwhelmed by Federals near Plantersville, Alabama, on April 1, Forrest killed a pursuing Indiana captain in hand-to-hand combat, whereupon he was surrounded by about half a dozen Yankee troopers slashing at him with their sabers. One sliced Forrest's arm, knocking his saber from his hand, but one of the Wizard's men shot the Yankee from his horse, giving Forrest time to draw one of his pistols and shoot another dead. A few days later he personally killed yet another Yankee at Selma, Alabama, probably the thirtieth individual Federal to die directly by his hand.[27]

The battle at Selma was lost, however, as so much was being lost to the Confederates all across the South. Afterward, Forrest's men killed a gang of Federal foragers they found attempting to rape two women, and, demanding that Forrest remain behind to witness it, wiped out thirty-five Yankee pickets, thereby ending their general's career with another charge of massacre. A Yankee officer who had previously met and respected Forrest now concluded that in extremis he revealed "all the brutal instincts of the slave driver" to which was now added "a sulky and guilty consciousness."[28]

Even victory would not expunge Northern outrage over the Fort Pillow massacre. Encamped on the Mobile and Ohio Railroad, James B. Lockney of the 28th Wisconsin Infantry was horrified by the news that Grant had generously extended paroles to rebel officers. "Oh can this be?" he asked. "Can our loved comrades who fill so many, many, southern graves lie still," while the men who had led the South into "a desperate & bloody effort to establish a despotism in which all who were poor of whatever color were to be subject to the proud, wealthy & aristocratic" go free? If so, he expected that the "U.S. Congress may yet restore Forrest to Citizenship & give him a gold medal bearing the motto Ft. Pillow!"[29]

As news of the Army of Virginia's capitulation began to circulate among his men, Forrest tried to buoy their sinking spirits by insisting that Lee could not have surrendered, that Johnston and Sherman had agreed simply to a truce, that in the wake of Lincoln's assassination Grant's army was deserting by the thousands, and that it remained "the duty of every man to stand firm at his post and true to his colors."[30]

The last Tennessee skirmish between Yankee and rebel was fought on April 18 at Germantown,[31] two days after what was left of the Confederate Army of Tennessee had surrendered near Durham Station, North Carolina. When, in early May, Grant demanded the unconditional surrender of the Western Confederacy's forces, some of Forrest's men proposed regrouping in Texas and fighting on. But Forrest wearily declined to lead them. "Men, you may all do as you damn please," he told a delegation of diehards, "but I'm a-going home." Pressing the war "would be nothing but murder," he told them. "Any man who is in favor of a further prosecution of this war is a fit subject for a lunatic asylum."

On May 4, he addressed his men directly, with no ghostwriter interceding. "We have made our last fight," he told them. They had been "good soldiers," and any man "who has been a good soldier can be a good citizen. I shall go back to my home upon the Mississippi River, there to begin life anew, and to you good old Confederates, I want to say that the latchstring of Bedford Forrest will always be outside the door."

Many of his men could not believe the old warhorse was actually sheathing his sword. Hadn't he bluffed and bamboozled his way all through the war? Surely he still had something left in his bag of tricks. But his final farewell message to his troops was even more conciliatory than Robert E. Lee's. "Neighborhood feuds, personal animosities, and private differences should be blotted out," he advised his men; "and, when you return home, a manly, straightforward course of conduct will secure the respect even of your enemies. Whatever your responsibilities may be to the government, to society, or to individuals, meet them like men."

"Where I live," Forrest confided to a reporter, "there are plenty of fish, and I'm going to take a tent along, and I don't want to see anyone for twelve months."[32]

GOING HOME
CONFEDERATE VETERANS

1865–1902

THE WEATHER SEEMED TO CONSPIRE AGAINST THE DEFEATED TEN-
nesseans as they slogged their way back home. In April 1865, almost simultaneous with the assassination of Lincoln and the first anniversary of the fall
of Fort Pillow, the lower Mississippi Valley was swept by a severe and peculiarly long-lasting flood that collapsed levees, inundated already devastated
towns, drowned livestock, and prevented men from putting in a crop. Men
"wading homeward through miles of destroyed and overflowed country,"
wrote the historian Robert W. Harrison, "felt little hope for the future" as
hundreds of families fled the lower Mississippi, "many never to return."[1]

In May 1865, W. H. Harris's horse gave out while he was on a scout with
his 8th Tennessee Cavalry. When he limped back into camp and asked
Colonel Wilson for a new mount, Wilson informed him that "the thing was
over." Woody Johnson and his Texas comrades rode off with Confederate
mules and wagons, one of each of which Johnson claimed for himself "as I
captured them from a negro." But that summer he decided he had better
turn them over to the Yankees, and "took the amnesty oath & have tried to
keep [it] till now."[2]

By the time Forrest surrendered, John Brownlow of the 19th was fighting and retreating on foot.* "My horse had died," and though he had tried to
lay claim to one of his company's wagon mules, his captain "would not let
me have one." However, his old friend Bob English let him ride his "old family horse," Charley. English doubted whether Charley could carry Brownlow

---

*Unless otherwise indicated, all regimental numbers refer to Tennessee cavalry units.

all the way home, "but he did," Brownlow fondly recalled. Some of the men who rode with Forrest had grown so attached to the equestrian life that they would never entirely dismount. A. W. McKay of the 19th, for example, went home and became a jockey. Others of Forrest's men tried to salve the psychic damage they had sustained by going west. T. W. Leigon of the 2nd grew up an impoverished hired hand and could never settle down after the war. "I have lived a roving life," he declared as an old man, "never satisfied any where."[3]

Hearing rumors that because of the Fort Pillow affair Forrest's men would not be paroled, Joe Weems, a scout for the 10th, decided he would flee to Mexico with a few of his comrades. But he got no farther than the Mississippi River, in whose churning depths several of his party were drowned. So Weems and the rest turned their "thin but spirited nags" around and headed home. A mounted infantryman named Victor Murat Locke started for Mexico, but got into "a fight with free Negroes on Texas/ Louisiana line" and rode instead to Oklahoma, where he became a cowboy and a teacher for the Choctaw nation.[4]

One of Forrest's men sought his fortune well south of Texas. In 1866, an American diplomat in Paraguay was approached by a tall, double-dealing fortune seeker who called himself James Manlove and claimed to have been a sharpshooter in Forrest's assault on Fort Pillow. Manlove "always denied that there was any massacre or any violation of the rules and customs of war." He said he was seeking a commission from the Paraguayan government to attack Brazilian ships and to split the profits of his piracy with the Brazilian government. Though "he was a man generally of courteous manners and of fair education, and of extensive reading and information," his violent, "ungovernable temper," a weakness he often "lamented," led him to quarrel "with nearly every foreigner that he had any intimacy with in the country." After being caught playing both sides against the middle, Manlove was executed by the Paraguayan police.[5]

Those few troopers who had received wages had been paid in Confederate tender that was now entirely worthless. So they had to work for their food as they made their way home. Ed Morris of the 4th "was so near starved" on his long journey home that he had to "sit down and rest every few minutes." Separated from his company, Jesse Shelton of the 4th was reduced by disease to a near skeleton when he started home from East Tennessee, and recalled the journey as "the lonesomest trip of my life."[6]

"On the trip home, we passed the towns and villages which were occupied by federal troops," recalled Bill Hazelwood of Forrest's Old Regiment. "In most places we were treated very friendly, and often when in passing

'Yankee' troops, some would ask, 'Where are you going, boys?' To which we would reply, 'Home.'. . . . Back in an instant would come the statement, 'I would to God we were going there too.'" Jim Lasley of the 2nd recalled encountering a Yankee colonel on his journey home. "You have made damn good soldiers," he told Lasley and his comrades. "Go home and make damned good citizens." And "we did," Lasley declared.[7]

J. W. Williams of the 4th returned home to find "everything was tore up: the fences and everything on the farm." Thomas Edward Bradley of the 8th Tennessee Infantry limped home to Smith County to find that the military governor had enfranchised his former slaves, "so I confess [to] Christ [I] got behind old [Beck's Bull Tongue] plow and went to work." When L. W. Travis of the 7th got home, he made a "fine crop" of the "cotton patches that the Negroes left." According to his son, John S. Howell of Forrest's Old Regiment came home to find "the fences all burned, his mother dead, his father broken in health and his wife an invalid, but he went to work on the farm and lived there the rest of his life."[8]

By the time M. B. Dinwiddie of the 20th returned from the war, he had lost his father, mother, and three brothers, and suffered a wound to his lung that disabled him for the rest of his life. He came home to find his county occupied by Federal troops and his father's farm in ruins: "no stock, no feed, nothing to work and nothing to work with." Only a few of his father's old slaves had remained, "and they stayed until they died, and I buried them. The bulk of the young ones went away." For three years his wound refused to "cure up" and ran constantly. But he "never applied for a pension," he wrote as an old man, "because I didnt need it." He said he had "plenty of this worlds goods to do me the rest of [my] lifetime, and my five children, after me."[9]

When Billy Matthews of the 9th went to war, he had a wife and two babies, five thousand dollars in cash, "seven horses, four cows, ten hogs." When he returned home after the war he had a wife, two babies, a sack of worthless Confederate money, "no bread, no meat"; and all of his father's slaves had gone over "to the Yankeys." Some men had a hard time returning to the measured rhythms of farm life, especially now that their slaves had fled. Bob McCalister of the 11th vowed that after the war he would rest for a few months "and try and get myself in shape to kick clods and hoe potatoes." He kept his promise to himself, and did not "hit the job untill the year following." Infantryman Joe McCorkle of the 10th Mississippi returned home to find that "my best Negro had staid at home & was making a crop," so McCorkle "didn't work much the balance of the year."[10]

Lem Tyree of the 19th found that he could not bear manual labor. "That is the last furrow I ever intend to plow," he declared one day, throwing down his plow.

"But boss," one of his hired hands inquired, "how is you going to make a living without plowing?"

Tyree replied that he was going to study law, and, after graduating from Princeton University, he did indeed become a lawyer and a probate judge. But as an old man, he took less pride in his Princeton law degree than in his Confederate parole, which he always kept framed on his office wall.[11]

There were plenty of diehards among Forrest's men who never could admit or adjust to defeat. Some were too ashamed to go home. After his company disbanded, John Russell Dance of the 2nd "did not want to go home." He said he "never wanted my people to see me" because "we had failed and laid down our arms." "I didn't go home for over a year," recalled Jasper Eldridge of the 16th, who tried to join up with the fugitive Jeff Davis and his escort, "but, hearing he was captured, I hired and went to work on [a] farm." Billy Nolen of the 2nd, however, "had the honor" of leading President Davis and what remained of the Confederate treasury into Georgia, where it was divided up among his escort. "Each one got $21.25 in silver and $5.00 in gold. I had my silver made into spoons, and the gold into a ring" that he later presented to his fiancée.[12]

When he returned home, Andy McLeary of the 12th gave his thick, contraband "Eskimo cloak" to his slave Ben, "who stayed at home and helped my mother take care of the children after father died. My mother gave Ben a horse when the war was over," McLeary wrote as an old man, "and we all have a good feeling now for any of Ben's relations." "On arriving home," wrote Jim Cochran of the 8th Mississippi, "the biggest hug was given me by my old uncle Ned, a servent."[13]

Jim Hendricks of the 17th Tennessee Infantry recalled his journey home as pleasant enough "until I got to Nashville," where the legislature was in session "denouncing 'Rebels,' etc. Three negroes [tried] to push me from the sidewalk into the street," but Hendricks "threw one of them into the gutter." On reaching home, "I found a negro siege headed by white soldiers" and rebel deserters. A Yankee captain and his black troops tried to take his farm from him, but Hendricks "knocked one of them down with an ax."[14]

Jack Reagan of the 6th recalled how hard it was for his comrades to adjust to the new, if temporary, order of things. At Nashville, his company spent a few days in a Federal penitentiary, awaiting transport home. When a passing black Union soldier called Reagan and his defeated comrades "Jefferson Davis's shinplasters," "we had to endure it." At the penitentiary Reagan and his comrades "had to file by a cook for our grub," but some of his comrades "would not fall in because a big buck negro forked out our meat and bread to us. I told them we had a negro cook at the old home, and I was used to it, and that I had plowed many a day side by side with negroes, and I was going to have my rations. It was good," he concluded, "to a hungry man."[15]

Rebels passing through Memphis after the war would risk reprisals at the hands of the black troops stationed at Fort Pickering, including the 11th USCI, to which Fort Pillow's black survivors had been assigned. The *New York Herald* reported that on May 21, the authorities uncovered "a negro plot to assassinate the paroled rebel prisoners at Memphis, of whom there has been quite an influx lately, in revenge for the Fort Pillow massacre. White troops were immediately put on guard, and on the attempt of the negroes to come out of the fort at a given hour, they were ordered back, when, refusing to obey, a sharp conflict ensued."[16]

On returning home, M. B. Dinwiddie found hired labor "much better labor than slaves: more satisfactory in every way." But however much his opinion of slavery changed, his estimation of Yankees did not. "I have never forgiven the Yankeys yet," he declared in 1922. "One reason [is], they havent asked forgiveness, [another is] I wouldnt give it if they did." When asked how he managed to overcome his animosity toward the Yankees, nonagenarian A. J. Grantham, who fought at Fort Pillow with the 5th Mississippi, "couldn't say" because he had not "got over it yet."[17]

Bob Mockbee of the 14th Tennessee Infantry moved to South Carolina after the war "and went through the 'Reconstruction period' under carpetbag, scalawags & Negro rule which was more trying than any of the experiences of the war." Between the time Thomas Carrick of the 21st surrendered and the day he reached home, Unionists had killed his father and burned down his grandfather's house. "Well," Carrick bitterly recalled, "the truth is, I and the yankeys got to hating each other so bad" that he kept away and "sta-y-e-d till the yankees left." When he finally did return, it was with his dukes up and his rifle cocked.[18]

At the age of eighty-four, B. P. Hooker of Forrest's artillery declared that he was "yet a lover of the South, for which we fought." "Though vanquished," declared Lee Yancey of the 7th, he was not "downhearted. I am still Southern to the core." Writing as an old blind man in 1922, Billy Matthews extolled his comrades along racial lines. "The world will never again see their equal in arms," he wrote. "The great war in Europe had its [Pershing], its clever Yank. But the south had its thousands of them." The rebel soldier "fought naked and hungry against great odds without hope of pay." The Confederate soldier was "the best blood in the world," he said, and fought "for a great principle he believed right and for humanity's good, and because he knew Bob Lee led them. The world will be poorer," he concluded, "when this thin line disappears."[19]

A lot of Confederates believed that emancipation would spell the doom of the Southern black. "Some who went to the wars with me came not back," wrote John Marshall Alley; "some have died at home and some have moved away. Most of the negro population have gone either to the grave, the army, or to live in filth and poverty in some hovel or camp whither they have repaired in search of freedom."[20]

The slave had been "a happy and child-like creature," wrote Frank Montgomery, who went on to serve as a Mississippi judge. "He had no wants not willingly supplied; he had no care; his day's work done, he slept secure. Crime was literally unknown to him. The planter left his wife and children on his place surrounded by his slaves; sure that they were safe from harm. Now, what is his condition?" Montgomery wanted to know. "Ask the jails, the penitentiaries, the lunatic asylums, which are filled not from the ranks of the old slaves, but their sons and daughters. No white man will now leave his family on his place, surrounded by negroes alone, and often when I have been on the bench, I have been constrained to excuse jurors for this reason."[21]

Other men were ready to put the war and its causes behind them. "As I look back at the situation, after 60 years," wrote Bill Carson of the 4th Louisiana, "the thing that impresses me is the singular lack of efficiency that attached to the institution of slavery. Neither master nor slave seems to have sought to economize in time or anything." "I was too young to be an enthusiastic soldier," recalled Ed Gardner of the 6th Mississippi, "and there was too much of misfortune, blood and suffering connected with that far-a-way time for me to remember it with pleasure. I never had a love for strife and carnage." And when he "realized what was being enacted" in World War I, he would lose "all taste for such things." As an old man, he still believed in patriotism "and would not hesitate to shoulder a gun even at my age if necessary to defend my country. But I utterly abhor the idea of war."[22]

"JEALOUSY, FALSEHOOD, AND FANATICISM"
FORREST'S GENERALS

1865–1905

Convinced the war was lost, McCulloch's division grew more brazen, stealing cotton, horses, mules, wagons, and slaves, and keeping the spoils for themselves. McCulloch and Neely were scolded for allowing their men to abandon guns and supplies while breaking up their camp at Tupelo. "The abandonment of these articles evinces a disregard of duty & an indifference to the interests of the service & the country which are disgraceful to all concerned." "Horse stealing," wrote an officer on March 15, 1865, "is a trade I believe they are all engaged in."[1]

By then their horses were so cut up that the army sent McCulloch and his Mongols south to recuperate. After surrendering to the Union army at Columbus, Mississippi, the two Bobs rode home together with what was left of the boys of Cooper County whom they had led into first border and then civil war half a dozen years before. After Colonel Black Bob's hair turned white, the cousins' nicknames fell into disuse. The colonel remained the grimmer of the two. An indomitable old buzzard with a withering gaze and a walrus mustache arching over a set jaw, he raised horses for the county's four-mile races, and "the memory of these game horses ridden by Negro mounts," wrote one Cooper County chronicler, "is a happy one to many." He served as county collector, sheriff, registrar of lands, and founder of the George B. Harper Camp No. 714 of the United Veterans of the Confederacy, eventually attaining a generalship as Missouri commander of the United Confederate Veterans, which trotted the old warrior out at dozens of reunions. It was said that at one such gathering, Robert E. Lee took the colonel's daughter aside to say that her father was the bravest man he ever knew. But in all likelihood this was Stephen D. Lee, not Robert E. Lee, who disliked such affairs and had never met McCulloch. In old age, Robert A. remained the more benign of the two McCullochs. With a full beard and a wistful tilt to his eyebrows, the former lieutenant colonel served as county judge for six years, retiring at last in 1880. "As a neighbor he is hospitable and kind," concluded his Cooper County biographer, "and as a man he is upright and honorable and above reproach."[2]

———————————

Charged by Chalmers with insubordination, severely wounded at Lindville, Tennessee, on Christmas Eve, the gigantic, tumultuous Brigadier General Abraham Buford was knocked out of commission for the rest of the war. He returned to his bluegrass "Bosque Bonita," his enormous Kentucky plantation and horse farm, and served in the Kentucky legislature. But after his wife and son died, he suffered a series of financial reverses that cost him his home and his racehorses. On June 9, 1884, in a rooming house in Danville, Indiana, the sixty-four-year-old warhorse put a pistol to his head and killed himself, leaving a suicide note requesting only that he be buried near his wife and son. "His mind became unsettled," wrote Mercer Otey, "it is thought through religious mania, and it eventuated in his driving a ball through his brain."[3]

Disabled by wounds received at Murfreesboro in December 1864, the Ohioan Clarke Russell Barteau of the 22nd Tennessee Cavalry made his peace with his brother Harry, who had served on the Union side. But the war had cost him his share of his father's property. In May 1864, he married a Mississippi woman who had tended to Forrest's wounded at Okolona. After studying for the bar, he eventually moved to Shelby County, Tennessee, and was a frequent speaker at veterans' reunions. As an old man he was a Democrat, but not "the narrow partisan sort," wrote Hancock, "for he abhors hypocrisy and mere expediency." Though he entered the war convinced that "the South was right—that the anti-slavery crusade was founded on jealousy, falsehood, and fanaticism," in his old age he accepted "in good faith the issues settled by the war," looked "only to the building up of the country," and always took "the side of right against wrong, of the weak against the powerful."[4]

The longest-lived of Forrest's brigade commanders, Tyree Bell was commissioned a brigadier general in February 1865, and after the war moved west: first to Fresno, California, and then to Los Angeles, where, working as a real estate broker, he was elected major general of the Pacific Division of the United Confederate Veterans of California. After visiting his old tobacco plantation in Sumner County and attending a veterans' convention in New

Orleans, he died of heat stroke on September 1, 1902, at the age of eighty-seven. His body was shipped back to California, and lies buried in a small cemetery near the little town of Sanger.[5]

On April 15, 1879, fifteen years and three days after the attack on Fort Pillow, former general James Ronald Chalmers, now a congressman from Mississippi, stood up in the chamber of the United States House of Representatives to defend himself against the resurrected charge that he was responsible for the massacre at Fort Pillow and had personally shot a young contraband boy in cold blood. Accused by an Ohio congressman of delivering an "insolent" speech denouncing Northerners as "traitors to their country," and characterized by the *Cincinnati Gazette* as "one of the notorious and bloody-handed butchers of the forever infamous Fort Pillow massacre," Chalmers demanded a full-fledged congressional investigation.

Failing to see how such an inquiry would "do any good either to him or the country," Congress denied his request but permitted him to enter his defense into the record. He addressed the stain that Fort Pillow had left on his reputation with an indignation garnished with gentility, as if his colleagues, knowing him to be a gentleman of high pedigree, exquisite refinement, prodigious accomplishments, and eloquent erudition, could not possibly suspect him of such outrages. He cast much of his argument in the subjunctive: not in terms of what he actually did, but what he trusted that his esteemed colleagues understood that a man of his breeding would not have done.

He said he had tried to answer the charges during his hotly contested congressional campaign in 1875, but had remained silent over the next four years because "the charges were so shocking to humanity, so incredible in my judgment, and had been so fully denied, that I did not believe there was a respectable man in the country who could give any further credence to them."

He cited a recent encounter with his former prisoner, Lieutenant Mack J. Leaming, who "sought an introduction to me for the purpose of returning his thanks for kindness I had shown him" while he was "a wounded prisoner at Fort Pillow"—a selective offering of water and medical care he had extended to Leaming as a fellow Mason—as proof he was blameless. He dismissed the story of his killing a child by pointing out that a witness said the culprit wore a star on his coat, which would have identified him as a major, and by claiming, falsely, that in any case there were no children at Fort Pillow left to kill.

He refuted accounts of his accepting a libation aboard the *Platte Valley* and vowing not to treat blacks and Homemade Yankees as prisoners of war by reminding his colleagues that he had permitted the Yankees to load their wounded black troops aboard the *Platte Valley*, although, in fact, he had been ordered to by Forrest, who had decided he could not entrust the task to Chalmers and his men and assigned it instead to Major Anderson. Besides, Chalmers continued, it was well known among his colleagues that he never touched alcoholic beverages. In disputing that there was a sufficient disproportion of casualties to establish that the battle was a massacre, Chalmers wildly overstated the number of Confederate casualties from his own command at 110, and an equal number from Bell's. He deemed the accusation that his men burned Akerstrom to death "so manifestly false that it needs no refutation," and to corroborate his version of events at Fort Pillow, entered into the record excerpts from Jordan and Pryor's authorized biography of Forrest, some of which were based on Chalmers's own account. (In his own tribute to Forrest, written two years after the Wizard was safely in his grave, Chalmers could not refrain from pointing out with aristocratic disdain that though Forrest was undoubtedly a great warrior, "he never rose to that greatness and dignity of soul which enabled Robert E. Lee at Gettysburg to assume the responsibility of a failure.")[6]

Chalmers's defense might have been more convincing had the former general not recently betrayed a capacity for precisely the kind of mayhem of which he now declared himself patently incapable. After the war, a few Mississippi planters, in cooperation with the Freedmen's Bureau, had drafted and honored labor contracts with their black employees, hoping that by providing decent pay and housing, they would attract good workers. But they lured the best hands away from less progressive planters, who regarded such fair dealing as treason to the white race. These conservatives organized themselves into a sort of militia that systematically murdered blacks working for moderate planters. During this period, white night riders conducted raids around Friar's Point, putting to the torch the plantation of a man who had defied his neighbors by renting his land to blacks.

In the mid-1870s, "Negro Riots," as Southern whites called them, broke out all across the state of Mississippi. As the financial panic of 1873 and the proliferating scandals in the Grant administration began to weaken the Republican Party's hold on the nation, the state's Democrats united behind what they called their "Mississippi Plan": a campaign to impose one-party rule by fair means or foul. The plan involved terrorizing black voters and candidates, stuffing ballot boxes, and destroying Republican ballots. It succeeded brilliantly, as whites rose up against local Republican governments from Vicksburg to Rolling Fork. The alarmed Republican governor, former

Union general Edelbert Ames, begged Grant for troops. But the president refused, and Ames was compelled to recruit a black militia under the command of a biracial immigrant from Oberlin College named John Brown.

In August 1874, hundreds of outraged blacks armed with rifles poured into the riverside town of Austin to protest the release of a white doctor accused of shooting a young black girl to death. After most of the town's whites, including its sheriff, fled Austin, looting ensued, and Chalmers swept down from Memphis with a force of about three hundred armed men to quell the disturbance. By the time he rode back to Memphis, thirty-three blacks had been captured, beaten, and imprisoned.[7]

At Friar's Point, Mississippi, in October 1875, Chalmers led an attack on Sheriff John Brown himself, who had been elected by a huge black Republican majority two years before. Despite Brown's reputation for rectitude, white Democrats had relentlessly tried to bring him up on a series of trumped-up charges, all of which were thrown out of court. On October 6, several hundred black Republicans from surrounding plantations began to converge on Friar's Point to hear Brown speak on the need for Mississippi's African Americans to defend themselves against the depredations of white night riders. The assembly alarmed local whites. Fearing bloodshed, Brown prudently asked his people to disperse and return to their homes. This they did, but three miles out of town they were surrounded by about one hundred "well-armed" whites under Chalmers's personal command. Among the night riders was Mississippi senator and former Confederate general James Lusk Alcorn, who confronted the blacks with a shotgun. The Little Un ordered his men to open fire, and as the blacks, the vast majority of them unarmed, retreated into the woods, the whites chased after them. Though Brown's supporters avoided being trapped by a flanking movement that Chalmers had no doubt picked up from the Wizard himself, the diminutive former cavalry commander and his men managed to kill about twenty-five blacks as they fled through the forest.

His own life in jeopardy, Brown escaped across the Mississippi to Helena, Arkansas, from which he telegraphed Governor Ames on October 8 that his people were "still finding the bodies of men that have been killed by the body of armed men led by Chalmers." Ames was powerless to help, however, and Brown ultimately fled west. In his place, the whites of Coahoma County elected as their sheriff Senator Alcorn's son.[8]

In 1876, as the Democrats regained control of the state, Chalmers was elected to the Mississippi legislature, and eventually to Congress from the "shoe-string district," comprising seven counties lying along 250 miles of the

Mississippi's eastern bank. But in his bid for reelection, he was defeated by the twenty-four-year-old biracial photographer John R. Lynch of Natchez, the son of a white planter and his slave.[9]

After losing to Lynch, a humiliated Chalmers sullenly returned to the law, serving as a special assistant to Mississippi's federal attorneys. Disgusted by the Democratic Party's feeble support, in 1883 he ran for Congress as an independent, but this time with the unlikely backing of Mississippi's Republican Party. He received a majority of votes but was almost cheated out of his victory by Mississippi's secretary of state, who gave a certificate of election to his Democratic opponent. Congress finally seated Chalmers the following June, but after losing a subsequent election, he retired from politics and moved to Memphis, where he died in 1898 at the age of sixty-seven.

Fort Pillow remained an obstacle to the Southern mythology of the Lost Cause and thus a special object of Dixie revisionism. The massacre tainted the Southern whites' campaign to romanticize and ennoble the Confederate cause, to deprecate slavery as its root, to wax nostalgic about the days when slave and slaveholder's "hearts were young and gay."

In 1896, the *Confederate Veteran* laid out the goals of Southern revisionism: "That the Confederate States may for all time live as a nation, born of, and battling for, constitutional rights won by so many revolutions against personal government," and that

> the victors shall not be left alone to publish to the world only such accounts as comport to their views, and sustain their acts pending and after the war. A conquered people seldom have the heart to write the history of their humiliation and defeat, and it is generally left to the victors, and if we consider the abuse and slanders that were heaped on us by northern writers, with accompanying degrading illustrations, it cannot be reasonably expected that they will hereafter, assign the true causes that led to the war, nor give their real motives in carrying it on, nor acknowledge the overwhelming power that eventually gave them success even in the pleasing language of fiction or much less in the plain language of truth.

"No nation ever rose so high," declared the *Veteran,* "and passed through battle and blood, and came forth from the ordeal so free from disparagement and guiltless of crime."[10]

The most notorious crime of which they contrived to prove the white

South guiltless was the massacre at Fort Pillow. In 1907 the United Confederate Veterans urged its members to befriend newspaper publishers and inundate the press with their reminiscences. Soon newspapers that had once condemned Forrest for Fort Pillow now declared that the charges of massacre were unfounded or embraced the Southern argument that the disproportion of deaths was the fault not of the Confederates but of the victims themselves. After Forrest's death, the *New York Times* would decree that the Fort Pillow massacre was a "malignant partisan falsehood" that should be "buried as deep as the dead Federal soldiers." The exaggerations of abolitionist and Union propaganda, combined with the white North's desire to reunite the country, suddenly put the massacre's witnesses on the defensive.[11]

In 1903, Forrest's old commander, Stephen D. Lee, served as chairman of the United Confederate Veterans History Committee, and saw fit to condemn an account of the massacre that had appeared in a contemporary schoolbook. "The committee is pained at this late date to see such paragraphs breathing all the bad blood of the bitterest war of the centuries," wrote Lee, "and endeavoring to undermine the respect of American youth for their ancestry, in a book which is generally fair in other respects. Until those paragraphs are expunged by the author, your committee states that the book should not be bought or allowed in the home of any Southern family, where Southern youth can read such a misrepresentation of history."[12]

Former Confederate general Thomas Jordan and an alcoholic journalist named J. P. Pryor worked in close consultation with Forrest and his senior officers to write what was in effect the Wizard's authorized biography. Published only four years after the war, *The Campaigns of Nathan Bedford Forrest and of Forrest's Cavalry* dismissed the massacre at Fort Pillow in a chain of arguments that boiled down to: there was no massacre; if there was a massacre, it was not Forrest's fault but Bradford's for refusing to surrender; the obstinate mongrel garrison of depredatious former slaves and Homegrown Yankees got what it deserved; and anyway, even if there was a massacre and all the stories of atrocities were true, they could not hold a candle to the crimes committed by the French and English on the Iberian Peninsula during the Napoleonic Wars. "We submit to the candid, and those who are capable of accepting the truth," Jordan and Pryor concluded, "that, in what occurred after the Confederates stormed the trenches, there was neither cruel purpose nor cruel negligence of duty, neither intention nor inadvertence, on the part of General Forrest, whose course, therefore, stands utterly devoid of the essence of outrage or wrong."[13]

In *That Devil Forrest,* John Wyeth, who served in Forrest's Old Regiment, regarded emancipation as "the unlawful and unjust sweeping away of private property," and characterized the joint subcommittee's report as "deftly woven out of the exaggerated testimony of two or three of the officers and some of the Negroes and whites who were of the garrison, much of which testimony was so self-contradicting as to prove its falsity, and all of which was *ex parte* and inadequate in establishing the trumped-up charges of a violation of the rules governing civilized warfare."[14]

Robert Selph Henry of Tennessee, a railway lawyer who served in World War I and eventually became president of the Southern Historical Society, gave the most considered critique of Wade and Gooch's report in his *"First with the Most" Forrest*. He conceded that newspapers on both sides had indulged in outlandish accusations of atrocity and barbarism. But he blamed the initial characterization of the Fort Pillow affair as a massacre on the Unionist *Memphis Bulletin,* accusing its editors of inventing its reports of rebels shooting wounded and unarmed men pleading for mercy. Though he wrote about the Civil War with rare restraint and evenhandedness, his account of the Fort Pillow affair was strangely injudicious. He claimed to find contradictions in the testimony where only the narrowest and most partisan reading could find any; indulged in a selective literal-mindedness that did not allow, for instance, for the possibility that not all the civilians—including women and children—had managed to scramble aboard the coal boat and escape; and gave disproportionate weight to the coordinated testimony that Wyeth collected from Forrest's officers. And Andrew Nelson Lytle's hagiographic *Bedford Forrest and His Critter Company* depicted Forrest as a champion of Southern agrarian values, innocent on all counts at Fort Pillow, and the wise leader of a just and gentlemanly Ku Klux Klan.[15]

Such was the context in which Southern critiques of the *Report of the Joint Subcommittee on the Conduct of the War* depicted the Fort Pillow affair. They were at least as propagandistic as the report itself, and even more afflicted by casuistry and glaring omissions, lack of eyewitness testimony, and selective use of evidence, all compounded by not only a reflexive contempt for black and Homegrown Yankee testimony but an intransigent belief in the inherent decency and nobility of the Confederate officer.

Forrest himself set the tone for his defenders. Shortly after the Wizard surrendered, a reporter asked him if he would "ever put upon paper a true account of the Fort Pillow affair."

"Well," said he, "the Yankees ought to know. They sent down their best men to investigate the affair."

"But," the reporter persisted, "are we to believe their report, General?"

"Yes," Forrest replied, "if we are to believe anything a nigger says."[16]

FULL CIRCLE

BLACK TROOPS

1865–1900

AMONG THE LAST FEDERALS TO ENLIST, MANY BLACK TROOPS WERE THE last to be mustered out. The army ordered that all black artillery units be dismounted and disarmed and returned to garrison duty to guard imprisoned Confederates. But with Yankee prisons emptying, officers did not know what to do with them all. In May, Sherman got word that officers were employing black troops from the 44th USCI as teamsters and body servants. "We have very easy times," a white infantryman wrote from Alabama, "as the guard duty is not hard, and we make the negroes do the work." Sherman ordered them returned to duty.[1]

It began to seem to these veterans of the pioneer corps and the contraband camps that they had come full circle. On June 5, 1865, two sergeants, a corporal, four privates, and a bugler of the 2nd USCLA were found guilty of mutiny, with sentences of three years of hard labor with, in the case of one of the sergeants, the addition of annual four-month terms in solitary confinement on bread and water.[2]

Tennessee's new constitution declared all slaves free, but hedged on their civil rights. Among other things, it forbade them to marry whites or send their children to the same schools with white children. Blacks were subject to the same penal code as white persons, except that "rape by a negro upon a white woman is punishable with death." No contract between a white and a black could be binding, "unless reduced to writing, and witnessed by a white person." Though "colored persons may be witnesses in all state courts for or against each other," they could not testify "in cases to which the parties are white." Thus, the *Christian Recorder* pointed out, a former rebel could assault the "widow or daughter of the husband that fell

at Fort Pillow" and shoot or stab her "in revenge for the South," and the legislature would shield him from effective prosecution.

"By the bleached and whitened bones of the thousands slain upon the
battle-fields of the Republic in the defense of Republican liberty," declared
the *Recorder,* "by the mangled corpses of our martyred braves at Fort Pillow—
by every attribute of common humanity, we demand that the government
shall do justice by the oppressed and loyal people who stood by the fortunes
of the country in her hour of darkest trial." But in many parts of Tennessee,
even the limited civil rights accorded the state's blacks were withheld by
farmers who kept their slaves in bondage "until the harvest came in that fall."[3]

"Fort Pillow showed no signs of either massacre or defense," wrote Whitelaw
Reid of the *Washington Tribune* shortly after the war. "In fact, one could see
nothing but a blank bluff, whence artillery might command a fine range up
or down the river." One evening he landed below the bluffs and, climbing up
the old ravine road, came upon "a row of the rudest cabins, ranged after the
fashion of the negro quarters on a plantation." In one hut he found a middle-
aged black woman holding a sick child close to a roaring fire. The cabin
contained "an old bedstead, nailed together by pieces of rough boards and
covered with a tattered quilt," a crude table "on which were the fragments
of a half-eaten, heavy, sodden corn-pone," a skillet with a busted lid in the
fireplace, an old box piled with broken dishes, and absolutely nothing else.

At the landing, Reid asked a group of black woodchoppers where they
came from. They replied they were refugees from the guerrillas who had
been raiding downriver cotton plantations. They said a white speculator had
established a wood yard for passing steamboats and paid them a dollar a
cord. "But the trouble is, sir," said one of them, "he done never pay us. He
say guerrillas sunk the steamboat his money come down on, and we got to
take goods for our pay. Then he sell us pork not fit to eat, at three bits a
pound, and the meanest cornmeal you ever see." The speculator had sold
them "brass rings at five or six dollars apiece, and gaudy cotton handkerchiefs for the head at three dollars," until they were all hopelessly in debt.

The post itself was "a lonely, desolate-looking spot" from which the
woodcutters were afraid to stray for fear of guerrillas, as if the ghosts of Fort
Pillow's Federal dead, or the occasional passing gunboat, would protect
them.[4]

Two years after the war, a white survivor of the massacre applied to protect and defend the ex-slaves and black veterans of West Tennessee. Shot in the head, six-foot two-inch Captain John L. Poston of 13/E had been captured by the rebels and held a prisoner for seven months in "various places." Nearly starved, inadequately clothed and sheltered, he developed bronchitis and heart trouble. Escaping in November, he recovered from his wound and the privations of prison life, and returned to duty with the 6th Tennessee Cavalry, to which the survivors of his company had been transferred.

In 1867, Poston accepted a position as an agent for the Bureau of Refugees, Freedmen, and Abandoned Lands. For fifty dollars a month, he oversaw a district encompassing not only the West Tennessee counties of Haywood and Tipton but Lauderdale itself: the very site of his harrowing ordeal at Fort Pillow three years before. As such, Poston was a firsthand witness to what the Civil War and the end of slavery had accomplished and failed to accomplish in the lives of West Tennessee African Americans.

The freed people of his district were "generally working for half of the crop," he wrote in his first report to headquarters, "the employer finding the land, team, & farming tools of every description. The freedmen board themselves & pay their own Duties Bill, cultivate the crop, gather it, & house it. Those who work per year, a few men who are extra good hands may get as much as $200 & a few women are employed for cooks &c. at not more than $50." Although this appeared to be the most profitable system "for the freed people, especially those who are industrious," white farmers had already learned that they could increase their share of the profits "by forcing contracts on their sharecroppers which obliged them to buy staples and supplies from their employers," plunging them into a cycle of debt in an early version of the sharecropping system that would trap former slaves and their descendants for impoverished generations to come.

Poston also bore witness to the first efforts of West Tennessee blacks to educate themselves. "There is but one school in my district that I have any knowledge of," he reported in May 1867, "and that is in Brownsville & numbers 42 students taught by Miss Harriett A. Turner. There is quite a number of children being taught the alphabet & speling & some few to read by the white families." Though he found "nothing that would amount to even Plantation Schools," he did know of "a very thrifty little country school in the northern portion of Haywood County taught by a colored man." But in early April "the house was burned & the school broken up" by a party of "Guerillas or out laws who have been prowling about in Gibson, Dyer, & the northern portion of Haywood County for several months & have committed many outrages upon freedmen in those counties" before Poston arrived in Brownsville to take up his duties. "While a majority of the white people claim to favor the education of the freed people, yet there is such a strong prejudice against [it] by one class of citizens & so few that take any active interest in it that it is almost impossible to organize or carry on any school out of Brownsville." Though there were some districts in Haywood County "where there is a strong loyal sentiment which favors freed mans schools," their opponents were "strong enough to deter any person from engaging in it" because prospective teachers could not "feel safe in their person."

Poston watched as the resurgent tide of white power eroded the freedmen's rights. Though most of the courts in Poston's district gave the freedmen "a fair & impartial trial," whites prevented African Americans "from applying to the courts" or the bureau "for a redress of wrongs by threats of violence," thereby forcing freedmen "to compromise for a trifle."

Poston feared that in areas of his district beyond the bureau's effective reach, emancipated blacks would be allowed to vote only "as their employers or a few ruffians may desire. I hear frequently of threats against those who may take any part in elections & it is to be found that those threats will be carried into execution."

His superior, Captain James Kendrick, warned Poston that the planters in his district intended to run their workers off their plantations in order to prevent them from voting in the elections that August. During the election, "small squads" of ex-Confederates gathered to "drive off or cruelly punish freedmen," and Poston was directed to arrest all such "lawless characters and have them brought to a speedy trial." Poston was to keep careful records of evictions, do his utmost to educate the freedmen about their rights, and urge them to vote, "whatever the immediate consequences may be." Should any freedmen be evicted, the bureau pledged to take care of them until they could find other employment.[5]

After the bureau was dismantled, Poston spent the rest of his life as a farmer and served for a time as Haywood County clerk. Though his own claim would be denied, he testified on behalf of his men's claims to a pension.[6]

———————————

As Congress wrestled with Reconstruction, Fort Pillow was invoked to counter the Democrats' argument that the United States was intended to be "a white man's government." When black soldiers "stood on picket on the cold, stormy night to guard you against surprise," asked a New Hampshire congressman, "did you creep up and warm their congealing blood with an infusion of the 'white man's Government?' . . . 'White man's Government,' do you say? Go to Fort Pillow; stand upon its ramparts and in its trenches, and recall the horrid butchery of the black man there because he had joined you against rebellion, and then say, if you will, 'This is the white man's Government.'"[7]

Fort Pillow was even invoked by the temperance movement. "Did we not charge upon the head of that confederacy, aye, upon the whole confederacy itself," asked a teetotaling delegate to Michigan's constitutional convention, "the assault upon Fort Pillow, and many of the similar crimes which were committed by those marauding and plundering chiefs? Why? Because they were acting under the commission, under the license, call it what you will, of that confederacy, and we and the civilized world held the confederacy responsible. Now what do we ask here? We ask that if certain men in our state shall go on serving intoxicating drinks, the State of Michigan shall not be held responsible for it."[8]

"In the center of the parade ground," a reporter for the *Memphis Argus* reported from Fort Pillow in September 1865, "there still stands the lofty pole from which, on that fateful morning, waved the stars and stripes of the Republic. The pole is bare now, and leans over toward the ditch as if still weeping over relics of the slain." Scattered throughout the fort he came upon "the debris of hats, boots, and clothing mixed with the whitening bones of their wearers. The fort and ditch are all overgrown with weeds," the reporter continued. On one headboard he saw "the name and fate of one, who had left the waving prairies of Iowa to fight his country's battles." Otherwise "no vestige of any of the buildings now remain, except the blackened posts that supported them, and the charred fragments of timbers that once constituted a part of the happy homes of inhabitants now scattered and gone."[9]

Perhaps it was the *Argus*'s bleak description of exposed bones that prompted Stanton to order the army to see to it that the bodies of the Federal dead at Fort Pillow were "properly cared for." Two days before Christmas, the Union army contracted with a Memphis undertaker to exhume, casket, and bury the bodies of the Fort Pillow dead, at a rate of seven dollars per corpse. On December 12, the army asked Mrs. Booth to leave her current home in Cincinnati and return to Fort Pillow to identify the remains of the 6th USCHA's dead. Assistant Quartermaster W. J. Colburn detailed a detachment of the 11th USCI, which now contained remnants of the 6th USCHA, to assist in the burial. An agent reported that at Fulton and Fort Pillow the graves of about three hundred soldiers were still distinguishable, but only about eighty of them—mostly men who had died under Wolfe's regime—had headboards. A Mr. Lea, to whom a disillusioned Edward Benton had apparently deeded his land, now sold to the army a forty-thousand-square-foot patch fifty yards southwest of the parapet to serve as a cemetery for the garrison's fallen, and contracted to build a picket fence around it.[10]

In January 1866, the army began to search what remained of the 13th's regimental records for the names of the fallen. But Mrs. Booth had still not come down to help identify the bodies of black troops. By mid-February, Assistant Quartermaster Colburn ran out of patience and asked permission to begin work without her, for he "could obtain as much information from men who were present at the massacre and whose services may be obtained as could be furnished by Mrs. Booth."[11]

Local people assisted in locating bodies and graves, and by April 9, three days shy of the massacre's second anniversary, Colburn and his crew had exhumed or recovered the bodies of 124 blacks and 134 whites that were found "scattered over a large area." They reburied them separately: the blacks in the western half of the cemetery, the whites to the east. Everyone acknowledged that these 258 graves did not represent all of the victims at Fort Pillow, for in addition to the disappearance of the bodies of the men who were shot in the river, Colburn reported that "nearly all the bodies of men who had been killed under the bluff and next to the river have been washed away by the high water during the past year." Among the bodies recovered, Colburn asserted, was that of Major Booth, "which was supposed to have been removed from its first resting place." But Booth's corpse was among those likely to have been washed away, and several men testified that the body Colburn claimed to be Booth's appeared to them to be the remains of a black.

Each grave was marked by a numbered oak stake corresponding to a list of the dead. But the bodies had been buried so shallowly that no blacks and only forty-one whites were actually identified, all but five of them Indianans, Iowans, New Yorkers, and civilians from the first Union garrison. Colburn had accomplished his mission at a cost of $2,145.65. But when an inspector from the quartermaster's office visited the cemetery, he saw that cows had broken through the feeble picket gates and grazed among the graves. "Little can be said in commendation of the work," he wrote. "As a temporary expedient to save the bodies from being washed away to protect them from destruction it can be tolerated, but as a permanent structure worth the martyred heroes, who have been laid within the enclosure, it is wholly inappropriate." Since, under the circumstances, "it would not be strange, if wanton desecration should be committed," he urged "the ultimate removal of those bodies to some larger and permanent cemetery to be established on the Mississippi river below."[12]

In January 1883, Ike Revelle, brother of Cordy and Hardy Revelle, would write his congressman to deplore the condition of the Federal graves at Fort Pillow. The letter was forwarded to Secretary of War Robert Lincoln, the late president's son, who gently replied that in fact the graveyard was empty, for all the bodies had been removed in 1866 and reinterred in a special "Fort Pillow Section" of the Memphis National Cemetery. Some black Memphians, however, insist that only the whites were buried at Memphis, and that the blacks were buried in a ditch just shy of the city where, in the mid-twentieth century, a road crew excavating for a highway came upon their remains.[13]

Fort Pillow itself was gradually stripped of artifacts from the garrison's fall. Hobbyists searched the ground for memorabilia; local black children dug minié balls out of the bluff and employed them as fishing weights. In August 1889, the town of Covington employed a six mule team festooned with flags to haul a nine-foot, six-thousand-pound spiked rebel cannon all the way from Fort Pillow. The old cannon was deposited in the courthouse yard, where it was installed as a monument to the Confederate dead. Not to be outdone, in 1906 the citizens of Ripley hauled away the last of Fort Pillow's spiked guns for display on their own courthouse square. But eventually Covington's gun was hauled off in a scrap drive during World War I, as was Ripley's during World War II.[14]

The Mississippi did its part in erasing evidence of the battle. By 1908, it had undercut the bluff so deeply that a huge section collapsed into the river. "The rending and groaning as the landslide took place was heard for miles," wrote the *Bolivar Bulletin,* "and caused consternation among the negroes of the vicinity." As it crumbled into the river, it caused an enormous wave that rolled across the river and beached the houseboats moored along the Arkansas shore. By 1930, the river had side-wound half a mile from the foot of the bluff, and a cottonwood forest had sprung up where the worst of the massacre transpired. "The flat top of the hill on which the guns were mounted that faced the river does not contain at present more than two acres of land," wrote a visitor. "This is now a cotton patch and the narrow valleys between these high ridges have been cleared and are in cultivation."[15]

In 1970, the state of Tennessee surveyed 1,242 acres of farmland and wasteland along the first Chickasaw Bluff and a year later purchased and dedicated the parcel as Fort Pillow State Park. Under the supervision of a young archaeologist named Robert Mainfort, the state initiated a dig aimed at locating and preserving the principal sites of the battle, and it is thanks to his efforts that an accurate picture of the fort can be approximated. The state's efforts protected the site from scavengers and developers, but not from the river, which in the spring of 1979 washed away another twenty-five acres. "We're losing park land to the river," the park's superintendent said, "in gulps and gobbles."[16]

"DELIVER ME FROM BLOODGUILTINESS"

FORREST

From 1865

Thirty-seven years after Forrest's death, deep in the era of Jim Crow, the white establishment in Memphis literally and figuratively resurrected the Wizard, disinterring his remains and burying him and his wife on a grassy city square they dubbed Forrest Park. On May 16, 1905, with thirty thousand Memphians looking on, the city's new white elite unveiled a handsome, life-size equestrian statue of Forrest. According to the *Memphis Commercial Appeal* the dedication was "one of the proudest moments of Peace," and marked the consolidation of white hegemony in West Tennessee.[1]

"It may be only a mirage of a war-loving brain that peoples the park again with spectral men in ghostly garb," the editorialist conceded, but white Memphians would be comforted by a depiction of Forrest as "that leader whose iron hand held the reins of safety over the South when Northern dominion apotheosized the negro and set misrule and devastation to humiliate a proud race."[2]

After Forrest's centenary in 1921, the Tennessee legislature made the Wizard's birthday a state holiday. In the summer of 1940, the *Memphis Commercial Appeal* favorably compared Hitler's blitzkrieg to Forrest's tactics. What Forrest did "on horses," the paper declared, "the Germans are doing in planes and tanks." But a year later, Northern National Guardsmen protested naming a Tullahoma, Tennessee, training facility after Forrest, citing his actions at Fort Pillow. Under the glare of the nation's spotlight, Memphians began once more to swell the crowds at Forrest Park to celebrate the general's birth and honor his sole grandchild, Mary Forrest Bradley, a large-boned ringer for her great-grandmother Mariam and the keeper of the

Wizard's bloodstained saber. But by the time of the civil rights movement of the 1950s and 1960s, Forrest had become a symbol of white supremacy.[3]

After Martin Luther King's assassination in Memphis, the local black community managed to have the Confederate flag removed from Forrest Park, and the Tennessee legislature erased Bedford's birthday from the state's holiday calendar. The community demanded more, however, and by 1988, a movement was afoot to demand the removal of Forrest's statue and the renaming of Forrest Park.[4]

Most prominent among Forrest's defenders was the novelist and historian Shelby Foote, who first expressed his admiration of Forrest as "the most man in the world" in his novel *Shiloh*; then in the third volume of his brilliant narrative history of the Civil War; and later, in his famous commentaries for Ken Burns's PBS series *The Civil War*. In interviews, Foote contended that Forrest had been not only a kindly slave trader but a force for moderation in the Ku Klux Klan. "The day that black people admire Forrest as much as I do," he declared, "is the day when they will be free and equal, for they will have gotten prejudice out of their minds as we whites are trying to get it out of ours." But local black leaders suggested that perhaps the esteemed Mr. Foote might keep trying a little harder. They inverted his prescription by suggesting that not until Foote had discarded his boyish worship of Forrest would he have rid himself of the racist prejudice that still oppressed the descendants of the Wizard's victims.

The *Southern Partisan* responded to the attack on Forrest Park by warning that, if pushed too far, the Wizard himself "may just come roaring out of the grave one day, eyes flashing, teeth clenched—and then you will see some well-fed, middle-aged black men run like they haven't run in years, on their way to catch the train to Yonkers, to confront the challenge"—presumably Northern racism—"they have so cravenly avoided for so long."[5]

In 1995, in defiance of black protesters, an enormous statue of Forrest seated on a rearing charger—said by its fabricator to be the largest equestrian statue in the world—was unveiled in the privately owned Confederate Flag Park near Brentwood, Tennessee, within unavoidable sight of Interstate 65. Disproportionate, bug-eyed, painted in glossy lacquer like an oversized toy soldier, it is surely the ugliest statue ever erected to a Civil War general, which is saying something. Black leaders in Tennessee decried this "overblown yard art" as another monument to Southern racism.[6]

The *Nashville Tennessean* tried to balance its coverage of the statue's dedication "so it would not seem that it was only whites who supported the NBF memorial, or only blacks who opposed it," wrote an observer, but "the skew of opinions clearly seemed to fall along those lines."[7]

Whether as a symbol of white pride, frontier pluck, or military genius, Forrest remained at the turn of the twenty-first century the defiant, hell-for-leather poster boy of the Lost Cause, and at Southern barbecues and re-enactments appeared on five times as many T-shirts as did Robert E. Lee.[8]

In May 1865, Forrest had ridden home with his battle-hardened son Will and tried to return to the quiet life of a planter. But rumors continued to circulate in the papers that he had fled the country, was organizing another uprising, or was in hiding from a government bent on punishing him for his atrocities. Stories circulated that he intended to drive west and south and conquer Mexico, and indeed the idea seemed to have intrigued him briefly, and may have been what lured his brother Bill to Texas, where he eventually died in a gunfight. Forrest claimed to have been promised twenty thousand muskets and thirty thousand men with which to conquer the country in six months, appoint military governors, and serve as king or president, whereupon he intended to open Mexico to immigration from Europe and the South. But that particular fever passed, and he published letters protesting his innocence and declaring his intention to stay in the country and "contribute all my influence toward strengthening the Government, sustaining its credit, and uniting the people once more in the indissoluble bonds of peace and affection." On March 13, seven days after Lincoln's deadline for his capture and indictment had passed, Forrest and his friends posted ten thousand dollars' bond to ensure his appearance September 3 in the United States Circuit Court for the District of West Tennessee to answer a charge of treason. After the arrest of a Confederate admiral, Forrest's friends told him he would surely be next and urged him to flee. "This is my country," he replied. "I am hard at work upon my plantation, and carefully observing the obligations of my parole. If the Federal government does not regard it, they'll be sorry. I shan't go away." On his next trip to Memphis, he decided to settle the matter once and for all, bursting into the adjutant general's office and demanding that the authorities put up or shut up. They shut up, and Forrest returned to his plantation, but it would not be until 1868 that a lame-duck Andrew Johnson formally dropped all charges.[9]

During the war, Forrest had poured much of his slave-trading fortune into equipping and supplying his men. Consequently he had little capital left to invest in his Mississippi plantation. Only eighteen of his former slaves abandoned him, but in late March, in the midst of a cholera epidemic, he weakened his hold on the rest by axing to death a former slave named Thomas Edwards. Forrest claimed that upon entering Edwards's cabin he

had caught him in the act of beating his wife; when Forrest tried to inter-
vene, Edwards attacked him with a knife.

Edwards's fellow blacks did not regard Forrest as Mrs. Edwards's deliv-
erer. Notoriously cruel—he once whipped a mule to death—Edwards was
nonetheless the leader of Forrest's labor force, and apparently just before
the encounter he had defied Forrest's order to drain a puddle behind his
house and stomped off to his cabin.

Perhaps this act of disobedience from a former slave was the last straw
for the Wizard of the Saddle. In any case, as his field hands lit bonfires and
surrounded the general's house to prevent his escape, it must have seemed
to Forrest like the ultimate nightmare of a servile insurrection. The general
armed and barricaded himself inside his house and greeted with relief the
arrival of a deputy to arrest him. Forrest was released on ten thousand dollars' bail, and though Edwards's wife testified that she had not been attacked, and another eyewitness could not testify to seeing a knife in
Edwards's hand, Forrest was exonerated, largely because the white judge
made sure that his charge to the jury was so narrowly framed that they had
no choice but to believe his plea of self-defense.[10]

Describing himself as "ruined by the war," Forrest sold off his land in
Mississippi and returned to Memphis to open an insurance agency. But his
fortunes continued to plummet. He joined in ill-fated partnerships with other
ruined Confederates, founded an insurance company that soon failed, joined
a Memphis street-paving firm, and by February was entirely bankrupt.[11]

––––––––––

In June 1868, the Wizard attended the Democratic National Convention as
a delegate-at-large from Tennessee. The mere sight of him in fighting lather
was still enough to send men flying. As his train paused for water en route
to New York, a local man burst into Forrest's car, vowing to thrash the
"butcher" of Fort Pillow. Forrest "bounded from his seat, and demanded to
know what the man wanted. Though taller and heavier than Forrest, he
could only gape and stammer at the sight of the general marching toward
him down the aisle. To the cheering of a local crowd that had assembled
outside, the man turned on his heels and fled."[12]

During his visit to New York, a woman awakened him by banging her
umbrella on his hotel-room door and demanding to know if it was true he
had killed "those dear colored people at Fort Pillow."

"Yes, madam," he blearily replied, standing in his bedclothes. "I killed
the men and women for my soldiers' dinner and ate the babies myself for
breakfast."[13]

Later, as Forrest stood on the convention platform after Samuel Tilden was nominated to run for the presidency against Ulysses S. Grant, a man pointed up at him from the crowd and shouted, "There is the butcher of Fort Pillow!"

Forrest rushed forward and pointed back at the man. "I have seen such men as you before," he snarled. "They were not in the war. If you will step down here in front of this stand, I'll give you a beating." But before the heckler could advance or retreat, a cadre of former Union soldiers had dragged him away.[14]

During the presidential campaign of 1868, Forrest became a target of political cartoonist Thomas Nast. Inventor of the Republican elephant, the Democratic donkey, and the American image of Santa Claus, Nast recognized an archetype when he saw one, and in his cartoons depicted Forrest as the very model of a recalcitrant, racist Southern Democrat fatuously cultivating the votes of his former slaves.[15]

In words that suggest that Major Anderson was still assisting his old commander as a ghostwriter, Forrest wrote to Andrew Johnson that he was aware "that I am at this moment regarded in large communities at the north with abhorrence, as a detestable monster, ruthless and swift to take life, and guilty of unpardonable crimes in connection with the capture of Fort Pillow." He said he was not surprised by "this misjudgment of my conduct and character; nevertheless, it pains and mortifies me greatly." But to cool the heated political atmosphere in Tennessee, he was "still willing to rest for a time longer under this heavy, wounding weight of undeserved obloquy." Eventually he intended to provide posterity with a "complete refutation" of the "ex parte proceedings" of Wade and Gooch's investigation, "with their manifestly leading questions and willing witnesses whose prompted evidence should, thenceforward, mislead no one." But he would "throw off the load of these widely believed and injurious calumnies," he told Johnson, only when it would not "in the least contribute to those sectional animosities which now rend the country." In the meantime he was willing to "waive all immunity from investigation into my conduct at Fort Pillow." But it never came to that.[16]

Though he would deny it before a congressional committee, it was not long after the war that Forrest added another item to his dismal civilian résumé. By May 1866, a number of ex-slaves had settled at Fort Pickering under the protection of one of the black regiments that the Union authorities had assigned the task of enforcing martial law in the city. Memphis's primarily

Irish police force bitterly resented their patrols, and as black troops were mustered out and disarmed, the police sought them out in the saloons of the black district and began to make arrests, severely beating several soldiers with their nightsticks.

The Southern press claimed that on May 21, a large body of blacks were incited to riot by "the teachings of Northern 'school marm's' in the nigger schools" and turned on the police, killing one of them.[17] But a congressional inquiry determined that they had merely gathered to protest the brutal treatment their comrades had received. After shots rang out from somewhere, a white mob armed with knives and revolvers began to rampage through Memphis's black neighborhoods, robbing and torching houses and murdering their inhabitants. The next day, in broad daylight, black men, women, and children were shot down "as if they were mad dogs," wrote an observer. "The sick were murdered in their beds—a young lady of rare promise as a teacher, & who had worked hard to get an education, undertook to flee [but] was met in her doorway, shot down—pushed back into the house, & the house set on fire." For the next two nights, Memphis was "brilliantly illuminated" by the flames from four black churches, twelve schools, and ninety houses. A local Northern mission to the freedmen lost $2,000 worth of property; the black community, $110,000. "This nation has set the black man free with the bayonet," wrote a Freedmen's Bureau agent. "Then let the nation if needs be protect his life with the same weapon."[18]

That fall, Forrest decided to meet the threat to white hegemony by joining—according to some accounts, founding—the Ku Klux Klan. He evidently saw the Klan as "a damned good thing," as he reportedly told one organizer, that they could use "to keep the niggers in their place." In October 1866, he attended a Klan meeting in Nashville at the Maxwell House Hotel, where he was elected Grand Wizard and commander of the Grand Dragons of the Realms: the chief arbiter of questions of "paramount importance." "He had done as much as any other man," declared an admirer, "to draw together into a compact resisting mass, soldiers of a thousand resisting battlefields, and he held them there until our civilization had been preserved, until some questions were settled, and until the Southern people"—white Southern people—"got control of their own states."[19]

In the spring of 1867, Forrest and his dragons launched a campaign of midnight parades; "ghost" masquerades; and "whipping" and even "killing Negro voters, to scare blacks off voting and running for office." By early June the Klan had established "realms" in Columbia, Franklin, Shelbyville, and Nashville, and was making headway in Gallatin and Pulaski as well. On

June 5, the Klan staged an enormous parade through the streets of Pulaski, marching in formation to the commands of a "Grand Cyclops" who blew on a mournful sounding horn. Its displays would recall the wartime stratagems of its Grand Wizard; marching through towns in a show of strength, Klansmen would wheel around from the front of their processions, gallop back down side streets, and rejoin their comrades at the rear, creating the impression of a never ending flow.[20]

"Of this order I was a loyal member," wrote John Carroll of the 21st Tennessee Cavalry, "and woe unto the insolent negro or turbulent white man who incurred its displeasure!" In Maury County gangs of Klansmen careened around the countryside, disarming Unionists, lashing blacks with hickory sticks, driving off the Northern missionaries and newly literate young African Americans who ventured out into the countryside to establish black schools. In late February 1868, Klansmen rode among the mourners at the funeral of a white man allegedly murdered by a black. The next day twenty of them entered the jail in Columbia, dragged out the accused, and hanged him from a tree. In Pulaski, one hundred Klansmen caught a black man accused of raping a white woman and left his bullet-ridden body in the street. In mid-July 1868, Klansmen made their first midnight parade through Memphis itself. Dressing in white hoods and gowns and silencing the clatter of their horses' shoes by wrapping their hooves in cloth, they terrorized the black section of town, sending scores of freedmen fleeing as if "the Devil himself were pursuing them." Though Forrest and his fellow Klansmen agreed to abide by emancipation, they urged the restoration "of a white man's government" and deplored "negro supremacy" and the enfranchisement of blacks as a "political crime" that would destroy both races.[21]

"I look for another war," Forrest wrote, "unless the people can be brought to a better understanding." With whip and gun, Forrest's followers were proving more successful during Reconstruction than during the war itself in upholding the old order: intimidating blacks and Yankees of both the imported and homegrown varieties and establishing the South as a bastion of white supremacy. During the election of 1868, Klan members rode through Giles, Lincoln, Franklin, Weakly, and Shelby counties, murdering one black and threatening anyone they could find who was even considering voting Republican. In Coffee County, the Klan gave a black man two hundred lashes for voting Republican, and so terrified black voters that Grant's plurality was significantly reduced. As Forrest's old friend and fellow Klansman Judge J. P. Young recalled, "squads of the K.K.K. went to the polls and dared the soldiers to molest them. Every Democrat who was 21 was legally voted and no protests made by the carpetbaggers. Ten days after the election, the Klan was disbanded by Gen. Forrest, because we knew it would not be needed again."[22]

"When you see men, things or demons on your premises, claiming to be me," read a Klan circular in Wilson County, "shoot them down, for you may be certain that we are not there." But masked riders continued to haunt the countryside. In Overton County they attacked African Americans in the streets, and after a white was killed in the altercation that followed, masked riders returned the next day and disemboweled his alleged slayer. They burned down freedmen's schools and churches, killed at least one school-teacher, and whipped and chased off scores more. Klansmen demanding "fried nigger meat" were fired upon and driven out of Shelbyville by the friends of a white schoolteacher the Klan had whipped the previous July. At Columbia, Klansmen dragged a Unionist detective off a train and lynched him, and even some of the most restrained members kept their paraphernalia in readiness for some future emergency. In 1871, Forrest testified coyly before a congressional committee investigating the Klan's activities. He denied ever having been a member, let alone the leader, and claimed that everything he knew about it was mere hearsay. "I lied like a gentleman," he confided afterward to a friend.[23]

One effect of the Klan's campaign was that the black survivors of the Fort Pillow massacre were afraid to reveal their service in the Union army. Long after the war a white resident of Rupellville, Alabama, named Robert A. Wardlaw would write the commissioner of pensions regarding Charles Mullins's fear of reprisals by former Confederate soldiers in the neighborhood. "This old colored soldier is peculiarly situated," Wardlaw reported. "Confederate soldiers living here threaten to finish up the work so nearly done at Ft. Pillow. To say the least of it, he is very timid, and we have a few reckless ex confederette soldiers" in the area who were "much opposed to Federal soldiers having Pensions and colored soldiers in particular." Black Union veterans lived in terror of "violence from a few bad and reckless men of our country," several of whom were said to have taken part "in the Confederate massacre at Ft. Pillow."[24]

Alarmed by the increasing number of former slaves emigrating north, Forrest began to envision a Southern labor force of African and Chinese immigrants. He saw no need for "a war of races," he said, for he wanted "the whole country to prosper." Indeed, by late 1868, Forrest began to alienate his die-hard compatriots with his tentative support for limited black enfranchisement and his pragmatic and entrepreneurial courtship of carpetbaggers and Unionists.

After an abortive term as president of the failing Selma, Marion, and Memphis Railroad, Forrest's setbacks seemed to seep into him. He became increasingly irascible, and once threatened to shoot his tailor "like a rat" for allowing moths to damage his suit. Disillusioned by his failed railroad venture, he volunteered his services and those of thousands of his former raiders to fight in Cuba. The prospect of Nathan Bedford Forrest and his men descending on Cubans frightened Republicans, but in the process of politely turning him down, Sherman called Forrest "one of the most extraordinary men developed by our civil war," and expected that if he did serve "he would fight against our national enemies as vehemently as he did against us, and that is saying enough."

In Trenton, Tennessee, in September 1873, after two white men had refused to pay for their servings at a black barbecue, outraged freedmen threatened to burn the town to the ground. A white posse arrested sixteen black men, whereupon about seventy-five whites—many of them die-hard renegade Klansmen—rode into town, dragged the blacks from jail, killed or mortally wounded six of them on Trenton's outskirts, and executed the remainder in the countryside. Forrest, who regarded white Reconstructionists as his primary foe, condemned the murders, and at an "indignation meeting" attended by Jefferson Davis declared that if he had the authority he would "exterminate the white marauders who disgrace their race by this cowardly murder of negroes." But the outrages continued. A black country schoolteacher named Julia Hayden was shot to death by masked marauders, and many country schools were burned to the ground. The Klan's depredations precipitated a sharp decline in enrollment at Nashville's Fisk University, the freedmen's school that strove to become the emblem of an egalitarian future for a reconstructed South, but was now an imperiled outpost of a dream white Americans North and South were fast discarding. In September 1874, Fisk's president reported a "reign of terror and blood in the state" that was "sad and fearful."[25]

In 1875, Forrest received a special dispensation from the city of Memphis to farm on President's Island, the former contraband camp where so many of his victims' families had languished during the war. To collect a workforce, he added yet another entry to his civilian résumé by pioneering the hiring of convicts from the state of Tennessee. Under conditions worse than anything that had obtained on his plantation in slavery times, Forrest incarcerated seventy-eight black and thirty-nine white prisoners in abandoned Federal buildings and put them to work on 1,300 leased acres. The island proved pestilential, and Forrest was so beset with recurrent fevers and debilitating bouts of diarrhea that at times he could hardly stand. His work gangs were composed of not just criminals but former slaves and Republican agitators scooped up by the city's police, and rumors spread through Memphis that Forrest had resorted in extremis to the lash.[26]

The election of 1876 that brought Rutherford B. Hayes into office saw such widespread intimidation of black and Unionist voters that it cost the Republicans perhaps a quarter million Southern votes. Claiming he was saving the country from a second civil war, Hayes agreed to remove Federal troops from the South in exchange for the Southern states' certification of his election. Thus did the Republicans reward the Klan's campaign of terror by giving away the South and leaving the matter of black enfranchisement to white Democrats.

Worn out by war, humiliated by defeat, nagged by persistent accusations about his role at Fort Pillow, Forrest turned, at his wife's urging, to the Bible. He became so unnaturally "mild," as one of his old comrades reported, that his men could hardly recognize him. Forrest had never been a practicing Christian. Once, during the war, he had remarked to an evangelizing officer that he didn't have time for religion while there was so much unholy fighting to do. But in his frailty he grew penitent and once burst into tears after a sermon, likening himself to the text's man who "built his house upon the sand." That night, after meditating on Psalm 51—"Deliver me from bloodguiltiness, O God, thou God of my salvation"—he emerged satisfied that "all is right," for he had "put my trust in my Redeemer." His faith seemed to affect him so much that his benignity disturbed the old comrades who visited him. One even went so far as to observe that the old warhorse now displayed "the gentleness of expression, the voice and manner of a woman." When a former aide suggested to Forrest that he didn't seem to be "the same man I used to know so well," the old rage flickered briefly.

"I hope I am a *better* man," Forrest snarled, grabbing his aide by the lapels. "I've joined the church and am *trying* to live a Christian life."

Anticipating Alabama governor George Wallace's ambiguous change of heart over a century later, Forrest defied, as he put it, the "jeers and sneers of a few white people" to attend an African American picnic in 1875, where he declared that he and his black audience "may differ in color but not in sentiment." Black and white came from "the same soil, breathe the same air, live in the same land," he said, so "why should we not be brothers and sisters?" He promised to "do all in my power to elevate every man" and "depress none," and declared himself "with you in heart and in hand."[27]

He was apparently sincere, at least to the extent that he had come to think of blacks as fellow Southerners (if of a decidedly inferior sort) who could help their former masters cast out "white radicals," as he called them. "I shall not shoot any negroes so long as I can see a white radical to shoot," he once declared, threatening that if all-out war returned to Memphis, "not one of them would get out of this town alive." Black and white were becoming "as one people, having a common interest," Forrest assured some Yankee investors he hoped to interest in yet another railroad scheme. He called on blacks to "stand by the men who raised you, who nursed you when you were sick, and who took care of you when you were little children." If they stood by their former masters, Forrest promised, "we will always stand by you, and do as much for you as any white man can do for you."[28]

In these his sunset years, however, it was said that Forrest made it a practice never to frequent the same black barber twice in succession for fear that between shaves one of them might muster the courage to slit his throat. In the double log cabin he had erected on his pestiferous island farm, Nathan Bedford Forrest wasted away to one hundred pounds. "Just here, I have an indescribable peace," he had told a visiting preacher from his deathbed, pointing to his breast with a skeletal finger. "I have led a life of strife and violence," he remarked as his life ebbed away. "I now want to die at peace with all men." According to a friend, his last words were "I trust not in what I have done, but in the Captain of my salvation."[29] Nathan Bedford Forrest died on October 29, 1877, at the age of fifty-six.

At his funeral, Jefferson Davis served as a pallbearer and expressed his regret that he had not recognized Forrest's genius earlier. Many whites took comfort in the fact that about five hundred black people came out for Forrest's funeral, and that several who were approached by Forrest's admirers expressed their respect for him.

Considering the fact that by 1877 African Americans made up almost half of the city's population, five hundred was not a large number, and no one knows exactly what compelled them to attend. Some may have turned up to greet imprisoned relatives from Forrest's plantation as they shuffled by "in convict garb." Others may have come out of respect, perhaps, but just as likely out of curiosity, relief, or a need to make damn sure that the former slave catcher, slave trader, scourge of Fort Pillow, Grand Wizard of the Ku Klux Klan, and pioneering convict-labor contractor was at long last dead.[30]

NOTES

Letters, special orders, and memoranda are given as author/recipient, order number, or title: date, source.

Volume and page numbers for multivolume sources that are available on CD or the Web are not included here because a researcher can use search engines.

All Web addresses begin with http:// unless otherwise indicated.

Abbreviations
Notes and sources contain the following abbreviations:

AMA   American Missionary Association (Microfilm at TSLA)

AS   *The American Slave: A Composite Autobiography,* George P. Rawick (Westport, CT, 1972–1979; CD version by MyFamily.Com)

BRFAL   Records of the Bureau of Refugees, Freedmen and Abandoned Lands (NARA)

CDF   Courtesy of Derek Frisby

CV   *Confederate Veteran*

CWAL   *The Collected Works of Abraham Lincoln,* ed. Roy P. Basler, 8 vols. and index (New Brunswick, NJ, 1953)

CWD   *The Civil War Dictionary,* Mark Mayo Boatner (New York, 1991)

CWH   *Civil War History Magazine*

FBP   Frederick Bancroft Papers (Columbia University, New York, NY)

FU   Fisk University (Nashville, TN)

LC   Library of Congress (Washington, DC)

MHCD   *Medical Histories of Confederate Generals,* Jack D. Welsh (Kent, OH, 1995)

MHUD   *Medical Histories of Union Generals.* Jack D. Welsh (Kent, OH, 1995)

MPL   Memphis Public Library (Memphis, TN)

NARA   National Archives and Records Administration (Washington, DC, and Seattle, WA)

NFWW *Naval Forces on Western Waters* (cdl.library.cornell.edu/moa/browse.
monographs/waro.html)

NPSSSS National Park Service Soldiers and Sailors System (www.itd.nps.gov/
cwss/)

OATTR Online Archive of Terry's Texas Rangers (www.terrystexasrangers.com)

OCA Oberlin College Archives (Oberlin, OH)

OK Oklahoma

ORCW *Official Records of the Civil War* (United States War Department,
Washington, DC, 1880–1901) (cdl.library.cornell.edu/moa/browse.monographs/
waro.html)

RJSCW *Reports of the Committee on the Conduct of the War: Fort Pillow Massacre
and Returned Prisoners* (United States Senate, Joint Subcommittee on the
Conduct of the War, Washington, DC, 1864)

RMC Robert Mainfort Collection (Privately held)

SHC/UNCCH Southern History Collection, University of North Carolina at
Chapel Hill

SHSP *Southern Historical Society Papers*

ST *Slave Testimony: Two Centuries of Letters, Speeches, Interviews and Autobiographies,* John W. Blassingame (Baton Rouge, 1977)

TCW *Tennesseeans in the Civil War,* 2 vols., Civil War Centennial Commission of
Tennessee (Nashville, 1964)

TCWVQ *Tennessee Civil War Veterans Questionnaires,* eds. Gustave W. Dyer and
John Trotwood Moore (Easley, SC, 1985)

THQ *Tennessee Historical Quarterly*

TSLA Tennessee State Library and Archives (Nashville, TN)

UHS *Unwritten History of Slavery: Autobiographical Account of Negro Ex-Slaves,*
Ophelia Egypt (Nashville, TN, 1945)

VT Virginia Tech, Special Collections Department, University Libraries (Blacks-
burg, VA)

WTHSP *West Tennessee Historical Society Papers*

"This Unnatural War": West Tennessee: 1682–1864

1. "had gone unanswered . . ." Henry, *The Story of the Confederacy,* p. 3.
2. "I am naturally anti-slavery . . ." Lincoln/A. G. Hodges: April 4, 1864, in *CWAL.*
3. "Abraham Lincoln . . ." Anonymous couplet in Silver, ed., *Mississippi in the
Confederacy,* p. 279.
4. Tilly, "Aspects of Social and Economic Life in West Tennessee before the Civil
War," pp. 7, 20.
5. Peters, *Lauderdale County,* p. 4; Goodspeed, *Lauderdale County History.*
6. Mills, "Fort Pillow"; Peters, *Lauderdale County,* p. 5.
7. Q'master Claims in Peters, *Lauderdale County;* Samuel B. and Hattie Lanier
File, RG 124 (Court of Claims) in NARA.
8. E. H. Wolfe/Henry Binmore: September 13, 1863, in 52nd Regiment Indiana
Infantry, Regimental Letters Sent in NARA; J. T. Jett/L. Polk: September 21,
1861 (RMC).
9. Henry, *"First with the Most" Forrest,* pp. 250–251; Officer of 2nd Tennessee Cavalry (CSA) in *Charleston Mercury,* May 2, 1864.

10. Mitchell Lafayette Davidson in *TCWVQ*; M. B. Dinwiddie in ibid. See also James D. Davis in Ballard, "James Dick Davis."

11. Mississippi's agent was state attorney general Thomas J. Wharton, who toured central and West Tennessee, warning that "at no distant day" the Republican Party would "inaugurate the reign of equality of all races and colors, and the universality of the elective franchise." Alabama's emissary warned Tennesseans that Republican policy would rob Southerners of not only their property and their liberty, but "the sacred purity of our daughters." With these sentiments they echoed every one of their counterparts who fanned out across the Upper South to fulminate before state legislatures and conventions, congregations and assemblies. (Thomas J. Wharton and Leroy Pope Walker in Dew, *Apostles of Disunion*, pp. 22, 27, 77–80; Felix Kirk Zollicoffer in *ORCW*.)

12. *New York Herald*, December 4, 1861; Burt, "Civil War Letters."

Bedford: Nathan Bedford Forrest: 1821–1864

1. "With his powerful frame . . ." Maury, *Recollections of a Virginian*, p. 208. "To another . . ." Hurst, *Nathan Bedford Forrest*, p. 247.

2. Mrs. Irby Morgan recalled how exhilarated Forrest was by the number of Yankees his sharpshooters killed. "After the battle he said he counted sixty killed in one place, and called on Col. Kelley to know if that was the number. He said their execution was wonderful and fearful to contemplate, the number killed was so great." (Morgan, *How It Was*, pp. 22–23.) Early on, Forrest threatened to hang eight captive Unionist ministers, "all on one pole," unless Illinois released some imprisoned Kentucky secessionists. (Montgomery, *Reminiscences*, p. 225.)

3. Blanton, "Forrest's Old Regiment."

4. Chalmers, "Lieutenant General Nathan Bedford Forrest."

5. Another of Buchanan's secretaries, Jacob Thompson of the Interior Department, was also accused of subverting the Union before slipping down the Atlantic coast as a secessionist commissioner to North Carolina in December 1860.

6. James R. Miles in *TCWVQ*.

7. Blanton, "Forrest's Old Regiment."

8. Donelson's fall . . . Pratt, *Civil War on Western Waters*, p. 6. Now the rebels Forrest C. Pogue Public History Institute, *The Civil War in the Jackson Purchase Region of Kentucky*. The bitterest blow . . . Moore, *The Rebellion Record*, pp. 37–38.

9. Frisby, "'Remember me to everybody.'"

10. Hill, *Diary*.

11. Mariam, used to administer . . . Rogers and Patterson in "Concerning the Nathan Bedford Forrest Legend."

12. "chewed tobacco . . ." Rogers, ibid.

13. Thus "settle" became "setl"; "done," "don"; and so on. "I never see a pen," he once said, "but what I think of a snake." Forrest and Lincoln bear comparing. Like the Lincolns, the Forrests were upright Anglo-Saxon yeomen who had moved west from Virginia.

14. The son of a Scottish immigrant, Joseph Williams Chalmers was born in Halifax County, Virginia, and studied for the bar. Positioning himself for the Mis-

sissippi land grab of 1836, he moved west in 1835 and four years later acquired a large plantation in De Soto County.

15. Chalmers, "Lieutenant General Nathan Bedford Forrest."

16. "The planter living upon his own lands," Montgomery continued, "surrounded by his slaves, a happy and childlike race in that day, dispensed a broad and generous hospitality; no one was ever turned from his door. For even the lowliest a place was found. . . . What pen can do justice to southern society as it was before the war, its wide influence for good all over the land; mine cannot." Neither can mine. (Montgomery, *Reminiscences of a Mississippian in Peace and War*, p. 20.)

17. It is believed . . . They included Mariam's uncle, the Reverend Cowan, who in 1845 sold two children to settle his debts; and Forrest's doomed Uncle Jonathan owned at least five "slaves for life" whom his creditors were always trying to seize.

18. "infested with gamblers . . ." Hurst, *Nathan Bedford Forrest*, p. 35.

19. A slave named Betty . . . Betty Simmons (Tennessee) in *AS*. In 1852 . . . Bancroft, *Slave Trading in the Old South*, pp. 250, 253, 367–368, 379.

20. FBP. In early 1849, Byrd Hill offered fifty blacks for sale "on Adams Street east of the American hotel. All likely Maryland and Virginia Negroes, men, women, boys and girls, some families . . . Don't be alarmed because of the cholera," he urged prospective customers. "These Negroes are all healthy." (*Memphis Commercial Appeal*, February 15, 1974.) On one trip home from Galveston, Forrest is said to have camped with Indians and hunted game among the grasslands. (G. W. Aelan [Atlanta, GA]/"Major": September 27, 1866, Papers of Leroy Nutt/ 2285/Folder 6 [SHC/UNCCH].)

21. *Memphis Eagle and Enquirer*, June 2, 1857, in FBP.

22. Eden, "Memoir"; Hurst, *Nathan Bedford Forrest*, p. 179.

23. An admiring Tennesseean . . . James Ralston in Rogers, "Concerning the Nathan Bedford Forrest Legend." "I remember one day . . ." Eden, "Memoir."

24. Hurst, *Nathan Bedford Forrest*, pp. 330–331.

25. *New York Tribune* in Hurst, *Nathan Bedford Forrest*, p. 179.

26. A Massachusetts soldier described her as "an elderly negro woman in a delapidated looking buggy, and wearing a long old fashioned sun bonnet, and driving with a rein in each hand." The Yankees "cheered her loudly, but she passed by perfectly unconcerned." H. N. Peters/Margaret Trueworthy: April 23, 1862, in Special Collections, University of Arkansas Libraries.

27. Douglas Turner Ward in Memphis *Commercial Appeal*, August 14, 2005.

28. Armstrong, *Old Massa's People*, pp. 260–261.

29. "childish indignation . . ." J. P. Young/Frederic Bancroft: December 28, 1920, and January 21, 1921, in FBP. According to a former slave . . . Hughs, *Thirty Years a Slave*, pp. 90–93, 98–99. Thomas Hooper . . . Pension file of Thomas Hooper.

30. Some Tennessee masters . . . Anonymous (née Caruthers) in *UHS*, p. 254. Another insisted . . . *Nashville Daily Gazette*, March 4, 1856. "no one responded . . ." Johnson, *Slavery Days in Old Kentucky*, pp. 10–11. A number of slave traders actually specialized in selling children. In South Carolina in 1851, a pair of dealers named Allen and Phillips sold a twelve-year-old boy away from his family, also "two likely boys, aged 11 and 6 years," and sought to buy "5 or 6 likely girls

from 11 to 20 years of age." (Nancy Gardner in *AS*, p. 160. See also Charlotte Brooks in Albert, *The House of Bondage*, p. 22; Robinson, *From Log Cabin to the Pulpit*, pp. 49, 70, 73.)

31. Owners sometimes purposely kept slave parents and their children in separate quarters in order to discourage escapes. "If their families could be cared for or taken with them," observed a Union army officer, "the whole slave population of Maryland would make its exodus to Washington." (Fields, *Slavery and Freedom on the Middle Ground*, p. 119.) (James Curry in *ST*, p. 129.)

32. As for Forrest, . . . George Ross and his fellow slaves enjoyed their stay in a Maryland jail, which was a great relief from slavery. "The jailer, seeing we were trusty servants, let us wait on tables, sweep the yard, and so on. I was married, & he said 'you may go home every night at 7 o'clock, and come back at 7 in the morning,' and so I did." George Ross in *ST*, p. 408. In any case, . . . Hughes, *Thirty Years a Slave*, pp. 92–93. "I knowed Mr. Forrest . . ." Hancock *Diary*, p. 473.

33. Neither the frontier . . . Forrest was repeatedly fined by his fellow aldermen for making remarks out of order. Declaring himself a "fighting man," Forrest once threatened a colleague with physical harm. He opposed Sabbath blue laws and championed public works, the railroads, and the rights of prisoners. "fierce and terrible . . ." Lafcadio Hearn in Carney, "The Contested Image of Nathan Bedford Forrest."

34. 1860 Census.

"Bonds of Wickedness": Slavery in Tennessee: 1820–1861

1. Schweninger, *James T. Rapier and Reconstruction*, p. 8.

2. The slave insurrectionist . . . Redford, *Somerset Homecoming*, pp. 142–143. "country bullies . . ." Brent in Gates, ed., *The Classic Slave Narratives*, p. 393. "The brightest and best . . ." Charity Bowen in *ST*, p. 267. (See also Goodstein, *Nashville, 1780–1860*, pp. 112, 140.)

3. *UHS*, p. 84; Cimprich, *Slavery's End in Tennessee*, p. 10.)

4. Woodward, *The Burden of Southern History*, pp. 54–56.

5. "cut darkies' heads off . . ." Anonymous (née Shaw?) in *UHS*, p. 296. In the late 1850s . . . *UHS*, p. 171.

6. Knox, *Slave and Freeman*, pp. 45–46; James Thomas/John Rapier Jr.: December 23, 1856, in Schweninger, ed., *From Tennessee Slave to St. Louis Entrepreneur*, p. 204.

7. Peter Cooper in McPherson, *The Negro's Civil War*, p. 65.

8. House slaves . . . James Thomas in Schweninger, ed., *From Tennessee Slave to St. Louis Entrepreneur*, p. 70; Escott, *Slavery Remembered*, p. 34. Thomas Rutling's mistress . . . Pike, *The Jubilee Singers*, p. 56. Even field hands . . . *UHS*, p. 5. (See also Frederick Douglass in Jordan, *Black Confederates and Afro-Yankees*, p. 149; *Chattanooga Confederate* in Wiley, *Southern Negroes*, p. 19 and nn; *UHS*, p. 269; Sarah L. Johnson and Frankie Goole in *AS*; "Reverend Green" in Johnson, ed., *God Struck Me Dead*, p. 80.)

9. Henrietta Matson to Whipple, November 21, 1867 (AMA).

10. First of all . . . James Curry in *ST*, p. 135. (See also Ambrose Headen in ibid., pp. 744–745; Lewis Clarke in ibid., p. 153; Unidentified slave in Escott, *Slavery*

Remembered, p. 112; Patsy Jane Bland in *AS*.) "The downtrodden slaves . . ." Hughs, *Thirty Years a Slave*, p. 78.

11. For many others . . . Lewis Clarke in *ST*, p. 153; Plomer Harshaw in *AS*; Anonymous in *UHS*, p. 250. We had a man on our place . . . Charlotte Brooks in Albert, *House of Bondage*, p. 40.

12. "We knowed freedom . . ." Felix Haywood in Botkin, *Lay My Burden Down*, p. 224. But some slaves understood . . . Charlie Davenport in Mellon, ed., *Bullwhip Days*, p. 376.

13. "Somebody from across the water . . ." Anderson Brown in Wiley, *Southern Negroes*, pp. 15–16. "Some of the old folks . . ." Cato Carter in Mellon, ed.; *Bullwhip Days*, p. 277. "It was the old story . . ." L. M. Mills in *ST*, p. 504. (See also Jordon Smith in *AS*; Brent in Gates, ed., *The Classic Slave Narratives*, p. 376.)

14. Orland Kay Armstrong in Wiley, *Southern Negroes*, p. 13 and nn; *UHS*, pp. 16, 135, 199.

15. "Why," a slave exclaimed . . . Wiley, *Southern Negroes*, p. 14. Among the fugitive slaves . . . *Brooklyn Daily Eagle*, May 12, 1862. Italics mine.

16. Escott, *Slavery Remembered*, p. 122.

17. "Lincoln freed us . . ." Patsy Perryman in *AS*. "throwed back his head . . ." Willie Doyle in Botkin, *Lay My Burden Down*, p. 235. (See also Maggie Pinkard in *AS*; Anonymous in *UHS*, p. 115.)

18. Sam Ward in Mellon, ed., *Bullwhip Days*, p. 343.

19. Caldwell, "A Brief History of Slavery in Boone County, Kentucky," p. 7.

20. Berlin et al., eds., *The Wartime Genesis of Free Labor: The Upper South*, pp. 39–400.

21. Nancy Gardner in *AS*.

22. "God's emmissary . . ." James Southall in *AS*. (See also Pinkey Howard in Botkin, *Lay My Burden Down*, p. 16, and Mollie Watson in *AL*.) "I thought he was . . ." Angie Garrett in Botkin, *Lay My Burden Down*, p. 240. (See also Annie Young in *AS*.) "He done more . . ." Charles Willis in *AS*. (See also George W. Harmon and William W. Watson in ibid.) But others . . . Tishey (Mrs. Baltimore) Taylor in ibid. "didn't care much . . ." Hannah McFarland in ibid. "It was the plans . . ." Escott, *Slavery Remembered*, p. 112.

23. "Master was too old . . ." Nicey Kinney in Botkin, *Lay My Burden Down*, p. 81. (See also Charley Williams in ibid., p. 114; J. W. Stinnett in *AS*.)

24. "I took my freedom . . ." Robert Davis in Davis and Gates, *The Slave's Narrative*, p. 55. (See also Bruce, *The New Man*, pp. 104, 114; James Thomas in Schweninger, ed., *From Tennessee Slave to St. Louis Entrepeneur*, p. 172; Knox, *Slave and Freeman*, p. 53.)

25. Rachel Cruze in Mellon, ed., *Bullwhip Days*, p. 215. (See also Wiley, *Southern Negroes*, p. 8 and nn.)

26. "Old mistress . . ." Katie Rowe in Botkin, *Lay My Burden Down*, p. 109. One slave owner . . . Robert H. Cartmell in Cimprich, *Slavery's End in Tennessee*, p. 31.

27. Bob Maynard's kindly master . . . Bob Maynard in *AS*. Tom Wilson's owner . . . Escott, *Slavery Remembered*, p. 134. "he don't want to live . . ." Anna Miller in Botkin, *Lay My Burden Down*, p. 234. (See also Annie Row in *AS*.)

28. "'The faithful slave' . . ." Wiley, *Southern Negroes*, p. 83. "The negroes care no more for me . . ." Mrs. W. H. Neblett in Wiley, *Southern Negroes*, p. 52nn. A

slave in Davidson County . . . Cimprich, *Slavery's End in Tennessee*, p. 121. (See also Louisa Alexander in *ST*, p. 119.)

29. Harriett Robinson in *AL*. One morning when . . . Anonymous in *UHS*, p. 253.

30. James Thomas in Schweninger, ed., *From Tennessee Slave to St. Louis Entrepreneur*, pp. 158, 175.

31. "That old Yankee . . ." "Reverend Green" in Johnson, ed., *God Struck Me Dead*, p. 80. When George . . . George W. Harmon in *AS*. Some sold their slaves . . . Wiley, *Southern Negroes*, p. 91.

32. Allen V. Manning in Botkin, *Lay My Burden Down*, pp. 97–98; Redford, *Somerset Homecoming*, pp. 119–120. Some slaveholders . . . Cimprich, *Slavery's End in Tennessee*, p. 29.

33. Escott, *Slavery Remembered*, p. 84. (See also James Curry in *ST*, p. 140.)

34. Slaves had developed . . . Bancroft, "A Letter from the Far South" in *FBP*. "anybody would come . . ." Scott Bond in *AS*; Anonymous (née Caruthers) in *UHS*, p. 257. (See also Plomer Harshaw in *AS*; Pension file of James Green; Mellon, ed., *Bullwhip Days*, p. 301; Bud Jones, Robert Burns, and Walter Rimm in *AS*; Heywood Ford in Botkin, *Lay My Burden Down*, p. 177; Anonymous (Robinson County) in Johnson, ed., *God Struck Me Dead*, p. 135; Escott, *Slavery Remembered*, p. 84; Charles Grandy in Perdue et al., eds., *Weevils in the Wheat*, p. 117.)

35. E. L. Davison Sr. in Baylor, *Early Times in Washington County*, p. 326.

36. The son of a slave owner . . . John G. Hawkens in Botkin, *Lay My Burden Down*, p. 193. "lay out in the woods . . ." Lee Guidon in Botkin, *Lay My Burden Down*, p. 65.

37. Colonel Douglass Wilson quoting "Uncle Si" in Albert, *House of Bondage*, pp. 134–135.

38. Cimprich, *Slavery's End in Tennessee*, p. 25.

39. William Colbert in Botkin, *Lay My Burden Down*, p. 170.

Hoosiers and Iowans: The First Union Garrison at Fort Pillow: 1862–1864

1. "Only ten remained . . ." *New York Herald*, June 12, 1862.

2. Moore, *Anecdotes, Poetry, and Incidents of the War*, pp. 14–15.

3. Their banner featured an angry eagle on a purple field under the motto "Clear the tracks."

4. F. A. Starring/Grenville Dodge: September 27, 1862, in *ORCW*.

5. Here and there . . . *Indianapolis State Journal*, September 27, 1862 (RMC). Determined to turn . . . Addison Sleeth in Mainfort and Coats, eds., "Soldiering at Fort Pillow: 1862–1864."

6. Robert Mainford Collection (RMC). My depiction of the orientation of these encampments is based on a map drawn by William D. Power of the 32nd Iowa that was obtained by Robert Mainfort and exhibited at Fort Pillow, from which it was later stolen. My copy is a computer-enhanced version of a color print Mainfort kindly provided for me. sixteen-by-twenty-two-foot . . . Ross Griffin in Samuel B. and Hattie Lanier File, Court of Claims in NARA.

7. Wolfe began to send . . . *Rushville* (IN) *Jacksonian*, September 12, 1862 (RMC). The oath . . . Cimprich, *Slavery's End in Tennessee*, p. 33.

8. Andrew Johnson in Moore, ed., *The Rebellion Record*, vol. 8, pp. 340–341.

9. "Some take . . ." Watkins, Diary (RMC). "Most locals . . ." Captain Griffiths in File of William Conner, Southern Claims Commission in NARA. Italics mine. It was common . . . Brayman/Hurlbut: February 15, 1863, in NARA. Some joined under assumed names to protect themselves from their secessionist neighbors. (H. W. Griffith/Hurlbut: March 21, 1863, in NARA.) In April 1863, General Asboth asked the assistant adjutant general's advice on whether two rebel prisoners who had recently had their legs amputated should be allowed to take the oath and go home. Asboth/"AAG" [Henry Binmore]: April 21, 1863, in RG94/E729A/Box 2 in NARA. (See also W. C. Stanbery (32nd Iowa Infantry/ E. H. Wolfe: April 23, 1863, in RG94/E729A/Box 3 in NARA; Frisby, "'Remember me to everybody'"; Britton, *The Aftermath of the Civil War*, p. 179.)

10. Richmond believed that cutting down on the supply of Southern cotton would force Britain to side with the CSA. It was Confederate gospel that Britain's economy could not survive unless its textile manufacturers received a continuing supply of American cotton. But even though the shortage did give Britain pause, it merely proved a boon to the proliferating cotton growers of Britain's newly established Indian empire.

11. "He has a permit . . ." Addison Sleeth in Mainfort and Coats, eds., "Soldiering at Fort Pillow, 1862–1864." Colonel Lake/Editor, *Buchanan* (MT) *Guardian*: November 22, 1862, in Anonymous, *The History of Buchanan County, Iowa*, p. 174. Transcribed by Tommy Joe Fulton and Peggy Hoehne at www.genweb.net/ 27th-Iowa/jedlake/nov221862.html.

12. Addison Sleeth in op. cit.

13. In December . . . E. H. Wolfe, Special Order No. 34: December 26, 1862, in 52nd Regiment Indiana Infantry, Regimental Orders Issued in NARA. "A goodly share . . ." Ryan, *Reminscences*. Trade was brisk . . . Watkins, *Diary* (RMC).

14. Willoughby, "Gunboats and Gumbo."

15. Willoughby, "Colonel Dawson and the Shadow War."

16. Chalmers, "Lieutenant General Nathan Bedford Forrest."

17. "What shall I do . . ." J. M. Tuttle/Hurlbut: January 3, 1863, in 16th Army Corps (Letters Received) RG98, Part 2, Entry 391, Box 7 in NARA.

18. Willoughby, "Gunboats and Gumbo."

19. A veteran of the war with Mexico, Scott had been taken prisoner with Cassius M. Clay in 1847. The frantic General Davies had apparently overstepped his bounds by ordering the 32nd to destroy New Madrid and come down to Fort Pillow, for Scott and New Madrid were part of Curtis's command, and Davies and Fort Pillow were part of Grant's. The result of his panic was that the Mississippi had been stripped of Union forces between Cairo and New Madrid. Scott was eventually exonerated. (Edward H. Mix/L. S. Coffin: January 13 and 20, 1863, in Regimental Record Books, 32nd Regiment Iowa Infantry, Regimental Letters Sent 1862–1865 in NARA.) Scott, ed., *Story of the Thirty Second Iowa Infantry Volunteers*, pp. 83–84. Among these contrabands, Scott recalled, was the family of a young boy named John Waller. "Probably very few of the comrades have any remembrance of this colored family," he would write long after the war, "who, with others, were furnished transportation to Central Iowa. It may interest them to know that the boy, John, is the identical John L. Waller, late Presidential Elector from Kansas; later, United States Consul in Madagas-

car; and at present, November 1895, enjoying the hospitality of a French prison, under a twenty-years sentence of a Military Court, for a political offence." Accused of assisting Madagascar natives in their efforts to prevent a French takeover, Waller was eventually released after President Grover Cleveland and the American Congress lodged formal protests.

20. "split 'shakes' . . ." Aldrich, "Incidents," pp. 82–83; Scott, *Story of the Thirty Second Iowa Infantry Volunteers,* pp. 100–101. Scott's headquarters . . . Alexander Cissell in Samuel B. and Hattie Lanier File, RG124 (Court of Claims), in NARA.

21. John Scott/H. Z. Curtis: April 29 and May 13, 1863, in Regimental Record Books, 32nd Regiment Iowa Infantry, Regimental Letters Sent 1862–1865 in NARA; Charles Aldrich/Commanding Officer of 32nd Iowa Infantry: May 12, 1863, in Regimental Record Books, 32nd Regiment Iowa Infantry, Regimental Letters Sent 1862–1865 in NARA.

22. Amos S. Collins/16th Army Corps: March 19, 1863, in 16th Army Corps, Vol. 4, Register of Letters Received 1863 in NARA. Drill was not neglected . . . Aldrich, "Incidents."

23. Ryan, *Reminiscences.* Ryan, of course, was not the only Yankee to recoil in horror from his own comrades' behavior. "Hit is a shocking sight," wrote a Union private from Camp Sill, Tennessee, "to see how the soldiers starve the farmers." He saw them "go in to a hous and take everthing they could lay thaer hands on, and then went for the chickens out a doors, and the worst of all hit was a poor widow woman with fore little children. I was mity sorry for her." Shiflitt, Letter.

24. Jewell, ed., *New Orleans.*

Contrabands: West Tennessee: 1861–1863

1. "What will you do . . ." Albert D. Richardson in Silver, ed., *Mississippi in the Confederacy,* p. 149. The first blacks . . . McPherson, *The Negro's Civil War,* p. 28.

2. Andrew Johnson . . . Cimprich, *Slavery's End in Tennessee,* p. 64. (See also McPherson, *The Negro's Civil War,* pp. 89–94.)

3. George E. Waring in Berlin et al., eds., *Free at Last,* pp. 28–29.

4. W. E. B. DuBois in Wharton, *The Negro in Mississippi: 1865–1890,* p. 26.

5. Cimprich, *Slavery's End in Tennessee,* pp. 41–45.

6. The farms that experienced the highest rates of desertion tended to be the large riverside plantations under absentee ownership. (Wiley, *Southern Negroes,* p. 65.) Cimprich, *Slavery's End in Tennessee,* p. 57.

7. J.C.C./*New York Jewish Messenger,* July 16, 1863.

8. Watkins, *Diary.*

9. "The question raised . . ." H. C. Cahe/E. H. Wolfe: February 19, 1863, and E. H. Wolfe/Asboth: February 21, 1863, in RG 393, District of Columbus in NARA. "Instructed to punish . . ." W. R. Rowley/Asboth: February 25, 1863, in RG 393, District of Columbus in NARA.

10. A brigadier general recalled that every master who called on him at Nashville presented himself as "a prodigy of patriotism and devotion to the Union. He wants his negro, as he says, not for his value, but to gratify a longing mother, who ardently desires that her son shall return to her and to slavery," and "the kind-hearted owner only wishes to oblige her." (Maslowski, *Treason Must Be*

Made Odious, pp. 98–99. See also Cimprich, *Slavery's End in Tennessee,* p. 30; Wiley, *Southern Negroes,* p. 167.)

11. E. H. Wolfe/W. H. Thurston: June 13, 1863, in RG94/E729A/Box 3 in NARA.

12. Aldrich, "Incidents"; Scott, ed., *Story of the Thirty Second Iowa Infantry Volunteers,* pp. 101. "Really a pro-slavery regiment . . ." Ibid., p. 102.

13. By January . . . E. H. Wolfe/Special Orders Number 66: January 19, 1863, in 52nd Regiment Indiana Infantry, Regimental Orders Issued in NARA. Local whites . . . But the Iowans . . . *Mason City* (IA) *Cerro Gordo Republican,* March 5 and 7, 1863 (RMC). "You will only . . ." *Davenport Gazette,* January 17, 1863. "Goddamn," one Yankee exclaimed to an elderly master grieving over the loss of his slaves, "these must be your grandchildren, the way you're carrying on about them!" (*UHS,* p. 199.)

14. "All the soldiers as a rule . . ." James Thomas in Schweninger, ed., *From Tennessee Slave to St. Louis Entrepreneur,* p. 165. "humiliating treatment . . ." Robinson, *From Log Cabin to the Pulpit,* p. 105. Addison Sleeth . . . Addison Sleeth in Mainfort and Coats, eds., "Soldiering at Fort Pillow, 1862–1864." In September . . . *Rushville* (IN) *Jacksonian,* January 18, September 2, October 8 and 28, and November 4, 1863. (See also Joel Grant/Professor Henry Cowles (Oberlin College): April 10, 1863, AMA in TSLA.) Many would have agreed with an Ohio private who wrote from Camp Sill that "this onholy war wood a bin over if oald Lincoln wood a let the negros alone. I wish he had forty the blackest negroes in the South tide to him." (Shiflitt, Letters.)

15. "Tha niger . . ." James Jenkinson/Orrin Stanley: April 20, 1863, in Orrin Elmore Stanley Papers, University of Oregon Library.

16. A Hoosier captain . . . *Rushville* (IN) *Jacksonian,* January 28 and February 13, 1863. An Iowan reported . . . Albert L. Towne/Clarissa Towne: undated, 1863, in RMC. (See also Cimprich, *Slavery's End in Tennessee,* p. 54.)

17. "Niggers are thicker here . . ." Joseph R. Edwards (12th Michigan Infantry)/ "Sister Mary": August 20, 1863, in John Gillette Collection, Michigan Historical Collections, Bentley Historical Library, University of Michigan at Ann Arbor.

18. Knox, *Slave and Freeman,* p. 63.

19. "Here, as in many places . . ." Allan Pinkerton in McPherson, *The Negro's Civil War,* p. 147. A Union soldier . . . Wharton, *The Negro in Mississippi: 1865–1890,* p. 21.

20. N. [B]. Buford/Hurlbut: June 5, 1863, in RG94/E729A/Box 2 in NARA.

21. "all negroes . . ." E. H. Wolfe/Special Order Number 155: October 22, 1863, in 52nd Regiment Indiana Infantry, Regimental Orders Issued in NARA. "a set of asses . . ." E. H. Wolfe/B. K. Logan: October 23, 1863, and E. H. Davis/Special Order Number 157: October 23, 1863, in 52nd Regiment Indiana Infantry, Regimental Letters Sent (NARA); seventy-nine Contrabands were sent upstream under the charge of Sergeant Shepard Whitcomb. (E. H. Wolfe/Special Order Number 159: October 24, 1863, and E. H. Wolfe/Special Order Number 174: November 3, 1863, in 52nd Regiment Indiana Infantry, Regimental Orders Issued, in NARA.)

22. "I would recommend the New Madrid bend as a proper locality for a larger settlement," wrote Asboth, "as it contains several thousand acres of rich farming lands, well timbered, and belonging to men not merely sympathizing with the

rebellion but being, many of them, in arms against the government." Though New Madrid was also near a nest of rebel guerrillas at Tiptonville, Asboth assured Memphis that "if properly fortified and garrisoned"—which must have made the 32nd Iowa downriver groan with dismay—it could provide "a desirable and safe place for a large Contraband Colony." (Asboth/Henry Binmore: May 6 and 11, 1863, in RG94/E729A/Box 2 in NARA.)

23. Frisby, "'Remember me to everybody.'"

24. Colonel John Beatty in Cimprich, *Slavery's End in Tennessee*, p. 35.

25. Berlin, ed., *The Wartime Genesis of Free Labor: The Upper South*, pp. 39–40.

26. "By and by . . ." Knox, *Slave and Freeman*, p. 49. One slave remembered . . . Anonymous in *UHS*, p. 191.

27. Colonel Wolfe . . . E. H. Wolfe: May 24, 1863, in 16th Army Corps, vol. 6, Register of Letters Received 1863 in NARA.

28. Stranded . . . John Scott/Special Order Number 5: May 16, 1863, in 32nd Regiment Iowa Infantry, Regimental Orders Issued 1862–1865 in NARA. After Captain Moore's . . . "Charges and specifications performed by Col. Edward H. Wolfe 52d Reg. Ind. Infty. Vol. Com'dg Post of Fort Pillow" (RMC). "French leave . . ." E. H. Wolfe/Special Order Number 45: May 30, 1863, in 52nd Regiment Indiana Infantry, Regimental Orders Issued in NARA.

29. Scott reported . . . John Scott/Hurlbut: June 1 and 8, 1863, in 16th Army Corps, vol. 6, Register of Letters Received, 1863 in NARA. It was charged . . . Z. S. Main/W. H. Thurston: June 13, 1863, in RG94/E729A/Box 3 in NARA.

30. John Scott/W. H. Thurston: June 14, 1863, in RG94/E729A/Box 3 in NARA.

31. John Scott/[W. H.] Thurston: June 13, 1863, in RG94/E729A/Box 3 in NARA.

32. Trying to keep the noise down . . . Asboth/Special Order Number 145: June 16, 1863, in RG393, Records of U.S. Army Continental Commands, Entry 992, District of Columbus, KY, General Orders, 1862, vol. 101/248A in NARA; T. J. Harris [Asboth]/Special Order Number 161: July 2, 1863, in 52nd Regiment Indiana Infantry, Regimental Orders Issued in NARA.

33. Nevertheless . . . Aldrich, "Incidents." "Hoosier colonel . . ." Capt. A. B. Miller/ ed.: June 22, 1863 in *Mason City* (IA) *Cerro Gordo Republican* (MC).

34. "and doing very irksome . . ." Aldrich, "Incidents." "The 32nd, which had hitherto . . ." Anonymous in *Dubuque Times*, April 28, 1864.

35. "not sufficient force . . ." E. H. Wolfe/Asboth: July 13, 1864, in 16th Army Corps, Vol. 6, Register of Letters Received 1863 in NARA. At last . . . E. H. Wolfe: July 27, 1863, in RG393, District of Columbus in NARA.

36. "The time is now . . ." Sherman/David Porter: January 19, 1864, in *ORCW*. "Hard War . . ." Sherman in Chalmers, "Lieutenant General Nathan Bedford Forrest."

37. My portrait of Hurlbut is based on Jeffrey N. Lash's excellent doctoral study of the general, since published by Kent State University Press as *A Politician Turned General: The Civil War Career of Stephen Augustus Hurlbut*.

38. "never had any orders . . ." Testimony of Stephen A. Hurlbut in *RJSCW*.

39. Sherman/Hurlbut: January 11, 1864, in 16th Army Corps (Letters Received) RG98, Part 2, Entry 391, Box 7 in NARA.

40. Alethea Sayers, "Fort Pillow: What the Federal Government Didn't Tell," *A Nation Divided* online magazine. www.ehistory.com/uscw.

41. E. H. Wolfe/Thomas H. Harris: January 2, 1864, in RG94/E729A/Box 7 in NARA.

42. The heavy guns . . . Hurlbut/A. J. Smith: January 16, 1864, in District of Columbus, Kentucky, vol. 93, Letters Sent 1862–1864 in NARA. To accomplish this . . . T. H. Harris/E. H. Wolfe: January 17, 1864, in 16th Army Corps, vol. 3, Letters Sent 1863–1864 in NARA. All of the contrabands . . . E. H. Wolfe/Special Order Number 15: January 18, 1864, in 16th Army Corps, vol. 3, Letters Sent 1863–1864 in NARA. Hurlbut had urged . . . Hurlbut/A. J. Smith: January 16, 1864, in District of Columbus, Kentucky, vol. 93, Letters Sent 1862–1864 in NARA. N. B. Buford/T. H. Harris: January 24, 1864, in 16th Army Corps (Letters Received) RG98, Part 2, Entry 391, Box 7 in NARA.

43. "horses, Mules . . ." E. H. Wolfe/Special Order Number 9: January 16, 1864, in 178th Regiment New York Infantry, Regimental Papers in NARA. "Twelve or thirteen Tennessee boys . . ." Addison Sleeth in Mainfort and Coats, eds., "Soldiering at Fort Pillow, 1862–1864." "left the keeping . . ." J. Hough/E. H. Wolfe: January 16, 1864, in ORCW. According to J. N. Lewis, the second garrison arrived at Fort Pillow on the twenty-second, not, as Harris and Hurlbut testified, on the twenty-fifth. J. N. Lewis/T. H. Harris: January 22, 1864, in 16th Army Corps (Letters Received) RG98, Part 2, Entry 391, Box 7 in NARA. The 52nd Indiana would spend the rest of the war in the 3rd Division of the 16th Army Corps under Colonel Wolfe's command, fighting at Tupelo and Oxford, and most notably in December at the Battle of Nashville, where they formed a line a couple of regiments down from their old nemeses—the Iowans of the 32nd—and, "with a shout," as Wolfe reported, "peculiar to this corps," charged the rebel works, capturing enumerable rebel guns and several Confederate officers, including Major General Edward Johnson, for which Wolfe was eventually breveted. After the war he would resume his mercantile business, accept a perhaps unwisely offered appointment as Indiana state auditor, and die in Rushville in 1916 at the ripe old age of eighty.

"We Soldiers Are Men": Black Troops: 1863–1864

1. In March . . . McPherson, *The Negro's Civil War*, p. 170. belated convert . . . Just a year earlier, *Harper's* said, Thomas had been "so 'sound'—as the phrase was—on the slavery question that he was even suspected of rebel sympathies." (*Harper's Weekly*, June 20, 1863.) "all officers and enlisted men . . ." L. Thomas/Stanton: October 5, 1863, in ORCW. (See also Asboth/General Order Number 34: May 29, 1863, in RG94/E729A/Box 3 in NARA.)

2. Several white soldiers of the 1st Kansas Volunteers, for instance, demanded the transfer of a man who, according to his colonel, was "full two thirds 'nigger,' too black to serve upon terms of equality with white soldiers," but insisted that he was not making this recommendation "out of disrespect for the nigger." (Aptheker, *To Be Free*, p. 100.)

3. "hot and sickly season . . ." Gideon Welles/C. H. Davis: April 30, 1862, in *NFWW*. Webb and Hennessy served on the *Black Hawk* and the *Great Western*, respectively. (NPSSSS. See also David D. Porter/Joshua Bishop: December 19, 1862 in *NFWW*.)

4. "The able-bodied negro . . ." R. B. Lowry/Gideon Welles: May 19, 1863, in *NFWW.*

5. one Union doctor . . . Melancthon W. Fish/R. Weeks: November 5, 1863, in RG94/E729A/Box 6 in NARA. (See also David D. Porter/General Order Number 76: July 26, 1863, and William D. Faulkner/Pennock: February 28, 1863, in *NFWW.*)

6. Chetlain in RG393/2911/vol. 36/66: General and Special Orders: Organization of Colored Troops, p. 10 in NARA.

7. L. Thomas/Stanton: April 4, 1863, at www.coax.net/people/lwf/ltr_lt4.htm.

8. Military Record of Lionel F. Booth, NPSSSS.

9. *Republican* [St. Louis] *Daily Missouri,* March 25, 1862.

10. Betts, "A Revelation of War."

11. Within a few days . . . Though Grant's injury was just a sprain, Smith's, compounded by jaundice, would claim his life by the end of April. Ibid.

12. William M. Thomas in *AS.*

13. "house was burned . . ." T. J. Welch in pension file of Peter Williams. But others . . . RG94 Collections of the Adjutant General's Office: 1780s–1917. Bounty and Claims Division: 1862–1878: Records of Slave Claims Commissions: 1864–1868 (Tennessee) in NARA. Apparently none of the masters of the slaves who joined what would become the 2nd United States Colored Heavy Artillery (USCHA) and 6th United States Colored Heavy Artillery (USCLA) were paid the three-hundred-dollar bounties they were supposed to receive if qualified, perhaps because their slaves were recruited from contraband camps and often under newly adopted names. The highest number of bounties claimed were paid out to Middle and East Tennessee masters, perhaps because Federal authorities in West Tennessee were understandably more suspicious of local masters' loyalty to the Union. (See Anonymous in *UHS,* p. 175.)

14. Peter Williams gives the slave dealer's name as "Boggers," but I am guessing that it was Thomas Boudant, one of the most prominent traders in New Orleans.

15. Pension file of Willis Ligon.

16. Glatthaar, *Forged in Battle,* p. 77.

17. J. G. Kappner/Henry Binmore: May 16, 1863, in RG94/E729A/Box 2 in NARA.

18. Robert Cowden in McPherson, *The Negro's Civil War,* pp. 170–171.

19. "Where the Negro . . ." James Thomas in Schweninger, ed., *From Tennessee Slave to St. Louis Entrepreneur,* p. 166. "Put a United States uniform . . ." Glatthaar, *Forged in Battle,* p. 79. At Columbus, General Oglesby despaired "of making anything out of the 1st West Tenn Infy. I think the best thing to be done with them is to send them to Union City." But the 1st would evolve into the 59th USCI. (Richard James Oglesby/Henry Binmore: June 2, 1863, in RG94/E729A/Box 3 in NARA.)

20. "You ought to seen them . . ." "All I hates about them Sarges and Lieutenants is they never did shave," White continued. "Them days all wore whiskers." Mingo White in Botkin, *Lay My Burden Down,* pp. 16–17. "I was in the field . . ." Anonymous (Williamson County) in Johnson, ed., *God Struck Me Dead,* p. 105.

21. Greene et al., *Missouri's Black Heritage,* p. 84.

22. Testimony and statement of Emanuel Nichols; "Daniel Tyler" in *Liberator*, July 22, 1864; Testimony and statement of Ransom Anderson.

23. Masters used to amuse themselves . . . Emperor Williams in *ST*, p. 621; James Thomas in Schweninger, ed., *From Tennessee Slave to St. Louis Entrepreneur*, p. 95. "My Master's name . . ." Bill Simms in *AS*. A slave named Jack . . . Redford, *Somerset Homecoming*, p. 169.

24. "The government seemed . . ." Martin Jackson in *AS*. (See also Lee Guidon in Botkin, *Lay My Burden Down*, p. 66.) Some chose the names . . . Redford, *Somerset Homecoming*, p. 89. (See also Anonymous in *UHS*, p. 109; Eliza Evens in Mellon, ed., *Bullwhip Days*, p. 341.)

25. Blain had been sold . . . Family records compiled by descendants of Blain-Hamner lines; Fayette County, Tennessee, 1830 census. "They used to run him . . ." Deposition of Sherry Blain in pension file of Robert Blain. For seven years . . . Aaron, Gundy, Lewis, and Bob Blain.

26. Pension file of Sherry Blain; Sherry Blain in pension file of Robert Blain; Abraham Huggins, Ellen Thornton, Allen James/Walker, and David Weston in pension file of Sherry Blain/Thornton; George Houston in pension file of Samuel Green; testimony of Aaron Fentis in *RJSCW*.

27. "I gave them my name . . ." Robert Jones in pension file of Allen James [Walker]. Among the men . . . NPSSS.

28. "a gun and blue clothes . . ." Pompey Williams in pension file of Peter Williams. (See also C. W. Foster/Josiah V. Meigs: January 9, 1864, RG94/Box 8: Records of the 2nd USCAL in NARA; A. B. Campbell/T. H. Harris: January 17, 1864; B. J. D. Irwin/Hurlbut: January 27, 1864; R. C. Wood/Hurlbut: January 16, 1864, in 16th Army Corps (Letters Received) RG98, Part 2, Entry 391, Box 7 in NARA; Edward C. Strode/Hurlbut: January 22, 1863, in RG94/E729A/Box 7 in NARA.) Reduced to drinking . . . John Baker/Company Orders 1: September 15, 1863, in RG94/E112–115/P1–17/vol. 5 in NARA; Robert Cowden in McPherson, *The Negro's Civil War*, pp. 170–71.) "The men have been drinking . . ." RG94/E112–115/P1–17/vol. 2 in NARA.

29. Brigadier General . . . Stevenson/Hurlbut: January 12, 1864, in 16th Army Corps (Letters Received) RG98, Part 2, Entry 391, Box 7 in NARA. To ease the congestion . . . A. M. [Tann]/Hurlbut: April 28, 1863, in RG94/E729A/Box 5 in NARA. "corralled" . . . J. W. Lewis/Henry Binmore: September 19, 1863, in RG94/E729A/Box 4 in NARA; Hurlbut/A. Severance Fisk: Undated [August 20–30], 1863, in RG94/E729A/Box 4 in NARA. A pension examiner would describe the "thousands of negroes—men, women and children" who had flocked to Union-occupied Corinth. "The eligible men were enlisted in the army, and the women and children and old men put into a contraband camp. A great many marriages took place during this year, some marrying their slave wives, others finding new companions or getting married for the first time. Nearly all of these women who had husbands in the army generally followed the fortunes of the regiment and were more or less known to all the company." (Pension examiner in pension file of Joseph Key. See also Lorenzo Thomas/T. E. Ellsworth: January 21, 1864, in RG94/9: Letter Book of Brigadier General Lorenzo Thomas in NARA; B. S. D. Irwin/Superintendent of U.S. Military General Hospitals: March 18, 1864, in 16th Army Corps (Letters Received) RG98, Part 2, Entry

391, Box 7 in NARA; Henry Beets, Isabella Cross, Jackson Green, Ambrose Jones, Hamilton Lee, Pius McHenry, in pension file of Charles Cross; Jacob Wilson in *RJSCW.*)

30. In about 1859 . . . Pension file of Thomas Hooper. Captain O. B. Hooper was Thomas Hooper's master.

31. "They may have . . ." W. Young in ibid. Rosa originally testified that they had received their masters' permission to marry, and several witnesses, including Thomas's brother Bush, testified to having been present at the wedding, but apparently their testimony was perjured. (I have therefore discounted the remainder of Bush's testimony in favor of the more reliable Alexander Nason's.) Rosa admitted that she had been put up to lying about the ceremony by a white lawyer and embezzler named Macomb who told her that the examiners would never accept her claim unless she invented a marriage ceremony. (R. E. Potts [chief of Criminal Section, Bureau of Pensions] in ibid.)

32. In their escape, the Hoopers were accompanied by another slave from the neighborhood named Henderson Van, who joined the black infantry and promptly died of smallpox. (Josephine Hooper Armstrong, Henry Condry, Bush Hooper, Rosa Spearman Hooper, Alexander Nason, R. E. Potts (chief of Criminal Section, Bureau of Pensions), Henry Weaver, in pension file of Thomas Hooper.)

33. This cook was probably Thomas Addison.

34. Willis Ligon's first master's name was Abner Ligon. As administrator of Bill's former master's estate, he sold him to Bobo's sister and his own sister-in-law. (Pension file of Willis Ligon; www.ssrc.msstate.edu/grr/coahm.htm.)

35. "I fought to free . . ." Anonymous in *UHS*, p. 144. One recruit trembled . . . Anonymous (Williamson County) in Johnson, ed., *God Struck Me Dead* p. 106. "Most cruelly" . . . Glatthaar, *Forged in Battle,* p. 70. "He treated me more cruelly . . ." Patsey [Wiley?] in Berlin et al., eds., *Free At Last,* pp. 400–401.

36. J. P. Harper Sr./Colonel of the 2nd USCHA: May 9, 1864. NA/RG393/Box 2/1/4/4723.

37. Anonymous (Williamson County) in Johnson, ed., *God Struck Me Dead,* p. 102. (See also Cimprich, *Slavery's End in Tennessee,* p. 30; Rachel Cruze in Mellon, ed., *Bullwhip Days,* p. 216.)

38. In June . . . Asboth/Special Order Number 151: June 22, 1863, in RG 393 Records of U.S. Army Continental Commands, Entry 992 District of Western Kentucky, General Orders, 1862, vol. 101/248A. "All officers will . . ." E. H. Wolfe/Special Order Number 69: June 25, 1863, in 52nd Regiment Indiana Infantry, Regimental Orders Issued (RMC).

39. But apparently . . . W. R. Roberts/Charles Adams: August 6, 1863, in RG 393 Records of the U.S. Army Continental Commands/Entry 991 District of Western Kentucky, Letters Received 1862–1865 (RMC). while Wolfe continued . . . E. H. Wolfe/Special Order Number 112: August 31, 1863, in 52nd Indiana Infantry, Regimental Orders Issued (RMC).

40. "Cromwellian fervor . . ." Robert Cowden in McPherson, *The Negro's Civil War,* pp. 170–171; Osofsky, ed., *Puttin' On Ole Massa,* p. 34. After a sermon . . . Marrs, *Life and History,* p. 24. After Richard Frisby of the 7th USCI was ar-

rested in a state of "religious excitement," he was court-martialed for "boisterous conduct after taps." (Court-Martial Proceedings, MM3244.)

41. "If he still alive, then they hang him. Wasn't that awful? Hang a man just because he could read?" (Cora Gillam in *AS*.)

42. Sarah Fitzpatrick in *ST*, p. 640.

43. Marrs, *Life and History*, pp. 21, 33, 58–59. (See also Aptheker, *To Be Free*, p. 90.)

44. "Nine of the murderers . . ." W. R. Roberts/Charles Adams: August 6, 1863, in RG 393 Records of the U.S. Army Continental Commands Entry 991 District of Western Kentucky, Letters Received 1862–1865 (RMC). In October 1863 . . . Thomas O. Bigney/Stearns: October 28, 1863 in Records of Colonel Robert D. Mussey, 1863–1864. RG393/Box 2 in NARA.

45. Frank A. Kendrick/L. H. Everts: October 21, 22, and 23, 1863, in RG94/E729A/Box 5 in NARA.

46. "My associates . . ." Deloz Carson/Thomas H. Harris: ca. October 20, 1863, in RG94/E729A/Box 5 in NARA. Other sergeants-turned-captains did not survive long as officers of black troops. A Captain Waller of Company F, 2nd Tennessee Heavy Artillery (Colored) was deemed "utterly worthless"; he was incompetent and lacked "energy and interest," and "if he does not disgrace the service, he certainly does it no honor." A. Burns/unknown (extract): December 10, 1863, in RG94/E729A/Box 6 in NARA.)

47. The army began . . . Isaac Hawkins/[Hurlbut]: September 20, 1863, in RG94/E729A/Box 4 in NARA. "Instructions for Agents . . ." Reuben D. Mussey/"Instructions for Agents Recruiting Colored Men for the U.S. Service": August 18, 1863, in Records of Colonel Robert D. Mussey, 1863–1864, RG393/Box 2 in NARA; Reuben D. Mussey/General Order Number 329: October 3, 1863, in Records of Colonel Reuben D. Mussey, 1863–1864, RG393/Box 2 in NARA.

48. At Paducah . . . Samuel Walker/Asboth: June 20, 1863, in RG94/E729A/Box 5 in NARA. "This is an enigma . . ." Asboth/James S. Martin: June 22, 1863, in RG94/E729A/Box 5 in NARA; James S. Martin/Special Order Number 68: July 22, 1863, in ibid.

49. "You say you will not fight . . ." Abraham Lincoln in McPherson, *The Negro's Civil War*, p. 192. "The Government . . ." Thomas O. Howard/[?]: August 15, 1863, in University of Oregon Library, Orrin Elmore Stanley Papers (RMC).

50. Greene et al., *Missouri's Black Heritage*, pp. 81–82.

51. C. P. Lyman/Z. P. Lyman: August 9, 1864, private collection.

52. [Agent]/Major George L. Stearns: October 13, 1863, in Records of Colonel Robert D. Mussey, 1863–1864, RG393/Box 2 in NARA.

53. Acting on complaints . . . Booth: General Battalion Order 1: February 17, 1864, in RG94/E112–115/P1–17/vol. 2 in NARA. "Is my condition . . ." Marrs, *Life and History*, p. 25.

54. "to perform any labor . . ." Aptheker, *To Be Free*, pp. 82–83. Trained infantry . . . Lovett, "The West Tennessee Colored Troops in Civil War Combat."

55. "accuracy in throwing shells . . ." Frank Kendrick: Report on the Battle of Moscow, December 14, 1863, in Lovett, "The West Tennessee Colored Troops in Civil War Combat." "After they fight . . ." Cornelius Garner in Perdue et al., eds., *Weevils in the Wheat*, p. 104.

56. The Union army's . . . Hurst, *Nathan Bedford Forrest*, p. 159; "inciting servile insurrection . . ." Williams, *A History of the Negro Troops*, p. 309. "Uneasiness is felt . . ." *Harper's Weekly*, June 20, 1863.

57. On June 16 . . . Richard James Oglesby/Hurlbut: June 16, 1863, in RG94/E729A/Box 3 in NARA. Joe Wheeler's men . . . Sarah Debro in Hurmence, ed., *My Folks Don't Want Me to Talk about Slavery*, p. 57.

58. "What disposition . . ." Col. John L. Logan/W. J. Hardee in Golden West Marketing, "4th Mississippi Cavalry at www.gwest.org/4thms.htm. Most rebel officers . . . Glatthaar, *Forged in Battle*, p. 157. Other commands . . . Goodrich, *Black Flag*, p. 50.

59. "They are raising . . ." Wooster, "With the Confederate Cavalry in the West." Affleck's father, Isaac, was the author of *Affleck's Southern Rural Almanac and Plantation and Garden Calendar* and a slave owner whose Ingleside plantation included the largest nursery in the lower South.

60. Abraham Lincoln in Williams, *A History of the Negro Troops*, p. 313.

61. Stanton's directive . . . E. D. Townsend/Lorenzo Thomas: March 10, 1864, in 16th Army Corps (Letters Received) RG98, Part 2, Entry 391, Box 7 in NARA. Within a week . . . RG393/2/2911 Vol. 36 Orders.

62. Jackson/General Order 3: March 17, 1864, in RG94/E112–115/P1–17/vol. 2 in NARA.

63. Booth/General Order 4: March 18, 1864, in RG94/E112–115/P1–17/vol. 2 in NARA.

Homegrown Yanks: Bradford's Battalion: 1863–1864

1. A. J. Smith/Thomas H. Harris: October 25, 1863, in RG94/E729A/Box 5 in NARA.

2. Hamer, *Tennessee: A History*, p. 285.

3. "main stand-by . . ." Thomas W. Harris/General [Jeremiah Cutler] Sullivan: November 28, 1862, in *ORCW*. Under the pretense . . . Jordan and Pryor in Morris, "Fort Pillow: Massacre or Madness?"

4. Daniel Stamps . . . Testimony and statement of Daniel Stamps; John T. Stamps and John H. Copher in pension file of Daniel Stamps; Daniel Stamps in pension file of John M. Condray. The oldest enlisted man . . . George L. Ellis in pension file of Alfred Middleton. Andrew McKee of Dyer County was thirty-eight years old when he joined Company C. Having borne him three sons and two daughters, his first wife died in 1857; a year later his second wife added another daughter to his brood. (John Copher [Cofer], John N. Green, and John T. Stamps in pension file of Andrew McKee.) By the time of the battle, thirty-eight-year-old Frank Alexander of Company B had been married for fifteen years and fathered five children. (Thomas Loftis in pension file of Francis A. Alexander and medical report of Francis A. Alexander.)

5. Their median age . . . *TCWVQ*. Perhaps the garrison's youngest enlistee was seventeen-year-old Fred Kelso of Company C, who would desert on the eve of the massacre. (Pension files of Frederick Kelso and Anderson Jones.) Robert McKenzie of Coffee County was only eighteen years old when he enlisted. (Pension file of Robert B. McKenzie.) Wiley Robinson of Company A was not quite

eighteen years old at the time of the attack on Fort Pillow but had already served, however briefly, in two other Union regiments. (Testimony of Wiley Robinson.)

6. At least 10 percent . . . Records indicate that fifty-seven or slightly less than 10 percent of the enlistees I researched were deserters from the CSA, but the actual number is undoubtedly higher.

7. He banned "promiscuous and straggling . . ." Order of Colonel George E. Waring Jr., 1st Brigade, 6th Division, 16th Army Corps. *Columbus* (KY) *War Eagle,* December 12, 1863 (CDF). The troops followed a classic cavalry routine: reveille at 6:00 a.m., stable call fifteen minutes later, guard mount at 8:20, drill at 9:00, recall at 11:00, stable call at 11:30, roll call at noon, drill call at 2:00, recall at 3:30, stable call at 4:00, retreat at sunset, tattoo at 8:45, and taps at 9:00. *Columbus* (KY) *War Eagle,* December 12, 1863 (CDF.)

8. The unit's proper title was the 14th Tennessee Cavalry, for there was already a 13th when Bradford began recruiting. The designation was officially changed to the 14th Tennessee Cavalry on August 22, 1864, and the survivors of the battle at Fort Pillow were consolidated with the 6th (Company E) on February 24, 1865, by Military Governor Andrew Johnson. The July 1864 regimental records for the 13th report two officers and forty men. Pension file of Thomas Loftis.

9. Thomas H. Harris in JSCW.

10. "Finding recruitment very difficult . . ." Thomas H. Harris in JSCW. "I think General Sherman . . ." Testimony of Mason Brayman in JSCW.

11. T. H. Harris/W. F. Bradford: February 2, 1864 in *ORCW*; Testimony of Hurlbut and Thomas H. Harris in RJSCW.

12. Chalmers, "Lieutenant General Nathan Bedford Forrest and His Campaigns," *SHSP,* October 1879; Isaac R. Hawkins/H. T. Reid: February 3, 1864, in *ORCW*; pension file of David H. Leonard; Forrest/Jefferson Davis: February 5, 1864, in *ORCW*; Mack J. Leaming in RJSCW.

13. William Sooy Smith/William Bradford: February 1, 1864, in *ORCW.*

14. A commissioned officer . . . Thomas H. Harris/Statement: April 26, 1864, in *ORCW*; D. Townsend: War Department Special Order 91: February 25, 1864, RG94/Box 8: Records of the 2nd USCLA in NARA. On March 7 . . . Lorenzo Thomas/Stanton: March 7, 1864, in RG94/9: Letter Book of Brigadier General Lorenzo Thomas in NARA.

15. Dona Alsobrook, H. T. Sumerow, and Isaac J. Winston in quartermaster's claim of James C. Alsobrook of Lauderdale County in NARA.

16. "Some of the worst . . ." Captain James Marshall in *Trade Regulations, & c.,* U.S. Senate Report 38-S, vol. 4, no. 142, part 3, serial set 1214, 35 (LC). "It was hard . . ." Thomas B. Curlin, John B. Harrison, Jasper W. Hoadfins[?], and Joseph F. Peck in quartermaster's claim of Lemuel Curlin, RG92/817 in NARA; pension file (1812) of Lemuel Curlin.

17. In early 1864 . . . James C. Alsobrook File, Southern Claims Commission Notes (NARA); Willoughby, "Rev. George Washington Harris: The Unordained Bishop of West Tennessee"; claims of James C. Alsobrook, Lemuel Curlin, Robert Medlin, and Hartwell D. Stovall, RG92/817 in NARA; Willoughby, Gunboats and Gumbo. Forrest demanded . . . Forrest/Buckland: March 22, 1864, in *ORCW.*

18. "depriveing me of the means . . ." Union Provost Marshals' File of Papers Relating to Individual Civilians, RG109/ALS, DNA in NARA; Simon, ed., *The Pa-*

pers of Ulysses S. Grant, vol. 10, p. 544. In early March . . . A. H. Polk/T. F. Sevier: March 3, 1864, in *ORCW.*

19. In February . . . Pension file of Theodorick Bradford. "Very young . . ." Hurlbut in *RJSCW.*

20. Bradford's broken promises . . . Joseph W. Byrns, J. A. Durham, and Jonathan W. McDonald in pension file of James D. Burcham. By February 20 . . . Henry M. Bunch and C. Underwood in pension file of Joseph M. Bunch; Joseph W. Byrns, J. A. Durham, and Jonathan W. McDonald in pension file of James D. Burcham; pension file of William L. Cope; Martin V. Day and Alfred Middleton in pension file of George L. Ellis; Ezekiel Arnold in pension file of Andrew J. Glass; pension file of John A. Halford; C. R. Allen, John N. Green, and Chapman Underwood in pension file of David H. Leonard; pension file of Hiram S. Neely; David Sneed in pension file of Thomas Ruffin; statement of Anne Jane Rufin [Ruffin]; testimony of William Cleary; pension file of Thomas J. Powell; pension file of William P. Stephens.

21. Ira Gifford/Harris: April 6, 1864, in 16th Army Corps (Letters Received) RG98, Part 2, Entry 391, Box 7 in NARA.

22. By the eve . . . Report for March of the 13th Tennessee Cavalry in 16th Army Corps (Letters Received) RG98, Part 2, Entry 391, Box 7 in NARA. En masse . . . Dr. John Fitch in Cimprich and Mainfort, "Dr. Fitch's Report."

23. Joseph and Rosa Johnson in pension file of William R. [Read] Johnson. Read Johnson would be captured on April 12 and taken to Andersonville. On December 2 he entered the prison hospital with scurvy, and he died two months later. With Johnson's back pay his father bought "a little homestead" in Obion County, but he eventually lost it to his creditors and spent the rest of his life doing odd jobs around Troy.

24. Gregory's mother was eventually driven from her home in Graves County, Kentucky, by Confederate guerrillas and lived in destitution behind Federal lines. (Pension file of Jonathan Gregory.) The murder may have been under investigation at the time of Bradford's death.

25. Pension files of Jonathan F. Gregory and James Park.

26. A. L. Gaskins, Pink W. Lee, and Pleasant Powers in pension file of James M. Moore.

27. Henry also stated that Company E had not been mustered in at the time of the massacre: something he could not have known unless he had been at Fort Pillow. (Pension file of William M. Henry.) Another of those who deserted that February was thirty-year-old Jack McConnell of Gibson County. McConnell developed chronic diarrhea at Union City "caused by exposure to bad weather" and "hard service" and went home to recover his health. He must have succeeded. Though later described as "stout, florid," and "robust," he apparently never returned to his regiment. (James W. Landowne and F. D. Lawrence in pension file of John C. McConnell.)

28. "and the very day . . ." Pension file of Anderson Jones. In fact . . . Report for March of the 13th Tennessee Cavalry in 16th Army Corps (Letters Received) RG98, Part 2, Entry 391, Box 7 in NARA. Twenty-one-year-old Sergeant John K. Tate of Company D, a native of Obion County, complained that the preceding winter had been hard, and the regiment "much exposed." Tate claimed to have

escaped the day of the fight, and that he was unable to return to his regiment. (John K. Tate in pension file of Isaiah Jones; pension file of John K. Tate.) Some men deserted to care for their families. Twenty-four-year-old Corporal Henry Williams of Company A was a family man by default. The son of a drunken adulterer, Williams was his mother's sole means of support. She followed him to Paducah, and when the regiment was ordered away to Union City he deserted, probably to remain behind and care for her. Though he was apparently not with the 13th when it was attacked at Fort Pillow, he was admitted to an army hospital in late April and died there on May 3 of smallpox. (Pension file of Henry H. Williams.) Other cases are less clear. George Box of Company C, for instance, was recorded as deserting shortly before the battle and not rejoining his comrades until July 20, 1864, whereupon he entered the hospital and deserted again two days later. But as an old man Box adamantly maintained that in early April 1864 he had received a medical discharge from Sergeant B. A. Hewatt, whom Bradford had placed "in charge of the hospittle at fort Pillar," because Box had lost his voice and breathed with difficulty. Unable to go home "because the country was so foul of the enemy," he eventually made his way north to Mound City, Illinois, where he camped "amongst the soldiers all the time." Governor Andrew Johnson's permit "to Carry arms for home protection" was "the only thing I have got of my war pappers. If a Discharge from the Sargent makes me a Dezerter, I am one. But I feel my Conchance Clear that I was as true to the government as any man." But the charge of desertion was never expunged and George Box received no pension. In 1892 he chided the pension office for the trouble and expense they were putting "a poor man" through to prove his claim. "I thought rather than take from a soldier," he wrote, "it was the motto to help them." (B. A. Hewatt and Thomas L. Raney in pension file of George Box.) Tom Powell was a wagoner for Company A, and was among the droves of 13th Tennessee Cavalrymen who deserted in February after Major Bradford betrayed Gregory. He claimed he was sent out on a scout a week before the battle, captured by the rebels at Hagersville, and then paroled. (Pension file of Thomas J. Powell.)

29. Fort Memoir in Memphis Public Library.
30. Testimony of Edward B. Benton; Anonymous in Jewell, *New Orleans*.
31. Musick, *6th Virginia Cavalry*; B. D. Hyam/Edward Stanton: January 18, 1864; A. Van Camp/Abraham Lincoln: January 10, 1865; deposition of Maria L. Van Camp, January 17, 1865; L. C. Turner (Judge Advocate)/Edwin Stanton: January 19, 1865; William P. Wood (Superintendent of "Old Capitol" Prison)/C. A. Dana (Assistant Secretary of War): January 27, 1865, RG94/3828, Records of the Adjutant General's Office, microcopy M797: Case Files of Investigations by Levi C. Turner and Lafayette C. Baker: 1861–1866 in NARA.

"Unequal Strife": Forrest's Cavalry: 1861–1864

1. *CV*, April 1908.
2. John Milton Hubbard in Henry, *As They Saw Forrest*, pp. 152–155.
3. My overview of Forrest's command derives primarily from the veterans of Forrest's command who responded to a questionnaire a sociologist circulated some fifty years after the war. Though the resulting survey, published in five volumes as *The Tennessee Civil War Veterans Questionnaires* (*TCWVQ*), provides a

unique window into the Confederate experience, the glass is somewhat fogged. Some respondents were losing their memory, and those who lived long enough to take part were probably more literate and more prosperous than their shorter-lived comrades. For many of them, the war came before the entire "burden" of slaveholding, as they liked to think of it, had descended upon their shoulders, and their recollections derived primarily from childhood. They were interviewed when the mythology of the Lost Cause was ascendant and veterans were determined to deprecate the part slavery played not just in the war but in antebellum society itself. Take this reminiscence, for example, from Captain Hampton Cheney of the 2nd Tennessee Cavalry. "As a general thing, the slaves were kindly treated by their masters." Cheney urged posterity to save its pity for the master, whose "burden of care" was "made heavy by the thought that he was responsible for [the] lives and happiness of so many human beings." His father's slaves "seemed to have no care or foreboding for the future. And why should they," asked Cheney, "when they knew they would be well cared for, as well in sickness as in health, and when old age came and found them helpless, that same care that had been given them all their lives, would be still given with perhaps added tenderness?" (Hampton J. Cheney in *TCWVQ*.) For their part, the slaves in Cheney's neighborhood had a song they used to sing: "You're selling me to Georgy," it began, "But you cannot sell my soul./Thank God Almighty,/God will fix it for us some day!/I hope my old grandma'll/Meet poor John some day./I knows I won't know him when I meets him/Cause he was so young when they sold him away." (Sarah Thomas in *AS*.) Thirty-nine listed Virginia as their native state, 33 North Carolina, 8 Tennessee, 2 South Carolina, 2 Georgia, 2 Alabama, 2 Maryland, 2 Kentucky, 1 New Jersey, 1 Massachusetts.

4. The greatest concentrations of slaves came from the counties of Wilson (14); Williamson (11); Henry (10); Fayette, Maury, and Weakley (9 each); and Bedford, Gibson, Lauderdale, and Madison (7 each).

5. "At least three-fourths of the men who carried guns in the battle-line of the Southern Confederacy," wrote Wyeth, "had no interest directly or indirectly in slavery, and would willingly have seen the negroes freed and colonized out of the country." (Wyeth, *With Sabre and Scalpel*, p. xv.) "That farmers did not own slaves did not necessarily mean that they did not work them," wrote Bob Street of the 10th. "Many small farmers hired slaves from their owners and worked with them in the fields, paying their wages to their masters." Robert Florence Street (*TCWVQ*).

6. "Some of my hardest work as a boy," recalled Lieutenant Dance of the 20th, "was trying to beat the fastest negro cotton picker." (John Russell Dance in *TCWVQ*. See also George Washington Brown, Hampton J. Cheney, Samuel Bond Clemmons, James Park Coffin, M. B. Dinwiddie, T. R. Ford, and Edwin Maximilian Gardner in ibid.)

7. "There were many acts . . ." John Russell Dance in ibid. (See also James E. Dickinson and John Prince Verhine in ibid.)

8. "the rich slave owners . . ." Meriwether Donaldson in ibid. "where the work on the plantations . . ." Hampton J. Cheney in ibid.

9. The cavalrymen's education . . . The men who answered the question about their schooling averaged less than two and a half years, with a median of two

years. But the average education was probably a good deal less, since over a quarter of the respondents, perhaps out of embarrassment, did not answer the question. "couldent spell to Baker . . ." William R. H. Matthews in ibid. Most boys who went . . . Zeke Ray of the 15th attended school off and on for a total of about one year, but his father had to pull him out "on account of the lack of funds to buy clothing and pay tuition." (See also Thomas F. Carrick, James Lindsy Cochran, M. B. Dinwiddie, Edwin Maximilian Gardner, James Hezekiah [Samuel Martin] Ray, in ibid.) "Men that owned . . ." James Patton Walker in ibid.

10. "Clan Allan . . ." Wyeth, *With Sabre and Scalpel*, pp. 7, 131. "In my boyhood days," wrote Wyeth, "you might be called a liar, and survive with something of character and reputation by promptly replying, 'You're another'; but when in a moment of excitement or anger one boy called another a damned liar he had to fight or go to Texas." An obstreperous patriotic strain . . . John L. McMurtry in *TCWVQ*. (See also Thomas Cheatham Little and W. H. Lamastus in ibid.) John W. Carroll . . . Carroll, "Autobiography and Reminiscences," p. 1.

11. "Forrest's recruiters rode . . ." Bess Ogilvie in Rogers and Patterson, "Concerning the Nathan Bedford Forrest Legend." At a single rally . . . R. M. Hughes in ibid. "heard the fife and drums . . ." Weatherred, "Wartime Diary."

12. "In the spring . . ." William Garrett Hight in *TCWVQ*. "Ran away . . ." Edward Perry Davis in ibid. Joe Weems of Anderson's scouts was knocked off his horse as a schoolboy by a gang of Yankee stragglers, and wished ever afterward he had been allowed to carry a pistol, so he "could have gotten one of them, anyway." (Philip Van Horn entry for Joseph Burch Weems in ibid.) "breakfast job . . ." R. M. Hughes in Rogers and Patterson, "Concerning the Nathan Bedford Forrest Legend." "I left home . . ." Jesse Harrison Green in *TCWVQ*. Though there was honor . . . Willoughby, "Colonel Dawson and the Shadow War."

13. "Some of us . . ." John Milton Hubbard in Henry, *As They Saw Forrest*, p. 142. "why men will pick up arms . . ." Robert Florence Street in *TCWVQ*.

14. Watterson-Marcosson, *Marse Henry*, pp. 83, 92–93.

15. "I was not in favor . . ." George Washington Brown in *TCWVQ*. "My sympathies . . ." Carroll, "Autobiography and Reminiscences," p. 19. Unlike World War I, wrote the 20th's M. B. Dinwiddie in 1922, during the Civil War the girls, "rich and the poor alike," cheered them on. "Go, in defense of our grand old South land," they called out as he and his regiment filed by. (M. B. Dinwiddie in TCWV; A. J. Grantham in Anonymous, "Aged Civil War Vet Says He Still Hasn't Overcome Animosity Toward Yankees," *Corpus Christi Caller Times*, October 6, 1940; D. S. Combs in Giles, "Terry's Texas Rangers.")

16. Mays, *Autobiographical Sketch of the Life of William Tapley Mays*.

17. William Alston Johnston in *TCWVQ*.

18. Carroll, "Autobiography and Reminiscences," pp. 25–27.

19. but in the end only 97 returned . . . At one point Johnston denounced Forrest for recruiting as far afield as Georgia. Lonn, *Desertion during the Civil War*, p. 56. "Terrible persecutions are said to be inflicted on the Southern people in Alabama who try to evade the conscription," wrote the less than impartial *New York Herald* in April 1864. "Hundreds of men, women and children are concealed in the swamps, and numbers die of starvation." (*New York Herald*, April

16, 1864.) "There is dissatisfaction . . ." John A. Crutchfield/Mrs. L. M. Crutchfield (20th): Undated, Gordon Browning Museum of the Carroll County Historical Society.

20. Slogging along the roadsides . . . Weatherred, "Wartime Diary." But the men . . . Chalmers, "Lieutenant General Nathan Bedford Forrest." "who fought indifferently . . ." Maury, *Recollections of a Virginian*, pp. 219–220. "We was mounted . . ." J. P. Wilson in *TCWVQ*.

21. "slender-built men . . ." C. P. Lyman/Edna Lyman: April 14, 1862 (Private Collection). "I look like a border ruffian . . ." Given Campbell/Sue Betti Woods: January 26 and May 11, 1862 in Given Campbell Papers (UNCCH).

22. Some cavalrymen . . . Wyeth, *With Sabre and Scalpel*, p. xv. "We have good clothing," wrote John W. Love of the 6th Texas Cavalry. "We have 3 good pair of pants 4 coats good boots though I believe our socks are about to run out. Send me a chew of tobacco & a pocket knife & all will be regular." (John W. Love/ Father: December 5, 1861. 6th Texas Cavalry at Texas Christian University. "My wife and mother . . ." Brownlow, "John Brownlow's First Published Memoirs." "clothing was our greatest want . . ." S. P. Driver in *TCWVQ*.

23. John W. Rabb/Mary C. Rabb: January 14, 1863, at OATTR.

24. "yanky over coates . . ." Brownlow, "John Brownlow's First Published Memoirs." "at the first step . . ." Robert Z. Taylor in *TCWVQ*. (See also Fitzhugh, "Terry's Texas Rangers.")

25. "War suits them . . ." Sherman in Brooksher and Snider, *Glory at a Gallop*, p. xvi. "The boy . . ." Wyeth, *With Sabre and Scalpel*, pp. 13–14, 18–19.

26. Wyeth recalled . . . Ibid., p. 19. "When three or four hundred of such men," wrote Giles of his fellow Texans, "charging as fast as their horses would go, yelling like Comanches, each delivering twelve shots with great rapidity and reasonable accuracy, burst into the ranks of an enemy, the enemy generally gave way." (Giles, "Terry's Texas Rangers.")

27. Almost as important as a good horse was a good saddle. The equipage made by Confederate saddlers was generally inferior to Union issue, however, so "it was a proud Confederate trooper who could boast of having a full set of Yankee tack and equipment." A wounded Andy McLeary of the 12th confessed to stealing a McLellan from a comrade who had in turn purloined it from a Yankee prisoner. "My old saddle was ruining my horse's back, and I felt I had as much right to that saddle as he had—at least I tried to get my conscience to help me see it that way." (Wyeth, *With Sabre and Scalpel*, pp. 15–16.)

28. "on mulberry leaves . . ." Charles Stephen Olin Rice in *TCWVQ*. "In times of stress . . ." Wyeth, *With Sabre and Scalpel*, pp. 6, 14, 18, 19. Forrest's cavalry's pride in their horsemanship was matched by their deep affection for their horses. "My horse Nipper is so fine and fat," exclaimed John Rabb, "and walks soft and runns so fast." (John W. Rabb/ Mellisa C. Rabb and Mary E. Rabb: undated.) Such was their attachment to their mounts that a number of Civil War troopers were actually court-martialed for having "congress" with their horses, manifesting a decided preference for gray mares. (Author's interview with Thomas P. Lowry.) "My poor horse . . ." Giles, "Terry's Texas Rangers." (See also Charles Stephen Olin Rice in *TCWVQ*; Edward O. Guerrant in Davis and Swentor, eds., *Bluegrass Confederate*, pp. 395–396, 398–399, 600.)

29. "We were armed . . ." Newton Cannon in *TCWVQ*. All of J. D. Hughes's . . . J. D. Hughes in ibid. "Alas! . . ." Samuel G. French in Silver, ed., *Mississippi in the Confederacy*, p. 42. (See also Fitzhugh, "Terry's Texas Rangers"; Wyeth, *With Sabre and Scalpel*, pp. 168–169, 200.)

30. Forrest's handpicked . . . Captain J. C. Jackson (Forrest's Escort)/General Thomas Jordan: June 4, 1867, Papers of Leroy Nutt/2285/Folder 8 (SHC/ UNCCH). Forrest himself . . . Hurst, *Nathan Bedford Forrest*, pp. 110, 154. "I doubt if any commander, since the days of lion hearted Richard," wrote Confederate lieutenant general Dick Taylor, "has killed as many enemies with his own hand as Forrest." (Richard "Dick" Taylor in Chalmers, "Lieutenant General Nathan Bedford Forrest.") But it did not take Forrest long . . . Maury, *Recollections of a Virginian*, pp. 219–220. None of Forrest's men were particularly adept with the saber. Few enlisted men bothered to carry them. Forrest himself had no formal knowledge of its use, and figured that he could stand up to "half-a-dozen expert *sabreurs* with his revolver."

31. Giles, "Terry's Texas Rangers." Pistols "circulated among the Rangers throughout the war as a sort of currency," wrote Fitzhugh, "probably a far more satisfactory medium of exchange than declining Confederate paper money." (Fitzhugh, "Terry's Texas Rangers.")

32. "Our necessities . . ." H. C. Coles in *TCWVQ*. "Sometimes . . ." Maury, *Recollections of a Virginian*, pp. 217–218. (See also Burney, "Shannon's Scouts.")

33. "In the cavalry . . ." Given Campbell/Bettie Woods: January 29, 1863, in Given Campbell Papers, 5033–7/Folder 2 in SHC/UNCCH. "The experance . . ." Robert Milton McCalister/McAllister in *TCWVQ*.

34. "By his captures . . ." John W. Morton in Henry, *As They Saw Forrest*, p. 271. (See also S. P. Driver and Edwin Maximilian Gardner in TCWVQ; Captain J. C. Jackson (Forrest's Escort)/General Thomas Jordan: June 4, 1867, Papers of Leroy Nutt/2285/Folder 8 in SHC/UNCCH.) "We were exposed . . ." M. B. Dinwiddie in *TCWVQ*. "life of hardships . . ." J. W. Shankle in ibid. During the retreat from Nashville, Dr. Sam Caldwell of the 21st would see "more superb courage displayed—more endurance of cold and hunger—than I thought possible." (Dr. Samuel H. Caldwell in King, *History and Biographical Sketches of the 46th Tennessee Infantry C.S.A.*)

35. "Camp life . . ." William James Sutton in *TCWVQ*. "Lived mighty hard in camp," agreed Rufus Ireland of the 2nd. (Rufus Ireland in ibid.) "the men and horses . . ." John Johnston in Henry, *As They Saw Forrest*, p. 67nn. "no ditches . . ." William G. Frazier in *TCWVQ*.

36. "I want to say . . ." Archelaus M. Hughes in *TCWVQ*. "sleeping places out of little poles . . ." George Booth Baskerville in ibid. (See also Rufus Morgan Ireland, James Monroe Jones, Christopher Wood Robertson, and W. A. Rushing in ibid; Carroll, "Autobiography and Reminiscences," p. 29.)

37. "mind so much the rains . . ." Wyeth, *With Sabre and Scalpel*, p. 201. "covered up in snow . . ." Sometimes they would wake up under a blanket of snow "so heavy that we could hardly get up." (George V. Payne in *TCWVQ*. See also Andrew Jackson Killebrew, Robert Green Pepper, and J. W. Andes in ibid.) "For want of bedding . . ." Robert Lucius Bowden in ibid.

38. "The bite . . ." Claiborne, "Claiborne's History of Terry's Texas Rangers." "thick enough . . ." Felix L. Walthall/Mary L. Lyons: July 4, 1863, McCain Library and Archives, University of Southern Mississippi: M290. "We drink . . ." J. C. M. Bogle/Bess Bogle: May 9, 1863; Carroll, "Autobiography and Reminiscences," p. 29.

39. www.psychiatrictimes.com/p980301b.html. (See also W. E. Turner in *TCWVQ*; McLeary, *Humorous Incidents of the Civil War*, p. 18.)

40. "eager to get . . ." John W. Rabb/Mellisa C. Rabb: December 5, 1861, at OATTR. Bill Wakefield of the 11th "had smallpox, measles, mumps." (William Leonandus Wakefield in *TCWVQ*.) Three weeks after . . . James S. Pearce in ibid. "There is a good deal . . ." Hugh Black/Mary Ann Black: June 27, 1862 at Robert Manning Strozier Library, Florida State University. Medical care ranged from none to worse than none. "We have been very badly treated by the chief physician of this brigade," wrote Rabb's comrade, Cyrus Love. Several officers remarked that "they would rather kill him than an enemy from the Lincoln Government." (Cyrus Love/Tea Love: January 8, 1862 at Texas Christian University.) When Jimmy Nail of the 2nd became ill, he chose to hire his own doctor. (James B. Nail in *TCWVQ*.)

41. "Our ambulance . . ." Newton Cannon in *TCWVQ*. The 4th . . . John Dillard Vaughan in ibid.

42. "hard eats . . ." John Tallant in ibid. "I have eaten raw corn . . ." Lee T. Billingsley in ibid. "Our rations . . ." Carroll, "Autobiography and Reminiscences," p. 29. (See also Rufus Morgan Ireland; William Leonandus Wakefield, Jesse Harrison Green, and John Russell Dance in *TCWVQ*; McLeary, *Humorous Incidents of the Civil War*, p. 11.) "Some of the boys . . ." Charles Stephen Olin Rice in *TCWVQ*. Scolded by his granddaughter for eating horse meat during the war, the 4th Mississippi's William Henry Womack replied, "Honey, when you're starving you'll eat anything." Golden West Marketing, "4th Mississippi Cavalry."

43. They slaughtered . . . "Pa," wrote one trooper, "I never hooked a hog in my life until I come up here. I have been compelled to kill them up here. We always took them from union men when we could get them." (John W. Love/Father: December 5, 1861 at OATTR.) Returning from home   " Samuel J. Martin in *TCWVQ*. (See also Wyeth, *With Sabre and Scalpel*, p. 202; Giles, "Terry's Texas Rangers"; F. F. Ward, William Roberts, John Wesley Young, and James Frederick Anthony in *TCWVQ*; Burney, "The Famous Terry Rangers"; Wyeth, *With Sabre and Scalpel*, p. 202; John W. Love/Father: December 5, 1861 at OATTR.)

44. "As to camp life . . ." Marcus Vines Crump in *TCWVQ*. "We were a jolly set . . ." McLeary, *Humorous Incidents of the Civil War*, p. 8. "We lived pretty hard . . ." R. W. Michie in *TCWVQ*. "Had a jolly good time," insisted Sol Brantley of the 7th. (See also Solomon Norman Brantley and Thomas Jefferson Evans in ibid.) "Forrest's Command . . ." Solomon Norman Brantley in *TCWVQ*.

45. "was hunting yanks . . ." Robert Edwin Rogers in *TCWVQ*. "A man who can show . . ." James Dinkins in Henry, *As They Saw Forrest*, p. 251. Homesickness afflicted men, many of them mere boys when they enlisted, wrenched from their family farms. (Charles Stephen Olin Rice in *TCWVQ*.)

46. Giles, "Terry's Texas Rangers."

47. What coherence such regiments sustained through the war they owed in large part to Forrest himself. "A sore backed horse was a felony in Forrest's command," wrote Tully Brown of Forrest's artillery; "a broken chain was to him a misdemeanor; and he ruled that command; while it was not lightly trained and drilled in an ordinary sense, yet Forrest, with his iron will and his great power over men," welded it into "almost an absolutely solid mass of men." (Brown, "Nathan Bedford Forrest.")

48. "Unless one were inherently loyal . . ." John K. Bettersworth in Silver, ed., *Mississippi in the Confederacy,* pp. 153–154. "A pack of hounds . . ." Rogers and Patterson, "Concerning the Nathan Bedford Forrest Legend."

49. "The people of Tennessee . . ." Claiborne, "Claiborne's History of Terry's Texas Rangers." Forrest complained . . . Lonn, *Desertion during the Civil War,* pp. 63–64. "Haystack Secessionists . . ." Eliot, *The Story of Archer Alexander,* pp. 45–46. "There are men . . ." Montgomery, *Reminiscences of a Mississippian in Peace and War,* pp. 234–235.

50. "true soldiers . . ." Montgomery, *Reminiscences of a Mississippian in Peace and War,* pp. 234–235. "I was never discharged . . ." James Harvey Hinson in *TCWVQ.* Lonn, *Desertion during the Civil War,* pp. 128, 228. Both sides did what they could to lure enemy soldiers away from their commands. The North offered to pay Confederate deserters for their equipment and grant them immunity from conscription, and the South offered to assist deserters from the Union army in returning to their homes.

51. "large numbers . . ." J. M. Tuttle/Hurlbut: January 3, 1863, in 16th Army Corps (Letters Received) RG98, Part 2, Entry 391, Box 7 in NARA. "I am sorry . . ." Montgomery, *Reminiscences of a Mississippian in Peace and War,* p. 234.

52. "quite a number . . ." M. B. Dinwiddie in *TCWVQ.* "Forrest had a standing order . . ." Wyeth, *With Sabre and Scalpel,* pp. 250–251. At Murfreesboro . . . Hurst, *Nathan Bedford Forrest,* pp. 240–241. At Pulaski . . . Jordan Riggs in Rogers and Patterson, "Concerning the Nathan Bedford Forrest Legend." "On two or three . . ." Claiborne, "Claiborne's History of Terry's Texas Rangers."

53. Hancock, *Hancock's Diary,* pp. 309–310; Hollis, "The Diary of Elisha Tompkin Hollis."

54. Brown, "Nathan Bedford Forrest."

55. "was an outrage . . ." Captain F. G. Terry (Co. G, 8th Kentucky Cavalry)/V. Y. Cook (Co. H, 7th Kentucky Mounted Infantry): November 9, 1918, Robert Selph Henry Papers (VT). "Forrest was cruel . . ." J. F. Rickman in Rogers and Patterson, "Concerning the Nathan Bedford Forrest Legend," pp. 46–47.

56. "From the first . . ." William James Sutton in *TCWVQ.* "born to die . . ." Given Campbell/Sue Betti Woods: January 26 and May 11, 1862, in Given Campbell Papers, Wilson Library, UNCCH.

57. The few comforts . . . "Lingering still in our memory was the sound of the fiddle and the banjo played by two darkies singing at intervals 'John Brown' and other songs to arouse enthusiasm of their young masters . . . These darkies, and many more, followed them to war as cooks and were faithful in loving care of them." (Lockhart, "Memories of the Civil War.") "My father . . ." John Russell Dance in *TCWVQ.*

58. Chalmers/Special Order 65: September 12, 1863, in RG94/Chapter 2/v.299 (Chalmers) in NARA. "The cooks & washermen will be regularly mustered & rations & forage will be issued for them. The cooks will be paid & transportation will be furnished them by the Quarter Master's Department. The washermen will be paid by those who employ them. Each negro employed as a cook or washer will be furnished by the Regimental Quarter Master with an axe for which he will be held responsible & which he will carry constantly when on a march . . . When on a march all the negroes attached to each Regiment or Battalion shall be marched between the main column and the rear guard under the charge of a suitable man detailed for that purpose who shall prevent them from straggling."

59. Otey, "The Story of Our Great War." "I told my boy Tom on several occasions that Mr. Lincoln's proclamation of January 1, 1863 pronounced him free, and at any time he was at liberty to go North, and I should put no obstacles in his way. I can never forget the expression on the face of this faithful and loved companion of my youth, as he candidly avowed his devotion to me, saying, 'Why, Marse Willie, you don't suppose I'm going to leave you. Didn't I promise old miss and old marster to always stay with you?' and he never did desert me through the whole war; but was always the warm-hearted, faithful creature under all circumstances." After the war was over, however, Otey and his slave "drifted away with the great stream of struggling soldiers who were scattering here and there, seeking to earn their daily bread. Whether the honest fellow is now alive or not I do not know, but, God knows, he could always share my crust and cot."

60. "I had with me a favorite . . ." Montgomery, *Reminiscences of a Mississippian in Peace and War,* pp. 112–113.

61. At the Battle of Brandy Station . . . Wiley, *Southern Negroes,* p. 140. An armed slave . . . Willoughby, "Bayonets and Bloomers." After the war . . . Thornton Forrest was born in Shelby County, Tennessee, around 1845 and claimed to have served at Forrest's headquarters. His application was accepted. Another former slave who claimed to have served at Forrest's headquarters was Ben Davis of Lafayette County, who was born March 4, 1836. His claim was also approved. Brogden, comp. *Tennessee Colored Pension Applications for CSA Service* (TSLA).

62. Later, when a company of Union soldiers tried to take his horse, Luke flourished his parole, whereupon a Yankee lieutenant declared, "Boys, we better let that Negro alone." (John Andrew Wilson in *TCWVQ.*)

63. "At least seventeen . . ." Alfred Duke, George Hanna, Henry Jackson, Howard Roach, Cal Sharp, and Earl Turner served in Forrest's Old Regiment, and Greer Jones in his Escort. Lewis Mussall, Henry Nelson, Smith Woods, and George Word applied from the 20th Tennessee, Henry B. West and Alex "Little Alex" Whorton from the 21st. Billy Musgraves served in the 8th Mississippi. (Brogden, comp., *Tennessee Colored Pension Applications for CSA Service* [TSLA].) "were very rough . . ." Knox, *Slave and Freeman,* pp. 50–52.

64. If slavery was so cruel . . . All of these slaves—their names, masters, and services—were chronicled by Edwin H. Rennolds in *A History of the Henry County Commands,* pp. 292–295. "In the four years . . ." William Witherspoon in Henry, *As They Saw Forrest,* pp. 72–73.

Duckworth's Bluff: Union City: Spring 1864

1. In the stasis . . . Maness, "A Ruse That Worked." An old friend . . . Joseph Russell Jones/Abraham Lincoln, January 7, 1863, in Abraham Lincoln Papers (LC).

2. W. M. Reed/Strange: March 21, 1864, in *ORCW*.

3. S. M. Winkler/Hurlbut: April 5 and 18, 1864, in 16th Army Corps (Letters Received) RG98, Part 2, Entry 391, Box 7 in NARA. Winkler prayed that Hurlbut himself "*may* never know what pang it brings to the heart of a man to be asked by his children for bread when he has none to give them."

4. "in greenbacks or Kentucky money . . ." Wyly M. Reed/J. P. Strange: March 21, 1864, in *ORCW*; Forrest/Buckland: March 22, 1864, in *ORCW*. Around the middle . . . Wyly M. Reed/J. P. Strange: March 21, 1864, in *ORCW*; Wyeth, *That Devil Forrest*, p. 339.

5. "scour the country . . ." B. H. Grierson/Fielding Hurst: January 20, 1864, in *ORCW*. "a roving commission . . ." Wyeth, *That Devil Forrest*, p. 339. Such a mandate would have met with Sherman's approval. On January 31, a question about the proper treatment of secessionist civilians in occupied territory elicited from Sherman a burst of Old Testament wrath. "The people of the South," he declared, had "appealed to war," and were therefore "barred from appealing to our Constitution, which they have practically and publicly defiled . . . To those who submit to the rightful law and authority," he continued, "all gentleness and forebearance; but to the petulant and persistent Secessionist, why, death is a mercy, and the quicker he or she is disposed of the better." (Sherman/R. M. Sawyer: January 31, 1864, in Moore, ed., *The Rebellion Record*, vol. 8, pp. 352–353.)

6. "after cutting off . . ." Wyeth, *That Devil Forrest*, pp. 339–340. After arresting . . . Wyly M. Reed/J. P. Strange: March 21, 1864, in *ORCW*.

7. Outraged . . . Forrest/Buckland: March 22, 1864, in *ORCW*. "not entitled . . ." Forrest/"To Whom It May Concern": March 22, 1864, in *ORCW*.

8. Forrest/General Order Number 1: January [?], 1864, in RG94/Chapter 2/v.295 (Chalmers) in NARA.

9. "a regular stampede . . ." Carroll, "Autobiography and Reminiscences," p. 20. "We felt it . . ." Blanton, "Forrest's Old Regiment," *CV* 3, no. 3 (February 1895).

10. "The difficulties . . ." Chalmers, "Lieutenant General Nathan Bedford Forrest and His Campaigns; Forrest/Jefferson Davis: February 5, 1864, in *ORCW*. By mid-February . . . Bob Richardson did not fare so well. "Relieved on account of charges preferred against him" by one of his subordinates, he was replaced by Colonel J. J. Neely and never commanded under Forrest again. (Henry, *"First with the Most" Forrest*, p. 237.)

11. Early in March . . . Jordan and Pryor, *The Campaigns of General Nathan Bedford Forrest*, p. 403. "They were so greatly reduced, however, all three together did not number more than seven hundred effectives, about one-third of whom had received horses already—the remainder were, as yet, to be horsed." (Wyeth, *That Devil Forrest*, pp. 299–300.) Forty-four-year-old Abraham Buford was a Kentucky turfman: a huge, pugnacious, square-faced man with the puffy eyes of a prizefighter and a beard that hung from his jowls like grandfather moss. Horses sagged under his weight; soldiers shuddered at his roar.

"One good *Abe*," a rebel admirer called him. (Edward O. Guerrant in Davis and Swentor, eds., *Bluegrass Confederate,* pp. 155, 416.) An indirect descendant of John Marshall and Thomas Jefferson, Abraham Buford had graduated next to last in his class at West Point, but served gallantly with the 1st Dragoons on the frontier and earned a brevet at Buena Vista in the war with Mexico. "He was born a fighter," wrote a biographer, "and so rigid a disciplinarian that he could not always resist the temptation to command in civil life." ("Shotgun" pseudonym, "Civil War Potpourri," in Alabama State Archives.) After resigning from the army in 1854, he returned to his estate in Woodford County, Kentucky, to raise race horses and cattle, and served for a time as president of the Richmond and Danville Railroad. Comfortably established at his horse farm Bosque Bonita, Buford had opposed secession, and many of his relatives, including his cousins John and Napoleon Bonaparte Buford, joined the Union army. (Both sides would try to hang another of Buford's cousins, the secessionist double agent Basil Wilson Duke of Missouri. Lawrence L. Hewitt in Davis, ed., *The Confederate General,* vol. 1, pp. 145–146.) But when the Confederates raided neutral Kentucky in 1862, Abraham joined the rebellion, rising to brigadier general in a matter of months. He had a curious career in the Confederate army: kicked about from command to command, none of which seemed to know what to do with him. He participated in engagements at La Vergne and Champion Hill and in the siege of Jackson, but it was Forrest who would unleash this raging buffalo of a man, whose strategy was akin to the Wizard's: "Fight," he would advise Forrest before saving the day for him at Tishomingo Creek, "and fight damn quick." (Otey, "The Story of Our Great War.")

12. Lawrence L. Hewitt in Davis, ed., *The Confederate General.* vol. 1, pp. 145–146; Henry, *"First with the Most" Forrest,* pp. 235–236; Dinkins, "The Capture of Fort Pillow"; Jordan and Pryor, *The Campaigns of Nathan Bedford Forrest,* pp. 403–404; Wyeth, *That Devil Forrest,* pp. 300–301; Chalmers, "Lieutenant General Nathan Bedford Forrest and His Campaigns."

13. Otey, "The Story of Our Great War."

14. George Waring in Willoughby, "Gunboats and Gumbo."

15. "My available force for duty [officers and men], as appears from trimonthly report of March 20, as follows: Paducah, 408; Cairo, 231; Columbus, 998; Hickman, 51; Island Number Ten, 162; Union City, 479." (Mason Brayman in *RJSCW.*) In addition, Fort Pillow boasted at the time a garrison of about 280 men.

16. Mason Brayman in *RJSCW.*

17. After Bradford's doomed battalion . . . This according to the returns of March 20. (Mason Brayman in *RJSCW.*) The Maury County native had studied for the bar before serving in the Mexican War. He returned to West Tennessee to hang his shingle in Carroll County, and in 1861 attended a conference in Washington, D.C., to try to devise a means of preventing civil war. By the time he entered the Union army, "the most gentlemanly" Hawkins had served for a year as circuit court judge, and even after obtaining his commission in the Union army he protested the treatment of West Tennesseeans by his fellow Federals.

(Willoughby, "Gunboats and Gumbo"; Biographical Directory of the United States Congress at bioguide.congress.gov.) Back in December . . . TCW, vol. 1, pp. 336–338.

18. Wyeth, *That Devil Forrest,* p. 303.

19. John W. Beatty and P. K. Parsons in *RJSCW.*

20. "a notorious scoundrel . . ." W. R. McLagan in *RJSCW.* Duckworth . . . Wyeth, *That Devil Forrest,* p. 301.

21. Duckworth knew . . . TCW, vol. 1, pp. 68–70. "You damn boys . . ." William Witherspoon in Henry, *As They Saw Forrest,* pp. 101–103.

22. As Duckworth . . . Jordan and Pryor, *The Campaigns of Nathan Bedford Forrest,* p. 407. So on they rode . . . William Witherspoon in Henry, *As They Saw Forrest,* pp. 101–103.

23. Hawkins told him . . . James H. Odlin in *RJSCW.* But after encountering . . . Thomas P. Gray in ibid. Doubling his pickets . . . Thomas P. Gray in "Official Statement of Facts Attending the Attack, Defense and Surrender of the U.S. Military Post at Union City, Tenn., on the 24th of March, 1864," in RG94/E729A/Box 7 in NARA.

24. James H. Odlin in *RJSCW.*

25. Maness, "A Ruse That Worked."

26. Captain Thomas Gray . . . Thomas P. Gray in *RJSCW.* "As soon as . . ." John W. Beattie in ibid. Captain P. K. Parson . . . P. K. Parsons in ibid.

27. "with but little difficulty . . ." Thomas P. Gray and John W. Beattie in ibid. "considerable loss . . ." Jordan and Pryor, *The Campaigns of Nathan Bedford Forrest,* pp. 407–408, 408nn; Thomas P. Gray in *RJSCW.* "After that . . ." Thomas P. Gray in ibid.

28. "curiosity or something else . . ." William Witherspoon in Maness, "A Ruse That Worked." But in fact . . . John W. Beattie in *RJSCW.*

29. A jubilant . . . Thomas P. Gray in *RJSCW.* "a great many . . ." John W. Beattie in ibid.

30. Thomas Gray in *RJSCW;* Kennedy Manuscripts, Southern Historical Collection (RMC).

31. John W. Beattie and P. K. Parsons in *RJSCW.*

32. Henry, *"First with the Most" Forrest,* pp. 238–239; John W. Beattie in *RJSCW.*

33. Maness, "A Ruse That Worked."

34. John W. Beattie in *RJSCW.*

35. Hawkins's officers may have overstated their opposition to the capitulation. According to William Witherspoon of the Confederate 7th Tennessee Cavalry, the sole Yankee officer to oppose surrender on any terms was the seniormost captain, "Black-Hawk" Hays. (Jordan and Pryor, *The Campaigns of Nathan Bedford Forrest,* pp. 408–409; Henry, *"First with the Most" Forrest,* p. 239.)

36. "The next thing . . ." John W. Beattie in *RJSCW.* "Curses loud and deep . . ." Thomas Gray in ibid.; Otey, "The Story of Our Great War."

37. Maness, "A Ruse That Worked."

38. Mason Brayman in *RJSCW.*

39. Willoughby, "Gunboats and Gumbo."

40. William Witherspoon in Henry, *As They Saw Forrest,* pp. 101–103.

41. "God damned coward . . ." P. K. Parsons in *RJSCW.* "These men . . ." John Milton Hubbard in Henry, *As They Saw Forrest,* pp. 152–155.

42. "until the second night . . ." John W. Beattie in *RJSCW.* "300 horses . . ." Maness, "A Ruse That Worked." "were marched two days . . ." John W. Beattie in *RJSCW.*

43. "were not guarded . . ." Thomas P. Gray in "Official Statement of Facts Attending the Attack, Defense and Surrender of the U.S. Military Post at Union City, Tenn., on the 24th of March, 1864," in RG94/E729A/Box 7 in NARA.

44. Holley, "The Seventh Tennessee Volunteer Cavalry: West Tennessee Unionists in Andersonville Prison," in *WTHSP,* 1988.

Paducah: Fort Anderson: September 6, 1861–March 26, 1864

1. Forrest C. Pogue Public History Institute, *The Civil War in the Jackson Purchase Region of Kentucky: A Survey of Historic Sites and Structures.* Much of the background material in this chapter is drawn from this survey. "As near as . . ." John Vance Lauderdale in Josyph, *The Wounded River,* pp. 89, 108, 110. See also Brayman/Sherman: May 2, 1864, in *ORCW.*

2. "Abatis of fallen timber . . ." Wyeth, *That Devil Forrest,* p. 305. Grant set aside . . . John Vance Lauderdale in Josyph, *The Wounded River,* pp. 89, 108, 110.

3. John Vance Lauderdale in Josyph, *The Wounded River,* pp. 89, 108, 110.

4. "Dangerous and Unreliable Men . . ." Henry Dougherty, "Dangerous and Unreliable Men" and "Unconditional and Perfectly Reliable Union Men": October 29, 1862, in RG94/E729A/Box 2 in NARA. The list of "Unconditional and Perfectly Reliable Union Men" was twenty names shorter. (See also Grant/Hurlbut: April 14, 1863, in 16th Army Corps (Letters Received) RG98, Part 2, Entry 391, Box 7 in NARA.) After Hurlbut . . . Their particular concern was continuing their lucrative trade in illicit whiskey, large quantities of which kept turning up in Columbus en route to Tennessee. "Whiskey are arriving here daily, siezed in transit to Tennessee, and shipped from Paducah without my Permit." (Asboth/Henry Binmore: May 13, 1863, in RG94/E729A/Box 2 in NARA, James S. Martin/Asboth: May 4, 1863, and James T. Bollinger/ Judge Green Adams and S. L. Casey: April 2, 1863, in RG94/E729A/Box 2 in NARA.)

5. "Southern rights men . . ." Henry Doughterty/W. H. Thurston: May 16, 1863, in RG94/E729A/Box 2 in NARA. "sharp nosed . . ." William Barber (Co. H, 21st Ohio Infantry)/Family: January 26, 1862, in Jerome Library, Bowling Green State University.

6. In May 1863, a Michigan congressman named F. W. Kellogg decried the treatment Union officers meted out to contrabands in Louisville, Kentucky. "Colored men from Arkansas, Tennessee, Miss. and other Rebel States who have Certificates of their freedom signed by Generals in the field are seized— imprisoned, and sold for costs &c," he said. (Berlin et al., eds., *Free at Last,* pp. 105–106.) A slave-owning Union sergeant saw it differently, and asked Lincoln's attorney general, Edward Bates, this loaded question: "Whether a Union Man who has lived & intends to live & die a Union man has the legal Right to arrest

& compel his slaves to serve him . . . ?" (E. Cheek/Edward Bates: May 6, 1863, in Abraham Lincoln Papers [LC].)

7. "for the purpose . . ." James S. Martin/Cunningham: April 23, 1863, in RG94/E729A/Box 5 in NARA. "To say . . ." Thomas B. Johnson in Cimprich, *Slavery's End in Tennessee,* p. 45. Italics mine.

8. Like Wolfe . . . James S. Martin/Asboth: May 4, 1863, in RG94/E729A/Box 2 in NARA. "such persons . . ." James S. Martin: Special Order 37: June 8, 1863, in ibid.

9. "come within our lines . . ." James S. Martin/Asboth: June 6 and 19, 1863, in RG94/E729A/Box 5 in NARA. Martin concluded . . . James S. Martin/Asboth: July 7, 1863, in ibid.; James S. Martin/Special Order 57: July 9, 1863, in ibid.

10. Apparently at the behest . . . Testimony of William H. Bunting: October 10, 1863, in ibid. Drake made it a practice to endorse all civil warrants for masters to retrieve their slaves. For example: "You are commanded to arrest Eliza, a woman aged about 28 years old, Henry & Palmer, runaway slaves belonging to V. A. M. Crutcher of Ballard County Ky." (Lieutenant Quincy J. Drake/Captain Burns: October 8, 1863, in ibid.) Nevertheless, the abductions . . . A. De Lezyuski/Lieutenant Colonel Allen: July 11, 1863, in ibid.

11. *Louisville Journal,* December 20, 1863, in 16th Army Corps (Letters Received) RG98, Part 2, Entry 391, Box 7 in NARA.

12. A veteran . . . Brayman/Sherman: May 2, 1864, in *ORCW.*

13. Hicks summoned . . . Testimony of Captain James H. Odlin in *RJSCW.* "lively" pace . . . Hancock, *Hancock's Diary,* p. 370; Cook, "Forrest's Capture of Col. R. G. Ingersoll," *CV* March 1907.

14. "the rebels took advantage . . ." James W. Shirk in in *RJSCW.* "women, children . . ." James H. Odlin in ibid.; Mrs. Hannah Hammond and Mason Brayman in ibid.

15. Forrest in Huch, "The Fort Pillow Massacre," p. 65.

16. James W. Shirk in *RJSCW.*

17. Stephen G. Hicks in ibid.

18. Brayman/Sherman: May 2, 1864, in Chicago Historical Society.

19. to the cheering . . . Fuchs, *An Unerring Fire,* p. 41. "Most of the inhabitants . . ." Testimony of General Mason Brayman in *RJSCW.* "shingles, brick chimneys . . ." Officer of 2nd Tennessee Cavalry (CSA) in *Charleston Mercury,* May 2, 1864.

20. "The negro troops . . ." Testimony of James H. Odlin in *RJSCW.* "conspicuous for his gallantry . . ." Moore, *Anecdotes, Poetry, and Incidents of the War,* p. 139.

21. "having muskets . . ." Testimony of James H. Odlin in *RJSCW.*

22. "first carried away . . ." Officer of 2nd Tennessee Cavalry (CSA) in the *Charleston Mercury,* May 2, 1864. Captain McKnight . . . Hancock, *Hancock's Diary,* p. 604.

23. "canister, grape . . ." Officer of 2nd Tennessee Cavalry (CSA) in *Charleston Mercury,* May 2, 1864. "I see . . ." Wallace, "A Trip to Dixie."

24. During the third charge . . . Morris, "Fort Pillow: Massacre or Madness?" "took shelter . . ." Stephen G. Hicks in *RJSCW.* "the thickening shades . . ." Officer of 2nd Tennessee Cavalry (CSA) in *Charleston Mercury,* May 2, 1864.

25. Stephen G. Hicks in *RJSCW.*

26. "held the town . . ." Forrest in *ORCW*. "loss in government stores . . ." Stephen G. Hicks in *RJSCW*; Morris, "Fort Pillow: Massacre or Madness?"
27. Lauchlan Donaldson in *TCWVQ*.
28. "I have been . . ." Hicks quoted in testimony of General Mason Brayman in *RJSCW*. "I cannot refrain . . ." Brayman/Sherman: May 2, 1864, in *ORCW*.
29. According to Chalmers . . . Forrest C. Pogue Public History Institute, *The Civil War in the Jackson Purchase Region of Kentucky*, p. 34; Stephen G. Hicks in *RJSCW*. See also Captain James H. Odlin in ibid.; Hurst, *Nathan Bedford Forrest*, pp. 161–162. "freed from official restrictions . . ." Officer of 2nd Tennessee Cavalry (CSA) in *Charleston Mercury*, May 2, 1864.
30. The next morning . . . *Charleston Mercury*, May 2, 1864.
31. Captain James H. Odlin in *RJSCW*.
32. "the iron heels . . ." Chalmers in *ORCW*.
33. Anderson, "The True Story of Fort Pillow."
34. Pension file of George W. Craig; George Craig in pension file of William H. Albritton; pension file of Thomas Loftis.

"All Is Quiet": Booth at Fort Pillow: March 28–April 12, 1864

1. In late March . . . *CWAL*, vol. 1, p. 407 and vol. 2, p. 205. As a young lawyer he had overseen the withdrawal of the Mormons from Illinois, rented part of Abraham Lincoln's property in Springfield, and in 1853 put Lincoln on retainer with the Illinois Central. (Ibid., vol. 2, pp. 397–398.)
2. "Our posts . . ." Brayman/Thomas H. Harris: April 2, 1864, in *ORCW*. "ridiculous nonsense . . ." Sherman in Henry, *"First with the Most" Forrest*, p. 243. There had been some minor effort made to recruit rebels in southern Illinois. Captain James W. Shirk would testify that on April 9, Captain Smith, commanding the *Peosta*, broke up a rebel recruiting office on board a trading vessel docked at Brooklyn, Illinois. Smith "destroyed the boat, but saved seven new rebel uniforms that were on it." (James W. Shirk in *RJSCW*. See also Captain R. D. Mussey/Major C. W. Foster: April 4, 1864, RG94/Box 8: Records of the 2nd USCLA in NARA.)
3. Hurlbut/Sherman: March 30, 1864, and April 10, 1864, in 16th Army Corps (Letters Received) RG98, Part 2, Entry 391, Box 7 in NARA.
4. "considered it hazardous . . ." Grierson/Harris: April 24, 1864, in 16th Army Corps (Letters Received) RG98, Part 2, Entry 391, Box 7 in NARA. Within ten days . . . Hurlbut/Sherman: March 30, 1864, and April 10, 1864, in 16th Army Corps (Letters Received) RG98, Part 2, Entry 391, Box 7 in NARA; Grierson/Harris: April 24, 1864, in 16th Army Corps (Letters Received) RG98, Part 2, Entry 391, Box 7 in NARA.
5. Mrs. Elizabeth Wayt Booth/Major General Cadwallader Colder Washburn: August 25, 1864, RG109/Microcopy M345/Union Provost Marshal's File of Papers Relating to Individual Civilians in NARA. With Forrest . . . William Smith in pension file of Thomas McClure; J. [Lewis]/Thomas H. Harris: March 28, 1864, in RG94/E729A/Box 6 in NARA.
6. Hurlbut/Booth: March 28, 1864, in *ORCW*.
7. Hurlbut/Bradford: March 28, 1864, in *ORCW*.
8. Regimental records of 13th Tennessee Cavalry, March 1864, in NARA.

9. In addition . . . Henry, *"First with the Most" Forrest*, p. 249. The 2nd's returns for March show thirty-three, but at the time of the battle at least two men from the 2nd were in the hospital. Seven men of Company D were officially listed as on detached service working with the quartermaster's office, but in fact the quartermaster had simply neglected to report their return to their company until early April. (Charles P. Brown/L. Methuly: April 2, 1864, in 16th Army Corps (Letters Received) RG98, Part 2, Entry 391, Box 7 in NARA.) Weighed down . . . Fuchs, *An Unerring Fire*, pp. 48–49.

10. Lionel Booth's Command on Departure from Memphis: Report dated March 29, 1864, in 16th Army Corps (Letters Received) RG98, Part 2, Entry 391, Box 7 in NARA.

11. One possible reason . . . Joseph K. Barnes/Stanton: March 30, 1864, in 16th Army Corps (Letters Received) RG98, Part 2, Entry 391, Box 7 in NARA. "I think . . ." William F. Bradford/Andrew Johnson: November 15, 1863, in Papers of Andrew Johnson (Microfilm) in TSLA.

12. John L. Poston in pension file of Neal Clark.

13. Deeming the garrison . . . Robert Mainfort in the *Memphis Commercial Appeal*, September 14, 1979. "Working his command . . ." Achilles V. Clark/George B. Halstead: April 19, 1864, in TSLA. It is likely . . . "Many of the slaves who had helped to build the fort for the confederates later ran away from their owners and went to Fort Pillow after it was occupied by the Union forces. They believed they would be safe here, for they had been told that nothing could capture it." Mills, "Fort Pillow."

14. After his men . . . Henry, *"First with the Most" Forrest*, p. 251. But his own men . . . Henry Weaver in *RJSCW*.

15. Mollie Pittman in *RJSCW*.

16. Kirkland, *The Pictorial Book of Anecdotes*, pp. 487–488. By another account, she had just proposed purchasing ammunition for Colonel F. M. Stewart of Forrest's 15th Tennessee Cavalry (in which her father's employer served) when the Yankees captured her and brought her to Fort Pillow. Brought before Booth, she refused to reveal where she had concealed the goods she had purchased for the rebels. According to this account, her husband was serving at Fort Pillow but refused to see her, "saying she had brought disgrace upon him and their family by aiding the enemies of their country," and asked "that their true names might not be given to the public." Yet another version has it that only after Captain Theodorick Bradford and several other Dyer County men identified her and threatened to hang her did she admit who she was. But Mollie herself claimed that before then her "mind and feeling had undergone a very material change from what they were when I started out in the war as to the character of the Northern people and soldiers and the merits of the controversy involved." Repulsed by an "utterly atrocious and barbarous" command she declined to specify, she quit Missouri's Southern League, telling its members "I would have nothing more to do with them." And yet she believed it would be "dishonorable" to desert the rebel cause entirely, until she was captured, when she decided to "do what I could to atone for the past and resolved to throw myself upon the Government." Willoughby, "Bayonets and Bloomers." Earl Willoughby has investigated "Mollie" Pittman's life with particular care.

17. Willoughby, "Bayonets and Bloomers."
18. Thomas P. Gray in *RJSCW*.
19. "take all the available . . ." Hurlbut/Grierson: March 31, 1864, in 16th Army Corps (Letters Received) RG98, Part 2, Entry 391, Box 7 in NARA. "The march must be . . ." Thomas H. Harris/B. H. Grierson: March 30, 1864, in RG94/E729A/Box 7 in NARA. He warned Grierson . . . Hurlbut/Grierson: March 31, 1864, in 16th Army Corps (Letters Received) RG98, Part 2, Entry 391, Box 7 in NARA.
20. "severely crippled . . ." Hurlbut/Sherman: April 1, 1864, in RG393/Box 1 in NARA.
21. Hurlbut/R. M. Sawyer: April 1, 1864, in RG393/Box 1 in NARA.
22. "to give life . . ." Sherman/McPherson: April 2, 1864, in *ORCW*; "a big bombshell . . ." Henry, *"First with the Most" Forrest*, pp. 243–244. See also Chalmers, "Lieutenant General Nathan Bedford Forrest."
23. "No matter what strength . . ." Sherman/Hurlbut: April 2, 1864, in *ORCW*. "and found them too strong . . ." Hurlbut/Sherman: April 4, 1864, in RG393/Box 1 in NARA. Declined . . . Hurlbut/Sherman: April 6, 1864, in ibid.
24. On April 4 . . . Grierson/Hurlbut: April 5, 1864, in 16th Army Corps (Letters Received) RG98, Part 2, Entry 391, Box 7 in NARA. "The enemy . . ." Hurlbut/R. P. Buckland: April 4, 1864, in RG393/Box 1 in NARA; B. H. Grierson/Hurlbut: April 6, 1864, in 16th Army Corps (Letters Received) RG98, Part 2, Entry 391, Box 7 in NARA. "purely guess work . . ." Hurlbut/B. H. Grierson: April 5, 1864, in RG393/Box 1 in NARA.
25. Ira Gifford/T. H. Harris: April 6, 1864, in 16th Army Corps (Letters Received) RG98, Part 2, Entry 391, Box 7 in NARA.
26. Benjamin Densmore (3rd Minnesota Infantry)/Brother: April 7, 1864, Benjamin Densmore and Family Papers (A0413), Minnesota Historical Society.
27. Hurlbut/Buckland: April 7, 1864, in 16th Army Corps (Letters Received) RG98, Part 2, Entry 391, Box 7 in NARA; Henry, *"First with the Most" Forrest*, p. 244.
28. Hurlbut/McPherson: April 10, 1864, in *ORCW*.
29. Sherman/McPherson: April 10, 1864, in *ORCW*.
30. The next day . . . W. T. Sherman in Chalmers, "Lieutenant General Nathan Bedford Forrest and His Campaigns." In any case . . . Sherman/McPherson: April 19, 1864, in *ORCW*.
31. Booth/Hurlbut: April 3, 1864, in RG393, Part 2, Entry 391, Box 7 in NARA.

"A Bitterness of Feeling": Forrest: March 28–April 12, 1864

1. The scouts' report . . . Jordan and Pryor, *The Campaigns of Nathan Bedford Forrest*, p. 419. "As we plunged . . ." Johnston, "Civil War Recollection."
2. "We fought . . ." William R. Kimbrell/Joseph Kimbrel: April 8, 1864 (TSLA). "mistresses . . ." James Ronald Chalmers in Morris, "Fort Pillow: Massacre or Madness?" Chalmers said Neely captured seventy-five men; Jordan and Pryor said thirty. (Jordan and Pryor, *The Campaigns of Nathan Bedford Forrest*, pp. 418–419.)
3. "not at all Suit . . ." Fielding Hurst/Andrew Johnson: April 29, 1864, in Graf and Haskins, *The Papers of Andrew Johnson*, vol. 6, pp. 685–687. But like it or not . . . Hatch/Thomas: May 13, 1865, in *ORCW*.
4. Jordan and Pryor, *The Campaigns of Nathan Bedford Forrest*, p. 415. According

to Wyeth, "not one took advantage of this opportunity to desert the cause in which he had enlisted." (Wyeth, *That Devil Forrest,* pp. 305–306.)

5. Unlike Chalmers . . . Wyeth, *With Sabre and Scalpel,* p. 175. Commissioned a captain . . . *TCW* vol. 1, pp. 97–99, 109; Willoughby, "Home-made Yankees"; M. B. Dinwiddie in *TCWVQ.*

6. Bell's brigade . . . Jordan and Pryor, *The Campaigns of Nathan Bedford Forrest,* p. 415. McCulloch's brigade . . . On April 1 they "were beautifully 'April fooled,'" wrote their scout, Dewitt Clinton Fort, "by a false alarm which caused us a whole day's hard march for nothing." (Fort, "Journal of Dewitt Clinton Fort"; Jordan and Pryor, *The Campaigns of Nathan Bedford Forrest,* p. 415.)

7. "to visit their friends . . ." Jordan and Pryor, *The Campaign of General Nathan Bedford Forrest,* p. 420. Part of this force . . . S. L. Woodward/Hurst: April 2, 1864, in *ORCW.*

8. Darting back and forth . . . Jordan and Pryor, *The Campaigns of Nathan Bedford Forrest,* pp. 420–422; Wyeth, *That Devil Forrest,* p. 306; Bates, *History of Pennsylvania Volunteers,* vol. 1, pp. 1–2. Delighted by yet another . . . Johnston, "Civil War Recollection."

9. Jordan and Pryor, *The Campaigns of Nathan Bedford Forrest,* p. 415; Henry, *"First with the Most" Forrest,* p. 242.

10. "well combed . . ." Britton, *The Aftermath of the Civil War,* p. 119. "'Twere useless . . ." Fort, "Journal of Dewitt Clinton Fort." "highly gratified . . ." L. Polk/Jefferson Davis: April 27, 1864, in *ORCW.*

11. N. B. Forrest in Wyeth, *That Devil Forrest,* pp. 306–307.

12. Forrest/Thomas M. Jack: April 4, 1864, in *ORCW.* Sherman once groaned that it was foolish to leave any horses in occupied territory because "Forrest would be sure to steal them." (Wyeth, *That Devil Forrest,* p. 299.) Cavalrymen had their preferences. "The western horse was no good to a Tennessee or Kentucky cavalry man." He required "medium size horses: keen and active." (William Gibbs Allen in *TCWVQ.*)

13. Wrote John Johnston, who did not fight at Fort Pillow, "this band of marauders who were about on a par with Hurst's men, had robbed and insulted the defenseless citizens at their pleasure." (Johnston, "Civil War Recollection.")

14. Barteau in *Detroit Free Press,* December 1, 1884.

15. Another local story . . . Bettie Davis/author: June 3, 2001. Tom Mays . . . Willoughby, "Under the Black Flag" and "Home-made Yankees." "negro stealing . . ." Hancock, *Hancock's Diary,* pp. 351–352. Judge Green, a neighborly planter who had been so hospitable toward the officers of the 32nd Iowa Infantry as to not only feed them but dissuade Confederate scouts from attacking them, fell out with the ever suspicious Bradford. (Scott, ed., *Story of the Thirty Second Iowa Infantry Volunteers,* p. 99.) The foraging parties of the 13th apparently found his prosperous spread with its vast icehouse, cotton mills, and sawmills an irresistible target. According to local lore, it was Green "who lit the fuse which led to the battle of Fort Pillow," after a party of foragers confronted the judge as he was riding home from Ripley, killed his horse, and robbed him of all his money. "That was when he decided to send a messenger to Jackson," wrote a man who grew up on Green's farm, "where Gen. Forrest was stationed, and let him know what was going on in Lauderdale County." After reading

Green's letter Forrest "rounded up his troops and headed west to Fort Pillow." Parker conflates the dates in his recounting of family lore: "Early in 1862, when Confederate Gen. Gideon J. Pillow, with his men, left the fort, the Federal army slipped in and took over. It soon ran short of money and food, and it was then Union soldiers began stealing and taking from people all over the county." But the story is plausible. Green would have been outraged by such treatment, especially after his kindness to Bradford's predecessors. (Albert F. Parker in *Lauderdale County* (TN) *Enterprise*, March 8, 1978.)

16. "to capture . . ." Johnston, "Civil War Recollection." "General Forrest was a man . . ." Brewer, "Storming of Fort Pillow," *CV*, December 1925. "A long course of brutal, infamous conduct on the part of Bradford's Battalion toward the non-combatant people of West Tennessee had determined General Forrest to break up their lair," wrote his authorized biographers Jordan and Pryor, "and capture or destroy them before leaving that section of the country for other operations." Robert Selph Henry concurred. (Jordan and Pryor, *The Campaigns of Nathan Bedford Forrest*, p. 424; Henry, *"First with the Most" Forrest*, pp. 249–250.) "attacking the fort . . ." Wyeth, *That Devil Forrest*, pp. 313–314.

17. Fort, "Memoir." The Tennessee historian Bobby L. Lovett writes that the three men were lynched after "having been accused of cooperating with the Yankees." (Lovett, "The West Tennessee Colored Troops in Civil War Combat"; *Memphis Bulletin*, April 2, 5, 6, 1864).

18. Forrest/Joseph E. Johnston: April 6, 1864, in *ORCW*.

19. "assume command . . ." Chalmers: Special Order 76: April 7, 1864, in RG94/Chapter 2/v.299 (Chalmers) in NARA. Forrest instructed . . . W. A. Goodman/J. J. Neely: April 8, 1864, in *ORCW*. Colonel John McGuirk . . . Wyeth, *That Devil Forrest*, p. 314; Henry, *"First with the Most" Forrest*, pp. 246–247. "executed these orders . . ." Chalmers in *ORCW*.

20. Fuchs, *An Unerring Fire*, p. 45; Henry, *"First with the Most" Forrest*, p. 243; Jordan and Pryor, *The Campaigns of Nathan Bedford Forrest*, p. 416; Wyeth, *That Devil Forrest*, p. 308.

21. In the meantime . . . Achilles V. Clark/Sister: April 14, 1864, in Cimprich and Mainfort, "Fort Pillow Revisited"; Hollis, "Diary of Elisha Tompkin Hollis." McCulloch's brigade . . . Fort, "Memoir"; Forrest/Chalmers: April 7, 1864, in RG94/Chapter 2/v.299 (Chalmers) in NARA. On April 8 . . . W. A. Goodman/J. J. Neely: April 8, 1864, in *ORCW*.

22. Together they would . . . Henry, *"First with the Most" Forrest*, p. 250. Bell . . . Hollis, "Diary of Elisha Tompkin Hollis"; Jordan and Pryor, *The Campaigns of Nathan Bedford Forrest*, p. 423; Achilles V. Clark/Sister: April 14, 1864, in Cimprich and Mainfort, "Fort Pillow Revisited." badly shot up . . . Hancock, *Hancock's Diary*, pp. 351–352. Otherwise, from the time . . . ibid.

23. Anderson, "The True Story of Fort Pillow."

24. Anderson had originally . . . Wyeth, *That Devil Forrest*, p. 594. "Soon after . . ." "Reunion of Forrest's Escort," *CV*, February 1894.

25. "I move . . ." Forrest/S. D. Lee: April 10, 1864, in *ORCW*. Be it . . . NPSSSS. But almost certainly . . . Robert Selph Henry, *"First with the Most" Forrest*, pp. 253–254. There is continuing debate about how many men Forrest sent to Fort Pillow. To intimidate the enemy and make himself shine in the eyes of Rich-

mond and the Southern public, Forrest tended to understate his own force and overstate the forces he defeated and the gains he won. A journalist who interviewed him after the war maintained that "any one hearing him talk would call him a braggadocio. As for myself, I would believe one half he said, and only dispute with him with my finger upon the trigger of my pistol." (Moore, *Anecdotes, Poetry, and Incidents,* pp. 350–351.) Jordan and Pryor, Forrest's authorized biographers, who might have been tempted to underestimate Forrest's strength in the wake of the massacre controversy, estimate that there were 1,500 in McCulloch's brigade and 1,700 in Bell's, for a total of 3,200. Some other estimates of Forrest's force that day: Charles Anderson (over 1,800) ("The True Story of Fort Pillow"); Hurlbut (hearsay) ("not less than 2,500") in *RJSCW;* James Bingham (3,500–4,000) in ibid.; Lieutenants F. A. Smith and William Cleary (hearsay) (5,000–7,000) in ibid.; Lieutenant Mack J. Leaming (7,000–10,000) in ibid.; N. D. Wetmore Jr. (hearsay) (7,000–8,000) (Wetmore/Editors, *Argus:* April 13, 1864 (*NFWW*). The following figures derive from regimental returns, though some were submitted before Forrest's reorganization and massive recruitment drive (and subsequent desertions): Escort, 80; 16th (Detachment), 100; 19th (Detachment), 100; Walton's Battery, 52; Forrest's Old Regiment, 139; 2nd Missouri, 300; 22nd (2nd) Tennessee, 300; 20th Tennessee, 300; 5th Mississippi, 300; 18th Mississippi, 250; Willis's Texas Battalion, 450: Total 2,371. These totals do not include the various partisans, scouts, slaves, local men, and stray Texans and Kentuckians who, if pension records and postwar correspondence are anything to go by, were intermingled with Forrest's troops. Men from the 2nd Kentucky; 2nd Mississippi; 7th, 9th, and 15th Tennessee; and McNeill's (Tennessee) Cavalry would also claim to have participated. Considering these factors, and Forrest's recruitment drive, Jordan and Pryor's estimate of 3,200 is probably the most accurate. (Forrest/Polk: April 15, 1864, in Wyeth, *That Devil Forrest,* p. 333; *TCWVQ; NPSSSS; ORCW.*)

26. Their saddlebags . . . Anderson, "The True Story of Fort Pillow"; Dyer [Forrest's Escort], Pocket Diary, MF91 in TSLA. Duckworth's 7th . . . William Lee Anthony in *TCWVQ.* Buford sent . . . Alexander M. Pennock in *RJSCW.* Buford himself . . . Jordan and Pryor, *The Campaigns of Nathan Bedford Forrest,* p. 416; James W. Shirk in *RJSCW;* James W. Shirk/Gideon Welles: April 12, 1864 (*NFWW*); LeRoy Fitch/David D. Porter: April 16, 1864 (*NFWW*).

27. At about two . . . Jordan and Pryor, *The Campaigns of Nathan Bedford Forrest,* pp. 424–425; Johnston, "Civil War Recollection." They set off . . . Notes of Captain Walter A. Goodman in Jordan and Pryor, *The Campaigns of General Nathan Bedford Forrest,* p. 425.

28. Dyer [Forrest's Escort], Pocket Diary, MF91, TSLA.

29. Also known as Jackson's Company . . . Thomas Cheatham Little in *TCWVQ.* "A splendid company . . ." Chalmers, "Lieutenant General Nathan Bedford Forrest and His Campaigns." See also J. C. Jackson/Thomas Jordan: June 4, 1867, in Papers of Leroy Nutt/2285/Folder 8 (SHC/UNCCH).

30. But it was a favorite . . . Captain J. C. Jackson (Forrest's Escort)/General Thomas Jordan: June 4, 1867, Papers of Leroy Nutt/2285/Folder 8 (SHC/UNCCH). Mustered into service . . . Goodspeed, *History of Tennessee Illustrated,* at www.homepages.rootsweb.com.

31. Anonymous, "Colonel Drew Wisdom," *CV,* May 1906.

32. Deposition of Samuel Hughes in pension file of Charles Macklin [Koon].

33. Deposition of Nicholas Hamer in pension file of Samuel Green.

34. Also riding . . . Otey, "The Story of Our Great War"; Wyeth, *That Devil Forrest,* p. 314. By some accounts Forrest's guide was a man named John Laney, a former Union sympathizer enraged by a squad of Bradford's boys who rode up to his house, shot three chickens, and carried them off, whereupon he offered to guide Forrest to the fort. But by the time Forrest got to Fort Pillow his men had already invested the place. (Mills, "Fort Pillow"; *Covington* [TN] *Leader,* July 28, 1932.)

35. Regimental records of the 6th Tennessee Cavalry (USA) in NARA; NPSSSS.

36. "learned that . . ." Fitch, "Monthly Report." Perhaps tipped off . . . Kelso returned shortly thereafter and convinced the provost marshal to let him off with a mere docking of his pay. After the war, Kelso acquired a wife and children, and died in 1898. (Pension file of Frederick Kelso.) "poor and worn out . . ." Five years later Walters remarried and eventually fathered eight more children, for a total of four daughters and seven sons, who lived with him in abject poverty until his death in 1894. (Pension file of John A. Walters.)

37. "Little 'Un . . ." Hancock, *Hancock's Diary,* p. 308; Terry Jones in Davis, ed., *The Confederate General,* vol. 1, pp. 169–171. See also McPherson, *The Negro's Civil War,* app. A; John K. Bettersworth in Silver, ed., *Mississippi in the Confederacy,* pp. 280–282; Wharton, *The Negro in Mississippi: 1865–1890,* pp. 17–18, 27.

38. One young gentleman-soldier . . . Unidentified officer in Hurst, *Nathan Bedford Forrest,* p. 230.

39. Henry, *"First with the Most" Forrest,* p. 237.

40. Polk ruled . . . Henry, *"First with the Most" Forrest,* pp. 236–237; Jordan and Pryor, *The Campaigns of Nathan Bedford Forrest,* pp. 406–407; Forrest: Special Order 33: March 13, 1864, in RG94/Chapter 2/v.299 (Chalmers) in NARA; Forrest/Special Order 77: March 17, 1864, in RG94/Chapter 2/v.299 (Chalmers) in NARA. Though Forrest himself was a teetotaler, his orders to destroy stills had less to do with his aversion to liquor than with the amount of valuable and increasingly scarce corn the stills used up. In April, the citizens of Clarksville implored the local Union commander to shut down eighteen local distilleries because "the scarcity of corn in the country is such that if the Distilleries are not Closed (at least until a new crop is grown) that the people will suffer for want of this necessary Article of food." A. A. Smith/B. H. Polk: April 11, 1864, *ORCW.* whereupon Forrest ordered . . . Wyeth, *That Devil Forrest,* p. 307. Chalmers reached Bolivar on the thirtieth, in time to furnish Colonel Neely with a guard to take charge of the Yankee prisoners he had captured the day before and escort them down to Corinth while Chalmers and the rest of his command ranged between Memphis and Jackson with orders to keep Forrest "'fully posted of all movements of the enemy from the direction of Memphis and Fort Pillow." (Charles W. Anderson [Forrest]/Chalmers: March 30, 1864, in *ORCW*; Jordan and Pryor, *The Campaigns of Nathan Bedford Forrest,* p. 419; Henry, *"First with the Most" Forrest,* pp. 242–243.)

41. John Wyeth described Russell as a "grim old colonel" whom he saw smile only once, at Anderson's Crossroads on October 2, 1863, when Forrest gave him the

command to advance with his 4th Alabama Cavalry. (Wyeth, *With Sabre and Scalpel*, p. 200.)

42. "Forrest will carry . . ." S. A. Hurlbut in *RJSCW*. "McCulloch's men . . ." Hancock, *Hancock's Diary*, p. 352.

43. "contemplating not only . . ." John Milton Hubbard in Henry, *As They Saw Forrest*, p. 217.

44. Frustrated by their failure . . . Some argue that Paducah could not have been preying on the minds of Forrest's men at Fort Pillow, because none of the men who served at Paducah fought at Fort Pillow. They are mistaken on two counts; first, both Forrest's Escort and Russell's 20th Tennessee Cavalry plus small squads or detachments from other regiments were engaged in both attacks; and second, the defeat at Paducah demoralized Forrest's entire command, not just the regiments who fought in both places. "Tho' hungry . . ." Fort, "Memoir."

45. "Those within . . ." Hubbard, *Notes of a Private*, p. 102. "The rebel . . ." *Franklin [VA] Repository*, April 27, 1864. Bell had a special . . . Moore, *Anecdotes, Poetry, and Incidents of the War*, pp. 450–451.

46. Wyeth, *That Devil Forrest*, pp. xxii, 338–339.

47. "Many of the citizens . . ." Brewer, "Storming of Fort Pillow." A. G. Grantham . . . A. J. Grantham in "Aged Civil War Vet Says He Still Hasn't Overcome Animosity toward Yankees," *Corpus Christi Caller Times*, October 6, 1940. By another account . . . Sayers, "Fort Pillow."

48. Dinkins, *Furl That Banner*, pp. 150–151.

49. Thomas P. Gray in *RJSCW*. When asked if Duckworth's men had said anything about "negro troops, &c." Gray's comrade, Captain Beattie, said "not much." (John W. Beattie in ibid.)

50. Stopping about a mile . . . Achilles V. Clark/Sister: April 14, 1864, in Cimprich and Mainfort, "Fort Pillow Revisited." As Wilson . . . Fuchs, *Unerring Fire*, p. 51; Hancock, *Hancock's Diary*, p. 354; Chalmers, "Official Report," *ORCW*. Captain Frank J. Smith . . . Mills, "Fort Pillow."

51. Jordan and Pryor, *The Campaigns of Nathan Bedford Forrest*, p. 425 and nn.

52. "Little Dixie . . ." Out of Missouri's 112 counties, Cooper had the eighth largest number of slaves in 1860. Robert McCulloch's grandfather was an Irishman who had immigrated to Virginia and served in the Revolutionary War. Regarding slavery in Cooper County, see also Melton, *History of Cooper County, Missouri*, pp. 70–71; Laura Lacenberry-Jackson in *AS*; Delicia Ann Wiley Patterson/Lucinda Patterson at www.rootsweb.com/~mocooper/Biographical/Home_Town-Sketches_PP_301_328.htm.

53. Through their early . . . In fact, military service had a curious history in Cooper County. Every year its militia used to don Continental cocked hats adorned with long red feathers and muster in Boonville. Musters were once rollicking occasions, an excuse for barbecues and binges, but as the white population increased and the fear of Indian attacks receded, people lost interest. In 1842, some local wags expressed their boredom by dubbing themselves the "Fantastic Company" and burlesquing the militia with mock military uniforms. The outraged militia responded with brickbats, but the Fantastic Company proved too much for them, and in the ensuing battle the wags killed their major and wounded their colonel before scattering into the countryside. almost every

man . . . "Slaves couldn't shoot," a former Cooper County slave named Joseph Higgerson recalled. "Was a law against it in slaves' times." (Joseph Higgerson in AS.) "whisky traders . . ." H. D. Benedict in Johnson, *History of Cooper County, Missouri*, p. 180.

54. "from Civilization to Sundown . . ." Anonymous, *Historical Atlas of Cooper County, Missouri*. See also Johnson, *History of Cooper County*, Missouri, p. 181.

55. Johnson, *History of Cooper County, Missouri*, p. 182.

56. In October 1863 . . . Chalmers/S. Cooper: October 22, 1863, in *ORCW*.

57. Anonymous, "Robert A. McCulloch," in *CV*, April 1905.

58. Whatever their differences . . . McCulloch initially trained his men to fight with sabers, but after one of his troopers saved his life by shooting McCulloch's saber-wielding assailant from his saddle, he became, like Forrest, a convert to pistols in close combat. Like Forrest . . . Richards, "The 'Arme Blanche' in Tennessee: The Battle of Middleburg." By the end . . . Anonymous, "McCulloch Cousins Survive Civil War Together."

59. It is possible . . . J. G. Deupree in Silver, ed., *Mississippi in the Confederacy*, p. 64. Or perhaps . . . Captain Thomas Henderson/Chalmers: March 15, 1865, in Chalmers Papers in NARA.

60. Its core companies . . . This is according to the Upton Hays Chapter of the United Daughters of the Confederacy. St. Louis Public Library/author: September 20, 2001. Slavery had been . . . "Gallant old Bob McCulloch," General Chalmers sighed, "never failed to come when needed, but never received the promotion he deserved." Chalmers, "Lieutenant General Nathan Bedford Forrest and His Campaigns."

First Fire: Fort Pillow: 5:30 A.M.–3:00 P.M., April 12, 1864

1. Tall and fair . . . *Columbus* (KY) *War Eagle*, December 12, 1863 (courtesy of Derek Frisby). But Bradford . . . John T. Young/Washburn: September 13, 1864, in *ORCW*.

2. Sounding the alarm . . . Fitch, "Monthly Report." Buttoning his coat . . . Achilles V. Clark/George B. Halstead: April 19, 1864, in TSLA; Chalmers, "Official Report," ORCW. Lieutenant Mack J. Leaming, William F. Mays, and W. P. Walker in *RJSCW*.

3. *Dyersburg* (TN) *States Gazette*, April 21, 1866; James McCoy in *RJSCW*.

4. James Marshall and Elvis Bevel in ibid.

5. Elvis Bevel in ibid.; *New Era* log, April 12, 1864, in Cimprich and Mainfort, "Fort Pillow Revisited." During the battle Johnson "was on a big island," she recalled, "where the gunboat men took us," and she would remain there "a part of two days and one night." (Rosa Johnson in pension file of Joseph Johnson and *RJSCW*.)

6. Allen Wells in *RJSCW*. Josephine Hooper Armstrong, Henry Condry, Bush Hooper, Rosa Spearman Hooper, Alexander Nason, R. E. Potts (Chief of Criminal Section, Bureau of Pensions), Henry Weaver, in pension file of Thomas Hooper.

7. Abner Buford, Rachel Parks, George Patterson, Jerry Steward, in pension file of Ransom Parks. Some recruits' marital arrangements were inscrutable. It is hard to tell, for instance, if Charles Macklin was ever married, for his sup-

posed widow's pension claim was contested by his nieces and rejected by the board. He stood out among his comrades in Company C of the 6th USC Heavy Artillery. Not only was he over six feet tall and of a gingerbread complexion, but from birth he sported a small patch of white hair near his temple. When "very young," Macklin was taken away from his parents by a man named Koon and sold to a Carroll County, Mississippi, planter named Macklin, whose name Charles chose for himself when he ran off in August 1863 with Jim Stokes and Moses and Alexander Nason and joined the Union army. A fellow slave testified that he had married one Mary Jane Hicks in about 1857, and that "it was the custom of slave owners to allow husbands to visit their wives on each Wednesday night, and on Saturday nights, and remain until Monday morning." Mary Jane claimed that they had four children—"Lizzie was born in fodder pulling time, Charlotte after a good frost, Mariah last of the winter, and Irene in hoeing cotton time"—and that Charles had been "fond of his family, and usually visited them when permitted." Mary Jane Hicks Purnell would explain that she never took Charles's name because in slavery "the wife did not take the name of her husband unless both belonged to the same person." But the pension examiner suspected that her employer was also her lover and put her up to filing a false claim. In the end the agent concluded, on little evidence, that she had been married instead to a man named Ned Koon. Hughes went off to serve as a cook for two local Confederate brothers named Gardiner. (Martha Colbert, Samuel Hughes, Alexander Nason, Mary Jane Hicks Purnell, and Jane and Sam J. Smith in pension file of Charles Koon [Macklin].)

8. Marshall shouted . . . Anne Jane Rufin in *RJSCW.* None of the wives . . . Abner Buford, Rachel Parks, George Patterson, Jerry Steward, in pension file of Ransom Parks.

9. First Lieutenant Nicholas Logan . . . He had been commissioned in December 1863, and mustered in at Columbus, Kentucky, the following month. (Isaac Hawkins and Mack J. Leaming in pension file of Nicholas Logan.) "About the time . . ." Chapman Underwood in *RJSCW.*

10. He bullhorned . . . "The evidence shows that only one of these women was shot. Dr. C. Fitch, who was surgeon of the Fort Pillow garrison at this time, says: 'Early in the morning all of the women and all of the noncombatants were ordered on to some barges, and were towed by a gunboat up the river to an island before any one was hurt.'" (*SHSP*, vol. 7, p. 439; Wyeth, *That Devil Forrest*, p. 589; Fitch, "Monthly Report"; Alexander M. Pennock in *RJSCW.*) "keeping underway . . ." James Marshall: Report: April 15, 1864 (*NFWW*); *New Era* log, April 12, 1864, in Cimprich and Mainfort, "Fort Pillow Revisited." Because of the strong wind . . . James Marshall in *RJSCW.*

11. Jacob Thompson . . . Pension file of Jacob Thompson and in *RJSCW.*

12. The hotelier John Nelson . . . John Nelson in *RJSCW.* The newly arrived merchant . . . Van Camp was among those transported to Memphis, where Hurlbut personally ordered that his wounds be dressed. At the urging of an army surgeon named Holston, his father sent him to Illinois and eventually to Corning, New York. In a letter to Lincoln dated January 10, 1865, Aaron Van Camp asked that his son be "released from banishment and protected from [the]

Draft." In the end he was allowed to return home to Washington, but his exemption was denied. Musick, *6th Virginia Cavalry*; B. D. Hyam/Edward Stanton: January 18, 1864; A. Van Camp/Abraham Lincoln: January 10, 1865; Deposition of Maria L. Van Camp, January 17, 1865; L. C. Turner (Judge Advocate)/Edwin Stanton: January 19, 1865; William P. Wood (Superintendent of "Old Capitol" Prison)/C. A. Dana (Assistant Secretary of War): January 27, 1865, RG94/3828, Records of the Adjutant General's Office, microcopy M797: Case Files of Investigations by Levi C. Turner and Lafayette C. Baker: 1861–1866 in NARA. The Minié "ball's" conical shape "bored through rather than bounced off tissue. As the lead further expanded upon striking its target, there was much internal damage and the consequent loss of velocity caused a larger exit wound, if it exited at all. On impact, it often slowed to a halt and remained in the body, shards of filthy clothing having been carried into the wound, spreading infection so quickly that some doctors wondered whether the enemy hadn't perhaps poisoned its bullets . . . Practically every Minié ball extracted from either a Union or a Confederate wounded was bent, twisted, and sometimes even split . . ." Josyph, *The Wounded River,* pp. 27–28. A clerk from upstate . . . James R. Brigham in *RJSCW.* "put on our blouses . . ." Hardy N. Revelle in ibid.; Charley Robinson/Family: April 17, 1864, in Mortimer Robinson and Family Papers (P352), Minnesota Historical Society. "behind a large stump . . ." Elvis Bevel in *RJSCW.*

13. Edward B. Benton in *RJSCW.*
14. William T. Smith in pension file of Thomas McClure.
15. Awakened by the rebel . . . Pension file of John G. Akerstrom; William Cleary in Anne Jane Ruffin, F. A. Smith, Major Williams in *RJSCW.* The closest any name comes to Akerstrom in Forrest's command is a trooper Adkersom of the 9th Tennessee Cavalry. (NPSSSS.) Rushing into the fort . . . Mack J. Leaming in *RJSCW.*
16. Achilles V. Clark/George B. Halstead: April 19,1864, in TSLA (RMC).
17. Deposition of Wilbur H. Gaylord in pension file of Samuel Green; pension file of Wilbur H. Gaylord; statement of Wilbur H. Gaylord.
18. "to occupy . . ." Hancock, *Hancock's Diary,* pp. 354–355. "They kept up . . ." Mack J. Leaming in *RJSCW.* "realizing their advantage . . ." Officer of 2nd Tennessee Cavalry (CSA) in *Charleston Mercury,* May 2, 1864.
19. "The Rebel sharp shooters . . ." Fitch, "Monthly Report." "to take his instruments . . ." Lieutenant William Cleary and James R. Brigham in *RJSCW*; Fitch, "Monthly Report."
20. Wounded while firing . . . James R. Brigham in *RJSCW.* Some accounts mistakenly give his name as Bingham. Dr. Fitch was impressed . . . Fitch, "Monthly Report."
21. Spurring their horses . . . Anderson, "The True Story of Fort Pillow."
22. Forrest turned . . . Mills, "Fort Pillow." The oak tree, traditionally associated with the attack on Fort Pillow, was destroyed by lightning in 1932. (*Covington* [TN] *Leader,* July 28, 1932.)
23. "From ten a.m. . . ." French in Hancock, *Hancock's Diary,* p. 591. "The enemy . . ." Dinkins, *Furl That Banner,* pp. 151–152."
24. Nicholas Hamer in pension file of Samuel Green.

25. Chalmers deemed . . . Johnston, "Diaries and Memoirs." "No matter . . ." Wyeth, *That Devil Forrest*, p. 317.

26. Charles Anderson in Wyeth, *That Devil Forrest*, p. 342.

27. Jordan and Pryor, *The Campaigns of Nathan Bedford Forrest*, p. 429.

28. Forrest was especially . . . Hugh Saunders/"Mother": March 28, 1864, in Saunders, Papers.

29. his hour's scout . . . Wyeth, *That Devil Forrest*, p. 318. In addition . . . Jordan and Pryor, *The Campaigns of Nathan Bedford Forrest*, p. 429.

30. Robert A. McCulloch in Wyeth, *That Devil Forrest*, pp. 316–317.

31. Forrest in Fuchs, *An Unerring Fire*, p. 53.

32. Wyeth, *That Devil Forrest*, p. 332.

33. "made the charge . . ." Henry, *"First with the Most" Forrest*, pp. 251–252; Jordan and Pryor, *The Campaigns of Nathan Bedford Forrest*, pp. 429–430. "to a position . . ." James J. White in *TCWVQ*.

34. William T. Smith and Henry F. Weaver in pension file of Thomas McClure; Litton, *History of Oklahoma at the Golden Anniversary of Statehood*, vol. 3, pp. 1028–1029.

35. Pension file of Tom Addison; G. W. Barrett, Gabriel Lane (aka Calvin McLellan), and Jesse Wilson in pension file of Tom Addison; Tom Addison in *RJSCW*. Emphasis mine.

36. Henry F. Weaver in *RJSCW*; F. A. Smith and William Cleary in ibid.

37. Hardy Revelle . . . Hardy N. Revelle in ibid. "He expired . . ." Wilbur Gaylord in ibid.

38. Command now fell . . . Mack J. Leaming in ibid. Though rebel sharpshooters . . . William T. Smith and Henry F. Weaver in pension file of Thomas McClure; Litton, *History of Oklahoma at the Golden Anniversary of Statehood*, vol. 3, pp. 1028–1029; Henry F. Weaver in *RJSCW*; Wyeth, *That Devil Forrest*, p. 316; Mack J. Leaming in Henry, *"First with the Most" Forrest*, p. 250. But Bradford . . . Wilbur H. Gaylord in *RJSCW*.

39. As rebel minié balls . . . *RJSCW*. It was the first . . . Carl A. Lamberg/I. G. Kappner: April 20, 1864, in *ORCW*. In any case . . . Second Lieutenant John C. Barr had transferred as a private from the 15th Illinois Cavalry and spent most of his service chasing after deserters. Wilbur H. Gaylord and Mack J. Leaming in *RJSCW*; Wyeth, *That Devil Forrest*, p. 589.

40. With Booth dead . . . Pension files of Charles J. Epeneter and Peter Bischoff; Autograph book in pension file of Thomas A. Cord. Now, just as Gaylord . . . Wilbur H. Gaylord in pension file of Samuel Green; pension file of Wilbur H. Gaylord; Wilbur H. Gaylord in *RJSCW*. The subcommittee's investigators referred to a "Captain Potter who is now lying here"—meaning at the hospital at Mound City, where Leaming was interviewed—"unable to speak." Leaming did not correct them about his rank, though the record suggests he was a lieutenant, not a captain. "Potter" may simply have been a mistaken transcription of Porter. There was a Captain Poston at Fort Pillow, but he was not at Mound City. A Crockett County Unionist, Porter had been married for ten years and was the father of two boys and two girls. Bill Stephens of the 13th, who served under Porter in 6/B, saw Porter shot in the head early in the fight, about the same time that Booth was killed. (John Poston and William J. Stephens in pen-

sion file of John H. Porter; Mack J. Leaming in *RJSCW; McNairy County* (TN) *Independent,* February 1, 1924; www.searches.rootsweb.com.)

41. Over the course . . . RG94/E112–115/P1–17/v.2 in NARA. Now Cothel . . . Moore, *Women of the War,* pp. 310–312.

42. Eli Falls . . . Pension file, testimony, and statement of Elias Falls; pension file of Jordan and Eli Irwin; Alsie Williams in pension file of Peter Williams. Henry Gibson . . . He left a widow, Caroline, but no children, for they had only just been married. (Sandy Addison, Caroline Gibson, and Frank Hogan in pension file of Henry Gibson.) Fighting alongside . . . Captain Adolf Lamberg (2nd USCLA)/Colonel Kappner: April 20, 1864, RG94/Box 8: Records of the 2nd USCLA in NARA.

43. While standing . . . Jackson's wife Rose Ann had married him in 1857 at the age of thirteen. The pension examiner refused to believe her, and demanded that she obtain proof of her marriage to Charles from her "late former owner" or "some other disinterested person." She apparently gave up. (James Collier, Rose Ann Adams Jackson, in pension file of Charles Jackson.) At forty-two . . . Harry Cox, Benjamin and Samuel Green, and Julia Williams in pension file of Jacob Jones.

44. Pension file of Samuel Green; Peter Bischoff in pension file of Charles Epeneter.

45. Willis never knew his father's name, "as I was taken away from my mother when I was quite small." After Clark Bobo's death, Willis was sold to Bobo's sister in Coahoma County, Mississippi. But the change apparently did not sit well with him, and in 1862, while still in his teens, he ran away from his new mistress's house, crossing the Mississippi to join the Union army's Pioneer Corps in Helena, Arkansas. "When I first went to the Yankees, they was planting the cotton crop," Willis recalled, and it was not until October 1863 that he was able to enroll in the 6th USC Heavy Artillery. Booth's recruiting examiner was not particularly selective, and ignored Willis's impaired hearing, even though his comrades remembered that at the time of his enlistment he was so deaf "he had to be hollered at." "The doctor did not have me take off my clothes," Ligon recalled. "He just took hold of my arms and bent them and examined me to see if I was afflicted in any way." Three days later he was mustered into 6/C and began to train on the heavy guns at Corinth. Though the entire regiment received instruction in the use of artillery, in the event of a battle most were assigned to act as artillery supports: infantrymen and sharpshooters trained to protect the gun crews from infiltration and rifle fire. But Willis rose to become a first-class fireman. (J. Altshul, Andrew Clopton, Abraham Huggins, Abner W. Ligon, David and Nelson Mooring, Alexander Nason, Monroe Wilson, Phillip Young, in pension file of Willis Ligon.)

46. "There were . . ." Henry Weaver in *RJSCW.* "Never did men . . ." Military, pension, and ration commutation files of Samuel Green; Reason Barker, Thomas Brown, Morning Clay, Felix Davis, Steven Davis, Wilbur H. Gaylord, Henry Gillespie, Benjamin Jones, Pearson Lee, Henry Meeks, J. C. Shearer, in pension file of Samuel Green; Samuel Green in pension files of Henry Dix and Jacob Jones. According to . . . *Missouri Democrat,* April 15, 1864. When a reporter . . . *Cairo News,* April 16, 1864.

47. James Brigham in *RJSCW.*

48. "Although our garrison . . ." Mack J. Leaming in *RJSCW.* Late in the morning . . . Mills, "Fort Pillow."

49. Jordan and Pryor, *The Campaigns of Nathan Bedford Forrest,* p. 430.

50. D. W. Harrison in *RJSCW.*

51. *New Era* log, April 12, 1864, in Cimprich and Mainfort, "Fort Pillow Revisited"; Anderson, "The True Story of Fort Pillow."

52. It should have . . . Henry, *"First with the Most" Forrest,* p. 254. Dodging fire . . . Barteau in *Detroit Free Press,* December 1, 1884. "and as useless . . ." Fort, "Memoir." "During the entire morning the gunboat kept up a continuous fire in all directions, but without effect." (Forrest/Jefferson Davis: April 24, 1864, in Wyeth, *That Devil Forrest,* p. 334; Hancock, *Hancock's Diary,* pp. 355–356.)

53. Anderson, "The True Story of Fort Pillow"; Chalmers in Fuchs, *An Unerring Fire,* pp. 54–55.

54. "Our men . . ." Wyeth, *That Devil Forrest,* pp. 317–318. The bluecoats . . . Dinkins wrote, "The negro soldiers had been given all the whiskey they could drink, and were told that no rebels could ever enter Fort Pillow." The charge that the blacks fought so bravely because they were inebriated will be addressed later in this account. Dinkins, *Furl That Banner,* pp. 151–152. "the desired position . . ." Forrest/Jefferson Davis: April 24, 1864, in *ORCW.*

55. "These positions . . ." Hancock, *Hancock's Diary,* pp. 356–357. By now . . . Henry, *"First with the Most" Forrest,* pp. 252–253.

56. Hurlbut/R. P. Buckland: April 12, 1864, in RG393/Box 1 (NARA); Alfred G. Tuther/I. G. Kappner: April 12, 1864, in *ORCW.*

57. Hurlbut/"Officer Commanding Force for Fort Pillow": April 12, 1864, in *ORCW.*

58. *CWAL,* vol. 7, p. 7:276.

59. Sherman/Hurlbut: April 12, 1864, in 16th Army Corps (Letters Received) RG98, Part 2, Entry 391, Box 7 in NARA.

60. "an eminence included . . ." Wyeth, *That Devil Forrest,* p. 318. Forrest therefore concluded . . . Jordan and Pryor, *The Campaigns of Nathan Bedford Forrest,* pp. 430–432.

61. A Nashville grocer when the war broke out, the native Ohioan suffered from a boyhood foot injury that caused him to limp. Captured at Tupelo and paroled six weeks later, he had fought with great daring at Mud Creek, where a Yankee minié ball shattered his right forearm. In October 1863, he had returned to his command.

62. A. H. French in Hancock, *Hancock's Diary,* p. 591.

63. A. H. French in ibid., p. 592; Wyeth, *That Devil Forrest,* p. 318.

"Yes or No": Truce: 3:00 P.M.–4:00 P.M., April 12, 1864

1. By 3:00 p.m. . . . Anderson, "The True Story of Fort Pillow"; Wyeth, *That Devil Forrest,* p. 318. The rebels . . . Fitch, "Monthly Report." Bell's men . . . Wyeth, *That Devil Forrest,* p. 318.

2. home.olemiss.edu/~cmprice/cavalry; Achilles V. Clark/Sister: April 14, 1864, in Cimprich and Mainfort, "Fort Pillow Revisited."

3. "We'd better . . ." Dinkins, *Furl That Banner*, p. 152. "It was the plain . . ." Barteau in *Detroit Free Press*, December 1, 1884.

4. As Bradford . . . Wyeth, *That Devil Forrest*, p. 319. "A man . . ." Chalmers, "Lieutenant General Nathan Bedford Forrest and His Campaigns"; Anderson, "The True Story of Fort Pillow."

5. Several similar versions of Forrest's surrender demand appeared after the battle. Jordan and Pryor give the following: "As your gallant defense of the fort has entitled you to the treatment of brave men"—or, as Jordan and Pryor put it, "something to that effect"—"I now demand an unconditional surrender of your force, at the same time assuring you that they will be treated as prisoners of war. I have received a fresh supply of ammunition, and can easily take your position." Jordan and Pryor, *The Campaigns of Nathan Bedford Forrest*, pp. 430–432.

6. "No doubt as to the meaning and scope of this proposition was ever expressed or intimated in any of the notes and conversations which followed it under the flag of truce." Jordan and Pryor, *The Campaigns of Nathan Bedford Forrest*, pp. 430–432.

7. Dinkins, *Furl That Banner*, p. 152. James Dinkins was apparently a witness to this conversation.

8. Flanked . . . Wyeth, *That Devil Forrest*, p. 319. drew to a halt . . . Jordan and Pryor, *The Campaigns of Nathan Bedford Forrest*, pp. 430–432.

9. Jordan and Pryor, *The Campaigns of Nathan Bedford Forrest*, pp. 434–435.

10. Mack J. Leaming in *RJSCW*.

11. Achilles V. Clark/George B. Halstead: April 19, 1864, in TSLA.

12. Sayers, "Fort Pillow."

13. Goodman cantered back . . . Wilbur H. Gaylord in *RJSCW*. By now . . . Mack J. Leaming in *RJSCW*.

14. Goodman mildly replied . . . ibid.

15. "who had remained . . ." Dinkins, "The Capture of Fort Pillow." Another Federal . . . John T. Young in *RJSCW*.

16. Dinkins, "The Capture of Fort Pillow."

17. "both remarked . . ." Dinkins, "The Capture of Fort Pillow." "that General Forrest . . ." John T. Young in *RJSCW*.

18. Wyeth, *That Devil Forrest*, p. 594; Anderson, "The True Story of Fort Pillow."

19. Forrest suspected . . . Henry, *"First with the Most" Forrest*, p. 253. "The gunboat . . ." Forrest/Jefferson Davis: April 24, 1864, in Wyeth, *That Devil Forrest*, p. 334.

20. Bradford was no longer counting . . . Anderson, "The True Story of Fort Pillow." "After our men . . ." Charley Robinson/Family: April 17, 1864.

21. "You have done . . ." Ibid. The boat . . . *New Era* log, April 12, 1864, in Cimprich and Mainfort, "Fort Pillow Revisited."

22. Shepley . . . Descended from a seventeenth-century Massachusetts pioneer and Indian fighter, Shepley was, like his counterparts along the Mississippi, an attorney by profession. As colonel of the 12th Maine Infantry, he was one of the first to occupy New Orleans, of which he was appointed acting mayor in May 1862. A month later he was promoted to the military governorship of Louisiana.

But even his Harvard law training and his nine-year stint as United States district attorney for Maine could not light his way through New Orleans, a rat's nest of counterfeiting, spies, profiteering, and fraud. A small man . . . Civil War Interactive at www.civilwarinteractive.com; the Political Graveyard at www.politicalgraveyard.com; History of the New Hampshire Federal Courts at www.nhd.uscourts.gov/ci/history/03-06e.asp.

23. George Foster Shepley in *RJSCW*.

24. Captain B. Rushmore Pegram . . . Charles C. G. Thornton and George Foster Shepley in ibid.

25. In fact . . . Hancock, *Hancock's Diary,* pp. 357–358. From their position . . . Anderson, "The True Story of Fort Pillow."

26. None of which . . . S. A. Hurlbut in *RJSCW*.

27. "The steamer was now in sight, and blue with troops coming down the stream toward the beleaguered garrison and the gunboat. If she had been signaled that a truce was prevailing, she did not respect the signal by stopping or putting about or sheering over to the Arkansas shore, but came steadily on. . . . She was in full view; the gunboat, also under truce, was bound by the obligations incurred in accepting a cessation of hostilities, and should have signaled the steamer that the truce was prevailing, that she must put about and not approach. That was the plain duty of Captain Marshall and Major Bradford. Forrest did not intend to be robbed or cheated out of his prey while it was nearly in his grasp. Moreover, there now appeared in sight two other steamboats coming up the river from the direction of Memphis, and the Confederate general had every reason to hasten matters to a conclusion. The Union commander had equally strong reason to secure delay in the hope of succor. . . . The movement diminished the assaulting [Confederate] column by four hundred men, for these men took no part whatever in the assault on the fort, and only fired on the Federals when they endeavored to escape." Wyeth, *That Devil Forrest,* pp. 319–322.

28. "The Confederate detachments . . ." Henry, *"First with the Most" Forrest,* p. 260.

29. George Foster Shepley in *RJSCW*.

30. "no doubt . . ." Charles C. G. Thornton in ibid.

31. Second Lieutenant John C. Akerstrom . . . Pension file of John G. Akerstrom; William Cleary, Anne Jane Ruffin, F. A. Smith, Major Williams in *RJSCW*. The closest any name comes to Akerstrom in Forrest's command is a trooper Adkersom of the 9th Tennessee Cavalry. (NPSSSS.) "Mr. Akerstrom was . . ." James McCoy in *RJSCW*. Other accounts . . . Colonel William Hudson Lawrence, who had his hands full with Buford's assault on Columbus that day, came as close to accusing Shepley of cowardice as he deemed prudent. He said that on the morning of the 13th Shepley had told him "he believed the fort had surrendered, and was at this time expecting an attack upon my post, and General Shepley offered me two batteries of light artillery, which he said were fully manned and equipped. I am informed there were some 200 infantry on board the steamer in addition to the artillery," to which Shepley responded with no mention of his artillery, with the air of a helpless bystander: "I left New Orleans, on the evening of the 6th of April, as a passenger in the Olive Branch, a

New Orleans and St. Louis passenger steamer *not in the service of the government,* but loaded with male and female passengers and cargo of private parties. The steamer was unarmed, and had no troops and no muskets for protection against guerillas when landing at wood yards and other places." Shepley in *ORCW.*

32. Burfford, "In the Wake of Fort Pillow with Forrest in Command." Burfford's account follows much of Anderson's and was probably based on it. "After their commander . . ." According to Hurlbut, Shepley reported "that as he approached Fort Pillow, fighting was going on; he saw the flag come down 'by the run,' but could not tell whether it was lowered by the garrison, or by having the halliards shot away; that soon after another flag went up in another place. He could not distinguish its character, but feared that it was a surrender, though firing continued." When Fitch began to pull away, "the firing was kept up, but not as heavily as at first," and "he was not certain how the fight was terminating." S. A. Hurlbut in *RJSCW.*

33. Jordan and Pryor, *The Campaigns of Nathan Bedford Forrest,* pp. 445–446.

34. Nathan Fulks in *RJSCW.*

35. "They feel quite proud of defending their fort so long against such overwhelming numbers, and declare that but for their treachery in stealing up while negotiations under flag of truce were going on, the rebels could not have taken the place in daylight." *Cairo News,* April 16, 1864. (See also John F. Ray, Elvis Bevel, Daniel H. Rankin, Jason Loudon, William B. Walker, William A. Dickey, William F. Mays, James R. Brigham, Hardy N. Revelle, F. A. Smith, William Cleary, [Private] Major Williams, Francis A. Alexander, John F. Ray, James McCoy, Edward B. Benton, Mack J. Leaming, Henry F. Weaver, James N. Tayor, William P. Walker, Thomas H. Harris, Charley Robinson, William B. Purdy, James Marshall in *RJSCW;* Jordan and Pryor, *The Campaigns of Nathan Bedford Forrest,* pp. 445–448; Achilles V. Clark/George B. Halstead: April 19, 1864, in TSLA.)

36. Daniel Stamps in *RJSCW;* John T. Stamps and John H. Copher in pension file of Daniel Stamps; Daniel Stamps in pension file of John M. Condray.

37. James N. Taylor [Tayler] in pension file of Isaac J. Ledbetter; James N. Taylor in *RJSCW.*

38. John F. Ray in *RJSCW.*

39. Carroll, "Autobiography and Reminiscences," pp. 28–29.

40. This is Charles Anderson's version, copied from the original in his possession. Another version, probably a paraphrase, comes from Mack J. Leaming. "Sir: I do not demand the surrender of the gunboat; twenty minutes will be given you to take your men outside the fort and surrender. If in that time this demand is not complied with I will immediately proceed to assault your works, and you must take the consequences." Mack J. Leaming in *RJSCW.*

41. Jordan and Pryor, *The Campaigns of Nathan Bedford Forrest,* p. 432.

42. Chalmers, "Lieutenant General Nathan Bedford Forrest and His Campaigns."

43. "another form . . ." Wyeth, *That Devil Forrest,* p. 344. But in every previous case . . . Lieutenant Van Horn testified that the first two communications were separated by a period of intense fighting, but no one else mentioned it, though

Thomas J. Jackson repeated this story in his account. But Jackson was not present during the battle and would prove an unreliable source, and after submitting a statement Van Horn was not called upon to testify before Wade and Gooch. (Lieutenant Van Horn in Wyeth, *That Devil Forrest*, pp. 590–591; Thomas J. Jackson/George B. [Halstead]: April 19, 1864, RG94, Regimental Papers, 11th USCI [New] in NARA.)

44. William Witherspoon in Henry, *As They Saw Forrest*, pp. 126–127.

45. Wyeth, *That Devil Forrest*, pp. 323–324.

46. Nevertheless . . . "Most of the fifty men who furnished affidavits to Dr. Wyeth mention the presence of whisky in the fort, and the evidences of its too-liberal use by the garrison. Barrels of whisky found along the parapet, with tin dippers attached, were kicked over and spilled by prudent officers of the attacking forces." Henry, *"First with the Most" Forrest*, pp. 264–265. "The troops in the fort had evidently been made drunk, for those we took were more or less intoxicated, and we found barrels of whisky and ale and bottles of brandy open, and tin cups in the barrels out of which they had been drinking. We also found water-buckets sitting around in the fort with whisky and dippers in them, which showed very clearly that the whisky had been thus passed around to the Federal troops." Clarke Barteau in Hancock, *Hancock's Diary*, p. 367. Fortifying . . . Mainfort, *Archaeological Investigations*.

47. "didn't know whisky . . ." "He did not use tobacco, neither smoked nor 'chawed,'" which accounted in part for his unusually fine teeth. Brown, "Nathan Bedford Forrest."

48. While the negotiations . . ." William P. Walker in *RJSCW*. "any amount . . ." Fort, "Memoir." "the moment . . ." Wyeth, *That Devil Forrest*, p. 338. "The enemy . . ." Fort, "Journal of Dewitt Clinton Fort." "While the flag of truce was being considered, I saw the enemy plundering our evacuated quarters and moving their forces up in bodies, getting them in position. We had been driving them all the morning. They were at the same time placing their sharpshooters in the buildings we had occupied as barracks." James N. Taylor recalled that "I plainly saw the enemy engaged in disposing their troops, plundering our camp, and stealing goods from the quartermaster's and other stores." (Jason Souden [Louden] and James N. Taylor in *RJSCW*.) "There is abundant testimony from Confederate sources that wide spread and almost general intoxication among the garrison contributed to the frenzy of the scattered resistance offered between the time the parapet was stormed and the time Forrest could restore order below the bluffs." Henry, *"First with the Most" Forrest*, pp. 264–265.

49. A. H. French in Hancock, *Hancock's Diary*, p. 591.

50. Anderson, "The True Story of Fort Pillow."

51. "Forrest sent . . ." A. J. Grantham in "Aged Civil War Vet Says He Still Hasn't Overcome Animosity Toward Yankees," *Corpus Christi Caller Times*, October 6, 1940. But as a matter of fact . . . Mack. J. Leaming in *RJSCW*.

52. Nathan G. Fulks in *RJSCW*.

53. If Forrest . . . Wyeth, *That Devil Forrest*, pp. 322–323. "Major Bradford . . ." F. A. Smith and William Cleary in *RJSCW*.

54. "would be able to hold . . ." Captain Adolf Lamberg (2nd USCLA)/Colonel Kappner: April 20, 1864, RG94/Box 8: Records of the 2nd USCLA in NARA.

"Up to this time . . ." Henry F. Weaver in *RJSCW*. Edward Benton . . . Edward B. Benton in ibid. Dr. Fitch . . . Fitch, "Monthly Report."

55. "Tell My Dier . . ." Pension file of Elam V. Cashion. Tom Cartwright . . . He was paroled on the thirteenth and released on a surgeon's certificate in July. Though unable to perform manual labor, he ran a contracting business in Arlington, Oregon. He died in 1897 of "dropsy of the heart" in Spokane, Washington, where he used to tug open his collar, show off his wound, and recount his experiences at Fort Pillow. He left his widow only "a horse buggy and harness and a few household effects and very few at that." She was described as "unusually devoted to the deceased during his lifetime," but Cartwright's doctor refused to testify that his death had anything to do with his old wound, on the grounds that the Cartwrights had never paid their bill. (Pension file and medical report of Thomas Cartwright.) Over six feet . . . Thomas Loftus [Loftis] and Daniel N. Rankin in pension file of Francis A. Alexander; pension file of Thomas Loftis.

56. "defiance and insult . . ." Clark Barteau in Hancock, *Hancock's Diary*, pp. 366–367. "called to us . . ." Clark Barteau in *Detroit Free Press*, December 1, 1884. "Provoking . . ." Dinkins, "The Capture of Fort Pillow."

57. Clark Barteau in *Detroit Free Press*, December 1, 1884.

58. Dinkins, "The Capture of Fort Pillow."

59. Clark Barteau in Hancock, *Hancock's Diary*, pp. 366–367.

60. Barteau . . . Clark Barteau in Hancock, *Hancock's Diary*, pp. 366–367. "shouted . . ." This was a version of the "They weren't massacred, and, besides, they had it coming" defense. (Wyeth, *That Devil Forrest*, p. 322.)

61. William Bradford in Morris, "Fort Pillow: Massacre or Madness?"

62. Mack J. Leaming in *RJSCW*.

"Bloody Work": The Final Assault: 4:00 P.M., April 12, 1864

1. "Go to hell . . ." A. J. Grantham in "Aged Civil War Vet Says He Still Hasn't Overcome Animosity Toward Yankees," *Corpus Christi Caller Times*, October 6, 1940. As the word . . . Fort, "Memoir."

2. "Bell's brigade . . ." Forrest/Jefferson Davis: April 24, 1864, in Wyeth, *That Devil Forrest*, p. 335. "The commanding ridges . . ." Jordan and Pryor, *The Campaigns of Nathan Bedford Forrest*, p. 436.

3. Anderson, "The True Story of Fort Pillow."

4. Sheppard, *Bedford Forrest*, p. 168.

5. Forrest/Jefferson Davis: April 24, 1864, in Wyeth, *That Devil Forrest*, p. 334.

6. Wyeth, *That Devil Forrest*, pp. 324–325; Jordan and Pryor, *The Campaigns of Nathan Bedford Forrest*, pp. 435–436.

7. "With a few . . ." Hancock, *Hancock's Diary*, pp. 358–359. "General Chalmers . . ." Robert Bufferd in Logan, "No Massacre by Forrest at Fort Pillow," *Memphis Commercial Appeal*, September 2, 1934. "the incarnation . . ." Dinkins, "The Capture of Fort Pillow."

8. "Our men . . ." Barteau in Hancock, *Hancock's Diary*, p. 367.

9. Sheppard, *Bedford Forrest*, p. 172.

10. A. J. Grantham in "Aged Civil War Vet Says He Still Hasn't Overcome Animosity Toward Yankees," *Corpus Christi Caller Times*, October 6, 1940.

11. Fort, "Memoir."

12. With the withdrawal . . . Wyeth, *That Devil Forrest*, p. 324. "The 13th was . . ." Charley Robinson/Family: April 17, 1864. All but a couple . . . Henry F. Weaver in *RJSCW*. "All along . . ." Wyeth, *That Devil Forrest*, p. 324.

13. "three bucks . . ." Davis, "What About Fort Pillow?" Woodford Cooksey testified that he was wounded with such a charge. Woodford Cooksey in *RJSCW*. "Being a courier . . ." *Memphis Commercial Appeal*, September 2, 1934.

14. It was almost 4:00 p.m. . . . Fort, "Journal of Dewitt Clinton Fort." Perhaps five minutes . . . Dinkins, "The Capture of Fort Pillow."

15. Dinkins, "The Capture of Fort Pillow"; Wyeth, *That Devil Forrest*, p. 325; Hancock, *Hancock's Diary*, pp. 360–361. "As soon as [the flag of truce] started back, the enemy immediately started up the hill on the double-quick, not waiting for the flag of truce to return. As soon as they came close to the fort and had their sharpshooters distributed through our barracks, (which were just outside the fort,) they opened fire upon the garrison, and then charged the works." William A. Winn in *RJSCW*.

16. "the first blare . . ." Dinkins, "The Capture of Fort Pillow." "It made an awful . . ." Fort, "Memoir." "The wild . . ." Wyeth, *That Devil Forrest*, p. 326. "could not rise . . ." Dinkins, "The Capture of Fort Pillow." "As the blue caps . . ." Wyeth, *That Devil Forrest*, p. 326.

17. Hardy N. Revelle in *RJSCW*.

18. "the main Confederate. . . ." Jordan and Pryor, *The Campaigns of Nathan Bedford Forrest*, pp. 435–436; Hancock, *Hancock's Diary*, pp. 360–361. "The sight . . ." "Memphis" pseudonym/Report: April 18, 1864, in Cimprich and Mainfort, "Fort Pillow Revisited." "The outside . . ." Dinkins, "The Capture of Fort Pillow." "the slanting bank . . ." Wyeth, *That Devil Forrest*, p. 325.

19. "Exterminated these reckless horsemen . . ." Wyeth, *That Devil Forrest*, p. 325; "guns and navy sixes . . ." Tyree H. Bell in ibid., p. 593.

20. Reed's name is often given as Wiley M. Reid, but after his death, his father protested that it was actually Wyly Martin Reed. (C. P. Reed/Major [W. H.?] Davis: June 3, 1867. Papers of Leroy Nutt/2285/Folder 8 [SHC/UNCCH].)

21. Dinkins, "The Capture of Fort Pillow."

22. Berry, *Four Years with Morgan and Forrest*, p. 269.

23. Barteau's . . . "As will be remembered, it was also the first to move up in close range of the fort. B. A. High was among the first to mount the works. Another man (whose name I have not been able to learn), in attempting to ascend rather in advance of High, was shot, and rolled back into the ditch a corpse, while High succeeded in going to the top, and captured a cannoneer, whose gun he soon after turned upon the Federal gun-boat, as previously mentioned. Several of Company C were close after High. Among the number was J. C. McAdoo, who was long enough to jump into the ditch but too short to leap out until Colonel Bell came to his assistance." (Hancock, *Hancock's Diary*, p. 365). "Colonel McCulloch and I . . . concluded that we entered the fort just about the same time. I could not say for myself which was first, but Captain Farris thinks the Second Tennessee was first." (Barteau in ibid., pp. 365–366.) Among the first . . . Hardy N. Revelle in *RJSCW*. Henry Claiborne-Armstrong of Com-

pany B, of the 2nd (22nd) Tennessee, told his son that "he was the first man over the wall at Fort Pillow. He always said there was absolutely no 'massacre' at Fort Pillow. Not a shot was fired after the white flag was raised. Report of 'massacre' he said, was pure Yankee propaganda to save face." Last Will and Testament of Louise Claiborne-Armstrong of Apopka, Florida (d. February 12, 1976) (RMC).

24. "from out of the very earth . . ." "Before the garrison, which had fired at the first apparition of the charging line, could reload, the second wave was over, to empty another 600 guns into the mass below them." Henry, *"First with the Most" Forrest,* pp. 254–255; Mack J. Leaming in *RJSCW.* "They had been told . . ." Dinkins, "The Capture of Fort Pillow." "it was like a terrible shock . . ." Fort, "Memoir." "Our troops never fired a gun until they landed inside the fort." Tyree H. Bell in Wyeth, *That Devil Forrest,* pp. 326, 593. "In making the assault our troops, being without bayonets, reserved their fire." Anderson, "The True Story of Fort Pillow." Some of the defenders . . . Samuel H. Caldwell/Wife: April 15, 1864, in Cimprich and Mainfort, "Fort Pillow Revisited."

25. "After the shotguns were fired, the guns were slung on the horns of our saddles and with our six shooters in hand we pursued those fleeing, either capturing or killing until they reached their reserved force." (Blackburn, "Reminiscences.") They usually loaded their rifles with shot. "You can see the style of the secesh cartridges," wrote Henry Eells, who as a U.S. surgeon had dug rebel lead out of scores of Union soldiers. Each had "a ball and three buckshot. The round bullets," he said, "are all secesh and so are the large conical ones." (Frisby, "'Remember me to everybody.'")

26. Wyeth, *That Devil Forrest,* p. 589.

27. "The charge . . ." Fort, "Journal of Dewitt Clinton Fort." As the rebels . . . Jordan and Pryor, *The Campaigns of Nathan Bedford Forrest,* pp. 326–327; Wyeth, *That Devil Forrest,* p. 325. "wounds almost . . ." Ibid., p. 589. "I was wounded . . ." Wilbur H. Gaylord in *RJSCW.* Daniel Rankin was shot . . . Daniel H. Rankin in ibid. James and Frank . . . James N. Taylor in ibid. John Haskins . . . Pension file of John Haskins.

28. "Memphis" pseudonym/Report: April 18, 1864, in Cimprich and Mainfort, "Fort Pillow Revisited."

29. Mack J. Leaming in *RJSCW.*

30. "In the shortest time . . ." Fort, "Memoir." Within five minutes . . . In less than five minutes after our men scaled the esplanade, the fort was cleared of the enemy, the main body of whom fled to the edge of the river leaving the fort colors still flying." Isham Harris in the *Charleston Mercury,* May 6, 1864.

31. "As we charged . . ." Fort, "Memoir." The black artillerists . . . Henry Weaver in *RJSCW.* Corporal William Dickey of the 13th claimed that the blacks were the first to flee. "After the rebs got inside, the white troops saw that there was no mercy shown, and they threw down their arms and ran down the bluff, too; and they were at the same time shot and butchered." (William Dickey in ibid.) Rankin claimed that "two companies of negro troops broke and ran down the bluff, which made an opening for the rebels to come in at, when they got possession of our works and indiscriminate slaughter commenced of both white and black." (Daniel Rankin in ibid.)

32. Peter Bischoff in pension file of Charles Epeneter; Private John Kennedy in report of Capt. Carl A. Lamberg, Company D, Second U.S. Colored Light Artillery, of the capture of Fort Pillow in *ORCW*.

33. Nathan Fulks in *RJSCW*.

34. "The niggers . . ." W. P. Walker in ibid. The disparity . . . "Regardless of which element of the garrison first broke, it is agreed that almost instantly the whole garrison, or such of them as had not been already killed or wounded, ran from their positions back through the little enclosure of the fort to the brow of the bluff above the river side, and plunged over." (Henry, *"First with the Most"* Forrest, pp. 254–255.) Civilians less invested . . . John Nelson in *RJSCW*. Dr. Chapman Underwood . . . Chapman Underwood in ibid. "Many post-war accounts tell of survivors running down to the river's edge to escape the Confederate onslaught," writes Sayers. "But this was virtually impossible, as the open side of the redan overlooked the Mississippi from a bluff with a sheer drop of eighty feet. And though a two-foot wide narrow footpath ran along the face of the bluff to the water's edge, attempting to escape via this route would have been suicide. Therefore, those surviving Union soldiers who ended up at the river's edge must have quit the fight early. When the defenders found little room for shelter, those that did attempt to escape over the bluff were fired on by Forrest's men, who had been stationed at the river's edge on the north and south extremes of the fortified area. Still, some plunged to their deaths in the eighty foot drop." (Sayers, "Fort Pillow.") The weaknesses of this novel analysis are many. Not just "post-war accounts" but virtually every witness on both sides testified that the garrison fled down the bluff, which was steeply sloped but eminently descendable, as evidenced by the fact that during the siege the Union wounded were constantly being littered down to Chapman's field hospital by the river. Only one participant testified that anyone died from a fall, and even his testimony is ambiguous. "Not one, however, would halt, unless a bullet caught him," wrote James Dinkins in 1925. "They ran to the high bluff and jumped over. Those who did never knew what the end was. They were too flat to bury." But he may have meant that they were shot as they descended and dead when they reached the bottom. (Dinkins, *Furl That Banner,* pp. 153–154.)

35. "What was called . . ." Mack J. Leaming in *RJSCW*. "the negroes . . ." William F. Mays in ibid.

36. Jordan and Pryor, *The Campaigns of Nathan Bedford Forrest,* pp. 327–328.

37. John Penwell in *RJSCW*. "Some negro soldiers were lying down in the wood floor tents," wrote one of Forrest's defenders. "We do not know whether they were sick or drunk—or merely trying to escape the battle. We do know that some of these men were shot during the engagement." Davis, "What About Fort Pillow?"

38. This claim was corroborated by two other survivors. (William F. Mays, Daniel Stamps, James N. Taylor in *RJSCW*.)

39. "If there was . . ." Robert Bufferd in Logan, "No Massacre by Forrest at Fort Pillow," *Memphis Commercial Appeal*, September 2, 1934. "Their fort . . ." Achilles V. Clark/George B. Halstead: April 19, 1864, in TSLA (RMC).

40. Some rebel . . . Anderson in Wyeth, *That Devil Forrest,* pp. 594–595; Brewer, "Storming of Fort Pillow." "found barrels . . ." Barteau in Hancock, *Hancock's Diary,* p. 367. "those of the garrison . . ." Wyeth, *That Devil Forrest,* p. 593. "The negroes were drunk, and, when Forrest's men got into the fort, the negroes continued to fight until they were overpowered. This is why so many of them were killed. . . . I never saw a man killed or a gun fired after the drunken negroes surrendered. The killed on the Union side was necessarily great, but it could not be helped. This fight was in no sense a massacre."(Dinkins, "The Capture of Fort Pillow.") Dewitt Clinton Fort also testified to the garrison's—and the attackers'—drunkenness. (Fort, "Memoir.") Dr. Fitch testified to the rebels' drunkenness later that night. (Fitch, "Monthly Report.")

41. "a cloud . . ." James McCoy and Chapman Underwood in *RJSCW.* The men fell back . . . Sheppard, *Bedford Forrest,* p. 170. "Lieutenant Van Horn . . ." Henry Weaver in *RJSCW.*

42. Dinkins, *Furl That Banner,* pp. 153–154.

43. "earthworks thrown up . . ." Joseph E. Harvey (9th Minnesota Infantry)/Mary: May 31, 1864, Minnesota Historical Society (ms. P591). "and ran down . . ." Daniel Stamps in *RJSCW;* John T. Stamps and John H. Copher in pension file of Daniel Stamps; Daniel Stamps in pension file of John M. Condray.

44. "The garrison . . ." Dinkins, "The Capture of Fort Pillow." "piled against . . ." Jordan and Pryor, *The Campaigns of Nathan Bedford Forrest,* p. 436; Charles W. Anderson in Wyeth, *That Devil Forrest,* pp. 594–595. "hemmed in . . ." John Nelson in *RJSCW.*

45. Of the thirty-six Union survivors to the battle who testified regarding when or whether the Federals threw down their guns, seventeen (ten out of fifteen black and four out of twelve white soldiers, and three out of eight civilians) did not specify when the men of the garrison threw down their weapons, only that they had thrown down their arms before they were shot. Fifteen (one black and nine white soldiers, and five civilians) claimed that the garrison first threw down their weapons and then fled. Though two eyewitnesses (the hotelier John Nelson and Jerry Stewart of 6/A) testified that a few of their comrades were armed when they got to the river, and one (Alexander Nason of 6/C, who was not among the thirty-six) made an ambiguous reference to comrades being shot "while they were fighting," only four (one black and three white soldiers) explicitly testified that at least some of the garrison first fled and then threw down their arms by the river. (James Walls in *RJSCW.*) Wade and Gooch: "Did you go back from the river after you were shot?" Nason: "No, Sir." W&G: "You remained there until you were brought away by the gunboat?" N: "Yes, sir. I saw several of our boys shot while they were fighting." But it is not clear who he meant by "they." (Alexander Nayron [Nason] in ibid.) "Negroes . . ." Wyeth, *That Devil Forrest,* pp. 328–329.

46. "enough to justify . . ." Wyeth, *That Devil Forrest,* pp. 328–329. "In the process . . ." Ibid., pp. 337–338. "the heavy loss . . ." Charles Anderson in ibid., pp. 594–595. Jordan and Pryor chalked up rebel excesses to chaos, anger, and nerves. "It should be remembered that the entrance of the Confederates into the work had been achieved by an impetuous rush over the parapet by each in-

dividual, and therefore, for some moments afterward, there was necessarily a general confusion and tumult, in fact, a dissolution of all organizations. Accordingly, as always happens in places taken by storm, unquestionably some whites, as well as negroes, who had thrown down their arms, and besought quarter, were shot under that *insania belli* which invariably rages on such occasions." Jordan and Pryor, *The Campaigns of Nathan Bedford Forrest,* pp. 438–440. "maddened by excitement . . ." Officer of 2nd Tennessee Cavalry (CSA) in the *Charleston Mercury,* May 2, 1864.

47. Ransom Anderson, Elvis Bevel, Eli Carlton, W. Ferguson, in *RJSCW;* Charley Robinson/Family: April 17, 1864; Berry, *Four Years with Morgan and Forrest,* pp. 269–271; Mills, "Fort Pillow." To refute testimony and popular illustrations of the massacre depicting rebel troops bayoneting their prisoners at Fort Pillow, Davis pointed out that "General Forrest's troops did not have a bayonet in the whole command." (Davis, "What About Fort Pillow?") An excavation in the early 1970s uncovered a bayonet, though it is not known from which occupation. (Mainfort, *Archaeological Investigations.*) Sergeant W. P. Walker (white): "I saw some knock them over the heads with muskets, and some stick sabres into them." Eli Carlton (black): "I saw them stick a bayonet in the small part of the belly of one of our boys, and break it right off; he had one shot [wound] then." Ransom Anderson: "I also certify that I saw Coolie Pride, of the same regiment and the same company, stabbed by a rebel soldier with a bayonet and the bayonet broken off in his body, after the said Coolie Pride had been taken prisoner by the Confederates." W. Ferguson (gunboat *Silver Cloud*): "We found bodies bayoneted, beaten, and shot to death." in *RJSCW.* It is possible that some of Forrest's new recruits had muskets fitted with bayonets. One rebel participant testified that "sheets of fire and flame, bayonets, clubbed muskets, revolvers, swords, flashed and rung among the maddened soldiers who shot the frantic negroes and slew the men who had urged the negroes to this rash act and who now rushed pell mell about and over the embankment and redoubts, only to be impaled on the bayonets of those outside the fort." (Berry, *Four Years with Morgan and Forrest,* pp. 269–271.)

48. Morris, "Fort Pillow: Massacre or Madness?"

49. "It is true . . ." Isham Harris in *Atlanta Confederacy,* quoted in *Charleston Mercury,* May 6, 1864. "No one . . ." Berry, *Four Years with Morgan and Forrest,* pp. 269–271.

50. "They made . . ." Barteau in *Detroit Free Press,* December 1, 1884. "Many of them . . ." DeWitt Clinton Fort in Morris, "Fort Pillow: Massacre or Madness?" And yet . . . Davis, "What About Fort Pillow?"

51. "unsuspectingly entered . . ." "This is the story of the famous 'Massacre of Fort Pillow,' as told me by Gen. Forrest after I had rejoined him at Jackson on my return from Memphis." Otey, "The Story of Our Great War." "the negroes . . ." Maury, *Recollections of a Virginian,* p. 217. The problem with these accounts is that they complicate Forrest's own assertion that at this stage there was in fact no white flag flying and hence no surrender; that all through the attack the Union flag continued to wave from the ramparts; and that the *New Era* and the passing steamboats gave the garrison no support. "The enemy made no attempt to surrender, no white flag was elevated, nor was the U.S. flag lowered until

pulled down by our men. Many of them were killed while fighting, and many more in the attempt to escape." (Chalmers.) "The Federal flag flying over the fort was not lowered until after the garrison had fled for refuge under the bluff immediately behind the works, and no surrender was made by any officer of the garrison. As the Federal soldiers rushed for the bluff they carried their guns with them, and many of them turned and fired at us as they retreated, and some continued to fire from the crowd below the bank." (Robert McCulloch in Wyeth, *That Devil Forrest,* p. 593.) "They had no thought of surrender then, and in defiance of Forrest they left their flag floating from the staff." (Ibid., pp. 326–329.) An intriguing question is whether Bradford raised a black flag. Private Major Williams of 6/B is the only witness to say he did. "Major Bradford brought in a black flag, which meant no quarter. I heard some of the rebel officers say: 'You damned rascals, if you had not fought us so hard, but had stopped when we sent in flag of truce, we would not have done anything to you.'" (Major Williams in *RJSCW.*) If Williams's testimony is anything to go by (and it probably isn't), it suggests a solution to some of the confusion about whether Forrest ordered Captain Theodorick Bradford—"that man with the black flag"—shot because he had been wigwagging to the *New Era,* or because Bradford was waving a black flag. It might also bear on whether it was Lieutenant Akerstrom who signaled the *New Era* and whether Bradford was not signaling in semaphore (which, in any case, would have required two flags) but flourishing a black flag to signify no quarter. James Brigham (eyewitness): "Captain Bradford, of the Thirteenth Tennessee, was engaged with a blue signal flag, in connection with gunboat No. 7. Captain Bradford was ordered shot by General Forrest, who said, 'Shoot that man with the black flag.'" Elvis Bevel (eyewitness): "Signals were given by Captain Bradford to Captain Marshall, of the navy commanding gunboat No. 7, to shell them from post No. 1, which is in sight of the fort, which was done by Captain Marshall." Lieutenants F. A. Smith and William Cleary (hearsay): "Captain Theo. F. Bradford, of company A, 13th Tennessee cavalry, was signal-officer for the gunboat, and was seen by General Forrest with the signal flags. The general, in person, ordered Captain Bradford to be shot. He was instantly riddled with bullets, nearly a full regiment having fired their pieces upon him." Jordan and Pryor (Forrest's authorized biographers): "Captain Bradford was the signal officer; it is plain he lived long enough to give the signal spoken of by Captain Marshall, and was found dead at the spot where the signal was made; he was doubtless shot by some one as the parapets were surmounted." Dr. Charles Fitch (eyewitness): "The Gunboat No. 7 [*New Era*] fired some 250 shells, at different points, as signaled by Captain Bradford, who was Detailed as the Signal officer." (Jordan and Pryor, *The Campaigns of Nathan Bedford Forrest,* p. 450; Fitch, "Monthly Report"; all other quotes from *RJSCW.*)

52. "the only men . . ." Chalmers in Wyeth, *That Devil Forrest,* p. 593. But the preponderance . . . Jacob Thompson in *RJSCW.* "the detachment from Barteau . . ." Anderson, "The True Story of Fort Pillow."

53. "the yells . . ." Clark Barteau in *Detroit Free Press,* December 1, 1884. "as soon as . . ." James R. Brigham in *RJSCW.* "We were followed . . ." Hardy N. Revelle in ibid.

54. "Upon them . . ." Anderson, "The True Story of Fort Pillow." "Thus being . . ." Hancock, *Hancock's Diary,* pp. 360–361.

55. "The bigger portion . . ." Edward B. Benton in *RJSCW.* "They had been promised . . ." Wyeth, *That Devil Forrest,* pp. 326–329. "Finding that the succor . . ." Hancock, *Hancock's Diary,* pp. 360–361.

56. Charles Anderson in Wyeth, *That Devil Forrest,* pp. 594–595.

57. "Hundreds were killed . . ." "Memphis" pseudonym/Report: April 18, 1864, in Cimprich and Mainfort, "Fort Pillow Revisited." "and hid myself . . ." Henry Weaver in *RJSCW.* "several hundred . . ." "Memphis"/Report: April 18, 1864, in Cimprich and Mainfort, "Fort Pillow Revisited."

58. Charles Anderson in Jordan and Pryor, *The Campaigns of Nathan Bedford Forrest,* p. 328. "cut off all . . ." F. A. Smith and William Cleary in *RJSCW.*

River Run Red: Massacre: 4:30 P.M., April 12, 1864

1. "it was General Forrest's orders . . ." Daniel Stamps in *RJSCW.* The 2nd Missouri Cavalry was the only regiment left at Fort Pillow that morning.

2. Testimony of James Walls; pension file of James Taylor; James Walls in pension file of Isaac J. Ledbetter.

3. Quote extrapolated from "saying he wanted them to kill niggers." William A. Dickey in *RJSCW.*

4. William A. Dickey in ibid.

5. Fitch, "Monthly Report."

6. "could not surrender . . ." F. A. Smith and William Cleary in *RJSCW.* "some five or six . . ." Fitch, "Monthly Report."

7. "none of them . . ." F. A. Smith and William Cleary in *RJSCW.*

8. David W. Harrison in *RJSCW; Missouri Democrat,* April 15, 1864.

9. Shelton saw them shoot five or six black troops on the hill. "They shot all they could find," he said. Afterward, under guard in a shack with the wounded, he saw the rebels drag out two black soldiers and shoot them, and watched as the rebels buried several dead soldiers in the ditch by the works. (John W. Shelton in *RJSCW.*)

10. Hardy Revelle in ibid.

11. "I was the second man . . ." Pension file of Elias Falls; Elias Falls in *RJSCW;* pension file of Jordan and Eli Irwin; Alsie Williams in pension file of Peter Williams. But he was . . . Duncan Harding in *RJSCW.*

12. Up to this point Tyler had not spotted a single rebel officer on the scene.

13. Testimony and military record of Daniel Tyler; Register of Courts-Martial: Records and Sentences Received: January 1865–January 1866, RG393/2/2898 in NARA; *Cairo News,* April 16, 1864; "Daniel Tyler," *Liberator,* July 22, 1864. The *Liberator's* account quotes from a probably fictitious letter Robert Hall was supposed to have sent to his wife after the battle, and recounts the April 13 death of Manuel Nichols, who in fact survived the battle to testify for the Joint Committee on the Conduct of the War ten days later. I prefer the Daniel Tyler who testified with such clarity before Wade and Gooch and joked with the reporter from the *Cairo News.*

14. "The officers . . ." Sandy Addison in *RJSCW.* "but the enemy . . ." Jerry Stewart

in pension file of Ransom Parks; pension file of James Winston; George Houston and Jerry Stewart in *RJSCW.*

15. "could see . . ." Charley Robinson/Family: April 17, 1864.

16. Mack J. Leaming in *RJSCW.*

17. "Many of the white men . . ." Wyeth, *That Devil Forrest,* pp. 326–329. "some darkeys . . ." Daniel Rankin in *RJSCW.*

18. The artillerists' . . . Jordan and Pryor, *The Campaigns of Nathan Bedford Forrest,* pp. 438–440. "The Mississippi's . . ." Blount, "Captain Thomas Blount and His Memoirs." Fleeing up Cool Creek . . . Anonymous, *History of Tennessee.* Joseph Ray . . . Nelson Payton in *RJSCW.* "saw one man . . ." Charles Key in ibid.

19. "They shot them . . ." Chapman Underwood in *RJSCW.* "I don't suppose . . ." James McCoy in ibid.

20. "seemed to seethe . . ." Berry, *Four Years with Morgan and Forrest,* pp. 269–271. "Numbers of the garrison . . ." Dinkins, *Furl That Banner,* p. 154. "wild with fright . . ." Jordan and Pryor, *The Campaigns of Nathan Bedford Forrest,* p. 328. "The actual loss . . ." Forrest/Jefferson Davis: April 24, 1864, in Wyeth, *That Devil Forrest,* p. 335.

21. "We surrender!" Brigham said he remained in the woods for two days and nights, but he must have been mistaken, for if, as he testified, he saw Akerstrom's remains it had to have been on the following day. James R. Brigham in *RJSCW.* "were shot . . ." Lieutenant Leaming used the same phrase. "Some of the colored troops jumped into the river," he testified, "but were shot as fast as they were seen." (Mack J. Leaming in *RJSCW.*) "One poor fellow . . ." Dickey also testified that he saw "negroes thrown into the river by rebels, and shot afterwards, while struggling for life." George Shaw was apparently one of them. (William P. Dickey and George Shaw in *RJSCW.*)

22. John Haskins in *RJSCW.*

"Kill the Last Damn One": Bradford's Battalion: 4:00 P.M.–7:00 P.M., April 12, 1864

1. William H. Albritton and Thomas Loftis in pension file of John C. Simmons; James P. Meador in *RJSCW;* John C. Simmons in pension file of James P. Meador.

2. "kneel down . . ." James P. Meador in *RJSCW.*

3. Wyeth, *That Devil Forrest,* pp. 338–339; D. Z. Alexander in pension file of Bryant Johnson.

4. *TCW.*

5. An old friend . . . T. J. Parr of Russell's 20th Tennessee Cavalry was assigned to guard Federal prisoners the night after the battle. He was stationed at the little church where Forrest's white prisoners were incarcerated on the night of the thirteenth; he later recalled talking to Johnson through an open window. But neither . . . Only two months after joining the 13th, he was charged with desertion from Company D for ducking off to see his family, but the charges were soon dropped, and Johnson was still with the regiment when it was transferred to Fort Pillow. (Military record of Bryant Johnson; D. Z. Alexander, A. W. Foster, T. J. Parr, and D. B. Silph in pension file of Bryant Johnson.)

6. Dr. Kellogg in medical report, and Mary Jane Cooksey in pension file of Woodford H. Cooksey; testimony of Woodford H. Cooksey. Italics mine. I have extrapolated a quote from the following verbatim testimony: "He had damned nigh a notion to hit me in the head on account of staying there and fighting with the niggers." (Woodford Cooksey in *RJSCW*.)

7. Jason Loudon in *RJSCW*; military record of Leonidas Gwaltney.

8. Robert Lincoln/L. C. Houk: February 6, 1883, Records of Office of Quartermaster General/Cemeterial/1828–1929/RG92/Box 56/NM81/576; statement of Hardy Revelle.

9. The next morning . . . Eli Cothel [Carlton] in *RJSCW*; pension file of Cordy B. Revelle; Lieutenants F. A. Smith and William Cleary in *RJSCW*. After a tour of Fort Pillow in 1883, Cordy and Hardy Revelle's brother Ike wrote Secretary of War Robert Lincoln to deplore the condition of the federal graveyard at Fort Pillow. Lincoln replied that all federal remains at Fort Pillow had been transferred to the federal cemetery at Memphis. (Robert Lincoln/L. C. Houk: February 6, 1883, Records of Office of Quartermaster General/Cemeterial/1828–1929/RG92/Box 56/NM81/576.) "about two minutes . . ." John Ray in *RJSCW*. "Since that time," testified McCoy, "I have been told that they wounded him and then nailed him to a door and burned him up, but I didn't see that myself." Leaming testified that he had "very good reason for believing that was the case, although I did not see it." (James McCoy and Mack J. Leaming in ibid.) Jack Haskins . . . John Haskins in ibid. "Here is . . ." Carlton, who had worked for Akerstrom, was told he had been burned to death. (Eli Carlton in ibid.)

10. William P. Walker in pension file of Daniel Rankin; William P. Walker in *RJSCW*.

11. "They were shooting . . ." Daniel Rankin in ibid. "Shot in the hip . . ." James N. Taylor [Tayler] in pension file of Isaac J. Ledbetter; statement and medical report of James N. Taylor. W. J. Mays quoted the same cry. The 2nd Missouri Cavalry was the only regiment left at Fort Pillow that morning. "Kill them . . ." "The general cry from the time they charged the fort until an hour afterwards was, Kill 'em. Kill 'em; God damn 'em, that's Forrest's orders, not to leave one alive.'" (W. J. Mays in *RJSCW*.)

12. Wiley Robinson . . . Wiley Robinson in *RJSCW*.

13. Paroled to Mound City, where he nearly died of "bowel trouble," Ledbetter was discharged in July. He became a Methodist minister and postal clerk and fathered six children. Probably the longest-lived of the survivors of the Fort Pillow massacre, Isaac J. Ledbetter died in Morrilton, Arkansas, in 1935. (Isaac J. Ledbetter in *RJSCW*; John L. Poston, James N. Taylor [Tayler], and James M. Walls in pension file of Isaac J. Ledbetter.)

14. Among the men . . . John L. Poston in pension file of Neal Clark. the already badly injured . . . Ezekiel Arnold in the pension file of Andrew J. Glass. Daniel Fields . . . Columbus R. Allen and John N. Green in pension file of Daniel B. Fields. Robert McKenzie . . . Pension file of Robert B. McKenzie.

15. Nathan G. Fulks in *RJSCW*.

**Black Flag: 6th USCHA and 2nd USCLA: 4:00 P.M.–6:00 P.M.,
April 12, 1864**

1. The few . . . William T. Smith and Henry F. Weaver in pension file of Thomas McClure; Litton, *History of Oklahoma at the Golden Anniversary of Statehood*, vol. 3, pp. 1028–1029. Though First . . . Daniel Van Horn/T. H. Harris: April 14, 1864, in ORCW.
2. Frank Hogan in *RJSCW*. Emphasis mine.
3. Henry Weaver in ibid. I have extrapolated this quote from Weaver's account: ". . . The rebel remarking that they did not shoot white men, but wanted to know what in hell I was there fighting with the damned nigger for."
4. Henry Weaver in ibid.
5. Wilbur H. Gaylord in pension file of Samuel Green; pension file of Wilbur H. Gaylord; Wilbur H. Gaylord in *RJSCW*.
6. Alfred Coleman in *RJSCW*.
7. Alexander Nayron [Nason] in ibid.
8. Achilles V. Clark/George B. Halstead: April 19, 1864, in TSLA (RMC).
9. The Confederates either lost track of him in his hiding place or simply left him for dead, but Edmonds survived somehow and was picked up the next morning and taken to Memphis, where he spent two months recovering from his wounds and was misidentified as Arthur Edwards by Wade's committee. Deemed unfit for duty, he was discharged in early November. After the war, Edmonds became an itinerant preacher, but his wife, Fannie, refused to travel with him, and divorced him in 1870. Preaching may have been about all he was fit for. The wounds to his head gave him a "swimming so that I cannot stoop," his right wrist was shattered, and his shoulder was so mangled by a burst of rebel buckshot that his arm merely hung by his side. He lived the rest of his life in a series of communities that suggest a decline: first Memphis, then Tupelo, then Delta Bottoms, Mississippi. (William Ellis, Thomas Greer, Shed James, Alexander Nason, Henry Robinson in pension file of Arthur Edmonds; Arthur Edwards [Edmonds] in *RJSCW*.)
10. George Shaw in *RJSCW*.
11. John F. Ray in ibid.
12. William Henry's wife's family owned 125. (Wade Pruitt, "The Bugger Saga"; Slave Schedules: 1860 Lauderdale County, Alabama; McDonald, "A Walk through the Past: People and Places of Florence and Lauderdale County, Alabama"; Hill, "History of Greenhill, Alabama and Surrounding Counties and 54 Cemeteries.") Ray's children, all of whom eventually entered the cattle business in Texas, would choose Jarrett for their last name as well. www.alabamawaterfowl.org/archive.
13. Pension file of Joseph Key; Jesse Smith, Taylor Jarrett, and Henry Garner in pension file of Joseph Key.
14. They arrived at Okolona with about 200 prisoners, "embracing 160 whites and 40 negroes, including women and children." *Charleston Mercury*, May 2, 1864.
15. Edward B. Benton in *RJSCW*.
16. "Yes," he said . . . William F. Mays in ibid. Elias Falls recalled hearing some of his comrades exclaim that the rebels "had killed two women and two children." Elias Falls in ibid. James Lewis . . . James Lewis in ibid. "The description of the

slaughter in the second principal point of the committee's report," wrote Henry, "is rhetoric. The aged, the women and children, and the civilians in the fort who did not wish to join in the fight, were placed in a coal barge early in the morning and towed by the *New Era* 'to a big island up the river,' as testified to by Captain Marshall and referred to by other witnesses. In a letter to Gen. Chalmers, then a member of Congress, the surgeon of the garrison at Fort Pillow, Dr. C. Fitch, referred thus to charges of the murder of 'babes': 'I don't believe there was a babe there for any one to kill, as early in the morning all of the women and all of the noncombatants were ordered on to some barges, and were towed up the river to an island by a gunboat before anyone was hurt.'" (Henry, *"First with the Most" Forrest*, p. 261.) Fitch, who soon after the massacre provided some of the most horrifying testimony about the massacre in his report, was strangely glib and conciliatory when, years later, Chalmers contacted him in an effort to defend himself against the charge, recently repeated by a senatorial foe, that he was the officer who ordered the boy dropped from the horse and shot. And his comrade . . . Thomas Addison in *RJSCW.*

17. Rachel Parks and Jerry Steward [Stewart] in pension file of Ransom Parks; pension file of James Winston; George Houston and Jerry Stewart in *RJSCW.*

18. Pension file of Tom Addison; G. W. Barrett, Gabriel Lane (aka Calvin McLellan), and Jesse Wilson in pension file of Tom Addison; testimony of Tom Addison (JCCW).

19. Pension file of Thomas Addison; G. W. Barrett, Gabriel Lane (AKA Calvin McLellan), and Jesse Wilson in pension file of Tom Addison; Testimony of Tom Addison in *RJSCW.*

20. Deposition of Sherry Blain in pension file of Robert Blain; Aaron, Gundy, Lewis, and Robert Blain in pension file of Sherry Blain.

21. Sandy Cole . . . Sandy Cole in *RJSCW.* Left by the rebels . . . Nathan Hunter in ibid.

22. His wound left a deep depression just behind his left ear. He spent the rest of his life as a Memphis teamster and "chore boy," collecting a pension of eight dollars a month. Dizzy, half deaf, he complained in old age that "most all the time I has a deadly pain on [the right] side of my head. It works down the leader of my back," he said, "and hurts me powerful." (Alexander Nayron [Nason] in *RJSCW;* Alexander Nason in pension files of Charles Fox, Thomas Hooper, Willis Ligon, and Charles Macklin [Koon]; Samuel Hughes in pension file of Charles Macklin [Koon]; pension files of John Cowan, Arthur Edmonds, Anthony Flowers, and Thomas Grier.)

23. Benjamin Robinson in *RJSCW.*

24. Jacob Thompson in ibid.

25. Struck over the head . . . Burgess apparently ascribed his subsequent mood swings to a case of syphilis he claimed to have contracted during the war, but his doctor could never find any evidence of it. Burgess's first wife, by whom he had eight children, died in 1906, whereupon this luckless old veteran married a woman named Lewisa who, within a few months of their wedding, was killed in Brinkley, Arkansas, by a cyclone. (Henry Gill and Joseph Waldrup in pension file of Armstrong Burgess.) Oliver Scott . . . Recovering after the fighting was over, Scott was kept a prisoner by General Forrest, who took him to Aberdeen,

Mississippi, from which place he escaped in the spring of 1865 and returned to his command at Memphis. After the war he lived in Memphis and then worked as a farm laborer in Osceola, Arkansas. The doctor who examined him in old age reported that "his injuries have so affected him as to affect his mind and cause frequent head aches in rainy" and also "in very hot weather." (James Murrell in pension file of George Washington Perkins; Benjamin Jones and Delgie [Scott] Simmons in pension file of Oliver Scott.)

26. Charley Robinson/Family: April 17, 1864.

27. "In many instances . . ." F. A. Smith and William Cleary in *RJSCW.* James Walls . . . James Walls in ibid. "saw them take . . ." Alfred Coleman in ibid.

28. Edward Benton in ibid.

29. Fitch, "Monthly Report."

30. Eli Carlton in *RJSCW.* I have extrapolated a quote from "A fellow who was ahead asked, 'if I surrendered.'" (John Penwell in ibid.)

31. Coming to . . . "Some negro soldiers were lying down in the wood floor tents," wrote one of Forrest's defenders. "We do not know whether they were sick or drunk—or merely trying to escape the battle. We do know that some of these men were shot during the engagement." Davis, "What about Fort Pillow?" Corporal Frank Hogan . . . Frank Hogan in *RJSCW.* John Kennedy . . . Lamberg/Kappner: April 20, 1864, RG94/Box 8: Records of the 2nd USCLA in NARA.

32. "fired into the hospital . . ." Wiley Robinson in *RJSCW.* "nearly all . . ." "I made a post-mortem examination, and found that the outer table of the skull was incised, the inner table was fractured, and a piece driven into the brain." (Horace Wardner in ibid.)

"I Thought My Heart Would Burst": Forrest: 4:00 p.m.–8:00 p.m., April 12, 1864

1. Jordan and Pryor, *The Campaigns of Nathan Bedford Forrest,* pp. 438–440.

2. dictionary sense . . . According to *Webster's New Twentieth Century Dictionary* (second edition) a massacre is "1. the indiscriminate, merciless killing of a number of human beings or, sometimes, animals: wholesale slaughter. 2. An overwhelming defeat, as in sports. [Slang]." Forrest's defenders . . . "Our men," wrote Clarke Barteau, "as by one impulse, seem to have determined they would take the fort, and that, too, independently of officers or orders, and had no command been given to 'charge,' I verily believe that after the insults given them during the truce they would have taken the fort by storm any way." (Barteau in Hancock, *Hancock's Diary,* p. 367.)

3. Forrest had watched . . . Hancock, *Hancock's Diary,* p. 363. One officer . . . Officer of 2nd Tennessee Cavalry (CSA) in the *Charleston Mercury,* May 2, 1864. Bruised from his earlier . . . Rumors circulated that Forrest "received four flesh wounds at Fort Pillow. He is concentrating all his force at Jackson," wrote Major J. Murphy of the 5th Tennessee Cavalry on April 20, "and has ordered them to be provided with ten days' rations; they are trying to make the impression that they are going to Memphis. One of my scouts assures me that he will cross the river. I think he will, and is watching his opportunity." (J. Murphy/R. Rowett: April 20, 1864, in *ORCW.*) James Brigham may have been the source. "The last attack was made by General Forrest in person, who headed the column. For-

rest was wounded in three places, and his horse shot under him." (James Brigham in *RJSCW.*)

4. Barteau ordered . . . Wyeth, *That Devil Forrest,* p. 329. "They would not, or at least did not, take down their flag. I ordered this done myself by my own men in order to stop the fight." (Barteau in *Detroit Free Press,* December 1, 1884.) "After I entered . . ." John Nelson in *RJSCW.* "Fortunately for those of the enemy who survived this short but desperate struggle," wrote Forrest, "some of our men cut the halyard"—Anderson said it was Forrest himself—"and the United States flag which floated from a tall mast in the centre of the fort came down. The force stationed in the rear of the fort could see the flag, but were too far under the bluff to see the fort, and when the flag descended they ceased firing; but for this, so near were they to the enemy, that few, if any, would have survived unhurt another volley." (Forrest/Jefferson Davis: April 24, 1864, in Wyeth, *That Devil Forrest,* p. 335.)

5. But if he paid . . . Jordan and Pryor, writing on Forrest's behalf, claimed that his first order "was to collect and secure the prisoners from possible injury, while details were made from them for the burial of the Federal dead." His first order of business, however, was to roll a Parrott gun into place and fire on the *New Era.* In any case, he apparently did not issue his "first order" until well after the battle had mutated into a massacre. (Jordan and Pryor, *The Campaigns of Nathan Bedford Forrest,* p. 440.) "We are hard pressed . . ." James R. Brigham in *RJSCW; Missouri Democrat,* April 15, 1864. "After he had . . ." *Cairo News,* April 16, 1864. "was instantly riddled . . ." Lieutenants F. A. Smith and William Cleary in *RJSCW.*

6. John Nelson in ibid.

7. "with several others . . ." Achilles V. Clark/George B. Halstead: April 19, 1864, in TSLA (RMC). The other account . . . Fort, "Memoir." Fort's defense of his comrades' actions at Fort Pillow is as intriguing for what it does not say as for what it does. "I was at Fort Pillow," he wrote, "and have never been so cowardly as to deny it. I did nothing there to shame any man, and saw nothing for which Genl Forrest could be justly blamed." Fort is merely denying that he engaged in the slaughter and denying Forrest's responsibility, not the massacre itself, which he seemed to regard as all for the best. "Thus terminated an affair which utterly destroyed that garrison: which greatly relieved West Tennessee for many miles around from frequent depredations, by robbing bands which periodically went out from this Hd Qrs under the absurd pretence of protecting that country against guerilla outrages." Fort described "hard fighting of about nine hours duration, and blood enough spilled to enrage both sides; the attacked determining even to be put to the sword rather than surrender; an assault successfully made, many killed and wounded on both sides, and many prisoners taken. Instead of this it was represented, published, promulgated, denounced and outlawed that an overwhelming force marched in and wantonly murdered a weak and unresisting garrison, refusing to take any prisoners, but cruelly putting every man to the sword. This version was published throughout the Northern states at that time and having since remained uncontradicted with the truth has been believed every where almost." But the Union casualties were comparable only up to the time of the truce. No one claims every man was put

to the sword, but it is clear that once the rebels entered the fort, rebel casualties ceased and Yankee casualties increased to enormous proportions.

8. Fitch, "Monthly Report." Italics mine.

9. "'Twas but the . . ." Officer of 2nd [22nd] Tennessee Cavalry (CSA) in the
Charleston Mercury, May 2, 1864. Lee H. Russ . . . "A puff of smoke, followed
by the almost deafening crash of the explosion, told that we were masters of the
situation. We watched the flight of this first shot, and found that it flew too
high and some three hundred yards to the rear of the gunboat. Again we loaded
and fired as before, the writer firing the blank charge into the touchhole of the
cannon, and, failing to get far enough to one side, was struck and knocked
down by one of the wheels as the gun rebounded. This shot proved to be better, and we were getting the range. This shot alarmed the crew on board the
gunboat, for immediately her signal bell was sounded, and, while we were reloading, her hoarse whistle began to answer, and by the time our gun was again
ready for action she began to move off upstream. This third also fell short, as
did the former ones, and, glancing on the water, it passed only a few feet to the
rear of the gunboat. Had the boat remained stationary, this shot would certainly
have struck her about the water line, something like one third her length. By
this time she was under a full head of steam, rapidly retreating up the river. We
loaded and fired as rapidly as we could, and succeeded in getting in two more
shots, though harmless ones, before she was lost to sight around a sharp bend
in the river." (Lee H. Russ, "Firing a Captured Cannon at Fort Pillow," *CV,* June
1904.) James Marshall was aware of only one Parrott gun firing at him. (James
Marshall in *RJSCW.*) But in some accounts, two Parrott guns were brought to
bear on the *New Era.* "As soon as we entered the fort," wrote Hancock, "two of
the captured guns were turned upon the gunboat, which caused her to move
further up the river in place of coming to the relief of the garrison, as her commander had distinctly agreed to do. (So well was one of these guns handled by
B. A. High (who was afterward made Orderly Sergeant, Company G, Second
Tennessee) [Forrest worked the gun with him, according to a Union survivor]
that Forrest offered to promote him to the rank of Captain and allow him to go
with the captured guns to Mobile, Alabama. He declined to take the command
of the battery from the fact that he was not willing to leave his comrades. He
would have accepted if Forrest had kept the battery with his own command.)"
(Hancock, *Hancock's Diary,* p. 360.) Brewer is mistaken when he asserted that
Captain Morton manned the guns. Morton was not present at Fort Pillow, and
Walton's battery of two guns was still positioned well east of the breastworks.
Brewer, "Storming of Fort Pillow."

10. Fitch, "Capture of Fort Pillow"; Fitch, "Monthly Report."

11. It took only five . . . Marshall counted two, Chapman Underwood three in
RJSCW. "over and around us . . ." James Marshall: Report: April 15, 1864
(NFWW). "a proud, exultant shout . . ." Officer of 2nd Tennessee Cavalry
(CSA) in the *Charleston Mercury,* May 2, 1864.

12. "I had to leave . . ." in Jordan and Pryor, *The Campaigns of Nathan Bedford
Forrest,* pp. 436–438. "part of our own men . . ." James Marshall in *RJSCW.*
Sergeant Henry Weaver of 6/C backed up Marshall, testifying that the *New Era*
could not have opened fire "without killing our own men" because "they were

all mixed up together." (Henry Weaver in ibid.) Forrest was also more under-
standing of Marshall's dilemma. The *New Era* "had, as I afterwards understood,
expended all her ammunition, and was therefore powerless for affording the
Federal garrison the aid and protection they doubtless expected of her when
they retreated towards the river." Forrest/Jefferson Davis: April 24, 1864, in
Wyeth, *That Devil Forrest,* pp. 335–336. "came to . . ." James Marshall: Report:
April 15, 1864, in *NFWW;* N. D. Wetmore Jr./Editors, *Argus:* April 13, 1864
(*NFWW*). Arkansas civilian . . . Elvis Bevel in *RJSCW.* "I saw the Union soldiers, black and white, slaughtered while asking for quarter; heard their
screams for quarter, to which the rebels paid no attention. About one hundred
left the fort and ran down the bank of the bluff to the river, pursued by the
rebels, who surrounded them; in about twenty minutes, every one of them, as
far as I could see, were shot down by the rebels without mercy. I left at this
time, getting on the gunboat."

13. 191 rounds . . . James Marshall: Report: April 15, 1864 (*NFWW*). "recreant at
this . . ." Hancock, *Hancock's Diary,* p. 360. "The naval commander . . ." Dinkins, "The Capture of Fort Pillow." "It would have been . . ." Anderson, "The
True Story of Fort Pillow." "steamed up the river . . ." William A. Winn in
RJSCW.

14. Fitch, "Monthly Report."

15. Several witnesses . . . Isaac Ledbetter was asked if he saw any rebel officers
while the shooting was going on. "None there that I know," Ledbetter replied.
"I did not see them until they carried me up on the bluff." James Walls: "I do
not know as I saw any officers about when they were shooting the negroes. A
captain came to me a few minutes after I was shot; he was close by me when I
was shot. . . . I did not hear a word of their trying to stop [the shooting]. After
they were shot down, he told them not to shoot them any more. I begged him
not to let them shoot me again, and he said they would not." Daniel Stamps
conceded, however, that he couldn't distinguish rebel officers "as I can our of
ficers. Their uniform is different." Wounded men like Benjamin Robinson who
never fled over the bluff testified to encountering a great many officers in the
fort: "lots of them," as he put it. The only general seen by the river was apparently Chalmers. (See also Jacob Thompson and William Cleary in *RJSCW* and
pension file of Jacob Jones.) "One rebel . . ." William F. Mays in *RJSCW.*

16. Aaron Fentis in *RJSCW.*

17. Isham Harris in the *Charleston Mercury,* May 6, 1864.

18. "six pieces . . ." Forrest/Jefferson Davis: April 24, 1864, in Wyeth, *That Devil
Forrest,* p. 336. "crackers, cheese . . ." Officer of 2nd Tennessee Cavalry (CSA)
in the *Charleston Mercury,* May 2, 1864. Jacob Thompson . . ." Jacob Thompson
in *RJSCW. "Did you see any rebel officers about there when this was going on?* Yes,
sir; old Forrest was one. *Did you know Forrest?* Yes, sir; he was a little bit of a
man. I had seen him before at Jackson." Critics of the Union version of what
transpired at Fort Pillow cite this exchange to discredit all of the black troops'
testimony. But the general Thompson saw was very likely Chalmers, who commanded the assault and was a pint-sized version of Forrest, down to his high
forehead, swept-back hair, and goatee. "Generals Chalmers and Bell . . ."
Wyeth, *That Devil Forrest,* p. 329.

19. "the mongrel garrison . . ." Chalmers in Willoughby, "Gunboats and Gumbo." General Chalmers "came by with his brigade and commenced killing everybody live and wounded," but "General Forrest stopped him." (Pension file of Jacob Jones.) "strong guard" . . . Fitch, "Monthly Report." Chalmers was compelled . . . Wyeth, *That Devil Forrest,* p. 329. "One Confederate within [Chalmers's] observation, who disregarded this order, he personally arrested and placed under guard for the offence." Wyeth, *That Devil Forrest,* p. 593. Dr. Fitch . . . Fitch, "The Capture of Fort Pillow."

20. "Both Generals . . ." Dinkins, "The Capture of Fort Pillow." "Generals Forrest and Chalmers," wrote Dinkins, "seeing the panic, called on the men to cease firing, and after a few minutes succeeded in restoring order." (Dinkins, *Furl That Banner,* p. 154.) Dr. Fitch would testify fifteen years later that Chalmers saved his life by threatening to shoot any rebel who molested him. Fitch, "The Capture of Fort Pillow."

21. "the flat of his sword . . ." Berry, *Four Years with Morgan and Forrest,* pp. 269–271. "and threatened him . . ." *Cairo News,* April 16, 1864. a story Union . . . Young "stated that General Forrest shot one of his own for refusing quarter to our men." N. D. Wetmore Jr./Editors, *Argus:* April 13, 1864, in *NFWW.*

22. Samuel H. Caldwell/Wife: April 15, 1864, in Cimprich and Mainfort, "Fort Pillow Revisited."

23. "to help . . ." Alfred Coleman in *RJSCW.* "Kill all . . ." Major Williams in ibid. And yet his men "kept on shooting. They shot at me after that," Williams testified, "but did not hit me; a rebel officer shot at me. He took aim at my side; at the crack of his pistol I fell." "There's another dead nigger," he said, moving on.

24. Manuel Nichols in ibid.

26. Military, pension, and ration commutation files of Samuel Green; Reason Barker, Thomas Brown, Morning Clay, Felix Davis, Steven Davis, Wilbur H. Gaylord, Henry Gillespie, Benjamin Jones, Pearson Lee, Henry Meeks, J. C. Shearer in pension file of Samuel Green; Samuel Green in pension files of Henry Dix and Jacob Jones. The general would probably have recognized the body of twenty-one-year-old Joseph Jackwood, who lived near his former home in sparsely settled Tippah County, Mississippi. (Pension file of Joseph Jackwood.)

26. J. Altshul, Andrew Clopton, Abraham Huggins, Abner W. Ligon, David and Nelson Mooring, Alexander Nason, Monroe Wilson, and Phillip Young, in pension file of Willis Ligon.

27. Dinkins, *Furl That Banner,* pp. 155–156.

28. The other CSA Middletons were Alva and John J., who served in Mississippi infantry regiments. (Peter Jolly; Elizabeth Middleton Jones; Arabella, George, Josephine, Steven, and Thomas F. Middleton; and George Oliver in pension file of Adam Middleton.)

29. Charles Macklin . . . Macklin ran away with Jim Stokes, and Moses and Alexander Nason; Martha Colbert, Samuel Hughes, Alexander Nason, Mary Jane Hicks Purnell, and Jane and Sam J. Smith in pension file of Charles Koon [Macklin]. Hughes's masters were Lieutenant Richard T. Gardiner and Private F. C. Gardiner of the 15th Tennessee. A slave belonging to Captain Thomas Buchanan of the 15th was armed and permitted to take part in the regiment's combat. (Willoughby, "Bayonets and Bloomers.") "the negroes belonging . . ."

Forrest: General Order 65: July 10, 1864, in RG94/Chapter 2/v.299 (Chalmers) in NARA. Consequently, they did not . . . Samuel Hughs in pension file of Charles Macklin.

30. "love and affection . . ." John H. Meeks/John C. Black: March 24, 1888, in pension file of Frank Meeks. Among the local men who might have recognized his body were Captain John R. Adams and Privates Thomas Benton Kendrick and R. W. Michie of the 19th Tennessee Cavalry; W. H. Harris, Company I, 16th Tennessee Cavalry; J. P. Wilson of Company A, 21st Tennessee Cavalry. James Lewis in *RJSCW.*

31. "Just after the firing . . ." Hancock, *Hancock's Diary,* pp. 363–364nn. Hancock conceded that "such was the animosity between the Tennesseans of the two commands, and as such is frequently the case in places taken by storm, some, no doubt, were shot after they had thrown down their arms and besought quarter; no such cases, however, happened to come under the immediate observation of the writer," who remained atop the bluff. Ibid., pp. 361, 363.

Plunder: Fort Pillow: 5:00 P.M.–Midnight, April 12, 1864

1. "some few . . ." Adolf Lamberg/Kappner: April 20, 1864, in RG94/Box 8: Records of the 2nd USCLA in NARA. Shot in the ankle . . . William Gaylord in *RJSCW.* "another man . . ." D. W. Harrison in ibid. Emphasis mine.
2. *Cairo News,* April 16, 1864.
3. Mack J. Leaming in *RJSCW.*
4. Burney, "Some Texas Rangers."
5. Less fastidious . . . Pension files of John Cowan and James Stokes; Benjamin Jones in pension file of Oliver Scott; Captain Adolf Lamberg (2nd USCLA)/ Colonel Kappner: April 20, 1864, RG94/Box 8: Records of the 2nd USCLA in NARA; John Cowan, Hardy N. Revelle, James Lewis, Daniel Tyler, W. P. Walker and Henry F. Weaver in *RJSCW.* Others . . . Hardy Revelle, W. P. Walker in *RJSCW.*
6. Charley Robinson/Family: April 17, 1864.
7. "When the fight . . ." Carroll, "Autobiography and Reminiscences," p. 28. "shooting and robbing . . ." William F. Mays in *RJSCW;* Mack J. Leaming in ibid. "I was wounded and knocked down with the but of a musket and left for dead, after being robbed, and they cut the buttons off my jacket." James Lewis in ibid. "They robbed . . ." Edward B. Benton in ibid.
8. Thinking Nathan Hunter . . . Nathan Hunter in ibid.
9. "They thought . . ." William P. Walker in ibid. "Yes, sir; they ran their hands in my pockets—they thought I was dead—they did all in the same way." John Haskins in ibid. Some rebels . . . "Thinking that if I should be discovered, I would be killed, I emerged from my hiding place, and, approaching the nearest rebel, I told him I was a citizen. He said, 'You are in bad company, G—d d—n you; out with your greenbacks, or I'll shoot you.' I gave him all the money I had, and under his convoy I went up into the fort again."(John Nelson in ibid.) Thomas Addison testified that as he played dead a rebel "searched my pockets and took my money. He said: 'God damn his old soul; he is sure dead now; he is a big, old, fat fellow.'" (Thomas Addison in ibid.) "Soon after . . ." (Mack J. Leaming in ibid.)

10. Fleeing to within . . . Carl A. Lamberg/I. G. Kappner: April 20, 1864, in *ORCW*. "I had some . . ." Emanuel Nichols in ibid.; "Daniel Tyler" in the *Liberator*, July 22, 1864; testimony and statement of Ransom Anderson.

11. "After the fight . . ." Samuel H. Caldwell/Wife: April 15, 1864, in Cimprich and Mainfort, "Fort Pillow Revisited." Forrest assessed . . . "Vidette" in *Atlanta Memphis Appeal*, May 2, 1864; Forrest/Jefferson Davis: April 24, 1864, in Wyeth, *That Devil Forrest*, p. 336.

12. Officer of 2nd Tennessee Cavalry (CSA) in the *Charleston Mercury*, May 2, 1864.

13. Edward B. Benton in *RJSCW*.

14. "and taken into the town . . ." Henry Weaver in ibid. "At the top . . ." Hardy Revelle in ibid.

15. Charley Robinson/Family: April 17, 1864.

16. James Brigham in *RJSCW*.

17. Hancock, *Hancock's Diary*, p. 400.

18. Forrest's defenders . . . *"You say they had bloodhounds; did you see any of them?* Edward Benton: Yes, sir; and not only I but others saw them. One other, Mr. Jones, was treed by them, and staid there a long time. *What Jones was that?* I don't know his given name. He lives on Island 34. I can find out his name. He is not any too good a Union man, but is rather southern in his feelings." Edward B. Benton in *RJSCW*; he made the same claim to General Rosencrans. (*New York Herald*: April 24, 1864.) But not only . . . Rogers and Patterson, "Concerning the Nathan Bedford Forrest Legend." "No man in all that country [West Tennessee] is safe," wrote Isaac Hawkins while Forrest's recruiters were active. "The confeds are conscripting: hunting men and boys down with hounds—and in some instances young men are so torn up by the dogs, as to be unable to travel." Isaac Hawkins/[Hurlbut]: September 20, 1863, in RG94/E729A/Box 4 in NARA; S. L. Phelps/A. H. Foote: December 10, 1861, in *NFWW*. In any case . . . Elvis Bevel in *RJSCW*.

19. "to complete the burial . . ." Jordan and Pryor, *The Campaigns of Nathan Bedford Forrest*, pp. 442–443. Some historians claimed that Forrest departed immediately after the firing stopped, but, like Henry, I take Major Anderson's word that he remained "into the late evening." Anderson, "The True Story of Fort Pillow." Chalmers commanded . . . Wyeth, *That Devil Forrest*, pp. 330–331. and follow Forrest . . . In asserting that any atrocities committed after dark had to have been the work of skulkers or local thugs, Wyeth wrote that "McCulloch, with Chalmers, followed at dark, leaving the fort entirely abandoned by the Confederates. The Federal wounded were left in charge of their surgeon. The rear guard of the Confederates encamped for the night two miles from the river. After dark that evening not a soldier of Forrest's command was nearer Fort Pillow than two miles, where General Chalmers went into camp. If the excesses charged by some of the survivors were committed after that time and before six o'clock of the following morning (April 13th), they were done by guerrillas, robbers, and murderers, with which this section of the country, as is well known, was then infested, and who, following in the wake of either army like hyenas, preyed without mercy upon the weak and defenseless." (Wyeth, *That Devil Forrest*, pp. 330–331.) But there is ample evidence that McCulloch

and his men did not leave until much later than nightfall, which, at that time of year, occurred around 7:00 p.m.; that the burial parties labored under rebel supervision at least until 10:00 p.m. ("They were burying pretty much all night," Woodford Cooksey in *RJSCW*); and that McCulloch's men camped not two miles away but no farther than one mile, from which point they could easily have slipped back during the night. ("Bell withdrew his brigade about one mile and a half east and encamped, while McCulloch's Brigade camped nearer the fort." Hancock, *Hancock's Diary,* pp. 363–364.) Finally, those who witnessed crimes that night invariably described the assailants as rebel soldiers.

20. Bell and his brigade . . . Hancock, *Hancock's Diary,* pp. 363–364. "Among the mass of sworn testimony examined by the author [Wyeth], it is shown that with but one exception, the perpetrator of which was arrested by General Chalmers on the spot and placed under guard, not a gun was fired or a prisoner injured after the flag of the garrison fell." But Wyeth must have entirely dismissed or failed to examine any of the Federal testimony. It is significant that in defending themselves against these charges, Forrest, his officers, and his biographers did not collect a single deposition from an enlisted man. He also neglected to remember that Chalmers himself recalled that Forrest had been forced to threaten one of his men for disobeying his cease-fire order. (Wyeth, *That Devil Forrest,* p. 329.) Bell claimed in a memorandum to Wyeth that his men camped fifteen miles from the breastworks that night, but he confused this night with the night of the thirteenth. (Tyree H. Bell in Wyeth, *That Devil Forrest,* p. 593.) By seven o'clock . . . Jordan and Pryor, *The Campaigns of Nathan Bedford Forrest,* pp. 442–443. Frank Hogan . . . Frank Hogan in *RJSCW.*

21. Alfred Coleman in *RJSCW.*

22. "earnest in his expressions . . ." Robert McCulloch in Wyeth, *That Devil Forrest,* p. 593. Perhaps McCulloch was hard of hearing. "They shot a great many that evening." (Thomas Addison in *RJSCW.*) "I heard guns away after dark shooting all that evening, somewhere; they kept up a regular fire for a long time, and then I heard the guns once in a while." (John F. Ray in ibid.) "The enemy carried our works at about 4 p.m., and from that time until dark, and at intervals throughout the night, our men were shot down without mercy and almost without regard to color." (Mack J. Leaming in ibid.) "I heard firing all night." (George Houston in ibid.) "the best fighting men . . ." Barteau in the *Detroit Free Press,* December 1, 1884.

23. "the unwounded . . ." Charles Anderson in Henry, *"First with the Most" Forrest,* pp. 256–257. Several survivors . . . Mack J. Leaming in *RJSCW.* "As fast as possible . . ." Hancock, *Hancock's Diary,* p. 362. "The most of our wounded . . ." Fitch, "Monthly Report."

24. "procure a skiff . . ." Forrest/Jefferson Davis: April 24, 1864, in Wyeth, *That Devil Forrest,* p. 336. "Sir," it said . . . Forrest in ibid., pp. 329–330.

25. "The object was . . ." Jordan and Pryor, *The Campaigns of Nathan Bedford Forrest,* p. 442; Henry, *"First with the Most" Forrest,* pp. 256–257. "taken off by citizens . . ." Charles Anderson in ibid.

26. After what Marshall . . . Forrest/Jefferson Davis: April 24, 1864, in Wyeth, *That Devil Forrest,* p. 336. "fearful . . ." James Marshall in ibid., p. 330.

27. Burfford, "In the Wake of Fort Pillow with Forrest in Command." Some of Burfford's account is very similar to Anderson's and was probably based on it.
28. Alexander Nason in *RJSCW.*
29. The officers' corpses . . . Hancock, *Hancock's Diary,* p. 363; Fitch, "Monthly Report"; Jordan and Pryor, *The Campaigns of Nathan Bedford Forrest,* p. 440. Most, but apparently . . . Eli Bangs in *RJSCW.* Some were buried . . . William B. Purdy in ibid. Major Booth . . . Benjamin Robinson in ibid. where a rebel trooper . . . "Major Booth and some of the other officers were burried in a separate grave. A Rebel soldier had taken off his Uniform, and was parading around with it on." (Fitch, "Monthly Report.") Sergeant Benjamin Robinson testified that "they took his clothes all off but his drawers; I was lying right there looking at them." (Benjamin Robinson in *RJSCW.*)
30. As the rebels . . . Fitch, "Monthly Report." "the unwounded . . ." Charles Anderson in Henry, *"First with the Most" Forrest,* pp. 256–257. Forrest described the details as "Federals and Negroes," thus denying the artillerists legitimacy as Union soldiers. (Forrest/Jefferson Davis: April 24, 1864, in Wyeth, *That Devil Forrest,* p. 336.) overall command . . . Captain O. B. Farris (Company K, 2nd Tennessee) superintended the burial of the dead. Hancock, *Hancock's Diary,* p. 363.
31. "They were all pitched in . . ." James Marshall, William B. Purdy, John W. Shelton in *RJSCW.* "Some had just been thrown . . ." Eli Bangs in ibid.
32. Black prisoners . . . Granville Hill (regiment unknown) testified to having been a slave of the same master—a man named Warren—as Thomas Davis of 2/B. He said he helped bury Davis on April 13. (Pension file of Thomas Davis.) Charles Williams . . . Carroll Harris, Granville Hill, and Mary Warren in pension file of Thomas Davis.
33. "there seemed to be . . ." Frank Hogan in *RJSCW.* "working his hand . . ." Benjamin Robinson in ibid.
34. "He laughs over his adventures, and says he is one of the best 'dug-outs' in the world." *Cairo News,* April 16, 1864.
35. Though a few . . . Deposition of Sandy Addison and Charles Williams in pension file of Robert Green testified that they were "detailed to return and help bury the dead." Corporal Reason Barker and Private Henry Miller in pension file of Harry Hunter testified that they buried Harry Hunter of 6/D. others who witnessed . . . John Shelton in *RJSCW.*
36. Dinkins, *Furl That Banner,* pp. 155–156.
37. For over four hours . . . Fitch, "Monthly Report." "left unattended . . ." Anderson in Henry, *"First with the Most" Forrest,* pp. 256–257. "After securing . . ." Officer of 2nd Tennessee Cavalry (CSA) in the *Charleston Mercury,* May 2, 1864.
38. A. W. Ellet/Porter: July 3, 1863 (*NFWW*).
39. In disputing . . . Jordan and Pryor, *The Campaigns of Nathan Bedford Forrest,* p. 443; Wyeth, *That Devil Forrest,* pp. 591–592. Billy Mays was taken for dead by a rebel arsonist. (William J. Mays in *RJSCW.*)
40. John Penwell in *RJSCW.*
41. James Walls and William J. Mays in ibid.
42. Nathan G. Fulks in ibid.
43. Ransom Anderson in ibid. Daniel Tyler and W. P. Walker testified that they did

not see anyone burned alive; James Walls and Isaac J. Ledbetter said they had been told about it by others. All in ibid.

44. "all other evidence . . ." Henry, *"First with the Most" Forrest*, pp. 265–266. Whatever the merits . . . Officer of 2nd Tennessee Cavalry (CSA) in the *Charleston Mercury*, May 2, 1864; Elias Falls in *RJSCW*.

"Walk or Die": Prisoners: From April 12, 1864

1. John Goodman: List of Prisoners Cap'd by Major General Forrest at Fort Pillow, & in Tennessee—Deserters, Men of Bad Characters, Flags &c. &c. Apl 12/64: undated (copied in Dept. 198—December 21, 1886) in RG249/107/896 in NARA.

2. C. R. Barteau in Wyeth, *That Devil Forrest*, p. 594.

3. L. T. Lindsay/McCulloch: April 19, 1864, in RG94/Chapter 2/v.289 (Chalmers) in NARA.

4. Jordan and Pryor published a list that included 53 black prisoners and 3 of their white officers: Epeneter, Bischoff, and Hennessy of 6/A. Pension and military records suggest that there were six more. ("List of Prisoners Captured at Fort Pillow," Jordan and Pryor, *The Campaigns of General Nathan Bedford Forrest*, p. 704.) Though Chalmers's own adjutant's list shows 155 white prisoners, including 141 men of the 13th, Chalmers later reported that "One hundred and sixty-four white men and 40 negroes were taken prisoners, making an aggregate of 273 prisoners. It is probable as many as half a dozen may have escaped. The remainder of the garrison were killed." (Chalmers/J. P. Strange: May 7, 1864, in *ORCW*.) "Seven officers and two hundred and nineteen enlisted men (fifty-six negroes and one hundred and sixty-three whites), unwounded, were brought off as prisoners of war, which, with the wounded, make an aggregate of those who survived, exclusive of all who may have escaped (it was said that about twenty-five escaped in a skiff), two hundred and ninety-six, or a little over half of the garrison." (Hancock, *Hancock's Diary*, p. 364) "Something over three hundred of them did so after having been convinced that further resistance was useless. Besides the wounded who were paroled we carried something over two hundred and fifty of them to Mississippi and I know that several made their escape. " (Fort, "Memoir.") My own count shows 62 blacks and 147 whites, for a total of 209; over half of the blacks (32) and 41 whites were wounded, most of them seriously. (Military, regimental, and pension records of the 2nd USCLA, 6th USCHA, and 11th USCI.) But by the time the prisoners reached Holly Springs there were only 104 white and 30 black prisoners. Some had escaped, some had been killed, and some were simply never heard from again. (Philip Young in *RJSCW*.)

5. Pension file of Samuel Green.

6. "saw officers . . ." James Brigham in *RJSCW*. "with a gun sling . . ." Captain Adolf Lamberg (2nd USCLA)/Colonel Kappner: April 20, 1864, RG94/Box 8: Records of the 2nd USCLA in NARA. Bob Winston . . . Harden Capers and Duncan Harding in *RJSCW*. Capers referred to him as Corporal Robert Winsent. Among the prisoners . . . *Charleston Mercury*, May 2, 1864. (See also "List of Prisoners Captured by Forrest at Fort Pillow," RG249/107/Item 896 in NARA.

7. five of them . . . They were D. Allgood ("a boy from Kentucky), W. T. Cameron

of Tennessee, George Washington Crafts of Minnesota, and J. Schaffer. Brigham testified that "there were from twenty-five to thirty black soldiers carried off as prisoners, and not over thirty to thirty-five white," which may have been all he saw or an attempt to exaggerate the scale of the massacre. (James Brigham in *RJSCW*; "List of Prisoners Captured by Forrest at Fort Pillow," RG249/107/Item 896 in NARA.) "were passing by us . . ." Fitch, "Monthly Report." "The Federals . . ." Howlett, "Dr. R. E. Howlett in the Civil War."

8. Wilbur H. Gaylord in *RJSCW*.
9. Manuel Nichols in ibid.
10. W. J. Mays in ibid.
11. Brown, *The Negro in the American Rebellion*.
12. "all the colored boys . . ." Jerry Stewart in *RJSCW*. "crawled down . . ." Benjamin Robinson in ibid. "they intended . . ." Philip Young in ibid.
13. Thomas Addison in ibid.
14. George Shaw in ibid. Emphasis mine. Henry Christian may have witnessed this same incident. "I saw two shot; one was shot by an officer. He was standing, holding the officer's horse, and when the officer came and got his horse he shot him dead." (Henry Christian in *RJSCW*.)

Paroled: Fort Pillow: April 12–13, 1864

1. In the night . . . Hollis, "The Diary of Elisha Tompkin Hollis."
2. Woodford Cooksey in *RJSCW*. (Emphasis mine.)
3. The 2nd Missouri Cavalry was the only regiment left at Fort Pillow that morning.
4. James Walls in *RJSCW*; pension file of James Taylor; James Walls in pension file of Isaac J. Ledbetter.
5. Brown, *The Negro in the American Rebellion*, pp. 246–247.
6. "one white woman . . ." Eli A. Bangs in *RJSCW*. "a gun . . ." Chapman Underwood in ibid.
7. At Mound City, Leaming "received good care and medical treatment in the U.S. general hospital." Leaming testified before Wade and Gooch in the hospital, with Lieutenant John Porter lying in the next bed, "unable to speak." The only other paroled officer to live long enough to reach Mound City, Porter would die of his wounds in June, "As to the course our Government should pursue in regard to the outrages perpetrated by the rebels on this as well as on a number of occasions during the existing rebellion," Leaming proposed the following January, ". . . some sort of retaliation should be adopted as the surest method of preventing a recurrence of the fiendish barbarities practiced on the defenders of our flag at Fort Pillow." (Mack J. Leaming in ibid.)
8. Daniel Stamps in ibid.
9. T. Pattison/Porter: April 13, 1864, in NFWW.
10. W. Ferguson (*Silver Cloud*)/T. Pattison: April 14, 1864, in NFWW.
11. Edmondson, Diary.
12. *Missouri Democrat,* April 15, 1864.
13. Pulling back . . . W. Ferguson (*Silver Cloud*)/T. Pattison: April 14, 1864, in NFWW. "some twenty . . ." W. Ferguson in *RJSCW*. Heaving the *Silver Cloud* . . . James Marshall: Report: April 15, 1864, in *NFWW*.
14. N. D. Wetmore Jr./Editors, *Argus*: April 13, 1864, in ibid.

15. Daniel Stamps in *RJSCW.*

16. Aboard the *Silver Cloud* . . . Wilbur H. Gaylord and Mack J. Leaming in ibid. Lieutenant Frank Smith of Company D was forty years old and spent much of his time in the 13th chasing deserters. "shoot one man . . ." William Cleary in ibid.

17. At Forrest's temporary camp . . . Peters, *Lauderdale County,* p. 47. Fearing that the *New Era* . . . Anderson, "The True Story of Fort Pillow." Elisha Tompkin Hollis was one of the men sent back. "Wednesday—April 13, 1864 Beautiful day, sent back to Fort and there remained most of the day under truce. In the evening we marched several miles out and camped." (Hollis, "Diary of Elisha Tompkin Hollis.") That Forrest felt . . . Wyeth, *That Devil Forrest,* p. 591.

18. Report of Major Anderson: April 17, 1864, in *NFWW.*

19. Anderson, "The True Story of Fort Pillow."

20. William Cleary in *RJSCW*; Anderson, "The True Story of Fort Pillow."

21. Charles W. Anderson/W. Ferguson: April 13, 1864 (*NFWW*).

22. Charles W. Anderson and W. Ferguson: Agreement: April 13, 1864 (*NFWW*).

23. The little general had just granted Dr. Fitch a parole, which read: "I Charles Fitch Asst Surgeon 13th Tenn. Cav. U.S. Volunteers, having been captured by the Confederate forces, do give my Parole of honor that I will not bear Arms, nor do any other Military service in any capacity whatsoever for the United States, until Exchanged, except to attend to the wounded of the U.S. Forces captured at Fort Pillow by the Confederate States forces." Fitch, "Monthly Report."

24. Anderson, "The True Story of Fort Pillow."

25. Chapman Underwood in *RJSCW.*

26. E. Nigh/T. H. Harris: January 24, 1864, in RG 393, Records of the U.S. Army Continental Commands: 1821–1920, General Records, 16th Army Corps, Letters Received, 1864. Box 1.

27. "in great stress . . ." Anderson, "The True Story of Fort Pillow." "It was a subject . . ." *Missouri Democrat,* April 15, 1864. The *Democrat* may have confused Young with Lieutenant Cordy Revelle, whose brother Hardy worked as a clerk in a merchandising firm at Fort Pillow.

28. Anderson, "The True Story of Fort Pillow."

29. "Those wounded . . ." N. D. Wetmore Jr./ Editors, *Argus*: April 13, 1864, in *NFWW.*

30. Thomas Loftus [Loftis] and Daniel N. Rankin in pension file of Francis A. Alexander; William H. Albritton, Emerson B. Eldridge, G. L. Ellis, Daniel N. Rankin, and John C. Simmons in pension file of Thomas Loftis.

31. James P. Meador and John C. Simmons in pension files of Thomas Loftis; William H. Albritton and Thomas Loftis in pension file of John C. Simmons.

32. William H. Albritton and Thomas Loftis in pension file of John C. Simmons; James P. Meador in *RJSCW*; John C. Simmons in pension file of James P. Meador.

33. George W. Craig, Thomas Loftis, and John C. Simmons in pension file of William Albritton; William Albritton in pension files of John C. Simmons and James P. Meador.

34. After suffering . . . Wiley Robinson in *RJSCW.* Jim McMichael . . . James McMichael in ibid. "They shot the most after they had surrendered," he gasped to Wade and Gooch. "They sent in a flag of truce for a surrender, and the ma-

jor would not surrender. They made a charge and took the fort, and then we threw down our arms; but they just shot us down."

35. Shot four times . . . William P. Walker in pension file of Daniel Rankin; testimony, statement, and pension file of William P. Walker. Wounded in the side . . . Testimony of Isaac J. Ledbetter; John L. Poston, James N. Tayler, and James M. Walls in pension file of Isaac J. Ledbetter.

36. Daniel Rankin in *RJSCW.*

37. Statement and testimony of Daniel H. Rankin; Martin V. Day and William P. Walker in pension file of Daniel H. Rankin; Daniel Rankin in pension files of Francis A. Alexander, Thomas Loftis, and Hartwell D. Stovall.

38. Testimony and statement of Daniel Stamps; John T. Stamps and John H. Copher in pension file of Daniel Stamps; Daniel Stamps in pension file of John M. Condray.

39. "About two o'clock . . ." Edward B. Benton in *RJSCW.* By now . . . Jewell, *New Orleans.*

40. Fitch, "The Capture of Fort Pillow"; Fitch, "Monthly Report."

41. Billy Bancom . . . Pension file of William A. Bancom. Frank Key . . . Frank Smith and Chapman Underwood in pension file of Franklin A. Key. Shot in the back . . . Testimony of David W. Harrison; *Missouri Democrat,* April 15, 1864.

42. Pension file of Tom Addison; G. W. Barrett, Gabriel Lane (aka Calvin McLellan), and Jesse Wilson in pension file of Tom Addison; Thomas Addison in *RJSCW.*

43. Still shaking . . . Ransom Anderson in *RJSCW.*

44. In 1903, at the age of about sixty, Sherry Blain impressed a pension agent as "rather dull and thick witted" but honest. Pension file of Sherry Blain; Sherry Blain in pension file of Robert Blain; Abraham Huggins, Ellen Thornton, Allen James (Walker) and David Weston in pension file of Sherry Blain (Thornton); George Houston in pension file of Samuel Green; Aaron Fentis in *RJSCW.*

45. His arm shattered . . . Moore, *Women of the War,* pp. 310–312; Eli Cothel in *RJSCW.* After the war . . . William Ellis, Thomas Greer, Shed James, Alexander Nason, Henry Robinson in pension file of Arthur Edmonds; Arthur Edwards [Edmonds] in *RJSCW.*

46. Statement of Hardin Capers, April 23, 1864, in Mason Brayman Papers, Chicago Historical Society.

47. Alexander Nayron [Nason] in *RJSCW;* Alexander Nason in pension files of Charles Fox, Thomas Hooper, Willis Ligon, and Charles Macklin [Koon]; Samuel Hughes in pension file of Charles Macklin [Koon]; pension files of John Cowan, Arthur Edmonds, Anthony Flowers, and Thomas Grier.

48. Emanuel Nichols in *RJSCW;* "Daniel Tyler" in the *Liberator,* July 22, 1864; Ransom Anderson in *RJSCW.*

Aftermath: Touring the Fort: April 13, 1864

1. F. A. Smith and William Cleary in *RJSCW.*

2. Anderson, "The True Story of Fort Pillow."

3. Pension file of John G. Woodruff and in *RJSCW.*

4. "I merely went on shore," he said, "but did not pretend to leave the boat." Chapman Underwood in ibid.

5. The corpses he saw were probably those of the men killed that morning, the rest having been buried or left smoldering in the rubble.

6. W. Ferguson in *RJSCW*.

7. Franklin, *Virginia Repository*, April 27, 1864.

8. N. D. Wetmore Jr./Editors, *Argus*: April 13, 1864, in *NFWW*.

9. "a handsome young fellow . . ." Maury, *Recollections of a Virginian*, pp. 216–217. "he could not control . . ." William Cleary in *RJSCW*.

10. By now . . . Captain J. W. Colburn in Quartermaster General's Office (endorsement): December 28, 1883, Records of Office of Quartermaster General/Cemeterial/1828–1929/RG92/Box 56/NM81/576 in NARA. "cheerfully and pleasantly . . ." Anderson, "The True Story of Fort Pillow."

11. Ferried across . . . Abner Buford, Rachel Parks, George Patterson, Jerry Steward in the pension file of Ransom Parks. Nancy Hopper . . . Rebecca Williams and Nancy Hopper in *RJSCW*; pension file of Daniel Hopper. Rosa Johnson . . . Rosa Johnson and Rebecca Williams in *RJSCW*; pension files of Joseph Johnson and William Read Johnson. Anne Jane Ruffin . . . David Sneed in pension file of Thomas Ruffin; Anne Jane Rufin [Ruffin] in *RJSCW*; William Cleary in ibid.

12. Nancy Hopper, Rosa Johnson, and Anne Jane Rufin [Ruffin] in *RJSCW*; Joseph E. Harvey (9th Minnesota Infantry)/Mary: May 31, 1864, Minnesota Historical Society (ms. P591).

13. For all that, Akerstrom remains a murky figure whose name was either Charles J. or John Charles, and whose widow's application was thrown out for lack of evidence of his ever having served. (William Cleary, James McCoy, Jane Rufin, and R. A. Smith in *RJSCW*; pension file of John C. Akerstrom; *RJSCW*.)

14. Jacob Thompson . . . Jacob Thompson in *RJSCW*. Common practice . . . Goodspeed Publishing Company, *History of Lincoln County*, pp. 367–368; Brown in Andrews, ed., *From Fugitive Slave to Free Man*, p. 34; McCandless, *A History of Missouri*, vol. 2, pp. 59–63; McReynolds, *Missouri*, p. 169. Nevertheless, what these . . . Anne Jane Rufin [Ruffin], Rebecca Williams, Nancy M. Hopper, and Jacob Thompson in *RJSCW*.

15. James Marshall: Report: April 15, 1864, in *NFWW*.

16. Thomas Clark and Robert Cribbs in pension file of Robin [James] Ricks.

17. Some artillerists . . . Henry Richardson in pension file of Daniel Ray. Sandy Addison . . . Sandy Addison and Charles Williams in pension file of Robert Green. The Greens had a daughter named Mary and a son named David.

18. N. D. Wetmore Jr./Editors, *Argus*: April 13, 1864, in *NFWW*.

19. Fitch reported . . . Fitch, "Monthly Report." Among these . . . John Poston and William J. Stephens in pension file of John H. Porter. Jordan died . . . Medical record of William Jordan [Jerdon].

20. *Mound City Dispatch*, April 14, 1864, in *Christian Recorder*, April 30, 1864.

21. Almost as disgraceful . . . William E. Johnson in *RJSCW*; neither Lieutenant Cleary nor James Marshall of the *Platte Valley* was among the officers who fraternized with the enemy. (William Cleary and James Marshall in ibid.) "Very free . . ." William Johnson in ibid. Astonishingly . . . John G. Woodruff in ibid.; *Owensboro* (KY) *Monitor*, April 20, 1864.

22. Anderson, "The True Story of Fort Pillow." "General," Woodruff would write Brayman, "since I left I see a scurlous attack on me in the Cairo 'Extra' news. I shall be back Monday when I will explain to your entire satisfaction." (Woodruff/Brayman: April 15, 1864, Brayman Papers.)

23. "I went on board . . ." John Penwell in *RJSCW*. "I thought . . ." Mack J. Leaming in ibid.

24. *Missouri Democrat,* April 15, 1864.

25. Chapman Underwood in *RJSCW*.

26. James McCoy in ibid. "Notwithstanding the evidences of rebel atrocity and barbarity with which the ground was covered, there were some of our army officers onboard the *Platte Valley* as lost to every feeling of decency, honor, and self-respect, as to make themselves disgracefully conspicuous in bestowing civilities and attention upon the rebel officers, even while they were boasting of the murders they had there committed. Your committee were unable to ascertain the names of the officers who have thus inflicted so foul a stain upon the honor of our army. They are assured, however, by the military authorities that every effort will be made to ascertain their names and bring them to the punishment they so richly merit." Report of the Subcommittee in *RJSCW*.

27. *Missouri Democrat,* April 15, 1864.

28. A little before 5:00 . . . Burfford, "In the Wake of Fort Pillow with Forrest in Command." Anderson assured . . . Anderson, "The True Story of Fort Pillow."

29. N. D. Wetmore Jr./Editors, *Argus:* April 13, 1864, in *NFWW*.

30. "The *New Era* . . ." James Marshall in *RJSCW*. "The *Red Rover* . . ." N. D. Wetmore Jr./Editors, *Argus:* April 13, 1864, in *NFWW*; Alexander M. Pennock in *RJSCW*; James Marshall: Report: April 15, 1864, and T. Pattison/Porter: April 13, 1864, in *NFWW*.

31. "We then mounted . . ." Anderson, "The True Story of Fort Pillow." Spurring their horses . . . Hancock, *Hancock's Diary,* p. 365; Wilbur H. Gaylord in *RJSCW*.

32. Wyeth, *That Devil Forrest,* pp. 587–588.

33. W. R. McLagan in *RJSCW*.

34. "a notorious spy . . ." Ibid. "The Rebel soldiers . . ." Fitch, "Monthly Report." The last Frank Hogan   Frank Hogan in *RJSCW*.

35. Fitch, "Monthly Report."

36. W. R. McLagan in *RJSCW*.

37. C. C. Washburn/Forrest: June 19, 1864, in *ORCW*.

38. "It was an act . . ." Jordan and Pryor, *Campaigns of General Nathan Bedford Forrest,* p. 455. "If he was . . ." Forrest/Washburn: June 25 [23], 1864, in *ORCW*. "there is nothing . . ." Wyeth, *That Devil Forrest,* p. 588.

39. With his father's "best horse and two pistols," eighteen-year-old Robert Z. Taylor joined Bell's brigade at Fort Pillow immediately after the battle and was assigned to guarding Forrest's prisoners. Robert Z. Taylor in *TCWVQ*.

40. Clarke R. Barteau in *Detroit Free Press,* December 1, 1884.

41. Peter Bischoff in pension file of John T. Young.

42. In the meantime . . . Forrest/Polk: April 25, 1864, in *ORCW*.

43. Washburn/S. D. Lee: July 3, 1864, in *ORCW*. Emphases mine.

44. *Memphis Daily Avalanche,* May 2, 1866. Phineas Thomas Scruggs was called Reverend in some records. Scruggs had a law degree and was a judge at some point in his career. A business associate and political ally of Forrest, he was born in Nashville on March 26, 1806, and died in Memphis in 1878. The commandant at Cahaba was Colonel H. C. Davis. (Gene Scruggs/Author: December 5, 2002 (e-mail); Nashville city directories.

45. John T. Young/Washburn: September 13, 1864, in *ORCW*; pension file of John T. Young.

46. *Cairo News,* April 16, 1864.

47. "geographical wedge piercing . . ." Forrest C. Pogue Public History Institute, *The Civil War in the Jackson Purchase Region of Kentucky.* But Cairo was . . . Dickson, Inspection Report, RG98/Box 93/4720 in NARA; John Rinaker (122nd Illinois Volunteer Infantry)/Semi-Weekly Return of Effective Force at the Post of Cairo: April 25, 1864, in NARA.

48. "to destroy the large . . ." Pennock/Welles: April 15, 1864, in *ORCW*. But on the night . . . Cairo was as plagued by dissension and accusations of disloyalty as Paducah was. Union agents were obliged to sift through calumnious letters from neighborhood gossips. A Mrs. H. S. Horn reported that Isaac and Mary A. Newton had abused and insulted her children for singing "sutch Union songs [as] Red White & Blue & Union Forever," and a cavalry orderly accused Mrs. Newton of singing "songs unbecoming a lady." (Forrest C. Pogue Public History Institute, *The Civil War in the Jackson Purchase Region of Kentucky;* T. H. Harris/[Hurlbut] April 17, 1864, in 16th Army Corps (Letters Received) RG98, Part 2, Entry 391, Box 7 in NARA; *U.S. v. Isaac Newton,* depositions of Mary A. Newton and F. G. Newell: June 8, 1864, in NARA.

49. Brayman: Report: May 2, 1864, in *ORCW*.

50. "Mary Bickerdyke was a one-woman whirlwind whose sole aim during the Civil War was to more efficiently care for wounded Union soldiers, no matter what. If improving the level of care meant scrubbing up after filthy, incompetent doctors, then she would scrub every surface in sight. If improving the level of care meant antagonizing the hospital staff by threatening to report drunken physicians, then she would antagonize them. If improving the level of care meant ordering a staff member who had illegally appropriated garments meant for the wounded to strip the clothes off, then she would order him to strip. Bickerdyke stepped on a lot of male toes, but she won most of her fights. One ruffled male appealed to General William Tecumseh Sherman to take action against her, but was disappointed by the reply he received: 'Well, I can do nothing for you; she outranks me.'" www.pinn.net/~sunshine/whm2002/c_war.html.

51. Horace Wardner in *RJSCW*.

52. "Dr. Wardner says . . ." *Cairo News,* April 16, 1864. But before the week . . . Horace Wardner in *RJSCW*. When an officer . . . Hurlbut: Special Order 97: April 18, 1864, in RG94/E112–115/P1–17/v.5 in NARA.

53. LeRoy Fitch/David D. Porter: April 16, 1864, in *NFWW*.

54. "captured by the enemy . . ." Marshall gives somewhat conflicting testimony about his maneuvers that morning. In one he mentions towing a coal barge to "Flower Island," a misnomer for Flour Island, which was located off Fulton, but then seems to suggest that he saw rebels racing around Coal Creek burn-

ing barges. My account is an attempt to reconcile his two accounts with the testimony of Ferguson, Fitch, and Pennock. "I put the refugees . . ." Report of Acting Master Ferguson: April 14, 1864, in *NFWW*. "and we followed them . . ." James Marshall in *RJSCW*. *Moose* and *Hastings* . . . James Marshall/David D. Porter: April 15, 1864, in U.S. Navy Records, M89/Box 132 in NARA; Pennock/Welles: April 14, 1864, in *NFWW*; LeRoy Fitch/David D. Porter: April 16, 1864, in *NFWW*.

55. "At last we hailed the Gun Boat which came & took us aboard & whose Officers treated us with every comfort the boat afforded. I stopped on the Boat all that day & as they were picking up wounded men & those who had escaped. I really was in hopes that George might have got away & that the boat would yet pick him up." (Charley Robinson/Family: April 17, 1864.)

56. All through the night . . . Major Williams in *RJSCW*. During the *Silver Cloud*'s . . . Duncan Harding in ibid.

57. Wilbur H. Gaylord in ibid.

58. On April 14 . . . Elvis Bevel in ibid. but a day later . . . USS *Moose* log, April 15, 1864. Charley Robinson . . . Charley Robinson/Family: April 17, 1864. As late as . . . LeRoy Fitch/David D. Porter: April 16, 1864, in *NFWW*. On April 17, the steamboat *Ike Hammett* accidentally rammed the already crippled *New Era* as she escorted her above Fort Pillow, forcing Marshall to return his gunboat to Cairo for repairs. (A. M. Pennock/Thomas Pattison: April 18, 1864, in U.S. Navy Records, M89/Box 132 in NARA.)

59. *Cairo News*, April 16, 1864.

60. Dinkins, "The Capture of Fort Pillow."

61. Berry, *Four Years with Morgan and Forrest*, pp. 269–271.

62. "With this affair . . ." Johnston, "Civil War Recollection." "West Tennessee . . ." Chalmers in Willoughby, "Gunboats and Gumbo."

63. Forrest, report dated April 15, 1864, in Wyeth, *That Devil Forrest*, p. 333.

64. It was "unfortunate" . . . Davis, "What about Fort Pillow?" But however inconvenient . . . Henry Smith Randle in *TCWVQ*.

65. *Memphis Daily Appeal*, May 2, 1864.

66. Jones, *A Rebel War Clerk's Diary at the Confederate States Capital* vol. 2, pp. 187–189.

67. Agnew also heard that Forrest was in a foul humor because Southerners had begun to pilfer the Union wagons he had captured, carrying away food and blankets. (Agnew, "Diary.")

68. "Out of 700 men . . ." *Charleston Mercury*, April 21, 1864. "I write with pleasure . . ." Officer of 2nd Tennessee Cavalry (CSA) in *Charleston Mercury*, May 2, 1864. "Your brilliant . . ." Polk/Forrest: April 24, 1864, in *ORCW*.

69. *Montgomery Mail* in *Macon Southern Confederacy*, January 19, 1865.

70. Hurlbut in Wyeth, *That Devil Forrest*, p. 314.

71. Fuchs, *An Unerring Fire*, p. 45.

72. Benjamin Densmore/[Brother]: April 15, 1864, Benjamin Densmore and Family Papers (A0413), Minnesota Historical Society.

73. Henry, *"First with the Most" Forrest*, pp. 244–245; Jordan and Pryor, *The Campaigns of Nathan Bedford Forrest*, pp. 416–417.

74. *Daily Missouri Democrat*, April 15, 1864.

75. After driving . . . David D. Porter/James W. Shirk: April 14, 1864, in *ORCW.* "As a part . . ." Wyeth, *That Devil Forrest,* p. 308.

76. Jordan and Pryor, *The Campaigns of Nathan Bedford Forrest,* pp. 416–417.

77. In late April . . . The regiments were the 9th Ohio and 7th Illinois Infantry. (James Jackson/Roddey: April 25, 1864, in *ORCW.*) "was about played out . . ." Forrest in Granville Moody/William J. Clark: April 24, 1864, in *ORCW.*

78. Forrest in Wyeth, *That Devil Forrest,* pp. 333–336.

79. Dinkins, *Furl That Banner,* p. 156.

Hellholes: Andersonville and Florence: From April 13, 1864

1. "we were formed . . ." Fitch, "Monthly Report." "had to sleep . . ." Several writers maintain that Forrest himself was kind to his prisoners. This may well have been true when he was personally escorting them. It was usually after he handed his prisoners over to his subordinates to convey them to prison that the abuse began. "I met the rebel commander, General Forrest, under a flag of truce," Abel Streight wrote of his surrender to Forrest, "when a stipulation was entered into between him and myself, whereby it was agreed that my command should surrender as prisoners of war, on the following conditions, to wit: 1. Each regiment should be permitted to retain its colors; 2. The officers were to retain their side-arms; 3. Both officers and men were to retain their haversacks, knapsacks, and blankets; and all private property of every description was to be respected and retained by the owner. The above terms were in a measure respected while we remained with General Forrest; but no sooner were we turned over to the rebel authorities than a system of robbing commenced, which soon relieved us of every thing valuable in our possession. The blankets, haversacks, and knapsacks were taken from my men at Atlanta. They were also robbed of nearly all their money, and most of them lost their overcoats at the above-named place. Here, too, the colors and side-arms were taken from us. My men were turned into an inclosure without shelter of any kind, destitute of blankets and overcoats, as I have before stated, and kept under guard for four days, during which time a most disagreeable cold storm prevailed; after which they were sent forward and soon exchanged." Streight's account recalls Duckworth's treatment of his prisoners after the fall of Union City. A. D. Streight/F. W. Kellogg in Moore, ed., *The Rebellion Record,* vol. 8, p. 451. "pressed all the conveyances . . ." Wilbur H. Gaylord in *RJSCW.*

2. John Goodwin/T. M. Mack: April 20, 1864, and S. J. Gholson/Polk: April 20, 1864, in *ORCW.*

3. Peter Bischoff in pension file of John T. Young in *RJSCW.*

4. Pension file of William R. Nail; Forrest's list of prisoners.

5. Frisby, "'Remember Fort Pillow!'"

6. Henry M. Davidson in Holley, "The Seventh Tennessee Volunteer Cavalry."

7. The pension agent concluded that since he had been absent without leave at the time of his capture, his family did not qualify for a pension. (James H. Clement, Nancy J. Mitchener, Samuel J. Murphy, and Green Ragsdale in pension file of George W. Babb.)

8. John L. Poston and John H. Stamps in pension file of Henry Clay Carter.

9. John Copher [Cofer], John N. Green, and John T. Stamps in pension file of Andrew McKee.

10. "black scurvy . . ." Statement of Rebecca Williams; pension file of Daniel Hopper; pension file of Benjamin W. King; Forrest's list of prisoners.

11. Private Ephraim L. Churchwell . . . Pension file of Ephraim L. Churchwell. Jim Clark . . . Pension file of James Clark; Barnett Cobb, J. M. Fields, G. J. Giles, Julia Anne Jenkins, T. M. Pierce, A. S. Russell in claim of John G. Fields. The date of Clark's death proved a major issue for the family, since he may have succumbed after his wife's death in September, which complicated their orphaned children's claim to his pension. Though Fields had a brother in the CSA, he was an avowed Unionist, and was allowed by the Federals to carry a gun to protect himself from rebel harassment.

12. Martin V. Day and Alfred Middleton in pension file of George L. Ellis.

13. Pension file of James M. Christenberg.

14. "If I cant liv by the help of man," he declared, "I will by the help of god as I have allways doon." (Sidney Kirk and James H. Welch in pension file of Doc Z. Alexander. Alexander was apparently no relation to Paton Alexander of the same regiment.)

15. Tom McMurry . . . Pension file of Thomas McMurry. Anderson Bailey . . . J. H. Copher and William A. Winn in pension file of Anderson Bailey. Paroled at Goldsboro, South Carolina, he was transferred along with the rest of the survivors of the 13th to the 6th Tennessee Cavalry (USA) and mustered out in July 1865. Bailey married after the war and fathered three children. But he never recovered from the privations of imprisonment and died of consumption in 1876.

16. George Dunn, Thomas Diggs, and George H. Dunn in pension file of Miles M. Deason. The rebel officers were Thomas Diggs of the 7th Cavalry CSA and Benjamin M. Turberville of the 9th Cavalry CSA.

17. Abner Long and Jesse M. Huffaker in pension file of John W. Long; *St. Louis Globe-Democrat*, May 6, 1888.

18. Ration compensation file of Martin V. Day.

19. At that time, Smith was trying to collect two deserters from the military prison at Columbus, one of whom, a man named Kelso, Jones had helped the local authorities to capture. But it took Smith a month to cut through all the red tape to get them released into his custody. In late October Jones accompanied a Captain Berry of the Kentucky State Guards on a scout. While chasing rebel guerrillas across a bridge, Jones was thrown from his horse and injured further when his mount stepped on his hand as it righted itself. "Tell me what you think 'honestly' of this claim," Jones begged the pension office after his applications were repeatedly returned as incomplete. "Don't flatter me but tell me the plain truth. I think the Govt. has treated me badly, as I furnished my own horse, bridle & saddle & when we were consolidated, we were dismounted & I was deprived of horse &c., for which I have never been paid a cent & then again when I reported back for duty after 7 mos imprisonment I was beat out of 7 mos service by enlisting me. But," he closed, as if with a sigh, "that is gone & I can't help it." (Pension file of Anderson Jones.)

20. "damned traitors . . ." Holley, "The Seventh Tennessee Volunteer Cavalry." Humphrey Jones . . . Pension files of James Antwine, Michael Cleek, and Turner A. Lunceford; Forrest's list of prisoners; military records of John Burrus, Allen Carr, and Humphrey S. Jones.

21. First Lieutenant Nicholas Logan . . . Isaac Hawkins and Mack J. Leaming in pension file of Nicholas Logan. G. W. Kirk . . . Pension file of George W. Kirk.

22. Holley, "The Seventh Tennessee Volunteer Cavalry."

Slaves Again: Black Prisoners: April 12, 1864–January 1865

1. Frank Smith and William Cleary in *RJSCW.*

2. Chalmers Papers: RG109/Entry 117/Box 2 in NARA.

3. "no negroes . . ." Anderson/Chalmers: April 13, 1864, in *ORCW.* Though Sandy Addison . . . Sandy Addison in *RJSCW.* Of Forrest's . . . These figures are based on my review of pension and ration commutation records.

4. Wyeth, *That Devil Forrest,* p. 337.

5. Badly wounded . . . Statement of Phillip Young in *RJSCW.* Colonel Barteau . . . Clarke R. Barteau in *Detroit Free Press,* December 1, 1884.

6. As their battle rage . . . Pension file of Henry Parker. Shot in the groin . . . In May 1865, Parker finally received a medical discharge and moved to Memphis, where he lived in part on a pension of four dollars a month. Two years later, he was married at Beale Street Church to an apparently irresistible former slave named Frances Ferguson, by whom he sired two children. But his wound never healed, and one fall day in 1877, a piece of bone emerged from his wound, along with a lot of decayed matter. "It turned black around the wound," recalled Marshall Lane, who nursed him in his final illness, "and smelt bad." Lane sent for a doctor, who, "without making an examination, looked at him and said that he was dying, as mortification had set in." He died on December 7. Left to her own devices, Frances fell victim to a "powerful wild" black con man named Hank Farrel who turned up one day claiming to be her late husband's old friend and lodge brother. She threw him out after he thrice forced himself upon her, but not before he had impregnated her. After she gave birth to his illegitimate child, she confessed her "sin" before her church and received its forgiveness. But her confession apparently excited the cupidity of a black lawyer named Slacker who offered to pursue her pension claim in exchange for her favors. (Samuel Green and Henry Parker in pension file of Henry Dix; John W. Brown, Marshall Lane, Frances Ferguson Parker in pension file of Henry Parker; Alexander Nason and Thomas Roy in pension file of John Cowan; John W. Brown and Marshall Lane in pension file of Henry Parker.)

7. By one account . . . John H. Baker: History of Company B, 7th USC Artillery (Heavy) during March and April 1864: undated in RG94/E112–115/P1–17/v.5 in NARA. On the night . . . Brayman/T.H. Harris: April 17, 1864, in *ORCW.*

8. Alfred Coleman in *RJSCW.*

9. Frank Hogan in ibid.

10. Phillip Young in *RJSCW.*

11. Henry Gill and Joseph Waldrup in pension file of Armstrong Burgess.

12. Pension file of Joseph Boyd.

13. Aaron Fentis, Samuel Green, Henry Parker in pension file of Henry Dix.

14. Pension file of Thomas Grier; Thomas Grier in ration compensation file of Charles Fox; Isaac Griffin and Alexander Nason in pension file of Thomas Grier.

15. Pension and ration commutation files of Elias Irwin.

16. He eagerly requisitioned . . . L. Polk/Jefferson Davis: April 27, 1864, in *ORCW.* "Put them to work . . ." Dabney H. Maury/S. Cooper: May 20, 1864, in *ORCW.*

17. Around Christmas 1864, Flowers was put on a train bound for Richmond but somehow managed to escape his guards, jump from his boxcar, and take to the woods. After traveling a circuitous route through Alabama and Mississippi, sleeping by day and traveling by night, he reached Memphis on February 19, 1865. Despite his wounds, Anthony Flowers remained with his company until it was mustered out in July 1865. He married a Fanny Simms in 1880, when he was in his midforties, and worked first in Memphis and then as a field hand in De Soto County, Mississippi, where a pension examiner found him living with his wife and deemed him "perfectly childish." (James Murrel, Alexander Nason, and Henry T. Weaver in pension file of Anthony Flowers.)

18. When he got to Memphis, Ligon was discharged for the wound to his head and his by now almost total deafness. After the war he moved from Memphis to Bolivar County, Mississippi, where in 1896 a local insurance agent reported that he was "unable to make a living on account of [his] disabilities." A pension examiner described this brave, resourceful, and resilient veteran as not having the intelligence of a ten-year-old, but he had the intelligence to collect not only a pension but compensation for the Union rations he did not receive while a prisoner of the Confederates. J. Altshul, Andrew Clopton, Abraham Huggins, Abner W. Ligon, David and Nelson Mooring, Alexander Nason, Monroe Wilson, Phillip Young, in pension file of Willis Ligon.

19. Ann Jennings Turner [Mrs. Green Patton] in pension file of Roach Turner; Phillip Robertson in ration commutation file of Roach Turner. After the war, Turner married twice and lived and worked in Hardiman County, Tennessee.

20. The brother was Private George M. Dallas Peevey of Company C.

21. Robert Jones in pension file of Allen James [Walker]. Among the veterans of Fort Pillow who greeted him were James Murrel, Robert Jones, and Sherry Blain.

22. Pension and ration compensation files of Charles Fox; Thomas Grier, Alexander Nason, and Charles Williams in ration compensation file of Charles Fox.

23. Military, pension, and ration commutation files of Samuel Green; Reason Barker, Thomas Brown, Morning Clay, Felix Davis, Steven Davis, Wilbur H. Gaylord, Henry Gillespie, Benjamin Jones, Pearson Lee, Henry Meeks, J. C. Shearer in pension file of Samuel Green; Samuel Green in pension files of Henry Dix and Jacob Jones.

Alarms and Flight: The North: From April 13, 1864

1. Hurlbut/James B. McPherson: April 13, 1864, in RG393/Box 1 in NARA.

2. Brayman in *RJSCW.*

3. "Fort Pillow has no . . ." Sherman/Brayman: April 14, 1864, in *ORCW*. Sherman groaned that Hurlbut had "plenty of force" if only he would "use it" to capture "some of Forrest's men that are now scattered from Paducah down to Memphis." Fort Pillow was taken . . . Brayman/Sherman: April 14, 1864, in *ORCW*.

4. "We have lost . . ." Hurlbut/Sherman: April 15, 1864, in RG393/Box 1 in NARA. "the enemy will not . . ." Hurlbut/Pattison: April 14, 1864, in *ORCW*.

5. "sacked Paducah . . ." Stanton/Grant: April 15, 1864, in ibid. "The Sioux Indians . . ." Washburn/Sherman: April 21, 1864, in ibid. "I don't understand . . ." Sherman/McPherson: April 15, 1864, in ibid. "I don't know . . ." Sherman/Grant: April 15, 1864, in ibid. "first fruits . . ." Sherman/Grant: April 14, 1864, in ibid. "has our men . . ." Sherman/John A. Rawlins: April 19, 1864, in ibid.

6. Realizing the full . . . Lash, "Stephen Augustus Hurlbut," pp. 116–161, 107–200. "marked timidity . . ." *CWAL* vol. 7, p. 327n.

7. Hurlbut demanded . . . *CWAL* vol. 7, p. 328n. Sherman detailed his frustration with Hurlbut and Grierson to Grant's chief of staff. "Grierson had 7,000 horses when I made up the Meridian count, and Smith and he reported the capture of some 4,000 animals, and yet now the excuse for not attacking Forrest is that he can mount only 2,400 men. . . . At Memphis are Buckland's full brigade of splendid troops, 2,000. Three other white regiments, one of black artillery, in Fort Pickering. 1,200 strong, about 1,000 men floating, who are camped in the fort, near 4,000 black troops; 3,000 enrolled and armed militia, and all of Grierson's cavalry, 10,983, according to my last returns, of which surely not over 3,000 are on furlough. Out of this a splendid force of about 2,500 well-mounted cavalry and 4,000 infantry could have been made up, and by moving to Bolivar could have made Forrest come there to fight or get out." (Sherman/John A. Rawlins: April 19, 1864, in *ORCW*.)

8. Hurlbut swung wildly. He accused one of his accusers of abandoning his family, seducing his sister-in-law, and living with her "in adultery in New York," and the other of lying for the first in exchange for a bribe; their names were Hirsch and Beman. "For about 18 months I have had nearly arbitrary power at the city of Memphis," Hurlbut wrote, "and thereby more or less on the Mississippi River. Many millions of dollars have depended on my action, many speculations depended for their success or failure on my Official Conduct," and yet he claimed to be "as poor a man as when I entered the service, with nothing made except the savings from the liberal compensation belonging to my Office," which savings must have been rather paltry considering how much of his pay he gambled and drank. Ever since he had taken command in November 1862, permits had been "given daily to all persons who proved themselves loyal, under 'General Orders' for reasonable amounts of family supplies." The job of inspecting the wagons and saddlebags that came and went fell to the Provost Guard. (Hurlbut/Stanton: April 29, 1864, and E. D. Townsend/Major General Canby: June 22, 1865, RG94/159/Box 27 in NARA.)

9. Sherman in Chalmers, "Lieutenant General Nathan Bedford Forrest and His Campaigns"; *CWD*.

10. "I have sent . . ." W. T. Sherman, Major General Commanding. Sherman in Chalmers, "Lieutenant General Nathan Bedford Forrest and His Campaigns." "Paducah, Cairo . . ." McPherson/Washburn: April 20, 1864, in 16th Army

Corps (Letters Received) RG98, Part 2, Entry 391, Box 7 in NARA. "All troops . . ." James B. McPherson/Brayman: April 19, 1864, in NARA. Many of the Union forts were in feeble condition. (Dickson: Report: April 20, 1864, in RG98/Box 93/4720 in NARA.)

11. "a deplorable affair . . ." James B. McPherson/Sherman: April 19, 1864, in *ORCW.* "This is the most infernal . . ." Chetlain/E. B. Washburne: April 14, 1864, in ibid. Chetlain's great concern was that Forrest might attack the Union garrison at Columbus, Kentucky. He urged Brayman to reinforce Columbus and Paducah if necessary, but otherwise to keep his men in readiness for a campaign up the Tennessee to frustrate Forrest's attempts "to induce us to make these detachments and prevent our concentrating in this quarter." (Sherman/Brayman: April 14, 1864, in *RJSCW.*)

12. "Slaveholding chivalry . . ." Bennett in Louisiana, *Constitutional Convention 1864.* "insatiate as fiends . . ." The *Herald* did not let Hurlbut off the hook, however. The capture of Fort Pillow, the *Herald* editorialized, "could not occur without the most culpable negligence on the part of the government. Why is a place occupied at all if it is not occupied by men enough to hold it? The force in this fort was too small to hold it, and too large to be lost in the attempt, and the same is probably true of every position in Forrest's way." (*New York Herald,* April 16, 1864.) "The whole civilized . . ." *Chicago Tribune,* April 16, 1864, in Frisby, "'Remember Fort Pillow!'"

13. "Mr. Daniel" in State of Maryland, *The Debates of the Constitutional Convention of the State of Maryland* (Annapolis, 1864), pp. 435, 635.

14. D. McCall in Post, ed., *Soldiers' letters, from camps, battlefield, and prison,* p. 365.

15. Edmondson, Diary.

16. Hurlbut/McPherson: April 17, 1864, in 16th Army Corps (Letters Received) RG98, Part 2, Entry 391, Box 7 in NARA; Hurlbut/Sherman: April 17, 1864, in 16th Army Corps (Letters Sent) RG393, 1864, Box 1.

17. "scared to death . . ." Alice Williamson, *Diary.* "The Yankees have . . ." *Columbus Times* in *Charleston Mercury,* June 11, 1864.

18. "contrary to the expectations . . ." Fredrick Douglass, "Address at Twelfth Baptist Church, New York City, April 14, 1864," *Liberator,* April 29, 1864, in Frisby, "'Remember Fort Pillow!'" "I ask you . . ." Kelley, *Replies of the Hon. William D. Kelley.*

19. "J.H.B.P." in *Christian Recorder,* June 11, 1864.

20. *Christian Recorder,* April 30, 1864. "Friendly soldiers, a word to you," wrote one of the *Recorder*'s female correspondents, "When and wherever hereafter you may be attacked by the enemy, remember Fort Pillow, and at the same time remember that you are fighting men who are enemies to you—those who are trying to destroy your manhood, and rob you of your God-given rights. Then fight with your whole soul, mind and strength, and die rather than surrender—for I would rather die the death of the brave, than to live the life of a coward." ("Lizzie H." in *Christian Recorder,* May 28, 1864.)

21. Despite such hopes . . . H. J. Maxwell/R. D. Mussey: March 1, 1864, in Records of Colonel Robert D. Mussey, 1863–1864, RG393/Box 2 in NARA. "out of the service . . ." *New York Herald,* April 19, 1864. "prevailing to an alarm-

ing . . ." Chetlain: General Orders: June 23, 1864, in RG393/2911/Volume 36/66: General and Special Orders: Organization of Colored Troops in NARA. By October . . . George L. Paddock/ Charles P. Brown: October 11, 1864, RG94/Box 8: Records of the 2nd USCCWAL in NARA.

22. Thomas Webster/Stanton: April 27, 1864, in *ORCW.*

23. Chetlain/Thomas: May 10, 1864, in RG393/2/2907 Letters Sent/Organization of Colored Troops in NARA.

24. *Anglo African,* April 23, 1864.

25. *New York Independent* in the *Liberator,* May 13, 1864.

26. Smith, "Gerritt Smith on the Fort Pillow and Plymouth Massacres," RG107: Records of the Office of the Secretary of War, Letters Received/File S-1146(130) in NARA. A quartermaster's clerk in Port Hudson, Louisiana, was tried for his remarks about Fort Pillow. "I would hang every damned Yankee and all their niggers," he was reported to have said. "The Rebels have no niggers in their army." (Court Martial Records, nn2155 in NARA.)

Wade and Gooch: The Joint Subcommittee on the Conduct of the War: April 15–May 5, 1864

1. "direct a competent officer . . ." Stanton/Sherman: April 16, 1864, in *ORCW.* Sherman promptly . . . Sherman/Brayman: April 16, 1864, in ibid. But no doubt . . . In his memoirs, Sherman would recall that at first he discredited the reports of a massacre at Fort Pillow because while preparing for the Meridian campaign he had ordered the post evacuated. "But it transpired afterward that General Hurlbut had retained a small garrison at Fort Pillow to encourage the enlistment of the blacks as soldiers, which," a disapproving Sherman observed, "was a favorite political policy at that day." Sherman never blamed Forrest for what he had "no doubt" was a massacre, because Forrest did not personally command the assault and "stopped the firing as soon as he could." Sherman had been assured by "hundreds of our men, who were at various times prisoners in Forrest's possession, that he was usually very kind to them." But Sherman conceded that Forrest had "a desperate set of fellows under him, and at that very time there is no doubt the feeling of the Southern people was fearfully savage on this very point of our making soldiers out of their late slaves, and Forrest may have shared the feeling." His friend Grant, however, blamed Forrest for the massacre. Sherman, *Memoirs,* pp. 12–13.

2. Sherman/Stanton: April 23, 1864, in *ORCW.*

3. *Malden* (MA) *Independent,* November 21, 1957. Courtesy of Rauner Special Collections Library, Dartmouth College.

4. "He declared that . . ." *New York Herald,* April 19, 1864. "I am glad . . ." Hal Wade in Tap, *Over Lincoln's Shoulder,* p. 195.

5. *RJSCW.*

6. Supplied with Stanton's letters . . . Stanton's note read: "This will introduce to you the Hon. Benjamin F. Wade and the Hon. Daniel W. Gooch, members of the Joint Committee of Congress on the Conduct of the War, who have been designated to inquire into and report upon the attack, surrender, and massacre at Fort Pillow. You will provide them while within the limits of your command

with quarters, subsistence, and transportation as may be required, and afford them such courtesy, assistance, and protection as may be within your power or required to facilitate the performance of their duties." Note that Stanton had already judged the battle a massacre. (Stanton/"Commanding Officers at Cairo" et al.: April 18, 1864, in *ORCW*; Frisby, "'Remember Fort Pillow!'") At 8:00 a.m. . . . Henry, *"First with the Most" Forrest*, p. 267.

7. "some of them pieced . . ." *New York Herald*, May 3, 1864. Some were too weak . . . A. M. Pennock: General report: April 28, 1864, in *NFWW*; Gooch/Stanton: April 22, 1864, in *ORCW*.

8. Charles Hicks, A. H. Hook, and George Mantell in *RJSCW*.

9. James Marshall in ibid.

10. S. A. Hurlbut and Benjamin Wade in ibid.

11. Sherman/Hurlbut: March 29, 1864, in RG93/4720 in NARA; Hurlbut and Benjamin Wade in *RJSCW*.

12. Hurlbut in *RJSCW*.

13. Hurlbut's interview . . . "That matters have been dreadfully mismanaged in this military Department I have already written you. You are also well posted as to the author of the mismanagement. The change in corps commanders will probably produce a change for the better." *Chicago Tribune*, April 27, 1864, in RG94/E729A/Box 7 in NARA.

14. On May 2 . . . Stephen Augustus Hurlbut/C. C. Washburn: May 2, 1864, in RG94/159/Box 27 in NARA.

15. Though he claimed . . . Lash, "Stephen A. Hurlbut"; Fuchs, *An Unerring Fire*, p. 50.

16. Daniel Gooch and Benjamin Wade in *RJSCW*; Davis, "What about Fort Pillow?" Some examples of bad grammar: Private Duncan Harding is quoted as saying, "when night come I came back to the river bank." Private Nathan Hunter: "I was down under the hill next the river." Private John Haskins: " They did all in the same way." *RJSCW*.

17. Edward Benton in *RJSCW*.

18. *Atlanta Confederacy* in *Charleston Mercury*, May 6, 1864.

19. Southern papers . . . Cimprich and Mainfort, "Fort Pillow Revisited." On May 13 . . . Forrest/S. D. Lee: May 16, 1864, in *ORCW*.

20. Confederate Congress: Joint Resolution: April 22, 1864, in *ORCW*. The British press also waded in. Quoth the pro-Confederate London *Times*, "The European reader will know what estimate" to place upon Wade and Gooch's "extravagant" accounts of Fort Pillow. "They remind one of the fables so extensively circulated [by Wade] just after the first battle of Manassas." But the stories might also have reminded the *Times* of the hysterical and inaccurate accounts it had printed of rebel atrocities in the Indian Mutiny seven years earlier. *Times* (London) in *Cairo* (IL) *Daily Journal*, June 19, 1864, in Frisby, "'Remember Fort Pillow!'" The Newcastle *Chronicle* took the opposite view, condemning the rebel press for failing to censure its army's atrocities. Reading their papers, and the copperhead press in the North, wrote a correspondent, a reader would think that "Quantrel is an energetic officer; Forrest is an able commander"; and warden John Henry Winder of the Confederacy's notorious

Richmond prison "is the mildest of jailers. Such is the way in which contemporary events are chronicled in England!" (Newcastle [England] *Chronicle* in *Christian Recorder,* July 30, 1864.)

"A Choice of Evils": Retaliation: May 1–25, 1864

1. *New York Herald,* May 3, 1864.
2. On May 5 . . . United States Congress, *Journal of the House of Representatives of the United States, 1789–1873* and *Journal of the Senate of the United States of America, 1789–1873*: May 5, 1864. "One of the most expert . . ." Williams, "Benjamin F. Wade and the Atrocity Propaganda of the Civil War." One Northerner suggested . . . Frisby, "'Remember Fort Pillow!'"
3. William H. Seward/Abraham Lincoln, May 4, 1864, in CWAL.
4. Secretary of War . . . Stanton/Lincoln: May 5, 1864, in CWAL. "arrest him . . ." Stanton/G. W. Berry and G. W. Berry/Stanton: May 7, 1864, in ORCW.
5. Gideon Welles/Abraham Lincoln, May 5, 1864, in CWAL.
6. Edward Bates/Lincoln: May 6, 1864, in ibid.
7. John P. Usher/Lincoln: May 6, 1864, in ibid.
8. Browne, *The Every-Day Life of Abraham Lincoln,* p. 584. After congratulating Lincoln for his "honesty, kindness, patience and intelligence," Thomas Worcester of Boston urged Lincoln to see to it that "until the Confederate Government requires its army to conform to the laws of civilized warfare in relation to our negro soldiers, our government ought not to be very strict in requiring our negro soldiers to conform to those laws in relation to the Confederate Army." (Thomas Worcester/Abraham Lincoln: May 16, 1864, in CWAL.)
9. Thomas H. C. Hinton in *Christian Recorder,* May 14, 1864.
10. Lincoln/Stanton: May 17, 1864, in CWAL.
11. "crowded out . . ." Nicolay and Hay, *Abraham Lincoln: A History,* vol. 6, p. 483. On September 5 . . . Lincoln/Marshal of the District of West Tennessee: September 5, 1864, in Robert Selph Henry Papers (VT).
12. Woodward, *The Burden of Southern History,* pp. 60–61.
13. Every major . . . *New York Herald* and *Daily Tribune,* May 7, 1864; *Franklin* (VA) *Repository,* May 11, 1864. Wade's wife received a letter from her aunt who found in the pages of the report "sufficient to convince one of the awful depravity of the slave holding system." She had read the report "with horror," and asked, "How long, O Lord, how long, shall the wicked rule?" (E. Hubbard/Caroline Wade, June 17, 1864, in Frisby, "'Remember Fort Pillow!'") "We have but one . . ." *Philadelphia Press,* undated. "The annals . . ." *Harper's Weekly,* April 30, 1864.
14. "Will our . . ." E. G. Conke/Henry Wilson: April 23, 1864, in CWAL. "Rebel Savagery . . ." *Franklin* (VA) *Repository,* April 27, 1864.
15. Washburn/Rawlins: April 23, 1864, in ORCW; Ward, *Our Bones Are Scattered;* Greeley, *The American Conflict,* vol. 2, pp. 619–620.
16. Benjamin Wade in Tap, *Over Lincoln's Shoulder,* p. 207.
17. Ibid.
18. Hurst, *Nathan Bedford Forrest,* p. 414n.
19. Unidentified transcript in Mainfort Collection.

20. Samuel Johnson: Affidavit: July 11, 1864 in *ORCW; New York Herald,* April 26, 1864.
21. Edward O. Guerrant in Davis and Swentor, eds., *Bluegrass Confederate,* pp. 542, 545, 547 and nn, 551.
22. L. Johnson/R. D. Mussey: October 17, 1864, in *ORCW.*
23. C. P. Lyman/Celia Lyman: August 29, 1864, in private collection.
24. "low diet . . ." Lieutenant C. D. Covington of the 45th Tennessee Infantry agreed that their black guards "were very brutal in their treatment." W. B. Allen, George Albright, C. D. Covington in *CV,* July 1899. "were actually . . ." Reverend J. W. Harding in *Christian Recorder,* November 26, 1864. "And then you should see these black troopers escorting their wives and little ones and sweethearts, each loaded on the head and in both hands with the spoils of the Egyptians, and the little smiling darkies who cannot march, nestling in the left arms of their protectors."
25. J. Holt/Stanton: July 3, 1865, in *ORCW.*
26. Stearns urged the Union army "to hang every one that claims to belong to that gang of outlaws." (Ezra Stearns/Ellen [Stearns] Brewer: April 30, 1864, in Ezra Stearns Papers, Schoff Civil War Collection: Letters 51, William L. Clements Library, University of Michigan.) The injustice of reprisals would be cruelly played out at Gratiot Prison in St. Louis by General William Starke Rosecrans. After guerrillas killed seven of his men, he ordered an equal number of rebel prisoners shot. "Never, so long as I live," wrote a fellow prisoner, "will I be able to forget or cease to hear the cries and pleadings . . . after the death warrant had been read." Because it was found that one of the men—a major—was a Mason, a local lodge persuaded prison authorities to delay his execution, and eventually drop it entirely. But the other men, including a member of McCulloch's 2nd Missouri Cavalry, were not so lucky. On October 29, 1864, they were taken out and tied to a post. After their sentence was read, Charles Minniken of Crabtree's Arkansas Cavalry was allowed to make one last address that would echo Lincoln's forebodings. "Soldiers, and all of you who hear me, take warning from me," he declared. "I have been a Confederate soldier four years and have served my country faithfully. I am now to be shot for what other men have done, that I had no hand in, and know nothing about. I never was a guerilla, and I am sorry to be shot for what I had nothing to do with, and what I am not guilty of. When I took a prisoner I always treated him kindly and never harmed a man after he surrendered. I hope God will take me to His bosom when I am dead. Oh Lord, be with me." Another man wrote the following to his wife: "I take my pen with trembling hand to inform you that I have to be shot between 2 & 4 o'clock this evening. I have but few hours to remain in this unfriendly world. There is 6 of us sentenced to die in [retaliation] of 6 union soldiers that was shot by Reeves men. My dear wife don't grieve after me. I want you to meet me in Heaven. I want you to teach the children piety, so that they may meet me at the right hand of God. I can't tell you my feelings but YOU can form some idea of my feeling when you hear of my fate. . . . Good-by Amy. Asey Ladd." "Confederate POWs and Prisons in St. Louis" at www.sterlingprice145 .org/prison.htm.

"Remember Fort Pillow": Black Federals and White Confederates: From June 10, 1864

1. William Witherspoon in Henry, *As They Saw Forrest*, p. 126.
2. "we kept on . . ." Solomon Norman Brantley (*TCWVQ*).
3. Hancock, *Hancock's Diary*, pp. 390, 399. "It was understood in this battle," wrote Tully Brown of Morton's Battery, "and correspondence having taken place between generals Johnston and Forrest, that there was not going to be any quarter [at Brice's Crossroads]: the black flag was raised. The regiments came out there under their battle flags, and 'Remember Fort Pillow'" on their lips. (Brown, "Nathan Bedford Forrest.")
4. Solomon Norman Brantley (*TCWVQ*).
5. "Here are the damn negroes!" Lovett, "The West Tennessee Colored Troops in Civil War Combat." "one of the hardest . . ." John A. Crutchfield/Mrs. L. M. Crutchfield: June 13, 1864, Gordon Browning Museum of the Carroll County Historical Society.
6. Wounded stragglers hid . . . William Witherspoon in Henry, *As They Saw Forrest*, p. 126. "as far as could . . ." Agnew, "Battle of Tishomingo Creek." "most of the negroes . . ." Agnew, "Diary."
7. "buried shallow . . ." Agnew, "Battle of Tishomingo Creek." But not all . . . Agnew, "Diary."
8. Sherman in Chalmers, "Lieutenant General Nathan Bedford Forrest and His Campaigns."
9. Forrest's horses . . . Agnew, "Diary." "After moving . . ." Cox, "Forrest's Men Captured at Parker's Crossroads," *CV*, August 1908.
10. Forrest/Washburn: June 14, 1864, in *ORCW*.
11. "In the expectation that the Confederate Government would disavow the action of the commanding general at the Fort Pillow massacre, I have forborne to issue any instructions to the colored troops as to the course they should pursue toward Confederate soldiers that might fall into their hands; but seeing no disavowal on the part of the Confederate Government, but on the contrary laudations from the entire Southern press of the perpetrators of the massacre, I may safely presume that indiscriminate slaughter is to be the fate of colored troops that fall into your hands." (Washburn/S. D. Lee: June 17, 1864, in ibid.)
12. "If you intend to treat such of them as fall into your hands as prisoners of war, please so state. If you do not so intend, but contemplate either their slaughter or their return to slavery, please state that, so that we may have no misunderstanding hereafter . . . If the latter is the case, then let the oath stand, and upon those who have aroused this spirit by their atrocities, and upon the Government and the people who sanction it, be the consequences." (Washburn/Forrest: June 19, 1864, in ibid.)
13. Forrest/Washburn: June 23, 1864, in ibid.
14. Forrest/S. D. Lee: June 24, 1864, in ibid.
15. S. D. Lee/Washburn: June 28, 1864, in ibid.
16. "If this remark . . ." Washburn/S. D. Lee: July 3, 1864, in ibid. "lenient and forbearing . . ." Washburn/Forrest: July 2, 1864, in ibid.
17. J. A. Seddons/Jefferson Davis: July 28, 1864, in ibid.

18. Jefferson Davis/J. A. Seddons: July 30, 1864, in ibid.

19. George W. Reed in *Christian Recorder,* May 21, 1864.

20. Coatsworth, *The Loyal People of the North-west,* p. 560.

21. Tap, *Over Lincoln's Shoulder,* pp. 204–205.

22. "You heard . . ." Charles Boardman/"Family": May 1864, in letter for sale on eBay by www.mikebrackin.com. "They stood us . . ." Allen E. Holcomb/James K. Bell: May 15, 1864, in RMC. (I have substituted "murderers" for "murders.")

23. Anderson/"Soldiers": June 28, 1864, in *ORCW.*

24. H. M. Turner in *Christian Recorder,* July 9, 1864.

25. McPherson, *The Negro's Civil War,* p. 222.

26. Cothern, *History of Ancient Woodbury, Connecticut,* pp. 1226–1227.

27. "The Colored Troops . . ." C. P. Lyman/Family: June 21, 1864 (private collection). One of their captains . . . Wiley Choate/Solon A. Carter: June 22, 1864, RG94/Box 8: Records of the 2nd USCLA in NARA. "To give orders . . ." L. Paddock/Charles P. Brown: July 19, 1864, RG94/Box 8: Records of the 2nd USCCWAL in NARA.

28. Perhaps the army's . . . William D. Turner/Editors, *Chicago Tribune*: July 6, 1864, in RG94/E112–115/P1–17/v.2 in NARA. But the survivors were not forgotten. Colonel William Turner was touched that the Sanitary Commission had provided his men with a Fourth of July supper. "Their enjoyment was much enhanced by the thought that our Country sympathized with the Colored Soldiers who fell at Fort Pillow," he wrote to the editors of the *Chicago Tribune,* "and encourages the Survivors, who were not forgotten on this day: the first anniversary to the Black Man of his real portion in the land of Washington." Despite . . . W. D. Turner: General Order 11: July 5, 1864, in RG94/E112–115/P1–17/ v.2 in NARA. "When the United States . . ." Brayman in Compiled Service Records, Records of the Adjutant General's Office, 1780s–1917, RG 94, in NARA.

29. In mid-November . . . R. D. Mussey/Charles P. Brown: November 14, 1864, in *ORCW.* It was their officers who disgraced them. On November 24, Lieutenant John Clancy of 2/B was dismissed from the service for riding around Norfolk and Portsmouth, Virginia, in a "beastly" state of intoxication. (But "this is evidently a mistake," wrote the sentencing officer, "as beasts do not get drunk.") Second Lieutenant William B. Gray of the 1st U.S. Colored Cavalry was also dismissed for riding to the rescue of Lieutenant Clancy and "drawing his saber and threatening to murder the Corporal of the Provost Guard." (Edward W. Smith: General Orders 147: November 20, 1864, in RG94/Box 8: Records of the 2nd USCCWAL in NARA.) "outside the pale . . ." Main, *The Third United States Cavalry,* pp. 304–307. In December 1864, officers of black troops would be urged to inform their men "that the Executive, Judicial and Legislative departments of the Government have manifested and continually manifest in their welfare the greatest interest, that they are disposed to afford them every facility in their progress from chattledom to an honorable manhood, and that with all the favor and assistance shown them, it is their own fault if they do not deserve the confidence of their friends, and prove themselves men." (R. D. Mussey/Memorandum: December 9, 1864, in Records of Colonel Robert D. Mussey, 1863–1864, RG393/Box 2 in NARA.)

30. Henry Pyles (OK) in *AS.*

Icons: Fort Pillow Myths: April 25, 1864–January 1865

1. "with a great many . . ." Horace Wardner in *RJSCW.* "I knew . . ." Daniel Tyler in ibid.

2. "With his one good hand . . ." Horace Wardner in ibid. Sergeant Ben Robinson testified to seeing a black man's hand working its way through the surface of the earth. Benjamin Robinson in ibid. Before dawn . . . Daniel Tyler in ibid.

3. "his quarters . . ." *Cairo News,* April 16, 1864. "My name . . ." *Harper's Weekly,* May 7, 1864.

4. He was not the only man to suffer harsh punishment at Fort Pickering. The commandant, Colonel A. G. Kappner, was repeatedly accused of unilaterally and capriciously arresting and imprisoning both black and white soldiers "without giving them the benefit of a court martial, or hearing of any kind whatever," despite the "repeated protests" of their officers." (J. M. Irvin/ George Mason: April 11, 1864, in *ORCW*; Charles Turner/E. D. Townsend: April 18, 1864, in 16th Army Corps (Letters Received) RG98, Part 2, Entry 391, Box 7 in NARA.)

5. Jonathan B. Simmons: "Prison Report of Inspection of 'Irving Block' Prison: May 21, 1863, in RG94/E729A/Box 2 in NARA.

6. Testimony and military record of Daniel Tyler; Register of Courts-Martial: Records and Sentences Received: January 1865 to January 1866, RG393/2/2898 in NARA; *Cairo News,* April 16, 1864; "Daniel Tyler," *Liberator,* July 22, 1864. I prefer the Daniel Tyler who testified with such clarity before the committee and joked with the reporter from the *Cairo News.*

7. There must have been at least four flags flying from the parapets that morning: a Union flag and the standards of the garrison's three regiments. Chalmers's adjutant general, Captain Walter A. Goodman, reported capturing four flags at Fort Pillow, including a large flag credited to Bell and his men, but he did not specify which ones they were, and though the flags were duly relayed to Richmond, they have since been lost. John Goodwin [Goodman]/Lieutenant Colonel Jack: April 21, 1864, in *ORCW.* Apparently Bell's brigade captured the Union flag. (John Goodman: "List of Prisoners Cap'd by Major General Forrest at Fort Pillow, & in Tennessee—Deserters, Men of Bad Characters, Flags &c. &c. Apl 12/64 (Copied in Dept. 198–Dec 21, 1886)" in RG249/107/896 in NARA.) In addition to the flags, Chalmers captured eight regimental pennants. (S. D. Lee/S. Cooper: May 27, 1864, in *ORCW.*)

8. In his testimony . . . Eli Cothel in *RJSCW.* It is curious . . . W. D. Turner/ Memorandum: September 29, 1863, RG94/E112–115/P1–17/v.2 in NARA.

9. Thomas J. Jackson/George B. Halstead: April 19, 1864, in RMC.

10. Elizabeth Wayt Booth/Washburn: August 25, 1864, RG109/Microcopy M345/ Union Provost Marshal's File of Papers Relating to Individual Civilians in NARA.

11. An account of this ceremony was included in a number of postwar books. Moore, *Women of the War,* pp. 311–312; Kirkland, *The Pictorial Book of Anecdotes and Incidents of the War of the Rebellion,* pp. 570–571; Brockett and Vaughan, *Women's Work in the Civil War,* p. 769. See also Brigadier General [Chetlain?]/Hurlbut: April 28, 1864, in RG393/2/2907 Letters Sent/Organization of Colored Troops in NARA.

12. Lincoln/Sumner: May 19, 1864, in *CWAL.*

13. "to provide suitable . . ." U.S. Congress, *Journal of the Senate of the United States of America, 1789–1873,* June 2, 1864. "according to the customs . . ." Quarles, *The Negro in the Civil War,* p. 202.

14. RG 393, Part 2, Entry 2872, 1 of 2, in vol. 10, District of West Tennessee in NARA; Michael Musick/Author: January 28, 2002.

15. Jonathan Phillips/Supt Prison: September 8, 1864, RG109/Microcopy M345/Union Provost Marshal's File of Papers Relating to Individual Civilians in NARA. Emphasis mine.

16. A back room . . . George A. Williams/Judge Advocate General: June 24, 1864, in RG94/E729A/Box 2 in NARA. In June . . . James A. Hardie/Washburn: June 20, 1864, in ORCW.

17. Mary Elizabeth Wayt Booth/Washburn: August 25, 1864, RG109/Microcopy M345/Union Provost Marshal's File of Papers Relating to Individual Civilians in NARA.

18. "an immediate thorough . . ." Elizabeth Wayt Booth/Washburn: August 14, 1864, RG109/Microcopy M345, Union Provost Marshal's File of Papers Relating to Individual Civilians in NARA. She did not go on to give the other reasons. The military reluctantly . . . General Order 45, Hdqrs. Dist. of West Tennessee, Memphis (RG 393, Part 2, Entry 2872, 1 of 2, in vol. 10, District of West Tennessee in NARA.)

19. While languishing . . . Judge Advocate R. W. Pike/Major W. H. Morgan: September 27, 1864, RG109/Microcopy M345/Union Provost Marshal's File of Papers Relating to Individual Civilians in NARA. John L. Wilson/Major W. H. Morgan: September 9, 1864, RG109/Microcopy M345/Union Provost Marshal's File of Papers Relating to Individual Civilians in NARA. Hurlbut/Washburne: April 24, 1864, RG94/Regimental Papers, 11th USCI (New) in NARA.

20. Weary of her protests . . . RG 393, Part 2, Entry 2872, 1 of 2, in vol. 10, District of West Tennessee in NARA; Michael Musick in NARA/Author: January 28, 2002. "In consequence . . ." Deposition of Mrs. Lizzie Booth: January 12, 1865, RG109/Microcopy M345/Union Provost Marshal's File of Papers Relating to Individual Civilians in NARA. But Lizzie . . . Note by Robert Mainfort in RMC.

21. F. Hastings/Lieut. Col. T. H. Harris: April 30, 1864, in RMC. "The affair at Fort Pillow . . ." L. M. Methudy/J. G. Kappner, and J A. Copeland/J. G. Kappner: April 28, 1864, in RMC; I. M Irwin/Col. Kappner: April 29, 1864, in RMC.

22. Kappner brought the matter . . . T. H. Harris/T. J. Jackson: April 28, 1864, in RMC. "It is currently reported that you have asserted in the presence of Officers of this command that the late Major L. F. Booth of your regiment, while commanding Fort Pillow, reported to Major General Hurlbut the necessity for additional troops at Fort Pillow, and that Major Booth made three applications to Genl. Hurlbut for reinforcements. You will at once report in writing whether you have ever made such or similar statements, and your authority for the same. By order of Major General S. A. Hurlbut." "I have never . . ." T. J. Jackson/T. H. Harris: April 28, 1864, in RMC. "Entertain any other . . ." Mrs. Mary Booth/Col. Harris: April 28, 1864, in RMC. "unfitted for the position . . ." A. L. Chetlain: Report: July 15, 1865, in RMC.

23. John Walker in *Christian Recorder,* June 9, 1866.

24. Thomas J. Jackson/Adj. Gen. Thomas: April 26, 1863, in RMC.
25. That, in any case . . . Hubbard, *Sketches of Ex-Soldiers.* "a silver jawbone . . ." A. G. Stacey, *Directory of the Kansas State Senate 1889* (Topeka, 1889) in RMC. "In the particular bunch . . ." *Hutchinson* (KS) *News* in *Kansas City* (KS) *Journal,* November 1, 1905, in RMC.
26. "I love . . ." Pension file of Thomas J. Jackson. "His right arm . . ." *Kansas City* (KS) *Journal,* November 1, 1905, in RMC. See also P. H. Coney/"Comrades": November 3, 1905, in RMC.

"Brave to Recklessness": The Memphis Raid: August 20–December 3, 1864

1. Hurst, *Nathan Bedford Forrest,* pp. 207–210.
2. Carroll, "Autobiography and Reminiscences," p. 31.
3. "too deeply interested . . ." Porter/Welles: May 31, 1864, in U.S. Navy Records, M89/Box 132 in NARA.
4. The cracks . . . White, "Stirring Up the Yankees"; Carroll, "Autobiography and Reminiscences," pp. 32–34.
5. James Dinkins in Henry, *As They Saw Forrest,* p. 257.
6. "considerable stream . . ." Carroll, "Autobiography and Reminiscences," pp. 32–34. Forrest and his troopers . . . McIlwaine, *Memphis Down in Dixie,* p. 138.
7. Arriving within sight . . . John Milton Hubbard in Henry, *As They Saw Forrest,* pp. 184–188. The expedition . . . Agnew, "Diary"; John Milton Hubbard in Henry, *As They Saw Forrest,* pp. 184–188.
8. "While we believed . . ." John Milton Hubbard in Henry, *As They Saw Forrest,* pp. 184–188. "A shot . . ." Carroll, "Autobiography and Reminiscences," pp. 32–34.
9. "like a scythe . . ." James Dinkins in Henry, *As They Saw Forrest,* pp. 263–265. "At one point . . ." John Milton Hubbard in ibid., pp. 184–188. Sergeant Benjamin Thacker . . . Lovett, "The West Tennessee Colored Troops in Civil War Combat."
10. "charged into the city . . ." Captain J. C. Jackson (Forrest's Escort)/General Thomas Jordan: June 4, 1867, Papers of Leroy Nutt/2285/Folder 8 (SHC/UNCCH).
11. Hurlbut in McIlwaine, *Memphis Down in Dixie,* p. 141; Carroll, "Autobiography and Reminiscences," pp. 34–35.
12. Among Forrest's prisoners were contrabands as well as soldiers. "During the war many federal soldiers took wives of the negro women where they were quartered," wrote Carroll. "Among our prisoners on this raid was a real fat Dutchman," a German who had "a negro wife, whom he carried along with him. The weather being very warm; water, scarce; both captors and captured became very thirsty. On coming to a bold running stream of clear water, our Dutchman rushed in and fell down to drink. A mule (on which some of our soldiers were mounted), standing in the water, happened to notice the Dutchman lying behind him." Raising one hoof, the mule kicked him in the head, "killing him instantly, at which the negro lamented very much. But the procession moved on." (Hurst, *Nathan Bedford Forrest,* pp. 218–220.)
13. Carroll, "Autobiography and Reminiscences," p. 30
14. Hancock, *Hancock's Diary,* p. 474.

15. Hurst, *Nathan Bedford Forrest*, pp. 221, 224.
16. At Pam Landing . . . After Forrest's quartermaster, Major A. Warren, refused to turn over to Brigadier General Alexander all the slaves he had captured on the Union transport *Maguffin*, Buford, in violation of Forrest's order, had some of them "issued to his command." When Forrest's staff confronted him, Buford, "in an angry & excited manner & in the presence of [diverse] officers & soldiers," apparently accused Chalmers of ungentlemanly conduct and claimed that he had insulted Chalmers to his face and gotten away with it. (Undated note in Chalmers Papers in NARA.) On October 16 . . . Neely and a lieutenant were cashiered, "conscribed & placed in the ranks of the C.S. Army," and the others were suspended from rank and pay for six months, which effectively put them out of action for the rest of the war. The court ascribed its "extreme leniency" to the fact that the accused had all acted "under a misapprehension of their legal right." (R. Taylor: General Order No. 132: October 16, 1864, in RG94/Chapter 2/v.299 [Chalmers] in NARA.)
17. Hurst, *Nathan Bedford Forrest*, p. 227. Washburn began to worry . . . C. C. Washburn/E. R. S. Canby: November 7, 1864, in ORCW. Forrest's reputation . . . Cleveland, *A Discourse*, p. 11.
18. Forrest and "Recorder" in *Macon* (GA) *Southern Confederacy*, January 19, 1865.
19. Brownlow, "John Brownlow's First Published Memoirs."
20. Though the Yankees . . . Hurst, *Nathan Bedford Forrest*, pp. 236–238. Though Confederate chaplain and later bishop Charles Todd Quintard believed that "in the grave all earthly distinctions cease," he could not "content my mind with the resting place which had been chosen by the sexton for our gallant dead," including Major General Cleburne and Brigadiers Strahl and Granbury. Quintard was distressed that they had been buried "in close proximity to the graves of soldiers—both white and black—of the Federal Army. I, therefore, made arrangements to have the bodies disinterred and moved to the Church yard at St. John's, Ashwood." (Quintard, *Diary*, Robert Selph Henry Papers [VT].) See also C. P. Lyman/Parents: December 17, 1864, in private collection.
21. Willoughby, "Gunboats and Gumbo."
22. Hurst, *Nathan Bedford Forrest*, pp. 240–241.
23. "The so-called Confederates . . ." Thomas B. Webster in *Christian Recorder*, January 7, 1865. "The 'bill' . . ." George Walthall/Mrs. B. W. Walthall: April 1, 1865, at University of Mississippi.
24. "allured by the siren . . ." Forrest/"Soldiers": [January 1, 1865] in ORCW. By now his hair . . . Hurst, *Nathan Bedford Forrest*, p. 247.
25. As he marched . . . Willoughby, "Gunboats and Gumbo." Forrest threatened . . . Hurst, *Nathan Bedford Forrest*, p. 245.
26. "Their hats . . ." John Milton Hubbard in Henry, *As They Saw Forrest*, pp. 212–213. "It was said at the time that this was intended as a deterrent to desertion. It may have had the effect intended. It would be passing over it most kindly to state that the affair caused a profound sensation. It would be nearer the truth to say that, with the rank and file, it met with pronounced condemnation." "Everybody in low spirits . . .", Benjamin T. Bondurant in Chester, "The Diary of Sergeant Benjamin T. Bondurant," *WTHSP*, 1985.

27. On March 6 . . . President/Marshal of the District of West Tennessee: Sep-
    tember 5, 1864, Robert Selph Henry Papers (VT). Overwhelmed . . . Hurst,
    Nathan Bedford Forrest, pp. 250–251.
28. Hurst, *Nathan Bedford Forrest,* pp. 252–253.
29. Lockney, Journal. userdata.acd.net/jshirey/cw1865mar.html#assassination.
30. Hurst, *Nathan Bedford Forrest,* p. 255.
31. The last . . . Willoughby, "Gunboats and Gumbo."
32. "We have made . . ." Forrest in Hurst, *Nathan Bedford Forrest,* pp. 255–258. This
    quotation is a modification of "where he lives, there are plenty of fish; and that
    he is going to take a tent along, and don't want to see any one for twelve
    months." (Bryan McAllister in Moore, ed., *Anecdotes, Poetry, and Incidents of
    the War,* p. 451.)

Going Home: Confederate Veterans: 1865–1902

1. Robert W. Harrison in Silver, ed., *Mississippi in the Confederacy,* pp. 216–217.
2. In May . . . W. H. Harris in *TCWVQ.* "as I captured . . ." Isaiah Woody Johnson in ibid.
3. "My horse . . ." Brownlow, "John Brownlow's First Published Memoirs." Some
   of the men . . . Alexander Washington McKay in *TCWVQ.* Others of Forrest's . . . Timothy Walton Leigon in ibid.
4. Hearing rumors . . . Joseph Burch Weems [Philip Van Horn Weems] in ibid. "a
   fight with free Negroes . . ." Victor Murat Locke in ibid.
5. Manlove was undoubtedly not his real name. Though Manloves served in various Mississippi infantry regiments, and a Pat H. Manlove served in the 1st Tennessee Infantry, for what it is worth, there is no record of a James Manlove in
   Forrest's service. But it is unlikely he would have lied about fighting at Fort Pillow in the course of a discussion with an American ambassador. (Washburn,
   The History of Paraguay, vol. 2, pp. 215–221.) See also S. P. Driver and Joe Wright
   in *TCWVQ.*
6. Those few troopers . . . William and Henry Witherspoon (7th) in *TCWVQ.*
   "was so near starved . . ." Edward Morris in ibid. "the lonesomest . . ." Jesse
   Ransom Shelton in ibid. "It was no pleasure trip," agreed John Bittick of the
   9th, "except at its end." (John Holland Bittick in ibid.)
7. "On the trip . . ." William E. Hazelwood in ibid. "You have made . . ." James
   Thomas Lasley in ibid. Having heard that their son, Billy Lillard of the 4th, had
   been shot through a lung at Fayetteville, North Carolina, his parents had given
   him up for dead. Lillard would never forget the day he arrived home, nor the
   face of his "angel Mother" as she ran to meet him. "The news of my arrival went
   like wildfire, and the next day there [were] sixty-five that took dinner and spent
   the day. Will never forget the first meal taken at home. Oh, that Rio coffee!"
   When his father caught sight of him, "he jumped over the dash board of his
   buggy" and embraced him. His father bought him a suit of clothes that was several sizes too big, declaring that now that Billy was a veteran, he should wear
   "men's clothing." (William F. Lillard in ibid.)
8. "everything was tore up . . ." J. W. Williams in ibid. "so I confess . . ." Thomas
   Edward Bradley in ibid. "fine crop . . ." L. W. Travis in ibid. "the fences all
   burned . . ." L. S. Howell in entry for John S. Howell in ibid. "When news came

that Lee had surrendered in Virginia and Forrest men were disbanding in Ala., we were allowed to go to our homes," recalled Ed Williams of the 6th Mississippi, who had watched the smoke and flames rising from his father's house in a battle at Harrisburg a year before. "My father put what little we had left in an ox wagon and with the negroes we had with us, we traveled the thirty or forty miles to our home, two miles west of Tupelo on the old Harrisburg battlefield and took temporary possession of an old house inside the Federal breast-works as our house was burned." (Edwin Maximilian Gardner in ibid.)

9. M. B. Dinwiddie in ibid.

10. "seven horses . . ." William R. H. Matthews in ibid. Some men . . . Robert Milton McCalister [McAllister] in ibid. "my best Negro . . ." Joseph Monroe McCorkle in ibid.

11. Lemuel Hiram Tyree in ibid.

12. "did not want . . ." John Russell Dance in ibid. "I didn't go home . . ." Jasper Washington Eldridge in ibid. "had the honor . . ." William S. Nolen in ibid.

13. "Eskimo cloak . . ." "He was the father of Jim and Calvin McLeary and an uncle of the well-known Henry McLeary, of Humboldt." McLeary, *Humorous Incidents of the Civil War*, p. 15. "On arriving home . . ." James Lindsy Cochran in *TCWVQ*.

14. James W. Hendricks in ibid.

15. John R. Reagan in ibid.

16. *New York Herald,* May 23, 1865.

17. "much better labor . . ." M. B. Dinwiddie in *TCWVQ*. When asked . . . Andrew Jackson Grantham in "Aged Civil War Vet Says He Still Hasn't Overcome Animosity Toward Yankees."

18. "and went through . . ." Robert Theodore Mockbee in *TCWVQ*. "the truth is . . ." "I came home and wrote the homemade yankees a nice little [letter] saying I was at home, and we could not breathe the same air together. They left, and I am still in Tennessee. In them days, I feared no living man, and I've always stood [for] law and order and have had some tussels with the few dirty whelps that [invaded] our country: horsewhipped some and drove some out of the country."

19. "yet a lover , , ," B. P. Hooker in *TCWVQ.* "Though vanquished . . ." Lee Franklin Yancey in ibid. "The world will never . . ." William R. H. Matthews in ibid.

20. Alley, "Memoirs." "I don't trust the negroes now," Kate Carney of Murfreesboro confided to her diary. "They have too much of the Yankees about them to suit me." (Carney, *Diary.*)

21. Montgomery, *Reminiscences of a Mississippian in Peace and War,* p. 21. Some of Forrest's men moved north, where even the erudite Dr. John Allan Wyeth had difficulty adjusting to Yankee mores in a New York hospital. "I determined to have two small, neat wards set apart for colored men and women, where they could be exclusive and away from the possibility of wounded sensibilities by reason of color and race prejudice. The very first patient admitted to the new hospital was a negro lad, who came accompanied by his father, who took the boy back home, refusing to let him go into a colored ward. I wrote the father, saying how sorry I was; that I was from the South and was naturally desirous of

helping any member of his race. He wrote in reply that he might have known I was a Southerner, for nobody else but a man from that country would come up North building 'Jim Crow' wards in a hospital!" (Wyeth, *With Sabre and Scalpel*, p. 451.)

22. "As I look back . . ." William Waller Carson in *TCWVQ*. "I was too young . . ." Edwin Maximilian Gardner in ibid.

"Jealousy, Falsehood and Fanaticism": Forrest's Generals: 1865–1905

1. McCulloch and Neely . . . W. A. Gorman/McCulloch and Neely: June 5, 1864, in RG94/Chapter 2/v.289 (Chalmers) in NARA. "Horse stealing . . ." Another man, J. Boone of the 9th Texas Cavalry, confessed to robbing a widow but insisted that he "only got ten dollars in counterfeit money," and besides, he was acting on orders. Thomas Henderson/Chalmers: March 15, 1865, in Chalmers Papers.

2. "the memory . . ." Levens and Drake, *A History of Cooper County*, p. 153. "As a neighbor . . ." National Historical Company, *History of Howard and Cooper Counties; Boonville* (MO) *Daily News*, January 7, 1976.

3. Charged by Chalmers . . . Lawrence L. Hewitt in Davis, ed., *The Confederate General*, vol. 1, pp. 145–146; Henry, *"First with the Most" Forrest*, p. 235; Wyeth, *That Devil Forrest*, p. 299; Evans, *Confederate Military History*, vol. 11, p. 228. "His mind . . ." Otey, "The Story of Our Great War."

4. "the narrow partisan . . ." Hancock, pp. 578–581.

5. *CV*, October 1902; Anne Bailey in Davis, ed., *The Confederate General*, vol. 1, p. 98–99; Lewis Publishing Company, *Memorial and Biographical History of the Counties of Fresno, Tulare, and Kern, California*, p. 315; Evans, *Confederate Military History*, vol. 8.

6. James Ronald Chalmers in United States Congress, *A Personal Explanatio by Hon. J. R. Chalmers of Mississippi, Delivered in the House of Representatives of the United States, May 7, 1879*. Washington, 1879. In his own tribute . . . Chalmers, "Lieutenant General Nathan Bedford Forrest and His Campaigns."

7. *Greenville* (MS) *Times*, August 15, 1874.

8. Harry Abernathy, "County's First Black Sheriff Served in 1874–75." Undated clipping from unidentified contemporary newspaper.

9. *Jackson* (MS) *Clarion Ledger*, September 21, 1952; *Jackson* (MS) *Daily News*, January 17, 1965.

10. S. G. French, editorials, *CV*, May and September 1896.

11. In 1907 . . . Henry, *"First with the Most" Forrest*, p. 267. "malignant partisan falsehood" . . . *New York Times*, November 1, 1877.

12. "Gen. N. B. Forrest," Lee continued, "was not only the most distinguished cavalry leader of the Confederacy, but his memory and that of his heroic followers have the respect and love of every true Southern man and woman, and no slander of that great American soldier can hold in any true American heart in our reunited country, now beloved by all of its citizens." (Stephen D. Lee, "Tribute to Gen. Bedford Forrest," *CV*, June 1903.)

13. Jordan and Pryor, *The Campaigns of Nathan Bedford Forrest*, p. 453.

14. Wyeth, *That Devil Forrest*, p. 341.

15. He conceded . . . Robert Selph Henry Papers (VT). And Andrew Nelson Lytle's . . . Carney, "The Contested Image of Nathan Bedford Forrest."

16. Bryan McAllister in Moore, ed. *Anecdotes, Poetry, and Incidents of the War,* pp. 450–451.

Full Circle: Black Troops: 1865–1900

1. "We have . . ." George Kryder/Elizabeth Sweetland Kryder: May 29, 1865. Sherman ordered . . . Sherman/Slocum et al.: May 28, 1865, RG393/Entry 2498, Letters Sent in the Field; April–May 1864, in NARA. On January 20, 1865, General George Thomas appointed Augustus Louis Chetlain commander of the District of Memphis. Chetlain suspected he was being kicked upstairs, and that his removal as commander of black troops in the department was intended to sabotage the black regiments he had recruited. "I do not wish to be placed in command of the Port of Memphis," he protested, "if that will relieve me from my present command. I have long been in command of Colored Troops and I desire to continue with them. I hope by next spring that enough Colored Troops will be ordered here to give me a command in the field." But Chetlain's protests were unavailing. (Chetlain/Thomas: January 7, 1865, in Generals Papers: Chetlain: RG94/Box 9/159 in NARA.)

2. Court-martial of Sergeants J. Hall and Anderson Tolliver; Corporal Jim Jones; Privates Bob Jones, George Bryant, William Cannon, and Cate McDowell; and Bugler Isaac Reeves, RG94/Box 8: Records of the 2nd USCLA in NARA.

3. "By the bleached . . ." "It seems strange, after all, that colored men can get along with their wives," wrote the *Christian Recorder,* "and colored parents with their children without much trouble, but white men, and especially Legislators, are so suspicious of their wives and daughters for fear of their admiring a black man instead of a white, that they have to be exposing their jealousy to the civilized world, by enactment with penalties, for a white man or woman marrying whom they prefer." (*Christian Recorder,* June 15 and 24, 1865.) "until the harvest . . ." Willoughby, "Gunboats and Gumbo."

4. Later, at Cairo, and "for the first and only time on the trip, save while we were under the Spanish flag, slaves waited on us at dinner. They were the last any of us were ever to see on American soil." Reid, *After the War,* pp. 292–294.

5. History repeated itself during the 1960 presidential election when black sharecroppers in Fayette and Haywood counties were forced out of their homes, blacklisted by local merchants, and corraled into a tent city by local merchants for having tried to register to vote. After Kennedy's election, the case resulted in the first federal lawsuit brought under the 1957 Civil Rights Act. www.jacksonsun.com. John L. Poston: Report: May 1, 1867, in BRFAL (Brownsville, Tennessee, 1867) RG105/52 in NARA; James Kendrick/John L. Poston: September 7, 1867, in BRFAL (Brownsville, Tennessee, 1867) RG105/52 in NARA.

6. William J. Stephens in pension file of John H. Porter; John L. Poston in pension files of Henry Clay Carter, Neal Clark, Isaac J. Ledbetter, and Robert Medlin. John L. Poston/Jonathan C. Poston: December 3, 1868, in pension file of Wiley Poston.

7. "When, with a wild hurrah, on the 'double-quick,' they rushed upon the enemy's guns, and bore your flag where men fell fastest and war made its wildest

havoc, where explosion after explosion sent their mangled bodies and severed limbs flying through the air, and they fell on glacis, ditch, and scarp and counterscarp, did you caution them against such bravery, and remind them that this was the white man's Government? . . . No, no, sir; you beckoned them on by the guerdon [reward] of freedom, the blessings of an equal and just Government, and a 'good time coming.'" (Representative Daniel Clark of New Hampshire in Barnes, *History of the Thirty-ninth Congress,* p. 390.) Republicans brandished Fort Pillow in their attacks on the Democratic Party. Not every Democrat was a Southern racist and bushwhacker, James A. Garfield conceded, but "every Rebel guerrilla and jayhawker, every man who ran to Canada to avoid the draft, every bounty-hunter, every deserter, every cowardly sneak that ran from danger and disgraced his flag, every man who loves slavery and hates liberty, every man who helped massacre loyal negroes at Fort Pillow, or loyal whites at New Orleans, every Knight of the Golden Circle, every incendiary who helped burn Northern steamboats and Northern hotels, and every villain, of whatever name or crime, who loves power more than justice, slavery more than freedom, is a Democrat." (James A. Garfield [1866] in *Weekly Standard,* December 4, 2000.)

8. "Mr. Willard" in State of Michigan, *The Debates and Proceedings of the Constitutional Convention of the State of Michigan,* p. 651.

9. "Visit to Historic Ground" in *Memphis Argus,* September 10, 1865.

10. Perhaps it was . . . Stanton/"MC": December 11, 1865, in RG 92, Quartermaster's Consolidated File: Fort Pillow in NARA. Two days before . . . W. J. Colburn/A. R. Eddy: December 23, 1865, RG92/Box 818/225 in NARA. On December 12 . . . Montgomery Cunningham Meigs/James Lowry Donaldson: December 12, 1865, RG92/225/5337 in NARA. Assistant Quartermaster . . . W. J. Colburn/A. R. Eddy: December 23, 1865, in Quartermaster's Consolidated File (Fort Pillow) RG 92 in NARA. An agent . . . W. J. Colburn/J. S. Donaldson: December 26, 1865 (two letters), NA/RG92/Box 818/225. A Mr. Lea . . . W. J. Colburn/J. S. Donaldson: December 26, 1865, in Quartermaster's Consolidated File (Fort Pillow) RG 92 in NARA.

11. In January . . . Meyers/Darling: January 31, 1866, in ibid. But Mrs. Booth . . . W. J. Colburn/A. R. Eddy: February 12, 1866, and W. J. Coburn/J. L. Donaldson: February 12, 1866, in Entry 576, RG 92, General Correspondence and Reports Relating to National and Post Cemeteries 1865–1890 in Records of the Office of Quarter Master General in NARA; "Quarter Master Gen"/Stanton: March 10, 1866, in Quartermaster's Consolidated File (Fort Pillow) RG92 in NARA.

12. Each grave . . . W. J. Colburn/M. C. Meigs: April 9, 1866, in Quartermaster's Consolidated File (Fort Pillow), RG 92 in NARA. "Little can be said . . ." Capt. E. B. Whitman: Report No. 237: Undated in Records of the Office of Quartermaster General; E. B. Whitman/J. L. Donaldson: April 29, 1866, in RMC; Register of Cemeterial Reports Received and Remarks made on the Reports by the Quartermaster General: January–August 1866, RG 92/Entry 640 in NARA.

13. Ike K. Revelle/L. C. Houk: January 24, 1883, and Robert Lincoln/L. C. Houk: February 6, 1883, in Records of Office of Quartermaster General/Cemeterial/ 1828–1929/RG92/Box 56/NM81/576 in NARA.

14. The old cannon . . . *Covington Leader,* August 20, 1889. Not to be outdone . . . Interview with Fred Montgomery (Henning, Tennessee); Peters, *Lauderdale County.* Working with a metal detector in the 1960s, a buff named Beverly M. DuBose Jr. of Atlanta was disappointed to find very few artifacts from the old fort, only "three minie balls, a few odd bits of tin, and I think one eagle button." He did find "a major piece of what appeared to be an exploded cannon ball" but it was too big to dig up and cart back to his car. (Beverly M. DuBose Jr./Robert C. Mainfort Jr.: September 15, 1978, in RMC.)

15. "The rending . . ." *Bolivar* (TN) *Bulletin* in *CV,* December 1908. By 1930 . . . Mills, "Fort Pillow."

16. In 1970 . . . Tennessee Department of Conservation, *Master Plan Report: Fort Pillow: State Historic Area* (Nashville, 1975). Under the supervision . . . Robert Henry in *Memphis Commercial Appeal,* June 19, 1979.

"Deliver Me from Bloodguiltiness": Forrest: From 1865

1. On May 16 . . . *Memphis News-Scimitar,* May 17, 1905; Carney, "The Contested Image of Nathan Bedford Forrest." "one of the proudest . . ." *Memphis Commercial Appeal,* May 17, 1905.

2. *Memphis Commercial Appeal* in Carney, "The Contested Image of Nathan Bedford Forrest."

3. In the summer . . . *Memphis Commercial Appeal,* July 13, 1940. But a year later . . . Frisby, "'Remember Fort Pillow!'" Under the glare . . . Carney, "The Contested Image of Nathan Bedford Forrest."

4. Carney, "The Contested Image of Nathan Bedford Forrest."

5. Most prominent . . . The author's brother, Geoffrey C. Ward, was cowriter of the documentary. Shelby Foote in Carney, "The Contested Image of Nathan Bedford Forrest"; Matthew Sandel, "Tilting at Statues."

6. *Nashville Tennesseean,* July 14, 1998.

7. A seventy-one-year-old South Carolina man who attended the unveiling was quoted by the paper as claiming that his experience of living in an integrated community for seventeen years had convinced him that "the mixing of the races doesn't work." He went on to attribute hate and crime to blacks, who, the South Carolina man was quoted as saying, "are primarily criminal as a group." (www.blueshoenashville.com/history.html.)

8. Horwitz, *Confederates in the Attic.*

9. Forrest in Hurst, *Nathan Bedford Forrest,* pp. 271, 293. On March 13 . . . U.S. District of West Tennessee: March 13, 1866, in Robert Selph Henry Papers (VT). "This is my country . . ." Maury, *Recollections of a Virginian,* pp. 222–223; Wills, *A Battle from the Start,* 342–349; Hurst, *Nathan Bedford Forrest,* p. 308.

10. Hurst, *Nathan Bedford Forrest,* p. 273–275. If Forrest was open to any criticism from his neighbors, it was that his overindulgence toward his former slaves had demoralized them.

11. "ruined by the war . . ." Forrest/William Brent (Wheeler): September 13, 1866, at http://www.nav.cc.tx.us/lrc/NB2.htm. But his fortunes . . . Hurst, *Nathan Bedford Forrest,* p. 292.

12. Basil W. Duke in Hurst, *Nathan Bedford Forrest,* p. 300.

13. Hurst, *Nathan Bedford Forrest,* p. 302.

14. Joe Curtis (*Memphis Commercial Appeal*)/Robert S. Henry: November 7, 1930, Robert Selph Henry Papers (VT).

15. *Harper's Weekly,* September 5 and 26, and October 3, 1868.

16. Forrest/Andrew Johnson in Hurst, *Nathan Bedford Forrest,* pp. 283–284.

17. *Memphis Avalanche* in B. P. Runkle/C. B. Fisk, May 23, 1866 in BRFAL.

18. On Saturday, a Northern schoolteacher named Tade went out "among the hills, where my flock was scattered, [and] called them by their names. They knew the voice & followed." E. O. Tade/ M. E. Stricky: May 21, 1866 (AMA); Taylor, *The Negro in Tennessee,* pp. 85–87; Chalfant, "Persecution in the South," *American Missionary,* October 1866. "This nation . . ." B. P. Runkle/C. B. Fisk: May 23, 1866, in BRFAL.

19. That fall . . . According to one account he later asked his former artillery commander John Morton if he could join, and after Morton drove him into the countryside to administer the oath, Forrest slapped him on the back and exclaimed, "Why, you damned little fool, don't you know I'm the head of the whole damned thing?" "damned good thing . . ." Hurst, *Nathan Bedford Forrest,* pp. 285, 287–288. "He had done . . ." Brown, "Nathan Bedford Forrest."

20. In the spring . . . Hurst, *Nathan Bedford Forrest,* pp. 290–291.

21. "Of this order . . ." Carroll, "Autobiography and Reminiscences," p. 44.

22. During the election . . . Hurst, *Nathan Bedford Forrest,* pp. 294, 297, 304, 306, 322–323, 325. "squads of the K.K.K. . . ." Joe Curtis (*Memphis Commercial Appeal*)/Robert S. Henry: November 7, 1930, Robert Selph Henry Papers (VT).

23. Hurst, *Nathan Bedford Forrest,* pp. 341–342.

24. Robert A. Wardlaw in the pension file of Charles Mullins.

25. "exterminate the white marauders . . ." Hurst, *Nathan Bedford Forrest,* pp. 325, 341–342, 353, 369. But the outrages . . . Julia Spence Chase/Spence: August 29, 1875, in Papers of Adam Knight Spence (FU). "reign of terror . . ." Richardson, *Christian Reconstruction,* p. 137. By commencement in 1874, the Nashville papers were so hostile to Fisk that usually friendly rags like the *Bulletin* and the *Banner* refused to publish the school's notices. (Julia Spence Chase/Spence: August 29, 1875, in Papers of Adam Knight Spence [FU].)

26. Carney, "The Contested Image of Nathan Bedford Forrest."

27. Hurst, *Nathan Bedford Forrest,* pp. 366–367.

28. Ibid., pp. 311–13, 327–331, 360–362, 370, 373, 376.

29. In these . . . McIlwaine, *Memphis Down in Dixie,* p. 153. "Just here . . ." Hurst, *Nathan Bedford Forrest,* pp. 378–379, 386. "I have led . . ." Maury, *Recollections of a Virginian,* pp. 223–224. John Milton Hubbard in Henry, *As They Saw Forrest,* p. 179.

30. Lafcadio Hearn in McIlwaine, *Memphis Down in Dixie,* p. 154.

SOURCES

Key
CV   *Confederate Veteran*
CWH   *Civil War History*
RMC   Robert Mainfort Collection
SHC/UNCCH   Southern History Collection, University of North Carolina at Chapel Hill
SHSP   *Southern Historical Society Papers*
THQ   *Tennessee Historical Quarterly*
TSLA   Tennessee State Library and Archives (Nashville)
WTHSP   *West Tennessee Historical Society Papers*

Adams, Virginia M., ed. *On the Altar of Freedom: A Black Soldier's Civil War Letters from the Front: Corporal James Henry Gooding*. New York, NY, 1991.

Adler, Mortimer J., Charles Van Doren, and George Ducas, eds. *The Negro in American History*. 3 vols. Chicago, IL, 1969.

Agnew, Samuel A. "Battle of Tishomingo Creek." *CV*, September 1900.

Agnew, Samuel. "Diary." SHC/UNCCH.

Albert, Octavia V. Rogers. *The House of Bondage, or Charlotte Brooks and other Slaves*. New York, NY, 1890.

Aldrich, Charles. "Incidents Connected with the History of the Thirty-second Iowa Infantry." *Iowa Journal*, January 1906.

Allen, W. B. with George Albright and C. D. Covington. *CV*. Letter to the Editor. July 1899.

Alley, John. "The Memoirs of John Marshall Alley." United States Civil War Center. Louisiana State University. Baton Rouge, LA.

American Missionary Association. *History of the American Missionary Association: Its Churches and Educational Institutions among the Freedmen, Indians, and Chinese, with Illustrative Facts and Anecdotes*. New York, NY, 1874.

————. Papers. TSLA.

————. *Twenty-fifth Annual Report of the American Missionary Association.* New York, NY, 1871.

Anders, Leslie. "Confederate Dead at Lone Jack." *Prairie Gleaner,* December 1989.

Anderson, Charles W. "Col. Wiley M. Reed." *CV,* March 1897.

————. "The True Story of Fort Pillow." *CV,* September 1886.

Andrews, William L., ed. *From Fugitive Slave to Free Man: The Autobiographies of William Wells Brown.* New York, NY, 1993.

————. *Army of the Cumberland.* Philadelphia, PA, 1863.

————. *Historical Atlas of Cooper County, Missouri.* Boonesville, MO, 1897.

————. *History of Rush County, Indiana.* 1888. Reprinted Knightstown, IN, 1966.

————. *History of Tennessee: From the Earliest Time to the Present; Together with an Historical and a Biographical Sketch of Lauderdale, Tipton, Haywood, and Crockett Counties; Besides a Valuable Fund of Notes, Reminiscences, Etc., Etc.* 1886. Reprinted Greenville, SC, 1997.

————. *Old Times in West Tennessee.* Memphis, TN, 1873.

Anonymous. "Capt. Thomas A. Bottom." *CV,* September 1900.

————. Editorial. *Anglo African,* April 23, 1864.

————. "James W. Joplin and Family: Six Sons Were Confederate Soldiers." *CV,* November 1896.

————. "McCulloch Cousins Survive Civil War Together." *Historical Society at Pilot Grove, Missouri.* Undated. [1885?]

————. "Rebel Atrocities." *Harper's Weekly,* May 21, 1864.

————. "Request for Information." *CV,* July 1909.

————. "Reunion of Forrest's Escort," *CV,* March 1894.

————. "Robert A. McCulloch." *CV,* April 1905.

————. "The Last Roll: Gen. Tyree H. Bell." *CV,* October 1902.

————. "Visit to Historic Ground." *Memphis Argus,* September 10, 1865. RMC.

————. "When Will Popa Come?" *CV,* September 1896.

Aptheker, Herbert. *To Be Free.* New York, NY, 1991.

Armstrong, Orland Kay. *Old Massa's People: The Old Slaves Tell Their Story.* Indianapolis, 1951.

Armstrong, William M. "Cahaba to Charleston: The Prison Odyssey of Lt. Edmund E. Ryan." *CWH,* June 1962.

Ash, Stephen V., ed. *Secessionists and Other Scoundrels: Selections from Parson Brownlow's Book.* Baton Rouge, LA, 1999.

Atkinson, J. H., ed. "A Civil War Letter of Captain Elliott Fletcher, Jr." *Arkansas Historical Quarterly* 22, no. 1 (1963): 49–54.

Atlanta Confederacy in *Charleston Mercury.* May 6, 1864.

Bailey, Fred Arthur. *Class and Tennessee's Confederate Generation.* Chapel Hill, NC, 1987.

Bailey, Robert. "The 'Bogus' *Memphis Union Appeal*: A Union Newspaper in Occupied Confederate Territory." *WTHSP* (1978).

Baker, Pansy N., and Charlotte S. Reynolds. *Weakley Remembered.* 3 vols. Bradford, TN, 1982.

Baker, T. Lindsay, and Julie P. Baker, eds. *The WPA Oklahoma Slave Narratives.* Norman, OK, 1996.

Ballard, Elsie Miner. "James Dick Davis: (1810–1880): A Genealogical Sketch." *WTHSP* (1975).

Ballard, Michael B. *A Long Shadow: Jefferson Davis and the Final Days of the Confederacy.* Jackson, MS, 1986.

Bancroft, Frederic. *Slave Trading in the Old South.* 1931. Reprinted New York, NY, 1959.

———. Papers. Box 11, Columbia University Special Collections.

Barber, William. Letters. Jerome Library, Bowling Green State University.

Barnes, William H. *History of the Thirty-ninth Congress of the United States.* 1866. Reprinted New York, NY, 1969.

Basler, Roy P. *The Collected Works of Abraham Lincoln.* 8 vols. New Brunswick, NJ, 1953.

Bates, Samuel P. *History of the Pennsylvania Volunteers, 1861–1865.* 4 vols. Harrisburg, PA, 1869.

Baylor, Orval Walker. *Early Times in Washington County.* Cynthiana, KY, 1942.

Beard, Augustus Field. *A Crusade of Brotherhood: A History of the American Missionary Association.* Boston, MA, 1909.

Bears, Edwin C. *Forrest at Brice's Cross Roads and in North Mississippi in 1864.* Dayton, OH, 1991.

Beckham, Elihu C. "Where Was I and What I Saw during the Late War." *Melbourne* [AR] *Times,* September 6, 1906.

Bedford County, Tennessee, Deed Book, January 15, 1833.

Bejach, Lois D. "The Journal of a Civil War 'Commanco'—DeWitt Clinton Fort." *WTHSP,* 1948.

Benton, Edward. Letter. *New York Herald,* April 24, 1864.

Berlin, Ira, ed. *The Wartime Genesis of Free Labor: The Upper South.* Series 1, volume 2 of *Freedom: A Documentary History of Emancipation: 1861–1867.* New York, NY, 1993.

Berlin, Ira. *Slaves without Masters: The Free Negro in the Antebellum South.* New York, NY, 1974.

Berlin, Ira, et al., eds. *Free at Last: A Documentary History of Slavery, Freedom, and the Civil War.* New York, NY, 1992.

Berndt, Jon S. "The Slagg Family of Wisconsin during the Civil War." www.hal-pc.org.

Berry, Thomas F. *Four Years with Morgan and Forrest.* Oklahoma City, OK, 1914.

Berwanger, Eugene H. *The Frontier against Slavery: Western Anti-Negro Prejudice and the Slavery Extension Controversy.* Chicago, IL, 1971.

Betts, Vicki. "A Revelation of War: Civilians in Hardin County, Tennessee, Spring, 1862." www.hardinhistory.com.

Billings, John D. *Hardtack and Coffee: The Unwritten Story of Army Life.* 1887. Reprinted Lincoln, NE, 1993.

Black, Hugh. Letters. Robert Manning Strozier Library. Florida State University.

Blackburn, J. K. P. "Reminiscences." OATTR.

Blassingame, John W. *Slave Testimony: Two Centuries of Letters, Speeches, Interviews, and Autobiographies.* Baton Rouge, LA, 1977.

Blanton, J. C. "Forrest's Old Regiment." *CV,* February 1895.

Blight, David W. *Race and Reunion: The Civil War in American Memory.* Cambridge, MA, 2001.

Blockson, Charles L. *Black Genealogy.* Baltimore, MD, 1991.

Blount, T. W. "Captain Thomas Blount and His Memoirs." *Southwestern Historical Quarterly.* July 1935.

Boardman, Charles. Letter. www.mikebrackin.com.

"Boatman." "Letter from Pillow Battery (Camp of Southern Guards: July 14, 1861)." *Memphis Avalanche,* July 16, 1861. RMC.

Bodnia, George, ed. "Fort Pillow 'Massacre': Observations of a Minnesotan." *Minnesota History* (Spring 1873).

Bogle, J. C. M. Letters. Crutchfield Papers. The Gordon Browning Museum of the Carroll County [TN] Historical Society.

Bohrer, Zene. Letter. Iowa in the Civil War. www.iagenweb.org/civilwar/.

Boime, Albert. *The Art of Exclusion: Representing Blacks in the Nineteenth Century.* London, 1990.

Boles, John B. *Masters and Slaves in the House of the Lord: Race and Religion in the American South, 1740–1870.* Lexington, KY, 1988.

Bolivar [TN] *Bulletin.* "Site of Fort Pillow in Mississippi River." *CV,* December 1908.

Botkin, B. A., ed. *Lay My Burden Down: A Folk History of Slavery.* Chicago, IL, 1969.

Branch, Mary Polk. *Memoirs of a Southern Woman "Within the Lines" and a Genealogical Record.* Chicago, IL, 1912. SHC/UNCCH.

Brandt, Nat. *The Town That Started the Civil War.* Syracuse, NY, 1990.

Brayman, Mason. Papers. Chicago Historical Society.

Breckinridge, John Cabell. John Cabell Breckinridge Collection. Chicago Historical Society.

Brewer, Thomas. "Storming of Fort Pillow." *CV,* December 1925.

Britton, Wiley. *The Aftermath of the Civil War Based on Investigation of War Claims.* Kansas City, MO, 1924.

Brockett, L. P., and Mary C. Vaughan. *Woman's Work in the Civil War: A Record of Heroism, Patriotism and Patience.* Boston, MA, 1867.

Brogden, John V., comp. *Tennessee Colored Pension Applications for CSA Service.* TSLA.

Brooksher, William R., and David K. Snider. *Glory at a Gallop: Tales of the Confederate Cavalry.* McLean, VA, 1993.

Brown, Andrew. "Sol Street: Confederate Partisan Leader." *Journal of Mississippi History* (July 1959).

Brown, Barbara W., and James M. Rose, eds. *Black Roots in Southeastern Connecticut, 1650–1900.* Detroit, MI, 1980.

Brown, Tully. "Nathan Bedford Forrest: Lecture Delivered at Vendome Theatre, Nashville, Tennessee, January 26, 1905." TSLA.

Brown, William Wells. *The Negro in the American Rebellion—His Heroism and His Fidelity.* Boston, MA, 1867.

Browne, Francis Fisher. *The Everyday Life of Abraham Lincoln.* Lincoln, NE, 1995.

Brownlee, Frederick Leslie. *New Day Ascending.* Boston, MA, 1946.

Brownlow, John. "John Brownlow's First Published Memoirs." *Columbia* (TN) *Daily Herald,* September 30, 1984.

Bruce, [Henry] C. *The New Man: Twenty-nine Years a Slave. Twenty-nine Years a Free Man.* York, PA, 1895.

Buch. *The History of Buchanan County, Missouri, Containing a History of the Coun-*

try, Its Cities, Towns, Etc., Biographical Sketches of Its Citizens, Buchanan County in the Late War, General and Local Statistics, Portraits of Early Settlers and Prominent Men. St. Joseph, MO, 1881.

Buckley, Gail. *American Patriots: The Story of Blacks in the Military from the Revolution to Desert Storm.* New York, NY, 2001.

Bull, Augustus F. Papers. Web Center for Archival Collections. Bowling Green State University.

Burfford, Robert (interviewed by S. H. Logan). "In the Wake of Fort Pillow with Forrest in Command." *Memphis Commercial Appeal,* n.d.

Burney, Thomas Sylvanus. "The Famous Terry Rangers." *Groesbeck* (TX) *Journal,* November 25, 1909.

———. "Shannon's Scouts." *Groesbeck* (TX) *Journal,* December 9, 1909.

———. "Some Texas Rangers." *Groesbeck* (TX) *Journal,* December 16 and 30, 1909.

Burt, Richard W. "Civil War Letters from the 76th Ohio Volunteer Infantry." Courtesy of Larry Stevens. www.my.ohio.voyager.net.

Butchart, Ronald E. *Northern Schools, Southern Blacks, and Reconstruction: Freedmen's Education, 1862–1875.* Westport, CT, 1980.

Cairo News, April 16, 1864.

Caldwell, Merrill S. "A Brief History of Slavery in Boone County, Kentucky: Read before a Meeting of the Boone County Historical Society: Florence, Kentucky: June 21, 1857." Mid-Continent Public Library. Independence, MO.

Campbell, Given. Papers. Wilson Library, UNCCH.

Cannon, Newton. Papers. TSLA.

Carney, Court. "The Contested Image of Nathan Bedford Forrest." *Journal of Southern History* (August 2001).

Carney, Kate S. Diary, April 15, 1861–July 31, 1982. SHC/UNCCH.

Carroll, John W. "Autobiography and Reminiscences." docsouth.unc.edu.

Carter, Joe. Papers. TSLA.

Cary, Victor, and Grantham, A. J. "Aged Civil War Vet Says He Still Hasn't Overcome Animosity Toward Yankees." *Corpus Christi Caller Times,* October 6, 1940.

Casstevens, Francis H. *Edward A. Wild and the African Brigade in the Civil War.* Jefferson, NC, 2003.

Castel, Albert. "The Fort Pillow Massacre: A Fresh Examination of the Evidence." *CWH* (1958).

Catteral, Helen Tunnicliff, ed. *Judicial Cases Concerning American Slavery and the Negro.* 4 vols. Washington, DC, 1926–1937.

Chalmers, James Ronald. "Lieutenant General Nathan Bedford Forrest and His Campaigns." *SHSP,* October 1879.

———. *A Personal Explanation by Hon. J. R. Chalmers of Mississippi, Delivered in the House of Representatives of the United States: May 7, 1879.* Washington, DC, 1879.

Chapin, L. W. Letter. *CV,* October 1895.

Charleston Mercury. March 22, April 7, May 2 and 23, June 12–13, August 4 and 18, November 7 and 13, 1862; August 4, 1864.

Chatham, William L. Letter. McCain Library and Archives. University of Southern Mississippi.

Chears, Nathaniel Francis. Papers. TSLA.

Chester, William W. "The Diary of Sergeant Benjamin T. Bondurant, CSA." *WTHSP*, 1985.

Chicago Tribune in *Anglo African*, May 7, 1864.

Christian Recorder. January 9, April 30, May 7, 14, 21, and 28, June 11, September 3, November 26, December 11, 1864; January 7, April 29, June 24, July 1 and 22, September 23, and November 11 and 18, 1865; June 9, July 9, and December 15, 1866.

Cimprich, John. *Slavery's End in Tennessee.* Tuscaloosa, AL, 1985.

Cimprich, John, and Robert C. Mainfort, Jr. "Dr. Fitch's Report on the Fort Pillow Massacre." *THQ* 44, no. 1 (Spring 1985).

———. "The Fort Pillow Massacre: A Statistical Note." *Journal of American History* 76, no. 3 (1989).

———. "Fort Pillow Revisited: New Evidence about an Old Controversy." *CWH* 28, no. 4 (1982): 293–306.

Civil War Centennial Commission [Nashville]. *Tennesseeans in the Civil War: A Military History of Confederate and Union Units with Available Rosters of Personnel.* 2 vols. Nashville, TN, 1964.

Claiborne, John M. "Claiborne's History of Terry's Texas Rangers: A Confederate Cavalry Regiment Engaged in the Unfortunate War between the States." *New Birmingham Times.* N. d., 1891. OATTR.

Clarke, Lewis, and Milton Clarke. *Narratives of the Sufferings of Lewis and Milton Clarke, sons of a soldier of the Revolution, during a Captivity of more than Twenty Years among the Slaveholders of Kentucky, one of the So Called Christian States of North America.* Boston, MA, 1846.

Clayton, W. W. *History of Davidson County, Tennessee, with Illustrations and Biographical Sketches of its Prominent Men and Pioneers.* 1897. Reprinted Nashville, TN, 1971.

Cleveland, J. P. *A Discourse Delivered at the Twenty-first Anniversary of the Society for the Promotion of Collegiate and Theological Education at the West. In the Second Presbyterian Church, Newark, NJ, November 14, 1864.* New York, NY, 1865.

Coatsworth, Stella S. *The Loyal People of the North-west, a Record of Prominent Persons, Places and Events, during Eight Years of Unparalleled American History.* Chicago, IL, 1869.

Cole, C. M. "Vivid War Experiences at Ripley, Miss." *CV*, June 1905.

Collins, James R. "James R. Collins Describes His Civil War Experiences." Edited by Ken Lee and Gene Shields. www.iowacounties.com.

Columbus (KY) *War Eagle,* December 12, 1863.

Cook, V. Y. "Forrest's Capture of Col. R. G. Ingersoll." *CV*, February 1907.

Coombe, Jack D. *Thunder along the Mississippi: The River Battles that Split the Confederacy.* New York, NY, 1998.

Copley, John M. "A Sketch of the Battle of Franklin, Tenn.; with Reminiscences of Camp Douglas." SHC/UNCCH.

Cornelius, Janet Duitsman. *"When I Can Read My Title Clear": Literacy, Slavery, and Religion in the Antebellum South.* Columbia, SC, 1991.

Cornish, Dudley Taylor. *The Sable Arm: Negro Troops in the Union Army, 1861–1865.* New York, NY, 1966.

Cothern, John W. *Confederates of Elmwood.* Bowie, MD, 2001.

Cothren, William. *History of Ancient Woodbury, Connecticut.* Waterbury, CT, 1879.

Covington Leader, August 20, 1889.

Cox, N. N. "Forrest's Men Captured at Parker's Crossroads." *CV,* August 1908.

Crawford, Charles W. *Weakley County.* Memphis, TN, 1983.

Croffutt, W. A. "Bourbon Ballads." *New York Tribune,* extra no. 52, n.d.

Crutchfield, James A. *Williamson County: A Pictorial History.* Nashville, 1980.

Crutchfield, John A. "Letters of Captain John A. Crutchfield, Company 'F': Russell's 20th Tennessee Cavalry Regiment." Gordon Browning Museum. McKenzie, TN.

Culp, F. M., and R. E. Ross. *Gibson County Past and Present.* Trenton, TN, 1961.

Cupples, Douglas W. "Memphis' Confederate Civil War Refugees." *WTHSP* (1995).

———. "Rebel to the Core: Memphis' Confederate Civil War Refugees." *WTHSP* (1997).

Currotto, William F. *Wizard of the Saddle.* Memphis, TN, 1996.

Curry, Richard O., ed. *The Abolitionist.* New York, NY, 1965.

Daniel, Larry J. *Soldiering in the Army of Tennessee: A Portrait of Life in a Confederate Army.* Chapel Hill, NC, 1991.

Davis, Abraham. "What about Fort Pillow?" Unpublished manuscript, Tucson, AZ, 1964. Memphis Public Library.

Davis, William C. *The Cause Lost: Myths and Realities of the Confederacy.* Lawrence, KS, 1996.

———, ed. *The Confederate General.* Vol. 1. Washington, DC, 1991.

Davis, William C., and Meredith L. Swentor, eds. *Bluegrass Confederate: The Headquarters Diary of Edward O. Guerrant.* Baton Rouge, LA, 1999.

Deaderick, Barron. *Forrest: "Wizard of the Saddle."* Memphis, TN, 1960.

Densmore, Benjamin. Family Papers. Minnesota Historical Society.

Deupree, J. E. "Capt. T. J. Kennedy." *CV,* June 1909.

Dew, Charles B. *Apostles of Disunion: Southern Secession Commissioners and the Causes of the Civil War.* Charlottesville,VA, 2001.

Dinkins, James. "The Capture of Fort Pillow." *CV,* December 1925.

———. *Furl That Banner: Personal Recollections and Experiences in the Confederate Army, 1861 to 1865 by an Old Johnnie.* Cincinnati, OH, 1897.

Doak, Henry Melvill. Papers. TSLA.

Donhardt, Gary L. "On the Road to Memphis with General Ulysses S. Grant." *WTHSP* (1997).

Douglass, Frederick. "Address at Twelfth Baptist Church, New York City." *Liberator,* April 29, 1864.

———. *Life and Times of Frederick Douglass. His Early Life as a Slave, His Escape from Bondage, and his Complete History.* New York, 1993.

———. *Narrative of the Life of Frederick Douglass, an American Slave. Written by Himself.* 1845. Reprinted New York, NY, 1968.

Duberman, Martin, ed. *The Antislavery Vanguard: New Essays on the Abolitionists.* Princeton, NJ, 1965.

DuBois, W. E. B. *Black Reconstruction in America 1860–1880.* New York, NY, 1935.

Dunnavant, Robert, Jr. *The Railroad War: N. B. Forrest's 1864 Raid through Northern Alabama and Middle Tennessee.* Athens, AL, 1994.

Dyer Heritage Committee. *A History of the Dyer, Tennessee, Community: The People and their Work.* Dyer, TN, 1986.

Dyer, G. W., and J. T. Moore, eds. *The Tennessee Civil War Veterans Questionnaires* [1915–1922]. 5 Vols. Easley, SC, 1985.

Dyer, W. R. Pocket Diary, 1864. TSLA.

Eden, Horatio. "Memoir." TSLA.

Edmondson, Belle. Diary. SHC/UNCCH.

Edwards, Joseph R. Letters. John Gillette Collection. Michigan Historical Collections. Bentley Historical Library, University of Michigan at Ann Arbor.

Ege, Thompson. *The History and Genealogy of the Ege Family in the U.S., 1728–1911.* Harrisburg, PA, 1911.

Eggleston, George Cary. *A Rebel's Recollections.* 1875. SHC/UNCCH.

Egypt, Ophelia Settle, ed. *Unwritten History of Slavery: Autobiographical Accounts of Negro Ex-Slaves.* Nashville, TN, 1945.

Eisenschiml, Otto, and Ralph Newman. *Eyewitness: The Civil War as We Lived It: The American Iliad.* New York, NY, 1956.

Eldred, Wellington. Letter. University of Missouri Western Historical Manuscript Collection at Rolla.

Eliot, William G. *The Story of Archer Alexander: From Slavery to Freedom: March 30, 1863.* 1899. Reprinted, New York, NY, 1962.

Elkins, Stanley M. *Slavery: A Problem in American Institutional and Intellectual Life.* Chicago, IL, 1967.

Escott, Paul D. *Slavery Remembered: A Record of Twentieth-Century Slave Narratives.* Chapel Hill, NC, 1979.

Evans, Clement A., comp. *Confederate Military History; a Library of Confederate States History, in Twelve Volumes, Written by Distinguished Men of the South.* 1899. Reprinted New York, NY, 1962.

Ewell, Leighton. *History of Coffee County, Tennessee.* Manchester, TN, 1936.

Faulk, W. L. Diary. Vicksburg National Military Park.

Faust, Drew Gilpin, ed. *The Ideology of Slavery: Proslavery Thought in the Antebellum South, 1830–1860.* Baton Rouge, LA, 1981.

Federal Writers Project. *American Life Histories: Manuscripts from the Federal Writers' Project, 1936–1940.* Library of Congress Online.

———. *Cincinnati: A Guide to the Queen City and Its Neighbors.* Cincinnati, OH, 1943.

Fedric, Francis. *Slave Life in Virginia and Kentucky; or, Fifty Years of Slavery in the Southern States of America.* London, 1863. SHC/UNCCH.

Fehrenbacher, Don E. *The Slaveholding Republic: An Account of the United States Government's Relations to Slavery.* New York, NY, 2001.

Fields, Barbara Jean. *Slavery and Freedom on the Middle Ground.* New Haven, CT, 1985.

Filler, Louis. *The Crusade against Slavery; 1830–1860.* New York, NY, 1960.

Fitch, Charles. "Capture of Fort Pillow—Vindication of General Chalmers by a Federal Officer." *SHSP* 7 (1879).

———. "Monthly Report." Charles Fitch file, Personal Papers of Physicians, RG94. NARA.

Fitzgerald, Ross. *A Visit to the Cities and Camps of the Confederate States.* London, 1865.

Fitzhugh, Lester N. "Terry's Texas Rangers, 8th Texas Cavalry, CSA: An Address by Lester N. Fitzhugh before the Houston Civil War Round Table March 21, 1958." OATTR.

Flanders, Edwin P. Papers. Michigan Historical Collections. Bentley Historical Library, University of Michigan at Ann Arbor.

Fletcher, Robert Samuel. *A History of Oberlin College: From Its Foundation through the Civil War*. Vol. 1. New York, NY, 1971.

Fletcher, Samuel. *The History of Company A, Second Illinois Cavalry*. Chicago, IL, 1912.

Foner, Eric. *Reconstruction*. New York, NY, 1988.

Forrest, C. Pogue Public History Institute. "The Civil War in the Jackson Purchase Region of Kentucky: A Survey of Historic Sites and Structures." Unpublished report.

Forrest, Nathan Bedford. "General Forrest's Report of Operations in December, 1863." *SHSP8* (1880): 40–41.

Forrester, Rebel C. *Glory and Tears: Obion County, Tennessee, 1860–1870*. Union City, TN, 1970.

Fort, Dewitt Clinton. Memoir. Transcribed by Greg Newby. Memphis Public Library.

Foster, Francis Smith. *Witnessing Slavery: The Development of Ante-Bellum Slave Narratives*. Madison, WI, 1979.

Franklin (VA) *Repository*, April 27, 1864.

Franklin, John Hope, ed. *The Diary of James T. Ayers: Civil War Recruiter*. Springfield, IL, 1947.

Frazier, E. Franklin. *The Negro Family in the United States*. New York, NY, 1951.

Freehling, William W. *The South versus the South: How Anti-Confederate Southerners Shaped the Course of the Civil War*. New York, NY, 2001.

Freehling, William W., and Craig M. Simpson, eds. *Secession Debated: Georgia's Showdown in 1860*. New York, NY, 1992.

Freemon, Frank R. "The Medical Challenge of Military Operations in the Mississippi Valley during the American Civil War." *Military Medicine* (1992).

Frisby, Derek. "'Remember Fort Pillow!': Politics, Atrocity, Propaganda, and the Evolution of the Hard War." Unpublished manuscript. Courtesy of the author.
———. "'Remember me to everybody': The Civil War Letters of Samuel Henry Eells, Twelfth Michigan Infantry." Unpublished manuscript. Courtesy of the author.

Frost, Griffin. *Prison Journal. Embracing Scenes in Camp, on the March, and in Prisons: Springfield, Gratiot Street, St. Louis, and Macon City, Mo., Fort Delaware. Alton and Camp Douglas, Ill. Camp Morton, Ind., and Camp Chase, Ohio. Also, Scenes and Incidents during a Trip for Exchange, from St. Louis, Mo., via. Philadelphia, Pa., to City Point, Va.* Quincy, IL, 1867.

Fry, Gladys-Marie. *Night Riders in Black Folk History*. Nashville, TN, 1975.

Fuchs, Richard L. *An Unerring Fire: The Massacre at Fort Pillow*. Cranbury, NJ, 1994.

Fulk, Martin. Letter to John Sprankel, December (20?), 1864. www.genealogy.org.

Futch, Ovid. "Prison Life at Andersonville." *CWH*, June 1962.

Gallagher, Gary W., and Alan T. Nolan, eds. *The Myth of the Lost Cause and the Civil War History.* Bloomington, IN, 2000.

Garrison, Webb. *Civil War Curiosities: Strange Stories, Oddities, Events, and Coincidences.* Nashville, TN, 1994.

Gates, Henry Louis, Jr., ed. *The Classic Slave Narratives.* New York, NY, 1987.

Gatlin, Jeffrey. "James D. Rowland—Galvanized Yankee." www.rootsweb.com.

Gauss, John. *Black Flag! Black Flag!: The Battle at Fort Pillow.* Lanham, MD, 2003.

Genovese, Eugene D. *The Political Economy of Slavery: Studies in the Economy and Society of the Slave South.* New York, NY, 1967.

———. *Roll, Jordan, Roll: The World the Slaves Made.* New York, NY, 1976.

Gerrzina, Gretchen Holbrook. *Black London.* New Brunswick, NJ, 1995.

Gilbert, Betty S. "Confederate Dead: 2nd Missouri Cavalry." *Pioneer Times,* January 1985.

Giles, L. B. "Terry's Texas Rangers." OATTR.

Gillette, William. *Retreat from Reconstruction, 1869–1879.* Baton Rouge, LA, 1979.

Gladstone, William A. *United States Colored Troops, 1863–1867.* Gettysburg, PA, 1990.

Glatthaar, Joseph T. *Forged in Battle: The Civil War Alliance of Black Soldiers and White Officers.* New York, NY, 1990.

———. *The March to the Sea and Beyond.* Baton Rouge, LA, 1995.

Golden West Marketing. "Fourth Mississippi Cavalry." www.qwest.org/4thms.htm.

Goldhurst, Richard. *Many Are the Hearts: The Agony and Triumph of Ulysses S. Grant.* New York, NY, 1975.

Goodspeed Publishing Company. *History of Knox and Davies Counties, Indiana.* Chicago, IL, 1886.

———. *History of Lincoln County, Missouri.* Chicago, IL, 1886.

———. *History of Tennessee Illustrated.* www.homepages.rootsweb.com.

———. *Lauderdale County History.* Chicago, IL, 1887.

Goodstein, Anita Shafer. *Nashville, 1780–1860: From Frontier to City.* Gainesville, FL, 1989.

Graf, Leroy P., and Ralph W. Haskins, eds. *The Papers of Andrew Johnson.* Vol. 6. Knoxville, TN, 1983.

Greeley, Horace. *The American Conflict: A History of the Great Rebellion in the United States of America, 1860–1864.* 2 vols. London, 1886.

Green, Nathaniel E. *The Silent Believers.* Louisville, KY, 1972.

Greene, Lorenzo, Gary R. Kremer, and Antonion F. Holland. *Missouri's Black Heritage.* Columbia, MO, 1993.

Grigsby, Melvin. *The Smoked Yank.* Sioux Falls, SD, 1888.

Grimsley, Mark. *The Hard Hand of War: Union Military Policy Toward Southern Civilians, 1861–1865.* New York, NY, 1995.

Gutman, Herbert G. *The Black Family in Slavery and Freedom, 1750–1925.* New York, NY, 1977.

Hamer, Philip M. *Tennessee: A History, 1673–1932.* Vol. 1. New York, NY, 1933.

Hancock, Richard Ransey. *A History of the Second Tennessee Cavalry, with Sketches of First and Seventh Battalion.* Nashville, TN, 1887.

Hardeman County Historical Commission. *Hardeman County Historical Sketches.* Dallas, TX, 1979.

Harding, Lewis A., ed. *History of Decatur County, Indiana.* Indianapolis, IN, 1915. RMC.

Harley, Sharon. *The Timetables of African-American History: A Chronology of the Most Important People and Events in African-American History.* New York, NY, 1995.

Harrison, Absolom. Letter to Susan Allstun Harrison, August 12, 1862. Private Collection.

Hart, Patrick, ed. *The Civil War Diaries of Capt. Noah H. Hart.* www.triadic.com. (Noah Hart was an officer in the 10th Michigan Regiment.)

Harvey, Joseph E. Letter to "Mary," May 31, 1864. Minnesota Historical Society.

Hayden, Hiram C., ed. *American Heroes on Mission Fields: Brief Missionary Biographies.* New York, NY, 1894.

Hearn, Lafcadio. *Occidental Gleanings.* 2 vols. New York, NY, 1925.

Henry County Historical Society. *Pen Sketches: Henry County, Tennessee.* Paris, TN, 1976.

Henry, Robert Selph. *As They Saw Forrest: Some Recollections and Comments of Contemporaries.* Wilmington, NC, 1987.

———. *"First with the Most" Forrest.* Indianapolis, IN, 1944.

———. Papers. Special Collections Department. University Libraries of Virginia Tech.

———. *The Story of the Confederacy.* 1931. Reprinted New York, NY, 1964.

Higginson, Thomas Wentworth. *Army Life in a Black Regiment.* Boston, MA, 1870.

Hill, Robert I. Diary, August 1861–June 1862. www.rootsweb.com/~mscivilw/hilldiary.htm.

Hinton, Thomas C. Letter. *Christian Recorder,* May 21, 1864.

Hirshson, Stanley P. *Farewell to the Bloody Shirt: Northern Republicans and the Southern Negro, 1877–1893.* Chicago, IL, 1968.

Holladay, S. W. Letters. Crutchfield Papers. Gordon Browning Museum of the Carroll County [TN] Historical Society.

Holley, Peggy Scott. "The Seventh Tennessee Volunteer Cavalry: West Tennessee Unionists in Andersonville Prison." *WTHSP* (1988).

Hollis, Elisha Tompkin. "The Diary of Elisha Tompkin Hollis." Edited by William W. Chester. *WTHSP* (1985).

Hopping, James Mason. *Life of Andrew Hull Foote, Rear Admiral United States Navy.* New York, NY, 1874. RMC.

Horwitz, Tony. *Confederates in the Attic: Dispatches from the Unfinished Civil War.* New York, NY, 1998.

Howard, Goldena Roland. *Ralls County.* New London, MO, 1980.

Howard, William T. Letter. Lionel Baxter Collection. University of Mississippi Library.

Howell, Robert Phillip. Memoirs. SHC/UNCCH.

Howlett, R. E. *"Dr. R. E. Howlett in the Civil War. Record of the Service in the Confederate Army of Dr. R. E. Howlett, Otterville, Mo., as Dictated by Him to George Zollinger, September 2, 1916."* Western Historical Manuscript Collection. University of Missouri/State Historical Society of Missouri.

Hubbard, H. R. *Sketches of Ex-Soldiers of the Kansas House of Representatives, Legislature of 1887.* Topeka, KS, 1887.

Hubbard, John Milton. *Notes of a Private*. St. Louis, 1913.

Huch, Ronald K. "The Fort Pillow Massacre: The Aftermath of Paducah." *Journal of the Illinois State Historical Society* (Spring 1973).

Hughs, Louis. *Thirty Years a Slave: From Bondage to Freedom; The Institution of Slavery as Seen on the Plantation and in the Home of the Planter.* 1897. Reprinted Miami, FL, 1969.

Hunter, J. N. "Forrest's Cavalry." *CV,* July 1913.

Hurmence, Belinda, ed. *Before Freedom, When I Just Can Remember.* Winston-Salem, 1989.

———, ed. *My Folks Don't Want Me to Talk about Slavery.* Winston-Salem, NC, 1993.

———. *We Lived in a Little Cabin in the Yard.* Winston-Salem, NC, 1994.

Hurst, Jack. *Nathan Bedford Forrest: A Biography.* New York, NY, 1993.

Ingersoll, Lurton Dunham. *Iowa and the Rebellion: A History of the Troops Furnished by the State of Iowa to the Volunteer Armies of the Union, Which Conquered the Great Southern Rebellion of 1861–5.* Philadelphia, PA, 1867. RMC.

Ingmire, Frances T. *Confederate POWs: Soldiers and Sailors Who Died in Federal Prisons and Military Hospitals in the North.* Washington, DC, 1915.

"J. C. C." *Jewish Messenger,* April 10, May 6, June 2, July 16, September 4, and November 19, 1862; May 6 and July 16, 1863.

Jackson, J. C. Letter to General Thomas Jordan, June 4, 1867. Papers of Leroy Nutt. SHC/UNCCH.

Jacobs, Lee. *The Gray Riders: Stories from the Confederate Cavalry.* Shippensburg, PA, 1999.

Jewell, Edwin Lewis, ed. *New Orleans, Including Biographical Sketches of Its Distinguished Citizens, Together with a Map and General Strangers' Guide.* New Orleans, LA, 1873.

Johnson, Adam Rankin. *The Partisan Rangers of the Confederate States Army.* 1904. Austin, TX, 1995.

Johnson, Clifton H., ed. *God Struck Me Dead: Voices of Ex-Slaves.* Cleveland, OH, 1969.

Johnson, Isaac. *Slavery Days in Old Kentucky.* 1901. Reprinted Canton, NY, 1994.

Johnson, W. F. *History of Cooper County, Missouri.* Topeka, KS, 1919.

Johnston, John. "Civil War Recollection." TSLA.

———. Diaries and Memoirs, 1860–65. TSLA.

———. "Forrest's March Out of West Tennessee, December 1863, Recollections of a Private." TSLA.

Joint Committee on the Conduct of the War [Wade]. *Report of the Joint Committee on the Conduct of the War at the Second Session, Thirty-eighth Congress.* Washington, DC, 1865.

Jones, J. B. *A Rebel War Clerk's Diary at the Confederate States Capital.* 2 vols. Philadelphia, PA, 1866.

Jones, Jacqueline. *Labor of Love, Labor of Sorrow: Black Women, Work, and the Family, from Slavery to the Present.* New York, NY, 1986.

Jordan, Ervin L., Jr. *Black Confederates and Afro-Yankees in Civil War Virginia.* Charlottesville, VA, 1995.

Jordan, Thomas, and J. P. Pryor. *The Campaigns of General Nathan Bedford Forrest, and of Forrest's Cavalry.* 1868. New York, NY, 1996.

Josyph, Peter, ed. *The Wounded River: The Civil War Letters of John Nance Lauderdale, M.D.* East Lansing, MI, 1993.

Kane, Joseph Nathan. *The American Counties: Origins of Names, Dates of Creation and Organization, Area, Population, Historical Data, and Published Sources.* 3rd ed. Metuchen, NJ, 1972.

Kaplan, Justin. *Mr. Clemens and Mark Twain.* New York, NY, 1966.

Katz, William Loren, comp. *Flight from the Devil: Six Slave Narratives.* Trenton, NJ, 1996.

Kelley, William Darrah. *Replies of the Hon. William D. Kelley to George Northrop, Esq., in the Joint Debate in the Fourth Congressional District.* Philadelphia, PA, 1864.

Kempshaw, John. Letter. TSLA.

Khan, Lurey. *One Day, Levin . . . He Be Free: William Still and the Underground Railroad.* New York, NY, 1972.

King, Stephen Lynn, comp. *History and Biographical Sketches of the 46th Tennessee Infantry C.S.A.: Henry County, Tennessee.* Bowling Green, KY, 1992.

Kirke, Edmund. *Down in Tennessee.* 1864. Westport, CT, 1970.

Kirkland, Frazar. *The Pictorial Book of Anecdotes and Incidents of the War of the Rebellion, Civil, Military, Naval and Domestic: Embracing the Most Brilliant and Remarkable Anecdotal Events of the Great Conflict in the United States.* Hartford, CT, 1866.

Knox, George L. *Slave and Freeman: The Autobiography of George L. Knox.* Edited by Willard B. Gatewood, Jr. Lexington, KY, 1979.

Kraditor, Aileen S. *Means and Ends in American Abolitionism: Garrison and His Critics on Strategy and Tactics, 1834–1850.* Chicago, IL, 1989.

Kryder, George. Papers. Center for Archival Collections. Bowling Green State University.

Kunhardt, Dorothy Meserve, and Philip B. Kunhardt. *Mathew Brady and His World.* Alexandria, VA, 1977.

Lamon, Lester C. *Blacks in Tennessee, 1791–1970.* Knoxville, TN, 1993.

Lash, Jeffrey N. "Stephen Augustus Hurlbut: A Military and Diplomatic Politician: 1815–1882." Ph.D. diss., Kent University, 1980.

Lauderdale County, Tennessee. Will Books. Lauderdale County Courthouse.

Lee, George R. *Slavery North of St. Louis.* Canton, MO, 2000.

Lee, Stephen D. "Tribute to Gen. Bedford Forrest." *CV,* June 1903.

Lee-Davis UDC Historical Society. *Families and History of Gibson County, Tennessee, to 1989.* Milan, TN, 1989.

Lester, Julius. *To Be a Slave.* New York, NY, 1968.

Levens, Henry C., and Nathaniel M. Drake. *A History of Cooper County, Missouri: From the First Visit by White Men, in February 1804, to the 5th day of July 1876.* St. Louis, MO, 1876.

Lewis Publishing Company. *Memorial and Biographical History of the Counties of Fresno, Tulare, and Kern, California.* Chicago, IL, n.d., ca. 1892.

Lindsley, John B. *Military Annals of Tennessee: Confederate—First Series.* Nashville, TN, 1886.

Litton, Gaston. *History of Oklahoma at the Golden Anniversary of Statehood.* 4 vols. New York, NY, 1957.

Litwack, Leon F. *Been in the Storm So Long: The Aftermath of Slavery.* New York, NY, 1980.

———. *North of Slavery.* Chicago, IL, 1961.

Lockett, James D. "The Lynching Massacre of Black and White Soldiers at Fort Pillow, Tennessee, April 12, 1864." *Western Journal of Black Studies* (Summer 1998).

Lockhart, Margaret Morphis. "Memories of the Civil War." *South Reporter,* January 8, 1942.

Logan, S. H. "No Massacre by Forrest at Fort Pillow Says One Who Rode with Him: Interview with Robert Bufferd [Bufford]." *Nashville Commercial Appeal,* September 2, 1934.

Lonn, Ella. *Desertion during the Civil War.* New York, NY, 1928.

Louisiana State. *Constitutional Convention, 1864.* New Orleans, LA, 1864.

Love, Cyrus. Letters. Tennessee Christian University.

Lovett, Bobby L., ed. *The Afro-American History of Nashville, Tennessee, 1870–1930.* Nashville, TN, 1981.

Lovett, Bobby L. "The West Tennessee Colored Troops in Civil War Combat." *WTHSP* (1980).

Lovett, Bobby L., and Linda T. Wynn, eds. *Profiles of African Americans in Tennessee.* Nashville, TN, 1996.

Lowell [Massachusetts] *Daily Courier,* April 30, 1864.

Lowry, Thomas. Index to Civil War Court-martial Records. NARA.

———. *The Story the Soldiers Wouldn't Tell: Sex in the Civil War.* Mechanicsburg, PA, 1994.

Lufkin, Charles L. "Not Heard From since April 12, 1864: The Thirteenth Tennessee Cavalry, U.S.A." *THQ* (Summer 1986).

———. "West Tennessee Unionists in the Civil War: A Hawkins Family Letter." *THQ* (Spring 1987).

Lyman, C. P. Letters and Diary. Private Collection.

Lyons, Mark. Letters to Amelia Horsler, February 1861–April 10, 1865. Alabama Department of Archives and History.

M'cann, James M. "The Song of Forrest's Men." *CV,* July 1908.

Macaluso, Gregory J. *The Fort Pillow Massacre: The Reason Why.* New York, NY, 1989.

MacDonald, Ward. "Sensations in the Kentucky Backwoods." *CV,* May 1895.

MacMillan, Isaac. Letter. Indiana State Library. RMC.

Macmurphy, G. L. Diary. OATTR.

Magness, Perre. *Past Times: Stories of Early Memphis.* Memphis, TN, 1994.

Main, Beverly M. DuBose. Letter to Robert C. Mainfort, Jr., September 15, 1978. RMC.

Main, Edward M. *The Story of the Marches, Battles, and Incidents of the Third United States Cavalry: A Fighting Regiment in the War of the Rebellion, 1861–5.* New Orleans, LA, 1908.

Mainfort, Robert. Letter. *Memphis Commercial Appeal,* September 14, 1979.

Mainfort, Robert C. *Archaeological Investigations at Fort Pillow State Historic Area, 1976–1978.* Nashville, TN, 1980.

Mainfort, Robert C., Jr. "A Folk Art Map of Fort Pillow." *WTHSP* (1986).

Mainfort, Robert C., Jr., and Patricia E. Coats, ed. "Soldiering at Fort Pillow, 1862–1864: An Excerpt from the Civil War Memoirs of Addison Sleeth." *WTHSP* (1982).

Maness, Lonnie E. "The Civil War: An Historiographical Essay—The Importance of the West and Tennessee." *WTHSP* (1990).

———. "The Fort Pillow Massacre: Fact or Fiction." *THQ* (1986).

———. "Fort Pillow under Confederate and Union Control." *WTHSP* (1984).

———. "A Ruse That Worked: The Capture of Union City in 1864." *WTHSP* (1976).

———. *An Untutored Genius: The Military Career of General Nathan Bedford Forrest.* Oxford, MS, 1990.

Marrs, Elijah P. *Life and History of Elijah P. Marrs.* Louisville, 1885.

Marshall, E. H. *History of Obion County.* Union City, TN, 1941.

Marvel, William. *Andersonville: The Last Depot.* Chapel Hill, NC, 1994.

Maslowski, Peter. *Treason Must Be Made Odious: Military Occupation and Wartime Reconstruction in Nashville, Tennessee, 1862–65.* Millwood, NY, 1978.

Mason City [IA] *Cerro Gordo Republican.* December 24, 1862; January 23 and 27, May 25, June 22, 1863.

Mathes, J. Harvey. *General Forrest.* New York, NY, 1902.

———. *The Old Guard in Gray.* Memphis, TN, 1899.

Matlock, Philip N. Letters. TSLA.

Maury, Dabney Herndon. *Recollections of a Virginian in the Mexican, Indian, and Civil Wars.* 1894. Electronic ed., 1998. SHC/UNCCH.

Mays, William Tapley. "Autobiographical Sketch of the Life of William Tapley Mays." www.rootsqeb.com/~tncarrol.

McAdams, Benton. *Rebels at Rock Island: The Story of a Civil War Prison.* DeKalb, IL, 2000.

McCandless, Perry. *A History of Missouri: Volume II, 1820 to 1860.* Columbia, MO, 1972.

McCorkle, Anna Leigh. *Tales of Old Whitehaven.* Memphis, TN, 1967.

McElroy, John. *Andersonville: A Story of Rebel Military Prisons.* Toledo, OH, 1879.

McFeely, William S. *Frederick Douglass.* New York, NY, 1991.

McIlwaine, Shields. *Memphis Down in Dixie.* New York, NY, 1948.

McKay, John. "Final Report of the American Freedman's Inquiry Commission: June 22, 1864." Records of the U.S. Senate, 38th Congress, NARA.

McLeary, Andrew C. *Humorous Incidents of the Civil War.* Privately published, n.d., ca. 1902.

McPherson, James M. *The Abolitionist Legacy from Reconstruction to the NAACP.* Princeton, NJ, 1975.

———. *The Battle Cry of Freedom: The Civil War Era.* New York, NY, 1988.

———. *The Negro's Civil War: How American Negroes Felt and Acted during the War for the Union.* New York, NY, 1965.

McReynolds, Edwin C. *Missouri: A History of the Crossroads State.* Norman, OK, 1962.

Mellon, James, ed. *Bullwhip Days: The Slaves Remember (An Oral History).* New York, NY, 1988.

Melton, E. J. *History of Cooper County, Missouri*. Columbia, MO, 1937.

Memphis Commercial Appeal, August 23, 1851; June 19, 1879; May 17, 1905; January 16 and February 29, 1929; July 13, 1940; February 15, 1974; December 10, 1975.

Memphis Daily Appeal (printed in Atlanta), May 2, 1864.

Memphis Daily Appeal (printed in Memphis), October 30, 1877.

Memphis News-Scimitar, April 30 and May 17, 1905.

Metcalfe, Frederick Augustus. Papers. Archives and Library Division. Mississippi Department of Archives and History.

Michigan, State of. *The Debates and Proceedings of the Constitutional Convention of the State of Michigan (1867)*. Lansing, MI, 1867.

Miles, Jim. *A River Unvexed: A History and Tour Guide of the Campaign for the Mississippi River*. Nashville, TN, 1994.

Miller, M. A. "Under Sentence of Death." *CV,* April 1905.

Miller, Randall M., ed. *"Dear Master": Letters of a Slave Family*. Ithaca, NY, 1878.

Mills, Theodore A. "Fort Pillow." Ca. 1931. RMC.

Monroe, Mosby. Parsons Papers, 1861–1862. Duke University Library.

Montgomery, Frank Alexander. *Reminiscences of a Mississippian in Peace and War*. Cincinnati, OH, 1901.

Moore, Frank. *Anecdotes, Poetry, and Incidents of the War: North and South, 1860–1865; Collected and Arranged by Frank Moore*. New York, NY, 1867.

———, ed. *The Rebellion Record: A Diary of American Events with Documents, Narratives, Illustrative Incidents, Poetry, Etc.* Vol. 8. New York, NY, 1865.

———. *Women of the War; Their Heroism and Self-Sacrifice*. Chicago, IL, 1866.

Moore, Kenneth Bancroft. "Fort Pillow, Forrest, and the United States Colored Troops in 1864." *THQ* (Summer 1995).

Morgan, Mrs. Irby. *How It Was; Four Years among the Rebels*. Nashville, TN, 1892.

Morison, Samuel Eliot. *The Oxford History of the American People*. New York, NY, 1965.

Morris, Roy, Jr. "The Committee on the Conduct of the War Was as Much a Foe of Wayward Union Generals as It Was of Confederates." *America's Civil War,* November 2000.

———. "Fort Pillow: Massacre or Madness?" *America's Civil War,* November 2000.

Morris, William. "The Tennessee River Voyages of U.S.S. *Peosta*." www.hardinhistory. com

Morton, John Watson. *The Artillery of Nathan Bedford Forrest's Cavalry*. 1909. Reprinted Marietta, GA, 1995.

Moses, Jefferson. "The Memoirs, Diary, and Life of Private Jefferson Moses, Company G, 93rd Illinois Volunteers." www.ioweb.com.

Musick, Michael. "Sixth Virginia Cavalry." Virginia Regimental Histories Series, 1990.

National Historical Company. *History of Howard and Cooper Counties, Missouri*. St. Louis, MO, 1883.

Ndilei, David. *Extinguish the Flames of Racial Prejudice*. Yellville, AR, 1996.

New York Herald, June 11, 1862; January 12, 1863; October 5, 1863; January 6, April 14, 16–17, 19, 21, 24, and 26, and May 3, 1864; May 23, 1865.

New York Journal of Commerce, undated clipping [April 1864?].

New York Times, October 31, 1877.

Nevin, David. *Sherman's March: Atlanta to the Sea*. New York, NY, 1986.

Newcastle (UK) Chronicle in *Christian Recorder*, July 30, 1864.

Nicolay, John G., and John Hay. *Abraham Lincoln: A History*. 10 vols. New York, NY, 1890.

Nutt, Leroy. Papers. SHC/UNCCH.

O'Connor, Mrs. T. P. *My Beloved South*. 1914. SHC/UNCCH.

Oates, Stephen B. *The Fires of Jubilee: Nat Turner's Fierce Rebellion*. New York, NY, 1975.

Oberlin College Alumni Files.

Olsen, Sue. *Memphis Commercial Appeal*, February 4, 1983.

Osofsky, Gilbert, ed. *Puttin' On Ole Massa: The Slavery Narratives of Henry Bibb, William Wells Brown, and Solomon Northrup*. New York, NY, 1969.

Otey, Mercer. "The Story of Our Great War." *CV*, March 1901.

Owensboro Monitor, April 20, August 31, and September 14, 1864.

Painter, Nell Irvin. *Exodusters: Black Migration to Kansas after Reconstruction*. New York, NY, 1992.

Pakenham, Thomas. *The Scramble for Africa, 1876–1912*. New York, NY, 1991.

Parker, Albert F. *Lauderdale County Enterprise*, March 8, 1978.

Patterson, Caleb Perry. *The Negro in Tennessee, 1790–1865*. 1941. Reprinted Spartanburg, S.C., 1974.

Patterson, Delicia Ann. Letter. www.rootsweb.com.

Payne, James E. "A Brave Missouri Boy." *CV*, September–October 1932.

Payne, W. O. *History of Story County, Iowa*. Chicago, IL, 1911.

Perdue, Charles L., Thomas E. Barden, and Robert K. Phillips, eds. *Weevils in the Wheat: Interviews with Virginia Ex-Slaves*. Charlottesville, VA, 1976.

Peters, H. N. Letter to Margaret Treueworthy, April 23, 1862. Special Collections, University of Arkansas Libraries.

Peters, Kate Johnson, ed. *Lauderdale County from Earliest Times: An Intimate and Informal Account of the Towns and Communities, Its Families and Famous Individuals*. Ripley, TN, 1957.

Phillips, Margaret I. *The Governors of Tennessee*. Gretna, TN, 1998.

Pickard, Kate E. R. *The Kidnapped and the Ransomed: Being the Personal Recollections of Peter Still and his wife "Vina," after Forty Years of Slavery*. Syracuse, NY, 1856.

Pike, [Gustavus Dorman]. *The Jubilee Singers, and their Campaign for Twenty Thousand Dollars*. Boston, MA, 1873.

Polley, J. B. "Texans Foraging for Christmas." *CV*, December 1895.

Pomeroy, Dan E., ed. "A Letter of Account: Sergeant Clark Tells of the Fort Pillow Massacre." *Civil War Times Illustrated*, June 1885.

Post, Lydia Minturn, Mrs., ed. *Soldiers' Letters, from Camps, Battle-field and Prison*. New York, NY, 1865.

Potter, Hugh O. *History of Owensboro and Davies County, Kentucky*. Owensboro, KY, n.d., ca. 1974.

Powers, Auburn. "Juno: aka 'Pinch': Henderson County, Tennessee." 1930. Parker's Crossroads Battlefield Association, Memphis (TN).

Pratt, Fletcher. *The Civil War on Western Waters*. New York, NY, 1956.

Proctor, Henry Hugh. *Between Black and White*. Boston, MA, 1925.

Puckett, Newbell Niles. *Black Names in America.* Boston, MA, 1975.

Quarles, Benjamin. *The Negro in the Civil War.* New York, NY, 1989.

Rabb, J. W. "The Civil War Letters of J. W. Rabb." OATTR.

Ransom, John. *John Ransom's Andersonville Diary.* New York, NY, 1988.

Rawlins, Richard, ed. *Black Southerners in Gray: Essays on Afro-Americans in Confederate Armies.* Murfreesboro, TN, 1994.

Redford, Dorothy Spruill, and Michael D'Orso. *Somerset Homecoming: Recovering a Lost Heritage.* New York, NY, 1988.

Rees, William. Letters. Rees Genealogy Homepage. www.members.aol.com/Shelveston/reeslets.html.

Reid, Whitelaw. *After the War: A Southern Tour.* New York, NY, 1866.

Rennolds, Edwin H. *A History of the Henry County Commands.* 1904. Reprinted Kennesaw, GA, 1961.

Richards, Charles H. "The 'Arme Blanche' in Tennessee: The Battle of Middleburg." *WTHSP* (1991).

Richardson, Joe M. *Christian Reconstruction: The American Missionary Association and Southern Blacks, 1861–1890.* Athens, GA, 1986.

Robbins, Faye Wellborn. *World-within-a-World: Black Nashville, 1880–1915.* Ann Arbor, MI, 1980.

Robertson, John E. L. "Paducah: Origins to Second Class." *Register of the Kentucky Historical Society* (1968).

Robinson, Charley. Fort Pillow 'Massacre': Observations of a Minnesotan." Edited by George Bodnia. *Minnesota History* (Spring 1873).

———. Letter. Mortimer Robinson and Family Papers (P352), Minnesota Historical Society.

Robinson, W. H. *From Log Cabin to the Pulpit, or Fifteen Years of Slavery.* Eau Claire, WI, 1913.

Robson, John S. *How a One-Legged Rebel Lives: Reminiscences of the Civil War; The Story of the Campaigns of Stonewall Jackson, as Told by a High Private in the "Foot Cavalry"; From Alleghany Mountain to Chancellorsville; with the Complete Regimental Rosters of Both the Great Armies at Gettysburg.* Richmond, VA, 1876. SHC/UNCCH.

Rogers, E. G. "Concerning the Nathan Bedford Forrest Legend." *Tennessee Folklore Society Bulletin,* September 1938.

Roman, Alfred. *The Military Operations of General Beauregard in the War Between the States, 1861–1865: Including a Brief Personal Sketch and a Narrative of Services in the War with Mexico, 1846–8.* New York, NY, 1884.

Ross, Fitzgerald. *A Visit to the Cities and Camps of the Confederate States.* London, 1865.

Royster, Charles. "Slaver, General, Klansman." *Atlantic Monthly,* May 1993.

Russ, Lee H. "Firing a Captured Cannon at Fort Pillow." *CV.* June 1904.

Rutling, Thomas. *Tom: An Autobiography.* London, 1907.

Ryan, John. "Reminiscences." Clarke Historical Library, University of Michigan.

Sage, Leland L. *A History of Iowa.* Ames, IA, 1974. RMC.

Sandel, Matthew. "Tilting at Statues." *Southern Partisan* (Summer 1988).

Saunders, Hubert. Papers, 1862–1865. Special Collections. Duke University Library.

Sayers, Althea. "Fort Pillow: What the Federal Government Didn't Tell." www
.civilwarweb.com.

Scarborough, Dorothy. *On the Trail of Negro Folk-Songs.* Hatboro, PA, 1963.

Scharf, J. Thomas. *History of the Confederate States Navy.* New York, NY, 1996.

Schweninger, Loren, ed. *From Tennessee Slave to St. Louis Entrepreneur: The Auto-biography of James Thomas.* Columbia, MO, 1984.

———. *James T. Rapier and Reconstruction.* Chicago, IL, 1978.

Scott, John, ed. *Story of the Thirty Second Iowa Infantry Volunteers.* Nevada, IA, 1896.

Scott, Samuel W., and Samuel P. Angel. *History of the Thirteenth Regiment, Tennessee Volunteer Cavalry, U.S.A.* Philadelphia, PA, 1903.

Sessel, Edwin H./"Cousin": August 14, 1862, in "Our Evacuation of Fort Pillow." *CV,* January 1898.

Sheppard, Eric William. *Bedford Forrest: The Confederacy's Greatest Cavalryman.* New York, NY, 1930.

Sherman, William T. *Memoirs of William T. Sherman.* Vol. 2. New York, NY, 1875.

Sherril, Charles A., ed. *Tennessee's Confederate Widows and Their Families.* Cleveland, TN, 1992.

Shiflit, Hillory. Letters. www.geocities.com.

Sifakis, Stewart. *Compendium of the Confederate Armies: Kentucky, Maryland, Missouri, the Confederate Units, and the Indian Units.* New York, NY, 1995.

———. *Who Was Who in the Civil War.* New York, NY, 1988.

Silver, James W., ed. *Mississippi in the Confederacy as Seen in Retrospect.* Baton Rouge, LA, 1961.

Simon, John Y., ed. *The Papers of Ulysses S. Grant.* Vol. 10, January 1–May 31, 1864. Carbondale, IL, 1998.

Sink, Elijah. Memoirs. Indiana State Library.

Stanchak, John E. "A Legacy of Controversy: Fort Pillow Still Stands." *Civil War Times Illustrated,* September–October 1993.

Starr, Stephen Z.. *The Union Cavalry in the Civil War: The War in the West 1861–1865.* Vol. 3. Baton Rouge, LA, 1985.

Stearns, Charles. *The Black Man of the South, and the Rebels.* 1872. Reprinted New York, NY, 1969.

Stearns, Ezra. Papers. Schoff Civil War Collection. William L. Clements Library, University of Michigan.

Stevenson, William G. *Thirteen Months in the Rebel Army.* New York, NY, 1862.

Stewart, Charles S. Letters. Archival Reference Librarian, Alabama Department of Archives and History.

Stokes, David M. "Feared and Revered: Bedford Forrest, Fort Pillow, and the Western Theater of the Civil War: A Bibliography." *Bulletin of Bibliography* (1998).

Stonesifer, Roy P. "Gideon J. Pillow: A Study in Egotism." *THQ* (1966).

Story County [IA] *Herald & Roland Record.* N.d., 1922. www.iowa-counties.com.

Sullivan, Marge Nichols, ed. *My Folks and the Civil War.* Topeka, KS, 1994.

Tadman, Michael. *Speculators and Slaves: Masters, Traders, and Slaves in the Old South.* Madison, WI, 1996.

Tap, Bruce. *Over Lincoln's Shoulder: The Committee on the Conduct of the War.* Lawrence, KS, 1998.

———. "These Devils Are Not Fit to Live on God's Earth: War Crimes and the Committee on the Conduct of the War." *CWH,* June 1996.

Taylor, Altrutheus A. "Fisk University and the Nashville Community, 1866–1900." *The Journal of Negro History,* April 1854.

———. *The Negro in Tennessee, 1865–1880.* Washington, DC, 1941.

Taylor, Jerome G. "Upper-Class Violence in Nineteenth-Century Tennessee." *WTHSP* (1980).

Taylor, Richard. *Destruction and Reconstruction: Personal Experiences of the Late War.* New York, NY, 1879.

Taylor, Susie King. *A Black Woman's Civil War Memoirs.* Princeton, NJ, 1988.

Tennessee Department of Conservation. *Master Plan Report: Fort Pillow: State Historic Area.* Nashville, TN, 1975.

Tennessee, State of. Civil War (Federal) Collection (TSLA).

Terrell, Kate Scurry. "Terry's Texas Rangers." OATTR.

Thomas, Hugh. *The Slave Trade.* New York, NY, 1998.

Thornbrough, Emma Lou. *Indiana in the Civil War Era. Vol. 3 of The History of Indiana.* Indianapolis, IN, 1965.

Tilly, Belle Baird. "Aspects of Social and Economic Life in West Tennessee before the Civil War." Ph.D. diss., Memphis State University, 1974.

———. "The Spirit of Improvement: Reformism and Slavery in West Tennessee." *WTHSP* (1974).

TNGenWeb Project. www.rootsweb.com/~tnlauder/.

Toney, Marcus Bearden. Diaries. TSLA.

Trudeau, Noah Andre. "Kill the Last Damn One of Them." *MHQ: The Quarterly of Military History* (1996).

———. *Like Men of War: Black Troops in the Civil War, 1862–1865.* Boston, MA, 1998.

Tubbs, William B. "A Bibliography of Illinois Civil War Regimental Sources in the Illinois State Historical Library." *Illinois Historical Journal* (Autumn and Winter 1994).

Turley, Thomas B. Letter. *CV,* July 1899.

Turner, William Bruce. *History of Maury County, Tennessee.* Nashville, TN, 1955.

Turnure, F. P. "Letter to Mrs. H. Green: Fulton Tenn Apr. 9, [1863]." Orrin Elmore Stanley Papers. University of Oregon Library.

United Daughters of the Confederacy [Missouri Division]. *Reminiscences of the Women of Missouri during the Sixties, Gathered, Compiled, and Published by Missouri Division, United Daughters of the Confederacy.* Jefferson City, MO, 1913.

United Daughters of the Confederacy [Nashville Division]. *Tennessee C.S.A.* Nashville, TN, 1998.

United States Army. *Proceedings of a Military Commission Convened at St. Louis, Mo. [October 16, 1864], by Virtue of [Special Orders 287].* Special Collections Division, University of Arkansas Libraries.

United States Census Bureau. Censuses for 1850, 1860, 1870. (Microfilm.) Washington, DC.

United States Congress. *Journal of the House of Representatives of the United States, 1789–1873*. Washington, DC, 1873.

United States Congress. *Journal of the Senate of the United States of America, 1789–1873*. Washington, DC, 1873.

United States Congress. *Ku Klux Conspiracy: Report of the Joint Select Committee to Inquire into the Condition of Affairs in the Late Insurrectionary States*. Washington, DC, 1872.

United States Library of Congress. *Recording of Slave Narratives and Related Materials in the Archive of Folk Song: Reference Tapes*. Washington, DC, 1981.

Van Vlack, A. A. "Cahawba Prison, Ala.: A Glimpse of Life in a Rebel Prison." Bentley Historical Library, University of Michigan at Ann Arbor.

Wallace, Frances. "A Trip to Dixie: Diary, March 19–August 25, 1864." Electronic edition 1998 at SHC/UNCCH.

Walthall, George. Letters. Lionel Baxter Collection. Department of Archives and Special Collections, University of Mississippi.

Walvin, James. *Questioning Slavery*. London, 1996.

Ward, Douglas Turner, in Thomas, Wendi C., "Forrest Descendant Has a Different Take." Memphis *Commercial Appeal*, August 14, 2005.

Ward, Geoffrey C., with Ric Burns and Ken Burns. *The Civil War: An Illustrated History*. New York, NY, 1990.

Warner, Ezra J. *Generals in Blue: Lives of the Union Commanders*. New Orleans, LA, 1964.

Warner, Liberty. Papers. Web Center for Archival Collections. Bowling Green State University.

Washburn, Charles A. *The History of Paraguay, with Notes of Personal Observations and Reminiscences of Diplomacy*. 2 vols. Reprinted New York, NY, 1973.

Washington Republican, undated clipping [1864].

Watkins, Cornelia Anderson. "Diary." Typescript at Fort Pillow Archives, Fort Pillow, TN. RMC.

Watterson-Marcosson, Isaac F. *Marse Henry—A Biography of Henry Watterson*. New York, NY, 1951.

Weatherred, John. "Wartime Diary of John Weatherred." www.jackmasters.net

Welsh, Jack D. *Medical Histories of Confederate Generals*. Kent, OH, 1995.

West Central Missouri Genealogical Society and Library. "Lafayette County Confederate Cemetery." *Prairie Gleaner*, March 1975.

Wharton, Vernon Lane. *The Negro in Mississippi, 1865–1890*. New York, NY, 1965.

Whetstone, Rea. "History of Knoxville College." N.d. Westminster College Archives. McGill Library.

White, Cora. "Stirring Up the Yankees." Edited by Bobby J. Mitchell. *The Gray Ghost*, July–August 1999.

Whitesell, Hunter B. "Military Operations in the Jackson Purchase Area of Kentucky, 1862–1865." *Register of Kentucky Historical Society* (1966).

Wickliffe-Preston Family Papers. University of Kentucky Special Collections and Archives.

Wiemholt, Mary, comp. *Memorabilia of Cooper County* [MO], Dallas, TX, c. 1990.

Wiley, Bell Irvin. *The Plain People of the Confederacy*. Chicago, IL, 1963.

————. *Southern Negroes, 1861–1865.* 1938. Reprinted New Haven, CT, 1965.

Williams, Edward F. III. *Confederate Victories at Fort Pillow.* Memphis, TN, 1984.

————. "Early Memphis and Its River Rivals: Fulton, Randolph, and Fort Pickering." *WTHSP* (1968).

Williams, Eric. *Capitalism and Slavery.* 1944. Reprinted Chapel Hill, NC, 1994.

Williams, George W. *A History of the Negro Troops in the War of the Rebellion, 1861–1865, preceded by a Review of the Military Services of Negroes in Ancient and Modern Times.* New York, NY, 1888.

Williams, Harry. "Benjamin F. Wade and the Atrocity Propaganda of the Civil War." *Ohio State Archaeological and Historical Quarterly,* January 1939.

Williams, James. *Life and Adventures of James Williams, a Fugitive Slave.* San Francisco, CA, 1873.

Williams, Walter, ed. *A History of Northeast Missouri.* Chicago, IL, 1913.

Williamson, Alice. Diary. Special Collections Library. Duke Univeristy. www .scriptorium.lib.duke.edu/williamson.

Willoughby, Earl. "Bayonets and Bloomers: The Secret Life of Mollie Pittman," "Church Grove, Camp Bell and Civil War," "A Cold Blue Wind: Waring's Brigade Sweeps through Dyer County in 1864," "Colonel Dawson and the Shadow War," "Gunboats and Gumbo: The First Six Months of 1862," "Rev. George Washington Harris: The Unordained Bishop of West Tennessee," "Under the Black Flag." *Dyersburg* [TN] *State Gazette.* www.stategazette.com/ scripts/search/topbox.php?query=Willoughby&x=5&y=2.

Wills, Brian Steel. *A Battle from the Start: The Life of Nathan Bedford Forrest.* New York, NY, 1992.

Wilson, Joseph T. *The Black Phalanx.* Hartford, CT, 1888.

Wilson, Peggy Stephenson, ed. *Nolensville, 1797–1987: Reflections of a Tennessee Town.* Nashville, TN, 1989.

Wilson, Mrs. Robert H. Letter. *Liberator,* June 10, 1864.

Winn, Ralph B., ed. *A Concise Lincoln Dictionary: Thoughts and Statements.* New York, NY, 1959.

Wish, Harvey, ed. *Slavery in the South.* New York, NY, 1964.

Wood, Betty. *The Origins of American Slavery: Freedom and Bondage in the English Colonies.* New York, NY, 1997.

Woodson, Carter G., ed. *Free Negro Owners of Slaves in the United States in 1830 Together with Absentee Ownership of Slaves in the United States in 1830.* 1924. New York, NY, 1968.

Woodward, C. Vann. *The Burden of Southern History.* New York, NY, 1968.

Wooster, Ralph A. "With the Confederate Cavalry in the West: The Civil War Experiences of Isaac Dunbar Affleck." *Southwestern Historical Quarterly,* July 1979.

Worley, William. Diary. Indiana State Library.

Worthing, John P. Letters. McCain Library and Archives. University of Southern Mississippi.

Wright, Louise Wigfall. *A Southern Girl in '61: The War-Time Memories of a Confederate Senator's Daughter.* New York, NY, 1905. SHC/UNCCH.

Wright, Marcus J. *Tennessee in the War, 1861–1865.* New York, NY, 1908.

Wubben, Hubert H. *Civil War Iowa and the Copperhead Movement.* Ames, IA, 1980.

Wyeth, John Allan. *That Devil Forrest: Life of General Nathan Bedford Forrest*. New York, NY, 1959.

————. *With Sabre and Scalpel: The Autobiography of a Soldier and Surgeon*. New York, NY, 1914.

Zack, Naomi. *Race and Mixed Race*. Philadelphia, PA, 1993.

Select Records Reviewed at the National Archives and Records Administration (Washington, DC)

Adjutant General's Office: "Generals' Papers and Books: Stephen Augustus Hurlbut: 1861–1865"

Book Records of the 11th USCT Infantry

Bureau of Refugees, Freedmen, and Abandoned Lands

Carded United States Army Medical Records

Chalmers Papers

Collections of the Adjutant General's Office: 1780s–1917; Bounty and Claims Division: 1862–1878 and Records of Slave Claims Commissions: 1864–1868 for Tennessee

Department of the Cumberland and Division and Department of the Tennessee, 1862–1870: Organization of U.S. Colored Troops: Records of Capt. R. D. Mussey, 1863–1864

Eddy, Colonel A. R. *History of Forts Pickering and Pillow, Tennessee*. Adjutant General's Office. NARA

Final Report of the American Freedmen's Inquiry Commission: June 22, 1864

Fitch, [Charles]. "Monthly Report": April 30, 1864, in Regimental Papers of the 11th USCI: Letters Received, RG94, Records of the Adjutant General's Office, 1780's–1917. NARA

General and Special Orders: Organization of Colored Troops

Generals' Papers (USA and CSA)

Letters Received, Ser. 360, Colored Troops Division, Adjutant General's Office. NARA

Inspection Report of Colored Troops, Department of the Cumberland

Letter Book of Brigadier General Lorenzo Thomas

Letter Books of Officers of the United States Navy at Sea, March 1778–July 1908

Office of Inspector General, Department of Tennessee: Letters Sent and Received

List of Prisoners Cap'd by Major General Forrest at Fort Pillow, & in Tennessee—Deserters, Men of Bad Characters, Flags &c. &c.

List of Wounded Received from the Rebels at Fort Pillow

Fawn Log

Medical Records of the 13th Tennessee Cavalry (USA)

Memphis Subdistrict of the Bureau of Refugees Military Departments, Letters Sent, Brig. Gen. James R. Chalmers's Brigade—February 1862–March 1863

Naval Records Collection of the Office of Naval Records and Library: Records of Citizens of the United States: March 1778–July 1908

Office of the Adjutant General Volunteer Service Branch

Office of the Provost Marshal, District West Tennessee

Papers of General E. A. Paine, Records of the Adjutant General's Office, 1780–1912

Pension Files for the 1st Alabama Siege Artillery, the 2nd USCLA, the 6th USCHA, the 11th USCI, the 6th and 13th Tennessee Cavalry (USA)

Prisoners in Military Prison in Fort Pickering Probably Detained without Sufficient Cause

Quartermaster General Claims

Ration Commutation Claims for the 2nd USCLA, 6th USCHA, 11th USCI and 13th Tennessee Cavalry

Records of Captain Robert D. Mussey, 1863–1864, Department of the Cumberland and Department of the Tennessee: 1862–1870, Organization of Colored Troops

Records of the 16th Army Corps

Records of the 1st Alabama Siege Artillery (Colored), the 2nd USCLA, the 6th USCHA, the 11th USCI, and the 13th (14th) Tennessee Cavalry

Records of the Adjutant General's Office

Records of the Department of the Tennessee

Records of the District of Columbus

Records of the District of Nashville

Records of the Office of Quartermaster General

Records of the Office of the Secretary of War

Regimental Papers of the 2nd USCLA, 6th USCHA, 11th USCI and 11th USCI (New), and the 13th (14th) Tennessee Cavalry

Register of Letters Received by the Commissioner for the Organization of Colored Troops

Report of an Inspection of the Fortifications on the Ohio & Mississippi River, April 20, 1864

Report of Court of Inquiry [into Cotton Speculation at Helena, Arkansas,] by Major General Irwin McDowell

Reports of Investigations of Conditions at the Irving Block Military Prison in Memphis, Tennessee April–May 1864

Reports on Loyal Citizens [Paducah, Kentucky]

Semi-Weekly Return of Effective Force at the Post of Cairo: April 25, 1864

Union Provost Marshal's File of Papers Relating to Individual Civilians

INDEX